Viticulture

VOLUME 2 PRACTICES

Viticulture

VOLUME 2 PRACTICES

edited by

B.G. Coombe and P.R. Dry

contributing authors

T.G. Amos, E.W. Boehm, G.A. Buchanan, I.J. Cameron, A.P. Chapman,
R.M. Cirami, B.G. Coombe, D.M. Davidson, P.R. Dry, G. Due, R.W. Emmett,
B.M. Freeman, R.P. Hamilton, A.R. Harris, P.F. Hayes, P.R. Hedberg,
L.D. Jones, M.G. McCarthy, J.K. McGechan, P.R. Nicholas, M.D. Rebbechi,
J.B. Robinson, R.E. Smart, E. Tassie, R.H. Taylor, R.T.J. Webber
and J.R. Whiting

WINETITLES

ADELAIDE 1992

First published in 1992
Reprinted 1993 with corrections
Reprinted 1995 with alterations
Reprinted 1997
Reprinted 1998

Winetitles
2 Wilford Avenue, Underdale SA 5032
Australia

National Library of Australia
Cataloguing-in-Publication data

Viticulture. Volume 2, Practices

Bibliography.
Includes index.
ISBN 1 875130 01 2 (v.2)
ISBN 1 875130 02 2 (set).

I. Viticulture − Australia. 2. Grapes − Australia.
I. Coombe, B.G. (Bryan George). II. Dry, P.R.
III. Title: Practices.

634.8 0994

Volume 1 − Resources
ISBN 1 875130 00 4
Front cover: Carina grapes for drying; hand prining, Victoria;
tractor-mounted hedger, NSW; trellis end assemblies and drip
irrigation, Victoria; mechanized pruning, South Australia.

Back cover: vines trained to the minimal pruning system
(MPCT), CSIRO, Merbein.

Wholly produced in Adelaide, South Australia
Designed by Michael Deves
Typeset in Perpetua
Printed and bound by Hyde Park Press, Adelaide

Contents

ACKNOWLEDGEMENTS

Many people have made important contributions to the writing of this book. The authors and publishers would like to gratefully acknowledge those who have helped in writing, reading and advising on the early drafts of chapters; their advice has helped to make this text more accurate and relevant.

Many people have contributed to individual chapters and the authors of these chapters would like to acknowledge these specific contributions:

Peter Bailey, Brenton Baker, Greg Baker, Tony Bass, Geoffrey Bishop, David Botting, Peter Buss, Rev Cant, E.T. Carroll, Max Casimir, Tony Chapman, Peter Christensen, Tony Devitt, Peter Dickinson, B.C. Dodd, Ralph Doepel, Claire Fowler, Geoff Furness, Jennifer Gardner, Ian Geard, Stephen Goodwin, Olga Goss, Jim Hardie, Harry Hawson, J. Heaton, Albert Heslop, Bill Jamieson, P.T. Jenkins, Fred Jensen, Russell Johnston, Graham Lavis, Keith Leamon, Paul Madge, Peter Magarey, Peter May, Vic Patrick, Chris Rudd, Andrew Sproul, Rob Stevens, Henry Tankard, Barry Tugwell, Ross Turkington, Keith Watson, Trevor Wicks, Neil Wilkinson.

Thanks are also due to those authors of this present volume who, in addition to the writing of their own chapters, have served in the refereeing of other chapters.

The publishers also would like to acknowledge the financial support provided for the publication of this book by the following bodies:

The (former) Australian Wine Board
The Australian Society of Viticulture and Oenology
The Australian Grape and Wine Research and Development Corporation
The Australian Dried Fruits Research Council
The Australian Dried Fruits Association

AUTHORS' AFFILIATIONS

T.G. Amos, Vic. Dept. of Conservation and Environment, East Melbourne, Vic. 3002
E.W. Boehm, PO Box 79, McLaren Vale, SA 5171
G.A. Buchanan, Vic. Dept of Food and Agriculture, Irymple, Vic. 3498
I.J. Cameron, WA Dept of Agriculture, Midland, WA 6056
A.P. Chapman, formerly S.A. Dept of Agriculture, Nuriootpa, SA 5355
R.M. Cirami, SA Dept of Agriculture, Nuriootpa, SA 5355
B.G. Coombe, University of Adelaide, Glen Osmond, SA 5064
D.M. Davidson, 18 Stanley St, Leabrook, SA 5068
P.R. Dry, University of Adelaide, Glen Osmond, SA 5064
G. Due, University of Adelaide, Glen Osmond, SA 5064
R.W. Emmett, Vic. Dept of Food and Agriculture, Irymple, Vic. 3498
B.M. Freeman, Charles Sturt University, Wagga Wagga, NSW 2650
R.P. Hamilton, SA Dept of Agriculture, GPO Box 1671, SA 5001
A.R. Harris, CSIRO Division of Soils, Glen Osmond, SA 5064
P.F. Hayes, Grape and Wine Res. and Dev. Corp., 2 Portrush Rd, Payneham, SA 5070
P.R. Hedberg, Univ. of New England, Orange Agricultural College, Orange, NSW 2800
L.D. Jones, Vic. Rural Water Commission, Armadale, Vic. 3143
M.G. McCarthy, SA Dept of Agriculture, Nuriootpa. SA 5355
J.K. McGechan, 340 Malton Rd, Epping, NSW 2121
P.R. Nicholas, SA Dept of Agriculture, Loxton, SA 5333
M.D. Rebbechi, Charles Sturt University, Wagga Wagga, NSW 2650
J.B. Robinson, Scholefield-Robinson, PO Box 145, Kingswood, SA 5062
R.E. Smart, Smart Viticultural Services, 37 Bellevue Drive, Port Macquarie, NSW. 2444
E. Tassie, Charles Sturt University, Wagga Wagga, NSW 2650
R.H. Taylor, 12 Corsewall Close, Hawthorn, Vic. 3122
The late R.T.J. Webber, formerly SA Dept of Agriculture, Adelaide, SA 5000
J.R. Whiting, Vic. Dept. of Food and Agriculture, Bendigo, Vic. 3550

FOREWORD

The origin and production of these two volumes on viticulture were described in the Foreword to Volume 1. The first volume on resources (1988) dealt with matters that concern pre-planting decisions before the establishment of a vineyard; this has been well received. This second volume concerns the practices involved in the establishment and operation of a vineyard. The emphasis is on what a grapegrower has to do to earn a living from the enterprise, but the treatment is from the direction of principles rather than the details of the practices themselves. Like the first volume, we have tried to help those who read, and who are seeking information on the 'how' and the 'why' as well as the 'what'. Despite the large volume of literature that has been published during the last two decades, there are many topics that have not been collated in this fashion before and, for this reason, these have been heavily referenced. While this detracts from the reading flow, it permits those so inclined to pursue their own further investigation of the subject. We view these volumes as a resource of background information.

The boundaries of this volume are the vineyard gate. We have tried to cover the decisions (other than financial) that the grapegrower has to make, including the endpoints of packing of tablegrapes, delivery of winegrapes, and drying of raisins. But we have excluded subsequent handling and also specialist matters that are not the normal province of growers, e.g. grape breeding, market surveys, and the like. As before, we have given attention to the choice and spelling of terms for the industry in the hope of providing a unifying influence.

The dramatic rise in export earnings from grape products during the last five years will, if stabilized, represent another expansionary phase, but this time driven by the imperative of high quality products coupled with a significant new requirement — the world's demand for clean food and sustainable agricultural methods. As said in Volume 1, our viticulture is innovative and largely unconstrained by legislative controls. Many new methods of establishment and cultivation have been developed and adopted, and new viticultural areas have been tested. These changes have brought with them many new problems that require solutions based on principles. It is our hope that these volumes will help in the finding of answers.

The overall editing has been influenced by the teaching of courses in the University of Adelaide at Roseworthy (viticulture by P.R. Dry) and at Waite (horticultural science by B.G. Coombe). The editors and authors are conscious of the long time that has elapsed since commencing this task. We do not list the multiplicity of causes but will point out that all of us had to treat the work as a spare time occupation, a scarce commodity for most. The authors have generously donated their royalties to a fund to help in the production of further publications that will benefit the grape industries of Australia.

BRYAN COOMBE and PETER DRY
Adelaide

This volume is dedicated
to the memories of

R.T.J. (Ron) WEBBER
the growers' mentor and friend

and

M.G. (Mike) MULLINS
a pioneering and productive researcher

CHAPTER ONE

Grapevine Propagation

P.R. NICHOLAS, A.P. CHAPMAN and R.M. CIRAMI

In its wild state, the grapevine reproduces sexually by means of seeds or asexually by adventitious roots which form when canes touch the ground and become covered with soil or plant debris. Under cultivation, grapevines may be propagated by seeds, cuttings, budding, grafting, layering or tissue culture. Seedlings grown from the seed of one vine may differ appreciably from the parent and from each other because of genetic variation. Because of this, and because seedlings are usually inferior to the parent in vigour, production and fruit quality, they are impractical as a means of propagation for commercial vineyards. Vegetative or asexual propagation, by cuttings, grafts or layers, produces vines that are identical with the parents in all varietal characteristics unless mutation or virus infections intervene (see Volume 1 Chapter 9).

In early grape production in Australia, vineyards were readily established by quite simple methods, often by growers taking their own cuttings and doing their own propagation. Now, the position is more complicated.

The propagation method chosen will depend on a number of factors such as: presence or absence of soil-borne pests (e.g. phylloxera or nematodes); climate and vineyard location; the expertise of the grower and availability of skilled labour; and the availability of propagation material and equipment.

1.1 Collection and storage of cuttings

The first stage in the propagation of both own-rooted and grafted vines usually involves making hardwood cuttings from dormant canes i.e. last season's shoots.

1.1.1 Selection of cuttings

Cuttings are best made from moderately vigorous, well-matured canes which have an ample supply of stored foods to nourish the developing roots and shoots until the new plant becomes self-sustaining (Hartmann and Kester 1983). Mature wood, when sectioned, normally has a small pith in relation to the wood portion (Figure 1.1). Cuttings may perform poorly if taken from vines that have been water-stressed, over-cropped, or defoliated by insects, frost or disease before the wood has matured (Winkler et al. 1974). The central and basal parts of a cane make the best cuttings; those made from the late-formed regions at the tips of canes grow weakly.

The nutritional status of the mother vines may also be important: cuttings from vines receiving

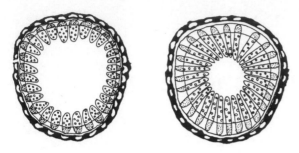

Figure 1.1. Transverse section of poorly matured cane (left) and well matured cane (right).

high nitrogen fertilization may root poorly (Pearse 1946, Alleweldt 1967); however high levels of N,P,K and zinc gave good rooting percentage in Israel (Samish and Spiegel-Roy 1957).

Cuttings for own-rooted vines
Cuttings for producing own-rooted vines should be about 8-12 mm in diameter and of medium internode length. Cuttings with long internodes from rapid growth often have low stored reserves. Canes which are flattened or immature or have dead sections are best avoided.

Cuttings for grafted vines
Similar quality requirements apply as for ungrafted vines, but size is more critical. Scion wood for bench-grafting should be straight, 7-10 mm in diameter, with internodes less than 7 cm; cuttings with longer internodes tend to be flattened in cross-section making them undesirable for bench grafting. Cuttings taken from machine harvested vines are unsatisfactory for bench-grafting.

In Australia, rootstock mother vines are generally grown sprawling on the ground i.e. they are not trellised. A method of trellising rootstock vines suggested for use in South Africa has been described by Pongracz (1978). Rootstock cuttings made for bench-grafting are best if straight, 7-10 mm in diameter and not flattened.

1.1.2 Taking cuttings
Cuttings may be taken at any time during the dormant period but are usually taken in early winter. Cuttings for own-rooted vines or scionwood are usually made 30-40 cm long. This length may vary slightly depending on the propagation method to be used. If the bottom cut is made at right angles just below a node and

the top cut is made about 3 cm above the top node, sloping away from the bud, then the polarity of the cutting is clear to those handling the cuttings: upside-down planting can be avoided. Rootstock cuttings are usually made longer (40-45 cm) so that when planted the graft union remains above soil level. Cuttings are usually tied in bundles of 50 or 100 with polypropylene twine or similar. Variety and clone should be indicated on an attached plastic label.

1.1.3 Treatment and storage
Cuttings required for an open ground nursery may be buried in a moist medium to allow callusing to proceed or they may be stored in a coldroom. Those required for bench grafting or as scionwood for budding are normally stored in a coldroom.

Chinosol® treatment
Cuttings to be stored in a coldroom are usually first treated with Hoechst Chinosol® (8-hydroxy-quinoline sulphate) as a protection against the grey mould *Botrytis cinerea*. Chinosol® which is water soluble has been found superior to other materials in its ability to penetrate the bark of cuttings and kill fungi and bacteria.

Bundles of cuttings for coldroom storage are first soaked in clean water for 1-2 days, until they sink (it may be convenient to place cuttings in jute bags prior to soaking). The cuttings are then soaked in a 0.5% solution of Chinosol® for at least 4 hours, although a slight increase in effectiveness will be obtained by soaking longer— up to 15 hours at 10-18ºC (Becker and Hiller 1977).

Chinosol® can form a dark precipitate when placed in contact with metals so non-metal containers, ties and labels should be used. If hard tap water is used, Chinosol® may come out of solution as a white precipitate, so the use of rain-water may be advantageous.

The concentration of active ingredient should be checked at regular intervals (using test strips supplied by the manufacturer) and the solution discarded when the concentration falls below 0.3%. Where large numbers of cuttings are processed it may be more economical to replenish the solution on a daily basis. The pH can be adjusted to 3.8 using sulfuric acid, the solution earth-filtered and more Chinosol® added.

Chinosol® treatment is most effective when cuttings are stored at 1°C. Cold storage has the added advantage that the metabolism of the cuttings is slowed and carbohydrate reserves are conserved. If cuttings are allowed to dry out during storage or if the temperature drops below 0°C and ice forms, the Chinosol® concentration may reach toxic levels. Cuttings can be heat-sealed in heavy duty polyethylene bags to prevent desiccation. They can then be stored in a cold room at 1-2°C and may still be viable after one year under these conditions. Cuttings can also be packed in bins of sawdust lined with polyethylene sheeting for cold-storage.

Hot water treatment (HWT)
Cuttings (or rootlings) can be immersed in hot water at a temperature high enough and for sufficient duration to destroy pests and pathogens, but not so high as to injure plant tissue. HWT can be used to inactivate phylloxera (Messenger 1948), nematodes (Lear and Lider 1959), flavescence doree (Caudwell 1966), Pierce's disease (Goheen *et al.* 1973), *Phytophthora cinnamomi* (Broemsen and Marais 1978) and crown gall (Burr *et al.* 1989). HWT of 50°C for 30 minutes may cause earlier budburst (Orffer 1977, Orffer *et al.* 1979) and delayed root initiation (Orffer and Goussard 1980); HWT at temperatures of 55°C for longer than 10 minutes may inhibit callusing (Goussard 1977) and can cause thermal death of cuttings (Goheen *et al.* 1973). Recent Australian experience suggests that HWT of rootstock cuttings may have little effect on strike rate, but HWT of *Vitis vinifera* cuttings can cause a reduction in strike. Cuttings should be immediately dipped in cold water following heat treatment.

Much of the propagation material presently used in Australia may be infested with crown gall, even though gall symptoms are not often seen (Ophel *et al.* 1988; 11.2.1). Rootlings of the rootstocks Dog Ridge and K51-40 frequently display root galls. HWT of vine cuttings to control crown gall involves immersion at 50°C for 30 minutes (Figure 1.2). This greatly reduces crown gall infestation but total elimination may not be achieved (Ophel *et al.* 1990). Cuttings should be soaked for several days prior to HWT. Care

Figure 1.2. Facilities for hot water treatment of propagation material.

must be taken not to allow vines which have had HWT to come into contact with untreated vines.

1.2 Propagation of own-rooted vines

It is possible to establish a vineyard of own-rooted vines by direct planting of cuttings (preferably callused) given favourable conditions, i.e. a warm, well-drained soil, adequate water and weed control and freedom from animal and insect predators. However, because of the risk of low cutting strike, one-year-old rootlings are generally preferred for planting.

Own-rooted grapevines are normally propagated by the rooting of cuttings in an open-ground nursery. Cuttings of most varieties form roots readily. Where propagation material is in short supply, various rapid propagation techniques may be used (1.2.2). Propagation by layering may also be used in some circumstances (1.2.3).

1.2.1 Open-ground nursery propagation.
One-year-old rootlings are produced in an open-ground nursery as follows.

Callusing cuttings
In some situations, cuttings for a nursery can be held in a coldroom and planted out when the soil is warm enough, but it is more usual to callus them before planting. An efficient method of callusing is to dig a trench 50 cm deep in a well-drained sandy soil, place the bundles of cuttings vertically in it (bottom down) and fill with soil, at the same time washing soil well into the cuttings to remove air pockets. The cuttings are then covered with 5 cm of soil and watered occasionally. Cuttings can also be callused above-ground in a container of moist, washed, sharp sand or hardwood sawdust. If callusing of stored

cuttings is delayed until late into spring it may be advantageous to callus cuttings upside down to inhibit shoot growth and hasten callus development with the warmth attained about 5cm below the surface of the sand or sawdust. When callus and root initials have developed, usually within 6 to 8 weeks, the cuttings are removed from the callusing bed and planted.

Choosing a nursery site

An ideal nursery soil is a deep, friable, sandy loam, which is fertile, well-drained and free of phylloxera, nematodes and pathogens. The site should be fairly level, protected from the wind but not shaded, and supplied with good quality irrigation water. Selection of a new site each year, or of land that has been fallowed for several years, will reduce nematode and infertility problems.

Nursery site preparation

The following is a satisfactory routine: the nursery site is ploughed well before planting, to a depth of 30 cm; raising of subsoil should be avoided. About 3-6 weeks later the soil is disced, harrowed or rotary-hoed to a fine tilth. If the soil is infested with nematodes, it should be fumigated by injecting a suitable fumigant into the soil at a depth of 15 cm. This is done with soil moisture at 'seedbed condition' when the soil reaches the temperature recommended for the fumigant (e.g. 15°C for EDB). The soil surface must be sealed immediately after treatment either by compaction with a roller or by application of a light sprinkler irrigation. Fumigation with methyl bromide or a methyl bromide/chloropicrin mixture is often used in nurseries for control of soil-borne pathogens and weeds. The soil must be covered at the time of treatment with a gas-proof sheet such as polyethylene. Nutrient deficiency problems have been experienced in some nurseries following the use of methyl bromide.

If rabbits are a problem, a wire mesh fence 1 m high can be erected around the nursery with the bottom of the fence buried. If the site is windy, it may be necessary to establish wind-breaks.

Planting

This is usually done from early to mid spring. At least 25% more cuttings than the number of rootlings required should be planted. A row

Figure 1.3. Planting cuttings in an open-ground nursery.

spacing of 1.2-1.5 m is suitable to allow access by a normal size vineyard tractor. A furrow is ripped along each row, water is applied along the full length of the furrow and the cuttings are pushed into the soil leaving at least two nodes exposed (Figure 1.3). Cuttings can be planted 5 cm apart but a wider spacing may be preferable for infertile soils or where irrigation is limited. A planting machine can be used which allows a person sitting on the machine to push cuttings into a furrow opened and closed as the machine progresses. Uncallused cuttings taken from a coolstore are well suited to machine planting. A heavy irrigation should be applied immediately afterwards to compact the soil around the cuttings. Different clones should be clearly separated by gaps and identified with labels (e.g. aluminium) so that mix-ups do not occur when lifting. A plan should be made of the nursery in case labels are lost.

In cool climate areas, rooting may be improved by planting the cuttings through polyethylene sheeting (Figure 1.4). This gives a higher soil temperature, reduces water loss, and eliminates competition from weeds. Rows are hilled up with friable moist soil and covered with polyethylene sheet about 60 cm wide which is stretched taut

Figure 1.4. Use of polyethylene sheeting in an open-ground nursery.

and its edges covered with soil. Holes are made through the sheet using a punching device similar to a rake with a vertical handle. Cuttings are pushed into the soil through the punched holes leaving at least two buds remaining above the sheet.

Care of the nursery

i. Irrigation

The provision of adequate, good quality water is probably the most crucial requirement during the growing season. The development of callus and adventitious roots are particularly sensitive to water stress. Soil should be maintained close to field capacity, but adequate soil aeration is also important. Regular irrigations are needed during the early part of the growing season, especially if the weather is hot and dry. Timing and rate of irrigations can be guided by indicators of soil water status used in the vineyard (see Chapter 6).

Overhead sprinklers are a good method of irrigation provided the sprinklers have a uniform distribution pattern and are mounted high enough to clear the foliage. Drip or biwall tube irrigation can be used (particularly beneath black plastic), but application of nutrients through the water may be important for success. Furrow irrigation may be used provided that slope and length of furrow are satisfactory. In sandy soils, length of furrows should not exceed 70 m and slope should be about 0.4-0.5%; with clay loam soils, length of furrow should not exceed 130 m and slope should be about 0.25%.

ii. Weed control.

In a vine nursery, weed control is essential as weeds compete for water, nutrients and sunlight and impede the lifting operation. Pre-plant soil fumigation with a methyl bromide/chloropicrin mixture will prevent germination of most weeds. Pre-emergence herbicides Devrinol® and Surflan® can be used safely in vine nurseries provided the soil is well prepared and a light irrigation is applied following herbicide application. Treflan® can also be used if it is lightly cultivated into the soil. In smaller nurseries, weeds may be controlled by hand hoeing or by use of a garden rotary hoe.

iii. Fertilizers.

Grapevine nurseries may require little fertilizer if the soil is reasonably fertile. On less fertile (e.g. sandy) soils, small quantities of urea or ammonium nitrate can be applied regularly during the growing season, but applications should be stopped at the end of summer to allow shoots to harden.

iv. Pests and diseases.

Nurseries are subject to the same pests and diseases as are vineyards. In fact downy mildew and oidium infections are favoured by the crowded conditions of the nursery. A protective copper-sulfur-based spray should be applied soon after budburst and regularly thereafter, depending on weather conditions, to control downy mildew, oidium, erinose and budmite (see Chapters 10 and 11). Control of vegetative growth by hedging up to three times per season can assist with disease control. Curculio beetle and cut worm can cause problems in heavy soils in late spring by attacking the stems at or just below soil level and ring-barking the vines. Carbaryl can be used to control these pests. Lightbrown apple moth and vine moth can be damaging and control by use of *Bacillus thuringiensis* (Dipel®) or other suitable insecticides may be necessary (see also 2.4.3).

Lifting, grading and storage of rootlings

i. Lifting.

Rootlings are usually lifted in late winter. Roots should be cut prior to lifting; a U-shaped digger fitted to a tractor can be used to cut the roots and lift the vines (Figure 1.5). The tops may be pruned back before lifting. To avoid mixing

Figure 1.5. A U-shaped digger for cutting and lifting vines in a nursery (above). A grapevine rootling trimmed for planting; usually internodes are shorter than shown here (below).

clones in the nursery, each clone should be bundled and labelled before starting the next clone.

ii. Grading.
Ideally, rootlings should have several major roots spreading in different directions and several shoots, 4-5 mm thick and 20 cm long (Figure 1.5). Poor quality rootlings should be rejected.

iii. Bundling and labelling.
Rootlings are conveniently bundled in lots of 50; if bundles are made too large, rootlings in the centre may dry out during sand storage. Each bundle should be tied with polypropylene twine and labelled with a plastic tag. Roots and canes may be trimmed to aid bundling, but root pruning should not be excessive since it may reduce initial growth of the rootling in the vineyard (Uys and Orffer 1983). Canes can be pruned back to one or two well placed 2-node spurs so the rootlings are ready for planting.

iv. Storage.
It is best to plant rootlings in the vineyard immediately after lifting if possible. Rootlings may

be kept for one or two days stacked in the shade under a tarpaulin and the roots sprinkled with water as necessary. To store for longer periods bundles can be heeled-in in a pit of moist sharp sand or in a sandy soil location; the sand is washed thoroughly between the roots and kept moist until the rootlings are removed for planting. Rootlings can also be soaked in a 0.1% Chinosol® solution for 15 hours and stored in sealed plastic bags at 1⁰C for as long as two years and still contain sufficient carbohydrate reserves to be successfully planted (Becker and Hiller 1977).

Treatment against nematodes
Freedom from nematodes is an important requirement of planting material. If pre-planting precautions have not been successful and rootlings have become infested, it is possible to disinfest them by treatment with hot water or nematicides. Rootknot nematodes are destroyed by submerging dormant rootlings in water at a temperature of 48⁰C for 30 minutes, 52⁰C for 5 minutes or 54⁰C for 2 min (Lear and Lider 1959). Suatmadji (1982) has found that a nematicide dip (fenamiphos at 1000 mg/L held at 24⁰C for 30 min) may be more effective than hot water treatment.

1.2.2 Rapid propagation techniques
The production of vine rootlings in an open-ground nursery is simple and economical, but a system that occupies a full 12 months may not be the best for all needs. The production of rootlings can be speeded up by heat-bed pro-pagation of hardwood cuttings, mist propagation of greenwood cuttings or micropropagation by tissue culture. These methods permit the production of new rootlings only a few months after taking cuttings. Several batches of rootlings may be produced in one year.

Mist propagation and micropropagation methods are costly and demanding of skill and attention and are usually confined to research stations or to large enterprises where there is an urgent need to propagate scarce material. They are especially useful when only a few mother vines are available for the supply of cuttings, as occurs with newly-introduced material, selected clones and clones freed from virus.

Heat-bed propagation of hardwood cuttings
The most important environmental factor which can be modified to hasten the propagation of

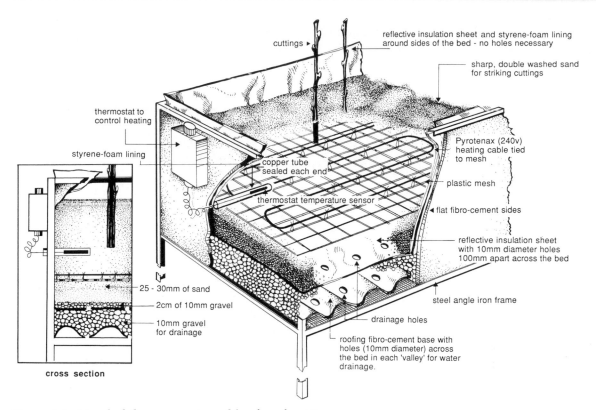

Figure 1.6. Heat-bed for propagation of hardwood cuttings.

cuttings is the application of bottom-heat. The optimum temperature for root initiation is 25°C. Soil temperatures in the field at depth are usually much lower than this. In a heat-bed placed outside in winter, the bases of the cuttings can be held at 25°C allowing root initiation to occur, but their apices are at low ambient temperatures, thus maintaining bud dormancy. Heat can be applied at the bottom of the bed by an electric heating cable (Chapman 1976); see Figure 1.6.

Cuttings may be as small as two nodes—one internode—in length, thus maximizing the number of vines produced from limited material. The cuttings are placed in sand at approximately 2 cm intervals, with the basal nodes 2.5 cm above the heating cable, and watered until there is free drainage from holes in the bottom of the bed. The sand should be kept moist during callusing and rooting. Roots are produced in 20 to 35 days and when they are 2 to 5 cm long the rootlings are ready for potting. If there is any delay in potting, the heat-bed should be switched off when root growth is sufficient, as long roots hinder potting. Rootlings from the heat-bed are normally potted

into plastic bags and grown-on in a glasshouse.

Plastic 'root trainers', cellular trays or cellular paper pots (which bio-degrade after six weeks), are all useful for heat-bed propagation. These are filled with a suitable medium, such as a peat/perlite mixture, to hold cuttings while in the heatbed and the rootlings removed later with little root disturbance. They can then be either repotted and grown on in plastic bags or planted directly into an open-ground nursery.

Mist propagation of greenwood cuttings
Roots can be initiated on greenwood cuttings in a glasshouse by using a mist propagator on a heatbed (Welch 1973, Hartmann and Kester 1983, Nelder and Cirami 1986). The following is a satisfactory procedure for mist propagation of grapevines:

i. Production of cuttings
Mother-vines are grown in large containers in a glasshouse or shadehouse. The shoots are de-fruited and trained vertically until they are about 1 m long. The vines are then pruned back to three nodes. The green shoots removed are cut into two-

node pieces with each piece cut directly below the basal node and 5 mm above the top node. A leaf is retained at the top node with the blade trimmed to reduce the crowding of cuttings during rooting. Cuttings taken from the middle of the shoot root best.

ii. Propagation of cuttings

Cuttings should be soaked in a suitable fungicide solution (e.g. Benlate® or Rovral®) for about 30 minutes. The base of each cutting may be treated with auxin to enhance rooting (1.3.1). The cuttings are then put in cellular propagation trays containing a moist medium, such as a peat/perlite or vermiculite/perlite mixture, and the trays placed on the heat-bed of a mist propagator (Figure 1.7). The temperature of the heat-bed is held at 24-28°C by thermostatic control and mist or 'fog' is applied intermittently to maintain greater than 95% relative humidity. A plastic tent is placed around the sides (not top) of the heat-bed.

Natural lighting is satisfactory in spring and summer but in winter it is necessary to provide a short period of light in the middle of the night or to extend the day length for growth to continue. The bed should be sprayed twice weekly with a fungicide (e.g. Ronilan® or Rovral®) to prevent botrytis infection.

Roots begin to appear after two weeks and the rootlings should be potted into plastic bags after three weeks. Any delay may lead to excessive leaching of nutrients (Good and Tukey 1966). The potted rootlings are gradually hardened-off on a mist bench by reducing mist frequency, removing plastic side covers and turning off bottom heat.

Tissue culture

The principles involved in the use of tissue culture for micropropagation have been reviewed by Hartman and Kester (1983). Tissue culture has the potential to produce several thousand plants from a single shoot tip between one growing season and the next. It can also be used to eliminate leafroll virus (Barlass *et al.* 1982) and crown gall (Burr *et al.* 1988).

Among several techniques which have been used for the micropropagation of grapevines, one commercial protocol follows the method of Barlass and Skene (1978). It involves the fragmentation of a 1 mm shoot tip under sterile conditions and growing the pieces in a liquid nutrient medium

Figure 1.7 Mist propagation of greenwood cuttings.

under defined conditions of light, temperature and daylength. Each fragment grows into a small leaf which when further cultured on a solid medium produces many shoots from the basal end. These shoots can be repeatedly multiplied to achieve the required numbers. Individual shoots are then placed on a different culture medium to encourage rooting. Actively-growing plantlets are taken from sterile surroundings, potted in a light mix and placed initially in high humidity conditions, then gradually hardened off (Figure 1.8).

Growing-on in the glasshouse

Vines produced by the above methods are normally repotted and grown-on in the glasshouse until the shoots reach 30 cm or longer. They can then be either planted in an open-ground nursery or held in a shadehouse for planting in the vineyard the following spring.

i. Potting mixes

The preparation of potting mixes has been detailed by Handreck and Black (1984). A light, free-draining, pasteurized mix is ideal. The mix can be pasteurized using aerated steam (Baker 1957) to kill weed seeds and pathogenic fungi, leaving saprophytic soil micro-organisms predominant. The temperature of the mix is raised to 65°C for 30 minutes, then cool air is passed through to lower the temperature to 25°C. Treatment with 'live' steam and fumigants such as methyl bromide are effective sterilants but destroy saprophytes as well, thus increasing vulnerability to later development of pathogens. Suitable mixes for repotting can also be purchased commercially.

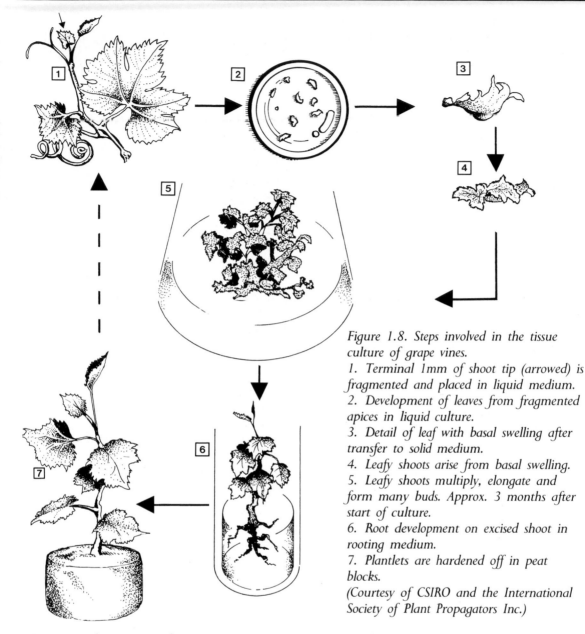

Figure 1.8. Steps involved in the tissue culture of grape vines.
1. Terminal 1mm of shoot tip (arrowed) is fragmented and placed in liquid medium.
2. Development of leaves from fragmented apices in liquid culture.
3. Detail of leaf with basal swelling after transfer to solid medium.
4. Leafy shoots arise from basal swelling.
5. Leafy shoots multiply, elongate and form many buds. Approx. 3 months after start of culture.
6. Root development on excised shoot in rooting medium.
7. Plantlets are hardened off in peat blocks.
(Courtesy of CSIRO and the International Society of Plant Propagators Inc.)

ii. Disease and pest control

The glasshouse environment provides good conditions for vine growth, but also favours the development of diseases and pests. A weekly spray schedule should be used to control diseases like botrytis, downy mildew, oidium and black spot. The use of different fungicides in rotation reduces the chance of resistant strains developing. For the same reason, insecticides and miticides should only be used when necessary and not on a routine basis. Plants should be checked regularly for mites by examining the leaves with a hand lens, and sprayed as required. Insects such as mealy bug, white fly, aphids, lightbrown apple moth, and vine moth should also be controlled with appropriate chemicals if they appear.

A disinfectant such as 0.5% sodium hypochlorite (40 mL 12.5% sodium hypochlorite to 1 L) can be used to sterilize floors, walls and benches. Other hygiene measures such as the use of foot-baths (e.g. copper oxychloride), keeping glasshouse doors closed where possible, removing dead vegetative matter and limiting traffic into the house will also assist in maintaining plant health.

1.2.3 Propagation by layering

As a means of propagation, layering has limited application in present day viticulture. It may however be used for the following.

Layering to replace missing vines

Misses in established vineyards may be difficult to fill by replanting because of competition. Layering is an alternative which can be used (Winkler *et al.* 1974, Pongracz 1978). In winter a long vigorous cane from an adjacent vine is bent down and pegged to the bottom of a trench 30 cm deep. The cane is positioned in the trench so that its tip projects above ground in the desired vine position and a shoot is trained to the wire. Development of the new vine is assisted if a wire is wrapped around the layered cane under ground between the mother vine and the new vine. As the cane grows, the wire acts as a girdle preventing the movement of 'foods' from the new vine back to the mother vine (Figure 1.9). The newly established layered vine should be allowed to bear only light crops for the first few years until it is large enough to compete successfully with the adjacent older vines.

Layering of varieties difficult-to-propagate from cuttings

The use of simple layers, trench layers and mound layers to propagate varieties whose cuttings strike poorly, e.g. *Vitis rotundifolia,* varieties has been discussed by Winkler *et al.* (1974). However, it may be easier to mist propagate these varieties if facilities are available.

1.3 Propagation of grafted vines

Grapevines are grafted for one or more of the following reasons (see Volume 1, Chapter 8):
i. To obtain vines of a fruiting variety with root systems tolerant to phylloxera, nematodes or other pests and diseases.
ii. To obtain vines with roots tolerant of certain soil conditions, e.g. limestone, salinity etc
iii. To advance or retard fruit maturity.
iv. To change the variety.

Grafting is defined by Hartmann and Kester (1983) as 'the art of connecting two pieces of living plant tissue together in such a manner that they will unite and subsequently grow and develop as one plant'. They define budding as 'similar to grafting except that the scion is reduced in size to contain only one bud'. Tukey (1937) called that part of the graft combination which is to become the upper position, the scion, and the part which is to become the lower portion or root, the stock. The union is where scion and stock come together.

Hartmann and Kester (1983) describe the usual sequence of events involved in the formation of the graft union as follows (Figure 1.10):
i. Freshly cut scion tissue capable of meristematic activity is brought into secure, intimate contact with similar freshly cut stock tissue in such a manner that the cambial regions of both are in close proximity. Temperature and humidity conditions must be such as to promote growth activity in the newly exposed and surrounding cells.
ii. The outer exposed layers of cells in the cambial region of both scion and stock produce parenchyma

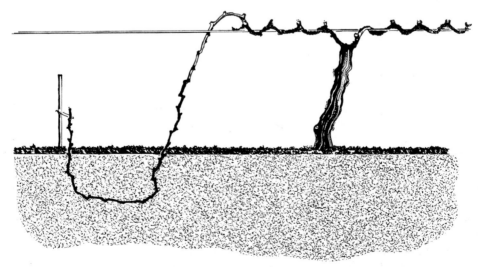

Figure 1.9. Layering to replace a missing vine.

10

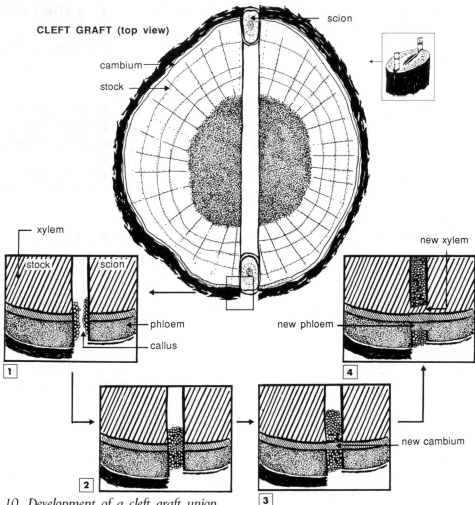

Figure 1.10. Development of a cleft graft union.

cells which soon intermingle and interlock. This is called callus tissue.

iii. Certain cells of this newly-formed callus in line with the cambium layer of the intact scion and stock, differentiate into new cambium cells.

iv. These new cambium cells produce new vascular tissue, xylem toward the inside and phloem toward the outside, thus establishing vascular connection between the scion and stock, a requisite of a successful graft union.

1.3.1 Factors that influence success

Environmental conditions

Favourable conditions of temperature, moisture and aeration are essential to enable the cambial layers of the stock and the scion to produce callus. With grapevines, temperatures of 24-30°C and relative humidities of 90-100% are optimal

for development of the graft union. It is difficult to obtain these conditions naturally and modifications to the environment at the union are necessary.

Compatibility

To ensure healing, the stock and scion must be compatible with each other. Compatibility and affinity are described in Volume 1, Chapter 8. Compatibility refers to the ability to form a sound union. Plants of the same species can usually be grafted readily to each other and varieties of *Vitis vinifera* present few problems when intergrafted. Occasional reports of incompatible combinations are usually attributable to virus infection. When *Vitis vinifera* varieties are grafted onto phylloxera- or nematode-resistant rootstocks, different species are involved and incompatibility can occur.

Development of roots on the rootstock
It is often more difficult to promote root development on rootstock cuttings than on *Vitis vinifera* cuttings. Ramsey rootstock in particular is known to have callusing and rooting problems (Goussard and Orffer 1979). Soaking of rootstock cuttings in water may enhance root development (Kracke *et al.* 1981, Bartolini *et al.* 1986). Growth regulators can also be used to promote root initiation; the use and methods of application of these has been summarized by Hartman and Kester (1983). Spiegel-Roy (1955) has noted that cuttings of the easily-rooted *Vitis vinifera* varieties contained high levels of auxins and low levels of a root-inhibiting compound. Treatment of *Vitis vinifera* cuttings with synthetic auxins had little effect on rooting but the difficult-to-root *Vitis berlandieri* hybrids (which have low levels of auxin and high levels of inhibitors until late in the dormant season) responded to synthetic auxins i.e. there was more rapid and prolific root initiation.

Of various synthetic auxins which promote root formation, indolebutyric acid (IBA) has been found the most effective for grapevines (Alley 1980). IBA may be applied as a concentrated dip, where the basal 2 cm of cuttings are dipped for a few seconds in a 2000 mg/L IBA solution (made up by dissolving 2 g of IBA in 500 mL of alcohol and adding 500 mL of water) or a dilute aqueous soak, where the basal 4 cm of the cuttings are soaked for 24 hours in a 200 mg/L IBA solution (prepared by dissolving 200 mg IBA in 10 mL ethanol and diluting with water to make up to 1 litre). These treatments result in better rooting of the difficult-to-root *Vitis champini* rootstocks e.g. Ramsey (Chapman and Hussey 1980); either can be used although the concentrated dip is often more convenient. Commercial formulations of IBA in talc may also be used.

1.3.2 Bench-grafting

A bench-graft is a graft made indoors (using dormant wood) instead of in the field and usually involves grafting single bud scions onto rootstock cuttings. Bench-grafting is the most commonly used method for grafting vines throughout the world as it is the most suited for mass production of grafted vines. Bench-grafting procedures used in Australia (Figure 1.11) have mostly been developed from those used in Europe, but have been modified for use with Ramsey, the most widely used rootstock in Australia. Typical methods used are as follows.

Preparation of stock and scion wood
Cuttings are stored in the coldroom (as described in 1.1.3), then removed prior to use and soaked for 1-5 days in a sodium hypochlorite solution (2 mg/L chlorine) made up with rainwater. Rootstock cuttings are usually soaked longer than scion cuttings. Soaking of the cuttings removes Chinosol® which can inhibit graft callus formation at high concentrations and it may also remove inhibitors which retard root development in many rootstock varieties. HWT of rootstock cuttings can be done at this stage.

The rootstock cuttings are disbudded with secateurs or a special disbudding knife (to minimize the risk of later suckering problems in the vineyard) and re-cut as close as possible below the bottom node. Scion wood is cut into one-node pieces about 50 mm long with less than 20 mm above the bud. Stock and scion cuttings are held in buckets of chlorinated water ready for grafting.

Machine grafting and preparation for callusing
The stock and scion cuttings are usually grafted with an omega cut machine. A twin-head revolving knife machine may be used, but this is slower (Figure 1.12). Some nurseries apply an IBA treatment to the base of the grafts at this stage. The completed grafts are packed vertically in a callusing medium in boxes, leaving a layer of medium below the grafts and with the tops all at exactly the same level. Shadecloth is placed on top of the grafts and is in turn covered with 50 mm of moist perlite or vermiculite.

Various box sizes may be used e.g. $0.3 \times 0.3 \times 0.5$ m, $1.2 \times 0.6 \times 0.7$ m or $1.2 \times 1.2 \times 0.7$ m holding between 200 and 3000 grafts. The boxes are lined with plastic sheet. A suitable callusing medium provides a high relative humidity around the union, but still allows sufficient aeration for callus development. Media which may be used include vermiculite, perlite, neutralized peat/perlite or sterilized sawdust. The medium must not be too wet; when squeezed by hand no water should be seen. The boxes of grafts may be kept at 1-$4^{\circ}C$ for several weeks until sufficient grafts are available to fill a callusing room.

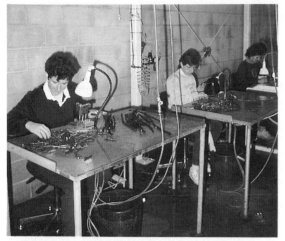

1. Machine grafting.

2. Packing grafts into a callusing box

3. Callusing room.

4. Bench grafts growing in a nursery.

Figure 1.11. Bench grafting procedure (Courtesy of S. Smith & Son Pty Ltd)

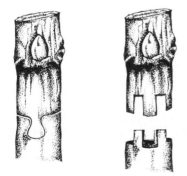

Figure 1.12. Omega cut graft (left) and revolving knife cut graft (right).

Callusing

Boxes of grafts are placed in a callusing room held at 28-29°C for about 2 weeks until there is a complete ring of callus 1-2 mm thick at the union. The shadecloth is lifted regularly to check progress. Excessive callus at the union is undesirable as unevenly-differentiated vascular tissue may result.

As shoots begin to grow, the shadecloth and medium above the graft may be removed and the boxes placed in a heated glasshouse so the shoots grow into light. This avoids etiolation by allowing photosynthesis to commence. The tops of the boxes are misted daily with chlorinated water and sprayed weekly with a fungicide (e.g. Ronilan® or Rovral®) to prevent Botrytis infection. The glasshouse temperature should be held at 18-20°C minimum and 28°C maximum for 4-5 days. Then the grafts are hardened-off for about 7-10 days by moving them firstly to a shadehouse then outdoors prior to planting.

Waxing and planting in a nursery
Grafts are removed from the callusing boxes and the shoots trimmed if too long. They are then dipped in a suitable grafting wax (held at 70-75°C) to give a thin (1-2 mm) coating over the scion and graft union. Small 'pin holes' in the wax should be avoided e.g. by ensuring there is no free moisture on the surface to be waxed. Grafts should be dipped into cold water immediately after waxing to cool them down. The bottom of the grafts can then be dipped in a fungicide (e.g. Terrazole® or Previcur®) as a protection against pathogen attack. There should be little root development at this stage as roots may break off during planting with consequent loss of reserves.

The grafts are planted in an open-ground nursery 5-7 cm apart, with 1.2-1.5 m between rows. It is usually advantageous to have wind-breaks in the nursery. The soil temperature of the nursery should be about 15°C at a depth of 20 cm at time of planting and this should be taken into consideration when deciding the time to start callusing. Thus callusing will normally be delayed till early spring but this will depend on a prior knowledge of temperatures at the nursery site. It may be advantageous to callus Ramsey last as the requirement for warm soil may be more critical for Ramsey than other rootstocks. Grafts should be planted and immediately watered in. The union should be located at least 5 cm above the soil. When the vines are lifted at the end of the growing season, they should be graded as for ungrafted vines; in addition, vines without a complete join at the union should be discarded.

Grafts can also be planted in pots and grown on in a shadehouse, but experience has shown that vines produced in this way may not be as strong as vines produced in an open-ground nursery.

Variations to this procedure
Prior to callusing, grafts may be wrapped with budding tape at the union, dipped for a few seconds in an IBA solution to encourage root growth (if necessary) and callused as above, but with the bases of the grafts enclosed in cellular paperpots or plastic root trainers containing a suitable medium, e.g. neutralized peat/perlite. The boxes are filled with callusing medium to the level of the scion buds and then sealed with a clear polyethylene sheet. The grafts are callused and placed in a heated glasshouse as before. When the shoots grow into light, the sheet is cut and progressively opened (Nicholas *et al.* 1984). This method is a little more labour-intensive but may be justified where a particular stock/scion combination has been found difficult to propagate or where it is intended to produce grafts before the nursery soil is warm enough to plant them out. The boxes can be designed so that the sides lift off allowing the callusing medium to be removed. The grafts are allowed to grow on in the containers until time of planting in an open-ground nursery.

1.3.3 Nursery budding and grafting
The budding of rootstock rootlings in an open ground nursery is a widely used method of producing grafted vines in Australia.

Production of rootstock rootlings
These are grown in a nursery using a method similar to that described for own-rooted vines in 1.2.1. However, prior to callusing, rootstock cuttings are re-cut immediately below the bottom

Figure 1.13. Callusing of rootstock cuttings in sawdust.

node and disbudded leaving only the top one or two buds. If considered necessary, the cuttings can be dipped in an IBA solution at this stage and then callused (Bass 1982). It is convenient to callus rootstock cuttings upright in damp hardwood sawdust — see Figure 1.13. As with bench grafts, the planting of rootstocks in an open-ground nursery should be delayed until the soil temperature at a depth of 20 cm reaches 15°C.

In the first year, rootlings may be trained to a single stem or allowed to sprawl depending on the method of budding or grafting to be used. If one-year-old rootlings are lifted and sold, the buyer usually plants and buds them in the same year.

Budding and grafting of rootstock rootlings
The stock should be growing strongly and the vine should have a high moisture status immediately prior to budding. Budding should be avoided in very hot or windy weather, as bud desiccation may occur. Scion material can be held in fresh water or an ice box. The scion is cut with a budding knife (or a hand-operated grafting machine), a matching cut is made in the stock and the bud is inserted so that the cambiums coincide. The bud is then tightly wrapped with PVC budding tape to provide high humidity around the union and ensure close contact between stock and scion. With most budding techniques, the top portion of the stock is removed after the scion bud begins to grow.

Table 1.1 gives reliable methods of budding and grafting. The range of techniques and types of scion wood that can be used allow the propagator flexibility to bud or graft vines from early September until March. The most commonly used methods are chip budding and T-budding.

i. Chip budding
This method (Nicholas and Bass 1979, Hodge

Table 1.1 A comparison of methods that can be used in a nursery or the vineyard for producing grafted vines

Method	Timing	Site of bud or graft	Type of scion wood	Shoot-training required	Rootstock desuckering required	Susceptibility to hot weather
Chip bud Dormant scion (Spring bud)	Early Sept to Dec	Original rootstock cutting	Brown (from coolstore)	Scion	No	Low
Green scion (Summer bud)	Mid Dec to late Jan	Original rootstock cutting	Green (current growth)	Scion	No	Medium
Matured scion (Autumn bud)	Mid Feb to Mar	Original rootstock cutting	Brown(current growth)	Scion	No	Low
Green graft Dormant scion	Late Oct to mid Dec	Green rootstock shoot	Brown (from coolstore)	Rootstock and scion	Yes	Low-medium
Green scion	Late Oct to late Nov	Green rootstock shoot	Green(current growth)	Rootstock and scion	Yes	High
T-bud Dormant scion	Late Nov to early Feb when bark lifts freely	Original rootstock cutting	Brown (from coolstore)	Scion	No	Low
Green scion	Late Nov to early Feb when bark lifts freely	Original rootstock cutting	Green(current growth)	Scion	No	Medium-high

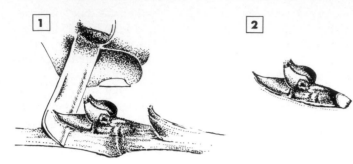

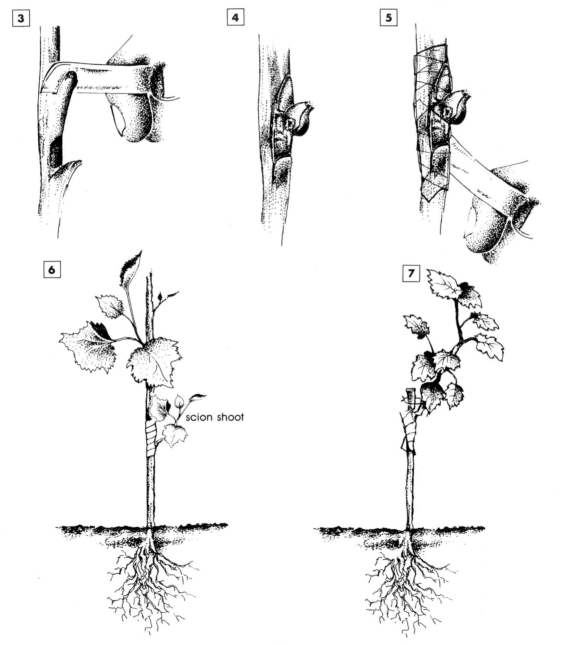

Figure 1.14. Chip budding.
1-2 Chip bud is cut from scion wood.
3. Matching cuts are made in the stock.
4-5. The chip bud is inserted and wrapped with tape.
6. Scion shoot begins to grow.
7. The top is cut off the rootstock and the budding tape is cut.

scion shoot

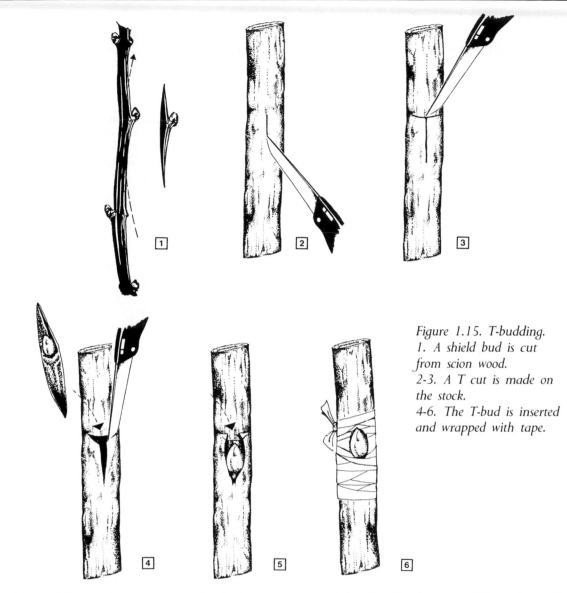

Figure 1.15. T-budding.
1. A shield bud is cut
from scion wood.
2-3. A T cut is made on
the stock.
4-6. The T-bud is inserted
and wrapped with tape.

and Bass 1989) involves inserting a chip bud into the main stem, i.e. what was the initial rootstock cutting (Figure 1.14). Buds for use from September to December are taken from cool-stored hardwood cuttings, summer buds are taken from semi-hardened green current season's growth and buds for use from mid-February to March are taken from mature, brown, current season's growth. Another method sometimes used is to insert a chip bud into a thick green rootstock shoot; this is most successful when vines are at least two years old.

ii. Green grafting
This method is not widely used. It is most successful in late October to mid December with vines at least two years old (Bass 1981). One- or two-bud scions taken from either cool-stored hardwood or green, 'springy' current season's growth are whip, whip-and-tongue or cleft-grafted onto a green rootstock shoot.

iii. T-budding
A bud is inserted into the main stem of the rootstock vine when the bark lifts easily in late November to early February (Bass 1981, Hodge and Bass 1989). Buds are obtained from thin, cool-stored, hardwood cuttings or green wood from the current season's growth. A traditional T-bud cut is used (Figure 1.15).

1.3.4 Field budding
In Australia, budding and grafting may be carried out in the vineyard although it is more common in an open ground nursery where it is easier to look after vines; water is readily available, windbreaks can be provided, and weeds, pests and diseases are more easily controlled. Budding or grafting in the vineyard does allow earlier establishment of the vine root system, but it can result in an uneven vineyard if some buds initially fail and their replacement takes several years.

1.3.5 Micrografting
Micrografting can be used to produce grafted vines from planting material in very limited supply, e.g. where stock and scion material have been freed of virus and crown gall by tissue culture. A method of micrografting developed in France has been described by Boubals (1987). This technique is being evaluated in Australia (Barlass and Possingham 1989).

1.4 Top-working

Grapevines require from three to six years after planting to reach full economic production. However, changes in demand may occur over a much shorter time, leaving the grapegrower with a variety in little demand. Replanting is costly. One solution is to graft another variety on top i.e. top-working or top-grafting. Off-types in a vineyard can also be corrected by this means.

1.4.1 Factors that influence success
Bleeding from the stock
This occurs when the stock is cut off during top-working. Callusing of the graft will not begin until bleeding ceases. Alley and Koyama (1978) showed that bleeding delayed budburst and reduced total scion growth on T-budded vines in California. Bleeding may be controlled by one or more of the following methods:
i. Grafting early before the vines begin to bleed
ii. Removing vine tops before grafting so that bleeding has ceased before grafting begins
iii. Cutting off the trunk at a 45° angle so that bleeding occurs on the low side away from the graft
iv. Making two diagonal saw cuts 5 mm deep on the opposite site of the trunk below the graft. Alley and Koyama (1978) found this to be most

effective when the cuts were made 15 cm above ground level as bleeding occurred at the cuts rather than at the graft union.

Delayed scion establishment
Suckers from the stock should not be allowed to compete with the new scion shoots and should be removed during periodic inspections in the season of grafting. The growth of suckers is very much reduced when a good union has been established, and the scion is growing vigorously.

The rate of growth of the young scion shoots can exceed 30 cm per week and wind damage can cause serious losses to grafts as the point of attachment is weak; hence shoots should be tied and trained regularly during the period of maximum growth (November–February).

It is important to bring grafted vines back into full production as early as possible, or the main advantage of top-working over replanting will be lost. As the vine still has its original root system, as many nodes as possible should be left at pruning, i.e. bud numbers retained should approach the original pruning level.

Pathogen infections
Pathogen infections are discussed in Chapter 11. Virus incompatability problems can cause significant reductions in take. Crown gall development in some situations may push the scion bud out and thus kill the bud. *Eutypa* infections can occur: when the trunks are cut, they are susceptible to infection by the airborne ascospores of *Eutypa*. This risk can be greatly reduced by treating the wound with a Benlate® paste.

1.4.2 Top-working methods
Historically, many methods have been used to top-work grapevines, such as:
— low level cleft and notch grafts (Alley 1964, Winkler *et al.* 1974),
— high level cleft and notch grafts (Jenson 1971, Alley 1975 and Dundon 1979),
— bark grafts (Jenson 1971, Winkler 1974),
— T-bud grafts (Alley 1977, Alley and Baron 1980),
— chip bud grafts (Alley 1979, Henschke and Dry 1982),
— side whip graft (Alley 1983).

Bass (1980) and Dry and Henschke (1982) have reviewed many of these methods. The high level chip bud, T-bud and cleft graft methods (using cold stored scion wood) are the ones now most commonly used in Australia. Vines can be chip budded or cleft grafted in early spring, but T-budding can only be commenced when the bark begins to slip in late spring. High level methods have a number of advantages over low level techniques. Desuckering is simpler, less training is required and the trunk is retained so that most of the new scion wood becomes potential fruiting wood for the following season.

Low-level cleft graft

The vine is cut off below ground level and the stump is split to a depth of 5 cm. Two scions, which can be one or two buds long, are cut to wedges at the base and inserted into the cleft. The scions are covered with damp sandy soil to provide the conditions required for callusing. A single scion shoot is then trained up and suckers from the

stock are removed. This method is now not widely used.

High-level cleft graft

Here the vine is cut off just below the crown and scions inserted in a similar way to the low-level cleft. The split in the stock between the scion pieces may be filled with paper and a grafting sealer is applied to all cut surfaces to prevent drying out. The grafting sealer is then coated with white paint (see Figure 1.16). This technique is most successful with trunks of diameter greater than 5 cm.

Chip budding

One or two chip buds are inserted into the trunk and the buds are tied with plastic tape as shown in Figure 1.17. The rootstock can be cut off either prior to budding or when the scion reaches about 10 cm. The method possibly works best on vines with a trunk diameter of less than 5 cm, but has been successfully used for larger diameter vines.

Figure 1.16. High-level cleft graft used to top-work vines.
1. The vine is cut off and the stump is split.
2-4. Scions are inserted and the graft is sealed.

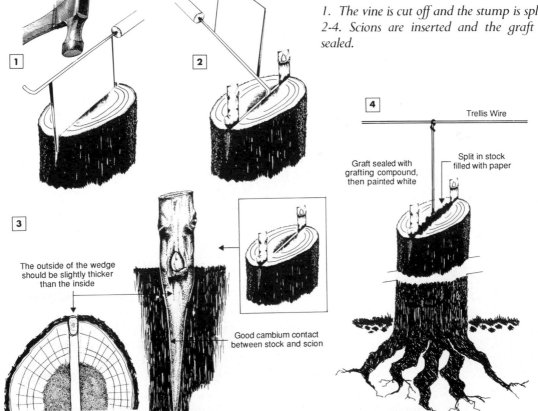

The outside of the wedge should be slightly thicker than the inside

Good cambium contact between stock and scion

Trellis Wire

Graft sealed with grafting compound, then painted white

Split in stock filled with paper

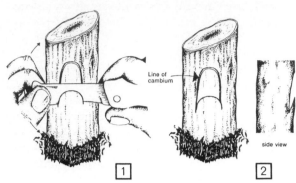
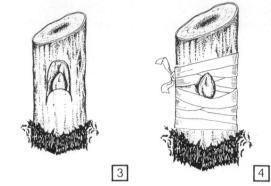

Figure 1.17. Chip budding used in top working. 1-2. Cuts are made in the stock.

3-4. A chip bud scion is cut, inserted and wrapped with tape.

T-budding.
A T-shaped cut is made in the bark high in the trunk. A bud shield is inserted behind the flaps of bark as shown in Figure 1.18. This method requires less skill than chip budding. It is not satisfactory with vines less than 2.5 cm trunk diameter. The top can be removed before budding or up to 2 weeks later.

1.5 Concluding remarks
Although grafted vines have long been used in phylloxera areas, in recent years there has been extensive demand for grafted vines in non-phylloxera districts, particularly in the warmer irrigated areas where grafted vines have not previously been used. This has required the widescale development of new expertise in bench-grafting and nursery grafting techniques. In the longer term the nursery industry must aim to supply grafted vines in the numbers and quality needed for the extensive vineyard rehabilitation program now required.

Vine improvement programs have been very successful. The widespread demand for quality rootstock material has resulted in the expansion of mother vine plantings of popular rootstock varieties. There is now a need to establish the optimum nutritional status and irrigation scheduling for these plantings so that the quality of cuttings produced will allow the best possible propagation success rates to be achieved. Another current problem is that the availability of scion wood is threatened by the use of new pruning techniques, e.g. minimal pruning, and by machine harvesting; to counter this, new source areas will be needed for the production of scion wood.

Greater use of hot water treatment of cuttings from vine improvement schemes is needed to combat infection by crown gall. Ultimately this material will be complemented by the multiplication in new source areas of pathogen-free material.

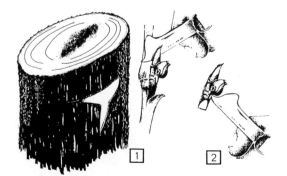
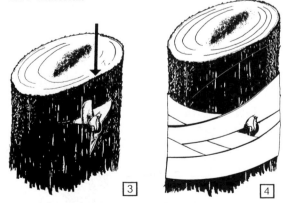

Figure 1.18. T-budding used in top working. 1. A T-cut is made in the stock.

2-4. A bud is cut, inserted and wrapped with tape.

Further reading

Hartmann, H.T. and Kester, D.E. (1983) Plant Propagation Principles and Practices. 4th Edition Prentice-Hall, Inc. Englewood Cliffs, New Jersey.

Pongracz, D.P. (1978) Practical Viticulture. David Philip, Capetown.

Weaver, R.J (1976) Grape Growing. John Wiley and Sons, New York.

Winkler, A.J., Cook, J.A., Kliewer, W.M. and Lider, L.A. (1974) General Viticulture. University of California Press, Berkeley.

Other references

Alleweldt, G. (1967) Einfluss der Unterlagssorte bei gleichzeitiger Variation der Stickstoff-und Wasserversorgung auf das Wurzel-und Kalluswachstum von Rebenstecklingen im Folgejahr. Z. Acker-und Pflanzenbau. 126, 19-32.

Alley, C.J. (1964) Grapevine propagation 1: A comparison of cleft and notch grafting; and, bark grafting at high and low levels. Amer. J. Enol. Vitic. 15, 214-7.

Alley, C.J. (1975) Grapevine propagation VII. The wedge graft—a modified notch graft. Amer. J. Enol. Vitic. 26, 105-8.

Alley, C.J. (1977) T-bud grafting of grapevines. Calif. Agric. 31 (7), 4-6.

Alley, C.J. (1979) Chipbudding of mature grapevines. Calif. Agric. 33 (9), 14-6.

Alley, C.J. (1980) Use of plant growth regulators in the rooting of grapevine cuttings. Proc. Grape and Wine Centenial Symposium. (Ed. A.D. Webb). University of California, Davis. pp137-42.

Alley, C.J. (1983) Side-whip grafting of grapevines to change over varieties. Calif. Agric. 37 (3), 8-9.

Alley, C.J. and Baron, D.H. (1980) Grapevine propagation. XV. Comparison of long and short bud shield below the bud; and standard and inverted cut in T-budding at high level. Amer. J. Enol. Vitic. 31, 95-7.

Alley, C.J. and Koyama, A.T. (1978) Vine bleeding delays growth of T-budded grapevines. Calif. Agric. 32 (8), 6.

Baker, K.F. (1957) The UC System for Producing Healthy Container Grown Plants. Univ. Calif. Agric. Exp. Sta. Ext. Serv. Manual 23.

Barlass, M. and Possingham, J.V. (1989) Towards a 'total clean concept' for new grapevine plantings. Aust. Grapegrower and Winemaker. No. 304, 55.

Barlass, M. and Skene, K.G.M. (1978) In vitro propagation of grapevine (Vitis vinifera L.) from fragmented shoot apices. Vitis 17, 335-40.

Barlass, M., Skene, K.G.M., Woodham, R.C. and Krake, L.R. (1982) Regeneration of virus-free grapevines using in vitro apical culture. Ann. Appl. Biol. 101, 291-5.

Bartolini, G., Topini, M.A. and Satini, L. (1986) Endogenous GA-like substances in dipping waters of cuttings of two Vitis rootstocks. Amer. J. Enol. Vitic. 37, 1-6.

Bass, A.W. (1980) Correct techniques essential for top working vines. Aust. Grapegrower and Winemaker. No. 196, 90-3.

Bass, A.W. (1981) Grafting methods looked at in detail. Aust. Grapegrower and Winemaker. No. 216, 15-7.

Bass, A.W. (1982) Handling and storing vine rootstock cuttings. Aust. Grapegrower and Winemaker. No. 226, 32-3.

Becker, H. and Hiller, M.H. (1977) Hygiene in modern bench grafting. Amer. J. Enol. Vitic. 28, 113-8.

Boubals, D. (1987) La culture in vitro et la production de plants greffes-soudes. Progres Agricole et Viticole 104, 13-14; 311-4.

Broemsen, S. von and Marais, P.G. (1978) Eradication of Phytophthora cinnamomi from grapevine by hot-water treatment. Phytophylactica 10, 25-7.

Burr, T.J., Katz, B.H., Bishop, A.L., Meyers, C.A. and Mittak, V.L. (1988) Effect of shoot age and tip culture propagation of grapes on systemic infestations by Agrobacterium tumefaciens. Biovar 3. Amer. J. Enol. Vitic. 39, 67-70.

Burr, T.J., Ophel, K., Katz, B.H. and Kerr, A. (1989) Effect of hot water treatment on systemic Agrobacterium tumefaciens biovar 3 in dormant grape cuttings. Plant Disease. 73, 242-5.

Caudwell, A. (1966) L'inhibition in vivo du virus de la flavescence doree par la chaleur. Etudes de Virologie. Ann. Epiphyties. n.h.s. 17, 61-6.

Chapman, A.P. (1976) Propagation of hardwood grapevine cuttings. Aust. Grapegrower and Winemaker. No. 148, 70-80.

Chapman, A.P. and Hussey, E.E. (1980) The value of plant growth regulators in the propagation of Vitis champini rootstocks. Amer. J. Enol. Vitic. 31, 250-3.

Dry, P.R. and Henschke, P.M. (1982) Further results with grapevine top-grafting. Aust. Grapegrower and Winemaker. No. 220, 16-8.

Dundon, C. (1979) Water stress reduces the success of grafting. Aust. Grapegrower and Winemaker. No. 184, 28-30.

Goheen, A.C., Nyland, G. and Lowe, S.K. (1973) Association of a rickettsialike organism with Pierce's disease of grapevines and alfalfa dwarf and heat therapy of the disease in grapevines. Phytopathology 63, 341-5.

Good, G.L. and Tukey, H.B. (1966) Leaching of metabolites from cuttings propagated under intermittent mist. Proc. Amer. Soc. Hortic. Sci. 89, 727-3.

Goussard, P.G. (1977) Effect of hot-water treatment on vine cuttings and one year old grafts. Vitis 16, 272-8.

Goussard, P.G. and Orffer, C.J. (1979) The propagation of Salt Creek. Deciduous Fruit Grower. Feb. 1979. 56-62.

Handreck, K.A. and Black, N.D. (1984) Growing Media for Ornamental Plants and Turf. New South Wales University Press, Kensington, NSW.

Henschke, P.M. and Dry, P.R. (1982) A modified method of chip-budding for top-grafting mature vines. Aust. Grapegrower and Winemaker. No. 220, 21-2.

Hodge, D. and Bass, A.W. (1989) Budding vine rootstocks. Dept. Agric. South Aust. Bull. 2/89.

Jensen, F. (1971) High level grafting of grapevines. Amer. J. Enol. Vitic. 22, 35-9.

Kracke, H., Cristoferi, G. and Marangoni, B. (1981) Hormonal changes during the rooting of hardwood cuttings of grapevine rootstocks. Amer. J. Enol. Vitic. 32, 135-7.

Lear, B. and Lider, L.A. (1959) Eradication of root-knot nematodes from grapevine rootlings by hotwater. Plant Dis. Reporter. 43, 314-7.

Messenger, A.P. (1948) Grape phylloxera policy. Calif. Dept. Agric. Q.C. Circular, No. 90.

Nelder, K. and Cirami, R.M. (1986) Mist propagation of grapevine rootstocks. Aust. Grapegrower and Winemaker. No. 268, 39-42.

Nicholas, P.R. and Bass, A.W. (1979) Chip budding nematode tolerant rootstocks. Aust. Grapegrower and Winemaker. No 184, 38-40.

Nicholas, P.R., Bass A.W. and Shepherd R.C. (1984) Successful commercial production of benchgrafted grapevines. Aust. Grapegrower and Winemaker. No. 244, 39-43.

Ophel, K., Burr, T.J., Magarey, P.A. and Kerr, A. (1988) Detection of *Agrobacterium tumefaciens* biovar 3 in South Australian grapevine propagation material. Australasian Plant Pathology. 17, 61-6.

Ophel, K., Nicholas, P.R., Magarey, P.A. and Bass, A.W. (1990) Hot water treatment of grape cuttings reduces crown gall incidence in a field nursery. Amer. J. Enol. Vitic. 41, 325-9.

Orffer, C.J. (1977) Hot water treatment of vine propagating material. Deciduous Fruit Grower. July 1977. 224-31.

Orffer, C.J., Goussard, P.G., Bosman, D.C., Morkel, D.C. and Wiese, J.J. (1979) The effect of hot-water treatment and growth regulators on budburst and rooting of cuttings of the grapevine rootstock cultivar USVIT 2-1. Deciduous Fruit Grower. Oct 1979. 340-4.

Orffer, C.J. and Goussard, P.G. (1980) Effect of hot-water treatments on budburst and rooting of grapevine cuttings. Vitis 19, 1-3.

Pearse, H.L. (1946) Rooting of vine and plum cuttings affected by nutrition of the parent plant and by treatment with phytohormones. Sth. Africa Dept. Agric. Science Bull. No 249.

Samish, R.M. and Spiegel-Roy, P. (1957) The influence of the nutrition of the mother vine on the rooting of cuttings. Ktavim. Records of Ag. Res. Station, Israel, 8, 93-100.

Spiegel-Roy, P. (1955) Some internal factors affecting rooting of cuttings. Rpt. XIV Int. Hortic. Congress.

Suatmadji, R.W. (1982) Control of rootknot nematodes, *Meloidogyne javanica*, in rooted stocks of grapevine, *Vitis vinifera* by immersion in nematicide solutions at different temperatures and in hot water. Nematol. medit. 10, 119-25.

Tukey, H.B. (1937) Stock and scion terminology. Proc. Amer. Soc. Hortic. Sci. 35, 378-92.

Uys, D.C. and Orffer, C.J. (1983) Changes in carbohydrates in nursery-grown rootstocks. S. Afr. J. Enol. Vitic., 4, 13-9.

Welch, H.J. (1973) Mist Propagation and Automatic Watering. Faber and Faber, London.

CHAPTER TWO

Vineyard Establishment

E.W. BOEHM and B.G. COOMBE

A vine planting commits the land to a pattern of use for many decades. The cost of both establishment and maintenance are high and each can be significantly influenced by the choice of site, grape variety and planting design. Once these choices are made, subsequent changes are costly, if not impossible. About two-thirds of the annual cost of operating a vineyard under current practices is for labour and management. The rising cost of labour increases the need for more mechanization of vineyard operations, especially with plantings over 10 ha. Therefore, care must taken that the site and design of a vineyard do not preclude the possibility of mechanization in the future.

A comprehensive feasibility study is a necessary preliminary to any other step in vineyard establishment. The vineyard planner must be satisfied that the planting has a prospect of producing satisfactory crops that will be saleable at an adequate price for an adequate period. Furthermore, a lapse of three or more years between planting and the first return imposes a large initial interest burden on the investment.

Costs of establishment are higher with vineyards in cold regions — currently ranging up to tens of thousands A$ per hectare during the first three years. Similarly costs of production are higher in cold regions and yields are lower (due to wind damage, poor setting and more disease, etc.); it is found that annual production costs per tonne of grapes are up to ten times greater in cold regions compared with hot (D.M. Davidson, pers. comm.).

Mistakes made during establishment may prolong development and add significantly to the costs. A check-list of some of the topics that need to be considered are shown in Table 2.1.

2.1 Vineyard design

Aspects of vineyard site selection were considered in Volume 1, Chapter 10. Section 10.4 deals with water supply, climate, soil, diseases and pests and the indications that are provided by local vegetation (see also Volume 1, section 3.5.2). Other factors listed as being important to site selection are cost of land, proximity to labour and resources, proximity to markets, demonstrated performance, community aspects and special factors such as the possibility of bird

Table 2.1 A check-list of topics that need to be considered in establishing a vineyard

Land suitability — soils, slopes, aspect, depth, drainage. pH, fertility, exchangable sodium

Soil conservation problems?

Pollution problems?

Water availability — quantity and timing

Water quality — salinity, sodium absorption ratio, Fe

Irrigation layout?

Farm plan — survey

Varieties and areas — marketable?

Planting plan — blocks, planting units, rows

Trellis design

Pre-plant soil treatment — ripping, liming, gypsum, organic matter, mulch, hilling or banking

Trellis strainers and intermediate posts

Planting

Post-planting care — water, nutrients (including Zn and Fe), foliar sprays, pests and diseases

Training

---

damage. Davidson (1989) discusses these matters together with financial aspects of vineyard establishment. The question of choice of varieties was dealt with in Volume 1, Chapter 6 and also Section 10.6. We now consider the matter of developing a patch of land into a vineyard.

2.1.1 Initial planning

A site plan is invaluable, especially if it shows the location of fixtures and topographical features to which can be added contour lines, drainage lines, wind information and the location of water points. Aerial photographs and contour maps are ideal as a basis. Multiple copies give freedom to work up the final integrated plan. In addition to surface fixtures it is helpful to have a soil evaluation (see Volume 1, Chapter 3). A soil auger indication of the depth of the surface horizons provides a valuable check against the position of topographical features; also zones of poor drainage can be noted.

2.1.2 Roads, blocks and rows

The location of buildings, dams and water lines, power lines, roads and other non-vine items are related to the areas actually planted to grapevines by considering topography, workability, costs and aesthetics. Road location is an early decision taking account of the needs for vehicular access and surface topography with special emphasis on space for focus points such as sheds and collecting areas; all-weather, stabilized access roads should be established as soon as possible to avoid subsequent soil damage. Headlands around individual blocks need to be integrated with road location and guided by the needs for passage of vineyard machinery and vehicles; the widest machine and largest turning circle determine road and headland widths. Congestion of the site is a common mistake in vineyard planning. Difficulty in turning machines frequently requires either costly trellis re-alignment, or the continued inconvenience and extra cost involved in a cramped working area; a headland space of at least 8 m at trellis ends is recommended. The above decisions need to be developed and integrated together; some are matters of personal choice.

Irrigation design imposes a large over-riding constraint on vineyard design. In addition to requirements associated with water supply, headworks and main lines, each irrigation method has its own effect on the details of the vineyard plan. For example, furrow and flood irrigation demand specific slopes along rows which in turn affects roads and blocks. Efficient irrigation management requires the matching of irrigation units to areas of soil with uniform water-holding capacity. 'Travelling irrigators' require lanes 4 to 5 m wide. Refer to Chapter 6 for details of these requirements.

Sheds, preferably with lighting, are best located centrally and, if possible, on least valuable soil (due to frost proneness, low fertility, stoniness, etc.). For winegrape vineyards a paved area for loading is needed, particularly if a mobile crane or fork-lift is to be used; this is most frequently incorporated in the farm centre and workshop area but, if the room here is inadequate, special provision should be made. A washing-down area with collection sumps is a valuable facility (see Chapter 13). For raisin vineyards, drying racks are ideally positioned on an elevated, hot, dust-free site (see Chapter 14). For tablegrape vineyards, packing and storage sheds are required (see Chapter 15).

Blocks

Vineyards are divided into units or blocks, often of one variety per block to simplify cultural requirements. Mixing varieties within a block complicates those vineyard operations that have timing constraints, such as spraying and harvesting. The size of each block is determined by the tonnage desired of that particular lot of grapes (total tonnes = area by expected yield per unit area). The shape of each block is determined by roads and the general design features selected for the planting.

The allocation of varieties to specific blocks requires a balance of the properties of particular varieties against features of each block ('terroir'), e.g. soil fertility, aspect, frost risk, slope — these are considered in detail in Volume 1, Chapters 3, 4, 6, 7 and 10. This matter is particularly important where highest quality winegrapes are to be grown since special management details will be required for each parcel. It is best if one marketable unit, e.g. 20 tonnes of winegrapes, is grown within one patch of vineyard with uniform soil type and uniform viticultural practices.

Row length

Row length is an additional decision that interacts with the determination of block boundaries. With long rows, less machine time is lost in turning at each end. Some of this advantage in machine time is countered in greater exit time as, for instance, when a spraying rig runs empty just after entering a row. This aspect is particularly important for harvesting and carting out loads of grapes. For vineyard workers, long rows aggravate tedium; this can be lessened by painting trellis posts in a line across the rows at intervals of say 200 m. There is a length limit for the straining of wires: a strain of 200 m is generally considered to be maximal, but for this purpose a trellis anchor and a headland are not necessary; wires may be tied at an intermediate trellis post and the next strain continued from the other side. Row lengths of 400m can be used provided the topography and soil type are uniform along the rows.

If the vineyard is to be furrow-irrigated then row length is governed by the needs for irrigation efficiency (see Chapter 6).

Row orientation

Row orientation may be pre-determined by irrigation needs (see above), soil type and topography. With parallel and narrow strips of different soil types it is useful to orient rows to minimize the number of soil changes along the rows. Contouring is a special requirement, considered in the next section. On gentle slopes, with reasonably straight contour lines, straight rows across the slope achieve an adequate protection against soil erosion. On steep slopes, greater than 10%, it may be necessary to run rows up-and-down the slope to reduce the danger of equipment over-turning. In such cases careful soil management is absolutely essential to reduce water erosion (Figure 2.1); precautions include:
- herbicide weed kill in the row line rather than tillage
- avoid ripping
- mulching the row line
- mowing herbage in the inter-row area.

Figure 2.1 Severe gully erosion due to a heavy December rain during planting activities on a steep slope.

If efficiency of vineyard operations is the uppermost criterion then long rows should be selected; this is achieved by planning for long blocks then running the rows parallel to the longest side. Detailed consideration should also be given to the way in which the vineyard is to be worked, particularly how it will be harvested. Row orientation can have a considerable impact on the efficiency of work-flow. For instance, if a block is to be planted in line with another there

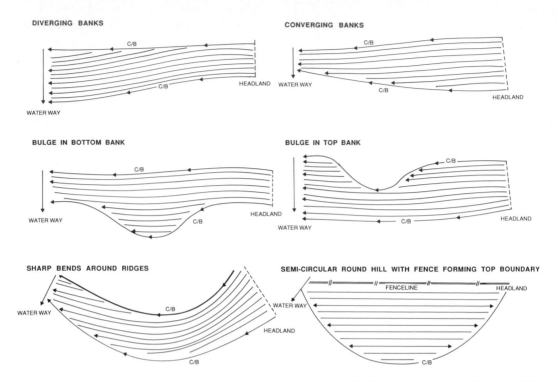

Figure 2.2 Six methods of pegging rows in relation to the check banks for contour vineyards under different circumstances (from Armstrong, 1980).

is an obvious advantage in matching the rows both in direction and spacing so that harvest and cultivation may eventually proceed across the headland which separates them and so reduce time for turning.

Row direction should preferably take account of its effects on canopy growth and micro-climate. North-south rows, by receiving morning sun on one side and afternoon on the other, are better displayed to maximize light interception; this effect is most apparent in spring and autumn and with narrow rows (Chapter 5). Against the advantage of best exposure to the sun it is found that, if the rows are oriented across the direction of the prevailing wind, foliage will blow to one side where it becomes fixed and will hamper machine harvesting and pruning. If canopies shift to one side, and thereby expose young berries to the sun, severe sunburn can result. This is less likely with rows that are parallel to the prevailing spring/summer winds. Such a direction is an advantage for speeding the drying out of a vineyard after rain where disease likelihood arises; for this effect the canopy needs to be 'ordered'

and with few leaves around the bunches (see Chapter 5). If warm air needs to be trapped between the rows, as in cool climates, then they should be at right angles to the wind.

2.1.3 Contouring
Since the advent of mechanical harvesting, and the adoption of grassing plus herbicide soil management , contour planting has lost favour. Nevertheless, if water erosion is at all likely, and if the slope of the land exceeds 10%, qualified advice should be sought on the advisability of contour planting and on the details of check-bank design and waterway and row positions (Armstrong 1974, 1980).

Check-banks are designed with a slight fall along the contour towards a waterway, at intervals down the slope (of about 40 m). It is important to adhere strictly to line; deviations may result in ponds of water which, if they break through the bank, can cause gullying. The initial marking may be done with any farm implement that leaves a visible furrow. At a convenient time a grader is used to build up a bank at least 50 cm high.

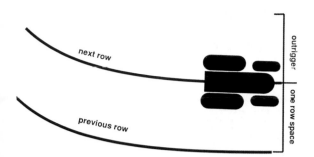

Figure 2.3 Diagram showing how contoured planting lines may be marked out.

Vine rows are marked in parallel between the check-banks, following a key line, which is usually at the top of one of the banks (Figure 2.2). Rows are marked using an out-rigger mounted on the front of a tractor. (Figure 2.3). Waterways should be graded so that water flows evenly across the whole width, then sown to a perennial grass, the commonest of which is rye grass (*Lolium* spp). Grading and paving may be necessary on roadways to give all-weather access.

Terracing by the construction of contoured walls, as used on steep land in parts of Europe, is rare in Australia; contour or near-contour plantings develop a degree of terracing because of the soil movement brought about by cultivation.

2.1.4 Density and spacing

Vine spacings throughout the world vary a great deal, with densities varying from as low as 500 per ha (e.g. 4 × 5 m) to as high as 50,000 per

ha (e.g. 0.4× 0.5 m); Table 2.2 illustrates the effect of row and vine spacing on vine number per ha. Spacing has generally been lower in Australian vineyards (e.g. 2,000 per ha) compared with European (usually between 3,000 and 10,000 per ha). This large difference is mainly attributable to differences in row widths — about 3.5 m in Australia versus 1 to 3 m in Europe. The tendency for wide rows in Australia, as in California, is explained by a number of factors: the lower cost of land relative to labour, the benefits of lower harvesting costs per tonne of grapes, and, above all, the use of the same wide tractors as used for agricultural crops.

During the 1970s the planting of vineyards in cooler regions of Australia brought with it an interest in denser plantings with rows between 2 and 3 m. A demonstration plot of 2 ha of Shiraz vines has recently been planted at Coonawarra, spaced at 0.75 × 1.5 m, to test the effect of high density on vine performance and wine quality (McCarthy 1988). European-style, upright trellises with narrow canopies and narrow or over-the-row tractors are being adopted in southerly areas. At the same time, an entirely different trend is developing in hot irrigated areas with the adoption of wider vine spacing in rows made possible by the high vigour of disease-free, clonal planting material, with vigorous rootstocks and better nutrition and irrigation (Possingham *et al.* 1990).

The choice of row spacing and vine spacing within the row is dictated by the costs weighed against the benefits over the life of the vineyard.

Table 2.2 Number of vines per hectare at different row and vine spacings*

Vine spacing (m)	Row spacing (m)				
	2.0	2.5	3.0	3.5	4.0
0.8	6250	5000	4167	3571	3125
1.0	5000	4000	3333	2857	2500
1.5	3333	2667	2222	1905	1667
2.0	2500	2000	1667	1429	1250
2.5	2000	1600	1333	1143	1000
3.0	1667	1333	1111	952	833

*Calculated by: 10,000 divided by (row spacing (m) × vine spacing (m))
To convert to 'vines per acre' divide by 2.47

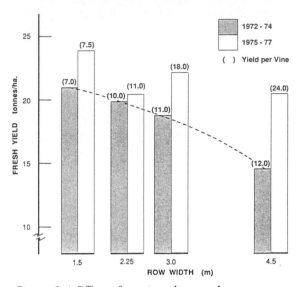

Figure 2.4 Effect of varying distance between rows on the early yields of Shiraz grapevines in Griffith, NSW (Hedberg and Raison 1982).

It is important to recognize that most establishment costs, e.g. ripping, planting, trellising, irrigation and training, are directly related to row length per ha and not vineyard area. This means that a decision to decrease row spacing from, say, 3.6 m to 3.0 m necessitates an increase of at least 20% in these costs. As well, there are many other costs e.g. pruning, harvesting and ground-spraying that are influenced as much by row length as surface area. All cost increases resulting from narrower row spacing must be justifiable and, in the absence of such justification, there is every reason for having vine rows spaced widely. Whatever the row space chosen, the benefits of having all rows of equal width, particularly within the one property, cannot be overemphasized.

Justifications for closer spacing are still being investigated, but the following points are relevant:

(i) the clearest benefit is the high early yields obtained with high density (Figure 2.4). McCarthy (1988) refers to a full crop in the third summer after planting with 8,888 vines per ha but not until the fifth summer with 1,633 vines per ha —such a difference has a large effect on cash flow;

(ii) dense plantings have a greater yield capacity due to the better spacing of shoots and a greater root density (Fisher and Pool 1988, Archer and Strauss 1989; the latter have shown that dense plantings use soil water faster);

(iii) the possibility of better winegrape quality (note that this benefit does not extend to raisins or tablegrapes); like all matters that affect wine quality this has not been extensively researched. A recent South African experiment showed that wine quality of Pinot Noir improved as density was raised from 9 m² per vine to 2 m² per vine (Archer and Strauss 1991). The authors comment on the probable variation of optimal spacing for optimal quality being dependent on soil fertility.

Crowding may increase the likelihood of disease development and there is a suggestion that fruit ripens earlier. Contrary to some opinions, problems of high vigour are not solved by increasing the vine density. On the contrary, to lessen shoot vigour, greater spacing is needed per vine using trellises that permit large numbers of shoots per vine, (presumably to raise the ratio of shoot number to root tip number on each individual plant — see section 5.4.1).

The spacing of vines within the row is determined by expected vine spread and cost. However, so far as cost is concerned, the effect of spacing along the row is not as significant as the spacing between the rows. Closer vine intervals directly affect the cost of planting and training, but, subsequently, the effect is minor. *The objective in within-row spacing is to achieve a regular dispersal of annual shoots along the trellis and to be assured of being able to maintain that distribution over the life of the vineyard.* With increasing trend to cordon-training, vine spacing becomes of decreasing importance. There are spacing differences dictated by the vigour of the shoots of different varieties (see Volume 1, Table 6.3 for a classification of vigour of grape varieties). Those that are vigorous, with long internodes, such as Sultana, Currant and Shiraz, should be spaced wider than less vigorous varieties of which Muscat Gordo is the extreme example (Figure 2.5); the same principle applies to invigorating rootstocks.

The choice of within-row spacing is also influenced by the style of pruning to be adopted. If to be cane-pruned from a vine head, the vines should be spaced so that 12-node canes coming from adjacent vines, when laid along the trellis wire, leave 10 to 15 cm between their ends. Closer spacing results in overlapping of the canes, tying is more difficult, and there is a clumping of foliage where the stronger, terminal growth arises from

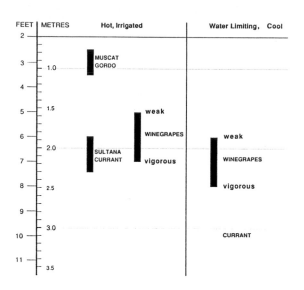

Figure 2.5 Ranges of within-row vine spacings currently used in Australian vineyards. Historically, spacings were wider than shown here.

the ends of the canes. If permanent cordons are to be established for spur pruning, care is needed that the spacing is not too wide lest spur positions are lost in later years producing gaps along the cordon.

If water is likely to be a limiting factor in a vineyard, vine spacings may be wide since the benefits from closer spacing cannot be exploited. If water is not limiting, yet for some reason vine vigour is expected to be lower than normal (due for example to nematode effects), then closer spacings within rows should be used; such has been the case with replanted vineyards unless nematode-tolerant rootstocks are used. Another incentive for closer spacing has been the expectation of die-back diseases, whatever the cause; greater vine density increases the chances of compensating for the loss of spur positions and maintaining the desired number and spacing of bearing buds.

The within-row spacings used in Australian vineyards are shown in Figure 2.5 and of the relationship between spacing and density in Table 2.1.

2.1.5 Windbreaks

Wind is a constant worry for grapegrowers in some regions as, indeed, for all horticulturists (Grace 1977). The damaging effects of wind are greatest during the establishment years, before the full canopies provide mutual protection. While all growers would like to gain some protection from wind, very few have been successful in devising inexpensive protection over broad areas.

Windbreaks, whether as physical barriers or as shelter belts of trees, reduce wind speed significantly both before and after the breaks. Wind speeds are reduced before the break for a distance equal to 10 times its height and after for a distance equal to 30 times its height (Figure 2.6). On the lee side of a moderately penetrable windbreak, wind speed may be reduced to ⅔, ½ and 1/5 of the unimpeded speed at distances of 5, 10 and 15 times the height of the break respectively. The degree of protection varies with the shape and density of the break. There is a danger of increased damage in areas where wind is accelerated as it swirls around the edge of a break (Caborn 1967).

Using the ratios quoted, and assuming a shelter belt 10 m tall, a break would be required every 200 m in the direction of the prevailing wind to reduce wind speed by 20% in the least protected areas. In a recent example (Anon. 1990), mechanical windbreaks were provided by a surrounding tall trellis of woven plastic cloth (Sarlon R) and internal breaks at every fifth row of a one metre strip of cloth at the top of the vine trellis. As a vineyard matures the need for internal protection decreases because of the large degree of self protection provided by the canopies of the mature vines; internal mechanical windbreaks could therefore be shifted to young plantings. However, the need for protection of edge vines still remains.

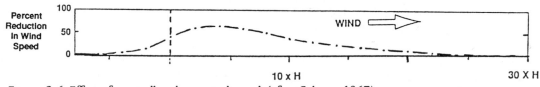

Figure 2.6 Effect of a windbreak on wind speed (after Caborn, 1967).

29

Against the benefits expected from windbreaks, it is necessary to weigh the following potential deficits:

- the productive value of the land allocated to the break
- the cost of establishing and maintaining the break
- the competition planted windbreaks give to adjacent vines (this could be reduced by watering the windbreak trees)
- the niche they provide for insect pests, particularly vine moth *Phalaenoides glycine*, and birds
- the obstruction to vineyard operations, particularly aerial spraying
- the possible increased frost hazard if the windbreak blocks the flow of cold air
- a possible increased disease incidence if the windbreak increases local humidity. The effects and financial benefits of windbreaks in vineyards are discussed by Ludvigsen (1989).

2.2 Preparation for planting

The nature of the soil and physiographic features influence the way in which a patch of land is prepared for planting. Special soil problems are best attended to before vines are planted (Sluggett and Adams 1989) particularly problems that entail the use of big machinery e.g. lime-slotting to adjust soil acidity (see Chapter 6, Kirchoff *et al.* 1991). In South African viticulture, elaborate soil preparation is recommended involving mixing, using a delve plough, and amelioration of the top 60 to 100cm of soil (van Zyl and van Huyssteen 1983).

2.2.1 Land new to vines

The first step in the preparation of a site for vine planting is the clearing of all trees, stones, old fences, wire and so on. There may sometimes be a reluctance to remove trees that have aesthetic value, but a decision to leave them is often regretted later; as well as competing with a surprisingly large area of vines, trees within or close to the edge of a vineyard are a harbour for vine moths and an obstacle for mechanization, especially aerial spraying. Isolated trees are of doubtful value as a windbreak. On the credit side, they may provide a habitat for predatory birds or a competing food source for bird pests, thereby lessening actual damage to the grape crop. Note

that some aspects of land clearing are subject to legislated control.

On some sites it may be necessary to grade waterways, a job which should preferably be done before vines are planted. Grading for flood or furrow irrigation must also be provided for at this initial stage.

Land which is timbered should be ripped after clearing to remove tree roots, which are not only an obstacle to subsequent planting and cultivating, but may also become a site for *Armillaria* spp., a fungal root-rot pathogen of vines. If heavy timber has grown on the site the land may have to be left for 12 to 24 months to allow settling where large stumps have been removed. The work required to clear a timbered site can be substantial.

As well as for the removal of tree roots, ripping may be necessary to break up a hard-pan or plough-sole in old cropping land. In the south-east of South Australia, the Uc6.13, Um6.24, Um6.43 and Uf5.31 soils (see Volume 1, 3.3.1) are underlain by limestone (calcarenite or calcrete) which is best broken up by ripping with heavy crawler tractors before planting. For these conditions a common practice is to peg out planting lines, then rip about 1 m deep along them. This operation raises limestone chunks which must be removed (e.g. by use of wind-rowing and rock-crushing equipment) before cultivation with a heavy disc plough. These operations are costly.

It has become common practice to rip along planting lines at shallower depths (40 to 50 cm) after pegging out, even when there is no general pan in the soil. Ripping establishes the planting line, removes unseen obstacles which may later be inconvenient in the vine row, and, in duplex soils, aerates the subsoil and traps moisture, thus encouraging better root development on the young vines. Ripping is done in the summer or autumn when the dry subsoil is more likely to be fractured; this effect is increased if the ripping tyne is fitted with a wing at say 85 cm depth. Following ripping, it is desirable to cultivate along the rip, e.g. with a rotary hoe, to reduce the rough surface to a tilth more amenable to the planting operations. Care should be taken to work in line so that the position of the rip, which is to be the future planting line, is not lost. Guidance of the ripper by laser beam helps maintain straight lines.

Ripping is not always advantageous. It may not improve root distribution, or, worse, may mix lower soil horizons that introduce toxic factors to the roots (e.g. boron). Ripping down slopes may aggravate erosion risks (Figure 2.1) and also produce underground 'mole-gullies'; the latter can be avoided by lifting the ripper out of the ground every 15-20 m thereby providing check barriers in any underground channel. Additional comments on up-and-down planting on hill slopes are made in 2.1.2 — row orientation.

The development of permanent planting banks by grading mid-row soil across to the planting line is being explored as a method of vineyard establishment. By this method the vineyard surface attains a serrated pattern with the vines elevated and the inter-row centre like a valley. The system has been used successfully for tree fruits such as apples and peaches.

Weeds in the planting line during the initial growing season of the new vines are detrimental to vineyard establishment Both translocated and pre-emergent herbicides have been valuable for reducing weed problems and have enabled minimization of cultivation. Nevertheless some tillage in addition to ripping is generally needed e.g. for rotary hoeing-in of lime or chicken manure and gypsum. In the case where irrigation is to be applied by furrow it will be necessary to work the interrow area into a tilth suitable for the formation of irrigation furrows at planting time. In other cases the inter-row may be left uncultivated for the winter and for the first growing season, provided there are no dangerous weeds present. High grass or other cover crops growing in this strip provides wind protection for the young vines and reduces wind blast from blowing sand; however, the possibility of increased frost risk should be watched. Perennial weeds such as convolvulus (Convolvulus arvensis), couch (Cynodon dactylon) and Johnson grass (Sorghum halepense), which are difficult to control amongst established vines, are best eliminated before planting, preferably before pegging out and ripping (see Chapter 8).

Land that has formerly grown vegetables, stone fruits, citrus or other crops may contain pests and diseases that might damage a new vineyard; these should be assessed and treated in the ways mentioned in 2.2.2.

2.2.2 Land formerly used for vines

Replanting of old vineyard land presents special problems additional to some of those mentioned above (2.2.1; Bakonyi 1988). When replanting is done in a designated 'irrigation district', the opportunity should be taken to review the irrigation and drainage design. It is desirable that any review take account of the whole vineyard even if only a part is to be replanted initially. A new co-ordinated design for both irrigation and drainage may incorporate irrigation and drainage methods that were unavailable originally.

Before any decision is made on varieties for replanting, the nematode status of the old vineyard should be assessed, especially if soil is sandy (Chapter 11). For such an examination, a nematologist needs to be provided with a soil sample. Fumigation of old vineyard land prior to replanting may also be recommended using such fumigants as DD or methyl bromide. This form of treatment has assumed greater significance since the nematode fumigant DCBP was deregistered and can no longer be used for fumigation in established vineyards. It must be remembered that nematodes on deep roots may not be killed by fumigation. There are examples in California's Napa Valley of virus-free, clonal vines planted on fumigated land formerly growing fanleaf infested vines, developing symptoms of this disease after about 5 years, presumably due to transmission by dagger nematode (Xiphinema index) of the disease persisting in old roots (see Chapter 11). The best long-term answer to nematode problems lies in the use of resistant rootstocks (see Volume 1, Chapter 9). However, the use of rootstocks adds appreciably to the cost of planting — present costs of grafted rootlings are 5 to 7 times those of ungrafted — a considerable input which must be accounted for.

The removal of the old vines involves cutting the trunks below the crown with a chain saw, then cutting the trellis wire and heaping tops and wires for burning . Finally the vine trunks are ripped out (with care to remove the least amount of soil) and heaped for burning using a small bulldozer.

From the viewpoint of improving the soil's fertility, it is desirable to leave the longest possible period between grubbing an old vineyard and replanting. This conflicts with the economic requirements which demand the loss of the fewest number of crops. Unless, grapegrowing is combined with some other enterprise for which the land can be used for a spell, the length of the period must be calculated by comparing the costs of delay with the benefits to the new planting. In infertile soils, spells from vines of up to five years may be beneficial, but such judgements are difficult to quantify.

2.3 Planting

It is most important that vines be planted in straight rows, not simply for the sake of appearance, but for efficiency in the subsequent mechanical operations. This is of increasing importance as more mechanization is applied to grapegrowing. Even with the curved rows of a contour planting it is still vital that the curves be smooth and regular. Row positions are surveyed and pegged. In some cases it is advantageous to put in the strainer posts before planting unless machine access is encumbered. If the planting is to be drip-irrigated the strainer posts and dripline support wires may be put in place before planting. This wire, combined with cross-rip lines, provides a very good base for planting and saves the time taken in shifting a planting wire after each row is planted.

Accuracy in vine spacing within the row is not as crucial as that between rows, but reasonable regularity is advantageous. Cross ripping at right angles to the vine rows along carefully pegged lines is one useful method. However, the most accurate is to use a planting wire prepared from a length of fence wire on which are fixed 'buttons' of solder at intervals equal to the vine spacing. The planting wire is stretched between the row ends with the first 'button' correctly located and then lightly tensioned as a planting guide. The vines are planted on the side of the wire away from the direction in which the wire will be moved to the next planting line.

2.3.1 Establishment by cuttings

The planting of rootlings is preferred over cuttings. However there are examples in Australia where, with careful management and good conditions, vineyards have been successfully established from cuttings; in fact, such vineyards may develop faster than those planted with rooted vines one year later. Favourable factors include warm, well-drained soil, good water and nutrient supply, freedom from weeds, pests and diseases, and use of callused cuttings (see 1.2.1).

The more usual outcome is an unacceptable percentage of failures with a consequent cost in replanting and a prolonged unevenness in the planting. The use of two cuttings at each vine site has been tried to increase the chances of success but, in the places where both cuttings take successfully, the unwanted vine is difficult to remove; it is more useful, and involves fewer cuttings, to use one per site and plant 30-50% cuttings in a nursery to provide fillers.

2.3.2 Planting of rootlings

Hand planting of grapevine rootlings is usually done with a spade. Louw and van Huyssteen (1992) recommend a square planting hole with rough (i.e. uneven and unsmeared) surfaces, large enough for roots to be spread out. The hole is refilled with the soil that was removed, and tamped lightly.

Alternatively, a dibber may be used if the roots are trimmed to about 10 cm, and the soil along the row is loosened to a depth of 30 to 40 cm by ripping; a useful dibber can be made from a D-type shovel handle pointed at its base. Where water is applied by furrow, vines are planted into the rip using either a spade or dibber, then water is run down the rip to consolidate the soil around the roots. At the same time, irrigation furrows are formed to continue the watering.

The water spear is a successful method of planting, commonly used in dry areas (Wall 1981a; Figure 2.7). The spear is made from 1 m of 18 mm galvanized iron water pipe fitted at one end with a jet system and, at the other, a T-handle and pistol grip valve which is, in turn, connected to a hose from the spray-rig behind the tractor. The tractor also carries the stock of rootlings to be planted, covered with wet bags. A planting team, consisting of tractor driver, two on spears and two planting, can plant 1 to 2 ha a day with this method. Under dry soil conditions this method has the advantage of supplying wet soil to set around the newly planted roots. On wet or heavy soils, care is needed to ensure that soil is back-filled around the roots, otherwise air pockets form and roots dehydrate. If the trellis has been installed prior to planting then very accurate vine placements can be achieved using spades or water spears.

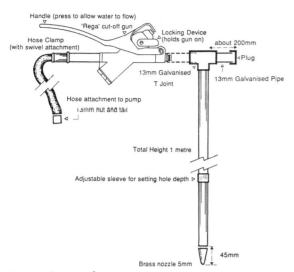

Figure 2.7 A planting spear.

Figure 2.8 A vine planter.

Planting by the use of explosives has been beneficial for fruit trees and might be useful in special circumstances for small vineyards. The materials required and the method of setting the charge are described by Gildare (1983) who refers also to the resultant benefits to root growth by the favoured physical and nutritional conditions in the root zone.

For large areas of new planting, it is desirable to acquire a vine planter fitted to the 3-point linkage of a tractor (Figure 2.8). (Note that trellising cannot precede machine-planting.) Various local engineering works in grapegrowing districts make suitable machines. A planting machine consists of a winged ripper to open up a furrow, behind which is mounted a seat for the operator and a box to hold the vines. Behind the planter are a pair of blades mounted on an angle to bank the edges of the burrow back onto the newly planted vine, and behind this again, on a hinged arm, a pair of motor car wheels, water-filled for weight, to run each side of the vine to press the soil down around it. On one side is mounted a third wheel selected with a circumference equal to the planting distance between vines. This wheel has, welded to the rim, a finger which strikes a bell at each revolution to indicate the planting spot. With care and straight driving, a regular planting can be made with such a machine. On a square planting, accuracy can be improved by cross ripping (as described above) and planting at the intersections. A vine planter is particularly useful for planting large areas of contoured vineyard where it is not possible to use sighters to locate vine positions; up to 4 hectares per day can be planted by a team of three men using a planter.

Roots are often trimmed before planting to facilitate the transport, storage and planting of rootlings. The use of a vine planter or water spear often requires quite severe root trimming. However, trimming removes stored reserves and could be detrimental (although scientific evidence for this is lacking). The best principle is to retain as much root as is commensurate with achieving a good spreading and spacing of the main roots since they are the basis of the future vine's structural root system (Figure 1.5). There have been examples of successful planting of untrimmed rootlings.

Vines on their own roots should be planted deeply, with roots pointing down, so that they are safe from damage during cultivation and slower to dry out between waterings; the sandier the soil the deeper should be the planting. When planting grafted vines, it is important to keep the graft union clear of the final undervine surface level to avoid root formation from the scion wood. It is important to take all possible means to protect the young vine from drying out from the time it is lifted from the nursery till it is finally watered into the planting hole since desiccation is the most likely cause of failure of a newly planted vine. For this reason, only two nodes should be left above the soil surface.

2.3.3 Timing of planting
Vines are usually planted in late winter and spring. The cuttings are kept dormant and non-

dehydrated, if necessary by cold storage of fungicide-treated (Chinosol R) bundles wrapped in plastic. Early establishment is desirable to maximize the length of the growing season and establish the biggest possible top on the vines before cool temperatures stop the growth. November to January are good development months. A disadvantage of early establishment is the shortening of the period when weed control can be most easily achieved by cultivating down the planting row. At this time of year weed growth is accelerating and there is considerable benefit from an extra few weeks with soil kept weed-free by the simpler methods available before vines are planted. Furthermore, soils become warmer and more favourable for root growth. On a poorly drained site, vines are prone to root rot if planted too long before growth commences. As a generalization, planting should commence in August on well-drained soil or later where drainage is poor; for best results, it should be completed by mid-September. However, if water supply and weed control are good, planting may be carried out as late as November/December (about grape-setting time), but with progressively diminishing success rate. Late planting reduces the length of the growing season for the young vines; if the planting is delayed it is preferable to leave the rootlings in cold storage (sealed and fungicided) for a further nine months and plant them the following spring.

2.4 Care of young vines

The period between planting of a new vineyard and the training of the vine frameworks is a difficult one. Inadequate attention to the young grapevine's water and nutrient requirements and to the detrimental effects of pests and weather extremes will prolong the establishment phase and thus increase establishment costs (Weste et al. 1979).

2.4.1 Irrigation and nutrition of young vines

The irrigation principles outlined in Chapter 6 apply also to young vines. However, adjustments are necessary to cater for the small, developing root system and the less robust nature of a plant adapting to its transplantation. In the early stages a young vine's root system occupies only a small part of the vineyard soil so a smaller amount of water is necessary. However, for the same reason, a young vine has a lower capacity to cope with hot, dry spells and therefore should be watered more frequently. In principle, the aim should be to keep moist all of the soil occupied by the roots, plus a safety margin. In the summer, and particularly during hot, dry periods, weekly watering is desirable if it is practicable.

The methods for frequent application of water to the discrete root-zone regions are dictated by water and land limitations: they include — furrows along the row, basins around one or a small group of vines, and drip irrigation; the latter has become a popular method. If all-over irrigation is the method used, attention needs to be given to the effects of the water applied to the non-vine area; a de-watering cereal crop may be needed.

A high level of mineral nutrition (along with water supply) is basic for good shoot growth in the establishment years. Fertilization of young vineyards differs from that used in mature vineyards (Chapter 9) in two ways:

(i) Heavy emphasis is placed on nitrogen; the high vigour resulting from high nitrogen is not the disadvantage it is in mature vines

(ii) restricted root distribution calls for localised fertilizer application.

It has become common practice to distribute a band of fertilizer into the planting furrow before vine planting. If this practice is adopted care must be taken to place the fertilizer deep enough to avoid burning by contact with young roots. Heavy dressings (1 tonne/ha) of superphosphate are frequently applied in this way. However, the method is not suitable for nitrogen because nitrogen is mobile and may be lost if placed at depth. Nitrogenous fertilizers are often applied as two or more side dressings beginning about November when root growth is active enough to withstand the resultant increase in osmotic pressure; care should be taken to avoid root burn in the first season. A young vineyard benefits from about 20 kg of nitrogen per hectare split into two to five small applications e.g. about 5 g (one heaped teaspoonful) of urea per vine. If vines are drip-irrigated, fertilizer can be applied through the system by injecting a concentrated solution at the control head. For very small plantings, urea, sulphate of ammonia or ammonium nitrate may be spread by hand along the row line; lumps of fertilizer may cause burning of the leaves of young vines. The need of young vines for micro-nutrients, especially zinc, should be considered (see Chapter 9).

2.4.2 Weed control

In the first growing season the young vine is particularly susceptible to weed competition. Adjacent weeds retard growth of the young vines either by competing for water and nutrients (dense grass clumps are particularly competitive) or by smothering the vine foliage. Removal of heavy weed growth close to the vines is expensive and inevitably results in the accidental loss of a proportion of vines. In the development of strategies against weeds it is useful to regard the soil of a young vineyard as having two territories: (i) the central inter-row areas (alleys), and (ii) a metre-wide strip along the vine rows. Weed growth between vine rows can be tolerated provided there is no frost risk; in fact, herbage growth of some sort is desirable if sand drift is likely during the summer months since sand can defoliate young vines in a high wind. Herbage also serves to dewater the inter-row space and permit traffic of vineyard machinery. By contrast, the space along the planting row should be weed free. Since soils are often too wet for cultivation at planting time it is necessary to begin weed control early in the winter using tillage or herbicide treatments (see also Chapter 8). The importance of early weed control in a new vine planting is paramount.

The recommended pre-emergent herbicides during the first two years (McCarthy 1981, Chapter 8) are napropamide (Devrinol®), oryzalin (Surflan®), oxyfluorfen (Goal®) and norflurazon (Solicam®) at specified rates. Trifluralin (Treflan®) is used as a preplanting treatment if weed pressure is heavy. These materials need to be mixed into the soil but, if the soil is wetted by rain or irrigation within 21 days, mechanical incorporation is then unnecessary. Where grasses are a problem, Fusilade® serves as a knockdown herbicide. Simazine® has been used as a pre-emergent herbicide on new plantings because it is cheap and does not need incorporation into the soil; however it can damage young vines, especially in sandy soils, and its use is not encouraged. Amitrol as an overall 'knockdown'

spray at 6-10 L per sprayed ha has been used as a 'rescue' treatment but it retards the young vines considerably.

Where herbicides are not used, early and frequent tillage along the planting line is needed to prevent weeds becoming a major problem. Tractor-mounted under-vine weeders with retractable arms are available for this purpose. A V-knife fitted to these machines is most useful in weed control in young vines. Such an implement works best if there is a slight bank (called 'berm' in USA) along the trellis line; this can be provided for at planting time. For small vineyards, and if labour is cheap and available, hand hoeing is an alternative.

2.4.3 Protection from environmental hazards and pests

Active shoots and leaves are a priority for good vineyard establishment and need to be protected. To be used legally, pesticides must be registered in each state; registration status is frequently modified and needs to be checked. For example, the pyrethroid alpha-cypermethrin has recently been registered in SA and will be available for use against cutworm, curculio, garden weevil, black beetle etc. Note that residue hazards are different in young, non-fruiting vines (see also 10.4).

Wind and water
The foliage of young vines, being low to the ground, is susceptible to damage from blown sand. Breakage of shoots and loss of leaves by wind jeopardizes the formation of the trunk and framework. It is desirable to develop herbage as a windbreak in the row centres. This may be volunteer, or planted as a covercrop; cereal rye (*Secale cereale*) serves well as a local windbreak. Planted cover crops have the added advantage of adding organic matter and lessening weed load.

Rabbits and hares
Chemical repellants or blood and bone are of limited use in deterring rabbits and hares from stripping the shoots off young vines. Trapping and poisoning may help but low electrified multi-wire fencing (1.8 mm) and boundary netting are the most effective methods. Effective control is particularly important in grafted vines because of the vulnerability of the scion growth. Be aware that birds and other animals may damage young vines.

Grasshoppers
A variety of grasshoppers (of which *Phaulacridium vittatum* and *Chortoicetes terminifera* are the most common) can be pests of vines in the initial years. Often they move in from neighbouring grass paddocks and it becomes necessary to spray a band at least 100 m wide around the vineyard using technical grade maldison at the rate of 0.55 L per sprayed ha. For spot spraying carbaryl, dimethoate or fenitrithion have been successful. A bait consisting of 42 mL of 50% maldison to 1 kg of dry bran, mixed and left overnight under polythene before scattering by hand or super spreader early next morning, is also useful against hoppers that are three parts grown (1 to 1.5 cm long).

Pink cutworm
The larva of pink cutworm, *Agrotis munda*, feeds from the edge of vine leaves to produce a smooth, scalloped feeding area. Larvae feed at night but during the day they may be found by scratching the surface of the soil within 25 cm of the base of the plant. One larva per plant is sufficient to retard growth. Young vines, especially those on sandy soils, should be monitored at least weekly from budburst until late December. Control should be started before 10% of young vines show symptoms. Pyrethroids prevent leaf feeding by pink cutworm when sprayed on the leaves, cane and soil at the base of the vine. If monitoring after spraying shows significant new damage, a second application may be necessary.

Curculio beetle, or apple weevil
Adults of curculio beetle, *Otiorhynchus cribricollis*, feed from the edge of vine leaves to produce a serrated feeding area. Like pink cutworms, they are night feeders and may be found during the day by scratching the surface of the soil. Densities in excess of about four adults per plant are sufficient to retard growth. The weevils are more likely to occur on heavier soils than sandy soils especially if formerly used for pasture. Monitoring and control is as for pink cutworm.

Garden weevil
Adults of garden weevil, *Phylctinus callosus*, produce feeding holes in vine leaves which appear as "shot holes" when feeding is intense. Adults feed at night but during the day they may be found sheltering under the bark of vines or in the litter

at the base of vines. Adults are flightless and must walk or be transported into a new vineyard. It is good practice to avoid planting near infested areas and carrying weevils on farm machinery. A weed-free or grassy fallow in the winter prior to planting helps break the life cycle. Monitor vines for damage during spring and summer. Pyrethroids will protect foliage against chewing for up to three weeks. Sprays applied at night are more likely to kill weevils by contact.

African black beetle
Adults of African black beetle, *Heteronychus arator*, chew the bark of young vines which may result in the sudden death of the vine. Adults may be found in soil at the base of vines. Vines are attacked by the summer generation of adults in January-February and need to be monitored for damage. Pyrethroids reduce damage but, since feeding may be underground, control by spraying may be difficult.

Bugs, vine moth and fungal disease
Several sap-sucking bugs, of which Rutherglen bug, *Nysius vinitor*, is the most common, cause wilted shoots. Like grasshoppers, these insects migrate from neighbouring pasture which may have to be sprayed as well as the vines to get control. Clean cultivation reduces this hazard.

Vine moth sometimes causes serious defoliation in autumn; for this carbaryl is effective.

Because of the small volume of growth in the first season the risk of damage by fungal disease is not great. At the same time the young vines have meagre reserves and may be badly stunted or even killed by an infection of downy mildew. Protective treatments may therefore be advisable if the risk of this disease is high; this is most likely in an area or season with frequent summer rains.

2.5 Training of young vines

Young vines are trained (Wall 1981b) by fashioning selected shoots into a predetermined framework. This framework provides the permanent structure on which are borne the nodes left after winter pruning which then give rise to the fruit-bearing shoots. The forming of a framework is difficult to describe in words. It is based on the art of choosing and fostering the growth of shoots that will become the frame, while suppressing or removing those which won't. The choices are

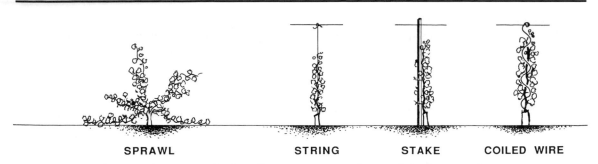

SPRAWL **STRING** **STAKE** **COILED WIRE**

Figure 2.9 Showing the systems for handling young vines during their first growth.

guided by the pruner's vision of the ultimate structure desired.

The types of framework are many and varied and are dealt with in the next chapter (Chapter 3); but basically each vine has a trunk leading to a head ('crown') with short side-arms or to cordons with extended side-arms (Figure 2.10, Figure 4.3). A great degree of flexibility is possible in the choice of framework shape, the chief limitation being the provision of a trellis structure. A framework may be enlarged readily at a later stage, but reduction is sometimes difficult. Errors and shortcuts in training have long-term detrimental effects that may be costly and difficult or impossible to correct at a later date.

The operations involved in achieving a particular framework are simple in theory but require care and patience in practice. They consist of a number of shoot manipulations: pruning and disbudding, directing and tying, and tipping or topping. These are 'hand' operations and involve attention to each vine at frequent intervals, as frequent as 1 - 2 weeks when growth is rapid. The application of these operations and the achievement of the desired shape is easier if the vine-to-vine variation is small and shoot growth is vigorous; hence the importance of the cultural practices outlined above (Section 2.4). Decisions

about training need to be made early in the planning of a vineyard and integrated with all of the other factors mentioned in this chapter. Once decided, vineyard operations are directed towards the achievement of the chosen shape (Chapter 3).

2.5.1 Formation of the trunk

At planting, grapevine rootlings are generally pruned to two or more nodes above ground level. Most of these buds are likely to burst and produce a shoot. Two methods of forming the trunk are in use, as shown in Fig. 2.9. Firstly, vines may be left to 'sprawl' during the first growing season. During the next winter, the strongest shoot is pruned to two nodes and all other buds are removed. The trunk is then formed from the best shoot that develops during the second season of growth. With weak vines, the procedure may even have to be repeated and the trunk formed in the third season. Secondly, the trunk may be formed in the season of planting; this is possible only with vines that grow for a sufficient length of time during the first 'leaf'. Objective comparisons are lacking to test whether vines trained by one or the other method differ in the size of their early crops or in long-term performance. Thus, the decision to form a trunk in the first season will

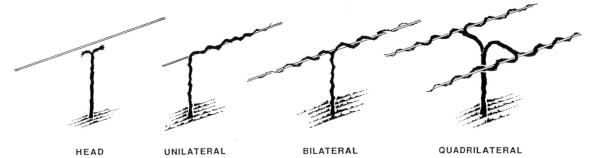

HEAD **UNILATERAL** **BILATERAL** **QUADRILATERAL**

Figure 2.10 Some framework forms used for the training of grapevines.

depend on whether growth is sufficiently vigorous and whether the trellising cost can be met beforehand and the labour input maintained. These early costs will be offset somewhat by the earlier cash return if the cropping is hastened. Success depends on having a large proportion of trunks formed together in the one season.

It is advantageous to have trunks straight, vertical and in-line. The shoot chosen for the formation of the trunk is usually the most vigorous provided its position and direction of growth is acceptable. The selected shoot is straightened vertically by twining it around a taut string or tying it to a support (a wooden or steel stake) or through a helically coiled wire (Figure 2.9). The string method is the most common method in Australian vineyards; to avoid 'strangling', the lower end of the string is tied to a dead (disbudded) spur and the upper to a wire. This may be the support-wire, a permanent foliage-wire or a temporarily placed training-wire (for T-trellis); it needs to be installed before the time of 'stringing'. If a drip-line support wire is installed before planting, the bottom of the string can be tied to it rather than to the vine. During tying, the strings are tensioned by slightly depressing the wire. Modern tying twine is a light-weight, degradable polymer.

The health of the growing point of the selected shoot is important for the success of trunk formation; this shoot should attain most of its length growth in 8-12 weeks. The higher the temperature the greater the length of internodes and hence shoots. Frequent attention is needed to ensure adequate water and nutrients and lack of damage or competition from wind, pests and weeds. Once the shoot has attained some flexibility it is wound on to its support and the laterals are regularly removed; the main leaves are kept. If the tip is damaged, removal of all but the terminal lateral helps the re-establishment of a new dominant apex.

Intriguing results have been obtained recently with the use of 'growing tubes' of translucent plastic set around the buds of the rootling's spurs (Gro-guard®, Due 1990). Stem growth is rapid and straight giving erect trunks without the need for tying; this type of performance is found even in water-stressed conditions indicating the favourable micro-environment for the shoot within the tube.

When the shoot has extended beyond the point of formation of the head or cordon it is topped to encourage bifurcation by the use of lateral shoots which are let develop at the apical two nodes.

The second node below the apical node, left after topping, becomes the crotch. Its height above ground level remains constant provided all lower internodes have completed elongation at the time of topping; this is the factor determining the earliest time topping can be done. The crotch needs to be 15 cm or more below the wire. The longer the 'internodes' (shoots more vigorous) the more important is the choice of topping position. A crotch close to the wire is more prone to splitting under fruit load later. It can also create problems with mechanical harvesting and pruning if the cordons grow over the top of the wire as they thicken.

Where a strong lateral develops without topping at the appropriate height the main shoot may be bent over and attached to the wire as one arm with the lateral as the other. Shoots developing too slowly during the first season to form mature laterals are not topped but cut to length during winter and the side-arms arise from the uppermost dormant buds; a greater amount of disbudding and deshooting are required in such a circumstance.

There is a wide variation in the time spent in training vines but as a guide it can be expected the attachment of strings will take about 6 hours per 1000 vines and the subsequent training during one season will occupy another 20 hours per 1000 vines.

2.5.2 Bush vines

The squat, vase- or goblet-shaped bush vine was common in Australian vineyards before the 1950s but is now rare because of the lower productivity and the operation and mechan-ization difficulties it presents. The system is still used in southern Europe. Each trunk is formed without the aid of a stake or twine and hence is kept short, say 20 cm, to maintain an upright, wind-resisting form. By shoot topping in summer and careful selection of spurs at winter pruning a vase shape of short bifurcating/radial arms is achieved over a number of years (Figure 2.11).

2.5.3 Formation of the head of head-trained vines

Head-trained vines may be developed to carry spurs or canes. Those which carry spurs are not common in Australia — cordons are generally preferred for spur pruning. Many cane-pruned systems are based on a head-trained framework (although again, cordons can serve this purpose); 'Sultana' has been the main example.

Such vines are formed by forking the supported trunk, at the height selected, into two or more short arms originating from lateral or latent buds forced into growth by summer or winter pruning (Figure 2.11). Vines trained to a head and pruned to spurs are mainly found in situations where growth is slow. The training of such vines is likely to extend over two or three seasons. If three to six arms are to be created per vine these are placed at about the same height and spread evenly around the trunk. Thus, not all can be formed from shoots developing from buds of the trunk; some proximal buds of these shoots have to be forced into growth

either during summer by tipping (and thus forcing laterals) or by winter pruning. Once the vines carry sufficient numbers of appropriately placed, mature shoots the arms are selected, pruned to a uniform height above ground and the remaining shoots are removed. At least the two uppermost buds of each arm are likely to produce shoots during the following season. Depending on the level of pruning to be adopted (see Chapter 4) the distal or both shoots are made into spurs and all other shoots are removed entirely during the next winter-pruning.

Head-trained vines carrying canes are also provided with arms, however, the arms are placed in the plane of the row only. They thus divert from the trunk in the form of a fan. Initially, each arm will carry one cane, but may carry more in later seasons. The shoots originating from the uppermost buds of the trunk may become the canes of the following season. However, it is useful to tip these shoots when young at the point where they reach the wire to ensure the development

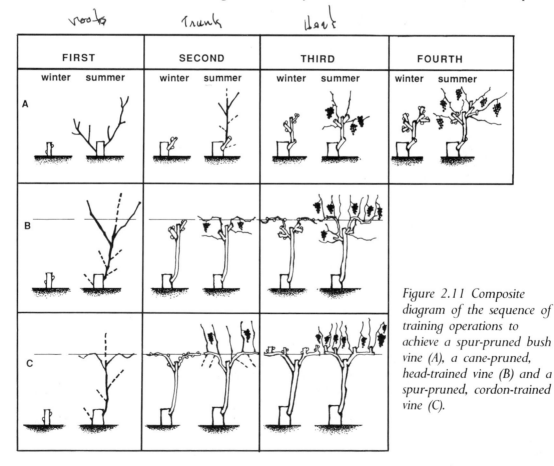

Figure 2.11 Composite diagram of the sequence of training operations to achieve a spur-pruned bush vine (A), a cane-pruned, head-trained vine (B) and a spur-pruned, cordon-trained vine (C).

of a mature lateral that can be cut to a spur during winter. Its buds will produce properly placed canes for the next winter-pruning.

2.5.4 Formation of cordons

Cordons are elongated, horizontal, permanent arms extending over the length of row allotted to the vine and carrying permanent, evenly-spaced, mainly upward-pointing side-arms that give rise to the annual fruiting-wood (generally spurs but canes are also possible) (Figure 2.11). In Australia, they usually are arranged in bilateral fashion, i.e. one cordon each on either side of the trunk along the length of the row (Figure 2.10); high bilateral cordons are also used for minimally-pruned vines (MPCT, Possingham *et al.* 1990). Mechanically-pruned vines are based upon this system; however, depending on the training method, the vines may carry from one to four cordons.

Generally, shoots selected to form cordons develop from the upper two nodes of the shortened trunk-shoot, i.e. at a height of 10-20 cm below the support-wire. They correspond therefore in their position and in the season of their formation to the arms of head-trained vines. Only strong shoots should be selected to form arms. Others are removed except for well-placed 'back-up' spurs designed to provide a replacement cordon if the original is damaged. The chosen shoots are lightly twisted along the cordon wire as they grow, to prevent wind damage. When they have extended beyond the space allotted to them by say 30-50 cm they are topped back to their specified length. Unilateral cordons may be useful in windy areas with the cordon directed away from prevailing winds.

The training during the following season determines the final form of the cordon. To keep it straight and to avoid breakage of the wire in later seasons it should be unwrapped and re-attached to the support-wire. The canes must carry sufficient numbers of upward-pointing shoots to ensure the proper spacing of the side-arms to which they give rise and which should be 15-20 cm apart. All shoots arising on the lower side of the canes are rubbed off at an early stage of their development. Downward shoots are selected for GDC training. Canes having gaps in the appropriate sequence of shoots due to the failure

of buds to burst (e.g. excessively long canes required by wide vine spacing) should be cut off beyond a strong shoot that is used to continue the developing cordon during the following season. Reducing the length of this cane and forming the cordon in stages will also lead to side-arms of uniform size and position. The shoots must be prevented from trailing under their own weight or from being blown sideways by the prevailing winds; otherwise, a misshapen vine with a bent trunk will result. To avoid this, at least some shoots of each vine may have to be attached to a permanently or temporarily placed foliage-wire. Without this the cordon may twist and grow upside-down.

The training of the cordon is completed during the following winter by establishing the side-arms. Only the shoots chosen to provide these arms are left on the cordons; they are pruned to two nodes. During this season, the first sizable crop will be produced even though some fruit may have been present during the preceding seasons. Care has to be taken to prevent excessive cropping due to light pruning during the formative years of the vine.

2.6 Concluding remarks

The establishment phase of a vineyard is a time of planning for the commitment of land, finance and time in a long-term and expensive enterprise. Decisions made during this phase are difficult to redress later. Success depends on the accuracy of the assessment of the resources at hand, and the wisdom of the decisions based on this assessment and on the judgement of the future trends. Profitability of the enterprise during the establishment phase is greatly dependent on the skill with which the vines are developed to their first big crop. Key factors are good genetic material, good soil conditions, water and nutrient supply and an abscence of pest effects.

Recommended reading

Boehm, E.W. (1971) Vineyard establishment. Sth. Aust. Dept. Agric. Special Bull. No. 1/71.

Winkler, A.J., Cook, J.A., Kliewer, W.M. and Lider, L.A. (1974) General Viticulture. Jacaranda Press.

Other references

Anon. (1990) Windbreak helps vineyard. Aust. Grapegrower and Winemaker 315, 27.

Archer, E. and Strauss, H.C. (1989) The effect of plant spacing on the water status of soil and grapevines. S. Afr. J. Enol. Vitic. 10, 49-58.

Archer, E. and Strauss, H.C. (1991) The effect of vine spacing on the vegetative and reproductive performance of *Vitis vinifera* L. (cv Pinot noir). S. Afr. J. Enol. Vitic. 12, 70-6.

Armstrong, F.W. (1974) Contoured vineyard development, Barossa Ranges, S.A. Leaflet No. 4020, S.A. Dept. Agric.

Armstrong, F.W. (1980) Pegging planting vines in contoured vineyards. Aust. Grapegrower & Winemaker, No. 197, 6.

Bakonyi, I. (1988) A guide to replanting winegrapes in the Riverland. S. A. Dept. of Agric., Murraylands Region.

Caborn, J.M. (1967) Shelter Belts and Microclimates. Dept. of For., University of Edinburgh, Bull. 29.

Davidson, D. (1989) Decision-making in vineyard establishment. Aust. N.Z. Wine Industry J. 4, 290-293.

Due, G. (1990) The use of polypropylene shelters in grapevine establishment - a preliminary trial. Aust. Grapegrower and Winemaker No. 316, 29-33.

Fisher, K.H. and Pool, R.M. (1988) Interaction between morphology and row and vine spacing effects on growth and yield of two grapevine cultivars. Proc. 2nd. Int. Cool Climate Vitic. and Oenol. Symp. N.Z. Soc. for Vitic. Oenol., Auckland, N.Z., 169-171.

Gildare, W.P. (1983) Better growth using explosives - by the A.G. method. Aust. Horticulture 81, 86-88.

Grace, J. (1977) Plant Response to Wind. Academic Press, London.

Hedberg, P. and Raison, M. (1982) Effect of vine spacing and trellising on yield and fruit quality of 'Shiraz'. Amer. J. Enol. Vitic. 33, 20-33.

Kirchhof, G., Blackwell, J. and Smart, R.E. (1991) Growth of vineyard roots into segmentally ameliorated acidic subsoils. 'Development in Plants and Soil Sciences', Kluwer Academic Publishers, Dordrecht, The Netherlands. In press.

Louw, P.J.E. and van Huysteen, L. (1992) The effect of planting holes on the root distribution of grapevines Aust. Grapegrower and Winemaker No. 340, 7-15.

Ludvigsen, K. (1989) Windbreaks — some considerations. Aust. Grapegrower and Winemaker, No 302, 20-22.

McCarthy, M.G. (1981) Chemical weed control in new non-irrigated vineyards. S.A. Dept. Agric. Fact sheet 11/81, Agdex 241/682.

McCarthy, M.G. (1988) Evaluation of a high density vineyard planting. Proc. 2nd. Int. Cool Climate Vitic. and Oenol. Symp., N.Z. Soc. for Vitic. Oenol., Auckland, N.Z., 172-173.

Possingham, J.V., Clingeleffer, P.R. and Cooper, A.M. (1990) Vine management techniques for the wine industry. Aust. Grapegrower and Winemaker No. 316, 85-89.

Sluggett, T. and Adams, T. (1989) Survey soil before developing or upgrading vineyards. Aust. Grapegrower and Winemaker No. 311, 32-33

Van Zyl, J.L. and Van Huyssteen, L. (1984). Soil and water management for optimum grape yield and quality under conditions of limited or no irrigation. Proc. 5th Aust. Wine Industry Tech. Conf., Perth, 1983.Aust. Wine Research Inst., Glen Osmond. 25-66.

Wall, R. (1981a) A water jet for planting vines. Vic Dept. of Agric. Agnote 1635/81, Agdex 241/21.

Wall, R. (1981b) Training young vines. Vic Dept. of Agric. Agnote 1646/81, Agdex 241/ 23.

Weste, H., Leamon, K. and Cadman, R. (1979) Care of young vines. Vic Dept. of Agric. Agnote 121/79, Agdex 241/20.

CHAPTER THREE

Training and Trellising

B.M. FREEMAN, E. TASSIE and M.D. REBBECHI

Grapevines, in the wild, are climbing plants, supporting their weak but twining stems by the action of tendrils on their annual shoots attaching to other plants and trees. Annual shoots vary hugely in length, occasionally reaching 10 m length in one summer. This ability is seen even in present day 'regulated' vineyards where occasional 'bull canes' are found, generally arising from the shaded parts of the vine. Most grapevines evolved in woodlands where they dominated the crowns of trees. Trees are still utilized for support in some grapegrowing areas in Europe but grape harvesting is difficult because most of the fruit is produced at the top of the tree due to apical dominance of the annual shoots.

Grapevines were domesticated from genetic material originating in the Caucasus and elsewhere. The natural growth habit of the vines was initially not exploited; rather, vines were trained along the ground or to a self-supporting vase or goblet shape; for this purpose short trunks were needed. In most cases vines have been trained using support systems, initially of stakes, later of posts and wire. The constant search for profitability and performance of vineyards has led to the development of a great variety of trellis forms.

Training is the design and development of a grapevine framework. A *trellis* is the structure that largely supports the framework. *Pruning* is the cutting away of a portion of the annual vegetative growth to maintain a desired number and spacing of nodes per vine. Training is strategic and pruning is tactical for the purpose of achieving a particular vine arrangement. The first section of this chapter concerns the principles behind the design of grapevine frameworks and supporting structures.

3.1 Principles of training and trellising

A trellised vine is one with an elongated trunk of varying length with either cordons or canes trained onto a support system. In some vineyards, vines are trained but not trellised, for example, head-trained, free-standing vines. Grapevines are not self-supporting when young and, if not trellised, inadequate grapevine training will limit grape production for several years until the trunk can support more shoots and fruit.

The basic aims of grapevine training and trellising are:

1. to maximize production;
2. to facilitate cultural operations in the vineyard—i.e. spraying, tillage, pruning, harvesting;

3. to improve canopy microclimate, to reduce disease incidence and optimize the quantity and quality of production;
4. to support the mechanical load of the grapevine.

The quantity and quality of the fruit will depend on the integration of trellising with initial grapevine training, canopy management and pruning (see Chapters 4 and 5). Because vineyards are long-term and usually trellised only once, the initial choice of a trellis system is a critical one; alterations are sometimes expensive. The management of vineyards is continually changing and this imposes different demands upon the trellis system. For example, mechanical harvesting requires high trellis systems and some vineyards with a low trellis have had to be retrained to accommodate the machines.

The major factors to be considered in selecting a trellis system are:
1. Simplicity; simple trellis systems are often the most economically viable but may restrict yield and quality.
2. Vine growth factors; the balance between vine vigour and capacity which influences yield and grape quality.
3. Economic factors; the cost-benefits of the more expensive trellis systems must be considered.
4. Environmental factors; temperature, rainfall, topography, soil, wind and potential frost risk.

These factors help determine the height and complexity of the trellis, e.g. the choice of a single wire trellis as compared with a more complex multi-wired system using foliage control. In a large-scale mechanized vineyard a simple, inexpensive and easily managed trellis may be the most appropriate system.

3.1.1 Vine vigour, capacity and yield
The function of the trellis is to support the vine to achieve an optimum production that is dependent on the capacity and vigour of the vine. *Capacity* is the productivity of the whole vine and *vigour* is the growth rate of its shoots.

Vine capacity, which is ultimately linked to the root contribution, often determines the choice of a trellis system. A simple training system is sufficient for a vineyard with low vine capacity: here there is no advantage in having a complex trellis system. Vines producing less than 1 kg of prunings per metre of row are unlikely to be more

productive on a complex trellis. Vineyards with a single cordon and narrow row spacing may be as productive as vines with a wide row spacing and a wide T-trellis (Hedberg and Raison 1982). However, vines with excess vigour, i.e. long shoots, extensive lateral growth and hence shading problems, indicate the need for a more extensive trellis system to permit retention of more nodes. Complex trellis systems have been developed in Australia, USA, France and New Zealand to accommodate high vine vigour (Shaulis et al. 1966, Coombe 1975, Carbonneau and Huglin 1982, van den Ende 1984, Smart and Smith 1988). However, devigoration may be achieved by minimal pruning or by reducing root contribution by, for example, the use of sod culture.

The ability of the trellis to accommodate the vine's capacity and vigour determines the microclimate and associated effects on photosynthesis and fruitfulness. Shading inside a dense canopy, e.g. in a vigorous vine on a simple trellis system, reduces fruitfulness and photosynthetic capacity. Choice of trellis system to optimize yield is one of a number of canopy management techniques available to the vineyard manager. The choice of an appropriate trellis system for a given vineyard situation is discussed in Chapter 5.

3.1.2 Trellis height
Trellis height is an important design criterion in the choice of a trellis system. The observation by Busby (1825) that 'from the dwarf vine, pruned to within a few inches, to that which overtops the elm to which it clings for support, there is every variety in the height of vines' is still relevant. All variations of trellis height exist today from low vines to overhead arbour systems. Modern vineyards depend on many mechanized practices, some of which, e.g. harvesters, determine the maximum height of a trellis.

Vines have been trained close to the ground in regions where extra heat was needed to ripen grapes and lower acid levels. This practice increases the risk of frost damage in spring. Higher yields may be produced on a higher trellis (Table 3.1). Some authors (e.g. Pongracz 1978) suggest that trunks longer than 1.4 m result in reduced fruitfulness, yield and drought tolerance. However, vines trained on overhead arbours are among the

Table 3.1 Summary of yield response to change in trellis.

Trellis change	% yield increase	Variety	Reference
Increase in trellis height (increase in height of fruiting wire(s))			
1.0 m to 1.4 m[a]	3	Chenin Blanc	Kasimatis *et al.* 1982
1.0 m to 1.5 m[b]	7	Sultana	May *et al.* 1973
1.4 m to 1.7 m[a]	No significant response	Crouchen	May *et al.* 1976
1.4 m to 1.9 m[a]	5 to 9	Concord	Shaulis *et al.* 1953
1.4 m to 2.0 m[a]	20	Sultana	Weaver and Kasimatis 1975, Weaver *et al.* 1984
Increase in trellis width (increase in width between fruiting wires)			
Single wire to 0.8 m T[c]	21	Sultana	Kasimatis *et al.* 1975
Single wire to 1.2 m T	26	Sultana	Weaver *et al.* 1984
0.3 m T to 1.5 m T	35	Sultana	May *et al.* 1973
0.9 m T to 2.25 m T	23	Shiraz	Hedberg and Raison 1982
Canopy division			
Single wire to GDC[d]	30 to 90	Concord	Shaulis *et al.* 1966
VSP[e] to Scott Henry	Up to 30	Various	Wood *et al.* 1989
VSP[e] to TK2T[f]	26 to 120	Various	Smart *et al.* 1990

a Single wire trellis   b 0.3 m T-trellis   c Plus foliage T   d Geneva Double Curtain
e Vertical shoot positioned   f Te Kauwhata Two Tier
Source: P.R. Dry, pers. comm.

most productive in the world and yields of 100 tonnes per hectare have been reported from South America and Israel.

Light interception increases as trellis height increases. Smart (1973) calculated that light interception is maximized on tall, closely-spaced, north-to-south rows. At very close row spacings, however, a high trellis will shade the base of the adjacent row, especially at high latitudes. Thus latitude is a factor influencing the choice of combination of row spacing and trellis height; for much of Australia, trellis height should not exceed row width (Smart 1973).

Hand pruning and harvesting of excessively high or low vines may cause worker fatigue. Optimal fruiting wire height for these practices appears to be in the range of 1.1 to 1.4 m; this is also suitable for mechanical harvesting.

3.1.3 Shoot orientation

Shoot orientation influences vine growth and yield. May (1966) found that vines trellised close to the ground with the shoots trained vertically upward were more vigorous, had a higher bud fruitfulness, and produced larger inflorescence primordia than vines with shoots trained horizontally. Downward-training of Cabernet Sauvignon shoots reduced shoot vigour, leaf size, internode length, lateral leaf number and dormant shoot weight compared with horizontal or upwardly-trained shoots (Kliewer *et al.* 1989). Upwardly-trained shoots flowered later but the bunches matured earlier compared with downwardly-trained shoots: this was attributed to the reduced leaf area of the latter. Hence a trellis system that trains shoots vertically upward has the effect of increasing shoot vigour and potential yield. Note however that an excess of shoot vigour may increase canopy density which may reduce yield and grape quality because the renewal area is at the bottom of the canopy and is most shaded.

Foliage wires help guide shoots upwards. With low to moderate capacity vines this may improve light interception by the whole vine. A 10% increase in yield was obtained in response to the use of a single foliage wire (Turkington 1978). High cordons are necessary for some training systems such as Hanging Canes (Sylvoz) to allow sufficient space for the canes and shoots to hang down. With wide T-trellises, standard tractors and row spacing may present a problem for machinery access. This has been overcome by increasing trellis height and shielding tractor wheels or by the use of low and narrow tractors.

3.1.4 Mechanization constraints

In pre-tractor days vine rows only needed 1 m space to allow for the passage of people and draught animals. With the introduction of tractors to Australian vineyards, row spacing had to be increased to allow their passage between rows. The constraints imposed by machine size and design, especially of tractors, have been a major determinant of vineyard and trellis design. Indeed the development of machines for harvesting and pruning during the last two decades has led to several major changes in spacing and trellis design.

Mechanical harvesters require a certain trellis design and the three major types of harvesters currently in use have different requirements (see Chapter 13.3.3). The horizontal impactor is adapted to a single wire or narrow T (< 0.3 m), the vertical impactor to the wide flexible T-trellis, and the pulsator harvester to a single wire with flexible vines. Most current commercial machines are unable to harvest bunches that are lower than 40 cm or higher than 1.75 m from the ground. The canes or cordons should preferably be at least 0.7 m from the ground as some bunches will hang 0.3 m below the fruiting wire. This distance varies with variety, internode length, cane angle and bunch length.

The increasing use of mechanical pruning in vineyards is another factor to be considered. The first machines were capable of pruning simple, single-wire systems. With the development of spring-loaded saws and sets of multiple cutter blades it is now possible to mechanically prune trellis systems with double cordons and/or foliage wires (Chapter 4).

3.1.5 Environmental factors

Environmental factors such as temperature, rainfall and soil type influence vine vigour and capacity and, in turn, the choice of trellis system. Very fertile sites encourage vigorous growth which requires a more complex trellis and other management strategies to balance vine growth.

Topographical factors may influence trellis type: at the bottom of slopes a higher trellis may reduce frost risk. In exposed, windy sites one or more foliage wires may be desirable to reduce shoot breakage and the rolling of the canopy to the lee side and consequent risk of sunburn damage to the berries.

A high canopy can improve air movement, reduce canopy humidity, and hasten the drying of the foliage after rain or overhead irrigation. A well-displayed canopy will also improve the effectiveness of fungicide spraying, and reduce possible disease incidence.

3.1.6 Economic considerations

There must be a balance between the potential benefits that can be obtained from trellis systems and their cost. Comparisons carried out in New Zealand with the standard vertical single cordon system (with foliage control) and two divided systems — Te Kauwhata Two Tier (TK2T) and Scott Henry (SH) — showed the yield advantages of the two divided systems (Table 3.1; Wood *et al.* 1989). Higher establishment costs of these divided systems result from extra wire and training costs. In addition, greater management expertise is required to instruct workers in the training of vines on more complex trellis systems. On the other hand, a simple trellis may be adequate in potentially high vigour sites if the shoot-devigorating characteristic of minimal pruning is used. It is necessary to assess the benefits and costs of new trellis systems.

3.2 Vine support systems

3.2.1 Evolution of support systems in Australia

Trellis systems have evolved in Australia from bush vines to quite sophisticated and complex systems. Most early plantings were bush vines. With increasing availability of trellis wire at the turn of the century and the replacement of horses and cross-ploughing with tractors in the 1920s, many vines were trellised to a low single fruiting wire at 0.6 m or less (virtually bush vines with a wire to support the canes). The wires are known as *fruiting* wires when they support the fruiting units, i.e. canes, or the cordons. *Foliage* wires were introduced later to support the foliage, either as a single wire or paired wires where the foliage is positioned between them. Additional fruiting wire and/or foliage wires were added, 0.2–0.3 m apart, particularly in irrigated vineyards.

In the 1950s the trellis height was generally increased, often to 0.9–1 m and then even up to 1.6 m. The reasons for these progressive changes were the greater ease of working and the yield response; increased yield with increased height (3.1.2). Higher trellises were also favoured with the introduction of mechanical harvesting and in frost-prone areas.

The *narrow T* —fruiting wires 0.3–0.45 m apart—were introduced in the 1960s and sometimes also had a foliage wire 0.3 m above the T. This change resulted in a slight yield response, and had the advantage of increasing the node number per vine on hand pruned vines. However, with the introduction of mechanical

pruning and harvesting it was more difficult to manage than the single wire.

The *wide T* —0.9–1.2 m wide—was also introduced at this time, primarily in the Riverland and Sunraysia districts. From the 1970s, flexible wide tees suitable for the vertical impactor harvester were installed, e.g. Waikerie and Padthaway. Advantages of the wider T were the greater yield response and better fruit recovery from the vertical impactor compared with the horizontal impactor harvester. More recently, flexible wide tees have fallen out of favour due to high maintenance cost.

Vertical trellises were also introduced in the 1960s and were either a 2 wire vertical (i.e. 2 fruiting wires for canes or 1 fruiting plus 1 foliage wire) or a 3 wire vertical system (2 fruiting wires and 1 foliage wire). A narrow fixed foliage T was sometimes used. The use of movable pairs of foliage wires for shoot positioning increased in the mid 1970s, particularly in cool climates and new vineyards. Vertical shoot-positioned trellises had advantages of improved canopies, better disease control, improved machinery access in narrow row vineyards, and facilitation of summer pruning operations. With the ongoing advances in technology, they are also suitable for mechanized pruning or harvest operations.

Divided canopy trellises, e.g. Geneva Double Curtain, Lyre or U, Scott Henry, Te Kauwhata Two Tier and Ruakura Twin Two Tier, started to be introduced in the mid 1970s but were developed in the 1980s. Their commercial use currently represents only a small percentage of trellised vineyards in Australia. The advantages of these trellises, discussed more fully in Chapter 5, are a large yield response with improved canopy management options, disease control and wine quality.

Minimal pruning and *hanging cane* systems both utilize higher single wire trellises; the former was introduced to large vineyards in the early 1980s.

3.2.2 Description of some support systems

Support systems can be classified according to their simplicity, use of foliage wires and orientation in space; they will be considered under the names by which they are commonly known; in Table 3.2 these names are classified into six groups according to specific training features.

Table 3.2 Classification of grapevine training systems according to the number and arrangement of trellis wires

Training feature	System name
No wire	Bush Staked
One wire	Single wire Hanging Cane Minimal Pruning
Multi-wire, vertical	Two-wire vertical Vertical shoot-positioned Vertical, divided - Te Kauwhata Two Tier - Scott Henry
Multi-wire, horizontal	T-trellis - narrow - wide Divided, flexible, e.g. duplex Divided, rigid - Geneva Double Curtain - U- or lyre - Ruakura Twin Two Tier
Multi-wire, sloping	Sloping
Multi-wire, overhead	Overhead

Bush (free-standing) vines

This is the oldest and least expensive system: it is still common in southern Europe and was originally most common in South Australia. The vines are trained to be self-supporting and are kept low. The low cost is offset by the low production, especially in the early years, as it takes many years to train the vines. The vines are usually spur-pruned and called 'bush vines' or 'goblets' (Figures 3.1a, 4.5), but they may be cane-pruned by tying the canes together to form a 'basket'. In the first year a single two-node spur is retained close to the ground, in some cases as low as 0.1 m. In the following years the crown of the vine is gradually increased to 0.3-0.5 m. By the fourth year it should be possible to have 5-6 two-node bearers that are distributed around the trunk.

The advantage of this system is that the vines are close to the ground and receive heat radiated from the soil, leading to earlier ripening in cool climates; in warm climates this could be a disadvantage. The system permits cross cultivation for weed control but with modern cultivation equipment and herbicides this is no longer needed. A major disadvantage of this system with wide rows is the small proportion of the vineyard

surface that is typically covered by the vine canopy, and hence low production. Surprisingly, bush vines deplete the soil moisture more rapidly than trellised vines because of increased airflow over the exposed canopies and increased soil evaporation (van Zyl and van Huyssteen 1980).

Staked vines

Staking represents an improvement over free-standing vines in that they can be higher above the ground and more readily pruned. The system was adopted widely in California but not in Australia. Vines are trained to form a crown 20-30 cm above the ground and 2-4 canes of about 8 nodes are fixed to the stake (Figure 3.1b). Alternatively, the vines are spur-pruned without a distinct crown but with bearers radiating from the trunk in the shape of a wagon wheel. The vines have a trunk 0.8-1.0 m high which is supported by a stake (usually 5 × 5 cm wood) driven into the ground next to the vine. These vines still have the disadvantage of a non-continuous row of foliage and a lower yield potential. Both self-supporting and staked vines are rarely planted in modern Australian vineyards, but some can still be found in Rutherglen, Barossa

Figure 3.1 Freestanding, staked and single wire systems.
a. A typical bush or goblet vine, head trained and spur pruned.
b. A staked vine, head trained and cane pruned.
c. A single-wire system, cordon trained and spur pruned.
d. A single-wire system, head trained and cane pruned.
e. A 'Hanging Cane' system—cordon trained with cane
   pruning (canes untied).

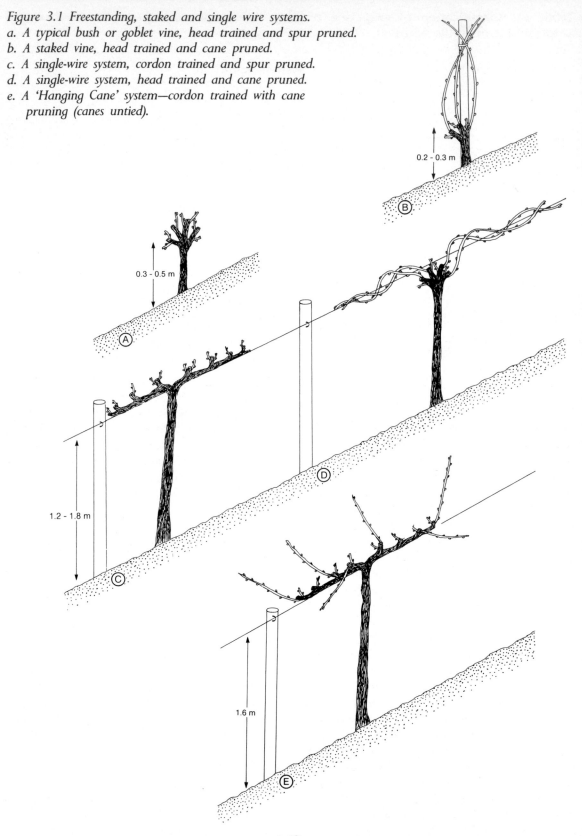

Valley and Southern Vales; there are large plantings in Europe (Spain, Portugal, southern France and Italy), South Africa and California.

Single wire

The simple single wire system has been extensively used in Australian vineyards (Figure 4.6). It has the advantage over bush vines of forming a continuous row of foliage and is relatively inexpensive to install and train. Similarly, in California the system has been widely adopted as a yield-increasing variant of the staking system. Initially, bush vines were often retrained onto a low single wire at about 0.3 m. In recent years however the wire height has been raised up to between 1.0 and 1.8 m to facilitate efficient mechanical harvesting and pruning, with the added advantage of decreased frost risk. Increase in trellis height of 1 m or less generally results in a yield increase of 12% or less (Kliewer 1982). This response is probably due to the greater interception of radiation as canopy height is increased. Smart (1973) showed that about 12% more light would be intercepted by exterior parts of canopies at 2 m height than at 1 m when the row spacing was 4 m.

Grapevines on single wire trellises can be cordon trained and spur pruned or head trained and cane pruned (Figure 3.1c and d). In Australia, a typical trellis would have intermediate posts every 3 to 5 vines, spaced 5 to 8 m apart depending on anticipated yield, wind strength, soil type and trellis height. Treated posts of 50-75 mm diameter, 1.7 m out of the ground, 0.4 m into the ground and spaced 8 m apart can support a crop of 25 t/ha. An alternative system is to have a stake, either of wood or galvanized steel, at each vine; the vine trunk is trained to each stake by tying (hence this may be more labour demanding than wrapping around a vertical string—see 2.5.1). Staked vines have straight trunks and low cordon sag. Rows with intermediate posts require stronger end assemblies than rows with staked vines.

Cordon-trained vines usually have the trunk divided 15 cm below the wire and a permanent cordon established. Head-trained vines have a crown established below the wire and usually between two and four canes of 10 to 15 nodes wrapped or fixed to the wire with two to four 2-node replacement spurs (see 2.5 for training). In spring when the shoots have developed there

is a tendency for the young cordons (or canes on cane-pruned vines) to roll so that the shoots hang down and the fruit may sunburn. This has led to the adoption of multiple wire trellis systems with a foliage wire to catch the shoots and stop the cordon or canes from rolling over.

Hanging cane

This is an adaptation of the Italian Sylvoz system. It has a permanent cordon at 1.6 m with 6 to 8 canes of 8 to 15 nodes spaced along the cordon that are left to hang down (Figure 3.1e). This spreads out the canopy and has the potential to increase the node number. Replacement spurs for each cane may also be maintained to supply replacement wood the following year. In the original Italian version of Sylvoz, the canes are tied to an additional wire at about 0.4 m below the cordon wire; there are 3 foliage wires above the fruiting wire to support the replacement wood that arises from the replacement spurs (one per cane). In the Friuli region of Italy, this system (known as Friuli or Casarsa) is much simplified and the canes are merely left hanging, as in the Australian version, known as Hanging Canes (Clingeleffer 1983). The cordon wire must be sufficiently high e.g. 1.5m to allow the canes to hang down and create a fruiting zone that can be mechanically harvested and permit other cultural operations.

Minimal pruning

In warm to hot regions, e.g. Riverland, a single wire at 1.5 to 2.0 m is often employed; in cool and/or windy regions, two wires, one at 1.2 to 1.4 m and the other at 1.6 to 1.8 m may be used (Clingeleffer 1989, Possingham et al. 1990). The cordon trained vines are either left unpruned or are skirted at the sides in winter and/or summer (see 4.7.3, Figure 4.13). Adequate trellis height is required due to the reliance of the system on mechanical harvesting and the extended fruit zone. Yields can be regulated by summer or winter skirting or by thinning the crop in midsummer with a mechanical harvester.

Multi-wired, vertical

Additional wires are used in some trellises to either add another fruiting wire or to position or catch the foliage. Multi-wired trellis systems vary from

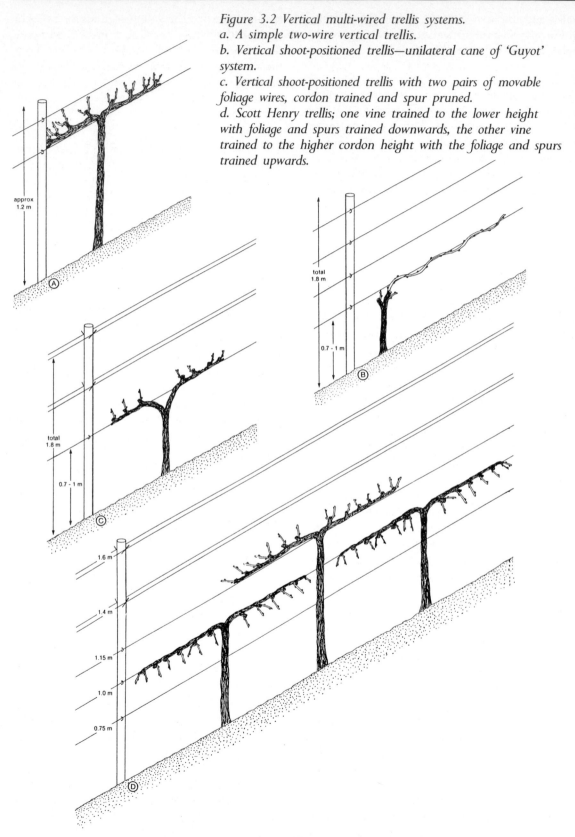

Figure 3.2 Vertical multi-wired trellis systems.
a. A simple two-wire vertical trellis.
b. Vertical shoot-positioned trellis—unilateral cane of 'Guyot' system.
c. Vertical shoot-positioned trellis with two pairs of movable foliage wires, cordon trained and spur pruned.
d. Scott Henry trellis; one vine trained to the lower height with foliage and spurs trained downwards, the other vine trained to the higher cordon height with the foliage and spurs trained upwards.

a single foliage wire to more complex systems with movable foliage wires. Foliage wires can be single or paired, moveable or fixed. Single foliage wires are often added above the fruiting wire to prevent wind damage or canopy rolling. Paired foliage wires are used to contain the foliage into a vertical curtain so as to improve light penetration and canopy shape and density.

Two-wire, vertical

The two-wire vertical is the most basic form of multi-wired trellis systems and is widely used throughout Australia. It consists of a single fruiting wire with a single foliage wire 0.3-0.5 m above (Figure 3.2a). The distance between the fruiting and foliage wire depends on the variety and environment. If the foliage wire is too high above the fruiting wire then most shoots will not become attached and may therefore 'droop'. If the foliage wire is too close to the fruiting wire the vine will grow above the foliage wire, especially a variety with long internodes such as Sauvignon Blanc when spur-pruned. If the foliage wire can hold up the shoots this will facilitate mechanical harvesting; however mechanical pruning may be more difficult as many canes become attached to the foliage wire by tendrils and do not fall to the ground. Pruning machines with spring-loaded saws that can prune up to and around posts are now available and other machines with multiple cutting blades can actually cut in between the foliage wires (Chapter 4).

In some cordon-trained vineyards, canes are fixed to a higher fruiting wire to increase the node number per vine. These canes are sometimes left to develop into a permanent cordon, but this is an undesirable practice as the upper cordon may shade out and devigorate the lower cordon. It is preferable to develop high and low cordons on alternate vines.

Vertical trellis systems with two bilateral cordons displaced vertically are found in some vineyards. If the cordons are close together (<0.3m vertically) the shoots from the lower cordon intermingle with those from the upper forming a single canopy. There are some examples where the system has been reasonably successful, usually where shoots are separated by virtue of adequate spacing between the cordons and the

'attitude' and length of the shoots. Generally, however, it is an inferior training method.

Vertical shoot-positioned

Systems with movable foliage wires have been developed to train the shoots into a narrow vertical canopy as is common in Europe. These trellis systems can be either cane-pruned (as in traditional Guyot; Figure 3.2b) or spur-pruned on unilateral or bilateral cordons (Figure 3.2c) with the fruiting wire at 0.7-1.0 m height (either single or double like a narrow T trellis) (Figure 3.2c). They may have either single fixed or pairs of foliage wires that may be dropped below the fruiting wire in winter. As the shoots grow in spring, wires are lifted up and attached to hooks at successive heights on either side of the posts. Hence, the shoots are retained in a narrow vertical canopy (Figure 3.2c). Up to 6 foliage wires can be used and the shoots may be trimmed at the top of the trellis above the top pair of foliage wires. Alternatively, shoots can be rolled over the top wire instead of being trimmed as practised in Italy, where the shoots are also often positioned before tying with twine and only fixed foliage wires are used. They are all suitable for narrow rows.

The *Guyot* system is one of the oldest examples, originating in France and now also used in Italy and in cool regions in Australia. It is a unilateral cane pruned system with a replacement spur. Variations of this include the double Guyot (bilateral) and arched cane system, which increase the node number per vine from the basic 14-20.

The standard New Zealand trellis also uses a vertical shoot positioned bilateral system with mostly cane pruning. The cane pruned version generally has four arms, i.e. two fruiting wires displaced horizontally 0.2 m apart with four canes of about 12 buds and 4, 2-node replacement spurs. Spur pruned versions usually have only 1 fruiting wire (Figure 3.2c).

With low to moderate vigour vines, vertical shoot-positioned trellises produce an efficient, well-exposed canopy. Since upward-growing shoots are more vigorous there is the possibility of poor setting. With high vigour vines the canopy may be too dense and leaf removal may be required to improve bunch exposure and reduce disease incidence (Chapter 5).

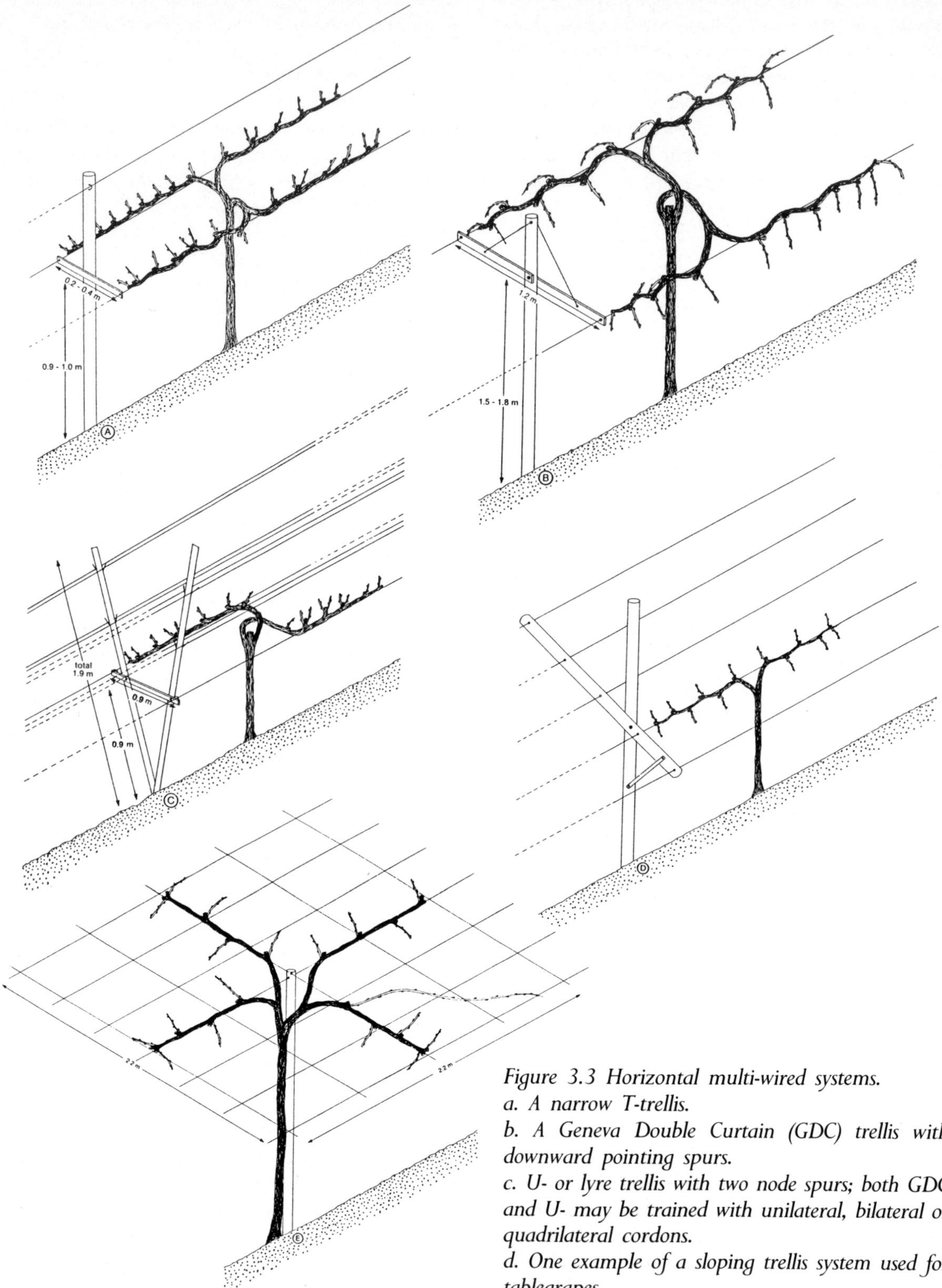

Figure 3.3 Horizontal multi-wired systems.
a. A narrow T-trellis.
b. A Geneva Double Curtain (GDC) trellis with downward pointing spurs.
c. U- or lyre trellis with two node spurs; both GDC and U- may be trained with unilateral, bilateral or quadrilateral cordons.
d. One example of a sloping trellis system used for tablegrapes.
e. Arbour or overhead trellis.

Vertical, divided

Vertical division of shoot positioned trellises into two distinct canopies produces a less dense canopy with concomitant advantages (Chapter 5).

Te Kauwhata Two Tier (TK2T)

The TK2T system was developed in New Zealand to overcome the problems of a dense canopy found with the standard vertical trellis (see 5.4.1.b). It consists of two vertically separated spur-pruned cordons, the first at a height of 0.4 m, the second at 1.2 m. Each curtain is trained upwards with two pairs of foliage wires, and is trimmed to 10-12 nodes with a gap of 0.2 m maintained between the two. Alternate vines are trained to different heights, but there may be maturity differences between the two cordons. Mechanical pruning and harvesting are possible.

Scott Henry

The Scott Henry system was developed in Oregon and promoted in New Zealand (Chapter 5). It also has two fruiting wires, one at 1.0 and the other at 1.15 m. The shoots on the higher wire are trained up between two pairs of foliage wires and the bottom foliage is turned downwards generally using one foliage wire (Figure 3.2d). The system can be spur- or cane-pruned (the former mechanically) and harvested by machine. Maturity differences are less obvious between the two levels than with the TK2T. Improved yield and decreased disease incidence have been recorded in these two divided systems over the standard New Zealand non-divided trellis and are attributed to a decrease in canopy density (Wood et al. 1989). The Scott Henry trellis has been adopted in some newer vineyards of Australia.

Multi-wired, horizontal

These trellises generally require wide rows, i.e. 3 m or more.

Single fruiting wire with foliage T

The foliage T was added above a simple fruiting wire to extend the canopy, increasing exposure to sunlight but avoiding excessive bunch exposure. However, canopy density is generally excessive with moderately vigorous vines. This system is not widespread in Australia but very popular in California.

T-trellis

T-trellises were developed so that more nodes could be retained at pruning, thus reducing the problems that develop in excessively dense canopies when single wire trellises are pruned lightly. A T-trellis has a horizontal cross-arm at each post which supports two fruiting wires (Figure 3.3a).

Narrow T-trellis

A narrow T-trellis has the fruiting wires 0.3-0.5 m apart at a height of 0.9-1 m. The crown of the vine is usually formed 0.15 m below the fruiting wires. A narrow T-trellis can increase yield by 7-11% compared with vines on a single wire trellis (Lyon and Walters 1941, Peterson et al. 1974). The yield increase is due to an increase in node number and hence bunch number; ripening is not necessarily delayed (Peterson et al. 1974). Foliage wires above the fruiting wires can support and spread the canopy. In some cases this has increased the yield (Turkington 1978) but in others there was no response (Baldwin et al. 1979). The narrow T-trellis does not divide the canopy into two separate canopies because the shoots tend to bridge across the T-trellis; mechanical pruning and harvesting are difficult because the shoots and bunches between the two wires are not very accessible. The yield increase is relatively small, and since the development of the wide T-trellis in the 1960s, the narrow T-trellis has not been favoured.

Wide T-trellis

The beneficial effect of increasing canopy width on yield by the use of fruiting wires separated by 0.9-1.2 m has been shown in many situations (Table 3.1). The trellis has traditionally not been shoot positioned and foliage tends to bridge the gap between wires. Vines with more than 1 kg of pruning wood per m of row can be expected to increase yields by up to 40% if converted from a single wire to a wide T (May et al. 1973, Turkington 1978). The increased yield is mainly due to an increase in vine capacity and number of nodes retained at pruning and not due to an increase in bud fruitfulness. The total amount of light intercepted by the wide T canopy is undoubtedly greater than the single wire canopy and would account for the increase in growth (Kliewer 1982). Despite the potential yield benefit, the fixed wide T-trellis has not been widely used in Australia. Until recenty, it was almost impossible to harvest by machine. The development of the 'combo head' harvester has made this trellis a more viable proposition (Botting and Dry 1989).

Divided, flexible
The Duplex trellis

The Duplex system, which is a variant of the wide T-trellis, was developed in California specifically for the vertical impactor harvester (Olmo *et al.* 1968, 13.3.4). The system was so named because the crop is produced on canes attached to the fruiting wires and the replacement canes are produced from the head of the vine. The machine harvester action requires flexible fruiting wires achieved by a combination of cane pruning and flexible T-piece. The latter is commonly constructed from flexible steel strapping and short wooden stays, but other materials have been used.

This trellis system was introduced to Australian vineyards along with the vertical impactor harvester in the 1970s and large areas were established, particularly in the Riverland, Sunraysia, MIA and Padthaway regions. Today, this harvesting method is rarely used and in many vineyards the flexible T-trellis has been either converted to another trellis type or it has become effectively a fixed wide T as the vines have been converted to cordon training and spur pruning (usually by machine). High costs of trellis repair and hand cane pruning have led to the virtual demise of this system. Most of the 'combo head' harvesting in Australia is done on converted duplex trellis (Botting and Dry 1989).

Divided, rigid
Geneva Double Curtain (GDC)

GDC is another variant of a wide T-trellis but with a divided canopy. It was developed in New York State, USA (Shaulis *et al.* 1966). The original work with Concord (*V. labrusca*) showed the beneficial effects of splitting the canopy of a wide T-trellis into two separate curtains of foliage thereby increasing budburst, bud fruitfulness and crop yields (Table 3.1). The improvement in yield per node has been shown to be mainly due to the improvement of the solar radiation environment in the vicinity of the renewal nodes (Kliewer 1982). Similar responses to GDC have been shown with *V. vinifera* varieties in many countries.

Training to GDC has generally increased yield by 30 to 90% for both *V. labrusca* and *V. vinifera* varieties (Kliewer 1982).

The GDC has fruiting wires 1-1.2 m apart and 1.5-1.8 m above the ground (Figure 3.3b). This height enables tractor wheels to pass under the cordons. The vines are cordon-trained and pruned to long, downward-pointing spurs. Shoots are positioned downwards—for *V. labrusca* varieties this can be achieved by hand or by mechanical brushing but for *V. vinifera* varieties with their more erect growth habit the use of movable foliage wires is often essential. Downward shoot positioning reduces shoot vigour and promotes exposure of renewal nodes and bunches. This system requires wide rows and can be mechanically pruned and harvested. The largest area of GDC in the world is found in northern Italy (Baldini 1982). The present area in Australia is small. The fixed wide-T can be readily converted at low cost by the introduction of shoot positioning.

U- or Lyre trellis

The U (lyre) system was developed in France (Carbonneau *et al.* 1978). It is a horizontally divided trellis with cordons at a height of 0.5-0.7 m preferably spaced 0.9 m apart to gain most advantage of the division (Figure 3.3c). The slightly inclined walls of foliage are shoot positioned upwards with 2 or 3 pairs of foliage wires and trimmed to about 15 nodes. This system can be established by using a square configuration and cross bars or by using two sloping posts that permit free passage in the centre of the trellis for trimming and foliage wire positionings. The lyre trellis has been shown to improve productivity and wine quality over non-divided shaded canopies (Carbonneau and Huglin 1982). It can be mechanically pruned and in France a suitable harvester has been developed. In Australia this trellis has been introduced to a few vineyards, mainly in cool regions.

Ruakura Twin Two Tier (RT2T)

The RT2T trellis was developed in New Zealand for high vigour sites (Smart and Smith 1988). It is a horizontal division of the vertically divided trellises—TK2T or Scott Henry—to create 4 discrete walls of foliage. With a row width of 3.6 m and a horizontal canopy spacing of 1.8 m, the RT2T has the same canopy configuration as the

TK2T or Scott Henry but a greater bud load per vine than those systems (Chapter 5). It is under trial in a limited number of sites in Australia.

Multi-wired sloping trellis

The most commonly used example of a sloping trellis relies on placement of the shoots along a sloping series of wires at 45° to 60° to the horizontal (Figure 3.3d). The aim is to maximize light interception by increasing the surface area of the canopy. Bunches hang freely below the foliage and are protected from too direct sun exposure. The slanting/sloping T-trellis, Y-trellis and factory-roof trellis are examples of this type and are mainly used for tablegrapes in Australia (see 12.1.3, Figure 12.2).

The *Link trellis* is an experimental modification of the sloping trellis that arranges the fruiting canes along a wire set above the cordons to promote apical dominance and hence more even budburst (Coombe 1975). Then, at flowering, the canes are lowered to bring the inflorescences below the canopy which promotes better fruitset; by this practice yields of 65 t/ha have been obtained.

The *Tatura trellis* developed for fruit trees has also been evaluated for winegrapes (van den Ende 1984). Grapevines planted at densities of 2,222 and 4,444 per ha were trained in a 60° V shape with 6 permanent cordons on each 2.6 m long arm of the V. Yields of 44 t/ha were produced due to the high population of evenly spaced shoots. The concept has not been developed commercially because of the high costs of trellis and training and the dominance of the top cordons over the lower cordons. The original design has been modified to overcome some of these problems (R.E. Smart, unpublished data).

The *swing-arm trellis* (Clingeleffer and May 1981) was designed for harvest pruning and trellis drying of Sultana vines. Two arms 90 cm long are attached to the post for the permanent cordon. The canes from the horizontal arm are removed and then the arms rotated so the vertical shoots become the horizontal fruit bearing canes for the following season. The 'Irymple trellis' (Gould and Whiting 1987) and the 'Ivan Shaw trellis' are similar (see also 14.7.1).

In north-eastern Italy the so-called 'pergola' is the most common form of sloping trellis (in Australia this term is used for flat, overhead trellises—see arbour trellises). The Italian single pergola is used on sloping sites and the double pergola on high vigour sites on valley floors; these structures resemble a 'saw-tooth' roof.

Multi-wire, overhead

The principle with overhead systems (arbour/pergola) is to have a complete cover of foliage at least 2 m above the ground (Figure 3.3e). All equipment can pass below the canopy and during the growing season the ground is shaded by the foliage canopy. This system is very productive and commercial yields of more than 100 t/ha have been achieved in Chile. In southern Italy a special design called the 'tendone' is used both for tablegrapes and winegrapes. The high cost of erecting and maintaining arbour trellises has precluded their use in Australia other than for tablegrapes, notably Ohanez (See Figure 12.1).

3.2.3 Training or re-training to different trellis systems

Establishment of trellis systems may require specific training after the initial formation of the trunk, head or cordon as described in Chapter 2, section 5. Basic principles of cane handling are used to establish the required trunk height and number of cordons. When changing from one trellis system to another, the conversion may require use of canes (including watershoots) from the head and extending them as required. With old established cordons it may be better to remove the old wood back to the crown and re-establish new ones in the required positions with appropriately placed canes. Treatment of large pruning cuts to avoid *Eutypa* infection is recommended (see 11.1.4).

Single wire systems
Training.

This is the simplest trellis for grapevines. The trunk is trained to a height just below the wire and the canes trained out along the wire for the establishment of the permanent cordons or, in the next year, are pruned to new canes thus establishing the head (4.7.1). Permanent cordons may be established in one or more seasons depending on vine capacity and the ability to establish spur positions at desired intervals along the cordon. For minimally pruned vines with two wires, a cordon is established on the lower wire and canes are subsequently wrapped onto the upper wire to provide a strong framework with cordons at two levels.

Re-training.
Conversion of old bush vines to a single wire trellis has been widely practised in Australia. Such vines were initially trained to low wires at about 0.3 m but are now being raised to higher wires, often using two canes to form two cordons or a new head. Conversion to minimal pruning is relatively simple, with the establishment of a single wire above the existing trellis. A typical conversion may take two or three seasons, depending on the nature of the original trellis. In the first year, as many strong canes as possible are lifted up from the crown area and tightly wrapped around the new wire.

Vertical systems
Training.
Simple two-wire vertical trellises require no special training. Non-divided shoot-positioned trellises, either spur or cane pruned, require the establishment of a cordon lower than in a single wire, non shoot-positioned system. Vertically divided trellises such as Scott Henry require training of cordons/head at two heights. The preferred system is to have alternate vines trained to two different heights rather than one vine at two heights. With the former method, each cordon spans two vine spaces. Downward-pointing spurs have proven useful on the lower cordon.

Retraining.
Methods of changing other systems to a Scott Henry system depend on the height of the old cordons and the flexibility and age of the vine. In relatively young vines it may be possible to lift the cordon of every other vine 0.15 m above its former position and then extend all cordons to meet along the main wires; a requirement for this is that cordon height is at 1 m and there is 0.8 m height above the cordon for foliage wires. In retraining, sufficient height of the posts and thus the supporting wires is necessary; for this, posts may need to be extended. The conversion of trellises to divided- and shoot-positioned trellises may become more popular with the introduction of machines that can position foliage by either tying it up or raising it and securing with pairs of foliage wires.

Horizontal trellis systems
Training.
T-trellis systems are established by division of the trunk to the two fruiting wires during the first year of training, given adequate vigour. For spur pruning, cordons are then taken along the two wires to become established, generally by the second year of training (unless vigour is low). For the establishment of T-trellis, GDC, or U-systems the vines may be trained to have either two cordons (Figure 3.3c) or four cordons (Figure 3.3a, b).

For any horizontal system, alternate vines can be trained to one side and then divided along the training wire to form a bilateral cordon.

Retraining.
From a single wire trellis, canes are taken across to form an additional cordon, or the old cordons are removed and new ones are established. Alternatively, alternate vines may be trained to opposite cordons, forming a 'V' along the planting line.

3.3 Structural aspects of trellising

A vine trellis is a structure having to support large and various loads. It is usually a significant expense during establishment of a vineyard. The temptation to reduce costs by reducing the strength of the trellis needs to take account of the possibility of trellis failure, since subsequent corrective measures can be expensive. An understanding of the loads on a trellis, and their relative distribution through the structure of the trellis, are factors that can help minimize costs yet maintain adequate strength.

3.1.1 Loads and forces
Loads on a trellis are:
(i) vertical (weight of fruit, shoots and wood, ice and the wire itself),
(ii) lateral (wind on trellis and canopy, machinery impact) and
(iii) longitudinal (tension of wires).
Each of these is affected differently by environmental factors (temperature and wind) and by the intrinsic properties of each part of the trellis structure. An additional complicating factor is that of ageing, both of the trellis itself and of the vines; the initial structure has to cope with the full load imposed by the developing vine structures. This

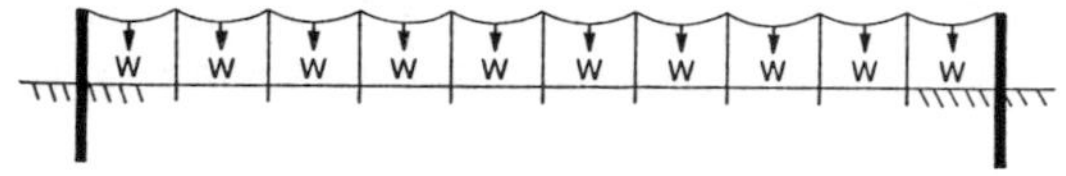

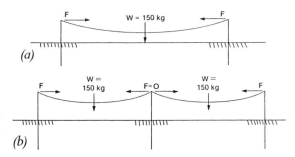

Figure 3.4 Relationship between vertical loads (W) and the total length of the trellis.

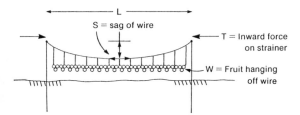

Figure 3.5 Vertical loads (W) on (a) a single panel and (b) two panels, demonstrating the balancing of internal forces (F) within the trellis.

Figure 3.6 Theoretical forces on a trellis wire, at equilibrium where tension (T) in a wire is a function of wire sag (S), distance between posts (L) and crop load (W).

load may diminish as the vine frameworks become woody and self-supporting and, in some cases, structurally entangled with the trellis wires.

Only the end (strainer) posts carry the longitudinal force of the wire tension. The intermediate posts carry the vine weight (W, Figure 3.4), which is mainly the fruit, vine cordon and new season's growth. The weight between the intermediate posts depends on vine weight and the spacing between posts such that the longitudinal force on an intermediate post is F (Figure 3.5a). But each longitudinal force F is balanced by the longitudinal force of the next panel. Hence there is no longitudinal force evident at each intermediate post (Figure 3.5b). Hence the longitudinal force is tranferred to the end post and the tension (T) in the wire equals the horizontal load at the end posts (Figure 3.6).

The tension (T) =
$$\frac{\text{weight (kg/m)} \times \text{panel length}^2 (\text{m}^2)}{8 \times \text{wire sag (m)}}$$

Put another way, a given load can be supported using a low sag with a high tension or a high sag with a low tension (or intermediate combinations). The amount of sag is influenced by diameter of the wire and its pre-tension at the ends. These principles mean that as little pre-tension as possible should be used consistent with the need to train straight trunks and for the needs of mechanical harvesting.

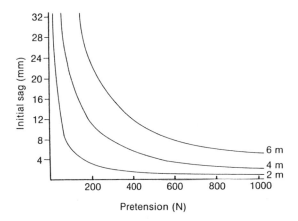

Figure 3.7 Relationship between sag in a wire, span between posts and pre-tension applied. The span between posts is 2, 4 or 6 m and the weight of wire is 0.1 kg/m.

It is easy to over-tension the wires of a trellis. The relationship between the sag in a wire and the amount of pre-tension applied to it (Figure 3.7) indicates that, after an initial rapid reduction in sag as the vine is trained, a situation is rapidly reached where a very large increase in strain (pre-tension) is required to get any appreciable reduction in sag. Visual assessment of sag, or the 'feel' of the wire, are poor indicators of wire tension. The solution is to measure tension directly; a simple tension metre can be constructed (Figure 3.8) in which the tension equals 25 times the force (p) required to deflect the wire by 10 mm.

Wire tension depends on wire diameter and the vertical load (Figure 3.9). The greater stretch of thinner wire leads to greater sag of the wires; this reduces the tension in the wire and the loads on the strainer assemblies.

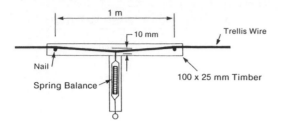

Figure 3.8 A simple tension meter for calculating wire tension. Wire tension is 25 times the force required to deflect wire by 10 mm.

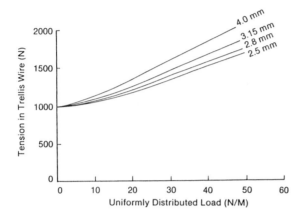

Figure 3.9 The effect of load on wire tension in wires with a span of 4 m, initial tension of 1000 N, and with diameters of 4.0, 3.15, 2.8 and 2.5 mm.

3.3.2 Temperature effects on trellis wires

A temperature reduction will shorten the wire or, if the wire is fixed at both ends, longitudinal tension increases: for example, the increase in force (tension) that follows a 10°C drop in temperature in wires of 4.0, 3.2 and 2.5 mm diameter is 276, 171 and 108 N respectively. In a grape trellis, with wire sag between posts, a temperature drop results in shortening of the wire and only a small reduction in the amount of sag. The temperature effects become less significant as the inherent sag increases; i.e. wires with large spans and heavy loads are least affected.

3.3.3 Wind loads on trellises

The forces caused by wind on a trellis are a function of topography, the reach conditions upwind of the vineyard, row direction and the type of vine canopy. The effect of wind on tension in trellis wire will increase with:

— increasing wind speed,
— higher initial wire tensions, i.e. low sag,
— increasing span between posts that resist cross wind (these are termed 'wind posts'),
— increasing vertical load,
— increasing wire diameter, and
— increasing canopy surface area.

The tension in the wires under wind load is quite sensitive to the post spacing of the 'wind posts'. Doubling the distance between them will cause a 50% increase in wire tension for a given wind load.

It is difficult to make specific recommendations to counter wind effects, but application of the following principles will reduce the likelihood of wind damage:

— use thin, high-tensile wire
— increase the frequency of posts that withstand lateral wind
— use low wire tensions
— install additional wires on the windward side of the trellis, especially on the windward rows

The effects of non-trellis windbreaks is referred to in Chapter 2.

3.3.4 Forces on strainer assemblies

The forces operating on, and within, trellises are greatly influenced by the strength of the strainer assembly, although this influence is lessened as the row becomes longer. This length effect is partly due to the effect of mature vines on the trellis strength, but also to the principle, derived from the study of wire fences, that loss of wire tension due to a specified inward movement of the strainer assemblies is smaller in long runs; Table 3.3 gives values of the tension loss in trellises of 100 and 200 m using wire of different diameters. Note that the effect of the 20 mm inward movement in this table equates to a temperature rise of 18°C in a 100 m trellis but only 9°C in a 200 m trellis (see 3.3.2).

The degree of movement in a strainer assembly depends on wire tension, trellis height, post diameter, depth of embedment and soil conditions. The load carried by the trellis wire is distributed through the buried part of the strainer post and

Table 3.3 Tension loss caused by a 10 mm inward movement of the strainer assemblies with 100 m/200 m long rows and different wire diameters

Wire diameter (mm)	Tension loss (N) with row lengths of:	
	100 m	200 m
4.00	502	251
3.55	395	198
3.15	311	156
2.80	246	123
2.50	196	98

Table 3.4 The effect of depth of post embedment on the load that can be sustained by a post

Depth in ground	0.75 m	0.9 m
Load at failure	20 kN	50 kN
Horizontal movement at 13 kN	40 mm	20 mm
Vertical movement at 13 kN	15 mm	10 mm

thence to the soil. The compressive stress (C) in the soil is inwards near the soil surface and away at the foot of the post (Figure 3.10). The stress is increased with higher wire loads (T) and trellis height (H) and decreased with broader post and the square of depth of embedment(D).

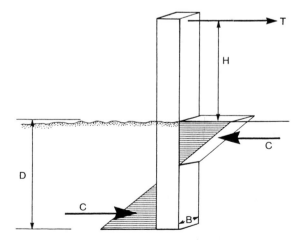

Figure 3.10 The effect of strainer post diameter (B), height (H), depth in the ground (D), soil forces (C) and the wire tension (T) that can be established.

The depth of embedment of the strainer post is critical as the stress is related to the square of the post depth. The load a strainer post can sustain will more than double with an increase in depth of embedment from 0.75-0.9 m (Table 3.4).

Conditions in the surface layers of soil are often poor for conferring strength to a strainer assembly. Surface horizons usually have lighter texture and higher organic matter content, and have been disturbed by tillage (Figure 3.11a). These layers tend to move into a mound as load is applied to the trellis wires. The effect of the zone of 'weak' soil is detrimental for two reasons: it increases both the 'effective height' and reduces the 'effective depth' of the post. The effective depth (D) is reduced (Figure 3.11b) and the effective height (H) depends on the strength and depth of the surface soils.

The load a strainer post can sustain can also be increased by:
— increasing post diameter,
— installing a bedlog near the surface to increase the bearing area where the soil is weakest (Figure 3.12),
— encasing the upper sections of the post in concrete, again to increase the bearing area, and
— placing the post deeper.

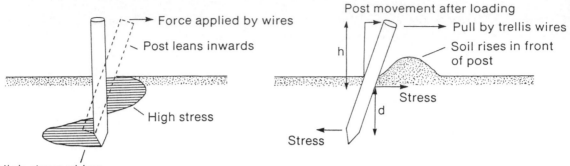

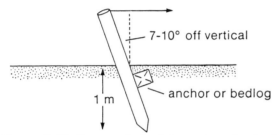

(a) Stress Distribution   (b) Soil Movement

Figure 3.11 The soil stress distribution around a strainer post, and potential soil movement.

Figure 3.12 One method of increasing the load capacity of strainer posts.

There are several other methods of increasing the strength of a strainer assembly, e.g. by using struts or bracing wires of various types; these are detailed in section 3.4.1.

3.4 Trellis material and construction

3.4.1 Strainer assembly construction

Strainers and strainer assemblies are the most important component of a trellis system. They anchor the trellis and provide the strength for tensioning the trellis wires, controlling wire sag between intermediate posts. A large number of trellis failures can be traced to the following causes:

— strainer posts inserted into the deep-ripped trenches for the vines
— excessive pre-tension of the trellis wires
— insertion of strainer posts to depths less than 1 m.

If these mistakes are made then the strainer assembly, regardless of design, is likely to fail. If these mistakes are not made, and given fair soil conditions, then quite simple assemblies will suffice. There are a number of straining systems, four of which are described here.

Single strainer posts
Single posts of a large diameter, 200mm or more, are frequently used as strainers. If the posts are less than 200mm diameter then some stabilization is required to reduce post movement; for this a rock or horizontal block of wood (referred to as a bedlog or 'dead man') is placed against the post on the 'pull' side (Figure 3.12). The post may be concreted into the ground but this is expensive and rarely done in commercial vineyards. This straining system relies for its strength on the depth of insertion and the resistance of the soil. The 'lean back' on the post (Figure 3.12) serves to compensate for the long term movement of the posts; it does not increase post stiffness.

The strength and resistance to movement of this system is a function of:

— the square of the depth of insertion into firm soil
— the diameter of the post
— the soil strength and in particular the depth of the disturbed top soil layer.

With a given post and soil type, the depth of embedment becomes the crucial and potent variable.

Strutted assemblies
The strength of a strainer post can be increased by a diagonal strut inserted between the post and the ground on the trellis side (Figure 3.13).

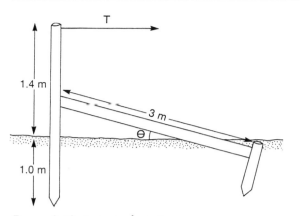

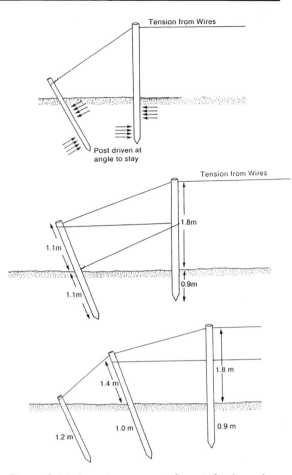

Figure 3.13 A strutted strainer post.

The strut acts by resisting compression. Its effect is such that smaller diameter strainer posts can be used. The positioning and length of the strut is important. The angle between the strut and the ground (θ in Figure 3.13) affects the distribution of forces. The smaller the angle (i.e. the lower the strut is notched into the strainer post) the lower the compression on the strut and the less the tendency for the post to be 'jacked' out of the ground. An adverse effect of a low angle, however, is the increased likelihood that the strainer will break or 'spin' out of the ground. Commonly used dimensions are with struts of 3 m or more in length at an angle of 25 to 30° to the ground. These decisions depend on the strength and length of the strainer post. It is essential that the base of the strut be supported on a suitable chock or base-plate set on firm ground below the level of any previous excavation; one suitable system is to butt the strut against the buried part of the first intermediate post.

Anchored strainers
An anchoring system confers considerable strength to a strainer post and is widely used in new plantings in Australia. This system is similar to the diagonal strut except the forces are reversed; here the post is being pushed down into the ground rather than tending to lift up. Anchors, either 1.2 m pointed pine posts, or steel stakes, are driven into the soil, generally angling towards the strainer as shown in Figure 3.14. The anchor is tied to the upper part of the strainer with an anchor wire which is then tightened. So-called 'duck-billed' anchors and screw anchors are now available in Australia. The system does, however, rely on a

Figure 3.14 A strainer post with a tie-back anchor system.

suitable anchor capable of resisting the tension in the anchor wire. The larger the angle of the anchor wire to the ground, i.e. the closer the anchor to the post, the greater the strength of the assembly. Steep anchor wires have the added advantage that less headland space is lost. Also greater 'lean back' of the strainer gives more usable trellis wire space which also lessens headland wastage.

Horizontal box strainer
This system was developed for taking greater loads than conventional straining systems. It consists of a horizontal post or 'rail' fitted between the tops of the end pair of posts, generally 2 to 3 m apart. A wire loop from the base of the end post to the top of the second post stabilizes the assembly (Figure 3.15a). The structural relationships are similar to the tension principle that operates in

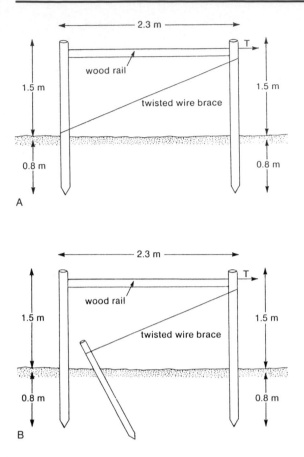

2.3 m

1.5 m

wood rail

twisted wire brace

1.5 m

0.8 m

0.8 m

A

2.3 m

1.5 m

wood rail

twisted wire brace

1.5 m

0.8 m

0.8 m

B

Figure 3.15 The forces on (a) a boxed strainer assembly and (b) a variation of the box which removes uplift on the near post.

anchored strainers. It has the additional advantage that both of the posts serve as cantilevers to cope with overloads. The horizontal box stay is expensive, and has failed in irrigated vineyards when the end post has pulled out of the ground, the rail collapsed or the end post snapped. If vines are trained into the end assembly the fruit is difficult to machine harvest. Hence the horizontal box strainer is not as popular as less expensive systems.

A further improvement to this system (at a higher cost) can be made by removing the vertical uplift on the rear post (Figure 3.15b) by attaching the wire loop to a separate post and not the strainer post.

3.4.2 Intermediate posts

The intermediate or line posts within the vine row are usually placed between vines and are not

utilized directly for vine training in Australia. Training of vine trunks against the posts, in the way vine stakes are used in Europe and California, presents several difficulties especially with large diameter or creosote-treated posts, and if they are installed using a post-hole digger. The intermediate posts are spaced between 4 and 8 m spanning 3 to 5 vines, the space depending on the anticipated crop yield and trellis system. A spacing of 6 m, using treated posts, is adequate for a single wire trellis, 1.2 m high, supporting yields of 20-30 t/ha. Larger T-trellis systems require the posts to be at least 100 mm diameter and spaced every 4 m. In newer vineyards with a vertical trellis, posts 180 cm out of the ground should be 75-100 mm diameter.

Trellis materials

Posts

Indigenous timbers such as belah, box, red gum and jarrah (*Eucalyptus* spp.) have been commonly used wherever the timber is available in split, sawn or log form. Longevity is important and timber should resist termites and rot fungi. The termite resistance of Murray pine (*Callitris*) made it popular for strainer posts in irrigated vineyards. Hardwood posts are more durable than softwood posts but the latter can be more effective once preserved with chemicals. In the last 20 years chemically-treated pine (*Pinus radiata*) posts have become popular; though more expensive, they are cheaper to install and readily available.

Pine posts are treated with either creosote or a mixture of copper, chromium and arsenic salts (CCA). For the latter, the posts are placed in a large cylinder under vacuum, all air pores evacuated and then the mixture is forced into the timber under pressure, until the point of refusal. The creosote treatment is similar but involves heating. Creosote, which has been used as a preservative for centuries, contains over 160 chemicals, many of which are insoluble in water and resistant to leaking out of posts. Creosote is toxic to humans and nodules of creosote from posts may contaminate grapes and, even at low concentrations, produce undesirable wine flavours. The salts in the inorganic preservative mixture (CCA) are water-soluble and highly toxic until bound in an insoluble form within the wood. Nevertheless, these chemicals can react with zinc and corrode galvanized wire causing wire breakage if the wires pass through holes in the posts. It is therefore helpful to use double-galvanized wire and fix the wires to the top or side(s) of the post.

There are relative advantages of the two differently treated pine posts. Creosote posts are unpleasant to work with, particularly with vaporization in hot weather. However, it has been reported that they are less likely to snap in the ground than CCA-treated posts.

Cambio-debarked posts with the knots of the wood retained are stronger than shaved posts. If shaved completely, it is preferable to select one size larger to get extra strength. Post dimensions are referred to in measurements (mm) of diameter; 50-75, 100-125, 125-150.

An important advantage of pine posts is the ability to be able to drive (hammer) them into the soil, for which purpose they are generally pointed. Treated pine posts, installed with a power driver, can take 50% greater load than posts set in an oversize hole with the soil rammed back; 'driving' compresses the soil, and increases post stability. The relative breaking load of treated posts, is greater than other posts or materials. A load of 2,000 kg is required to break a 125 mm treated post which is much greater than the 400 kg load for a concrete post and 100 kg for a steel post. The stability of a post is related to the depth set in the ground; an increase in the depth of set by one-third will double the load bearing capacity.

Polypropylene posts have been developed in Europe and are being evaluated in Australia. Steel star-posts or 'droppers' have been used but may bend with heavy crops under windy conditions and sink into the ground after irrigation or heavy rain. Since the 1970s, the use of metal stakes at each vine has been evaluated as a vine support system in Australia. Individual stakes at each vine results in greater vine flexibility and improved efficiency of mechanical harvesting, especially with the pulsator harvester. The stakes are easy to install but are more expensive than timber posts every 3 to 4 vines.

Wire
The length of wire in a vineyard can be considerable. A planting with 3.3 m rows and a single wire trellis requires 3 km of wire per ha.

This is relatively inexpensive ($200/ha in the early 1990s) but with trellis systems of up to 8 wires the costs may exceed $1,500/ha. A narrow row spacing of 2.5 m with 7 wires per row will need a total of 28 km of wire per ha, a large component in the cost of establishment. High-tensile wire is better value than soft wire; for example 2.5 mm high tensile wire is 50% less expensive than 4 mm soft wire but has the same load-bearing capacity.

The durability of wire depends on the galvanizing, the environment and the handling during construction. Galvanizing protects wire from corrosion and greatly increases the life of the wire. The wire is dipped in molten zinc which forms the protective layer. The thickness of the zinc determines durability and two grades of galvanizing are available in Australia, standard and heavy, the latter having treble the zinc and treble the life. Dragging of galvanized wire over the ground wears away some of the zinc layer; this can cause the wires to rust and break prematurely. The damage to the zinc can be avoided by transporting and unravelling the wire from a spool or 'spinning jenny'.

The wire can be fixed to end posts with patented wire fasteners or tied around the end post and strained using wire strainers. The wire fasteners are expensive but easy to use, although only the end panel can be strained once the cordons of the vines are established on the wire. Thus it is essential to establish an adequate tension in the first year for cordon trained vines or unwrap the vines and retension the wire at the end of the first year of cordon establishment. It is not necessary to strain the foliage wires because the extra height of the wires increases the risk of strainer post failure. However knots represent a weakness in a length of wire with all wire types and thicknesses.

The wires may be placed in a slot cut into the intermediate posts or fixed with staples. It is necessary to use barbed staples with CCA treated posts as these posts tend to dry out and the staples can fall out, especially during machine harvesting. If the staples contaminate the grapes this may cause a problem with some grape presses. This problem does not occur with creosote posts.

3.5 Concluding remarks

The training and trellising of grapevines has seen considerable advances in the short history of

Australian viticulture. The evolution of different trellis systems has been initiated by the drive for higher yields, the requirements for increasing mechanization in the vineyard, and the desire to improve fruit quality. Choice of an appropriate system is determined by these factors and production and environmental constraints, with an over-riding judgement of the profitability as a deciding factor that must be evaluated in terms of the economic risk involved in major changes in the trellis design. The most economic system may be the lowest cost system but this should be evaluated in terms of grape yield and expected returns related to grape quality.

Further reading

Kliewer, W.M. (1982) Vineyard canopy management—a review. In: A.D. Webb (ed.) Grape and Wine Centennial Symposium Proceedings 1980; University of California, Davis, pp.342-52.

Mollah, M.R. (1989) Review of trellis structures for horticultural crops. Tech. report series no. 177, Department of Agriculture and Rural Affairs, Vic.

Smart, R.E. and Robinson, M. (1991) Sunlight into Wine. A Handbook for Winegrape Canopy management. Winetitles, Adelaide.

Vogt, E. and Götz, B. (1987) Weinbau, Ulmer, Stuttgart.

Other references

Baldini, E. (1982) Italian experience of double curtain training systems with special reference to mechanization. In: A.D. Webb (ed.) Grape and Wine Centennial Symposium Proceedings, 1980. University of California; Davis, pp.195-200.

Baldwin, J.G., Bleasdale, G.E., Cadman, R.S. and Keens, J.L. (1979) Comparison of trellises and pruning levels for Sultana vines in the Murray Valley. Aust. J. Exp. Agric. Anim. Husb. 19, 634-640.

Botting, D. and Dry, P.R. (1989) Mechanically harvesting the wide tee trellis: some recent developments. Aust. Grapegrower and Winemaker 310, 39-40.

Busby, J.A. (1825) A treatise on the culture of the vine and the art of making wine. Sydney 1825 (reprinted by the David Ell Press 1979).

Carbonneau, A. and Huglin, P. (1982) Adaption of training systems to French regions. In: A.D. Webb (ed.) Grape and Wine Centennial Symposium Proceedings, 1980; University of California, Davis, pp.376-85.

Carbonneau, A., Casteran, P. and Leclair, P. (1978) Essai de determination, en biologie de la plante entiere, de relations essentielles entre le bioclimat naturel, la physiologie de la vigne et la composition du raisin. Ann. Amelior. Plantes 2, 195-221.

Clingeleffer, P.R. (1983) CSIRO Sultana vine management research. Aust. Grapegrower and Winemaker 232, 7-17.

Clingeleffer, P.R. (1989). Update : Minimal pruning of cordon trained vines (MPCT). Aust. Grapegrower and Winemaker 304, 78-83.

Clingeleffer, P.R. and May, P. (1981) The swing-arm trellis for Sultana grapevine management. S. Afr. J. Enol. Vitic. 2, 37-44.

Coombe B.G. (1975) The link trellis—a new concept in grapevine training. Aust. Grapegrower and Winemaker 12(136), 13-4.

Gould, I.V. and Whiting, J.R. (1987). Mechanization of raisin production with the Irymple trellis system. Trans. ASAE 30, 56-60.

Hedberg, P.R. and Raison, J. (1982) The effect of vine spacing and trellising on yield and fruit quality of Shiraz grapevines. Amer. J. Enol. Vitic. 33, 20-30.

Kasimatis, A.N., Lider, C.A. and Kliewer, W.M. (1975) Influence of trellising on growth and yield of Thompson Seedless vines. Amer. J. Enol. Vitic. 26, 125-9.

Kasimatis, A.N., Lider, C.A. and Kliewer, W.M. (1982) Trellising and training practices to influence yield, fruit composition and growth of Chenin Blanc grapes. In: A.D. Webb (ed.) Grape and Wine Centennial Symposium Proceedings, 1980; University of California, Davis, pp.386-9.

Kliewer, W.M., Bowen, P. and Benz, M. (1989) Influence of shoot orientation on growth and yield development in Cabernet Sauvignon. Amer. J. Enol. Vitic. 40, 259-64.

Lyon, A.V. and Walters, D.V. (1941) Production of dried grapes in Murray Valley irrigation settlements. 1. Viticulture, CSIRO, Australia Bulletin No. 143.

May, P. (1966) The effect of direction of growth on fruitfulness and yield of Sultana vines. Aust. J. Agric. Res. 17, 479-90.

May, P., Sauer, M.R. and Scholefield, P.B. (1973) Effect of various combinations of trellis, pruning and rootstocks on vigorous Sultana vines. Vitis 12, 192-206.

May, P., Clingeleffer, P.R., Scholefield, P.B. and Brien, C.J. (1976) The response of the grape cultivar Crouchen (Australian syn. Clare Riesling) to various trellis and pruning treatments. Aust. J. Agric. Res. 27, 845-56.

Olmo, H.P., Studer, H.E., Kasimatis, A.N. and Grape Farm Advisors of Fresno, Kern, Madera and San Joaquin Counties (1968) Training and trellising grapevines for mechanical harvesting. Calif. Agric. Ext. Ser. AXT 274, 1-15.

Peterson, J.R., Turkington, C.R. and Evans, J.C. (1974) Pruning and trellising trials with the *Vitis vinifera* cultivars Shiraz and Semillon under irrigated conditions. Aust. J. Exp. Agric. Anim. Hub. 14, 418-24.

Pongracz, D.P. (1978) Practical Viticulture. David Phillip, Capetown.

Possingham, J.V., Clingeleffer, P.R. and Cooper, A.M. (1990) Vine management techniques for the wine industry. Aust. Grapegrower and Winemaker 316, 85-89.

Shaulis, N., Kimball, K. and Tomkins, J.P. (1953) The effect of trellis height and training systems on the growth and yield of Concord grapes under a controlled pruning severity. Proc. Amer. Soc. Hortic. Sci. 62, 221-7.

Shaulis, N., Amberg, H. and Crowe, D. (1966) Response of Concord grapes to light exposure and Geneva double curtain training. Proc. Amer. Soc. Hort. Sci. 89, 268-80.

Smart, R.E. (1973) Sunlight interception by vineyards. Amer. J. Enol. Vitic. 24, 141-7.

Smart, R.E., Robinson, J.B., Due, G. and Brien, C.J. (1985) Canopy microclimate modification for the cultivar Shiraz. I. Definitions of canopy microclimate. Vitis. 24, 17-31.

Smart, R.E. and Smith, S.M. (1988) Canopy management: identifying the problems and practical solutions. Proc. 2nd Int. Sym. Cool Climate Vitic. and Oenol. Auckland, New Zealand.

Smart, R.E., Dick, J.K., Gravett, I.M. and Fisher, B. (1990) Canopy management to improve grape yield and wine quality. Principles and practices. Sth. Afr. J. Enol. Vitic. 11, 3-17.

Turkington, C.R. (1978) Pruning and trellising of Shiraz. Abstract 1385, XXth Int. Hort. Congr., Sydney, 15-23 August.

van den Ende, B. (1984) Tatura trellis, a system of growing grapevines for early and high production. Amer. J. Enol. Vitic. 35, 82-7.

van Zyl, J.L. and van Huyssteen, L. (1980) Comparative studies on winegrapes on different trellis systems. I. Consumptive water use. Sth. Afr. J. Enol. Vitic. 1, 7-14.

Weaver, R.J. and Kasimatis, A.N. (1975) Effect of trellis height with and without crossarms on Thompson Seedless grapes. J. Amer. Soc. Hort. Sci. 100, 252-3.

Weaver, R.J., Kasimatis, A.N., Johnson, J.O. and Vilas, N. (1984) Effect of trellis height and crossarm width and angle on yield of Thompson Seedless grapes. Amer. J. Enol. Vitic. 35, 94-6.

Wood, P.N., Smart, R.E. and Morgan, L.A. (1989) Yield responses with conversion to new training systems. In: Proceedings of Vintage '89 Seminar, Hawkes Bay, New Zealand, 46-56.

CHAPTER FOUR

Pruning

E. TASSIE and B.M. FREEMAN

Pruning is defined as the removal of living shoots, canes, leaves and other vegetative parts of the vine (Winkler *et al.* 1974). It does not include removal of inflorescences or bunches. Pruning may be carried out at any time during the growing season or the dormant period. This chapter exclusively describes pruning during the dormant period ('winter pruning'). Pruning during the growing season ('summer pruning') may be used as a technique of canopy management (see 5.4.2) or tablegrape production (see 12.2.4).

Traditional manual pruning is one of the most important cultural operations carried out in the vineyard and, after harvesting, is the most expensive and labour consuming. Pruning has important implications for vine function as it influences:
– the form and size of the vine
– the balance between vegetative and fruit growth in the vine
– the quantity and quality of fruit production.

Neat, skilful pruning is aesthetically pleasing and is a prized art. Grape pruning competitions were a feature of Agricultural Bureau activities in dryland grape areas of South Australia during the winter months of the 1940s and 50s. Many books were published early this century as can be seen by the list in Further Reading. Their popularity is illustrated by the fact that the 6000 copies of the 6th edition of Quinn's book, printed in 1921, were sold out within a few years.

Over the last twenty years, there have been significant developments in pruning methods: pruning severity has been markedly reduced, mechanization has been introduced and widely implemented, the range of pruning systems has been increased and traditional ideas have been challenged.

4.1 Aims of pruning

The aims of pruning may be defined as:
(i)   To establish and maintain the vine in a form that will facilitate vineyard management.
(ii) To produce fruit of a desired quality.
(iii) To select nodes which produce fruitful shoots.
(iv) To regulate the number of shoots and hence bunch number and size.
(v)   To regulate the vegetative growth of the vine.
These aims are achieved by adjusting the *number* and *position* of nodes during the pruning operation.

4.1.1 Node number
Increasing the number of nodes per vine (*lighter* or *less severe pruning*) will result in a larger number of shoots and bunches, and reduced shoot vigour.

This may lead to problems of imperfect ripening of fruit if the vine is overcropped. Reducing the number of nodes per vine (*heavier* or *more severe pruning*) will result in excessive removal of crop with fewer shoots of excessive vigour and associated problems of shading (see Chapter 5). This reduces vine capacity by decreasing early-season leaf area development.

To obtain a balanced vine with an 'optimum' shoot vigour, pruning level should be between these two extremes. This 'optimum' vigour level for many varieties is represented by shoots of about 1 m in length and 7 mm in diameter at the seventh internode (B.G. Coombe pers. comm.). At this level of vigour, vines have only moderate lateral shoot growth.

Shoot vigour is also influenced by management factors, other than pruning level, which influence grapevine capacity, e.g. irrigation and fertilizer application.

4.1.2 Node position

Node selection recognizes the qualitative difference between nodes and the importance of shoot and node position in the canopy (Chapter 5). This may be more important in cool climates and is also variety dependent.

Differential fruitfulness of buds along the cane is an important constraint on pruning method. Cane, or long pruning, is a requirement with varieties such as Sultana that have low fruitfulness at basal nodes. Bud, and hence shoot position in the canopy, must allow sufficient irradiation for inflorescence primordium initiation, efficient leaf photosynthesis and subsequent fruit development. The shoot distribution determines microclimate and hence affects disease incidence, temperature and hydrature of the berries, and fruit composition.

4.2 Pruning terms

When describing pruning of the grapevine, the following definitions are commonly used:

Apical dominance
Apical dominance is the phenomenon whereby distal (apical) buds on a cane, i.e. at the apex, burst prior to and inhibit the growth of the proximal (basal) buds. Apical dominance is also seen within annual shoots by the effect of the growth of the shoot apex in inhibiting lateral shoot growth;

removal of the apex by summer pruning will stimulate growth of lateral shoots. Apical dominance is most obvious in early spring when, in cane-pruned vines, the most distal buds of the cane burst early and grow vigorously, while those in the middle of the cane grow weakly. Some practices employed in an attempt to overcome this include arching the cane and, most recently, application of hydrogen cyanamide.

Basebud
A bud at the base of a cane, not classified as a bud at a count node. Such buds do not normally burst in the same season as buds at count nodes but may remain latent on old wood for many years; if stimulated by severe pruning, they produce water shoots.

Bearer or fruiting unit
One-year-old cane or spur with fruitful buds which will produce the current season's shoots and fruit.

Bud
A compound bud (winter bud or eye) at the nodes of grapevine shoots. These buds appear single but, in fact, comprise at least three 'true' buds. Pruning levels are often referred to as 'buds per vine'; however 'nodes per vine' is more correct because there is more than one bud per node.

Budburst
Budburst is the emergence of a new shoot from a bud during spring (Volume 1, Chapter 7). Percentage budbreak can be expressed as:

$$(a) \quad \frac{\text{No. shoots per vine}}{\text{No. count nodes per vine}} \times 100$$

or (b)

$$\frac{\text{No. count nodes with one or more shoots}}{\text{No. count nodes}} \times 100$$

(a) is used more on a per vine basis, and (b) for count nodes on individual bearers.

Bud fruitfulness
A 'fruitful bud' has one or more inflorescence primordia which give rise to bunches. One measure of fruitfulness is the number of bunches per shoot. Fruitfulness is an inherited characteristic which is also influenced by environmental factors,

especially irradiation, at the time of inflorescence primordium initiation, at about flowering time (Volume 1, Chapter 7). Yield per node is different from fruitfulness as it is a function of the number of shoots per node, the number of bunches per shoot, the number of berries per bunch and the size of the berries.

Cane (or rod)
A mature one-year-old shoot from the previous growing season. A shoot becomes a cane after periderm formation. A long bearer generally with more than 6 count nodes is called a 'cane' or 'rod'.

Capacity
The total growth of the vine including the total production of crop, leaves, shoots and roots. Capacity of each vine is indicated by its total weight of fruit and shoots. Capacity increases with an increase in root growth, shoot number and leaf area. A very young vine may be vigorous but have a low capacity, whereas a mature vine with a large number of nodes can have low vigour but a high capacity.

Cordon
A permanent arm, usually horizontal, arising from the trunk to form a part of the framework and support the bearers or fruiting units.

Count nodes
Nodes that are deliberately retained at winter pruning which are 'counted' to determine pruning level. The first count node on a bearer is the first clear node separated from the base of the bearer by an internode 5mm or longer.

Count shoot
A shoot arising from a count node.

Crown or 'head' of a vine
The central region at the top of the trunk where the main trunk branches to form the cordons or, on cane pruned vines, where the canes originate.

Internode
The section of a shoot between two adjacent nodes.

Laterals
Shoots that arise from prompt buds in the axils of true leaves on a main shoot. Lateral growth is promoted by topping the main shoot. Compound (winter) buds are axillary to the basal 'leaves' of prompt buds.

Non-count shoots
Shoots arising from base buds (i.e. from the base of canes and spurs) plus the water shoots.

Prompt buds
Axillary buds that develop into lateral shoots in the same season that the bud is produced; the lateral shoots may vary in length from a few mm to a metre or more.

Spur
A short bearer; the basal section of a cane which is cut back to one to three, generally two nodes. These are used in spur pruning to provide fruiting nodes for the current year and also in cane pruning to provide the replacement canes for the following year. Spurs should be left longer for less fruitful varieties—e.g. Sultana—or, in the case of a very fruitful variety such as Muscat Gordo Blanco, may be pruned to just one node.

Sucker
A water-shoot that emerges from the base of the established trunk of the vine.

Trunk
The main thickened stem from the ground to where branching begins.

Vigour
The *rate* of shoot growth measured by the change in shoot length over time. It is inversely proportional to the number of shoots per vine and to crop load.

Watershoots
Non-count shoots that arise on wood older than one year, i.e. from the trunk, crown or cordons of the vine, and originating from base buds. Generally they are less fruitful than count shoots and are removed at pruning unless required to provide replacement fruiting wood.

4.3 Pruning principles

Certain principles of grapevine pruning have been outlined by Winkler *et al.* (1974). They can be summarized as follows:

Grapevines have a fixed capacity
A vine in any one season can ripen only a certain quantity of fruit and support only a certain number of shoots. This is dependent on the capacity of the vine. In turn, the capacity of the vine varies with variety, climate, soil and vineyard manage-

ment practices. Appropriate pruning will allow expression of the yield potential intrinsic in a vine's capacity.

Pruning tends to depress growth

The elimination of shoots removes carbohydrate that potentially may be utilized to increase capacity. Severe pruning restricts shoot and leaf number and delays production of maximal leaf area, thus limiting early season photosynthetic capability. Light pruning results in many shoots and a maximal leaf area earlier in the season. Severe pruning increases vine vigour but reduces vine capacity. Vine capacity varies directly with the shoot number and the total leaf area. The greater the area of actively-photosynthesizing leaves, the greater the amount of carbohydrate that is available for reserves and for current growth. A vine with more shoots (having been pruned less severely) will produce more fruit, as well as greater total leaf area. Fruit production is reduced with severe pruning because fewer, although vigorous, shoots are produced.

Production of crop depresses vine capacity

A high crop load depresses the vigour in one season, which in turn reduces carbohydrate reserves laid down and hence capacity. A change to lighter pruning usually leads to a heavier crop in that year and a lighter crop in the following year.

Fruitfulness varies with shoot vigour

Conditions that lead to an extreme in vigour—i.e. very low or very high vigour—do not favour fruitfulness (Winkler *et al.* 1974). Therefore to ensure a good level of fruitfulness, intermediate shoot growth is advisable. Huglin (1986) showed that as shoots increase in size the number of their inflorescences increases but by diminishing amounts, i.e. tending to a maximum number (Figure 4.1). Studies on the effect of shading on yield (May and Antcliff 1963, Smart *et al.* 1982) have shown a reduction in yield per node due to shading of the node and/or the leaf that subtends that node. Lower yield per node attributed to high vigour may be a consequence of an indirect effect of an altered microclimate. Temperature and light intensity effects have also been noted: increased temperature and light

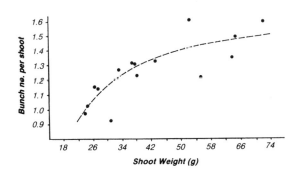

Figure 4.1 Correlation between shoot vigour and bud fruitfulness (Gewuerztraminer, 1979, INRA Colmar; After Huglin 1986).

intensity have increased bud fruitfulness (Buttrose 1970).

Shoot vigour varies inversely with shoot number and crop load

High crop load reduces individual vine vigour, as does a large number of growing points. A severely pruned vine will produce few shoots of high vigour. Conversely, no pruning results in many shoots of low vigour (as illustrated by the effects of minimal pruning—see 4.7). Crop load effects are illustrated in Winkler *et al.* (1974) who cite examples of average shoot lengths of 1.36 m from vines with no crop and 1.0 m from vines with crop.

Vine capacity is proportional to total potential growth

Large vines have a greater potential for growth than small vines and can therefore support a greater number of nodes (lighter pruning level). This principle reiterates the importance of vine capacity when determining pruning level.

Vines can self-regulate

Severe pruning will result in a high proportion of non-count shoots. Vines with a large number of nodes retained will not produce shoots from all count nodes. Reducing pruning severity will increase yield in the first year but by the third year the production level will have become stabilized (Freeman 1982). The vine regulates production by reducing the number of shoots per node, the proportion of shoots that fully develop, and bunch weight (fewer berries per bunch and reduced berry weight) (Freeman *et al.* 1979). This principle has been shown with mechanical, minimal and nil pruning.

Direction of growth influences type of growth
Shoots growing downwards tend to be devigorated.

4.4 Timing of pruning

Pruning usually refers to the removal and trimming of vine canes during the dormant or winter period but can also refer to trimming and other operations carried out during the growing season; the latter is referred to as 'summer pruning' and is discussed in Chapter 5.

Winter pruning normally takes place after leaf fall and before budbreak, when there is no appreciable transfer of carbohydrates from the shoots to the roots (Antcliff *et al.* 1957). The phloem is inactive during the dormant stage and the sieve plates are covered with callose: pruning at this stage has no effect on carbohydrate storage. Before leaf senescence, carbohydrates are translocated to the woody parts of the vine and pruning at this time may decrease this important process.

Late pruning, i.e. just prior to budburst or even after apical buds have burst, may delay subsequent budburst by several days or even weeks. This strategy may be used to avoid frost damage and other adverse climatic conditions at critical phenological stages, e.g. flowering. If yield is increased it is usually a consequence of improved fruit set (Coombe 1964). In regions with relatively warm winters, e.g. Margaret River (WA), late pruning can significantly increase yield (Whittles 1986).

Double pruning is a new technique that has been found to lead to profound changes in grape composition. With this method, normal pruning in winter is followed by a second pruning in December to early January after inflorescence primordia have been initiated but before buds become dormant. Grape maturity is delayed up to 3 months with increased grape acidity, colour, aroma and flavour profiles (Dry 1987); this is advantageous in hot districts although yields are reduced by 50–60%.

4.5 Yield components

The natural state for the grapevine is unpruned. As such, it has an inherent self-regulating

Table 4.1 Yield components and the period in which they are determined

Yield components	Determined at
No. of vines/ha	Planting
No. metres canopy/ha	Trellis construction and vine training
No. bunches/shoot	Bunch initiation previous growing season
Bunch stem weight	Year before cropping
No. nodes/vine	Pruning level—winter before growing season
No. flowers/bunch	Before budbreak
No. shoots/node	Budbreak ⎫ current
No. berries/bunch	Fruit set ⎬ growing
Berry weight	Berry growth ⎭ season

mechanism that dictates the balance between shoot and fruit growth, with a certain yield. Within the range of pruning levels commonly used in commercial hand pruning, yield increases with increased node number; however a point is eventually reached beyond which there is no further increase in yield due to the compensating effects of other yield components. The factors that determine yield — 'yield components' — are determined in both the previous and the current season (Table 4.1). Changes in seasonal conditions and management techniques—particularly pruning—influence yield components. Knowledge of these components and how they are influenced can be used to assess the potential yield in any one season.

The first component, number of vines per hectare, or vine density, is set at planting. For divided canopies, it is more useful to refer to the metres of canopy per hectare and therefore express yield as kg crop per metre of canopy. The number of bunches per shoot (fruitfulness) and bunch weight are potentially determined in the previous season. The number of nodes per vine and shoots per node are determined by pruning level and subsequent budbreak respectively. The remaining components are determined later, i.e. actual bunches per shoot, berries per bunch and berry weight.

Table 4.2 Yield components of Shiraz grapevines averaged over 5 years (1973–1977). Berry weights are from 1975 and 1977 only (Freeman et al. 1979)

Node number retained at pruning	20	40	80	160
Shoot number in spring	81	89	104	181
Shoot number in following winter*	26	41	77	103
Pruning weight (kg/vine)	2.2	3.6	3.1	2.8
Cane weight (g/shoot)	102	77	40	27
Yield (kg/vine)	5.9	11.2	15.3	16.3
Bunch number/vine	37	74	118	167
Bunch number/shoot	2.4	1.8	1.5	1.6
Bunch weight (g/bunch)	157	151	130	99
Berry weight (g/berry)	1.28	1.22	1.17	1.15
Berry number/bunch	150	154	118	99
Yield/pruning weight ratio	2.2	3.6	5.0	5.9

* Difference due to shoot thinning during growing season.

Yield component compensation

Yield component compensation dictates that as the level of one yield component is changed, the level of one or more of the others will also change. For example, if more nodes are retained at pruning, yield will not increase proportionally because one or more other components will be reduced, e.g. budburst, fruit set or berry size. The component most under control of management from year to year is pruning level and the effect of varying this component has been thoroughly investigated.

The phenomenon of yield component compensation was clearly illustrated by a pruning experiment conducted at Griffith, NSW during the 1973–1977 growing seasons in which Shiraz vines were pruned to 20, 40, 80 and 160 nodes (Freeman et al. 1979). Yield increased with node number up to 80 nodes, beyond which there was no significant increase (Table 4.2). Yield increased as a result of more mature shoots and a consequent increase in bunch number. At the higher pruning levels there were significantly higher shoot numbers, but relatively few shoots grew more than 5–15 cm, and many did not develop bunches. In addition, at higher pruning levels, there was a reduction in average shoot weight that compensated for the increased shoot number.

Studies in New York State have shown that increased node number leads to an increase in shoots per vine, but a non-linear increase in yield

(Smart et al. 1982). The increased number of shoots leads to crowding and subsequent shading in the canopy, which results in a reduction in shoots per node, bunches per shoot, berries per bunch and weight per berry. Canopy division permits retention of increased shoot numbers per vine without crowding and results in yield increases of 40–90% (Shaulis et al. 1966). The increase in yield per vine is a consequence of an increase in yield per node which is attributed to improved irradiation of the subtending leaf in the previous growing season (see Chapter 5).

Yield for a typical non-divided canopy can be calculated as:

Yield (t/ha) = no. vines/ha × no. count nodes/vine × no. shoots/no. count nodes × no. bunches/shoot × bunch weight (g) × 10^{-6}

where
no. shoots = total number of shoots per vine i.e. count shoots plus non count shoots.

bunch weight (g) = (no. flowers/bunch × no. berries/no. flowers × weight/berry (g)) + bunchstem weight (g)

Factors affecting yield components

Cultural factors and a physiological sequence of events influence the yield components as follows;

Planting density

This determines the number of vines per hectare. In Australia, about 1500 vines per ha is typical for traditional, wide-row plantings (see 2.1.4). Increase in productive canopy area can be achieved by closer row spacing or canopy division (Chapter 5). A low vine density with a divided trellis can have the same canopy length per ha as twice the planting density with a simple trellis (see Trellis design). The influence of planting density on other yield components is closely related to site and trellis factors.

Trellis design
The length of canopy per hectare can be doubled by dividing the canopy in two e.g. GDC, U- and Lyre, Scott-Henry systems. The canopy length can be increased four-fold with the RT2T trellis (Chapters 3 and 5).

Bunch initiation
This takes place during the previous season beginning around flowering time and potentially determines the number of bunches per shoot, bunch weight and thus yield per node. Within-canopy shade will decrease fruitfulness, and hence yield, and this can be manipulated via pruning and canopy management techniques (Chapter 5).

Winter pruning
Determines the number of nodes retained per vine. Shoot number per vine is potentially determined by pruning level, but modified by percentage budburst, in itself a function of pruning level. Severe pruning produces a higher percentage budbreak.

Budburst
The result of severe pruning of vines with the capacity to support more growth will be an increase in percentage budburst (even to more than 100%). This is due to shoot growth from 'non-count' nodes and multiple shoots at count nodes. Conversely, very light pruning will lead to lower percentage budburst.

Flowering
The number of flowers per inflorescence is potentially determined just prior to and during budbreak (Srinivasan and Mullins 1981).

Fruit set
The proportion of flowers that develop into berries is regulated by both climatic and endogenous factors. Fruit set is highest with fewest bunches per vine. A low percentage set is an important means of regulating yield for vines that are very lightly pruned. Set can be improved by decreasing competition from the shoot tip through the use of growth regulators e.g. CCC (Coombe 1973).

Berry development
Climatic conditions (both macro- and micro-climate), management practices (irrigation, nutrient status, pruning severity, trellis) and genetic characteristics determine berry weight. Coombe (1980) has shown that berry volume at maturity can be indicated by berry volume at veraison. Lighter pruning typically results in smaller berries due to an increase in bunch number.

4.6 Pruning level

Pruning level can be quantified as the number of nodes left after pruning. This number may be expressed as nodes per vine, nodes per metre of row, nodes per metre of canopy or nodes per unit area of vineyard surface. Classification of a pruning system as severe or light is not a simple matter because what may be severe in terms of nodes per vine may not be in terms of nodes per hectare. For example, individual vines in high density vineyards may be regarded as severely pruned (e.g. 15 nodes per vine) but at 10,000 vines per hectare, there are 150,000 nodes per hectare. By comparison the same number of nodes per hectare can be achieved with lighter pruning (100 nodes per vine) in a wide-row vineyard with 1500 vines per hectare. Nevertheless, an individual vine responds to the number of nodes per vine (see 5.4.2; Smart and Robinson 1991).

For wide-row vineyards (3 m or more) in Australia, the following classification of pruning level may be useful:

Severe—Less than 20 nodes per m row
This is typical of non-irrigated vineyards in traditional regions like the Barossa and the Hunter. Such vines would usually be pruned to two canes per vine.

Moderate—20–75 nodes per m row
Representative of irrigated vineyards in the traditional regions above and in the Riverland, MIA

and Sunraysia regions. Winegrape varieties are typically cordon-trained and spur-pruned whereas Sultana is cane-pruned (e.g. 8, 15-node canes).

Light—Greater than 75 nodes per m row
This includes mechanically pruned (hedged or minimal) or non-pruned vineyards, mainly in the Riverland, Sunraysia, MIA, Padthaway and Coonawarra.

Severe pruning will result in relatively few, long, thick shoots and few bunches. There is likely to be an imbalance in favour of vegetative growth at the expense of fruit production, particularly in moderate to high vigour vineyards. Conversely very light pruning will result in a large number of short, thin shoots and many small bunches; the fruit may not ripen to desired commercial standards.

4.6.1 Balanced pruning
Balanced pruning is the concept of equating the nodes retained at pruning with vine capacity, the aim being to maintain a balance between vegetative growth and fruit production. It was first investigated experimentally by Shaulis and co-workers in New York State, USA, in the late 1940s. Although not commonly used in commercial grapegrowing (Winkler *et al.* 1974) it has been used in viticultural experimentation. The basic aim of balanced pruning is to prune according to the capacity of each vine; in effect it quantifies the intuitive process of an experienced pruner. Most often, a specified number of nodes are retained for every kg weight of prunings. For the American variety Concord, Kimball and Shaulis (1958) suggested a formula of 30 + 10, that is, 30 nodes per vine for the first lb of prunings and 10 nodes for each additional lb of prunings. However, for the European varieties Gamay and Chardonnay growing at Oakville, California, a more suitable formula was 10 + 10 (Lider *et al.* 1973). Thirty to forty nodes retained per kg pruning weight has been recommended generally for Australian conditions (Smart and Robinson 1991).

4.6.2 Determination of pruning level
The pruning level to be adopted each year depends on the balance of vegetative and fruit growth of the previous year. To determine whether or not a vine is 'in balance', the following parameters can be assessed:

Yield to pruning weight ratio
The ratio of fruit weight to pruning weight (Y/P) gives an indication of the balance between fruit production and vegetative growth (Bravdo and Hepner 1987). These values will vary according to variety and environment. Work by Ravaz in France indicated that this ratio varied between 4–15 for very productive varieties with relatively small shoots, e.g. Cinsaut, and between 3–8 for less productive varieties with long or thick shoots, e.g. Shiraz, Grenache (Champagnol 1984). A value of 5–10 appears to be optimal for a wide range of vineyard situations in Australia (Smart and Robinson 1991).

Pruning weight
Previously, 1 kg pruning weight per metre of canopy was said to be the level beyond which canopy division was recommended. (May 1973). Smart *et al.* (1989) give a range of 0.3–0.6 kg/m of canopy as optimal.

Shoot or cane weight
Mean shoot weight is a good index of vigour; excessive vigour is indicated by long, thick shoots or canes with extensive lateral growth. Measurements in New Zealand on Cabernet Franc showed moderate vigour shoot weights of 20–30 g; more severely pruned vines had shoots of 70 g (Smart and Smith 1988). Recent findings indicate 20–40 g as the optimal value (Smart *et al.* 1989).

These and other measurements suggest that pruning level can, within limits, be used to improve canopy characteristics (Chapter 5). In vigorous vineyards with a restrictive trellis system, it may be necessary to increase nodes per vine and at the same time modify the trellis system to avoid excessive crowding of shoots.

4.7 Pruning systems
4.7.1 Hand pruning
Hand pruning encompasses a vast number of systems used around the world. The systems can be classified on the basis of:
1. Amount and arrangement of wood older than two years. Vines may be head trained where the apex of the vertical trunk forms the support for the fruiting units (Figure 4.2) or cordon-trained where a permanent arm or cordon supports spurs and/or canes (Figure 4.3).

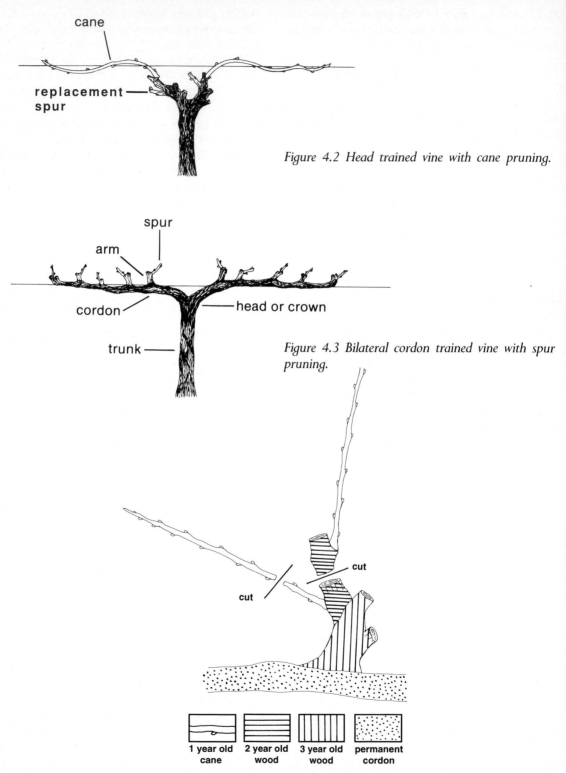

cane

replacement spur

Figure 4.2 Head trained vine with cane pruning.

spur

arm

cordon

head or crown

trunk

Figure 4.3 Bilateral cordon trained vine with spur pruning.

cut

cut

1 year old cane	2 year old wood	3 year old wood	permanent cordon

Figure 4.4 Spur pruning: at pruning the mature shoot most distant from the permanent cordon is generally removed and the closest one cut back to a two node spur. However, the distal shoot may be preferred if it is positioned better and if the lengthening of the arm is not a disadvantage.

Cordons may be horizontal or vertical and unilateral, bilateral or quadrilateral (Figure 2.10).

2. Length of bearers or fruiting units—i.e. short bearers (spurs) or long bearers (canes).
3. Position and arrangement of bearers—trained up or down, flat or arched. This will in turn depend on the height of the cordon or head of the vine.

In Australia, the two most common systems are:

1. Cordon-training, spur-pruning with spurs pointing upwards.
2. Head-training, cane-pruning with one replacement spur for each cane and canes wrapped horizontally along a trellis wire.

Spur pruning

Spur pruned vines may be either head- or cordon-trained, but more commonly the latter. Generally two-node spurs are retained as bearing units. At pruning the distal node and shoot is removed and the shoot at the proximal node is retained to become the new two-node spur (Figure 4.4). The vines require a rigid framework to support the spurs (Chapter 3).

Bush vines are head-trained with no trellising and may still be found in the older established vineyards of Australia, e.g. Barossa Valley, Southern Vales and Rutherglen (Figure 4.5).

With the introduction of trellising, a permanent cordon, generally bilateral, was introduced (Figure 4.6). Once the vines are mature, the number of spurs retained tends to be constant from year to year as pruners tend not to cut into wood older than two years. Spur pruning suits most varieties except for those with low fruitfulness at basal nodes, e.g. Sultana. One-node spurs may be used with fruitful varieties such as Muscat Gordo Blanco, but generally two-node spurs are preferred.

To increase node number per vine, spurs longer than 2 nodes may be used. However, to avoid excessive development of secondary cordons, long spurs, e.g. 3–6 nodes, are often used in combination with 2-node spurs—this is commonly referred to as 'finger and thumb' pruning. Long spurs (4–6 nodes) have been successfully used with Sultana (May *et al.* 1982).

Spur pruning is now preferred to cane pruning in most areas of Australia because it is quicker

Table 4.3 Average pruning costs and time for a typical large-scale vineyard

Pruning	Relative Cost/ha (approx.)	Hours/ha (approx.)
Hand—spur	550	95
—cane	1150–1580	130*
Mechanical	260	20
Minimal	100	10

* This figure incorporates the 3 operations
—cutting off 80 hrs/ha
—pulling out 25 hrs/ha
—tying on 25 hrs/ha
—tying on 25 hrs/ha

and thus more economical (Table 4.3). Pruners can be more readily taught to spur prune and a vine can be pruned in less than half the time required for cane pruning. Preferable spur positions are those close to the vine framework heading either up or out rather than downwards: GDC and spur-pruned Scott Henry systems are exceptions.

Cane pruning

This system utilizes long bearers (canes) of about 8–20 nodes usually accompanied by 2-node replacement spurs (Figures 4.2, 4.7 and 4.8) which can provide the canes for the following season. The vines are generally head trained with the canes arising from one central region. Canes may also arise from cordons. When head trained, there may be from 1–8 canes per vine: the number and length of canes is dependent on the capacity of the vine and the desired node number. The length of the internodes and the intervine distance may determine the cane length as it is desirable to fill the wire along the row.

For cane pruning, the vine framework is essentially non-rigid and the vine shape is more readily preserved than with spur pruning. Most varieties are suited to cane pruning. One problem typically encountered is that of 'apical dominance' whereby the terminal nodes burst first and develop more strongly at the expense of those in the mid-portion of the cane. A number of solutions have been suggested: these include 'cracking' or 'arching' the canes. Recent experience with cyanamide e.g. Dormex® promotes better

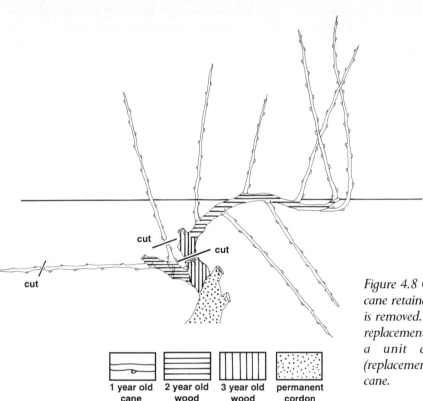

1 year old cane | 2 year old wood | 3 year old wood | permanent cordon

Figure 4.8 Cane pruning: at pruning the cane retained during the previous winter is removed. The mature shoots from the replacement spur are cut so as to produce a unit comprising a two node (replacement) spur and a 10 to 15 node cane.

budburst if applied after pruning and 3-4 weeks before normal burst (Dry 1992; also 12.2.6).

Cane pruning in commercial vineyards is usually divided into three distinct operations:

1. 'Cutting off' or 'cutting-out'—pruning off the unwanted wood and selection of the most desirable canes and replacement spurs.
2. 'Pulling out'—removal of the cut canes.
3. 'Rolling on', 'wrapping' or 'tying'—securely attaching the canes onto the vine.

Canes should be wrapped around the wire, cut through the end node and attached just before that node to avoid strangling the end shoot.

Wood selection

Selection of the most desirable cane depends on the cane quality and position. A fruitful, good quality cane has the following characteristics: well matured or ripened cane with respect to colour, hardness, and the wood-to-pith ratio; average length internodes 60–80 mm; brown colour to the tip; an average diameter of about 7 mm; and rounded rather than flattened internodes. There are differences between canes that have been well

exposed ('sun canes') and those that have grown in less exposed positions ('shade canes'); the latter tend to have flatter internodes, be lighter in colour and less well matured. The appearance of the cane has been shown to be more important for fruit production than its position of origin on the vine (Antcliff *et al.* 1958).

Alternative cane pruning systems

A popular system of cane pruning in Italy is the Sylvoz—it consists of a high cordon (1.6 m) with canes of 8–15 nodes at regular intervals along the cordon. The canes are attached to a lower wire. A 2-node replacement spur is retained for each cane and there are 3 single foliage wires above the cordon for support of replacement growth. The system has been tried in New Zealand (Wood *et al.* 1989). A modification of the Sylvoz is used in Australia: popularly called 'hanging canes' it is so-called because the canes are not attached to a lower wire but are allowed to hang freely. As the season advances, the weight of shoots and bunches causes the canes to hang vertically. The vines can be mechanically harvested

Figure 4.5 Spur pruned bush vine (Barossa, SA).

Figure 4.6 Spur pruned vine with bilateral cordon — before pruning (Riverland SA).

Figure 4.7 Cane pruned vine with head training.

readily and pruning can be partly mechanized.

Other systems being tried include cane-pruned versions of Scott Henry and Te Kauwhata Two Tier (Chapter 5). Cane pruning is decreasing in popularity with increasing mechanization. It is more common in cool climates, where spur pruning is claimed to result in poor budburst and fruitfulness may be low with spur pruning.

Hand pruning tools
Short-handled secateurs (or snips) are used for hand pruning. Recent innovations of roll handles may decrease fatigue. Similarly, pneumatic and hydraulic secateurs have facilitated pruning where continuous cuts are necessary as in the case of spur pruning. They reduce repetitive strain injury and fatigue, as well as time and cost of pruning by about 20% (Rice 1976). One pruning unit (a self-propelled power source with air compressor or hydraulic pump) can service four pruners, and can be operated by remote control by one of the pruners. There are also electric secateurs with power packs available. If using normal hand secateurs, a pair of long-handled secateurs is also useful for cutting into two-year-old wood. Large cuts should, however, be avoided where possible to prevent the possibility of *Eutypa* infections—if necessary, they should be treated with fungicide (Chapter 11). 'Prepruning' with cutter bars can aid the spur pruning operation.

4.7.2 Mechanical pruning
After mechanization of harvesting, hand pruning remains as the largest single cost factor in vineyard operations. However, the push for the introduction of mechanized pruning came initially from a threat of labour shortage rather than from cost considerations, particularly in the Coonawarra and Sunraysia areas (Patrick 1983). Australia has led the world in the development of mechanical hedging of grapevines. This has been such a radical departure from hand pruning that some growers now refer to the practice as vine 'sawing' rather than pruning.

Two different approaches have emerged with mechanical pruning: one that attempts to simulate hand pruning as much as possible, and the second that assumes that increased node numbers are acceptable, i.e. 'hedging'.

The first attempt at machine pruning involved positioning the canes so they could be easily cut or machines that simulated hand pruning (Freeman 1977, Hollick 1977). Machines and pruning systems are still being developed in Europe that will simulate hand pruning, such as the system of 'Creneaux alternes' (Sevila 1983, Sevila *et al.* 1979). In hedging, not only are node numbers increased, but there is also a change in the type of cut and the length of the bearer. The length of the bearing unit may be from zero count nodes, i.e. retaining only the base buds, to some multiple number depending on the position of the cutter. With repeated hedging, spur crowding and accumulation of old wood may be expected to create problems. However, hedging experiments at Griffith found that a mechanical method of node selection via offset rectangular hedging had no advantage over non-selective hedging (Freeman 1982). After 5 years of hedging, vines hedged to different levels had the same capacity.

Similar results were found with GDC-trained vines in Italy, where the alternate up-down system was compared with the standard down system (Intrieri and Marangoni 1982). Smart *et al.* (1979) studied the response to increased node numbers with mechanical pruning compared to normal hand pruning. An increase of 100% in node numbers resulted in only a 25% increase in shoots per vine due to reduced percentage budburst. The number of bunches per vine increased by 39%, but, due to poorer set and fewer berries per bunch, bunch weight was decreased by 10%. The yield increase was 21% on mechanically pruned vines illustrating the effect of yield component compensation (Table 4.4).

Over time, the yield of mechanically pruned vines is similar to hand pruned vines unless the vines had initially been hand pruned too severely (Dry 1983). Changes in yield components in mechanically pruned vines after three seasons compared with hand pruned vines showed that, although node numbers were retained at a high level, decreases in shoots per vine and bunches per vine resulted in a decrease in yield compared to the initial increase of more than 120% over hand pruning (Dry 1983). These and other trial results clearly show the capacity of the grapevine to regulate the amount of crop by adjusting yield components such as percentage budburst and fruit set.

Table 4.4 Effect of pruning method on yield components in the first year for Shiraz vines growing at Angle Vale, SA (after Dry 1983)

Yield component	Hand pruning	Mechanical pruning	Change relative to hand pruning (%)
Node number per vine	106	212	+102
Shoot number per vine	120	150	+25
Budbreak (%)	115	72	-37
Bunch number per vine	189	263	+39
Bunch weight (g)	76	68	-10
Berry weight (g)	1.4	1.4	0
Berry number per bunch	55	49	-11
Yield (t/ha)	15.7	19.0	+21

Mechanical pruning is now used in more than half of Australian vineyards, particularly in large vineyards (Figure 4.9). Advantages include reductions in cost, time and labour requirements (Table 4.3). For a 40 hectare vineyard annual pruning costs will be reduced by 50% (England 1976). An annual hand clean-up is recommended by some vineyard operators; others recommend a clean-up every three years. The conversion of hand to mechanical pruning requires the reshaping of old cordons, or their complete removal and replacement with new cordons (Figure 4.10).

Mechanical pre-pruning, usually with cutter bars and followed up by hand pruning, is used where some degree of control over node number and/or spur spacing is required. The latter is required to regulate shoot spacing. Examples include vineyards with high planting density and/or divided canopies, e.g. Scott Henry training system. The total time required can be less than 30 hours per ha including 5 hours per ha for the mechanical pre-pruning (R.E. Smart, pers comm).

Mechanical pruners

These generally consist of cutting tools: circular saws, reciprocating cutter bars or revolving blades mounted on tractors (Figure 4.11). The saws are more efficient for hedging old vines with large spur arms but are potentially dangerous and the operator must be protected by a wire screen and a 'dead-man' switch. Cuts in two-year-old wood may become infected by *Eutypa* and appropriate protection with fungicide is necessary, e.g. benzimidazole.

Cutter bars perform well on one-year-old wood

and are safer than saws. Revolving blades need continual sharpening. For pruning of typical Australian single-wire or T-trellis vineyards, the blades are arranged in an inverted L or U shape so that two or three cuts can be made with one pass. For vertical, shoot-positioned trellis systems, cutter bar systems with swing back mechanisms have been recently introduced. Any number of cutters can be attached to allow cutting of the canes in between foliage wires. A machine using multiple circular rotating blades mounted one on top of another has recently been imported into Australia (Figure 4.11d): this permits pruning of vertically trained trellis systems with foliage wires and the chopping-up and removal of canes from foliage wires.

4.7.3 Minimal pruning

The concept of 'minimal pruning' was developed by the CSIRO at Merbein, Victoria following long-term observations on non-pruned vines, particularly Sultana (Clingeleffer 1983). The CSIRO has coined the term 'Minimal Pruning of Cordon Trained Vines' (MPCT) for the vine management system for winegrape production. Minimally pruned vines are, to all intents and purposes, non-pruned vines which have been skirted below the cordon to either facilitate cultural operations, e.g. spray application, or achieve some degree of control of crop load. Skirting may be done in winter when the vines are dormant and/or in summer. 'Minimally pruned' vines are grown on a single or two wire vertical trellis (see 3.2.2). Canes growing

Figure 4.9 Mechanical hedge pruning (Griffith, NSW).

Figure 4.10 Grapevines on a low trellis converted from hand cane pruning to mechanical hedging (Barossa, SA).

Figure 4.11 Mechanical pruning machines
(a) Circular saws (b) Rotating knives (c) Reciprocating cutter bars (which can be used for both winter and summer pruning) (d) Pellenc®

Figure 4.12 Comparison of canopy development in spring with
(a) hard spur pruned vines
(b) minimally pruned vines

Figure 4.13 The typical appearance of minimally pruned grapevines in winter after many years with this pruning method.

downward may be cut but are often wrapped around the permanent cordons to avoid pruning and to maximize shoot numbers; the top growth is not pruned. Over successive seasons, both the cordons and the unattached canes grow into a large permanent structure (Figures 4.12, 4.13).

The success of minimal pruning relies on the grapevine's capacity for 'self-regulation' when pruning is eliminated or significantly reduced. Shoots are shorter than those of conventionally pruned vines with fewer nodes and shorter internodes. Node number per cane is reduced naturally by abscission of terminal shoot growth which fails to mature and lignify during autumn (Possingham *et al.* 1990). The leaf surface area is greater in the early part of the season (as much as *twice* the area of hand pruned vines in the first month after budburst; Figure 4.12). Minimally pruned vines have more shoots and bunches per vine than conventional vines, and smaller bunches and berries; mechanical harvesting is necessary. Minimal pruning is claimed to have the advantage over annual mechanical hedging of the creation of a stable vine architecture which requires little adjustment in subsequent years. Over time, mechanical hedging tends to increase the density of old wood resulting in excessive shading and congestion.

Minimally pruned vines have out-yielded traditionally pruned vines in many cases, but the difference varies according to variety and region. In warm regions it has been successful with traditionally cane-pruned varieties such as Sultana which have low basal-bud fruitfulness. Similarly, in cooler regions it is well suited to Sauvignon Blanc. Fruitful varieties such as Riesling, Shiraz and Chardonnay may require careful monitoring of cropping levels, particularly in cool regions, to ensure satisfactory ripening, especially in early years of conversion. Crop levels can be successfully adjusted with winter and/or summer skirting or by thinning the crop in January with a mechanical harvester to alter the leaf-to-crop ratio (Clingeleffer 1988, Possingham *et al.* 1990). In warmer climates, crop control by thinning is seldom required.

In regions of high shoot 'vigour' where environmental conditions do not induce growth cessation by the time of veraison, uncontrolled growth will lead to associated canopy crowding and shade problems. This has been found in some areas of New Zealand, with problems of uneven ripening and unacceptable levels of maturity (Smart and Robinson 1991). On the other hand, minimally pruned vines may be more susceptible to environmental stresses as a consequence of their larger crop load and/or leaf area. Additional irrigation will usually be required, particularly for certain varieties on their own roots, e.g. Shiraz (Possingham *et al.* 1990)

It is a successful technique in the hot intensively irrigated regions and in the southeast of South Australia and is being tried in many other regions.

4.8 Concluding remarks

Traditional hand pruning adheres closely to the principle of retaining appropriate node numbers per vine according to vine vigour and capacity. It aims to obtain a balance between vegetative and productive vine growth to optimize and maintain quantity and quality of fruit production.

This chapter has outlined the principles used in determining the appropriate pruning level and discusses the place of pruning as a determinant of yield. Increasing the node numbers per vine by lighter pruning does not however lead to a proportional increase in yield due to compensation of the other yield components.

Since the early 1970s there has been a move in Australia towards lighter pruning and less strict control of node numbers. The introduction of mechanical and minimal pruning in the grape industry has borne out the fact that, within certain parameters, the vine has the ability to regulate growth and crop load.

In un-mechanized winegrape vineyards, pruning and harvesting together make up a major part of the cost of production and large reductions in cost result if mechanization of these two operations is adopted. However mechanization of pruning is dependent on prior mechanization of harvesting. This is especially true with minimal pruning.

The machines used for pruning have been relatively simple in concept but are evolving and improving as new technology is applied. It is possible that, in future, methods may become available for all types of grapes (wine, drying and table) except those which need cane pruning.

Further reading

Busby, J.A. (1925) A Treatise on the Culture of the Vine and the art of Making Wine, Sydney (Reprinted by the David Ell Press, 1979).

Kelly, A.C. (1861) The Vine in Australia, Melbourne (Reprinted by the David Ell Press, 1980).

Perkins, A.J. (1895) Vine Pruning; its Theory and Practice. Vardon and Pritchard: Adelaide.

Perold, A.I. (1927) A Treatise on Viticulture. McMillan and Co. Ltd: London.

Quinn, G. (1901) Fruit Tree and Grape Vine Pruning. Govt. Printer, Adelaide. 12th edition 1945 by Robertson & Mullens. Melbourne.

Smart, R.E. and Robinson, M.D. (1991) Sunlight into Wine. A Handbook for Winegrape Canopy Management, Winetitles' Adelaide.

Winkler, A.J., Cook, J.A., Kliewer, W.M. and Lider, L.A. (1974) General Viticulture, Univ. Calif. Press; Berkeley.

Other references

Antcliff, A.J., Webster, W.J. and May, P. (1957) Studies on the Sultana vine. V. Further studies on the course of budburst with reference to time of pruning. Aust. J. Agric. Res. 8, 15-23.

Antcliff, A.J., Webster, W.J. and May, P. (1958) Studies on the Sultana vine. VI. The morphology of the cane and its fruitfulness. Aust. J. Agric. Res. 9, 328-38.

Bravdo, B. and Hepner, Y. (1987) Water management and effect on fruit quality in grapevines. In: Proc. Sixth Aust. Wine Industry Tech. Conf. Aust. Industrial Publ. pp.150-158.

Buttrose, M.S. (1970) Fruitfulness in grapevines: The response of different cultivars to light, temperature and daylength. Vitis. 9, 121-5.

Champagnol, F. (1984) Elements de physiologie de la vigne et de viticulture generale. Saint-Gely-du-Fesc, France.

Clingeleffer, P.R. (1983) Minimal pruning—its role in canopy management and implications of its use for the wine industry. Proc. Fifth Aust. Wine Industry Tech. Conf., Aust. Wine Res. Inst., Glen Osmond, SA 5064, pp. 133-40.

Clingeleffer, P.R. (1989) Update: Minimal pruning of cordon trained vines (MPCT). Aust. Grapegrower and Winemaker. No. 304, 78-83.

Coombe, B.G. (1964) The winter treatment of grapevines with zinc and its interaction with time of pruning. Aust. J. Exp. Agric. & An. Husbandry; 4, 241-6.

Coombe, B.G. (1973) The regulation of set and development of the grape berry. Acta Hortic. 34, 261-73.

Coombe, B.G. (1980) Development of the grape berry. I. Effects of time of flowering and competition. Aust. J. Agric. Res. 31, 125-31.

Dry, P.R. (1983) Grapevine response to mechanical pruning. In: Lester, D.C. and Lee, T.H. (eds) Coonawarra Viticulture: Proceedings of a Seminar. 8 June, Coonawarra, Sth Aust. Aust. Soc. Vitic. and Oenol., Glen Osmond, SA 5064., pp. 7-12.

Dry, P.R. (1987) How to grow 'cool climate' grapes in hot regions. Aust. Grapegrower and Winemaker. No. 283, 25-6.

England, P. (1976) The economics of mechanical pruning aids and fully mechanical pruning aids and fully mechanical pruning. In: R.E. Smart and P.R. Dry (eds) Workshop on Grapevine Pruning. Roseworthy Agric. College, p. 15-14

Freeman, B.M. (1977) Griffith experiments in mechanical pruning. Third Wine Ind. Tech. Conf., Aust. Wine Res. Inst., Glen Osmond, SA 5064. p. 55.

Freeman, B.M. (1982) Experiments on vine hedging for mechanical pruning. In: A.D. Webb (ed.) Grape and Wine Centennial Symp. Proc. June 1980, Davis Calif., University of California, Davis. pp. 261-3.

Freeman, B.M., Lee, T.H. and Turkington, C.R. (1979) Interaction of irrigation and pruning level on growth and yield of Shiraz vines. Amer. J. Enol. Vitic. 30, 218-23.

Hollick, R.R. (1977) Machine use in mechanical pruning. Third Wine Ind. Tech. Conf., Aust. Wine Res. Inst., Glen Osmond, SA 5064. pp. 54.

Huglin, P. (1986) Biologie et Ecologie de la Vigne. Editions Payot Lausanne. Technique and Documentation, Paris.

Intrieri, C. and Marangoni, B. (1982) The alternate 'up-down' mechanical pruning system: experiments on vines GDC trained (V. vinifera cv. Montuni). In: A.D. Webb (ed.) Grape and Wine Centennial Symp. Proc. June, 1980 Davis, Calif. University of California, Davis, pp. 266-9.

Kimball, K. and Shaulis. N.J. (1985) Pruning effects on the growth, yield and maturity of Concord grapes. Proc. Amer. Soc. Hortic. Sci., 71; 167-76.

Lider, L.A., Kasimatis, A.N. and Kliewer, W.M. (1973) Effect of pruning severity and rootstock on growth and yield of two grafted, cane-pruned wine grape cultivars. J. Amer. Soc. Hortic. Sci. 98, 8-11.

May, P., Clingeleffer, P.R, and Brien, C.J. (1982) Pruning of Sultana vines to long spurs. Amer. J. Enol. Vitic. 33; 214-21.

May, P. (1973) Trellising in relation to vine performance. Proc. Second Aust. Wine Ind. Tech. Conf. Tanunda, 1973, Aust. Wine Res. Inst., Glen Osmond, SA 5064.

May, P. (1987) The grapevine as a perennial, plastic and productive plant. Proc. Sixth Aust. Wine Ind. Tech. Conf., Adelaide, 1986. pp. 40-9.

May, P. and Antcliff. A.J. (1963) The effect of shading on fruitfulness and yield in the Sultana. J. Hortic. Sc. 38; 85-94.

Patrick, V. (1983) Mechanical pruning trails in Coonawarra. In: D.C. Lester and T.H. Lee (eds) Coonawarra Viticulture: Proceedings of a Seminar. 8 June, Coonawarra, Sth Aust. Aust. Soc. Vitic. and Oenol., Glen Osmond, SA 5064.

Possingham, J.V., Clingeleffer, P.R. and Cooper, A.M. (1990) Vine management techniques for the wine industry. Aust. Grapegrower and Winemaker No. 316, 85-89.

Rice, D. (1976) Performance of pruning aids. In: R.E. Smart and P.R. Dry (eds) Workshop on Grapevine

Pruning. Roseworthy Agric. College, p. 13.

Sevila, F., Carbonneau, A., Casteran, P. and Dumartin, P. (1979) Etude de la faisibilite d'une mecanisation de la taille de la vigne en France. Prog. Agric. Vitic. 96, 360-5.

Sevila, F. (1983) The 'alternate crenel' and a computerized growth model for the grapevine. A robot for the pruning of the grapevine with the 'alternate crenel' method. Proc. Int. Workshop on Mech. Pruning of the Grapevine. pp. 75-124.

Shaulis, N.J., Amberg, H. and Crowe, D. (1966) Response of Concord grapes to light, exposure and geneva double curtain training. Proc. Amer. Soc. Hortic. Sci.; 89, 268-80.

Smart, R.E., Kyloh, S.R. and Brien, C. (1979) Roseworthy experiences with mechanical pruning. In: R.E. Smart and S.R. Kyloh (eds) Proceedings of a Workshop, Mechanical Pruning of Grapevines, Roseworthy Agric. College. pp. 14-7.

Smart, R.E., Shaulis, N.J. and Lemon, E.R. (1982) The effect of Concord vineyard microclimate on yield II. The interrelations between microclimate and yield expression. Amer. J. Enol. Vitic.; 33, 109-16.

Smart, R.E. and Smith, S.M. (1988) Canopy management: identifying the problems and practical solutions. In: Smart et al. (eds) Proc. Second Int. Symp. for Cool Climate Vitic. and Oenol., Auckland, New Zealand. pp. 109-15.

Smart, R.E., Dick, J.K., Gravett, I.M. and Fisher, B.M. (1989) Canopy management to improve grape yield and wine quality principles and practices. South African J. of Enol. and Vitic.; 11, 3-17.

Srinivasan, C. and Mullins, M.G. (1981) Physiology of flowering in the grapevine—a review. Amer. J. Enol. Vitic.; 32, 47-57.

Whittles, J.G. (1986) The effect of time of winter pruning on the production of winegrapes. In: Proc. of the Winter Pruning Field Day, Te Kauwhata Res. Stn. Oenol. and Vitic. Bulletin No. 48, 9-14.

Wood, P.N., Smart, R.E. and Morgan, L. (1989) Yield responses with conversion to new training systems. In: Proc. Vintage '89 Seminar, Te Kauwhata Res. Station, New Zealand. pp. 46-56.

CHAPTER FIVE

Canopy Management

R.E. SMART

The concept of canopy management is a relatively recent addition to the list of commercial viticultural practices. Vineyard responses to other management practices such as irrigation, nutrition and pest and disease control have long been recognized and are now accepted as part of good vineyard husbandry. It is only over the last few decades that the particular contribution of canopy microclimate to vineyard productivity, including fruit composition and disease incidence, has been identified by experimentation. The phrase 'canopy management' has come into vogue to describe a range of practices aimed at avoiding within-canopy shade and poor ventilation.

While scientific explanation of canopy management concepts is only relatively recent, vineyard observation over at least two millenia has provided adages related to recent findings, especially in relation to wine quality, e.g. 'Bacchus amat colles' comes out of ancient Roman viticulture. 'Bacchus loves the hills' is a literal translation, but the phrase suggests that wine quality is higher on less fertile, hillside soils. 'A struggling vine makes the best wine' and 'high yields give low quality' are two further examples from recent European viticultural experience. The association between vine vigour and yield, canopy microclimate and wine quality is explored in this chapter.

Pioneering scientific studies in canopy management were made by Shaulis and co-workers in New York State during the 1960s. The Geneva Double Curtain training system arose from studies of canopy factors limiting yield of Vitis labruscana var. Concord in New York vineyards (Shaulis et al. 1966). Within-canopy shade was reduced by dividing dense canopies on wide row spacing into two pendant curtains, and yield was almost doubled. Similar principles were developed in a hot climate for V. vinifera var. Sultana when Shaulis worked with CSIRO researchers at Merbein, Victoria (Shaulis and May 1971). Carbonneau et al. (1978) extended these principles to demonstrate deleterious effects of shade on wine quality in Bordeaux for Cabernet Sauvignon, and subsequent studies at Roseworthy College (Smart 1982) produced similar results with the red winegrape Shiraz in the hot climate of Angle Vale, SA.

These publications, among others, have stimulated research activity in this area so that at the time of writing canopy management concepts are relatively well developed and commercial adoption is now beginning. For this reason this chapter will emphasize techniques to assess canopies and possible techniques to correct deficiencies, as a guide to further commercial developments. The theory and practice of winegrape canopy management has been described in Smart and Robinson (1991).

5.1 Definitions and concepts

5.1.1 Definition of canopy management

A canopy is defined as the leaf and shoot system of the vine. It is described by both dimensions of the boundaries in space (i.e. width, height, length) and the amount of shoot system within these boundaries (typically leaf area). Where foliage from adjacent vines intermingles and there are no large gaps down the row, canopies are described as *continuous*; if canopies are separated from vine to vine they are *discontinuous*. Where canopies of one vine (or adjacent vines) are separated into discrete foliage walls the canopy is termed *divided*. Canopies are described as *crowded* or *dense* where there is a large leaf area within the volume bounded by the canopy surfaces; dense canopies are associated with high values of shoot density (shoots per m canopy), ratio of leaf area per canopy surface area (LA/SA), or of leaf layer number (LLN). (These indices are subsequently defined, see 5.3).

The term *canopy management* embraces a range of techniques which a viticulturist imposes on a vineyard resulting in altered position or amount of leaves, shoot and fruit in space to achieve some desired arrangement. In actuality the term has broad implications for many viticultural practices. For example, shoot vigour control is an important component in maintaining a desired canopy microclimate, so that for example irrigation practice to achieve devigoration may in fact be rightly considered a component of a 'canopy management' program. In a similar fashion 'canopy management' includes the practice of shoot positioning and trimming, with the associated concomitant benefit of facilitating mechanized winter pruning, and also the practice of fruit-zone leaf removal to facilitate disease control.

A scheme showing the interaction of cultural practices with soil and climate conditions in affecting vine physiology is shown in Figure 5.1.

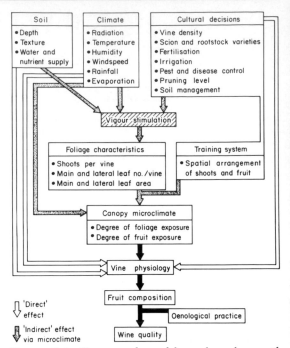

Figure 5.1. Conceptual model to show how soil, climate and cultural practices can affect wine quality via effects on canopy microclimate (From Smart et al. 1985a). This model also applies for tablegrape production but needs alteration for raisins.

This figure emphasizes that soil, climate and management factors can have 'direct' effects on vine physiology, as well as 'indirect' effects. The indirect effects result from vigour stimulation altering canopy microclimate, which in turn affects vine physiology. Note the interaction of vigour and training system which affects canopy microclimate. This interaction will be explored further in this chapter.

It could be argued that any practice that affects the position or amount of grapevine canopies in space is 'canopy management'. This chapter will however concentrate on canopy management techniques to avoid shade and produce a desirable canopy microclimate.

5.1.2 The concept of canopy microclimate

The presence of a grapevine canopy alters the climate relative to that which would have existed at that position in space had the canopy not been present. Canopy microclimate is the climate within and immediately adjacent to the canopy. Figure 5.2 gives a diagrammatic representation of differences in values of the climatic factors sunlight, wind, humidity, temperature and

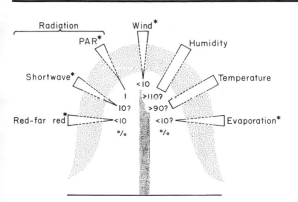

Figure 5.2. Diagrammatic representation of climate attenuation by grapevine canopies. The values within the canopy are percentages of the ambient, above-canopy values (from Smart 1984).

evaporation from the inside to the outside of a dense, non-shoot-positioned canopy. Note that of these climatic variables, sunlight, wind and evaporation are the most attenuated (altered) by the canopy presence. Leaf area is the most important canopy component which attenuates sunlight and wind, and in turn causes yield, quality and disease incidence responses.

5.2 Canopy Microclimate

Canopy microclimate is the climate within and immediately around the canopy and depends upon the attenuation of the above-canopy climate by the canopy elements (parts). The term *microclimate* is often incorrectly used to describe a vineyard site (see Volume 1, section 10.1.1 for definitions of macro-, meso- and microclimate.)

5.2.1 Canopy attenuation

Sunlight

The sun emits electromagnetic radiation (sunlight) over the waveband 300-1500 nm, termed 'shortwave' radiation. Only about half the available energy is used for photosynthesis (the waveband 400-700 nm is termed 'photosynthetically active'). Figure 5.3 shows a curve of the spectral distribution of sunlight for sunny and overcast conditions, and Figure 5.4 the absorption, reflection and transmission spectra for Traminer leaves.

Grapevine leaves, as for other plant species, strongly absorb radiation in the 400-700 nm or photosynthetically active waveband. For this

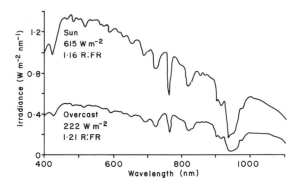

Figure 5.3. Spectral distribution of sunlight measured at Te Kauwhata, New Zealand. 'Sun' refers to measurements on 11 March 1986 (3/8 cloud) and 'Overcast' to measurements on 25 February 1986 (8/8 cloud) (from Smart 1987a).

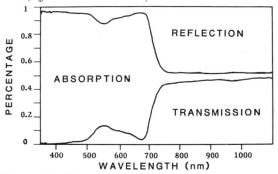

Figure 5.4. The spectral characteristics of a grapevine leaf var. Traminer (from Smart 1987a).

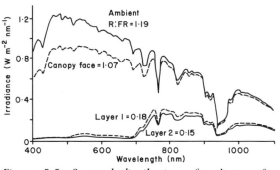

Figure 5.5. Spectral distribution of radiation for ambient sunny conditions, at the exposed vertical canopy face, and for leaf layers 1 and 2 in the canopy. R:FR values are shown for each (from Smart 1987a).

waveband, absorption is 87%, reflection 7% and transmission 6%. Therefore light measured within grapevine canopies is relatively depleted in the photosynthetically active waveband relative to the near infrared waveband (700-3000 nm) (Figure 5.5). The amounts of photosynthetically-active-radiation are maximal above a canopy on a sunny day with values of 2000 μE m^{-2} s^{-1}. Values at the centre of a dense canopy however may be as low as 15-30 μE m^{-2} s^{-1}, or less than 1% of above-canopy values. As well as being of reduced quantity, shadelight has altered quality (spectral distribution) (Figure 5.5). The ratio of red to far-red light (R:FR or 660 nm:730 nm) affects the plant's phytochrome system which triggers some plant responses to shade. The R:FR ratio above canopies for either sunny or overcast conditions is 1.0 to 1.2, but within dense canopies measured values of 0.1 or less are common.

Temperature

Exterior leaves and berries are heated by sunlight absorption. The amount of temperature change in leaves and berries caused by this heating depends on the counteracting effects of convection due to wind, and, especially for leaves, of transpiration. When well-supplied with water and transpiring freely, leaf temperatures for sunlit leaves are within 1-2°C of air temperature. Droughted vines show a substantial increase in sunlit leaf temperature over ambient, whereas leaves on well-watered vines, if not exposed to direct sunlight, may be up to 2°C below air temperature. Berries are only slightly cooled by transpiration, so that dark berries exposed to bright sunlight and low wind speed may heat up to 15°C above ambient. At night, exterior leaves and fruit may be cooled by longwave radiation emission to 1 to 3°C below air temperature. Generally interior leaves and fruit are at about air temperature both day and night.

Humidity

Transpiration by leaves can cause increases in the humidity within dense canopies, although increases of less than 10% relative humidity have been recorded. The extent to which this buildup occurs depends on canopy ventilation (windspeed), which in turn depends on canopy density.

Wind

Leaves and other vine parts reduce the momentum of the air so that wind velocity is reduced in the centre of crowded canopies. Wind velocity in the centre of dense Shiraz canopies at Angle Vale, SA has been measured at less than 20% of above-canopy values (Smart 1982). Studies with Semillon

canopies in New Zealand have shown within-canopy velocities at 10% to 20% of above-canopy measurements, varying with canopy density.

Evaporation

Evaporation rates in the centre of dense canopies are reduced compared with those outside, due to lower levels of radiation, windspeed and slightly increased humidity. Therefore plant parts wetted by rainfall or dew will dry more slowly in the centre of dense canopies, an important factor contributing to development of fungal diseases.

Rainfall

Initial rainfall is intercepted during 'wetting up' of the foliage, and subsequent rain tends to be concentrated in 'drip zones' along the edges of dense canopies. There can be interaction between rain direction and canopy configuration, so that the inter-row space receives 50% more rain than the soil under the vines (Smart and Coombe 1983). Intense rainfall and/or low-density canopies will reduce these differences.

5.2.2 Solar radiation microclimate and vine physiology

Because of the overwhelming importance of sunlight effects on vine physiology, this section elaborates on the solar radiation microclimate.

Photosynthesis

Photosynthesis is the light-dependent process whereby atmospheric CO_2 is converted to sugars in green plant tissues. Grapevines show a 'light saturated' photosynthetic rate at irradiance levels above about one-third of full sunlight (ca. 700 μE m^{-2} s^{-1}); the compensation point at which there is zero rate of net photosynthesis is low (ca. 30 μE m^{-2} s^{-1}) (Figure 5.6). Leaves that have commenced to yellow in plant shade photo-synthesize slowly even when exposed to high light levels; such leaves senesce and fall off earlier than if they had received full sunlight.

Because of the attenuation of light within dense grapevine canopies, it is essentially the exterior leaves that contribute to canopy photosynthesis. Studies with dense, irrigated canopies of Shiraz at Griffith (Smart 1974) showed that less than 30% of direct sunlight penetrated more than 10 cm from the canopy surface. Profiles of leaf area, diffused light levels and estimated photosynthesis

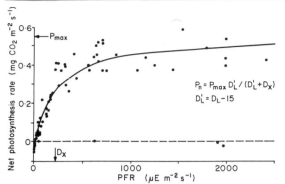

Figure 5.6. *The light response curve for photosynthesis for Traminer leaves. The four points near the line for zero photosynthesis correspond to yellow leaves removed from the canopy interior and exposed to light of different intensities (from Smart 1985b).*

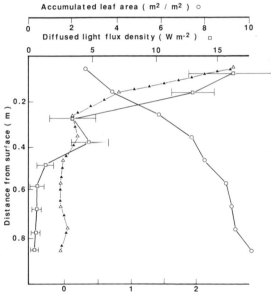

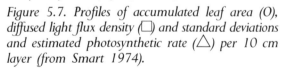

Figure 5.7. *Profiles of accumulated leaf area (O), diffused light flux density (□) and standard deviations and estimated photosynthetic rate (△) per 10 cm layer (from Smart 1974).*

photosynthesis as a function of distance from the surface of dense Shiraz canopies are shown in Figure 5.7. Interior leaves are less likely to receive direct sunlight, and are exposed to low levels of diffuse sunlight and as a result contribute little to canopy photosynthesis.

Phytochrome

Phytochrome reactions are important in regulating plant growth and development, especially in response to shade. Shade light is characterized by a lowering of the R:FR ratio but the significance

of this control system for grapevines is less studied than for photosythesis. Studies with Cabernet Sauvignon (Smart *et al.* 1988) showed that anthocyanin and fruit sugar levels were raised by enhanced R:FR ratios indicating a phytochrome reaction. Further experiments with Cabernet Franc (Kliewer and Smart 1989) confirmed these effects, and showed a phytochrome control of the important fruit ripening enzymes PAL and invertase. Thus it appears that fruit composition responses to a shaded canopy are in part due to phytochrome as well as photosynthetic control (Smart 1987a).

Thermal influences

Excessive leaf temperatures beyond 30°C can inhibit photosynthesis, and similarly high temperatures can adversely affect fruit ripening (Coombe 1987). Sunburn produces round necrotic spots on berries under certain conditions of high sunlight and air temperatures and low wind velocity. Fruit conditioning to exposure, i.e. gradual acclimatization, is important for avoiding sunburn damage — fruit that has developed in an exposed position shows tolerance of conditions that would otherwise cause sunburn. Thermal effects on fruit other than sunburn include berry shrivelling, suppression of colour development and increased juice phenolic levels in both red and white varieties.

Water relations

Exterior leaves are more water-stressed than interior leaves due to higher transpiration rates. Stomatal opening of interior leaves is reduced by low light levels.

Solar radiation microclimate at the canopy exterior

Sunlight interception at the canopy surface depends on interaction of the solar position and the degree of cloudiness with vineyard row orientation, shape and size. The majority of Australian vineyards are characterized by sunny conditions (Volume 1, Chapter 2), and so direct sunlight has a dominating influence.

The sun's position in the sky varies with time of day and season, and a grapevine's shape and size alters during the season as a consequence of shoot development. Computer simulation of the interaction between sun position and grapevine form (Smart 1973) has demonstrated that radiation

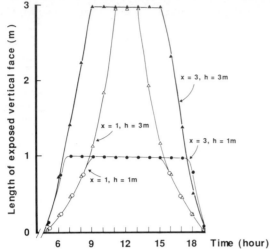

Figure 5.8. Model-simulated values of the vertical length of canopy exposed to direct sunlight for combinations of two vine heights (h = 1 and 3 m) and two distances between foliage walls (x = 1 and 3 m). Vertical vine walls, 1 m wide canopy, north-south rows, December 22, latitude 35°S (from Smart 1971).

interception is about 60% for wide-row vineyards (spacing 3-4 m). This value can be increased by decreasing row spacing, by increasing foliage height and by north-south row orientation. However with decreased distance between foliage walls, i.e. decreased row spacing, there is increased likelihood of cross-row shading. This effect is shown by a comparison of exposed vine-side length for foliage walls of 1 and 3 m height in combination with distance between vertical foliage walls of 1 and 3 m (Figure 5.8). Vine side exposure to direct sunlight is maximal for widely-spaced, short foliage walls, and is minimal for closely-spaced, tall foliage walls. Similar principles apply to diffused sky-light interception.

A balance is therefore required between wide row spacing and low vines, which intercept radiation inefficiently, and narrow row spacing and tall vines where shading of the canopy base is excessive. Measurements of light profiles of canopy exteriors have led to a rule-of-thumb (Smart 1985b) that distance between foliage walls should not be less than their height (Figure 5.9). For leaves located deep within the enclosure formed by the canopy walls of the 'U' trellis, shade levels were increased, and also for exterior leaves at the base of overhanging walls. This was not the case for leaves towards the top of the enclosure, where

the height:distance between walls ratio was less than one, or for vertical walls on the Te Kauwhata Two Tier trellis.

Solar radiation microclimate of the canopy interior
Dense grapevine canopies cause within-canopy shading, and sparse ones do not. This obvious distinction can be translated into terms of shoot density per unit length of row (or per unit length of curtain of foliage in the case of divided canopies). High shoot numbers per metre, say 30 or more, lead to shoot crowding and shading. Low shoot densities on the other hand, (say less than 5 shoots per m) cause excessive gaps in the canopy and much sunlight is not intercepted by the canopy. For example, the R:FR, shortwave radiation and photosynthetically active radiation (termed PPFR or photosynthetic photon fluence rate) in the most shaded part of Traminer canopies with vertically trained shoots at a range of shoot densities are shown in Figure 5.10. Canopies of less than 10 shoots per m had more than 30% gaps, and interior radiation values were similar to those measured above the canopy. For shoot densities greater than 20 shoots per m, the proportion of canopy gaps was less than 5%, and interior light measurements corresponded to deep shade. These results were for moderate-vigour Traminer shoots; high vigour shoots would need to be more widely spaced to achieve a similar light microclimate.

5.2.3 Viticultural implications of canopy microclimate
Variation in canopy microclimate has implications for grapevine yield, fruit composition and quality, and disease incidence.

Yield
High yield potential attaches to vineyards intercepting a high proportion of sunlight, and with a large canopy surface area per ha. A vineyard with close rows (or its equivalent achieved with canopy division) and with thin foliage walls can have over double the exposed canopy surface area of an overhead pergola (Smart 1985a). The greater the exposed canopy surface area, the higher is the interception of sunlight, and thus the potential photosynthesis and yield.

Shading within the canopy affects each of the yield-forming processes of budbreak, fruit bud

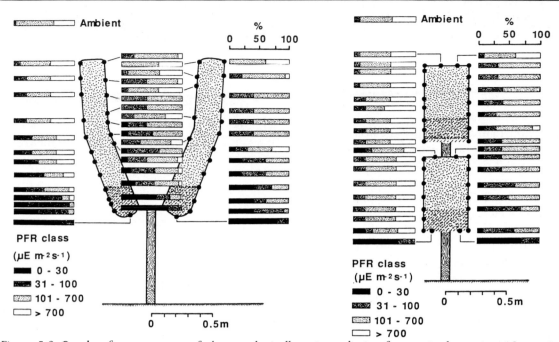

Figure 5.9. *Results of measurement of photosynthetically active radiation for exterior leaves over 10 occasions on 7 February 1984. (a) U trellis, (b) the Te Kauwhata Two Tier (from Smart 1985b).*

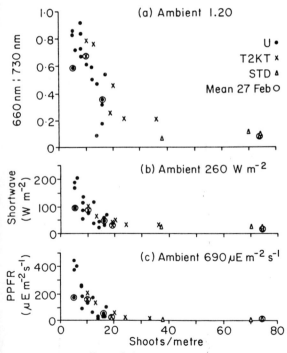

Figure 5.10. *Effect of shoot spacing on R:FR ratio, shortwave radiation 400-100 nm and photosynthetically active radiation for most shaded part of the canopy. U, TK2T, GDC refer to trellis systems (from Smart 1988).*

initiation and development, fruitset and berry growth. While early Australian studies have emphasized effects of shade on bud fruitfulness for Sultana (May 1965), it is now evident that shade reduces many yield components. In particular shade has recently been identified as contributing to poor fruitset due to a physiological process called Early Bunchstem Necrosis or EBSN (Jackson and Coombe 1988). Poor fruitset is often observed in the centre of dense canopies.

These shade responses are localized in the vine. For example, adequate sunlight exposure of the renewal zone is of paramount importance for high fruitfulness. (The renewal zone is the base of the shoots that are retained at pruning in winter; in dense, non-shoot-positioned canopies, the renewal zone is at the canopy centre and is the most shaded.)

Fruit composition and quality

Within-canopy shading has been established as an important factor in affecting grape composition for a range of cultivars and over a range of climates (see literature cited in Smart 1985a, Smart et al. 1990). While exposed fruit may be warmed during the day and be cooler by night, it is commonly assumed that the responses listed below are more likely to be influenced by light than by temperature effects. Shading of berries increases their size relative to exposed berries, and, as a consequence of dilution, decreases their sugar and tartrate concentration. Low sugar is associated with higher K concentration and higher juice pH. There are higher malate levels which may be due to lowered berry temperatures. Shading also causes lowered absolute amounts of phenols, lower than is due to dilution (Crippin and Morrison 1986); this means decreased dermal anthocyanin levels, important for both winegrapes and tablegrapes.

The monoterpene flavourants of Traminer have been found to be depressed by fruit shading (Reynolds and Wardle 1989) and experienced wine tasters have recorded a reduction in fruit character in wine for Shiraz vines from shaded canopies (Smart 1982). Overall quality was found to be reduced for wines from shaded canopies (Carbonneau et al. 1978, Smart 1982, Smart et al. 1990). Undesirable 'herbaceous' odours and flavours have also been associated with shaded canopies.

Disease incidence

Two of the major fungal diseases of grapevines are known to be affected by canopy microclimate: powdery mildew (oidium) and bunch rot. Powdery mildew overwinters inside dormant buds or on the vine surface. Early shoot growth is infected in the spring as spores are spread by wind. Importantly, sunlight inhibits germination of spores, and so low sunlight levels in the centre of dense canopies promote powdery mildew infections.

Bunch rot due to *Botrytis* and other fungi can cause major yield and quality losses. Flower parts can be infected before capfall, and after veraison any damaged berries are subject to infection. Spore germination requires free water and high humidity. Fruit in dense canopies is more prone to bunch rot infection since bunches wet by rain or dew dry out more slowly. Thus substantial reductions in bunch rot losses have been noted in New Zealand due to improved training systems and also to leaf removal in the fruit zone. During the wet 1990 vintage in the Hunter Valley it was apparent that well-exposed fruit on improved training systems was less affected by bunch rot, and thus could be left until normal maturity. Disease control is further facilitated with open canopies

since sprays penetrate better to the canopy centre and fruit and leaf surfaces are more effectively protected.

5.3 Canopy assessment and problem diagnosis

The techniques for canopy assessment that are described here are taken from the handbook of grapevine canopy management by Smart and Robinson (1991).

5.3.1 Canopy shape and size

Canopy shape and size is readily determined by sketching the outline, then by measurement of dimensions as shown, for example, in Figure 5.11. Row length (L) per ha is calculated from spacing between rows (R) by

$$L \text{ (m/ha)} = 10,000 \text{ m}^2/R \text{ (m)}$$

Exposed canopy surface area per m length of row is then established from the outline sketch, and exposed canopy surface area per ha can be readily calculated. Values of about 20,000-25,000 m²/ha are optimal, indicating high proportions of sunlight interception and thus yield potential. Lower values lead to lower yield potentials, and higher values indicate excessive cross-row shading (Smart et al.1990).

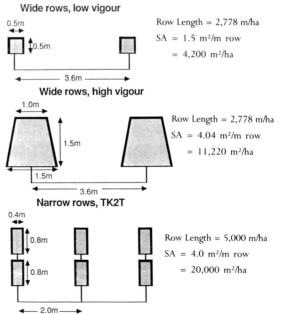

Figure 5.11. Scale diagrams showing calculation of exposed canopy surface area. Outlined surfaces are considered exposed.

Some precautions need to be exercised in calculations of this type. The calculation should not be made where canopies are not continuous. Where the canopy surface is irregular, occasional protruding shoots should be ignored. For example, calculate the canopy boundaries so as to include say 90% of the canopy leaf area. If canopy surfaces are not on the top or sides they should not be included as they will not be well exposed to sunlight — for example, ignore the underside of the Tatura trellis.

The value for exposed canopy surface area of about 21,000 m² per ha (or 2.1 m² canopy surface area per m² land area) appears to be the maximum obtainable for commercially acceptable trellis systems with upwardly trained shoots. The Te Kauwhata Two Tier trellis with a 2 m row spacing gives this value (Figure 5.11). Note the lower values for vineyards at wide row spacing, being about 4,200 m² per ha and 10,200 m² per ha for low and high vigour vineyards respectively.

5.3.2 Shoot characteristics
Grapevine shoots can be described by their length and leaf area. Vigorous shoots are long, have large leaves and considerable lateral shoot growth. Lateral shoots develop at each node to varying degrees, and their growth is stimulated when the shoot tip is removed, i.e. by topping or trimming. Lateral leaf area on vigorous shoots can be greater than the area of the primary leaves, i.e. on the main shoot. Measurements of leaf area for vigorous Shiraz shoots at Roseworthy are shown in Figure 5.12.

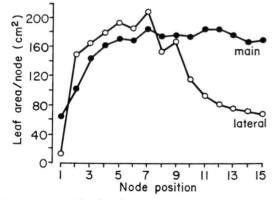

Figure 5.12. The distribution of main and lateral leaf area at each node position on vigorous Shiraz shoots sampled mid December at Roseworthy, South Australia (from Smart 1985a).

Table 5.1. Some measurements characterizing shoot vigour, var. Cabernet Franc

	Low vigour	High vigour
Mean cane weight in winter (g)	~25	~60
Length of 5th internode (mm)	60	180
Diameter of 5th internode (mm)	4	12
Yield/pruning weight ratio	~7	~2
Mean main leaf area (cm²)	~100	~170

There are several measurements that can be made to describe shoot vigour (Table 5.1). Shoot length, main node number and shoot leaf area are good indicators. Other useful vigour measurements are the ratio of lateral to total leaf area, shoot internode length and shoot diameter (a good internode to use is that above the bottom bunch). Shoot vigour is also measured by the weight of one-year-old canes at winter pruning. This value will be altered if the vines were trimmed during the summer. Cane weight may be expressed as pruning weight per unit row length (or per unit canopy length), or as the average weight of a cane. The ratio of shoot leaf area to shoot length (termed gamma, γ, by Smart 1985a) is an index of shoot leafiness, and can be used to calculate relations between shoot spacing and canopy density. Knowing the number of shoots per vine and vines per ha also allows calculation of total leaf area per ha (LA). This can be divided by canopy surface area/ha to give an index of canopy shading (LA/SA) (Smart 1985a).

5.3.3 Techniques of canopy assessment
Point quadrat
This technique employs a long, thin, rigid, pointed metal rod (e.g. 1 m × 2-3 mm) that is inserted into the canopy. The rod can be assumed to simulate a beam of light, so that contact with canopy components represents light absorption. Contacts with leaves and fruit are recorded, and in this way canopy structure can be described. Shoot, petiole and peduncle contacts may be ignored. Normally, 50-100 insertions are made to describe a canopy, either at random or using

some predetermined sampling interval. Measurements are usually made in the fruit zone as description of fruit exposure is important.

Where the canopy is very dense or wide, it may be necessary to penetrate only to the centre. Where canopies are tall and thin, as for those shoot-positioned vertically, then the rod can be inserted parallel to the ground and normal to the canopy wall. Where canopies have a wide top, as is common with vigorous, non-shoot-positioned canopies, then the rod may be inserted at an angle, say 60⁰ to the horizontal. From the recordings can be calculated the percent canopy gaps (where the rod makes no contact), the leaf layer number (LLN, the mean number of leaf contacts per insertion) and the proportions of interior leaves and fruit.

Visual scoring
The concept of visual assessment of canopies was first described by Smart *et al.* (1985) in a study of Shiraz canopies at Angle Vale, SA. The basic premise of the scorecard is that canopy characteristics that are important in affecting microclimate, productivity and fruit composition can be quickly assessed, and with sufficient accuracy, by visual observation alone. The scorecard is used between veraison and harvest. The scorecard has been modified several times; the most recent version (Smart and Robinson 1991) uses eight characters, each assessed out of ten points (Table 5.2). Of these, three characters describe characters which affect microclimate (canopy gaps, canopy density and fruit exposure) while the remaining five describe the growth status of the vine (leaf size, leaf colour, shoot length, lateral growth and growing tip presence).

The scorecard is particularly designed to assess canopy attributes as they affect the potential to produce desirable fruit composition for winemaking. In principle, it is likely that the same assessments would apply with advantage to tablegrape quality, but it is difficult to anticipate applications to canopies for drying grapes. Characters chosen for assessment were selected because of their association with vineyards of recognized wine quality, either experimentally- or empirically-derived, and also for ease of assessment. The scorecard as presented should be regarded as a preliminary approach — it is recognized that the equal 'weighting' of characters

is possibly superficial, as is the 'additive' nature of the scorecard, and that for different varieties and/or climates the 'weightings' could be modified. Despite these considerations, the concept is being found useful as a guide to vineyard management, and has been the basis for isolating sources of high quality red and white winegrapes in commercial vineyards (R. Gibson, Penfolds Wines, Nuriootpa, pers. comm.)

The scorecard favours low density canopies with a high proportion of gaps, a high degree of fruit exposure and with low leaf-layer number. Similarly, vine features associated with moderate vigour are favoured, as noted by leaf colour and size, shoot length, lateral growth extent and the activity of growing shoot tips. Note that the scorecard should not be used for severely stressed vineyards, as false indications of quality potential will result.

Sunfleck measurements
Measuring the number and length of sunflecks incident on a thin rod of known length in the centre of the canopy gives an estimate of canopy gap frequency. This approach is similar to a visual inspection of canopy shadows on the ground, which can also be quantified. There is an important effect of the sun's position on the measurement, as this will affect the length of canopy traversed by a sunbeam and hence the probability of interception; therefore, the time of day for measurement should be standardized.

Other vineyard measurements
During winter pruning, it is convenient to count canes that grew in the previous season, and also weigh one-year-old canes removed at pruning. This allows mean cane weight to be calculated (pruning weight divided by cane number) as well as shoot spacing per m of row or per m of canopy.

5.3.4 Towards a definition of an ideal canopy
The following remarks are directed towards specification of an ideal canopy, especially for winegrape production with quality in mind. A fuller development of these principles can be found in Smart *et al.* (1990). Similar principles of yield maximization apply also to table- and drying grapes, though considerations for quality may be

Table 5.2. Vineyard scorecard used for assessing potential winegrape quality (from Smart and Robinson 1991).

Note: If majority of shoots are less than 30cm long, or if these vines are clearly diseased or chlorotic or necrotic, or excessively stressed, DO NOT USE SCORECARD.

A. Standing away from canopy

1. CANOPY GAPS (from side to side of canopy, within area contained by 90% of canopy boundary)

* about 40% — 10
* about 50% or more — 8
* about 30% — 6
* about 20% — 4
* about 10% or less — 0

2. LEAF SIZE (basal-mid leaves on shoot exterior). For this variety are the leaves relatively:

* slightly small — 10
* average — 8
* slightly large — 6
* very large — 2
* very small — 2

3. LEAF COLOUR (basal leaves in fruit zone).

* leaves green, healthy, slightly dull and pale — 10
* leaves dark green, shiny, healthy — 8
* leaves yellowish green, healthy — 6
* leaves with mild nutrient deficiency symptoms — 6
* unhealthy leaves, with marked necrosis or chlorosis — 2

B. Standing at canopy.

4. CANOPY DENSITY (from side to side in fruit zone), mean leaf layer number
* about 1 or less — 10
* about 1.5 — 8
* about 2 — 4
* more than 2 — 2

5. FRUIT EXPOSURE (remember that the canopy has two sides normally — that fruit which is not exposed on your side may be exposed to the other side)

* about 60% or more exposed — 10
* about 50% — 8
* about 40% — 6
* about 30% — 4
* about 20% or less — 2

6. SHOOT LENGTH
* about 10-20 nodes — 10
* about 8-10 nodes — 6
* about 20-25 nodes — 6
* less than about 8 nodes — 2
* more than about 30 nodes — 2

7. LATERAL GROWTH (normally from about point where shoots trimmed. If laterals have been trimmed, look at diameter of stubs).

* limited or zero lateral growth — 10
* moderate vigour lateral growth — 6
* very vigorous growth — 2

8. GROWING TIPS (of all shoots, the proportion with actively growing tips — make due allowance for trimming).

* about 5% or less — 10
* about 10% — 8
* about 20% — 6
* about 30% — 4
* about 40% — 4
* about 50% or more — 0

Total point score /80 = %

less important with the latter. To some extent these guidelines are tentative, a reflection of the newness of this technology.

The ideal canopy form might consist of:

(i) closely-spaced curtains of foliage preferably oriented north-south to promote radiation interception. (This canopy should develop as quickly as possible in spring);

(ii) canopies as thin as possible to maximize exposed surface area (in practice 30-40 cm is the minimum thickness of a canopy obtained when shoots are in a straight line);

(iii) curtains need to be about as far apart as they are high to minimize cross-row shading at the base of canopies;

(iv) canopies should be vertical or almost so to reduce shading by overhanging foliage;

95

(v)   wherever possible the renewal/fruiting zone should be near the top rather than the canopy base, to promote fruitfulness and fruit exposure.

Within-canopy shade is avoided by:

(i)   ensuring adequate spacing between shoots so that the canopy has sufficient gaps to promote adequate leaf and fruit exposure, yet not so many gaps that the canopy is inefficient in sunlight interception. For medium-vigour Traminer vines this level is achieved with about 15 shoots per m (Smart 1988). From a physiological point-of-view, canopies should consist of shoots in balance between vegetative and fruit growth, i.e. with the minimum length and leaf area to adequately ripen fruit, generally about 10 cm^2 leaf area per g fresh weight of fruit, or 10-12 mature main leaves for shoots with two medium-sized bunches. This corresponds to a yield:pruning weight ratio of about 6-10:1, and a mean cane weight of 30-40 g.

(ii) shoots with no vegetative growing point activity between veraison and harvest, to promote ripening.

Mechanization is promoted if:

(i)   similar canopy components occupy a similar zone in space, i.e. trimming is facilitated by having shoots of uniform length trained in one plane, as is also leaf removal of the bunch zone, and mechanical prepruning in winter.

5.4 Techniques of canopy management

Traditional Australian vineyards are widely spaced (3.3-3.6 m), with short posts (up to 1.3 m), and no vertical shoot positioning (Chapter 3). If vigour is low, as may occur in dryland vineyards, shoot growth is terminated by water stress at about 1 m or less, and shoots are more or less erect. When vineyards are well supplied with water, either by irrigation or rainfall, shoots grow longer and then are generally incapable of supporting their own weight. The resulting canopy is bell-shaped, often with shoots extending to the ground. The fruit zone in the interior of such canopies is often heavily shaded.

Canopy management typically has two components. The first includes increasing canopy surface area, using canopy division techniques for existing vineyards and canopy division or close

row spacing for new vineyards. The second component relates to reducing within-canopy shade by considering such variables as shoot positioning, pruning level (shoot spacing), trimming and leaf removal.

5.4.1 Canopy size and form management

Planting distances

Traditional Australian vineyards have had relatively wide between-row spacings (3.3-3.6 m) and within-row spacings (1.5-2 m). The wide between-row spacings is a reflection of wide (>2 m) vineyard equipment used. Over the last decade narrow-row or occasionally over-row equipment has permitted narrower row spacings. In newly established vineyards, especially in cooler southern regions, there has been a tendency towards use of higher density plantings. In large part this practice has been encouraged by the supposition that restricted per-plant yields combined with high plant density will lead to improved productivity and wine quality (McCarthy 1988). Some proponents argue that high plant density will lead to desirable devigoration, although European experience would indicate that this is only likely for low fertility sites. An alternative viewpoint is to combine low vine density with light pruning and canopy division to devigorate (Smart *et al.* 1989) — further experience is required to evaluate these two approaches. Certainly the costs of vineyard establishment vary directly with planting density, especially if grafted plants rather than own-rooted vines are planted.

Trellis systems

Grapevine trellis systems are discussed in Chapter 3. Here it is only necessary to review their role in canopy management and to outline those systems of commercial interest. There is no doubt that, for Australian viticulturists, the adoption of altered trellis systems is the principal means of improving canopy microclimate, hence yield and quality. The present slow commercial adoption of altered trellis systems may be due to shortage of capital, mechanization problems (especially harvesting) and lack of appreciation of the benefits.

Summarized below are the most common trellis systems being presently evaluated in Australian vineyards. Dimensions of these systems and management procedures are outlined in Smart and Robinson (1991). It will be several years before firm recommendations can be made. In the majority of cases, these systems can be 'retrofitted' to existing vineyards. Order of presentation is from the simple to the more complex. Most experience is with winegrapes, but many of the systems have application for tablegrapes and perhaps drying grapes.

In general, trellis systems with larger canopy surface area are suited to sites with potentially high vigour.

NON-SHOOT POSITIONED CANOPY (NSP)

This is the current, 'traditional' Australian canopy, and is also common in California. Its widespread adoption in these two typically hot and dry climates is probably a reflection of low fungal disease pressures (in cooler, more humid climates it is difficult to control disease in such canopies). Also, the system is simple and cheap.

When NSP canopies are grown on wide rows they have a restricted canopy surface area, and the fruit/renewal zone is at the centre of the canopy. For vines of low to moderate vigour, with shoots of say 1 m length, the canopies can be quite open, as the canopy exterior is rough. Individual shoots can support their own weight and are relatively erect, so the canopy has a 'spiky' appearance. Fruit and leaf exposure can be adequate, though yield is typically restricted. Some moderate-vigour vineyards can produce high yields with open canopies if spurs are widely spaced, for example, by using 'finger-and-thumb' pruning.

With increased vigour, yield is higher but the canopy microclimate is often shaded as larger shoots are incapable of self-support and fall across the canopy, forming many leaf layers. Such canopies are typically bell-shaped and give poor fruit exposure even if one or more fixed foliage wires are added. Such vineyards are often unbalanced in terms of ratios of vegetative to fruit growth, and are responsive to retrofitting with a divided canopy. Yield responses of the order of 50% or more can be expected for the first harvest following conversion.

VERTICAL SHOOT POSITIONING (VSP)

This system is common in Europe and New Zealand, and is now being adopted in cooler southern regions of Australia. Shoots arising from a mid height (ca. 1 m head or cordon) are trained vertically upwards between two pairs of movable foliage wires (Figure 3.2c). This requires a total of 20-30 h per ha labour, and several passes through the vineyard. Trimming the canopy top, and occasionally the sides, maintains a rectangular shape. The system can be mechanized for pruning, harvesting, trimming and also leaf removal. For low to medium vigour vineyards the canopy density can be satisfactory, but for high vigour situations shading is common, so yield and wine quality are less than the potential.

SYLVOZ, HANGING CANES

This system is an undivided canopy, but canopy surface area increases slightly due to increased height and sometimes width. It may be established with a high cordon (at say 1.5 m or higher) or with a mid-height cordon (at say 1.0-1.2 m). Pruning is to canes of 5-15 nodes which are either tied vertically downwards (Sylvoz) or left untied (hanging canes); with the latter the canes position themselves downwards during the growing season through the weight of shoots and fruit (Figure 3.1e). With the mid-height cordon version, the above-cordon canopy part is essentially for production of renewal canes, and should be kept to low density.

The advantages of this system are increased canopy surface area and generally reduced canopy density with increased fruit exposure, though this depends on retained node number. Disadvantages include a dispersed fruit zone (which hinders operations such as bunch zone leaf removal) and the problems of avoiding shading where vigour is high. Shoots, being non-positioned, can grow along the canopy summit and readily form a 'cap' of leaves. Experience in New Zealand has shown that this problem can be reduced for the high cordon version by shoot positioning downwards with movable foliage wires, and close trimming to the top of the cordon. The system can be mechanically prepruned (to a variable extent depending on configuration) and can be readily machine-harvested.

MINIMAL PRUNING (MPCT)

This system has been developed in Australia by CSIRO research (Clingeleffer 1989). Vines are established on a high single cordon wire, and winter pruning consists of 'skirting' to a predetermined level (Figure 4.13). Node number retained at 'pruning' is very high and as a result shoot density can be very high, e.g. over 100 shoots per m. The system provides for increases in canopy surface area, as the vine form becomes wider with time, and gives marked shoot devigoration. Whether canopy shading is increased or not depends on the balance between these two factors. In warmer climates, especially in association with water stress, shoots can be so devigorated that fruit exposure can be improved compared to the shade-inducing standard trellis (NSP). Favourable effects on both yield and wine quality have been reported (Clingeleffer 1989). In cooler climates with well-watered vines the shoot devigoration may be less evident, in which case canopies may become excessively dense contributing to delayed ripening, increased bunch rot incidence and reduced wine quality. In such canopies fruit composition is heterogeneous with significant differences recorded from the canopy exterior to interior.

GENEVA DOUBLE CURTAIN (GDC)

This horizontally-divided system was developed in New York State for the variety Concord (Shaulis *et al.* 1966). The fruiting zone is at the top of the canopy, and shoots are vertically shoot-positioned downwards — this causes shoot devigoration (Figure 3.3b). Vertical shoot positioning downwards is facilitated by pruning to downward pointing bearers (2-4 nodes long), and by using a movable foliage vine to 'sweep' shoots downwards near flowering. The two canopies must be at least 1 m apart, and shoot growth across this gap must be avoided. The system can lead to excessive fruit exposure and hence excessive wine phenol levels (Carbonneau *et al.* 1978).

Fruit exposure may be reduced by the training and securing of current season shoot growth along the cordon to produce an 'umbrella' of leaves. The system lends itself to machine-pruning and, with suitable trellis construction, can be machine-harvested. It is highly productive due to high shoot fruitfulness, and yields in excess of 25 tonne/ha are possible even for normally medium-yielding winegrape cultivars on potential high fertility sites.

U OR LYRE SYSTEM

This horizontally-divided canopy was developed in Bordeaux (Carbonneau *et al.* 1978). Shoots are trained upwards between two pairs of foliage wires so the fruit-renewal zone is basal, and canopy walls are inclined slightly outwards (Figures 3.3c, 5.9). Shoots typically require trimming at the top of the canopy, to about 15-20 nodes. The canopy wall at the base should be at least 90 cm apart, or yield is reduced (Smart 1985b). The system is productive and gives better wine quality than shaded canopies. Machine pruning is feasible and a machine harvester for the system has been developed in France (A. Carbonneau, pers. comm.).

TE KAUWHATA TWO TIER (TK2T)

This is a vertically divided trellis developed in New Zealand (Smart 1985b). There are two tiers of upward-growing vertical shoots, trimmed to 10-12 nodes and with a 10-15 cm gap between the two (Figures 5.9, 5.11). Shoots from both tiers are held in place by two pairs of movable foliage wires. The base of the bottom tier is at ca. 40 cm height, the top at 120 cm. Adjacent vines are trained to different heights, and spur pruning is required. The system can be mechanically pruned and harvested. Shoots need to be trimmed shorter with this system than to either U or GDC, and repeated trimming may be necessary to prevent regrowth from the bottom tier invading the fruit zone of the top tier. There is a potential difference in yield and fruit composition between the tiers.

SCOTT HENRY

This system was originally developed in Oregon by a grower (Mr Scott Henry) and has been further refined in New Zealand (Smart 1987b). It resembles TK2T in being a vertically divided system, with the exception that shoots on the bottom tier are trained downwards (Figure 3.2d). Two pairs of foliage wires are required for upward-trained shoots from the top tier and a single wire for downward-trained shoots. Some growers prefer to use only one pair of movable foliage wires to train upwards. However, such canopies are not as tidy and regular, and make trimming and leaf removal operations difficult. The two fruit zones are relatively close together, leading to less difference in fruit composition between tiers than with the TK2T, and higher yield potential of the bottom tier. The system can be cane pruned and, if spur pruned, adjacent vines should be trained to alternate tiers. Shoots growing downwards from the lower tier are devigorated. The system can be machine pruned, and machine harvested.

RUAKURA TWIN TWO TIER (RT2T)

This system was developed in New Zealand (Smart and Smith 1988) and is suitable only for high fertility sites. The initial version (RT2TA) used vines on wide rows (3.6 m minimum) trained to form four discrete curtains of upward-pointing, vertical shoots which are kept trimmed to 10-12 nodes. These curtains are 1.5 m or more apart. Alternate vines are trained to high or low curtains. Vines are pruned to large node numbers to assist devigoration. The system must be spur pruned and therefore can be readily mechanized. At present the form as originally described cannot be machine harvested, though existing machines could be modified for this. Modifications to the system under evaluation include inverting the bottom tier to a configuration like the Scott Henry (RT2TB). This reduces ripening delays of the bottom tier, and also increases yield potential. Also, replacing a central line of posts and vines in 3.6 m rows with widely spaced vines in 1.8 m rows will allow harvesting with existing machinery. In this case the system resembles a close-row, wide in-row vine spacing version of TK2T (for RT2TA) or Scott Henry (for RT2TB).

Choosing trellis systems

As for any other aspects of vineyard management there are no blanket recommendations for choice

Table 5.3. The suitability of trellis systems to vineyard potential and row spacing.

Trellis	Vineyard Potential			Minimum (m) row spacing[a]
	Low	Medium	High	
NSP	✓	✓		3.0
VSP	✓	✓		2.5
Scott Henry		✓		2.5
TK2T		✓		2.5
U		✓		2.5
GDC		✓	✓	3.0
RT2T			✓	3.5
Sylvoz		✓	✓	3.0
MPCT		✓	✓	3.0

a This is the minimum suitable row spacing determined by microclimate considerations.

of trellis system. The suggestion as to the most appropriate system can vary from vineyard to vineyard, and even within the one vineyard. There are many factors to be taken into account in the decision, and the major ones are listed here. Some of these factors are summarized in Table 5.3.

Vineyard factors

Among the more important determinants of the optimal trellis system are vineyard factors, principally vine capacity. Simple trellis systems are suited to low potential vineyard sites, and more complex systems with larger surface area and requiring more foliage control are appropriate to those of high potential. Typically the best way to characterize vine capacity is to measure winter pruning weights, and to express these relative to unit row length. Low capacity vines might be characterized as about 0.5 kg prunings or less per metre, while high capacity vines will have 1.5 kg per metre or more. Table 5.1 shows other measures of shoot vigour which can help assess vineyard vigour, as can also more indirect methods of canopy assessment previously mentioned.

Since trellis changes are commonly made to existing vineyards (the so-called 'retrofitting' approach) the dimensions and training of the existing vineyard present important limitations. Narrow row spacing precludes use of horizontally divided canopies such as the U, GDC or RT2T, as well as wide, non-positioned canopies like minimal pruning. Traditional Australian vineyards have a wide row spacing of 3 m or more, and so can accommodate most systems (Table 5.3). Vineyard machinery dimensions can also be a problem as older tractors are typically wide (more than 2 m) and high. Recently, narrow tractors (about 1 m width) with lower height have become available with sufficient power for vineyard use.

The training of existing vineyards is also an issue to be considered. Of paramount importance is the head or crown height. Dimensions of newer training systems are critical, and are given in detail by Smart and Robinson (1991). A head height of 1.0 m or so allows retrofitting of most systems.

The ability to mechanize is a factor dominating trellis choice. Many operators will only countenance conversion to systems for which mechanical harvesters are readily available. Vertical shoot positioning and Scott Henry are therefore favoured. Other systems can be mechanized but require machine modifications. Pruning can be mechanized to a greater or lesser degree for all systems presented.

Socio-economic factors

More complex trellis systems have more components which cost more for materials and installation. A simple single wire trellis with posts 1 m high and an inclined post end assembly may be suited for low potential vineyards. A system like the RT2T has 16 wires for each row and requires a substantial end assembly with tall, closely spaced intermediate posts. Obviously there needs to be greater yield and/or reduced maintenance costs to make such an investment necessary, and any such financial decision will be sensitive to interest rates. New Zealand studies have shown that for high potential vineyards the conversion to elaborate trellis systems is economically beneficial in comparison to more conventional systems. There is an extra cost for shoot positioning which for most trellis systems normally is about 30 hrs per ha; these costs may be offset by mechanizing hand pruning at say 70 hrs per ha.

Vineyard performance is also important. If the goal is to minimize labour input, then either Sylvoz or Minimal Pruning have much to recommend their adoption. Other systems will probably give higher yields and quality but there is unfortunately a lack of experimental data at present. Evidence from published studies indicates that fruit composition and wine quality are improved with open canopies and good fruit exposure (e.g. Smart 1985b, Smart and Smith 1988, Smart et al. 1990). In addition yield increases have followed the conversion of high capacity, undivided canopies to more elaborate trellis systems; in very shady and vegetative canopies the yield responses may be up to 200-300%.

5.4.2 Shoot density management

Shoot positioning

Training shoots upwards (or downwards) brings 'order' to the canopy and facilitates mechanization. For example, summer trimming of shoot tips is facilitated as they are within a well defined zone, and so is leaf removal in the bunch zone. Vertical shoot positioning and constant summer trimming is a feature of vineyards grown in climates with a high incidence of fungal diseases

i.e. Europe, New Zealand. While adoption of this procedure in Australian vineyards would assist mechanization as noted above, it may also contribute to increased canopy shading as canopy surface area will probably be less than for a non-positioned canopy (Smart 1987b). The practice should therefore be adopted with caution and should preferably be combined with other canopy management procedures.

Trimming (summer pruning, slashing)

Trimming frequency depends on vine vigour. If mid-season water stress develops and prevents lateral regrowth, then no trimming, or only one, may be needed. For vineyards well supplied with water during the growing season, up to six trimmings may be necessary. Shoots should not be trimmed to less than 10-12 nodes as fruit ripening may be impaired. Trimming can improve the microclimate for non-positioned canopies (Smart 1982) but is most effective where shoots are positioned. Studies with the variety Sangiovese in Northern Italy have shown that trimming 25 days after flowering encouraged lateral growth and improved fruit composition due to lower pH and K^+ (Solari et al. 1988).

Early trimming (topping) improves fruitset (Coombe 1959) but also increases the incidence of primary bud-axis necrosis with some varieties e.g. Shiraz (Dry 1986). Late season trimming should be avoided: if not performed previously, young healthy leaves are removed from the canopy exterior, exposing previously shaded, senescing old leaves. Fruit maturation delays can be expected. Further, late trimming may also stimulate lateral growth, again to the detriment of fruit ripening.

Shoot removal (deshooting, desuckering)

Shoot removal can be an effective means of controlling shoot spacing. 'Crown suckering' (removal of shoots in the head of the vine) is often practised in Australia, particularly for tablegrapes, but removal of non-fruitful shoots along the cordon or canes is not common. Many varieties produce 'watershoots' from the trunk early in the season, and these are sometimes removed.

Where shoot density is too high, deshooting can help produce an optimal shoot spacing. This is best done early in the growing season, when shoots are less than 15-20 cm long. In this way, non-fruitful shoots can be selectively removed. This practice should be applied with caution, as shoot thinning has been shown to be associated with poor set on the remaining shoots; this effect has been noted for Traminer vines in New Zealand, and Chardonnay and Pinot Noir in the Adelaide Hills. It is probable that this disorder is due to early bunchstem necrosis (EBSN, Jackson and Coombe 1988) and related to invigoration of the remaining shoots. Primary bud-axis necrosis may also be induced by this treatment (Dry 1986).

Vigour control

Shoot vigour and shoot spacing are the major determinants of canopy density (Smart 1988). Dense canopies are typically found in high vigour situations, where the vineyard is poorly trellised. Shoot vigour may be reduced in a number of ways — these include lighter pruning (see Chapter 4), or by imposed nutrient (Chapter 9) or water stress (Chapter 6), or even by the effects of pests (Chapter 10) or diseases (Chapter 11); the latter two are insufficiently controllable to be regarded as acceptable for devigoration.

The techniques offering most promise in Australia are through management of pruning and/or irrigation levels. Recent studies in New Zealand (Smart *et al.* 1989, Smart *et al.* 1990) have shown that a combination of light pruning (to say 160 nodes per vine) in combination with an adequate trellis leads to shoots sufficiently devigorated and yet sufficiently fruitful to produce high yielding vines with open canopies. Shoot vigour can be measured in several ways — Table 5.2 shows values associated with high and low vigour shoots for the variety Cabernet Franc. To achieve large node numbers per vine and to avoid shade requires low vine planting density and divided canopies.

Similarly, restricting irrigation during the growing season can reduce shoot vigour. But this has several drawbacks: firstly, in regions of winter rainfall it is difficult to generate water stress early in the growing season for the inhibition of early shoot growth. Secondly, a reduction in shoot vigour is often accompanied by some yield loss. Moderate water stress applied after veraison is the most effective method for stopping shoot growth, with less effect on yield.

Leaf removal

Leaf removal in the bunch zone can markedly improve fruit exposure, with benefits of improving fruit composition and reducing disease incidence, especially botrytis bunch rot (Smith *et al.* 1988). Normally only one or two leaves need be removed per shoot, and about 60% fruit exposure gives adequate results. While the operation is tedious to perform by hand, requiring about 50 hours per ha, machines are available that perform the job satisfactorily at less than 5 hours per ha. These machines require a flat and preferably vertical canopy surface to perform well, and are not suited to non-positioned canopies, or where the fruit zone is widely spread.

Leaf removal gives best results when done several weeks before veraison. Benefits include lowered malic acid and pH, higher colour, phenols and sugar, and improved fruit flavour. Yield may also increase slightly.

Growth regulators

A number of growth regulators have been shown to be effective in reducing shoot vigour. These include maleic hydrazide, CCC, Alar, ethephon and paclobutrazol (Lavee 1987). Often their use is associated with undesirable side effects e.g. ethephon reduces photosynthetic rate, or the devigoration effect is associated with reduction in internode length, not leaf number. There seems no reason to introduce further chemicals into the vineyard ecosystem while alternative methods are available.

5.5 Concluding remarks

Canopy management is a relatively new concept which follows on from the adoption of improved management practices outlined in other chapters of this volume. Such changes invariably lead to vine invigoration, so that modern vineyards are characterized by dense grapevine canopies. The resulting shade leads to a loss in yield and worsened fruit composition, especially for winemaking.

Recent studies have shown viticultural and oenological benefits of open canopies and this may be achieved using a number of manipulations in the vineyard. Of these the most significant are use of an improved trellis system, which provides for a large canopy surface area, and appropriate shoot spacing to avoid within-canopy shade. There has been limited commercial adoption of these ideas but sufficient experimental evidence exists to encourage further evaluations.

Further reading

Smart, R.E. (1985a) Principles of grapevine canopy microclimate manipulation with implications for yield and quality: a review. Amer. J. Enol. Vitic. 35, 230-9

Smart, R.E. (1987b) Canopy management to improve yield, fruit composition and vineyard mechanization. In: Lee, T.H. (ed.) Proc. Sixth Australian Wine Industry Technical Conf., July, 1986, Adelaide, SA: Australian Wine Research Institute, Adelaide, SA, 205-11

Smart, R.E. and Smith, S.M. (1988) Canopy management: identifying the problems and practical solutions. In: Smart, R.E. et al. (eds.) Proc. Second Int. Symp. Cool Climate Viticulture and Oenology, January, 1988, Auckland, New Zealand; NZ Soc. for Vitic. and Oenol., Auckland, NZ, 109-15

Smart, R.E., Dick, J.K., Gravett, I.M. and Fisher, B. (1990) Canopy management to improve grape yield and wine quality. Principles and practices. S. Afr. J. Enol. Vitic. 11, 3-17

Smart, R.E. and Robinson, M.D. (1991) Sunlight into Wine: A Handbook for Winegrape Canopy Management. Winetitles, Adelaide.

Other references

Carbonneau, A., Casteran, P. and Le Clair, P. (1978) Essai de determination en biologie de la plante entiere, de relations essentielles entre le bioclimat natural, la physiologie de la vigne et la composition du raisin. Ann. Amelior. Plant 28, 195-221

Clingeleffer, P.R. (1989) Update: minimal pruning of cordon trained vines (MPCT). Aust. Grapegrower and Winemaker 304, 78-83

Coombe, B.G. (1959) Fruit set and development in seeded grape varieties as affected by defoliation, topping, girdling, and other treatments. Amer. J. Enol. and Vitic. 10, 85-100

Coombe, B.G. (1987) Influence of temperature on composition and quality of grapes. Acta Horticulturae 206, 23-35

Crippen, D.D. and Morrison, J.C. (1986) The effects of sun exposure on the compositional development of Cabernet Sauvignon berries. Amer. J. Enol. Vitic. 37, 235-42

Dry, P.R. (1986) Primary bud-axis necrosis of grapevines. M. Ag. Sc. thesis, University of Adelaide

Jackson, D.I. and Coombe, B.G. (1988) Early bunch stem necrosis — a cause of poor set. Proc. Second Int. Symp. Cool Climate Viticulture and Oenology, January, 1988, Auckland, New Zealand. NZ Soc. for Vitic. and Oenol., 72-5

Kliewer, W.M. and Smart, R.E. (1989) Canopy manipulation for optimizing vine microclimate, crop yield and composition of grapes. In: Wright, C. (ed.). Manipulation of Fruiting. Proc. 47th Easter School in Agric. Sci. Symp. April 1988, Univ. Nottingham. Butterworths, London, 275-91

Lavee, S. (1987) Usefulness of growth regulators for controlling vine growth and improving grape quality in intensive vineyards. Acta Horticulturae. 206, 89-108

May, P. (1965) Reducing inflorescence formation by shading individual Sultana buds. Aust. J. Biol. Sci. 18: 663-73

May, P. and Clingeleffer, P.R. (1977) Experiments on mechanical pruning of grape vines. In: Proc. Third Aust. Wine Industry Tech. Conf., August, 1977, Albury, NSW, Aust. Wine Res. Inst. 50-3

McCarthy, M.G. (1988) Evaluation of a high density vineyard planting. Proc. Second Int. Symp. Cool Climate Viticulture and Oenology, January, 1988, Auckland, New Zealand. NZ Soc. for Vitic. and Oenol., 172-3

Reynolds, A. G. and Wardle, D.A. (1989) Impact of various canopy manipulation techniques on growth, yield, fruit composition, and wine quality of Gewurztraminer. Amer. J. Enol. Vitic. 40, 121-9

Solari, C., Silvestroni, O., Giudici, P. and Intrieri, C. (1988) Influence of topping on juice composition of Sangiovese grapevines (V. vinifera L.). Proc. Second Int. Symp. Cool Climate Viticulture and Oenology, January, 1988, Auckland, New Zealand. NZ Soc. for Vitic. and Oenol., 147-51

Shaulis, N.J., Amberg, H. and Crowe, D. (1966) Response of Concord grapes to light, exposure and Geneva Double Curtain training. Proc. Am. Soc. Hortic. Sci. 89, 268-80

Shaulis, N.J. and May, P. (1981) Response of Sultana vines to training on a divided canopy and to shoot crowding. Amer. J. Enol. and Vitic. 22, 215-21

Smart, R.E. (1973) Sunlight interception by vineyards. Amer. J. Enol. Vitic. 24, 141-7

Smart, R.E. (1974) Photosynthesis by grapevine canopies. J. Appl. Ecol. 11, 997-1006

Smart, R.E. (1982) Vine manipulation to improve winegrape quality. Proc. Grape and Wine Centennial Symp., June 1980, Davis, Calif. Univ. of Calif. 362-75

Smart, R.E. (1984) Canopy microclimates and effects on wine quality. Proc. Fifth Australian Wine Industry Technical Conf., November-December, 1983, Perth, WA. Australian Wine Research Institute, 113-32

Smart, R. (1985b) Some aspects of climate, canopy microclimate, vine physiology and wine quality. Proc. First Symp. Cool Climate Viticulture and Oenology, June 1984, Eugene, Oregon. Oregon State University, 1-19

Smart, R.E. (1987a) The influence of light on composition and quality of grapes. Acta Horticulturae 206, 37-47

Smart, R.E. (1988) Shoot spacing and canopy light microclimate. Amer. J. Enol. Vitic. 39, 325-33

Smart, R.E. and Coombe, B.G. (1983) Water relations of grapevines. In: Kozlowski, T., (ed.). Water deficits and plant growth. Vol. VII. Academic Press, NY, 137-96

Smart, R.E., Dick, J.K. and Gravett, I.M. (1989) Shoot devigoration by natural means. Proc. Seventh Australian Wine Industry Technical Conf., August, 1988, Adelaide, SA. Australian Industrial Publishers, 58-65.

Smart, R.E., Robinson, J.B., Due, G.R. and Brien, C.J. (1985) Canopy microclimate modification for the cultivar Shiraz. I. Definition of canopy microclimate. Vitis 24, 17-31

Smart, R.E. and Sharp, K. (1989) Handbook for canopy management workshop. Viticultural Bulletin 54. MAF Ruakura Agricultural Centre, Hamilton, New Zealand, 45pp

Smart, R.E., Smith, S.M. and Winchester, R.V. (1988) Light quality and quantity effects on fruit ripening of Cabernet Sauvignon. Amer. J. Enol. Vitic. 39, 250-8

Smith, S.M., Codrington, I.C., Robertson, M. and Smart, R.E. (1988) Viticultural and oenological implications of leaf removal for New Zealand vineyards. Proc. Second Int. Symp. Cool Climate Viticulture and Oenology, January, 1988, Auckland, New Zealand. NZ Soc. Vitic. and Oenol. 127-33

CHAPTER SIX

Irrigation - Principles and Practices

M.G. McCARTHY, L.D. JONES and G. DUE

In Australia, the irrigation of vineyards developed in a major way in areas along the Murray and Murrumbidgee Rivers (Volume I Chapter 1). These were government and privately-sponsored settlement schemes with centrally organized works for water supply and dispersal of drainage water. Developments since the 1950s have mainly been by private individuals or co-operative groups who divert water directly from a water source thus avoiding the complex and high capital infrastructure of the older irrigation districts. The traditional rainfed grapegrowing regions were formerly not irrigated but irrigation has become widely adopted to avoid the effects of drought and maintain yields at a level to cover increasing costs of production. For example, in 1947 only about 38% of the total vineyard area in South Australia was irrigated (Figure 6.1), but by 1990 nearly 74% of the total area received some irrigation. Since the mid-1970s there has been a steady decline in vineyard area in South Australia, mainly due to the removal of unirrigated vineyards. Many growers would now be reluctant to establish a new vineyard unless some irrigation was in prospect.

At the same time there is an increasing competition for supplies of good quality water arising from other rural pursuits, secondary industries, urban water supplies and recreational activities. The wider community is more aware of the environment and the need for its conservation. Irrigators will have to ensure they are not responsible for land degradation as a result

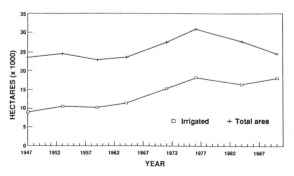

Figure 6.1 Total vineyard and irrigated area for South Australia 1947-1990

of irrigation mis-management leading to loss of soil fertility and productivity.

As most vineyards are now irrigated the rational design of irrigation systems and water use is increasingly important.

6.1 Irrigation principles

6.1.1 Soil as a reservoir of water

Water is held in the soil as films around soil particles and temporarily in pores. When all pores are filled with water and air has been displaced the soil is saturated. If the soil is then allowed to drain freely, some water moves out under the influence of gravity. When drainage ceases, usually after a day or so, the soil is at **Field Capacity (FC)** or the **Drained Upper Limit (DUL)**. Although water can be added to the soil profile in excess of the DUL it is likely that waterlogging will occur. The water content of the soil falls further as plant roots absorb water. Eventually a level of soil water is reached when plants can no longer extract enough water and they begin to wilt. When plants wilt by day and fail to recover at night, the soil is at **Permanent Wilting Point (PWP)** or the **Lower Limit (LL)**. **Plant Available Water (PAW)** is the amount of water held in the soil between DUL and LL and is the water that can be used by the plant. It can be expressed as a depth of water in mm per metre of soil; the amount of available water that a soil profile can store depends on its texture ranging from 33 to 208 mm per metre (Table 6.1).

The application of an equal amount of water to soils of different texture wets each to a different depth, provided that they are all initially at DUL, e.g. 100 mm of water wets a coarse sand to 150 cm and a clay to 70 cm. Consequently, variations

Table 6.1 The amount of available water (between DUL and LL) held by soils of different textures expressed in millimetres of water per metre of soil.

Soil texture	Available water in soil profile	
	Range mm/m	Average mm/m
Coarse sand	33-42	36
Medium to fine sand, loamy sand	62-83	67
Moderately coarse sandy loam, fine sandy loam	83-125	104
Medium fine sandy loam, sandy clay loam, silt loam	125-192	158
Moderately fine clay loam, silty clay	146-208	175
Fine sandy clay, silty clay, clay	133-208	167

(from Shockley 1956)

in soil texture down the profile should be taken into account in calculating the amount of water required to rewet the rootzone (Table 6.2).

Although a sandy soil holds only about one third of the amount available water per unit depth of soil as does a loam or a clay, the available water is not so tightly held and therefore is more readily and completely extracted by plant roots. The majority of the available water in a sand is extracted by plant roots at a tension of 100 kPa (1 bar) or less. In contrast, tensions of 400 kPa (4 bars) or higher are required to remove a similar amount of available water from loam and clay soils.

Table 6.2 Calculation of the available water present in the rootzone of a specific soil based on Table 6.1 and the amount of water needed to refill the rootzone to Drained Upper Limit.

	Texture	Depth cm	Available Water (DUL- LL) mm	Estimated water content based on feel of the soil	Amount of water required to refill soil to DUL
	Sandy loam	0-30	31	1/4 DUL	23
Depth of	Sandy Clay loam	30-70	63	1/2 DUL	31
rootzone (1 m)	Clay loam	70-100	52	3/4 DUL	13
	TOTAL		146		67

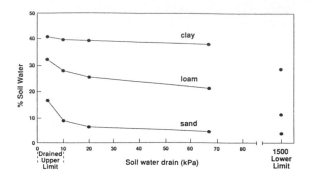

Figure 6.2 Water retention curves for a sand, loam and clay soil.

These differences are illustrated in Figure 6.2 showing the water retention curves for several soils with different textures.

Water is not equally available to plant roots between DUL and LL and the vigour and performance of plants falls off markedly as LL is approached. Water stress symptoms and loss in yield usually become apparent when more than about 50% of the available water has been extracted.

6.1.2 Water movement in soil and roots

The hydraulic resistance of soils depends very much on water content and structure. As soil dries, the hydraulic resistance increases and at the lower limit the resistance to water movement is extremely high. Water flow, as from a water table to a root in dry soil, is therefore restricted.

Water flows through the soil and into the interior of the root along a gradient of increasing water tension, the rate of flow being determined by the extent of this gradient and the various hydraulic resistances of soil and root. In moist soils, soil hydraulic resistance is low and the root surface itself presents the resistance which limits uptake. At normal levels of soil water, soil hydraulic resistance is high, especially near the root where local drying occurs, and the resistance between the soil and the root surface is the major limit to uptake.

6.1.3 Water stress effects during periods of grapevine growth

Water stress affects the grapevine in different ways depending on the vine's stage of development. It is convenient to consider these over four intervals,

between the phenological stages of budburst, flowering, veraison and harvest.

Budburst to flowering

This period of intense vegetative growth sets the pattern of the vineyard canopy for the whole growing season. Also, the development of the inflorescences and individual flowers influences the number of flowers and the way setting and berry growth progress. These growth processes are sensitive to water stress; dry conditions can lead to irregular budburst, short shoots and fewer flowers. However, in most of Australia, and in most years, water supply is not as important as low temperature during this interval. As in South Africa (Van Zyl 1984), the effects of irrigation are small except in areas that depend on a full irrigation schedule. In fact, excessive soil water, leading to waterlogging and hence oxygen deficiency, is a detrimental factor in some vineyards causing slowed shoot growth, leaf yellowing, and death (Hale 1959).

Flowering to veraison

Flowering and setting are sensitive stages because abscission and cell division processes are involved. Water stress (and/or cold conditions) at this time leads to poor setting and small berries (Alexander 1965, Hardie and Considine 1976). In irrigated areas, growers ensure that soil water is adequate before flowering starts, and in those rainfall areas where water supplies are limited, an irrigation for the flowering period is given high priority. The first flush of root growth occurs during this period and may be inhibited by drought (Van Zyl 1984) or waterlogging (Hale 1959, Freeman and Smart 1976).

After flowering, the canopy develops rapidly towards its final form and, with rising temperatures and lower humidities, the consumptive water use of the vineyard rises steeply. Added to this, the continued growth of the shoots and the early development of the berries are sensitive to water stress. Therefore irrigations between setting and veraison have large effects on the overall development of the canopy and crop. When the berries enter their lag phase, and shoot growth slows, the effect of water stress lessens, the main effect of severe stress being a delay in ripening.

Veraison to harvest

During fruit ripening, the vine can withstand a considerable amount of water stress; foliage will wilt and older leaves will senesce and drop, but berry sugaring proceeds. The production of valuable winegrape material in some vineyards, albeit in very low yield, attests the drought resistance of the grapevine. However, if the aim of the grower is to ensure maximum crop and maximum sugar per hectare, then adequate soil water during the whole of the ripening period is essential. This is the best strategy for raisin production. Soil water supply is a major factor influencing the size of the crop and the way berries ripen. This, in turn, alters berry composition and quality (see 6.4.2); it is a key aspect of the establishment of the 'controlled labelling' system adopted for some European winegrape areas. The effects of irrigations during ripening, as before, depend on the depth of the rootzone, the water storage characteristics of the soil, the efficiency of the irrigation system, and the climate of the area. On shallow soils with a low water holding capacity, and in districts with high evaporation, irrigations need to be frequent. Vineyards with deep soils and extensive root systems may produce well with few or even no irrigations provided the soil is charged with water at the beginning of ripening.

Postharvest and dormancy

In hot, irrigated districts some tablegrape and winegrape varieties may be harvested in late December-early January. This leaves up to 3 months during which time irrigation is still necessary, albeit at a reduced amount, to ensure maximum accumulation of carbohydrate reserves.

Dry soils after harvest inhibit the second flush of root growth and cause early leaf fall, thus limiting the build-up of carbohydrate and nitrogen reserves in the wood of the vines essential for bud and shoot growth during winter and spring. If autumn rains are limited or delayed, and soils are droughted, irrigations are desirable (but not if they cause a late growth of terminal lateral shoots which reduce wood reserves). After leaf fall, vines are little affected by waterlogging or drought. However, if the soil is very dry during later winter or early spring, a 'straggly' budburst may result causing uneven shoot growth, as occurred in the

Barossa Valley after the 1982-83 drought (McCarthy, unpublished data).

6.2 Water supply and use

6.2.1 Water supply

Water is a valuable resource and permission is normally required from government authorities before water can be diverted from rivers or ephemeral streams or an underground source can be tapped. An increasing number of grapegrowing districts in Australia are subject to controls over the quantity of water growers are allowed to use from such sources. These controls may be as a volume per hectare or area controls based on a reference crop such as is used in the South-east of South Australia. The Murray/Murrumbidgee/Darling river system is the major source of vineyard irrigation water in eastern Australia, where about 80% of Australia's winegrapes and nearly all of the dried grapes are produced. A wide variety of water sources are used in other areas. In the rainfed districts groundwater is the predominant source of water additional to rain.

In areas with suitable surface catchment large dams have been constructed such as in the Barossa Ranges. These dams are often built in water courses and fill naturally, others are filled with large flood pumps during times of high flow and low salinity. Surface water runoff can be increased with the use of engineered catchments. Moore (1990) reported a 33% annual runoff of rain over a five year period for a small engineered catchment in the Barossa Valley and demonstrated the possible economic advantages of storing this water. In Langhorne Creek (SA) winter flood waters from the adjacent creek are diverted through vineyards by a series of weirs; water is retained in each vineyard for a sufficient time to fill the relatively deep soil to the DUL thus allowing heavy crops to be grown without the need for additional irrigation in the summer. Reticulated water for domestic use is expensive but, where available, it is sometimes profitable to irrigate vineyards with it at strategic times such as during vineyard establishment or in periods of drought. Wastewater such as sewage effluent has also been used effectively (McCarthy 1981, Gamble 1986).

The choice of water source is often limited. Factors to consider include quantity (especially

Figure 6.3 Catchment dams used for drip irrigation of a vineyard in the Barossa Valley.

availability in drought years when needed most) quality (both seasonal and long term salinity) and cost (initial and annual costs). Other factors which may need to be considered are whether it is a shared supply or private, channel or piped supply, long term availability due to competing demands, pollution etc. Often the use of a variety of water sources is the best approach as this ensures flexibility.

6.2.2 Water use within vineyards

Grapevines can survive under a wide range of soil moisture conditions. In Australia, vines are grown in areas with annual rainfall ranging from about 270 mm to over 1100 mm; average district yields vary from about 8 to over 22 t/ha (Volume I, Chapter 1). Actual vineyard water use (soil evaporation + plant use) is reported to be as low as about 250 mm (McCarthy - unpubl.) to more than 800 mm (Prior and Grieve 1986). Grapevine vegetative growth and yield are determined by total water use (Figure 6.4) and a large increase in yield is possible with small amounts of additional water.

The sensitivity of growth and yield to water supply is influenced by many factors and varies between sites. For example, the following yield increases per 10 mm irrigation have been quoted:
— 0.16 t/ha with Thompson Seedless in California (Williams and Grimes 1986)

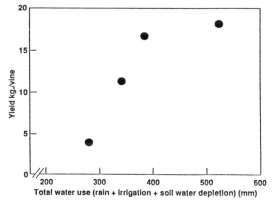

Figure 6.4 The influence of total water use on yield of Shiraz in the Barossa Valley. (McCarthy, incomplete data)

— 0.37 t/ha with Shiraz in the Barossa Valley (McCarthy *et al.* 1983),
— 0.33 to 0.7 t/ha with Chenin blanc in South Africa (van Zyl and Weber 1977),
Greater than 1 t/ha is suggested by the initial rise in Figure 6.4.

The drought tolerance on the one hand, yet responsiveness to irrigation on the other, is in part due to the grapevine's control of leaf water loss and the nature of its root system. A grapevine has a sparse root system compared with other perennial plants and this feature may help conserve moisture and distribute it over the growing season (Freeman 1983). The proportion of fine roots and the vertical distribution of roots have a role in determining the drought tolerance of rootstocks.

6.2.3 Plant water use

Water stored in the soil is lost by evaporation from the soil surface (Es) and loss of water from vine foliage (transpiration, Ef). As both processes involve the use of radiant energy they are collectively called evapotranspiration (Et = Es + Ef).

Evaporation

The extent to which evaporation from the soil surface contributes to evapotranspiration depends on the frequency of wetting of soil, the area of soil surface wetted, and the proportion of the wetted soil surface that is shaded. The rate of evaporation from bare soil remains high as long as the surface is wet — Es may exceed Et (Freeman cited in Hayes *et al.* 1992) but once the surface soil dries, the rate rapidly decreases, reaching a negligible level. Air temperature, humidity, and wind speed at ground level also affect evaporation from the soil surface.

Transpiration

Water vapour in the air spaces within leaves diffuses to the outside air through numerous valve-like pores (stomata) on the surface of the leaves. The stomata give the plant control over its water loss. When the stomata are closed, e.g. at night or when leaf cells are under water stress, transpiration is greatly reduced. Transpiration of water from the grapevine is related to leaf area, the evaporative power of the air (determined by wind speed, temperature and relative humidity), the availability of water in the soil and the light intensity. As grape berries have few stomata the majority of water lost by the vine is through leaf surfaces.

6.3 Water quality

6.3.1 Water quality effects on grapevines.

Grapevines are classified as moderately sensitive to salinity based on yield and foliar symptoms; in comparison, stonefruits are classified as sensitive.

Salts in irrigation water can affect grapevine performance in several ways (Prior 1993):

(i) Dissolved salts in the rootzone can reduce the availability of water in proportion to its salinity. This is called the osmotic effect and can be measured as the force (osmotic potential) the plant has to overcome to extract water from the soil. If the osmotic effect reduces water availability for significant periods of time reduced growth and yield can be expected.

(ii) Specific ions may be present which are toxic to grapevines at relatively low concentrations and can have greater affects on performance than the osmotic effect.

Chloride and sodium: Reduction in shoot growth and yield are among the first symptoms of toxicity, and losses may be large at the relatively high levels of stress at which foliar symptoms first appear (Alexander and Woodham 1968). It is difficult to distinguish between foliar symptoms of sodium and chloride; most commonly the two occur together under Australian conditions. Foliar symptoms of sodium and chloride toxicity begin with a yellowing of leaf margins which progresses inwards as stress increases until ultimately the leaves senesce and fall prematurely. In extreme cases grapevines may die.

Boron: Boron injury is indicated by cupping of the leaves with dark brown or black spots scattered about the leaf margin. At high concentrations premature defoliation and depressed growth may occur. Boron levels of less than 0.5 mg/L in irrigation water are considered to be safe for grapevines and fortunately, most irrigation waters in Australia are low in boron. Murray River water has less than 0.1 mg/L. Drainage water in some areas, such as the Australian Mallee, contain up to 5mg/L of boron and should therefore be kept separate from irrigation water. The recommended maximum level of boron in petioles taken at flowering is 0.03% D.Wt. (see Chapter 9), and this level is relatively unaffected by contingent factors.

6.3.2 Water quality criteria for grapevines

No exact standards for EC_w (electrical conductivity of irrigation water – Table 6.3) can be given since the effect of saline irrigation water depends largely on soil type and on management practices such as irrigation method, variety and rootstock. The classification of water quality given in Table 6.4 has been used as a guide for vineyard

Table 6.3 Symbols, and the relationship between units used to measure the salinity of water.

EC_w = Electrical conductivity of irrigation water.

The standard method of measuring salinity is by electrical conductivity in micro-siemens/cm (μS/cm) at 25°C. In Australia the term EC units is commonly used.

[1 deci-siemen/metre (dS/m) = 1 milli-siemen/cm (mS/cm) = 1000 μS/cm]

TDS = Total dissolved solids as milligrams per litre (mg/L) [mg/L $\approx$ ppm]. TDS can be determined by chemical analysis or estimated from -

$$TDS = EC_w \times 0.6$$

0.6 is an approximate conversion factor for many water sources.

Chloride
The standard measurement milliequivalents per litre (meq/L)
Milligrams per litre (mg/L) = meq/L x 35.5

---

irrigation water, but exceptions have been described: Prior *et al.* (1992) showed some yield loss with <1 dS/m water applied at every irrigation, whereas Stevens and Harvey (1990) found no effect from water of 3.5 dS/m applied during a single 2-month period each year.

Varietal tolerance to salt
Varieties differ in their sensitivity to chloride. Alexander and Woodham (1968) found that Muscat Gordo Blanco was more sensitive to sodium chloride than Sultana, Currant and Waltham Cross, (each of which had similar tolerances) and in each case growth depression occurred before the onset of symptoms. In a number of irrigated areas varietal differences to chloride symptoms have been observed under field conditions. Varieties such as Muscat Gordo Blanco, Doradillo and Merlot appear to be the most sensitive while Ohanez, Currant and Shiraz are the least sensitive.

Some rootstocks are able to keep the concentrations of sodium and chloride in the scion at non-toxic levels by a mechanism called salt-exclusion (see Volume I Chapter 8), and scions and own-rooted vines show different degrees of tolerance to salinity. Sauer (1968) found that Sultana on its own roots contained much more chloride in leaf petioles than the same Sultana grafted onto different rootstocks. The degree of reduction in leaf petiole chloride level was greater that 50% for Dog Ridge and 1613 and about 75% for Ramsey and 101-14. Environmental factors affect the ability of a vine to cope with salinity. The saline environment is often poorly drained, and waterlogging impairs the salt-excluding capabilities of a rootstock in an unpredictable way (West and Taylor 1984). The recommended maximum level of sodium and chloride in petioles at flowering are 0.5% and 1.5% (dry weight) respectively (see also Table 9.13).

6.3.3 Water quality effects on the soil
Very low salinity irrigation water (EC_w < 0.2 mS/cm) can result in soil permeability problems because it will dissolve soluble salts including calcium causing finer soil particles to disperse. Similarly irrigation water with a high sodium concentration can cause severe permeability problems. Damage arises as sodium displaces calcium and magnesium from soil colloids, causing them to disperse and lose structure or physical condition. The result is a reduction in soil aeration, infiltration rate, restricted root growth and tillage is made more difficult. The most commonly used method that has been used to evaluate the sodicity hazard of irrigation water is the Sodium Adsorption Ratio (SAR). SAR is sometimes reported by the symbol RNa.

$$SAR = \sqrt{\frac{Na^+}{\frac{Ca^{++} + Mg^{++}}{2}}}$$

where the concentration of the Na^+, Ca^{++}, and Mg^{++} ions are given in milliequivalents per litre (meq/L). Conversion factors for units are given in Table 6.3. Soil stability is maintained if the SAR of irrigation water is below 6, but may be degraded by waters with an SAR of between 6 and 9. Higher SAR can cause severe structural problems. Changes in soil permeability are also related to the carbonate (CO_3^{--}) and bicarbonate (HCO_3^-) content of the irrigation water. When drying of

Table 6.4 Guidelines for interpreting laboratory data on water suitability for grapes

Potential irrigation problem	Units	Degree of restriction on use		
		None	Slight to Moderate	Severe[1]
Salinity[2] *(affects water availability to crops)*				
ECw	dS/m	< 1	1.0 - 2.7	> 2.7
Toxicity (specific ions which affect growth of crop)				
Sodium (Na^+)[3]	meq/L	< 20	-	-
Chloride (Cl^-)[3]	meq/L	< 4	4 - 15	> 15
Boron (B)	mg/L	< 1	1 - 3	> 3
Miscellaneous				
Bicarbonate (HCO_3^-)[4]	meq/L	< 1.5	1.5 - 7.5	> 7.5
Nitrate-nitrogen (NO_3-N)	mg/L	< 5	5 - 30	> 30

[1] Special management practices and favourable soil conditions are required for successful production.
[2] Assumes that rainfall and extra water applied owing to inefficiencies of normal irrigation will supply the crop needs plus about 15% extra for salinity control.
[3] With overhead sprinkler irrigation, sodium or chloride in excess of 3 meq/L under extreme drying conditions may result in excessive leaf absorption, leaf burn and crop damage. If overhead sprinklers are used for cooling by frequent on-off cycling, damage may occur even at lower concentrations.
[4] Bicarbonate (HCO_3^-) in water applied by overhead sprinklers may cause white deposits on fruit and leaves which reduces market acceptability, but is not toxic to the plant.

(Source - Ayers and Westcot 1976)

the soil occurs between irrigations, Ca^{++} and Mg^{++} are removed by precipitation with CO_3^{--} and HCO_3^- causing an increase in the relative proportion of sodium. To account for these changes in soil water composition the use of adjusted SAR (adj. SAR) is recommended.

$$adj.\ SAR = \sqrt{\frac{Na^+}{\frac{Ca^{++} + Mg^{++}}{2}}} \rightleftharpoons [1 + (8.4 - pHc)]$$

Where pHc is a calculated value based on Na^+ + Ca^{++} + Mg^{++}, Ca^{++} + Mg^{++}, and CO_3^{--} + HCO_3^- (Ayers and Westcot 1976).

The SAR may be lowered by adding calcium, usually as gypsum, either directly to the irrigation water or to the soil. Murray River water generally has SAR readings of less than 4.

6.4 Irrigation systems

Irrigation systems used in vineyards in Australia can be broadly classified as pressurized and non-pressurized types. The main non-pressurized methods are flood and furrow, although their use is declining. Pressurized systems comprise both over-canopy (fixed and travelling sprinklers) and under-canopy (sprinklers, micro-jet and drip) methods. With most systems the basic aim is to distribute water uniformly over the whole vineyard area in order to wet all the soil in the rootzone. Drip systems, however, are based on the principle of more frequently wetting a limited soil volume. The choice of an irrigation system is dependent on many factors, some of which are summarized in Table 6.5.

Regardless of the irrigation system chosen there are certain design constraints that apply to all. These can be summarized thus:
(i) The irrigation system should be designed with a high degree of flexibility within the limits of installation costs. Irrigation headworks should have sufficient capacity to allow for maximum projected water demand during extended periods of hot weather or to allow new developments to be watered more

Table 6.5 Criteria to consider in selecting a vineyard irrigation system

Criteria or feature to consider	Furrow	Fixed overhead sprinkler	Under-canopy systems	Drip
Soil texture	Medium to heavy textured soils	All soils	All soils	All except very light textured soils
Slope of land	Flat or gently sloping	Suitable for most slopes	Suitable for most situations	Suitable for all situations
Capital cost	Low	High	High	High
Operating costs	Low	High	Medium	Medium
Labour requirements	High	Low	Low	Low
Potential for automation	Low	High	High	High
Efficiency of application	Medium	Medium to high	High	High
Potential for frost protection	Not suitable	Suitable with correct design	Not suitable	Not suitable
Potential for frost prevention through soil wetting	Suitable	Suitable	Suitable	Not suitable
Interval between irrigations	Large	Medium	Medium (depending on soil water storage)	Small
Limited total water supply	Not suitable	Rarely suitable	Rarely suitable	Well suited
Limited rate of supply	Not suitable	Not suitable	Dependent on design	Well suited
Water salinity	Reasonable with adequate drainage	Least tolerant	Tolerant	Well suited
Water cleanliness	Few problems	Some filtration	Fine filtration	Fine filtration, often chlorination

frequently. High yielding varieties may need to be watered more often than low yielding, and late maturing varieties will need to be watered later into autumn than early varieties such as Chardonnay. Table grapes need to be watered on a different schedule to wine and drying varieties. Post harvest irrigations may also need to be programmed.

(ii) Although difficult to design with flood and furrow systems, each irrigation shift should correspond to blocks of similar plant water availability. This is determined from soil auguring or pits dug on a grid through the proposed or existing vineyard. Readily available plant water can be calculated from information on soil texture, depth of each textural layer and rootzone depth. Irrigation shifts are programmed such that blocks of similar soil water availability are watered together. Several advisory services in Australia now offer this systematic approach to the design of irrigation systems.

(iii) For furrow irrigation the length and slope of irrigation runs should be within specified limits. Generally the finer the soil texture the longer can be the length of the irrigation run.

Table 6.6 Relationship between soil texture and length and slope of irrigation run.

Soil texture	Slope	Length of irrigation run (metres)
Sand	1:250 - 1:200	60 - 80
Sandy loam	1:400 - 1:250	100
Clay loam	1:400	120 - 140

Table 6.6 gives the recommended lengths and slopes of irrigation runs for different soil textures. Each irrigation run should theoretically consist of one soil type with respect to infiltration rate, but this is often difficult to achieve.

6.4.1 Flood irrigation

This method of irrigation is not common in Australian vineyards as large quantities of water are needed to flood irrigate effectively. The Langhorne Creek district (SA) is the only area still using flood irrigation; vineyards are irrigated in winter by diverting flood waters from the local rivers through vineyards by a system of levee banks and weirs. Water up to a metre deep is retained in each vineyard for sufficient time to fill the deep alluvial soils to the drained upper limit. The water is then released to flow into the next downstream vineyard. Unintentional flooding of vineyards located adjacent to creeks and rivers sometimes occurs and provided this does not happen close to harvest the result may be beneficial.

6.4.2 Furrow irrigation

Surface or 'gravity' systems operate at almost zero pressure and include many systems; only furrow is discussed here. Furrow irrigation was the most commonly used system of vineyard irrigation in Australia but this method is declining because of the high labour requirement and low irrigation efficiency. The chief advantages of gravity systems are their low capital outlay and low pumping costs. A large amount of foreign matter in the water is tolerated. The chief disadvantages are:
– the need for water distribution systems to be designed to cope with the maximum flows required, as in the spring when the soil is trashy following the incorporation of the cover crop and prunings.

Figure 6.5 Use of broad based furrows levelled by laser equipment to achieve uniform water distribution along the vine row.

Figure 6.6 Underground pipeline fitted with water control valve permits accurate regulation of furrow flows.

– large inputs of skilled labour are needed.
– irrigation efficiency can be low.
These latter disadvantages can be substantially overcome on a suitable site which has been prepared with laser grading techniques (Figure 6.5); laser equipment is available for levelling existing vine rows. Pipelines have largely replaced earthen ditches or concrete channels fitted with slide outlets, as valves on risers allow easy control of the flow rate (Figure 6.6).

Efficient furrow irrigation requires medium to fine textured soils. Very fine textured soils with low infiltration rates need unrealistically low flow rates while coarse textured soils need high flow rates which cause erosion. Deep soils are preferred, because the interval between irrigations can be long.

The objective of good furrow irrigation is to have water over the full face of the furrow from one end of the furrow to the other for approximately the same period of time. Given this, and provided the soils along the row have similar infiltration rates, there should be a uniform depth of wetting beneath each furrow. The evenness of distribution of water from furrows is influenced by furrow shape, slope, spacing and furrow length. Soil characteristics such as initial water status, surface trash and the roughness also determine the flow rate. In calculating irrigation requirements an efficiency of 40% to 60% is usually used although it can be higher. The skill of the irrigator has a major influence on irrigation efficiency.

A single furrow can be used if irrigation is only seasonal or occasional, since it is less important to wet the entire root zone. Furrows are normally V-shaped but, where salinity is a problem, as much of the soil surface as possible should be wetted and broad-based furrows are preferred (Figure 6.5). Broad-based furrows are also preferred in heavier soil types and for primary/secondary irrigation techniques (see below) because the secondary flow is lower and easier to judge. In sandy soil, furrows should be spaced closer together to achieve a good spread of water across the inter-row space without excessive depth of wetting and consequent leaching, as may occur with broad-based furrows.

A common system of furrow irrigation used in the Murray Valley is the primary/secondary flow method. This is well suited to sites where the slope along the row exceeds 1:250 (0.4 metre fall in 100 metre distance). This consists of a high initial or primary flow in which water travels rapidly to the end of the irrigation run covering the full face of the furrow, without eroding the soil. The flow is then cut back to a secondary or soakage flow which just maintains water across and along the entire length of furrow. The secondary flow is maintained for a specified soakage time, which depends on the infiltration rate of the soil and the depth of wetting required.

Maintaining uniform infiltration rates along the row is of key importance in furrow irrigation. This will ensure uniform water distribution and minimization of problems due to dry patches, salinization and waste. Careful soil management will avoid soil compaction, as will correct timing of vineyard machinery operations.

The efficiency of standard furrow irrigation can be improved by surge irrigation. Some of the claimed advantages of this method of furrow irrigation are more even water distribution along the length of the furrow, lighter applications of water and energy and water savings. A higher level of management of unskilled labour may be required and surge valves need to be adequately maintained and protected to prevent mechanical damage, especially if solar powered.

6.4.3 Travelling irrigators

In large vineyards and where a plentiful supply of good quality water is available, travelling irrigators or water winches provide an effective system of water distribution without the high capital cost of alternative systems. Travelling irrigators need frequent moving and this makes their use labour intensive. Pumping costs are high as the units operate at 550-800 kPa and, because of the higher pressures used, attention should be given to supply lines, seals, joints and pumps. The irrigator requires maintenance, and care of grassed walkways is required to avoid damage to the high pressure delivery hose by small sharp stones. Delivery is about 30L/s with about a 50 m radius of throw, a typical unit delivering about 75 mm to 3.5 ha in 24 hours, and serving about 60 ha. High application rates mean soil water infiltration

Figure 6.7 Travelling irrigator or water winch. Note the grassed walkway.

Figure 6.8. Fixed overhead sprinklers for vineyard irrigation.

rates should be sufficiently high to ensure ponding or erosion are kept to a minimum. For large travelling irrigators sprinkler walkways need to be wider than normal rows and have to be incorporated into the initial vineyard design. Water tapping points are located mid-way along the walkways (see 2.1.2).

Travelling irrigators offer little frost protection although they can be used to quickly wet the soil surface during dry periods when frost risk is greatest. Water distribution can be severely affected by cross winds. Units need to be checked regularly to ensure they are tracking correctly as the larger units will pull out trellis posts and vines if they travel off-line.

6.4.4 Fixed overhead sprinklers

Piping for sprinkler systems comprises the main supply lines, sub-mains and laterals which are normally installed underground at a depth of about 0.5 m. With some systems laterals are laid on the surface to reduce installation costs, especially where trenching is expensive. Polyvinylchloride (PVC) and polyethylene (PE) pipe have mainly replaced the use of asbestos-cement and concrete pipe. Pipe sizes are selected to give a reasonable balance between the initial capital cost and acceptable hydraulic design. Small diameter pipes, although less expensive, cost more to operate because of higher friction losses. Experience has shown that friction losses should only be $\pm 10\%$

of the total operating head in the system. Water filtration is usually necessary to avoid sprinkler blockages. Each sprinkler is fitted at a height of about 2.5 m on a vertical riser of galvanized iron pipe, PVC, PE or polypropylene. The vertical riser is normally securely fastened to a post to absorb vibrations caused by the operation of the sprinkler.

Sprinklers should be placed on an equilateral triangular spacing with the distance between rows being 86% of the distance between sprinklers. The number of sprinklers per hectare is determined by jet size, water pressure, operating conditions and to a lesser extent vine row spacing, but there should be between 27 and 35 sprinklers per hectare. The main sprinkler used is the impact type fitted with single or double jets operating at a pressure of 250 to 300 kPa and having a discharge rate between 0.5 and 0.75 L per second.

The rate of application is determined by the average sprinkler discharge at the operating pressure and sprinkler spacing and should be matched to the infiltration rate, slope and condition of the soil surface. Water applied too slowly prolongs wetting and aggravates disease problems. Water applied at a rate greater than the soil infiltration rate may cause run-off and erosion. In practice the application rate varies between about 4 and 12 mm per hour.

The efficiency of a sprinkler system can be assessed using two indices:

Christiansen's coefficient of uniformity (CU) is a measure of the uniformity of water distribution from a pattern of sprinklers. A commonly accepted standard is a CU equal to or greater than 84%.

Distribution uniformity (DU) is an indicator of the magnitude of the distribution problem of sprinklers and emphasizes the risk of low quarter precipitation. DUs of greater than 75% are considered acceptable, with values less than 67% being unacceptable. DU has greater usefulness in semi-arid, saline areas as it emphasizes the risk of soil salinization

Figure 6.9 Under-canopy microjet system.

The maintenance of fixed overhead sprinklers is relatively simple owing to the large diameter of jets. As with other systems, the flow rate should be checked when the system is turned on. The condition of sprinkler heads should be checked annually. Regular field checks are necessary to ensure all sprinkler heads have similar rotation speeds. Springs and washers should be regularly checked (Harvey 1990). In vigorous vineyards sprinkler heads are sometimes fouled by vine tendrils.

6.4.5 Under-canopy sprinklers and microjets

Under-canopy sprinklers and microjets have a place in situations where water quality is suspect and foliage wetting should be minimized to reduce salt uptake. Berry splitting and fungal disease problems are reduced and fruit appearance optimized with under canopy irrigation. For these reasons it is the favoured system for table grape production in the irrigated districts. Under-canopy systems are preferred to drip irrigation in situations where a greater area of the vineyard soil surface needs to be wetted such as for the growing of cover crops or where soils are shallow. Coarse soils that give very little lateral spread of water with drip irrigation are better irrigated with under-canopy sprinklers or microjets. Both systems require a high level of management as blockages caused by ants, snails and grit can be a problem. Damage can sometimes be a problem with machine harvester catchers and weed slashing where stone is present. Lateral lines need to be flushed periodically and chlorination may be necessary to prevent algae growth. Lateral lines should be drained during winter shut-down. The successful operation of these systems is dependent on having a high trellis, a herbicide-treated under-vine bank and periodic removal of low hanging foliage to prevent interference to the normal watering pattern of sprinklers or microjets. As most under-canopy sprinklers and microjets have a low angle of trajectory, weed growth and cover crops need to be kept short to permit even water distribution.

Sprinklers
Under-canopy sprinklers are installed every second or third vineyard row. Sprinklers are spaced on a triangular design with sprinkler heads about 30 cm above ground level. Sprinkler heads lower than this are likely to be fouled with grit and other debris splashed from the vineyard floor. Under-canopy sprinklers have a lower operating pressure requirement (150-250 kPa) than over canopy systems and, because wind velocity is less under the canopy, sprinkler spacing of 0.7 of the sprinkler diameter is used. Water filtration requirements are less than for microjet or drip. High soil water infiltration rates are necessary to avoid run-off and to reduce water splash into the canopy.

Microjets
Microjets are normally installed every vine row and most have no moving parts. Operating pressures are lower (75-125 kPa) than for under-canopy sprinklers but because of the smaller jet sizes additional filtration is needed. Under S.A. River Murray conditions, mesh screens with perforations of about one third of the minimum orifice size in the emitters are required. There is a wide range of microjets available; some produce a circular wetting pattern, others give a 180⁰

wetting pattern, both with varying wetted diameters. The wide range of jets available permits the matching of application rate to most soil types. Some microjets deliver fingers of water while others give a spray pattern. Where microjets are directly attached to the lateral, rigid support of laterals is necessary to ensure jets remain vertical. If plastic stakes are used to support microjets the PE laterals can be laid on the surface.

6.4.6 Drip irrigation

Drip irrigation was developed during the 1950s to irrigate crops grown under unfavourable conditions such as harsh climate, poor soil and limited or marginal-quality water supplies. It was found that crops grew and yielded well under drip irrigation and there were significant water savings, not because the crops used any less water with drip irrigation, but because wastage of water was minimized. The advantages of drip irrigation over other systems are low labour requirement, close individual control of water supply, efficient use of water, and good performance with saline water. Against these advantages are high capital cost, the need for pretreatment of water and attention to maintenance such as checking for blockages, damage to drippers and filter and dosing pump performance. Some modern installations are highly automated.

Drip emitters have been commonly placed at the same spacing as the vines. For disease reasons they should preferably not be adjacent to the trunk. Salt accumulates at the edge of the wetted area and this hazard can be minimized by spacing emitters according to soil texture, not vine spacing. This ensures that in normal operation the wetted areas coalesce to form a continuous band under the vine.

Because drippers have very small openings they are prone to blockages and the success of a drip irrigation system is very much dependent on avoiding such blockages. Chemical analysis of irrigation water will normally highlight any potential precipitation problems. The water should be tested for pH, calcium, magnesium, iron, carbonate and bicarbonate, sulphides and sulphates and for some water sources, manganese. The quantity and size of particulate matter should also be known as this will determine the aperture size of any screen filters. The size of the screen opening should be between 10-14% of the dripper orifice diameter. Preventative maintenance is the essential part of any micro-irrigation system as once blockages occur they are difficult to remove other than by physical methods. The irrigation system should be turned on at least monthly during the winter to prevent the drying out of any sediment and reduce the build up of ants and other insects in dripper outlets. Many blockages are attributable to organic matter, algae and bacteria which form organic slimes and bond colloidal and inorganic matter into particles that block outlets. Algae and bacterial slime problems can be largely overcome by chlorination, either applied continuously at low concentration or in 'slug' doses which must be flushed out thoroughly. A chlorine concentration of 1 ppm continuously injected will normally keep laterals and dripper outlets clean. Swimming pool test kits are widely used to test the chlorine concentration. Slug dosing at 10-20 ppm for 30 to 60 minutes on a regular basis during the irrigation season will also help prevent blockages. Organic matter blocking drippers can be removed with chlorine at 500 ppm if it is retained in laterals for periods of up to 24 hours prior to flushing. Sodium hypochlorite is preferred to calcium hypochlorite as the latter form may cause calcium and magnesium precipitation in the drippers. If nutrients are applied through the system, it is important to thoroughly flush and chlorinate following application in order to prevent bacteria growing in the lines (Black 1976).

Iron, a less common form of blockage, is one associated with the use of bore water rather than river or dam water and is a difficult form of blockage to overcome. The problem is due either to bacteria in the water converting dissolved or colloidal iron into a rusty-coloured slime, or to the precipitation of iron. Iron concentrations greater than about 0.1 ppm in the irrigation water will require treatment by either removing it from the water or by retaining it in solution until it passes through the dripper outlet. Iron concentrations greater than 0.4 ppm are likely to cause severe problems. Chemical precipitation can occur if the concentration of iron is above 1.0 to 1.5 mg/L. Aeration of water will oxidize soluble ferrous oxide to insoluble ferric oxide which can be settled in holding ponds prior to irrigation. Costs are manageable if aerated water is used as a post-irrigation flush for about 20 minutes (M.J. Sheridan, per. comm.; see also Hayes *et al.* 1992).

Chlorine injected into the irrigation system at a rate equal to the iron concentration will also precipitate ferric oxide. The precipitated iron is then removed by sand filtration. Injection of hydrochloric acid to lower the pH of the irrigation water to about 4.0 for a period of 30 to 60 minutes will help maintain the iron in solution or it may be used periodically to dissolve iron sediments. Calcium salt precipitation can similarly be treated by pH control.

6.4.7 Special uses of irrigation

Leaching
As water is removed by vine roots and evaporation most of the salts added with irrigation remain in the rootzone. These may accumulate and reduce plant water availability or cause toxicity problems (6.3.1). To minimize this accumulation additional irrigation is applied to leach salt from the rootzone. The amount of leaching is referred to as the leaching requirement (LR). It is defined as the fraction of the total amount of water applied that drains below the rootzone to keep rootzone salinity within the limit that a given crop can tolerate. The leaching requirement is defined and discussed in the context of the reclamation of saline soils in Chapter 7 (7.7.2).

Cole (1980) reported the practical application of reduced leaching requirements in Israel and its possible application to South Australian conditions. In practice the actual LR can only be determined by monitoring soil and plant salinity and vine performance. In some situations winter rainfall or deficiencies in the irrigation system may result in sufficient leaching. High leaching requirements that may cause a water-table to rise into the root-zone for extended periods of time are potentially hazardous and must be avoided. Methods of disposal of drainage water are discussed in Chapter 7.

Frost protection
Whilst overhead sprinkler irrigation for frost protection is widely used in the frost prone areas of California, its use for this purpose in Australia is mainly limited to vineyards in the south-east of South Australia and in north-east Victoria. Frost protection from sprinkler irrigation results from the release of latent heat when droplets of water on the grapevine reach $0^{\circ}C$ and begin to freeze. As long as the freezing continues there is a release

of latent heat which prevents leaves from freezing. Adequate frost protection can be achieved with water application rates between 2.5 and 3.5 mm per hour. Higher application rates, while effective, may lead to waterlogging, drainage problems, poor trafficability and inefficient use of power and water. Undervine and surface irrigation can have a small effect on vineyard temperature but are not as effective as overhead irrigation. The usual practice is for sprinklers to be turned on when air temperature in the vineyard has dropped to $1^{\circ}C$ and to run continuously until the air temperature outside the sprinkled area is above $0^{\circ}C$ and the ice has melted from the shoots; this can sometimes be after sunrise. The extent of frost protection obtainable with specially designed and operated sprinkler systems can be as high as $3-4^{\circ}C$. The speed of rotation and application rate should be sufficient to ensure there is always free water to freeze and release latent heat.

Most of the sprinkler systems installed for vineyard frost protection in the south east of South Australia are a compromise between frost protection systems and the ability to use the same sprinkler head for irrigation during the growing season. Typical systems have a precipitation rate of about 6 mm per hour but, because soils are permeable, waterlogging is generally not a problem.

Heat suppression
Trials conducted by the University of California in the San Joaquin Valley have shown that evaporative cooling of grapevines during the heat of summer can be accomplished by the intermittent use of overhead sprinklers. In field experiments Aljibury *et al.* (1975) showed that intermittent sprinkling resulted in a reduction of air, leaf, fruit and soil temperatures of $5-10^{\circ}C$ compared with uncooled treatments and that the effect extends well into the night. The reported effects of evaporative cooling during the ripening period (veraison to maturity) on varieties like Chardonnay, Semillon and Chenin Blanc are a stimulation of grapevine growth, an increase in fresh weight of berries, a delaying of ripening by 2 to 3 weeks, and a reduction in the level of total soluble solids. However, it remains to be determined whether cooling of varieties more adapted to the warmer regions or tablegrapes could produce fruit with higher acid and lower pH without loss of sugar or any delay in maturity.

Fertigation

The addition of fertilizer to irrigation water is called fertigation. In the case of drip irrigation it is now generally accepted as a necessity because of nutrient leaching. In general, nutrients with poor mobility (such as phosphorus) are added at the beginning of the season, more mobile nutrients being added later. Research is continuing on the most efficient method of application of nutrients through drip systems; the question of the efficiency of continual dosing of low concentrations of highly mobile nutrients compared with strategically-timed larger amounts has yet to be resolved. Flocculation and precipitation of chemicals is a hazard with drip systems requiring special forms of chemicals, careful pH control (Finkel 1983) and a particular sequence for the application of chemicals (Black 1976). Fertilizers are often corrosive, and the system should be corrosion-resistant and flushed thoroughly at the end of a cycle. Application of nitrogenous fertilizers through drip systems has the potential of causing soil acidification and monitoring of changes in soil pH is recommended.

Herbicide and pesticide application

These chemicals can be applied by irrigation sprinkler and drip systems (Jensen 1980). With drip systems it is important to consider the mobility of herbicides, and this is greatly increased if puddling occurs (Gerstl and Albasel 1984). Sprinkler systems require some special features, including a high distribution uniformity, to be an effective means of applying pest and disease control chemicals such as herbicides and nematicides (Herrington and Morgan 1973). Backflow prevention devices to prevent pollution of the water source are a mandatory requirement if chemicals or fertilizer are injected into irrigation water.

6.5 Irrigation scheduling

Irrigation scheduling should aim to optimize the soil water content so that vine water deficits are controlled and roots are not water-logged. Maximum efficiency of applied irrigation water will occur if all applied water is used to produce the potential harvestable crop of the desired quality. The occurrence of stress induced by either an excess or deficit of water is likely to result in a reduced efficiency or changed fruit quality. High

pumping costs, volumetric water allocations or limited water, salinity and drainage problems and the value of the crop all make irrigation scheduling an important management practice.

6.5.1 Plant-based methods

Appearance of the vine

Although irrigation timing based on appearance of the grapevine lacks the precision of some other methods, with experience and close observation it is possible to detect early signs of water stress. When there is adequate water the rapidly growing shoots appear soft and yellowish-green. However, as water stress develops shoot growth is noticeably reduced, internode growth is reduced and the growing tips become harder and appear darker green or greyish green in colour. Smart (1974) found that as stress increases the angle between the leaf blade and the petiole decreases and the blades tend to point towards the ground. He also showed stress causes a reduction in the diameter of the vine trunk. A slowing of the growth rate of immature internodes and tendrils is also a sensitive guide to water status but such measures have not been used for timing of irrigation. Although several years of data are necessary before any detailed interpretation is possible, measurements of vegetative growth and yield components such as pruning weight, percent budbreak, bunches per shoot, berry weight at veraison, berry and bunch weight at harvest, and shoot and berry growth rate may give useful information on general irrigation management. Factors such as pruning level, crop load, temperature and wind influence these measures but they are useful guides if monitored over the season.

Measurement of vine water status

Water potential is a generalized form of pressure. Water flows from high to low potential (i.e. from high to low 'pressure'). The more negative (i.e. smaller) the water potential, the greater the drought stress of the plant. The terms moisture or water 'tension' or 'suction' are also often used and may be less confusing as the more positive (i.e. larger) the water tension, the greater the drought stress. Water potential is used to express plant water status while water tension is commonly used to describe soil water status.

As obvious symptoms do not appear until after

Table 6.7 Feel and appearance of soils at different available water content

Percentage of available water removed from soil	Sand and Sandy loams	Loam	Clay and clay loams
Saturated (above DUL)	Free water appears on surface when a ball of soil is bounced in the hand or squeezed.	Free water can be squeezed out.	Soil is sticky.
Zero (at DUL)	No free water when squeezed but a ball leaves a wet outline on the hand.	Soil is sticky. No free water when a ball is squeezed but wet outline appears on hand. Possible to roll long thin rods 2mm diameter between finger and thumb.	As for loams
0-25	Slightly coherent. Forms weak ball under pressure but breaks easily.	Soil is coherent and pliable. Will not form 2mm ribbons.	Soil is coherent and ribbons out between fingers easily. Has a slick feeling.
25-50	Appears dry; ball will not hold together.	Soil is coherent and will form a ball under pressure.	Forms a ball and will just ribbon out between thumb and forefinger.
50-75	Appears dry and will not form a ball.	Forms crumbly ball under pressure.	Will form a ball but will not ribbon out.
75-100 (to LL)	Soil is dry and loose and will flow through fingers.	Crumbly, will not form a ball. Small crumbs will powder.	As for loams.

DUL - Drained Upper Limit.   LL - Lower Limit

the proper time for irrigation, a rapid technique which enables sensitive monitoring of water status is needed. Direct measurement of vine water status (water potential) has the advantage that no assumptions need be made about root distribution or the relationships between soil water content and uptake. The use of a pressure bomb to measure leaf water potential pre-dawn is useful only as a research tool. The thermal measurement of xylem sap movement to estimate plant water loss by transpiration has been used in several woody species, including grapevines. The technology of sap flow measurement has made rapid advances in recent years and no doubt will continue to improve. Unit cost is still too high to be used for other than a research tool. Although much experimental work still needs to be undertaken, irrigation scheduling using sap flow remains a possibility. Aerial infra-red photography

is useful to locate problem areas in a large vineyard or an irrigation district and canopy temperature measurements using far-infared have recently shown promise (van Zyl 1986). Direct measures of vine water status are rarely used in practice and other indirect methods have been developed. When correlated with yield or vegetative growth, electronic measurement of trunk diameter and berry expansion may provide valuable irrigation scheduling tools.

6.5.2 Soil-based methods
By feel
The feel of soil provides a good idea of its water content. It involves augering the soil at several sites in the vineyard and feeling the various layers of soil in the profile. Table 6.7 can be used to assess the amount of available water in each soil layer. Data in Table 6.1 can then be used to determine

how much should be applied. Particular attention should be given to the soil with the greatest concentration of feeding roots; this is usually the upper 50 cm of the profile, but needs checking by use of a soil auger or by digging.

Soil water sensors

Both water tension and water content are used to assess soil water status, and if desired conversions can be made using a moisture release curve (Figure 6.2). The placement of moisture sensors is important and locations representative of the predominant soil type (or similar water holding capacity) within the vineyard must be chosen. Sensors should be placed at depths appropriate to the root distribution.

Tensiometers

A tensiometer is a porous ceramic cup buried in the soil with an airtight connection to a vacuum gauge via a short column of water. Water in the tensiometer and in the pores of the cup is continuous with the water film around soil particles. As water is drawn from the cup by tension, a partial vacuum is created in the tube, thus enabling the tension to be measured by the vacuum gauge. Tensiometers are simple and cheap but cannot measure the entire range of available water in all soils. They operate satisfactorily up to tensions of about 85 kPa, above this air enters the pores in the cup and the vacuum is broken. Tensiometers are best for use in coarse textured soils, as a large part of their available water is held at tensions of less than 100 kPa. For medium textured soils (light sandy clay loams to clay loams), irrigations should be applied before tensions in the rootzone reach 35-50 kPa (the lower value for coarser textured soils). In comparison, at a similar tension in a clay soil there is still a considerable amount of plant-available water. In this soil profile, irrigation need not be applied until tensions in the rootzone reach at least 60 kPa, or higher, otherwise the vineyard would tend to be over-watered.

Tensiometer readings reflect the soil water tension only, i.e. they indicate the wetness of the soil surrounding the cup. They do not provide direct information on the amount of water held in the soil. Water retention curves for soils are needed to convert tension readings into amounts of water required (Figure 6.2) to bring the rootzone to the DUL. Several tensiometers at different locations and depths are necessary to assess the water status and the drying pattern of the rootzone in a vineyard.

In light-textured soils tensiometers placed at the bottom of the rootzone are of benefit in determining the effectiveness of leaching irrigations. If the reading on such a tensiometer falls to less than 10 kPa after an irrigation it indicates water movement and leaching of salt below the rootzone.

Moisture blocks

Moisture blocks (electrical resistance instruments) give an indirect measure of tension. They consist of two electrodes embedded in a block of gypsum, fibreglass, nylon or a mixture of fibreglass and gypsum. The electrodes are connected by wires to a battery and a resistance meter which measures the electrical resistance of the block. They are particularly useful in finer textured soils such as loams and clays where tensiometers are unsuitable. As with tensiometers, the success of moisture blocks depends on their location within the vineyard and in obtaining close contact between the moisture block and the soil. Moisture blocks are not very sensitive in the lower tension range (0-100 kPa) but, if used in conjunction with tensiometers, provide a means of measuring the entire range of available water. In the presence of soluble salts, nylon and fibreglass blocks give less reliable readings than gypsum blocks, but the latter are short-lived in saline soils. Blocks made of a mixture of fibreglass and gypsum have the advantages of both materials. As the variation in response between blocks can be large they should be calibrated prior to use. Moisture blocks are not widely used in Australia.

Neutron moisture meter

Although the neutron moisture meter (neutron probe) has been used mainly as an experimental tool in the past, there is increasing use of the neutron probe as a tool for irrigation scheduling and for defining management problems. Once calibrated the probe is accurate over a wide range of soil water content but has a high purchase cost and is demanding of time. An advantage of the probe is its ability to assess soil water content at any depth whenever required. Computer programs permit the rapid interpretation of data and

Figure 6.10 Neutron probe being used to assess soil water status in the profile to a depth of 120cm.

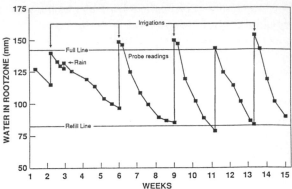

Figure 6.11 Soil water content during the drying and wetting of a sandy soil. Soil water content was measured with a neutron probe but tensiometers or gypsum blocks can be used in conjunction with the appropriate soil moisture release curve. (Data courtesy of Irrigated Crop Management Service - Loxton)

allow estimates to be made of rootzone depth, water infiltration rate, water distribution, etc. Operators have to be licensed by State health authorities and radiation monitoring badges worn.

Electronic sensors

Soil water sensors currently available cannot be efficiently used to generate real-time assessment of soil water storage and movement. The inability of irrigators to monitor and collect soil water data in a cost effective way has been a major reason why they have not widely adopted objective scheduling techniques. Developments in micro-processor technology have resulted in a range of sophisticated soil moisture sensors. These sensors offer the possibility of cheap, reliable and if necessary, continuous soil water data logging. Capacitance and heat pulse methods are now available for monitoring of soil water content. With some of the new systems, the data can be displayed so as to provide the irrigator with a graphical description of thresholds and trends to help formulate the most appropriate scheduling decisions. These systems offer a high degree of automation and can be used to control water applications.

6.5.3 Weather based modelling

Pan evaporation

Experimentally, evapotranspiration can be measured directly by growing grapevines in large lysimeters (a large pot sealed at the bottom and embedded in the ground). This, however, is both difficult and expensive. Plant water use can be estimated using mathematical models based on weather records. The evapotranspiration of a reference crop (ET_o), which is usually a stand of

actively growing, well-watered lucerne, is estimated by either the Penman (and modified Penman), pan evaporation, radiation or Blaney-Criddle methods. Evapotranspiration can fortunately be more simply calculated from pan evaporation and a pan co-efficient (K_p):

$$ET_o = E_{pan}K_p$$

The U.S. Weather Bureau Class A pan has been adopted as the standard evaporation pan in Australia (Figure 6.12). The pan is usually fitted with a wire mesh bird guard which is reported to decrease evaporation by about 13%.

Depending on pan location the value of K_p can vary between about 0.35 and 0.85. Crop evaporation (ET) is calculated using a crop coefficient k_c.

$$ET = k_c\ ET_o$$

Values of k_c vary from 0.25 to 0.9 depending on growth stage, ground cover and weather conditions (Doorenbos and Pruitt 1977).

Further improvements in accuracy can be made by including a coefficient to quantify the increase in water retention power of the soil as it dries. The value is small for grapevines growing in soil which has lost most of its available water but is close to 1 for a period following irrigation or heavy rain and the soil is near the DUL.

The most common and simplest method of calculating vineyard evapotranspiration is to use

Figure 6.12 US Weather Bureau Class A Evaporation Pan. Evaporation readings are used to estimate vineyard irrigation requirements. The pan is screened to exclude fauna.

Pan evaporation and a 'crop factor' (F) where

$$F = K_p k_c$$

and

$$ET_{crop} = F\ E_{pan}$$

Irrigation requirement is calculated by including the area (A) in square metres occupied by the vine.

Irrigation requirement (litres per vine) =

$$E_{pan} \times F \times A$$

Refinements to this method incorporate allowances for effective rainfall and vine growth stages. In irrigated districts the crop factor for September is between 0.2 and 0.3, rising steadily during the growing season and falling in autumn (Table 6.8). In the cooler grapegrowing districts

where the period of irrigation is much shorter, crop factors as low as 0.2 can be used (McCarthy *et al.* 1983).

For vineyards in Australia evaporation during the growing season (October-March) ranges from 911 mm in cooler areas such as the Yarra Valley to over 1500 mm in hot dry areas such as Sunraysia (Volume I Chapter 2). Within each district and within vineyards there are variations in the amount of water lost by evapotranspiration and these depend on the size and vigour of grapevines, the method and frequency of irrigation and other management practices. Irrigation scheduling based solely on evaporation can therefore be unreliable.

Water budgeting or accounting
Water budgeting is a quick and convenient means of estimating when to apply irrigation and how much to apply. The water budget is started on the day after an irrigation or heavy rain when the rootzone is fully recharged with water.

Information needed to operate a water budget is as follows:
(i) The total amount of available water in the rootzone in mm. This can be calculated from Table 6.1.
(ii) An acceptable maximum soil water deficit. Pre-veraison this is usually about 50% of available water in the rootzone but may be greater between veraison and maturity.
(iii) Actual evapotranspiration (E_a) calculated

Table 6.8 Calculation of evapotranspiration (E_a) based on E_{pan}, crop factor (F), and adjustment for soil moisture status 'p' using US Class A pan evaporimeter readings from Loxton, SA for the months irrigation is required. (Derived from Cole 1974).

Month	Aug	Sept	Oct	Nov	Dec	Jan	Feb	Mar	Total
E_{pan}(mm)	70	102	165	229	254	254	229	190	1493
Crop factor (F)	0.2	0.3	0.5	0.7	0.8	0.6	0.5	0.3	
Soil moisture factor 'p'	1.0	1.0	0.9	0.8	0.8	0.8	0.8	0.8	
Evapotranspiration mm $E_a = E_{pan} \times F \times p$	14	31	74	128	162	121	91	46	667

from evaporimeter readings multiplied by the appropriate crop factor (F), see Table 6.8.

(iv) Amount of effective rainfall. Falls of rain of less than 12 mm are not likely to be effective unless closely followed by irrigation or moderate to heavy rain. However, light falls lower the rate of evapotranspiration because of an increase in the relative humidity. After heavy rain an estimate of runoff and deep percolation or drainage below the rootzone needs to be made.

The budget method estimates water depletion from the rootzone due to evapotranspiration, with an allowance being made for any water inputs (irrigation and effective rainfall). It is a simple task to computerize a water budget; an example is given in Table 6.9.

Value of using several methods

The final choice of a method suitable for use with a particular vineyard involves assessing many of the factors mentioned above. No one method is ideal. It is better to use two or more methods, at least initially. If, for example, soil sensors are used it is sensible to assess the soil water content by augering and feel. This gives confidence in assessing the soil water status by the simple 'feel' method. Alternatively if sensors are used at the same time as water budgeting or modelling, confidence in the reliability of the latter methods can be gained. Soil water sensors, especially electronic types, can generate large amounts of data which by itself is of little value. The task of the grapegrower or advisor/consultant is to interpret these data by integrating it with other information such as vine appearance, water availability, soil type, yield, quality objectives, previous block performance, etc.

6.5.4 Special scheduling considerations

(i) Age of vines - young vines in the establishment phase require more frequent irrigation.

(ii) Vineyard operations - irrigations need to be timed to fit in with cultural operations such as pest and disease spraying, herbicide applications, cultivation, harvesting, sowing of cover crops etc.

(iii) Capacity and economics of operation of water reticulation systems. In many community irrigation districts, which irrigate on a roster

Table 6.9 An example of a soil water budget

Day	E_p (mm)	Crop use (Ea) (mm)	Adjust- ments (mm)	Daily water change (mm)	Avail- able soil water (mm)
0					127
1	6.2	3.1		-3.1	123.9
2	7.2	3.6		-3.6	120.3
3	5.2	2.6		-2.6	117.7
4	5.8	2.9		-2.9	114.8
5	7.0	3.5		-3.5	111.3
6	8.2	4.1	3[a]	-4.1	107.2
7	8.4	4.2		-4.2	103.0
8	7.0	3.5		-3.5	99.5
9	6.2	3.1		-3.1	96.4
10	6.4	3.2		-3.2	93.2
11	5.0	2.5	12[b]	+9.5	102.7
12	5.4	2.7	4[b]	1.3	104.0
13	6.8	3.4		-3.4	96.6
14	8.0	4.0		-4.0	92.6
15	6.6	3.3		-3.3	89.3
16	5.8	2.9		-2.9	86.4
17	5.6	2.8		-2.8	83.6
18	7.0	3.5		-3.5	80.1
19	6.4	3.2		-3.2	76.9
20	7.2	3.6		-3.6	73.3
21	6.2	3.1		-3.1	70.2
22	6.4	3.2		-3.2	67.0
23	5.6	2.8		-2.8	64.2
24	5.8	2.9	63[c]	+60.1	124.3
25	7.0	3.5		-3.5	120.8
26	7.0	3.5		-3.5	117.3

a. Rainfall, but discounted because ineffective
b. Rainfall added: the 4 mm rain on day 12 can be considered effective as the soil surface was wet from previous day's rain. Otherwise rainfall less than 10 mm should probably be disregarded.
c. Irrigation added

system, the timing of irrigation is influenced by the capacity of channels of pipelines and the cost of operation of capital works. It affects the quantity of water that can be supplied at each irrigation and the minimum interval between irrigations.

6.6 Responses to irrigation

The effects of irrigation on grape quality vary with the purpose for which they are grown, i.e. whether for drying, table or wine purposes. Vine response to irrigation is a much researched area and there is a plethora of literature on the subject (e.g. see Smart and Coombe 1983, Williams and Matthews 1990). The majority of this work has been done in irrigated grapegrowing regions such as the Central Valley of California, Israel, South Africa and the Murray-Darling basin of Australia. In recent years more research attention has been directed towards vine response in the rainfed irrigation regions such as south-eastern Australia, the Napa and Salinas Valleys of California and parts of South Africa.

Effects on drying grapes
With drying grapes, Sultana, Currant and Muscat Gordo Blanco, the objective is to produce a maximum dried weight per hectare at harvest time unless bonuses for quality justify lesser yields. In order to achieve this, grapevines should be adequately supplied with water up to harvest. If irrigation is withheld during the ripening period berry size is reduced, maturity is hastened and the yield of dried fruit per hectare is lowered. Irrigation strategies for drying grapes should also aim to minimize pest and disease damage.

Effects on tablegrapes
Berry size and texture are very important in tablegrape quality. To ensure large, turgid fruit it is necessary to use more water than with wine grapes. During ripening a shortage of soil water reduces yield mainly through its effect on berry size and sugar content. Vaadia and Kasimatis (1961) showed that water applied after veraison does not enable undersized berries to grow to normal size. Tablegrape appearance is brighter and more attractive when ample but not excessive water is provided during ripening (Winkler 1962). Drought stress causes several faults, including the impaired development of berries at the bottom of the bunch ('tailing'), wilted fruit (Kasimatis 1966), and depressions in the surface of berries ('thumbing'), or sunburn through exposure of bunches to the sun. Ohanez and Purple Cornichon are especially susceptible to 'thumbing'.

There is evidence that the interval between irrigations needs to be shorter for table grapes than for drying and wine grapes prior to the fruit ripening stage. However, once ripening commences, mild water stress is needed to accelerate maturation without causing the fruit to wilt

(Kasimatis 1966). van Rooyen (1980) recommended soil water tensions in sands of between 10-15 kPa prior to ripening and 5-10 kpa during the ripening stage. In finer textured soils (clay loams to clays) soil tensions of 25-40 and 20-35 kPa respectively should be maintained. Excessive irrigation can lead to an increase in loose berries during cold storage (Van Rooyen, Weber and Levin 1980). Hendrickson and Veihmeyer (1950) found that Emperor grapes from wet and dry soil treatments showed little difference in storage quality.

Irrigation management of tablegrapes grown in glasshouse and polyhouse structures is more demanding than field grown tablegrapes. High temperatures and large leaf areas contribute to very high transpiration rates. Irrigation during the ripening phase has to be carefully controlled to ensure berry splitting does not occur.

Effects on winegrapes
Historically Australian winegrape growing areas have been divided into irrigated (hot) and unirrigated (cooler) areas and grape prices set accordingly with fruit from irrigated areas being of perceived lower quality, receiving a lower price per tonne. Over time this led to the assumption that irrigated areas could not produce high quality winegrapes and almost a de facto acceptance that the long-term future of the irrigated vineyards in the Murray-Darling basin would be based on the production of fruit for the 'bulk' market. Changes in consumer demand in the late 1980s, both in the domestic and international market, increased the demand for fruit for the premium bottled wine market. This change, linked with both governmental and community pressure to improve irrigation efficiency, has added to the yield versus quality debate. The lack of objective measures of wine quality however means financial reward for producing high quality fruit is often inadequate.

Control and management of vegetative growth is now recognized as integral for the production of high quality fruit. There is general consensus that once veraison is reached the irrigation program needs to be modified to create a mild water stress or controlled deficit in the grapevine during the ripening phase. This has the effect of checking vegetative growth and preventing excessive fruit shading and a delay in the maturity of the crop. If irrigation stimulates excessive

Table 6.10. An irrigation scheduling strategy for the production of high quality table wines (after Hardie and Martin 1990)

Development phase	Soil water status
1. Budburst - flowering	Winter and spring rain is usually predominant. Maintain soil water tension below 30 kPa. Avoid waterlogging.
2. Flowering - fruit set	Maintain soil tension at 10 kPa throughout the rootzone
3. Fruit set - veraison	Allow rootzone soil water tension to increase to a maximum of 80 kPa. If irrigation is necessary, wet no more than 25% of the rootzone to 10 kPa.
4. Veraison - harvest	If irrigation water is readily available, maintain rootzone soil water tension at 80 kPa. If water is scarce, allow rootzone soil water tension to increase to a maximum of 200 kPa.
5. Harvest - leaf fall	Autumn rain is usually predominant. Avoid rootzone soil tension greater than 200 kPa.
6. Dormancy	Winter rain is usually predominant. Avoid soil water tension greater than 200 kPa. If rootzone soil water tension is greater than 30 kPa shortly before budburst, thoroughly wet the rootzone to 10 kPa. Avoid waterlogging

vegetative growth it may need to be slowed before veraison to prevent excessive fruit shading.

An irrigation strategy which seeks to reconcile grape yield with quality objectives for table wine by maximising bud fruitfulness and berry set while restricting berry size and vegetative growth was proposed by Hardie (1985) and is outlined in Table 6.10.

Although the strategy was originally proposed for grape production in the cool higher rainfall areas of southern Victoria, its subsequent implementation in vineyards in other regions of Victoria (e.g. King Valley (cool, not arid) and (Swan Hill (hot, arid) has confirmed its more general applicability. Details of this approach have been provided by Hardie and Martin (1990). The limits, described in terms of soil water tension, are intended to control the growth of shoots and fruit while avoiding severe photosynthetic stress under most soil and climatic conditions in which grapes are grown. In situations where soil hydraulic conductivity is slow and/or evaporative demand is high the maximum allowable soil water tension should be lower.

McCarthy (1986) suggested that for the Barossa Valley, replacement of only 0.2 of Class A pan evaporation would result in an economic yield increase without any detrimental effects on wine quality. Results from a drip irrigation experiment (Goodwin and Macrae 1990) in a Southern Victoria vineyard showed vines irrigated at 0.25 of Class A pan evaporation could be additionally stressed during defined periods of fruit maturity with no adverse effects on yield or quality. Pre-veraison soil water tension of about 200 kPa measured at 20 cm depth had no effect on vine performance but stressing vines to a tension of about 460 kPa approximately three weeks after veraison significantly reduced berry fresh and dry weight and fruit was of lesser maturity at harvest. The avoidance of severe water stress close to harvest was recommended.

Research on 'regulated deficit irrigation' — RDI — of peaches and pears has shown higher yields, larger fruit and significant water savings (Chalmers et al. 1981). The effects of RDI on grape berry development, vegetative growth and winegrape quality have not been clearly defined (Goodwin and Macrae 1990) but further experimental work is underway in the Australian Murray Valley.

The adoption of management strategies involving RDI or those proposed by Hardie (1985) to improve fruit quality will be dependent on payment for quality. High fruit quality and management of cropping level to achieve this goal will only be achieved by the use of irrigation systems which can be precisely controlled; these have been discussed in the preceding pages.

6.7 Concluding remarks

In recent times there have been a number of

important developments and trends in vineyard irrigation.

Firstly there is increased pressure on grapegrowers to make more efficient use of limited supplies of water. There are several reasons for this increased pressure:

(i) increasing competition for supplies of good quality water from secondary industries, urban areas and other rural pursuits.

(ii) the environmental consequences of faulty irrigation practices e.g. degradation of the landscape resulting from erosion, salting and seepage.

(iii) loss of soil fertility and productivity resulting from irrigation mis-management.

(iv) the rising costs of water and energy.

Secondly there is an increased use of water for irrigation in dryland vineyard areas of unreliable rainfall and the importance of obtaining consistent yields of high fruit quality.

Thirdly greatest improvements in vineyard irrigation efficiency are most likely to result from better timing of irrigations based on accurate assessment of soil water depletion and better control over the reticulation and distribution of water so that the correct amount of water is delivered to all parts of the vineyard. Advances in micro-processor control will probably be the catalyst for these improvements. Payment based on fruit quality rather than solely upon yield will be an added incentive for improved irrigation practices.

Further reading

Cornish, J.B., Murphy, J.P. and Fowler, C.A. Eds. (1990). Irrigation for profit: Water Force Victoria. Irrigation Association of Australia.

Finkel, H.K. Ed. (1982). CRC Handbook of Irrigation Technology Vol 1 CRC Press: Boca Raton, Florida.

Jensen, M.E. (1980). Design and Operation of Farm Irrigation Systems. American Society of Agricultural Engineers: St. Joseph, Michigan.

Hayes, P.F., Freeman, B.F. and Davidson, D.M. (Eds.) (1992) Advances in irrigation. Proc. ASVO Seminar, Mildura. Aust. Soc. Vitic. Oenol. Inc., Glen Osmond, S.Aust.

Smart, R.E. and Coombe, B.G. (1983) Water relations of grapevines. In: Water Deficits and Plant Growth. Ed. T.T. Kozlowski, Vol VUU, 137-196. Academic Press : New York.

Williams, L.E. and Matthews, M.A. (1990) Grapevine. In Monograph No. 30 "Irrigation of Agricultural Crops" Amer. Soc. Agron., Madison, 1019-1055.

Other references

Alexander, D. McE., and Woodham, R.C. (1968) Relative tolerance of rooted cuttings of four Vitis vinifera varieties to sodium chloride. Aust. J. Exp. Agric. Anim. Husb. 8, 461-465.

Alexander, D. McE. (1965) The effect of high temperature on short periods of water stress on the development of small fruiting sultana vines. Aust. J. Agric. Res. 16, 817-823.

Aljibury, F.K. et. al. (1975) Grape response to cooling with sprinklers. Amer. J. Enol. Vitic. 26, 214-217.

Ayers, R.S., and Westcot, D.W. (1976) Water quality for agriculture. FAO Irrig. Drain. Paper 29. Note also revision 1, 1985.

Black, J.D.F. (1976) Water treatment for trickle irrigation. Irrigation Farmer. Vol. 3, No. 1, 2-3.

Chalmers, D.J., Mitchell, P.D., and van Heek, L.A.G. (1981) Control of peach tree growth and productivity by regulated water supply, tree density and summer pruning. J. Amer. Soc. Hort. Sci. 106, 307-12.

Cole, P.J. (1974) Water budgeting for grapevines. S. Aust. Dept. Agric. Loxton Research Centre.

Cole, P.J. (1980) Salinity and irrigation - management in Israel. S. Aust. Dept. Agric. Soil Conservation Branch report S15/80.

Doorenbos, J., and Pruitt, W.O. (1977) Guidelines for predicting crop water requirements. FAO Irrig. Drain. Paper 24.

Freeman, B.M. (1983) At the root of the vine. Aust. Grapegrower and Winemaker 232, 68-64.

Freeman, B.M., and Smart, R.E. (1976) A root observation laboratory for studies with grapevines. Amer. J. Enol. Vitic. 27, 36-39.

Gamble, J. (1986) A trickle irrigation system for recycling residential wastewater on fruit trees. Hortscience 21, 28-31.

Gerstl, Z. and Albasel, N. (1984) Field distribution of pesticides applied via a drip irrigation system. Irrig. Sci. 5, 181-193.

Goodwin, I., and Macrae, I. (1990) Regulated deficit irrigation of Cabernet sauvignon grapevines. Aust. & N.Z. Wine Industry Journal. 5, 131-133.

Hale, C.R. (1959) Response of grapevines to prolonged flooding of the soil. M.S. Thesis, University of California, Davis.

Hardie, W.J. Irrigation scheduling for optimum yield and fruit quality in southern Victoria. Grapevine canopy management in southern Victoria; 11 July 1985; Knoxfield, Victoria. Vic. Dept Agric. & Rural Affairs; 1985. Agdex 241.

Hardie, W.J. and Considine, J.A. (1976) Response of grapes to water-deficit stress in particular stages of development. Amer. J. Enol. Vitic. 27, 55-61.

Hardie, W.J. and Martin, S.R. (1990) A strategy for vine growth regulation by soil water management. In: Williams, P.J., Davidson, D.M., Lee, T.H. (Eds) Proc. 7th Aust. Wine Ind. Techn. Conf. Adelaide, SA, 13-17 August 1989. Publ. Winetitles 1990. 51-57.

Harvey, M. (1990) Failure of sprinklers in vineyards. Aust. Grapegrower and Winemaker 323, 20-22.

Hendrickson, A.H. and Veihmeyer, F.J. (1950) Irrigation experiments with wine grapes. Calif. Agri. Exp. Sta. Bull. 728.

Herrington, P.J., and Morgan, N.G. (1973) Pest and disease control in blackcurrants and apples by the use of overhead irrigation sprinklers. Pestic. Sci. 4, 729-736.

Kasimatis, A.N. (1966) Vineyard irrigation. Univ. Calif. Agric. Ext. Serv. Circ. AXT-99.

McCarthy, M.G. (1981) Irrigation of grapevines with sewage effluent. I. Effects on yield and petiole composition. Amer. J. Enol. Vitic. 32, 189-196.

McCarthy, M.G., Cirami, R.M., and McCloud, P. (1983) Vine and fruit responses to supplementary irrigation and canopy management. S. Afr. J. Enol. Vitic. 4, 67-76.

McCarthy, M.G. (1986) Irrigation management for quality wine. Proceedings of the I.A.A. Annual Conference. Tanunda, SA, March, 1986. 58-66.

Moore, S. (1990) Harvesting water from an engineered catchment for the supplementary irrigation of vines. Aust. Grapegrower & Winemaker. 323, 29-30.

Prior, L.D., and Grieve, A.M. (1986) Water use and irrigation requirement of grapevines. In: Lee, T.H. (ed). Proc. 6th Aust. Wine Ind. Tech. Conf., 14-17 July, 1986, Adelaide, SA; Aust. Wine Res. Inst. 165-168.

Prior, L.D. (1993) Sodium, chloride and boron toxicity. In : P.R. Nicholas (Ed.). Grapevine Nutrition. Winegrape Production Manual. S. Aust. Dept. Agric., Loxton. In press.

Prior, L.D., Grieve, A.M. and Cullis, B.R. (1992) Sodium chloride and soil texture interactions in irrigated field grown sultana grapevines. I Yield and fruit quality. Aust. J. Ag. Res. 43, 1051-1066.

Sauer, M.R. (1968) Effect of vine rootstocks on chloride concentration in sultana scions. Vitis. 7, 223-226.

Shockley, D.G. (1956) The influence of moisture holding characteristics upon sprinkler irrigation design. Sprinkler irrigation manual, Wright Rain, 45-50.

Smart, R.E. (1974) Aspects of water relations of the grapevine (Vitis vinifera). Amer. J. Enol. Vitic. 25, 84- 91.

Stevens, R.M. and Harvey, G.C. (1990) Grapevine responses to transient soil salinization. Proc. Symp. Management of Soil Salinity in South East Australia. Aust. Soc. Soil Sci. Riverina Branch, NSW, 211-9.

Vaadia, Y. and Kasimatis, A.N. (1961) Vineyard irrigation trials. Amer. J. Enol. Vitic. 12, 88-98.

Van Zyl, J.L. (1984) Response of Columbar grapevines to irrigation as regards quality aspects and growth. S. Afr. J. Enol. Vitic. 5, 19-28.

Van Zyl, J.L. (1986) Canopy temperature as a water stress indicator in vines. S. Afr. J. Enol. Vitic. 7, 53-60.

Van Zyl, J.L., and Weber, H.W. (1977) Irrigation of Chenin blanc in the Stellenbosch area within the framework of the climate-soil-water-plant continuum. International symposium on the quality of the vintage. Cape Town. South Africa. 14-21 February, 1977. 331-350.

Van Rooyen, F.C. (1980) Table grapes: The scheduling of irrigation in the winter rainfall area. Farming in South Africa. D.1.

Van Rooyen, F.C., Weber, H.W., and Levin, I. (1980) The response of grapes to manipulation of the soil-plant atmosphere continuum. I. Growth, yield and quality responses. Agrochemophysica 12, 69-74.

West, D.W., and Taylor, J.A. (1984) Response of six grape cultivars to the combined effects of high salinity and rootzone waterlogging. J. Amer. Soc. Hortic. Sci. 109, 844-851

Williams, L.E., and Grimes, D.W. (1986) Modelling vine growth - development of a data set for a water balance subroutine. In: Lee, T.H. (ed). Proc. 6th Aust. Wine Ind. Tech. Conf., 14-17 July, 1986, Adelaide, SA; Aust. Wine Res. Inst. 169-174.

Winkler, A.J. (1962). General Viticulture. (University of California Press: Berkeley)

CHAPTER SEVEN

Drainage and Soil Salinity

R.T.J. WEBBER and L.D. JONES

Drainage is the removal of surface and subsurface water from land thereby creating a favourable soil environment for growth of plants and facilitating the movement of tractors and machinery through the planting. Drainage must be considered in the layout of all vineyards (Chapter 2), no matter whether the vineyard receives the bulk of its water from rain or from irrigation. However, drainage and salinity problems are usually worse in vineyards in arid and semi-arid areas that are intensively irrigated. It is a truism that better irrigation management reduces the chance that artificial drainage need be installed.

7.1 The purpose of drainage and its forms

The main reasons for drainage of vineyard land are:
(i)   to remove unwanted surface water,
(ii) to lower the watertable fast enough and deep enough to avoid crop damage due to waterlogging of the root zone, and
(iii) to help keep the salinity in the soil profile below a level which causes damage to grapevines.

7.1.1 Effects of poor drainage
Excess water in the root zone, i.e. waterlogged conditions, lowers grape production and affects vineyard operations in a number of ways.
(i)   It reduces the level of aeration (oxygen), especially in the subsoil and in so doing limits both root growth and depth of rooting. It has been suggested that the air porosity of soil should be kept at levels above 10% to ensure adequate diffusion of oxygen into the soil layers (Wesseling and van Wyk 1957). The effect of waterlogging depends on the time of the year: during winter, the dormant grapevines can withstand many weeks of submersion (Hale 1959) but, in

spring and summer, saturation of the root zone for a short period (2-3 days) can result in reduced growth and yield.

(ii) Salt builds up in the root zone, especially where the groundwater is shallow and saline. (Good irrigation and drainage practices lessen the chance of salination and the need for reclamation.)

(iii) Wet spots hamper movement of tractors and machinery through the vineyard, thus interfering with vineyard operations such as spraying for disease control.

(iv) Lime-induced chlorosis is usually aggravated by waterlogged conditions.

(v) Some pathogens and diseases will cause damage to plants in waterlogged conditions.

(vi) Waterlogging can lead to changes in pH, which may alter the availability of nutrients (e.g. too much manganese and not enough other nutrients).

7.1.2 Forms of drainage

There are two forms of drainage, surface and subsurface. They are complementary to one another in that removal of water from the surface helps to lessen subsurface drainage problems.

Surface drainage

Vineyards need some form of surface drainage. Provision should be made for surplus water to drain from the vineyard into natural waterways or storage dams. In furrow-irrigated vineyards, the gradient along the rows usually provides adequate surface drainage, however, in undulating rain-fed or sprinkler-irrigated vineyards some grading may be needed to prevent excess surface water from ponding in low-lying areas. The gradient along rows should be below that which causes erosion.

There are three main methods for collecting and conveying surface water from vineyards, namely:

(i) an open channel: suitable for flat grades, low flows and clay soils that do not easily erode.

(ii) a grassed waterway: ideal for steeper grades and to convey large peak flows after rain storms.

(iii) pipe drains: used for small amounts of run-off in undulating country.

As the runoff water from vineyards is usually of good quality, i.e. low in salt, there is increasing interest in storing this water in dams and using it for irrigation.

Subsurface drainage

Subsurface drainage is used to control the height of the saturated zone in the soil, i.e. the watertable, and is the main subject of this chapter.

7.2 Groundwater and its effects

The relationships between groundwater, watertable, capillary fringe and root zone are shown in Figure 7.1. A knowledge of the terms used is basic to an understanding of drainage.

(i) *Groundwater:* is the body of water within the saturated zone in the soil. Groundwater may be confined within permeable strata layers with low permeability above and below; often this groundwater is under pressure e.g. artesian waters. In other cases the groundwater is not confined and therefore not under pressure.

(ii) *Watertable:* is the upper surface of the saturated zone of free groundwater which is water that is neither confined by artesian conditions nor subject to the forces of surface tension. At the watertable the water pressure is at atmospheric pressure. In effect the watertable is the imaginary surface separating the capillary water (under tension) from the free groundwater below. A perched watertable is the upper surface of a body of groundwater which is located on a restricting layer, somewhere above the main body of groundwater. The restricting layer may be sufficiently permeable for the water to find its way to the permanent groundwater and for the perched watertable to fall slowly.

(iii) Capillary fringe: is the zone of soil above the watertable that grades from near saturation at the bottom to below field capacity at its top. This can be described as the zone of capillary influence. Although water contained in the capillary fringe is under slight tension, it can contribute a significant proportion of the groundwater that moves toward subsurface drains — as much as 20% or more under some conditions.

7.2.1 Movement of water in saturated soil

Groundwater moves in a saturated soil when there is a difference of hydraulic head (pressure) between two points in the soil. The principles of water

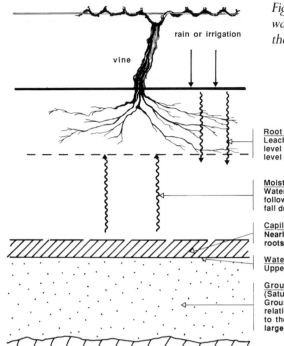

Figure 7.1. Relationship between ground water, watertable, the capillary fringe and the root zone.

rain or irrigation

vine

Root zone
Leaching necessary to keep salt level in root zone at tolerable level for grapevine growth.

Moisture and salt accession
Watertable and capillary fringe rise following heavy rain or irrigation and fall due to natural or artificial drainage.

Capillary fringe
Nearly saturated - too wet for roots to grow in.

Watertable
Upper surface of free groundwater.

Groundwater
(Saturated soil conditions)
Groundwater may be perched on a relatively impervious clay layer close to the surface or could be part of a large water-filled aquifer.

movement are illustrated in Figure 7.2. The difference in hydraulic head (H_1-H_2) divided by the distance between the two points (L) is called the hydraulic gradient

i.e. hydraulic gradient = $\dfrac{H_1\text{-}H_2}{L}$

The volume of water flowing across a unit area of soil in unit time depends on the hydraulic gradient and the hydraulic conductivity of the soil.

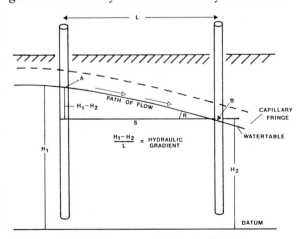

Figure 7.2. A difference in hydraulic head between two points causes water to flow; the steeper the hydraulic gradient the greater the rate of water movement.

Hydraulic conductivity, a numerical value for permeability of the soil, varies greatly with different soils the most important factor being the percentage of non-capillary pores (macro-pores) in the soil, i.e. pores that are greater than 10 micrometres (0.01 mm). Sandy soils, which have a high proportion of macro-pores, have a much higher hydraulic conductivity.

7.2.2 Measurement of hydraulic conductivity

There are laboratory methods as well as field methods for measuring hydraulic conductivity. If there is no watertable near the ground surface, the hydraulic conductivity can be determined by outflow from an auger hole rather than inflow.

Several 'pumped-hole' techniques have been developed to measure the hydraulic conductivity of the soil layers below the watertable. The techniques consist of:

(a) digging or boring a hole of suitable diameter in the range between 10-20 cm to some distance below the watertable.

(b) allowing time for the water level in the hole to reach equilibrium with the watertable in the soil.

(c) quickly lowering the level of water in the hole with a bailer or pump.

Figure 7.3. Measurement of hydraulic conductivity using the auger hole method. Water is baled or pumped from the hole and the rate of re-entry is measured with the specific equipment shown. Knowing this and a number of other parameters the hydraulic conductivity is calculated. (Photo — RWC)

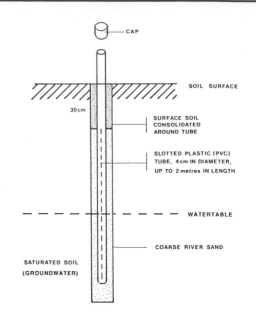

Figure 7.4. Test or observation well. This is used to monitor the movement of the watertable.

(d) measuring the rate of rise of water in the hole. From this value, and the diameter of the hole, the hydraulic conductivity of the soil layers penetrated by the auger hole below the watertable can be calculated (Figure 7.3). The method has its greatest value in deep, uniform soils. A highly permeable layer in the profile may bias the results.

7.3 Detecting watertables and determining the need for drainage

The existence and behaviour of a watertable can be monitored by installing a number of observation or test wells throughout the vineyard. A simple form of test well consists of a 40 mm diameter perforated plastic pipe inserted in an auger hole (Figure 7.4). The test well should reach to just above the restricting layer in a shallow soil or to a maximum of 2 m in a deep soil profile.

Test wells should be located away from traffic in the vineyard to avoid damage, i.e. they are best placed under rows of vines and close to trellis posts. On flat land, and in areas with a fairly uniform soil, 2 or 3 test wells per hectare are generally sufficient. However, in vineyards containing several soil types, and on sloping land, it is advisable to locate test wells just above soil type changes and throughout the low-lying areas. All test wells should be numbered and their location marked on a plan of the vineyard.

The level of water in the test well indicates the level of the watertable; its depth below the soil surface can be measured with a tape and sounding whistle or with a thin graduated rod.

7.3.1 Use of test well readings

The pattern of the watertable movement throughout the year helps to determine whether drainage is needed or not. The frequency of reading test wells depends on the following:

(i) where a watertable has not been found previously in the vineyard, the wells need only be read at the end of winter, after heavy rains or after irrigation in the spring.

(ii) where water is found in the bottom of the test wells during the growing season, or is known to be close to the bottom of the test wells, readings are needed more frequently, say monthly.

(iii) where the watertable comes within a metre of the soil surface, systematic readings taken throughout the growing season are used to decide whether subsurface drainage is necessary. Starting in the spring, the readings need to be recorded after each irrigation or heavy rain. In the first week, the readings should be at 2 to 3 day intervals and once per week thereafter. Additional readings may be desirable in the following year if the growing season has been abnormally wet or dry.

In vineyards which already have a drainage system installed, the test wells are best placed midway between drains and in any undrained areas where watertables are suspected. Test wells may also be placed along the rows adjacent to the drains to monitor the performance of the drains.

In interpreting test well readings, it is necessary to take account of:

(i) the potential depth of the root zone: In most soils used for grape growing the bulk of the feeding roots are in the top 60 to 90 cm of soil.

(ii) the salinity of the groundwater: The more saline the groundwater the greater the depth to which the watertable must be lowered and maintained to prevent harmful concentrations of salt from rising by capillarity and accumulating in the root zone. There is a lower safe level (about 2 m) below which salination of the surface soil is unlikely.

(iii) the depth to the impermeable soil layer.

7.3.2 Behaviour of the watertable

Where the watertable is within 2 m of the soil surface, it usually rises following an irrigation or heavy rain, reaches a peak shortly after, then begins to fall. The rate of fall depends on the ability of the groundwater to seep away and the rate of evapotranspiration. Ideally the watertable should fall to below the active root zone within 2 or 3 days of completion of irrigation or rain. This ensures that the root zone quickly resumes an adequate level of aeration. The watertable should then fall progressively to a safe depth. In high rainfall areas, where groundwater is normally of low salinity, the watertable can be regarded as safe if it remains 20 to 40 cm below the root zone, although greater depths are preferable. For grapevines growing in Mallee soils, empirical criteria based on rates of fall of the watertable have been developed for the maintenance of good vine health (Table 7.1).

7.4   Methods of subsurface drainage

7.4.1 Natural drainage

Natural drainage is the movement of excess water by downward or lateral percolation. Where natural drainage is good the water escapes at an adequate rate to avoid the development and retention of a high watertable. Natural drainage occurs in two ways:

(i) deep percolation: excess water moves downwards through the deeper soil strata beyond the root zone eventually reaching porous sand beds (aquifers).

(ii) down-slope seepage: commonly occurs in vineyards planted on hill slopes or on the slopes of sand ridges in the Mallee areas.

Groundwater which accumulates in the subsoil on the higher contours moves laterally down the slope thus preventing a high watertable forming on the upper slopes. However, where the

Table 7.1   Empirical drainage criteria suggested for grapevines growing in Mallee soils. The watertable needs to fall at or beyond the rates and depths indicated in order to maintain good vine health (From Anon 1970).

Soil Type	Days after irrigation				
	0	7	14	21	28
	Depth of the watertable in cm				
Deep light sand or sandy loam	40	90	120	140	150
Shallow heavy loam or clay loam	30	75	100	115	120

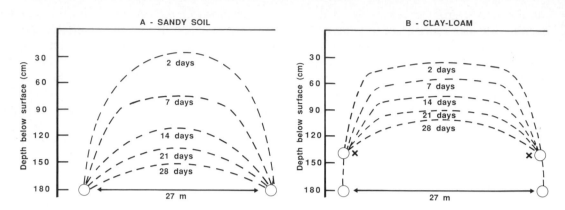

Figure 7.5. Pattern of watertable fall in (A) a sand and (B) a clay loam, following an irrigation.

slope flattens and the groundwater flow reaches soil that is less permeable, seepage areas may appear at the surface and act as discharge areas, necessitating the installation of artificial drains.

7.4.2 Artificial drainage

The principle of artificial drainage is to place a sink or drain, in the form of a channel or horizontal or vertical pipe, below the watertable so that a hydraulic head is created between the watertable and the drain. The rate of flow of water to the drain point is influenced by the hydraulic conductivity of the soil and the hydraulic gradient. The effects of these two factors are illustrated in Figure 7.5 which shows the pattern of water movement toward the drains in a sandy soil and in a clay-loam. In both situations the drains are 27 m apart and 1.8 m deep. In the sandy soil the watertable falls rapidly until it is almost at drain level, while in the clay-loam soil the rate of fall of the watertable is slower and falls no further

than 1.35 m. Below this level, the hydraulic conductivity is so low that it may be regarded as impermeable and the drains function as if they were at a depth marked X. Thus in the case of B, drains should be installed at a depth of 1.35 cm instead of 1.8 m and at a closer spacing. This results in a faster 'draw-down' or fall of the watertable (Figure 7.6).

There are four main types of artificial drainage; open ditch, pipe, mole and groundwater pumping.

Open ditch drains
Are used as collectors for both surface and subsurface water in some areas e.g. in the Murrumbidgee Irrigation Area in NSW. Ground water may also seep into the ditches if the water level in the drain is below the level of the surrounding watertable. Open ditches can be used where the subsoil has a high lateral hydraulic conductivity. There is very limited scope for using open drains in vineyards because of the area of

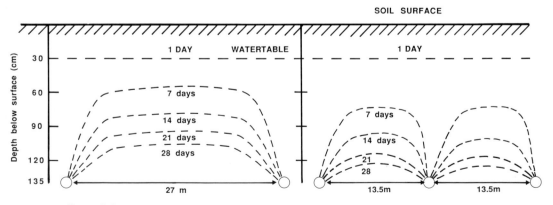

Figure 7.6. Effect of drain spacing on the rate of fall of the watertable.

Figure 7.7. Mole drain digger.

land taken up by the ditches, the physical obstruction to vineyard working, the cost of maintenance caused by silting, erosion, and weed growth and the cost of erecting bridges or crossings.

Pipe drains
Are used to construct a permanent network of subsurface drains. They are the most widely used form of drainage in Australian vineyards, and are described in detail in Section 7.5.

Mole drains
Are made by pulling a torpedo-shaped mole through the subsoil (Figure 7.7). The mole is 30 to 60 cm long and 5 to 8 cm in diameter and is attached to a sharply-wedged steel blade. A short cylindrical metal rod or ball slightly larger in diameter than the mole is attached to the rear of the mole by a short chain; this cleans and smoothes the walls of the drain. The vertical blade above the mole is an important part of the implement as it creates cracks in the soil, facilitating the flow of water down to the mole drains. Mole drains are rarely deeper than 80 cm because of the large tractor power required to pull the mole through the soil. In practice, the length of a mole drain is limited to 60 to 100 m with a gradient between 1 in 66 and 1 in 100.

The use of mole drainage is confined to certain types of soils. They need to have a high clay content (35 to 50%) and be low in sand (less than 20%). The stability of the clay is also an important feature. Constructing mole drains needs to be carried out when the soil is at the right soil moisture content. If the soil is too dry, it is too difficult to pull the mole through the soil. Although mole drainage is relatively inexpensive, there are many constraints to its successful application, and practical experience is considered to be the most satisfactory method for determining its likely success in any situation.

Mole drains are constructed by starting from an open drainage ditch and working up the slope. Mole drains can also start from a pipe drain trench which has been back-filled with very permeable soil.

The spacing of mole drains depends on the depth and texture of the soil and in practice ranges from 2 to 10 m apart. Under ideal conditions mole drains can remain effective for 10 to 15 years, but usually their life is much shorter. Forms of plastic lining are now being marketed and these show promise in considerably extending the life of mole drains.

Groundwater pumping
In certain geomorphic situations it is cheaper and more effective to lower the watertable by pumping directly from an aquifer or sand bed than by pipe drainage installed closer to the surface.

The conditions under which groundwater pumping is preferred to pipe drainage are:
(i)   where an aquifer or sand bed exists close to ground level, i.e. generally within about 15 m of the surface.
(ii) where the transmissibility of the aquifer is adequate to lower the watertable over an economically acceptable area. The ideal situation is one in which the confining layer above the aquifer is semi-permeable thus allowing pressure relief in the aquifer to be transmitted to the perched watertable above.
(iii) where there is a suitable way of disposing of the groundwater. In Mallee areas groundwater may be so saline that it must be pumped to an evaporation basin. Non-saline groundwater, on the other hand, can be used for irrigation if necessary.

Choice of drainage method
The choice whether pipe drainage or groundwater pumping is used should be based on either:
(i)   experience: If pipe drainage or groundwater pumping has been successfully used in the area, such as pipe drainage in Sunraysia, then that practice should be preferred.

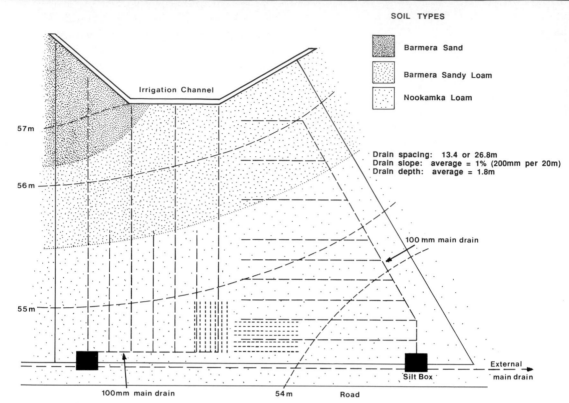

SOIL TYPES

Barmera Sand

Barmera Sandy Loam

Nookamka Loam

Irrigation Channel

57m

56m

55m

Drain spacing: 13.4 or 26.8m
Drain slope: average = 1% (200mm per 20m)
Drain depth: average = 1.8m

100 mm main drain

External
main drain

Silt Box

100mm main drain

54m   Road

Figure 7.8. Plan of furrow-irrigated vineyard showing contours (height above sea level — AHD), soil types and the spacing, slope and depth of pipe drains. Some of the vine positions are drawn to illustrate dimensions; vine spacing is 1.67 x 3.35m.

(ii) geohydrological investigation: If there is no experience of subsurface drainage in the area, then underground exploration must be carried out. It should identify whether a suitable aquifer exists and whether the water tables are perched or regional.

The capital cost of groundwater pumping is much lower than pipe drainage, but the maintenance and operating costs are higher. In situations where either method could be used, the choice depends on calculation of the capital and operating costs over the life of the vineyard. There may be a few situations where the regional groundwater and perched watertable are close to the surface and a combination of pipe drains and pumping from the aquifer may be needed to protect the vineyard.

7.5 Designing a pipe drainage system

Information used in planning and designing a subsurface pipe drainage system includes:

— a contour map of the area
— a land use map and soil survey information on the area giving details of soil profile characteristics which affect drainage, e.g. depth to clay, textual and structural features of the various layers and presence of restricting layers
— location of a suitable site for an outfall or a drainage disposal area
— a grid of test wells over the vineyard to identify areas in need of drainage

With the help of the items listed above, the following are developed:
— a drainage layout to suit the topography of the area
— determination of the correct depth and spacing for the drains
— a drainage construction plan setting out all relevant details e.g. the location and depth of outfall; location, depth and slope of main drains and lateral drains; position of sumps, etc. (see Figure 7.8)
— survey plans covering details for the installation of individual drains.

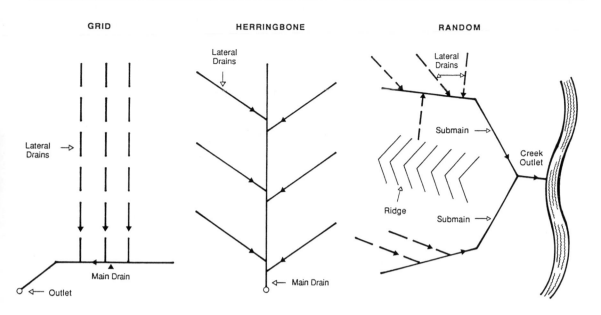

Figure 7.9. Types of layouts used for subsurface drainage.

7.5.1 Drainage layouts

The four main drainage layouts used within vineyards are grid, herringbone, random and interceptor. The choice is based on the topography and the planting design as shown in Figure 7.9. A cut-off or interceptor drain can also be used adjacent to a vineyard rather than within it.

Grid pattern—has parallel lateral drains which are at right angles to the main drains. This is used in flat or gently sloping land and in vineyards of regular shape. Ideally the laterals should run across the slope and the main drain down the slope, as this increases the water-carrying capacity of the main drain and the faster flow that results helps keep the main drain free of silt and sand deposits.

Herringbone pattern—has parallel lateral drains which enter the main drain at an angle, usually from both sides. It is best suited to a situation where the main drains run along a slight depression with vine plantings on both sides.

Random pattern—is used in undulating country with distinct valleys and ridges. The main drains are installed along the valleys or depressions and lateral drains are run into wet spots as required.

Cut off or interceptor drain—is installed along the upper side of an area to be protected. It is oriented at right angles to the down slope flow of groundwater resulting from irrigated highland, channel seepage or springs. An interceptor drain is usually effective for a considerable distance downslope of the drain but has only a limited effect on its upslope side (Figure 7.10). For best results, an interceptor drain needs to be installed as deep as practicable, preferably just above the impervious or restricting layer. It is also important that the drain be enveloped with coarse river sand or gravel and that the back-fill be very permeable. Modern drain digging machines are able to place a narrow band of coarse sand or gravel over the drain extending it upwards through the drain trench to surface layers of soil, thus facilitating the interception and flow of water to the drain.

7.5.2 Depth and spacing of pipe drains

Determination of the depth and spacing of drains is a first step in the planning and costing of a drainage system:

Depth

The drains are placed as deep as the soil profile characteristics and the depth capacity of the machine permit. Within reasonable limits, it might be preferable to modify the drain design to suit

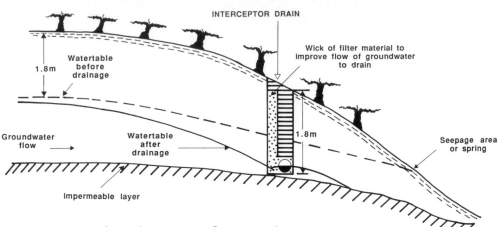

Figure 7.10. Interceptor drain showing its influence on the watertable both up-slope and down-slope of the drain.

the machine available. The present practical limit for lateral drains is about 2 m. As a general rule, deeper drains permit wider spacing between drains thus lowering the cost of drainage per unit area. Where there is insufficient soil survey information, the correct depth of drainage can be assessed by examining the soil profile at a number of sites in the vineyard. A 10 or 15 cm diameter open-mouthed auger is used to remove successive layers of the soil and the following features are noted:
— texture of the various layers of soil
— structure of the undisturbed samples of soil and particularly the number and size of visible pores
— presence of any obvious restricting layers. These can be detected by increased resistance to the 'bite' of the auger and a perceptible change in the texture of the soil. A dense rubbery or plasticine-like clay usually indicates poor drainage characteristics.
— where a perched watertable is present in the soil, it is often possible to identify the restricting layer beneath the saturated soil
— presence of anaerobic or reducing conditions. Subsoil layers with low permeability or poor aeration frequently contain the reduced oxide forms of manganese and iron. Manganese oxide shows as black flecks around soil particles at the top of the restricting layer, while hydrated iron oxide gives a yellow or mottle colour to the clay. In the irrigation areas of the Mallee, drainage contractors often look for black flecking (the 'black line') and use this as the drainage layer.

Spacing
The depth and spacing of drains for the various soil types have been derived from local knowledge and experience. By observation of grapevine health and watertable behaviour with different drain spacings, empirical relationships were developed for the depth and spacing of drains covering a range of soil types in the Mallee Irrigation districts (Table 7.2). From this sort of information, drain spacing formulae have been developed by Hooghoudt (1940), Ernst (1956) and Toksoz and Kirkham (1961) and have found general practical application.

In using these formulae it is necessary to determine the depth of the impermeable layer and the hydraulic conductivity of the soil. One can then select the maximum permissible height of the watertable midway between drains and the quantity of excess water to be removed during critical wet periods. Massland and Haskew (1957) used the auger hole method to calculate the hydraulic conductivity of the horticultural soils in the Murrumbidgee Irrigation Area and this approach formed the basis for designing on-farm drainage systems.

It has been estimated that, under furrow irrigation conditions, a drainage discharge of 50 kL/ha/day (5 mm/ha/day, i.e. an equivalent of 5 mm depth of water) provides a satisfactory rate of 'draw-down' of the watertable assuming a maximum height of watertable of 45 cm from the soil surface. Under sprinkler irrigation, where there is greater control over the depth of irrigation

Table 7.2. Empirical criteria for depth and spacing of drains in vineyards in the irrigated Mallee soils. (Adapted from Lyon and Tisdall 1942).

Soil Type	Drainage Depth (m)	Spacing (m)	Comments
Deep sands e.g. Winkie, Murray, Berri sands	1.8-2.0	27-40	Normally have good drainage (down slope) by virtue of their location on dune ridges. Over-watering is the most common cause of drainage problems.
Sandy and deep sandy loams e.g. Barmera sand, Barmera sandy loam, Moorook sandy loam	1.7-1.8	27	Shallow phase of these soils may need a closer spacing e.g. 20m
Sandy loams: Coomealla, Loveday, Bookmark sandy loams	1.4-1.5	13.5	
Deep loams: e.g. Sandilong loam, Nookamka sandy loam, Tatchera sandy loam	1.2-1.4	13.5	
Loams: e.g. Coomealla, Nookamka, Mildura, Benetook, Irymple loams	1.2	13.5	Early drainage of these soils is advisable
Clay loams and clay: e.g. Merbein clay loam, Boeill loam, Belar clay loam, Pomona clay	1.1-1.2	6.7-13.5	These are shallow heavy textured soils. Early drainage is necessary to maintain a safe salt level

water applied, Hall (1973) found that a drainage discharge rate of 20 kL/ha/day (i.e. a 2 mm depth of water) with a maximum height of watertable from the soil surface of 1 m, as suitable criteria under Mallee soil conditions. Spacing of drains may need to be closer than calculated if rapid reclamation is desired (Section 7.7).

7.5.3 Design considerations

Drainage rate
Smith (1974) states that a drainage runoff of 0.56 L/sec/ha of drained land (48 kL/ha/day or 4.8 mm/ha/day) provides a satisfactory basis for the design of drains in irrigated Mallee soils, with two notable exceptions:
(i) in topographical depressions where the piezometric pressure of the groundwater is above drain level,

(ii) where groundwater is moving in from other areas.

Pipe size and gradient
Slotted corrugated plastic pipe is marketed in 20 m rolls and is available in 2 sizes—65 mm diameter which is used for lateral drains and 100 mm diameter which is used for main drains. The recommended minimum grade for the 65 mm diameter pipe is 1 in 300 (3.3 mm per m) and for 100 mm pipe 1 in 400 (2.5 mm per m). Where drains are to be installed on less than the minimum grade recommended, special precautions are required:
— use of larger diameter pipes, especially for main drains
— avoidance of poor alignment of pipes and undulations in the drain
— installation of sumps at regular intervals along

the drain to trap silt and for inspection and cleaning purposes.

The size of earthenware tile pipes and the minimum gradients recommended for them are:

75 mm diameter: 1 in 300 (3.3 mm per m)
100 mm diameter: 1 in 400 (2.5 mm per m)
125 mm diameter: 1 in 500 (2.0 mm per m)
150 mm diameter: 1 in 800 (1.2 mm per m)

If accurate laser grading is used, relatively flat grades are possible, up to 1 in 1000. Smaller diameter pipes still need to be used on steeper grades.

Envelope requirement
To prevent or control the entry of soil material into the drain pipe, an 'envelope' should be installed around the pipe. The envelope provides improved hydraulic conditions around the pipe. The envelope is also useful in that it stabilizes and protects the pipe during installation, particularly in wet conditions. Where the soil is well-structured and stable, an envelope may not be required except to stabilize the pipe. If the soil has a high silt or fine sand content, or is sodic and 'non-cohesive', there is a risk that these particles will be carried to the drain by the moving water. Where these soils are present, a properly selected envelope should be used which has a permeability 10 times that of the soil.

A wide range of materials can be used for envelopes. They can be mineral (sand, gravel, crushed rock or slag) vegetable (coconut fibre, peat moss or straw) or artificial (fibre glass or other plastics known as 'geotextiles'). Artificial envelopes can be thin or voluminous. The best envelope material is a suitably graded coarse sand or gravel, but these are not always readily available, and transport costs can be high. A range of 'geotextiles' to suit most soil conditions is already available overseas, and is becoming more easily obtained in Australia. Plastic drainpipe can be supplied pre-wrapped with these surrounds. The envelope is selected to suit the type of soil, not for the gradient of the drainpipe.

Drain capacity
The water-carrying capacity of drains running full can be calculated using a modification of Manning's formula (Smith 1974).

$$Q = \frac{1000 \; r^{2/3} \; S^{1/2} \; A}{n}$$

where Q = litres per sec
n = roughness coefficient (0.014 is the figure used for tile pipes)
r = hydraulic radius
$= \dfrac{\text{internal diameter in metres}}{4}$
S = grade in metres per metre
A = cross sectional area of pipe in sq. metres

In studies of tile drainage systems, Lyon and Tisdall (1942) found that 100 mm diameter main drain on a gradient of 1 in 300 to 1 in 400 was capable of handling the drainage flow from 2000 m to 3000 m of lateral drains (75 mm diameter). This length of lateral would normally drain 4 to 8 ha of furrow irrigated Mallee soil depending on the hydraulic conductivity of the soil and hence the drain spacing.

7.6 Installing a pipe drainage system

7.6.1 Surveying and sump installation
Survey information is required for the design of the drains and to ensure that the depth and slope of the drains are adequate. Levelling is best done by laser but, if not used, construction pegs are placed every 20 metres along the proposed drain lines and survey levels are taken. Sighting (boning) rods are then set up on a predetermined grade so that the drain installer can check the depth and slope of the trench bed (Figure 7.11). Where

Figure 7.11. Drain contractor setting up sighting or 'boning' rods using survey data. Sighting rods enable a uniform trench bed at correct depth and gradient to be formed. Laser levelling is preferred.

Figure 7.12. Mechanical diggers used for drain installation in Australian vineyards. A, B and C are three types of trench digging machines. D is a trench-less drain layer. A back-hoe, which digs a wider trench, has more limited use (See Figure 7.13).

laser equipment is used to control the depth of the digging machine a peg at the start of the drainage line and at each change of slope is all that is required. More pegs should be used to check the accuracy of the laser equipment.

At the outlet to the drain a concrete pipe set vertically is used as a sump to trap silt from the drains. The pipe is 60 to 90 cm in diameter and the bottom of the silt trap 30 to 50 cm below the lowest inlet pipe. The sump is installed before any of the drains to provide a collecting point from which water can be disposed as the drainage pipes are being laid. In some irrigation areas e.g. the Riverland of South Australia, sumps or inspection pits are installed at strategic points along the drainage system to provide a means of inspecting the performance of the drains and for drain cleaning purposes.

Figure 7.13. Tile pipes being laid on a well prepared trench bed. Note that pipe laying commences at the main drain and that the drain installer works up the slope of the drain. (Phone: CSIRO Merbein)

7.6.2 Excavating the drain trench

Formerly, trenches were dug by hand using a shovel but this method is now used only in confined areas. Mechanical equipment has replaced hand digging, the main types of machine being the endless-chain digger, the wheel digger, 'trenchless' machines that instal pipes following a ripper (Figure 7.12) and the back-hoe. With trenches dug by hand or with a back-hoe the trench bottom is finished with a shovel to produce a smooth and even grade. The depth of the trench is checked either with laser equipment or by lining up a sighting mark on the handle of the shovel with the sighting rods. A slight groove is made in the trench bed to assist the laying of the pipes. The trench width is usually 45 cm to allow a man to stand and work in the trench. In some States, regulations to protect the safety of drain layers working in drain trenches have been enacted.

The wheel and chain diggers normally dig a narrower trench (about 30 cm wide) and finish the trench bed ready for pipe laying. These machines are better suited for installing plastic pipe in long lengths and lay the pipe and envelope material in the same operation.

7.6.3 Pipe laying and back-filling

Plastic pipe has almost completely replaced tile pipes as the overall cost of drainage using plastic pipe is less because of the lower digging and laying costs.

The plastic pipe used for drainage is corrugated and flexible and has rows of holes on the inside of the corrugations. It is available in rolls and is suitable for laying automatically behind narrow trench diggers.

Tile pipes are laid on the prepared bed of the trench starting at the sump or, in the case of laterals, from the main drain and working up the slope (Figure 7.13). Tile pipes are butted end-to-end and are fitted as neatly as possible so that there is a gap of 1 to 2 mm between them. The last pipe on each drain is plugged with cement to prevent sand and silt entering the drainage line. The pipe joints, through which water enters the

Figure 7.14. Strips of porous fibreglass mat or felt are used to partly or completely cover the tile pipe joints. Under some conditions the pipes are bedded on and covered with a 5 to 7 cm thickness of coarse river sand. These measurements help to prevent entry of silt and facilitate movement of drainage water to the pipe joints. (Photo: RWC)

Figure 7.15. A mechanical digger which has been adapted to place a layer of coarse river sand over the pipes and to automatically backfill the trench.

drains, are covered with a filter material to prevent entry of silt: in non-riverine soils, they are partly or completely covered with a strip of fibreglass mat or felt (Figure 7.14) and then with a layer of coarse river sand or surface soil. In riverine soils the fibreglass mat is not used because iron oxide deposits may block both the mat and the joints. Filter material consisting of coarse sand or gravel is used with a thin piece of brown paper as a temporary cover over the pipe joints; the brown paper decomposes as the filter and back-fill material settles.

Chain and wheel-diggers often have a conveyor attached to replace the soil directly behind the pipe-laying section of the machine (Figure 7.15). In other instances back-fill can be placed in the trench with a front-end or side-loader. Where back-filling is separate from digging and laying, such as with hand digging or when using the back-hoe, top soil is cut from the side of the trench to cover the pipes with 20 to 30 cm of more permeable surface soil. The remainder of the soil is then replaced, usually becoming mixed during the process. Gypsum should be incorporated with the back-fill if the soil is saline or is expected to become sodic once reclamation proceeds. Although the back-fill in the trench quickly settles following irrigation or rain, it does not consolidate to its original state and remains reasonably permeable. This facilitates the movement of groundwater to the drain.

7.7 Reclamation of saline soils

Drainage is the key to successful reclamation of saline soils. The approach to reclamation varies according to whether or not alkalinity compounds the salinity problem. The diagnosing of salinity and alkalinity problems and the reclamation measures used are shown in Table 7.3. Relevant details are also presented in Chapter 6 Section 6.3.

After drains have been installed, the way is open to remove excessive salts from the soil profile by leaching i.e. by the application of additional water, in excess of plant needs, by irrigation or by rainfall provided the volume and timing is suitable.

During and following an irrigation or rain, when the soil is at or near saturation, water is free to move through the large and small pores in the soil. When water moves through the soil, there are two mechanisms involved in the removal of salt (Talsma 1967); these are:

(i) the mixing of leaching water and soil water and its subsequent movement downwards; this occurs when there is slow movement of water through the small pores (micropores) and there is adequate 'contact' time for diffusion of salt or water molecules to take place.

(ii) the displacement of saline water contained in the larger pores by incoming leaching water.

7.7.1 Efficiency of leaching

Leaching efficiency is the fraction of drainage water that consists of displaced soil water (Boumans and van der Molen 1964). It is affected by many soil and irrigation factors and ranges from a ratio of about 0.2 in some clay soils to about 0.6 in sandy soils (Bouwer 1974). Factors that tend to increase leaching efficiency are:

(i) a high proportion of micro-pores in relation to macro-pores.

(ii) systems of irrigation that have a low application rate resulting in a large proportion of macro-pores remaining empty e.g. drip irrigation or low output sprinkler systems.

(iii) the presence of natural or artificial restricting layers at some depth in the profile. These reduce the rate of water movement through the root zone and increase the 'contact or

Table 7.3 Classification of saline and alkali soils (After USDA Salinity Handbook 60)

Features	Saline	Saline-alkali	Non-saline alkali
Electrical conductivity of the saturation extract in millisiemens per cm	More than 4	More than 4	Less than 4
Exchangeable sodium percentage (E.S.P.)	Less than 15	Greater than 15	Greater than 15
pH	8.5 or less	8.5 or less	8.5 to 10
State of clay	flocculated	flocculated	dispersed
Permeability	high	medium	low
Appearance	White crust on the surface	Similar to saline soil	Black alkali on surface. Sometimes there are 'slick spots'
Predominant ions	chlorides and sulphates of calcium, magnesium	chlorides and sulphates of magnesium and sodium	sodium, chloride
Method of reclamation	Drainage alone	Drainage with addition of gypsum to replace sodium followed by leaching	Difficult to reclaim. Drainage plus heavy and frequent application of gypsum, followed by leaching

diffusion time' thus increasing the efficiency of leaching. A similar result occurs when drains are plugged during irrigation and are unplugged on completion of the irrigation.

(iv) uniform water application in contrast to poor water distribution.

7.7.2 Leaching requirement

By varying the amount of irrigation water that moves through the root zone it is possible to regulate both the average and maximum concentration of salts in the soil water to some desired level. The term 'the leaching requirement' (LR) is defined as the fraction of applied water that must pass through the active part of the root zone to prevent the soil solution from exceeding a specified salinity, which is related to the salt tolerance of the crop.

Crop tolerance to salt is expressed as the electrical conductivity of the saturation extract (EC$_e$) of the soil in the root zone at which some reduction in production occurs. The conductivity is measured in decisiemens (dS) per m at 25^{0}C. The EC$_e$ value for grapevines that gives a 10% yield reduction is 4 dS/m and that for a 50% yield reduction is 8 dS/m (Bernstein 1965). In calculating LR it is customary to equate the salt tolerance of the crop with the maximum concentration of salts that can be permitted in the drainage water, i.e.

$$LR = \frac{EC_{iw}}{EC_{dw}}$$

where EC$_{iw}$ = salinity of the irrigation water in dS per m

and EC$_{dw}$ = the maximum permissible salinity of soil water draining from the root zone (in dS per m)

The value of EC$_{dw}$ used in the equation must ensure that a tolerable level of salt is maintained in the active part of the root zone.

The question of what value of EC$_{dw}$ to use in calculating LR still has to be resolved. Historically, EC$_e$ values that produce 50% yield reduction in forage and vegetable crops and 10% yield reduction in fruit crops have been used to give reasonable estimates of EC_{dw}. This, however, assumes that plants respond primarily to the average salinity in the root zone and not to the higher salinity found below the root zone. Bernstein and Francois (1973) found that crop yields were influenced more by the low salinities in the soil water of the upper root zone and were relatively unaffected by the higher salinities found below the root zone. On this basis they recommended that conventional EC_e values be increased four-fold before substitution for EC_{dw} in the LR equation.

Apart from the need to establish a realistic and practical value for EC_{dw}, Bouwer (1969) suggested that, in determining the irrigation requirement, due allowance be given to the factors that affect leaching efficiency viz: soil texture, irrigation method, rate of water application, depth of crop rooting, uniformity of water application and the spacing of drains.

In attempting to meet the LR of a crop and to remove from the root zone at least as much salt as is added in the irrigation water, it is necessary to take account of the drainage capabilities of the particular soil, i.e. 'the leaching fraction' (LF). The LF is the amount of extra water, over that required to replace water lost by evapotranspiration, which can be drained through the root zone using a specific irrigation method and expressed as a fraction of total water applied. If the LF is greater than the LR, then it is possible to drain sufficient water from the root zone to maintain a satisfactory salinity level. However, if the reverse is the case, salinity will have to be controlled by:
(i) increasing the LF by altering irrigation practices, or by installing additional drains or by modifying properties of the soil.
(ii) decreasing the LR by replacing the present crop with varieties/species that are more salt tolerant.

So far, the LR has been considered on the basis of total salinity and the osmotic effect that it produces. However, grapevines are sensitive to chloride (Cl^-) and tend to show the effects of Cl^- toxicity in advance of the osmotic effects due to total soluble salts. For this reason it is necessary to estimate separate leaching and drainage requirements based on Cl^- levels, viz.

$$\text{L.R.} = \frac{Cl_{iw}}{Cl_{dw}}$$

where: Cl_{iw} = concentration of Cl^- in irrigation water in meq/L, and
Cl_{dw} = maximum permissible concentration of Cl^- in drainage water in meq/L.

The tolerance limits to Cl^- in the soil solution for some grapevine varieties are 50 meq/L for Thompson Seedless (Sultana) and Perlette and 20 meq/L for Cardinal and Black Rose (Bernstein 1965). Where the LR based on Cl^- is greater than the value based on total salts, the former value should be adopted.

7.8 Drainage maintenance

Subsurface pipe drains have a long life; there are reports from overseas of tile drains lasting for over 200 years and there are tile drain systems in Sunraysia over 80 years old. However, some maintenance is needed from time to time.

7.8.1 Blockages

Blockages occur through the entry of roots and silt, and are most frequent where drains are laid on an uneven bed so that water lies in the depressions, or the pipes are misaligned. Water flowing continuously in a drain, due to inflows from other areas, will encourage the entry of roots from tree species growing close to drains, e.g. eucalypts, willows and poplars.

Blockages can also be caused by the incorrect selection of material for the envelope, and by chemical deposition. Intrusion of groundwater that has a different chemical composition from the soil water can also reduce water entry into drains. Groundwater high in bicarbonate often causes a sealing of pipe joints, or slots, with deposits of calcium and magnesium carbonates, while groundwater high in iron or sodium may greatly reduce the permeability of the back-fill around the drain pipes and in the drain trench. There is no simple answer to these particular problems; the best approach is to lower the watertable by groundwater pumping.

A blockage often shows as a wet patch on the surface along the line of a drain trench. Root blockages can be cleared in tile pipes using drain cleaning rods fitted with an auger head. A hole is excavated on the downstream side of the blockage and the drain cleaning rods are manually pushed and propelled up the drain. A screen is placed over the pipe downstream of the site to collect silt and roots freed by the cleaning rods and to prevent them lodging in lower parts of the drain. With plastic pipe a hydraulic jet is preferred for drain cleaning. A pressure of 1500-3500 kPa is required to sever roots that have entered the drain.

Where the drains need to be cleaned frequently, inspection pits are required, for example, every 100 metres along the drain to observe flows and provide easy access for cleaning. Where tree roots are a constant problem in main drains it is advisable to use a sealed pipe in that part of the drainage system. Silt blockages are more difficult to clear and remedy. Entry of silt is usually due to poor laying with large gaps between tile pipes or unsuitable filter material. Silt blockages can be cleared in the same way as root blockages. However, repeated siltation of the drains suggests that the drain should be relaid.

7.8.2 Trench sealing

Where the subsoil is sodic, drains may not operate effectively in the first few years. This is due to an increase in the sodicity of the back-fill material and a consequent loss of structure and permeability. Gypsum added during back-filling of the trenches reduces this problem. Where drains are already installed slaked lime applied to the surface will improve the permeability of the back-fill.

7.9 Drainage disposal and legislative aspects

With increasing emphasis on environmental pollution, laws are being developed to control the disposal of drainage water. In future, disposal of surface and subsurface drainage water may be an important cost factor in the drainage of vineyards.

There are several methods of drainage disposal that can be used, namely:
(i)   Re-use as irrigation water. Where drainage waters are non-saline, i.e. conductivity less than 0.5 dS/m, the water can be used for irrigation of grapevines. However, when drainage water has a higher salt content then it needs to be mixed with low salinity water to dilute it to a suitable level or, alternatively, left undiluted and used to irrigate other more salt tolerant crops such as lucerne. However, eventual salination is likely.
(ii) If the salinity of drainage water is high, i.e. above 2.5 dS/m, or toxic ions such as boron are present, then drainage water should be diverted into evaporation basins or to the sea. Drainage basins with an impermeable bed have a long term evaporative potential in arid areas of about 5 ML/ha.
(iii) Disposal into unsaturated aquifers can be used in some areas. However, this method has limitations because of the possible filling or pollution of the aquifers with drainage water.

The level of drainage runoff from irrigated mallee soils generally varies with the method of irrigation. Drainage runoff following furrow irrigation frequently ranges from 20 to 30% of the volume of irrigation water applied (Blainey 1960), while with sprinkler irrigation values of 8-12% have been recorded. Drainage after drip irrigation is usually nil except after the periodic leaching irrigations used to reduce salt that has built up to dangerous levels at the 'wetted front'.

7.10 Concluding remarks

Good drainage is essential for the continuing health and productivity of a vineyard. Without it, grapevines may be injured by waterlogging and /or the effects of salt. With greater use of irrigation in rain-fed vineyards to supplement natural rainfall, there is likely to be an increasing need to install drains to avoid seepage areas and to ensure effective salt management. This will apply particularly where irrigation water is of marginal quality.

Trial-and-error approaches to the design and installation of drainage systems have given way to scientific methods for determining the most appropriate form of drainage and the most effective depth and spacing of drains. The advances in technology and mechanical installation methods have made drainage systems more reliable, effective and cost efficient. However, there can be a problem when using broad-acre drain installation machinery within the confines of the vineyard.

The increasing difficulties and costs associated with the disposal of drainage water from individual vineyards in private vineyard areas suggest that there may be a need for co-operative drainage schemes. Such schemes are an essential feature of the Government-sponsored irrigation schemes.

With the current emphasis on the treating of drainage and salinity problems at their source, the concept has arisen of land-holders having to retain drainage water within their property.

Further reading

American Society of Agricultural Engineers (1982) Advances in Drainage. Proc. 4th National Drainage Symposium. Amer. Soc. Agric. Engineers. St Joseph, Michigan.

Houston, C.E. (1967) Drainage of irrigated land. Univ. Calif. Agric. Exp. Stn. Ext. Circular 504.

Luthin, J.N. (1957) Drainage of agricultural lands. Amer. Soc. Agron., No. 7. 620 pp

Luthin, J.N. (1966) Drainage Engineering. John Wiley and Sons, New York.

Smedena, L.K. and Ryecroft, D.W. (1983) Land Drainage. Batsford Academic and Educational Ltd., London.

Van Schilfgaarde, J. (Ed) (1974) Drainage for Agriculture. Amer. Soc. Agronomy, Madison. No. 17. 700 pp.

In this reference note in particular:

Bernstein, L. Crop growth and salinity, pp. 39-50.

Bouwer, H. Developing drainage design criteria, pp. 67-79.

Donnan, W.W. and Schwab, G.O. Current drainage methods in the USA. pp. 93-114.

Rhoades, J.D. Drainage from salinity control. pp. 433-461.

Wesseling, J. Crop growth and wet soils. pp. 7-37.

Withers, B. and Vipond, S. (1983) Irrigation: Design and Practice. Chapter 7-Drainage. Batsford Academic and Education Ltd., London.

Other references

Anon. (1970) Drainage of Soils in Sunraysia. Prepared by Officers of Vic. Dept. Agric. and State Rivers and Water Supply Commission Leaflet H 195.

Bernstein, L. (1965) Salt tolerance of fruit crops. USDA. Inf. Bull. 292. 8 pp.

Bernstein, L. and Francois, L.E. (1973) Leaching requirement studies. Sensitivity of alfalfa to salinity of irrigation and drainage waters. Soil Sci. Soc. Amer. Proc., 37, 931-43.

Blainey, J.M. (1960) The problem of excessive irrigation and drainage at Red Cliffs and Merbein. State Rivers and Water Supply Commission of Victoria Tech. Bull No. 10.

Boumans, J.H. and van der Molen, W.H. (1964) Ontwateringsbehoefte van bevloeide gronden in verband met hun zouthiushouding. Landbouwk. Tydschrift 76, 800-87.

Bouwer, H. (1969) Salt balance, irrigation efficiency and drainage design. Amer. Soc. Civil Eng., Proc. 95 (IR 1), 153-70.

Ernst, L.F. (1956) Calculation of the steady flow of groundwater in vertical cross sections. Neth. J. Agr. Sci. 4, 126-31.

Hale, C.R. (1959) Responses of grapevines to prolonged flooding of the soils. M.S. Thesis, University of California. Davis.

Hall, D.B. (1973) Drainage and water use in a sprinkler irrigated vineyard. State Rivers and Water Supply Commission of Victoria Mimeo 11 pp.

Hooghoudt, S.B. (1940) Algemene beschouwing van het probleem van de detailontwatering en de infiltratie door middel van parallel lopende drains, greppels, sloten en kanalen. Versl. Landbouwk. Onderz 46, 515-707.

Lyon, A.V. and Tisdall, A.L. (1942) Production of dried grapes in Murray Valley irrigation settlements. 2. Irrigation, drainage and reclamation. Bull. Counc. Sci. Ind. Res. Aust. No. 149, 35 pp.

Massland, M. and Haskew, H.C. (1957) The auger hole method of measuring the hydraulic conductivity of soil and its application to tile drainage problems. Water Conserv. Irrigation Comm., NSW Bull. No. 2.

Talsma, T. (1967) Leaching—the rinsing of undesirable salts from the soil. Irrigation Research and Extension Committee Farmers Newsletter No. 97. pp 2-17.

Toksoz, S. and Kirkham, D. (1961) Graphical solution and interpretation of a new drain spacing formula. J. Geophys. Res. 66, 509-16.

Smith, K.G.A., van der Lelij, A. and Poulton, D.C. (1988) Design practices of covered drains in an agricultural land drainage system. Int. Comm. on Irrigation and Drainage — Australian National Committee. Eng. Water Supply Dept., Adelaide.

U.S. Salinity Laboratory Staff. (1954) Diagnosis and improvement of saline and alkali soils. USDA Handbook 60. 160 pp.

Wesseling, J. and van Wyk, W.R. (1957) Soil physical conditions in relation to drain depth. In: J.N. Luthin (ed) Drainage of Agricultural Lands. Agronomy 7, 461-504. Amer. Soc. Agron., Madison.

CHAPTER EIGHT

Soil Management and Frost Control

M.G. McCARTHY, P.R. DRY, P.F. HAYES and D.M. DAVIDSON

The way in which the soil in a vineyard is managed influences its long term productivity, both physical and economic. The aims of vineyard soil management are to:

(i) create and maintain a soil environment favourable for optimal growth and functioning of grape roots in both the short and long term.

(ii) facilitate other vineyard operations.

(iii) induce a favourable aboveground micro-climate.

(iv) avoid soil erosion, soil degradation and spoilage of the environment.

The first aim is paramount: along with irrigation and mineral nutrition, soil management is the principal method of influencing the root environment. The important soil properties are those which influence the supply to roots of adequate oxygen, water and minerals plus a freedom from adverse physical, chemical and biological factors in the root zone.

The selection of soils for grapegrowing is covered in Volume 1, Chapter 3. An appropriate soil management strategy must be designed for each individual vineyard site — the components of the choices that collectively contribute to this are shown in Figure 8.1.

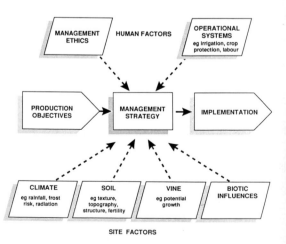

Figure 8.1. Formulation of a soil management strategy (after Hardie 1988).

In this chapter, the role of soil in root growth, maintenance and improvement of soil fertility and vineyard soil management systems are examined. The question of frost control in vineyards is also discussed.

8.1 The role of soil in root growth

A strong and viable root system is essential for a healthy vine as there is an important interdependence between the root system and shoot growth. The roots absorb water and nutrients from the soil and these, together with many essential organic compounds synthesized specifically in root tips, are distributed throughout the plant, particularly to the shoots. Woody parts of the root and shoot systems store reserves (ultimately derived from photosynthesis in green tissues) which contribute positively to the longevity and continued productivity of the grapevine.

As well as water and minerals, the root system provides anchorage for the vine. In order to be able to fulfil all of its roles, the roots must be able to grow freely through the soil, continually branching and forming new root tips. Many factors affect root development and the viticulturist can manipulate soil conditions to influence or control the growth and function of both root and shoot systems.

8.1.1 Soil texture and structure

Coarse-textured soils such as sands or sandy loams favour root growth as the roots can readily grow between their larger sized particles. More finely textured soils, such as silts and clays, restrict root growth because the pores between each particle are smaller. The size and extent of the pores (soil porosity) is considered to be the major factor controlling the distribution and growth of grapevine roots. Soil structure is determined by the manner in which particles aggregate together and confounds the texture effect of soils. A well-structured clay will be more favourable for root growth than a sand in which the particles are fused together. This is because structured clays have a high proportion of crumbs giving large pores which permit root entry and oxygen diffusion, while the crumbs themselves form a convenient water store.

8.1.2 Soil moisture

Infiltration of water into the soil is determined by the presence of stable pores and cracks in the surface soil. A uniform distribution of relatively large pores and cracks from the surface to depth is necessary for water movement through the soil profile. The rate of water movement is determined by pore size, being rapid through soil pores greater than 0.5 mm in diameter, but slow through pores less than 0.08 mm diameter. Moderate to large sized soil aggregates provide relatively large soil pores. However even low percentages of small particles from easily dispersed clays can act to seal pore spaces between aggregates and restrict infiltration.

Root elongation is favoured by moderately dry soil. Main roots spread widely and penetrate to depth. In wetter soils roots branch more frequently provided aeration is adequate (Richards 1983). A soil water potential lower than -50 kPa has little effect on the rate of root elongation, but few roots grow in soils drier than -1500 kPa (wilting point) (Richards and Cockcroft 1974). The ability of grapevines to cope with dry conditions may be attributed to their capacity to explore a large volume of soil with a system of deep roots, rather than to an inherent tolerance of dry soil (van Rooyen 1980). In general, vine size, capacity and yield is correlated to the vine's consumptive water use.

8.1.3 Soil aeration

Aeration of plant roots is by gaseous diffusion through soil pores. About 10% air-filled porosity is required for optimal root growth. Root systems develop less in water-logged soils, not only because less oxygen can diffuse to the root zone but also because there can be a build-up of carbon dioxide and ethylene, both of which are inhibitory to root growth and function. If cover crops are incorporated into wet soils creating anaerobic conditions, micro-organisms produce ethylene which inhibits root tip activity (Perret and Koblet 1984). Nutrient uptake may be decreased in water-logged soils and the chance of aluminium and manganese toxicity is increased. Wet soils favour many root diseases and increase susceptibility to pathogen attack (Chapter 11). Prolonged anaerobic conditions kill terminal meristems, although new lateral roots do develop. Well-structured soils drain to the drained upper limit within 1-2 days of an irrigation or rainfall (6.1.1). The rate of drainage is affected by soil profile and porosity, organic matter content and topography. The absence of impeding layers to 1-2 m under natural rainfall, or 3 m under irrigation, is necessary to avoid waterlogging unless natural surface drainage is satisfactory or subsoil drains are installed (Volume 1, Chapter 3). The rise of a water table into the rootzone for prolonged periods, will seriously affect root functioning; some varieties have roots that are especially sensitive e.g. Ramsey rootstock.

8.1.4 Impervious or unfavourable layers
Although soils differ widely in origin, depth and structure, most vine roots occur in the top one metre. Individual roots, may however, penetrate to depths of 6 m or more. The fine lateral roots comprising the majority of the absorptive surface area are concentrated in the upper zone (10-60 cm). Root depth is restricted if the soil profile contains unfavourable layers such as ironstone, calcrete, water tables, massive clays, saline or acid zones (Richards 1983). Zones of unfavourable soil pH (both high and low) will restrict root penetration. Both shoot and root growth of grapevines decrease with increasing soil compaction. Roots readily penetrate soils of bulk densities less than 1.1-1.2 g/cm³, but penetration markedly declines at values greater than 1.5 g/cm³ (Richards 1983). Restricted root growth was observed in soil with a bulk density exceeding 1.6 g/cm³ (van Huyssteen 1988). Although there is no critical value above which root growth is fully restricted, good vineyard soils probably should have bulk densities of less than 1.5 g/cm³.

8.1.5 Soil temperature
Roots grow best at temperatures between 15 and 30°C. Woodham and Alexander (1966) reported poor growth of potted vines when roots were maintained at 11°C; vines with roots at 20°C stopped growth at flowering while vines with roots kept at 30°C made the best growth and set the most fruit. As cold and wet soils discourage root growth it is not advisable to plant cuttings or rootlings until the soil is warmer than 12°C; this may not be until late spring in some districts. Unshaded topsoil can become too hot for root growth: it is not uncommon for the surface of dark-coloured clay soils or dry sand to reach

temperatures of 60-70°C. Subsoil temperatures are relatively low with little diurnal or seasonal fluctuation, e.g. temperatures at 60cm depth at the Waite Institute average 17°C with amplitudes of ±6°C yearly and ±1°C daily.

8.1.6 Mineral nutrients
The grapevine is considered to have greater adaptability to varying nutrient supply than many other horticultural crops (Winkler *et al.* 1974). Nevertheless, symptoms of nutrient deficiency or excess are frequently exhibited (Christensen *et al.* 1978). Nutrition of the grapevine is covered in Chapter 9; however, the impact of soil on nutrient availability and root growth is relevant to this chapter and especially the effect of soil pH (Figure 9.13). In alkaline soils there is a reduced availability of nitrogen, calcium, magnesium, manganese, iron, copper and zinc. In acid soils the availability of manganese and aluminium is increased, and these two elements, and sometimes copper, may become toxic. Acid soils are commonly found in high rainfall areas and have been diagnosed in vineyards in the Hunter and Hastings Valleys (NSW), Yarra and King Valleys, Great Western (Vic) and Mt Lofty Ranges (SA). Aluminium toxicity causes severe stunting of roots which are short, stubby, relatively unbranched and dark-coloured (Smart *et al.* 1991). The availability of all other minerals, with the exception of iron, is reduced at low pH. Calcium and boron may be in short supply in acid soils. A boron deficiency results in root distortion and death of root tips, but growth will return to normal when boron is supplied. As is general in perennial crops, root branching in grapevines is highly dependent on the available nitrogen and phosphorus levels (Richards 1983).

8.1.7 Biological factors
The soil is home to a distinct and diverse flora and fauna that interacts strongly with grapevine roots — directly and indirectly, positively and negatively. The organisms represent a large biomass and therefore a significant sink of mineral nutrients, e.g. dressings of straw lead to a temporary nitrogen deficiency because of the increase in numbers of straw-degrading organisms. At the same time this biomass influences the rate of availability of nutrients to the roots, e.g. some of the nitrogen in organic material is converted to plant-available nitrate ions, i.e. mineralization.

The uptake of phosphorus and zinc by vine roots from the soil is improved if mycorrhizal fungi grow in association with the root surface. Some fauna degrade organic material and benefit soil structure. Earthworms in particular benefit soils by tunnelling and cycling of nutrients and soil particles through the profile, thereby improving air and water movement and ultimately root penetration. Of course some flora and fauna are pathogenic to grapevine roots, e.g., the fungi rhizoctonia, pythium and phytophthora and the pests phylloxera and nematodes (See 11.1.8). Finally the roots of other plants affect grapevine roots either indirectly by altering or competing for soil resources (water, minerals, soil atmosphere) or directly by providing negative and positive growth signals i.e. allelopathic and companion plants.

8.2 Maintenance and improvement of soil fertility

Soil fertility embraces all those factors that contribute to the long term sustainable productivity of soil. Some of the features of a fertile soil are high organic matter content, balanced nutrient and water availability, good structure and other factors listed in 8.1. Vineyard soil management should aim to maintain or improve soil fertility, in a manner that is compatible with other vineyard operations. Favourable soil conditions encourage healthy roots and hence healthy vines.

8.2.1 Organic matter

Organic matter (OM) comprises the residue of plants and animals, including their excretions and secretions. It is part of the soil fabric, complementary to the mineral matter. Some of the benefits of OM are:
— contributes fabric to the soil (fibres and colloids)
— stabilizes soil aggregates
— cellulosic components add to the soil's cation exchange capacity
— adds to the matric water storage capacity
— plays a role in ligand binding of metals
— provides a reservoir of nutrient elements, especially N, P and S
— provides a substrate for micro-organisms and soil fauna

— helps reduce the rate of heat flow through the soil
— lowers soil bulk density.

Application of organic material to unstable soils can reduce the undesirable effects of slaking. Slaking occurs when dry unstable aggregates are unable to withstand the forces associated with the rapid intake of water (Emerson 1977); entrapped air is rapidly forced from the aggregate causing it to explode and collapse ('slake') into small aggregates. Maintenance of soil porosity, water movement and aeration is dependent on the soil aggregates being stable when wetted. As micro-organisms degrade the organic matter, they produce binding substances to stabilize soil aggregates (Tisdall et al. 1978). Typically, surface layer aggregates are prone to suffer slaking because they are subject to more extreme drying-wetting cycles than aggregates at depth.

Organic matter levels in surface soils may also be low as a result of cultivation. This leads to a crusty surface which has low air and water permeability. Such soils can be boggy when wet, with a high risk of water run-off and erosion. Growing plants may be used to stabilize aggregates against slaking. Ryegrass plants grown for 30 weeks and then desiccated with herbicide resulted in 34% of the soil being water-stable aggregates (greater than 2 mm diameter) 22 weeks after herbicide treatment (Tisdall and Oades 1979). Addition of both raw and composted poultry manure in a 45-year-old vineyard on a sandy loam soil significantly increased water infiltration rate (Bhangoo et al. 1988). Application of straw mulch allows earthworms to incorporate straw with the soil, create earthworm channels and improve soil macroporosity and water infiltration (Table 8.1). Trees planted into a killed fescue sward established more rapidly than when planted into cultivated or herbicide treatments. Water infiltration rate and macroporosity was greater with killed sward and bulk density of the soil was lower than with other treatments. Run-off with killed sward was lower than with herbicide-treated or cultivated soil (Glenn and Welker 1989).

A carbon:nitrogen (C:N) ratio of applied organic matter in excess of 10:1 tends to reduce N availability to the grapevines because of the demands for nitrogen by micro-organisms as they begin to digest the material. The incorporation

Table 8.1. Effect of soil management on earthworm population and soil structure in a peach orchard (adapted from Green 1979).

Soil management	Earthworm number per m²	Percent volume as large pores	Infiltration rate (mm per minute)
Standard cultivation	151	5	0.6
Tatura system[a]	2000	19	50

[a] See 8.3

of OM into the soil can, under some circumstances, have inhibitory effects on grapevine root growth; OM plus anaerobic conditions may lead to increased ethylene levels which inhibit root tip activity.

8.2.2 Effects of surface cover

A bare soil surface is subjected to many influences, most of which are damaging (Tisdall and Huett 1987). In comparison to soils with a cover of organic matter, bare soils have greater evaporative water loss on the surface (due to higher soil temperatures), develop lower infiltration rates, higher bulk densities, smaller soil pores, are prone to wind and water erosion, have lowered organic matter contents and fewer earthworms. Lack of herbage growth often has serious consequences for the development of flora beneficial in the biological control of pests.

These negative effects need to be weighed against the positive aspects of bare soil such as simple management, less interference with irrigation and other equipment, and less competition for minerals. Except in special circumstances, soil management systems that maintain bare soil surfaces are not favoured in Australian viticulture. Rather one, or combinations, of the methods listed below are chosen.

Cover crops

A cover crop can be defined as any plant species, used singly or in a mixture, which is deliberately sown between vine rows (alleys). Vineyard cover crops are usually only grown in the alleys in vineyards (8.3.2, Figure 8.2). They may be grown

to provide organic matter for the soil or for mulch, and to increase infiltration rate and nitrogen status. Cover crops will help control erosion, reduce dust, and provide wind protection in young vineyards. They also dry out and stabilize the soil in wet areas, facilitating machinery access, and act as a host for predators of harmful insect pests. Cover crops have some disadvantages:

— unless direct drilling is used the soil must be cultivated to prepare a seed bed
— they can be expensive to sow and maintain
— legume cover crops may be a more expensive form of nitrogen than nitrogenous fertilizer
— if allowed to grow after budburst they may increase the frost risk and compete for water and nutrients.

Mown sward

This is also known as sod culture or 'grassing-down' (Figure 8.3). A sward is defined as a closely grazed or mown area; it may comprise introduced (sown) species or, less often, volunteer growth. For mown sward systems, either annual or perennial, grasses or legumes are used. For annuals, they should be, if possible, early and self-seeding. Mowing may be used on both vine strips and alleys for control of volunteer growth or sown herbage provided the additional water demand can be compensated. A mown sward surface improves soil structure, water infiltration and traffic flow (Cock 1985). On sloping sites where contour planting has not been used, mown sward may be the only viable option to prevent soil erosion, even for young vineyards. Soil acidification can occur under legume-dominant, grazed or mown sward. However where clippings are returned to the soil surface, the recycling of cations will counteract

Figure 8.2. Winter Cover crop grown in the alley combined with herbicide-treated vine strip.

Figure 8.3. Undervine mound with mown sward.

this effect (Haynes and Goh 1980). Weed-free soil may become acidified with time because of lack of nutrient cycling (Table 8.2); this acidification can be reduced if sward clippings are transferred over its surface.

Maintenance of herbage may serve to provide a habitat for beneficial insects, and reduce dust to assist in mite control (Flaherty *et al.* 1981). Herbage may harbour beneficial insects (parasites and predators) thus reducing insect pests in vineyards (Williams 1981); however couch grass, (*Cynodon dactylon*) is a host for several nematode pests including *Meloidogyne* spp. (Flaherty *et al.* 1981). Plant roots may interact in ways which are not clearly understood to stimulate or inhibit the growth of adjacent plants ('allelopathy') (Rice 1984); little is known about the role of allelopathic plants in viticulture.

The clearest detrimental effect on vineyards of herbage growth, whether volunteer or planted, is through competition for water and mineral nutrients (Smart and Coombe 1983, Tan and Crabtree 1990). The relative significance of each will depend on the local soil and environmental conditions.

For instance, in a six year trial in South Africa, mown sward led to unacceptably low pruning weights and yields compared with cultivation and straw mulch (van Huyssteen 1990, Table 8.3). Competition from mown sward not only decreased vine yield, but also caused a significant decrease in nitrogen status of the vine sufficient to decrease wine quality because of the effect of 'stuck' fermentations (van Huyssteen 1990). In contrast, a mown sward of perennial rye grass in the alleys of a non-irrigated vineyard in Oregon

153

Table 8.2. Soil pH[a] in the undervine herbicide strip and grass sward alley 10 years after establishing the sward; clippings not transferred (from Haynes 1981).

Soil depth units (cm)	Herbicide (Strip)	Grass sward (Alley)	
0-5	4.6	6.3	sig.[b]
5-10	5.3	6.3	sig.
10-20	5.7	6.1	sig.
20-30	5.9	6.0	ns
30-40	6.0	6.1	ns
40-50	5.9	6.0	ns

[a] pH measured in distilled water.
[b] sig. significantly different at 5% level, ns = non significant.

only slightly suppressed shoot growth but significantly reduced root growth in the upper 10 cm (Lombard *et al.* 1988). Although mown sward used up to 33% more water than was lost from a bare soil surface, it was suggested that deeper roots were able to meet the grapevine's requirement for water under their conditions. Mown sward almost eliminates grape roots from the upper 20cm of soil (Giulivo *et al.* 1988, Freeman and McLachlan 1988, Figure 8.4).

Where sward becomes too competitive for water despite regular mowing, selection of less competitive species may be desirable, however such species may be expensive and difficult to establish and maintain, and may not compete well against invading weeds. Alternatively, mown sward can be suppressed by low rates of knockdown herbicide from budburst onwards. The decreased yield reported with mown sward must be offset against the higher operating costs of cultivation

and any increased environmental risk from herbicides. The competition from mown sward may be too great for young vines (Table 8.4) and alternative options should be used, where possible, until the vines mature. Mown sward may not be a viable option where irrigation water is limited, or for sites with shallow soils.

Mulch
There is now ample evidence from many grapegrowing areas of the value of undervine mulch in developing favourable root environments. Mulch is applied to vine strips (the under-vine area) or alleys (the inter-row area) (van Huyssteen and Weber 1980, Godden and Hardie 1981, Adem 1988) but the former is currently more common in Australia. Mulch helps control weeds, reduce evaporation and improve soil structure through the activity of soil micro-organisms. This improvement of soil physical conditions allows an

Table 8.3. Effect of soil management on performance[a] of Chenin Blanc grapevines under dryland conditions (adapted from van Huyssteen 1990).

Treatment	Yield	Pruning weight	Juice total soluble solids
	(t/ha)	(t/ha)	(^{0} Brix)
Straw mulch	13.0	1.8	21.2
Herbicide	11.1	1.5	22.7
Cultivation	10.0	1.2	22.9
Mown sward	3.7	0.4	23.6
LSD (P = 0.05)	3.2	0.5	2.3

[a] Mean of six seasons.

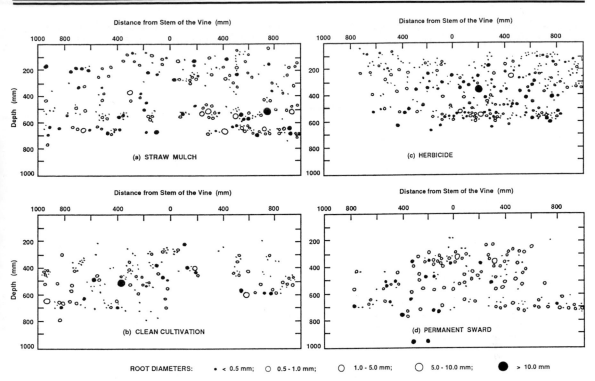

Figure 8.4. Root distribution under different soil management systems (from van Zyl and van Huyssteen 1984).

increase in root branching (Richards 1983), and as soil surface temperatures are lower and more constant, root growth is encouraged in surface layers (van Huyssteen and Weber 1980, McLachlan *et al.* 1989; Figure 8.4). Other benefits include decreased herbicide use, increased infiltration (hence less erosion), decreased water

evaporation from the surface, increased earthworm activity (Table 8.5), increased shoot growth (Table 8.4), and increased yield (Pool *et al.* 1990, Code 1990).

There can be some disadvantages in using mulch, such as (a) increased frost risk if vines are trained low and the area is frost prone, (b) a

Table 8.4. Effect of soil management system of growth of Shiraz grapevines in the first growing season[a] (adapted from Code 1990).

System		Total shoot
Vine strip	Alley	length per vine (mm)[b]
Straw mulch	Herbicide[c]	2509
Plastic fabric[d]	Herbicide[e]	2179
Plastic fabric[d]	Mown sward	1550
Straw mulch	Mown sward	1522
Herbicide[e]	Herbicide[e]	1367
LSD (P = 0.05)		273

[a] Vines planted in September 1988 at Milawa (Vic). Treatments applied just after planting. Weeds in untreated controls included barnyard grass (*Echinochloa* sp), couch (*Cynodon dactylon*) and water couch (*Paspalum paspaloidis*). Shoot length of controls not measured.
[b] Measured in April 1989. [c] Oryzalin/simazine mixture. [d] Weedmat® . [e] Oryzalin.

Table 8.5. Number and weight of active earthworms in the soil profile (0-60cm) after 3 years of different soil management systems (adapted from Haynes 1980).

System	Number per m³	Total weight (g per m³)	Mean weight per worm (g)
Grass sward	837	341	0.41
Herbicide	141	36	0.26
Cultivation	6	2	0.33

Figure 8.5. Poor infiltration with excessive cultivation.

temporary nitrogen deficit may be induced depending on the carbon: nitrogen ratio (see 8.2.1) and extra nitrogenous fertilizer may be necessary in the first year, (c) increased fire risk primarily in the first year but the problem is reduced as the mulch consolidates and (d) mulch may also provide shelter for some pests, e.g. crickets, although this is generally not a major concern. The soil cooling effects of straw mulching need investigation.

8.2.3 Effect of cultivation

Until growers gained confidence in the use of herbicides, cultivation was the most widely-used soil management practice in Australian vineyards (Robinson 1990). Although cultivation has beneficial effects on soil water conservation by the elimination of weeds, it has many undesirable effects on soil. It prevents a continuous buildup of dead and decaying organic material. It can readily destroy soil structure, especially if it is carried out when soil is not at a suitable water content. Conventional tillage, whilst increasing total porosity, results in a few, large, irregular and elongated pores. Non-tillage produces more pores in the soil thus providing better growing conditions for roots (Pagliai *et al.* 1984). As structure deteriorates, soil pore size may be reduced, slowing water infiltration (Figure 8.5); root growth is restricted. The positive effects on soil organic matter derived from the incorporation of a cover crop are not necessarily obtained if the soil is subsequently cultivated, particularly in warmer climates (Robinson 1990). Earthworm populations are lower in cultivated soils than with grass or herbicide (Haynes 1981; Table 8.5). The frequency and depth of cultivation affects root distribution and results in root growth in the surface layers being suppressed. When roots are cut they actively regenerate; this is one means of decreasing root overlap and rejuvenating root systems close to the vine (Barnard 1932). However, the value of root pruning is debatable as it may upset the balance between root and shoot growth.

Cultivation increases the mineralization of organic nitrogenous compounds to plant-available nitrate ions. From work on the monitoring of nitrate in soil solution, Swiss and German researchers have found that the problem of nitrate pollution of ground water can be mitigated by delaying vineyard cultivation until grape roots are active and able to take up the released nitrate; they recommend delaying cultivation until after shoots have six separated leaves (P. Perret, pers. comm.).

High bulk densities can develop at the interface between surface-cultivated soil and the underlying undisturbed soil following repeated cultivation at a constant depth; such a condition is termed a plough sole, hardpan or tillage pan (van Huyssteen and Weber 1980). The problem is exacerbated if the same implement is used at a constant depth over a number of seasons. This compacted layer will restrict root growth. The use of a subsoil cultivator may be beneficial as it can break up a hardpan without greatly disturbing the topsoil. Ripping to break up a plough sole must be done when the soil is relatively dry otherwise the required shattering effect will be replaced by a shearing and the soil will not be improved.

8.2.4 Herbicides

Herbicides do not cause the structural and root damage that cultivation does and, as large areas can be rapidly treated, they are often more economical than alternatives. As most herbicides are non-specific and must be correctly applied, more operator skill is required. Additional management skill may be needed to ensure herbicide programs do not result in major changes in weed flora (so called 'escape weeds' that may build up rapidly) or detrimental changes to surface soil structure. Some growers employ contractors for weed spraying because of their awareness of methods and problems. Continued use of herbicide may reduce soil pH, possibly due to reduction in organic matter and cation exchange capacity (Atkinson 1979, Robinson 1990). The effect of a herbicide on weed flora will depend on the nature of the chemical, the species present and the method and rate of application. The weed growth stage, rate of growth and environmental conditions at the time of spraying will also determine selective pressure. The term 'selectivity' is often misused in relation to herbicides, implying that it is only the target weed that is affected and not the crop. This may be an over-simplification because many 'selective' herbicides are non-selective at high rates.

Herbicides are classified into three groups based on their mode of action: residual, systemic or contact.

Residual herbicides

Also known as pre-emergent herbicides, these are applied to the soil surface and then leached into the top 5 cm or so of the soil by rainfall or irrigation or, less commonly, incorporated by cultivation. To allow maximum contact with the soil, the surface at the time of application should be relatively free of herbage and/or trash. The active ingredients in these herbicides have low solubility and are adsorbed onto the clay and organic particles in the surface soil where they persist for long periods. They are effective against germinating seeds and seedlings, with little or no effect on established weeds or grapevines at the application rates normally used. Some 'residuals' should not be used near young vines and/or on sandy soils because of their potential to damage the vines.

Residual herbicides are decomposed by micro-organisms in the soil and, if used at correct rates, no problem should arise from accumulation in the soil. No significant accumulation of simazine in the upper layers of vineyard soil was seen after 14 years of repeated use (Damanakis and Daris 1981). In a review of the long term effects of herbicides on soil micro-organisms Greaves (1979) concluded that the effects are likely to be complex. If organic matter is high, e.g. crop residues or mulch present, then micro-organism activity is likely to be maintained; however where organic matter content is low, micro-organisms and worm populations are likely to be suppressed because of poor energy and nutrient availability.

Although residual herbicides generally kill a wide spectrum of weed species, some are more effective against grass weeds and others more effective against broadleaved weeds. Table 8.6 lists some of the weeds controlled by residual herbicides. Residual herbicides currently registered for use in Australian vineyards include: napropamide, diuron, simazine, oryzalin, oxyfluorfen and trifluralin.

Systemic herbicides

Also known as translocated herbicides, they are absorbed by foliage and move through plant tissue causing physiological damage. Their modes of action include destruction of chlorophyll, prevention of root growth and distortion of leaf and stem growth. They are usually slow acting and include selective and non-selective types; for example, fluazifop is selective against grasses whereas amitrole and glyphosate are effective against both broadleaf and grass species. Great care with spray application is required with this group

Table 8.6. Weeds found in vineyards controlled by currently registered residual herbicides; P = pre-emergent control, S = seedling control (adapted from Jenkins 1988).

Weed	Common Name	Diuron	Oryzalin	Oxyfluorfen	Simazine	Trifluralin
Amaranthus spp.	Amaranth	P			P	S
Amsinckia spp.	Yellow burrweed			PS		
Arctotheca calendula	Capeweed	P		PS	P	
Avena fatua	Wild oats	P			P	PS
Brassica spp.	Wild turnip, Indian mustard	P	PS[a]			
Bromus spp.	Bromegrass				P	
Capsella bursa-pastoris	Shepherd's purse			PS	P	
Cenchrus spp.	Spiny burrgrass, Innocent weed		P			S
Chenopodium album	Fat hen	P	P	P	P	
Cucumis myriocarpus	Prickly paddy melon		PS[a]			
Datura spp.	Thornapple			P		
Digitaria ciliaris	Crabgrass, Summer grass		P	P		S
Echinochloa spp.	Barnyard grass	P	P	P		S
Eleusine indica	Crowfoot grass	P		PS		
Emex australis	Spiny emex, Threecornered Jack	P				
Eragrostis cilianensis	Stinkgrass			PS		
Eragrostis spp.	Lovegrass		P	P		
Galinsoga parviflora	Potato weed, yellow weed				P	
Geranium spp.	Geranium, cranesbill				P	
Hordeum leporinum	Barley grass	P		P	P	
Lamium amplexicaule	Deadnettle		P	S	P	
Lolium spp.	Ryegrass	P		P	P[b]	P[b]
Malva parviflora	Marshmallow			S		
Oxalis corniculata	Creeping oxalis				P	
Phalaris minor	Lesser canary grass					S
Poa annua	Winter grass	P			P	PS
Polygonum aviculare	Wireweed	P	P	P	P	S
Portulaca oleracea	Pigweed, munyeroo, purslane	P	P	PS		S
Raphanus raphanistrum	Wild radish	P		PS		
Setaria spp.	Pigeon grass		P	P		
Solanum elaeagnifolium	Silverleaf nightshade		PS[a]			
Solanum nigrum	Black berry nightshade	P	PS[a]	P		
Sonchus spp.	Sowthistle	P	P	PS	P	
Sorghum halepense	Johnson grass					P
Stellaria media	Chickweed			P	P	
Tribulus terrestris	Caltrop		PS[a]	P		S
Urochloa panicoides	Liverseed grass			PS		P
Veronica spp.	Speedwell				P	

[a] Control may range from poor to excellent depending on factors such as soil temperature, time of germination, weed seed depth.

[b] Wimmera ryegrass

as it is important to avoid drift onto foliage, young wood and even fresh pruning cuts. Systemic herbicides currently registered for use in Australian vineyards include amitrole, glyphosate and fluazifop. Although the phenoxy group (MCPA, 2,4-D) are systemic herbicides effective against broad leaf weeds, they can cause severe damage to grapevines through volatilization and drift onto foliage. As drifts of many kilometres are possible, they should not be used in situations close to vineyards.

Contact herbicides
These chemicals kill or desiccate the tissue with which they come into contact. Normally fast-acting, they are not translocated through plants

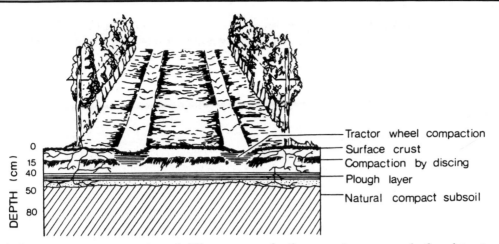

Figure 8.6. Diagrammatic presentation of different types of soil compaction commonly found in vineyards (from van Zyl and van Huyssteen 1984).

and are inactivated on contact with soil. They are most effective on young and actively growing annual weeds but can be used to retard the growth of perennial weeds. Diquat and paraquat, used singly or mixed, are the only common contact herbicides currently used in Australian vineyards. Contact herbicides are unlikely to cause problems for vines unless there is spray drift onto green tissue but, even then, the effect is localized. Some operators prefer not to use diquat and paraquat because of human toxicity. In the industry, both contact and systemic herbicides are sometimes called 'knockdowns'.

8.2.5 Effects of traffic

The passage of machinery along rows causes soil compaction which is an inevitable part of operating a vineyard. Soil compaction, which restricts root growth, is greatest below the wheel tracks and is determined by soil conditions and the weight of the machine per unit area in contact with the soil. There were ten times more peach roots in the noncompacted soil of the tree line than in the compacted soil of the traffic area (Richards and Cockcroft 1974).

Most present day tractors have four wheels spread wide for stability, the width being a compromise between the slope, safety, convenience and alley width. As the wheel lines tend to be near the vine line the resulting compaction can remove a high proportion of the total soil volume from root access (Figure 8.6; van Huyssteen 1988). A practical solution to this problem is to increase the potential root volume

close to the vine by shifting topsoil from the alley to the vine row ('mounding') as in the Tatura system (Cockcroft 1978, Adem 1988, Macrae 1991; Figure 8.3).

Soil compaction can be lessened by using lighter machinery and avoiding its use when the soil is wet. The trend toward smaller tractors, perhaps with smooth tyres, low-volume spray equipment and minimum tillage has obvious benefits for the soil. Compaction could also be lessened by transferring machinery weight to a single track in the centre of the alley: this would require substantial redesigning of alley-travelling tractors and implements or, alternatively, a change to over-row tractors.

8.2.6 Gypsum application

Dispersion is the breakdown of soil aggregates in water to individual sand, silt and clay particles. Clay dispersion is usually greatest in sodic non-saline clay soils. Clays with a high proportion of exchangeable calcium (calcic clay) do not undergo such dispersion and swelling.

Gypsum (calcium sulphate) is a moderately soluble calcium mineral which is frequently used to reduce dispersion of surface soils and to minimize swelling of sub-surface soils. Calcium ions from the gypsum replace exchangeable sodium and to a lesser extent magnesium on the clay particles. The sodium cations released into the soil solution must be leached below the rootzone otherwise salinity damage may result. Gypsum applied to the surface of hardsetting or crusting clays will reduce dispersion, resulting in improved water infiltration and trafficability after rain or irrigation, and a more friable topsoil for seedbed preparation. Subsoil gypsum application will reduce clay swelling and dispersion and result in improved permeability and aeration. Subsoil treatment is difficult as gypsum must be placed at depth either by ripping, trenching or soil slotting, all of which are expensive.

Rates of gypsum required must be adequate to replace sufficient sodium and magnesium ions to obtain the desired effect. Although laboratory analysis can be used to define gypsum requirements (Brown et al. 1980) the recommended rates are usually uneconomically high. The likely response to added gypsum can be tested 'on-farm' by adding some air-dry aggregates to a small container of deionised water (distilled water or rain water will suffice). Leave undisturbed for about two hours. If there is a murky cloud around the aggregates the soil is likely to respond to gypsum; if the water is clear a gypsum response is unlikely. Test areas of different gypsum rates, either surface-applied or ripped-in, are often the most practical way of determining the gypsum requirement. Either mined or by-product gypsum can be used provided it is of adequate fineness and purity. The sodium chloride content of the gypsum should be less than 1.2% wet weight (Abbott and McKenzie 1986).

8.2.7 Lime application

Naturally-acid soils occur in many parts of the high rainfall areas of Australia (Smart et al. 1991). Soil acidification may result from the use of herbicides to keep soils bare and/or by the use of nitrogenous fertilizers; these effects are possibly exacerbated by use of some low salinity water sources (Merry 1990; Robinson 1990).

Lime (calcium carbonate) is a water-insoluble product that is found naturally in various forms and with a range of purities. Other liming materials used are burnt lime (quicklime), slaked lime, magnesite and high quality dolomite. Lime quality is assessed by measuring its neutralizing value, calcium and magnesium content, and fineness (Weir 1987). It is primarily used to increase soil pH although its calcium content will also achieve some structural improvement in soil with high exchangeable sodium percentage (ESP).

It is best to correct soil pH with lime before planting as it is only very slowly active if applied to the soil surface. Deep incorporation in established plantings damages vine roots. Incorporation of lime to 30-40cm is advocated although deeper incorporation and localized slotting may require less lime to achieve a similar result (Blackwell et al. 1988).

Liming is recommended if the pH (1:5/soil:water) for vineyard soil is less than 5.5. The quantity of lime required to increase the pH of some acidic soils in Australia may be considerable: as much as 10 - 15 tonne/ha, although such rates would not be applied as a single application. Regular maintenance applications of lime may be required, particularly to counter the effects of soil acidification by nitrogenous fertilizers. Soil tests can be used to monitor pH. Alternatively, maintenance dressings of lime can be used to take account of the specific fertilizer which has been used - the calculated lime requirements necessary to neutralize the acidifying effect of some commonly used nitrogenous fertilizers are shown in Table 9.3.

8.2.8 Other factors

Improvement and maintenance of the nutrient status of the soil is covered in Chapter 9, provision of artificial drainage in Chapter 7 and maintenance of the soil at optimal moisture levels for root growth in Chapter 6.

8.3 Soil Management Systems

Soil management can be defined as 'the method of providing as near as possible the ideal environment for root growth' (Cockcroft 1978). Since root production is a function of both the volume of soil available for root growth, and the concentration of roots that can develop in a given volume of soil, soil management practices should aim to maximize both components. Slightly modified from Cockcroft (1978), the components of a good soil management system will be:
— minimal or no cultivation
— elimination of weeds during the growing season
— mounding of surface soil along the vine row
— addition of organic matter
— avoidance of soil water content greater than the 'drained upper limit'

Table 8.7. Mean root distribution with depth and grapevine performance under different soil preparation methods on an acid sandy clay loam soil, Stellenbosch, South Africa (adapted from van Huyssteen 1990).

Treatment[a]	Total number of roots	Root distribution (% of total) Depth interval (cm)					Grapevine performance (kg/vine)	
		0-25	25-50	50-70	75-100	100-125	Fruit Weight	Pruning Weight
A. Shallow ploughed	271	50	31	12	6	1	5.5	0.7
B. Ripped	356	38	34	16	10	2	6.6	0.8
C. Delve ploughed	527	33	29	30	7	1	8.1	1.0
D. Delve ploughed + straw	563	25	36	31	7	1	8.2	1.0
E. Delve ploughed + compost	595	18	31	37	13	1	8.2	1.1

[a] A: Shallow ploughed, 22 cm deep
  B: Ripped, zone loosening to depth of 70 cm
  C: Delve ploughed, 70 cm deep
D: Delve ploughed, 70 cm deep + 25 t/ha straw
E: Delve ploughed, 70 cm deep + 23 t/ha compost

— mulching and/or shading the soil surface
— stabilizing the subsoil and avoiding hardpans
— maintenance of surface soil as aggregates
— achieving optimal nutrient status.

One of the primary objectives of soil management should be to improve levels of organic matter in the soil as this leads to better aggregation of soil particles and an improved soil structure. This in turn enables better root exploration, water penetration and enhanced fertility and microbial activity and, above all, better oxygen supply. The choice of an appropriate soil management system for a particular vineyard site must take into account the principles outlined in 8.2.

The Tatura soil management system was designed to achieve these principles in peach orchards in the Goulburn Valley. Using this system, orchards produced four times more yield than orchards with the standard soil management of the region (Cockcroft 1978). Adem and Tisdall (1988) reported a four-fold increase in yield in the first year that the Tatura soil management system was used in a vineyard in north-east Victoria.

Some soil management practices such as deep ripping, incorporation of lime and mounding are best applied before planting; others can be used in established vineyards, and may be desirable every few seasons, e.g. sub-surface ploughing and

incorporation of gypsum and organic matter.

8.3.1 Pre-plant treatments

Deep ripping
Establishment of young vineyards on sites with heavy or impenetratable subsoils is aided by deep ripping as this allows deeper root penetration (Saayman and van Huyssteen 1980). This also applies to sites with impervious layers of rock or calcrete (Figure 8.7). Ripping depth varies according to site and is normally between 0.3 and 1.0 m. Deep ripping when soil is dry, as in autumn, achieves an extensive fracturing effect of 'tight' subsoil layers. Ripping of wet soils is not likely to be effective.

Deep ploughing
With deep ripping, only soil adjacent to the rip line is loosened but the effect is not long-lasting (Figure 8.8). In South Africa, deep ploughing is used to loosen the subsoil and to mix soil horizons; Table 8.7 shows the yield response to different soil preparation treatments (van Huyssteen 1990). Such treatments are rarely used in Australian vineyards but should be tested, especially in dryland vineyards to increase the effective root volume. A recent adaptation of deep ploughing — soil slotting — may provide an alternative. This technique was developed for acid soils to create

Figure 8.7. Deep ripping to break break through the calcrete layer for vineyard establishment.

Figure 8.8. Inadequate soil loosening with a ripper leads to poor utilization of the potentially available soil volume as roots are confined mainly to the loosened zones (from van Huyssteen 1988)

Figure 8.9. Total cultivation (vine strip and alley).

Table 8.8. Factors affecting choice of soil management option. (+ + = Highly recommended, + = Recommended, − = Not recommended)

Soil and environment factors	Cultivation	Herbicide	Mulch or suppressed sward	Mown sward
Rainfall — low (a)	+	+	+ +	−
— high	−	+	+	+ +
Poor structure	− (b)	+ (c)	+ +	+ +
Poor drainage	−	−	+	+ +
Poor infiltration	− (c)	−	+ +	+ +
Steep terrain	−	−	+	+ +
Frost-prone site	+ (d)	+ (e)	− (f)	− (f)
Beneficial effects on soil flora/fauna	−	+	+ +	+ +
Restricted root zone	−	+ (g)	+	−

a Even in low rainfall areas intense rainfall may result in significant erosion
b May be suitable for some soil types.
c Surface compaction may occur with some soil types.
d Suitable if also compacted with a roller.
e Soil surface needs to be kept bare.
f May be suitable if mown very short and/or frost risk is only low to moderate.
g Higher temperature of surface layer may restrict root growth if soil surface is directly exposed to radiation.

zones of modified soil (slots) in which the surface and sub-soil are mixed with amendments such as lime and gypsum. The aim of slotting is to improve root growth in the subsoil, thus increasing plant access to water and nutrients which were previously inaccessible. The slots are 15 cm wide, up to 80 cm deep and normally about 1m apart. In an experiment conducted in an established vineyard at Port Macquarie (NSW), slotting to 40 cm depth and incorporation of lime at 2 t/ha resulted in an increase in soil pH from 4.3 to 5.0 at 40 cm depth. Roots which had been restricted to about 15cm depth increased in length ten-fold (Kirchhof et al. 1990)

Incorporation of soil amendments
Organic matter, gypsum, lime or fertilizers can be mixed with the surface soil by conventional tillage to the depth of the topsoil, or deep ploughing (Table 8.7). Unlike gypsum, lime is insoluble and thus surface-applied lime has little short-term impact on acidic subsoils.

Soil mounding
Mounding has been used successfully where there is a shallow surface layer over a restrictive subsoil

(Figure 8.3). The initial preparation may involve incorporation of soil amendments. Mounds or banks are then formed along the vine lines with soil delved from the alleys. A high proportion of the topsoil is thus located where it is less likely to be compacted by machinery. Surface drainage and trafficability are improved because surface water flow is confined to the base of the V in the alley centre. To stabilize the mound and avoid erosion the alleys are usually sown to a permanent sward (Figure 8.3).

Herbicides
Perennial weed problems such as couch grass and convolvulus should be controlled before planting. Some residual herbicides can be applied along the intended vine-line before planting.

8.3.2 Established vineyards
Because the vine strip may be treated differently to the alley, a soil management system will often be a combination of two options. The most widely used system in Australian vineyards at present is the combination of alley cultivation (tillage) and vine strip herbicide. Another system becoming

Table 8.9. Comparison of some vineyard soil management systems (+ + + = High, + + = Moderate to High, + = Moderate, — = Low to Moderate, —— = Low, ——— = Nil to Low, 0 = Nil).

System		Costs				Damage	
Alley	Vine Strip	Time	Machinery	Chemicals	Total	Soil	Root
Cultivation	Cultivation	+ + +	+ + +	0	+	+ + +	+ + +
Cultivation	Herbicide	+	+	+	+	+	+
Cultivation	Mulch	+	+	— — —	+ +	+	+
Mown sward	Herbicide	— —	— —	+	+	— —	— —
Mown sward	Mulch	—	— —	— —	+	— —	— —
Herbicide	Herbicide	— —	— —	+ + +	+[a]	—	— —
Mulch	Mulch	—	—	— — —	+ +[b]	— —	— —

[a] Low to High
[b] Material costs may be high

popular is vine strip herbicide plus mown sward in the alley. Other methods used are total herbicide, mowing and chemically-suppressed sward. There are many factors influencing the choice of system (Table 8.8), and the advantages/disadvantages of the most common soil management systems are listed in Table 8.9.

Cultivation
Some dryland vineyards in winter rainfall regions use total cultivation (vine strip and alley; Figure 8.9) and winter cover crop involving up to 10 tractor passes per row per annum. The detrimental effects of such a program are discussed in 8.2.3; but, despite these bad effects, alley cultivation is still common because there is a low skill requirement. Cultivation is the preferred option for alleys in furrow-irrigated vineyards because of the need to form/reform irrigation furrows and in frost-prone sites where a bare, compacted soil surface is maintained and herbicide is not a favoured option.

There has been a heartening trend in recent years away from cultivation: for vine strips, the currently preferred alternative is herbicide, although the use of mulch and undervine mowing is increasing. For alleys, mowing and herbicide are replacing cultivation. The choice of an appropriate system is important even in the formative years of a new vineyard: the first crop from Shiraz vines with undervine straw mulch and alley herbicide was 8 times higher than that from

an untreated vine strip plus mown sward in the alley (Code 1990).

Periodic cultivation may be required in herbicide-treated or mown alleys to overcome surface compaction and sealing with some soil types — in such cases, sub-soil ploughing with the AgrowPlow® or similar is preferred. Cultivation is normally used to prepare seed beds for covercrops — however, the development of narrow direct-drilling machinery has overcome this requirement. Subsoiling may still be necessary to minimize the development of a hard pan beneath the seeding and cultivation implements.

Herbicides
Herbicides can provide economical, long-term weed control with better conservation of soil structure and less root destruction than cultivation. Whereas herbicides are now the most popular vine strip treatments in Australian vineyards (Figure 8.2), their use in alleys is less widespread, being largely confined to flat sites with self-mulching soils — for example, Coonawarra where the resulting bare soil reduces frost risk (Figure 8.10). This option will be unsuitable for sloping sites because of the possibility of erosion if the soil is kept bare. With hard-setting soils, compaction and sealing of the surface layers may occur with subsequent reduction in infiltration if organic matter is not encouraged during the winter months.

Recommended programs can be found in extension bulletins (Baker and McCarthy 1981)

Figure 8.10. Total herbicide (vine and alley).

Figure 8.11. Herbicide-treated vine strip; volunteer growth in the alley killed with knockdown herbicide applied with a controlled-droplet-applicator (CDA) unit at budburst.

Figure 8.12. Winter-grown cover crop mown at budburst; knockdown herbicide will be applied later with a CDA unit.

and other sources (Beckingham 1988, Bates and Macgregor 1991). Herbicide use during vineyard establishment is discussed in Chapter 2. A typical herbicide program for vine strip treatment in a mature vineyard in a winter-rainfall area will comprise a contact or systemic, with or without a residual herbicide in late autumn/early winter after an initial weed germination, followed by a residual, with or without contact or systemic, in mid-winter to early spring. The aim of such a program is to produce a weed-free strip (usually about 1m wide) along the vine line through the winter (Figure 8.2) so that the residual in the second spray is applied to relatively bare soil — this residual should produce a weed-free strip for the remainder of the growing season. Additional sprays of contact or systemic herbicide may be required during the growing season for particular problem weeds, e.g. couch grass. Weed control with herbicides in the sandy soils of the Australian Murray Valley presents additional problems because of potential leaching of herbicide to the rootzone. Crop safety, escape weeds and short term control with some residual herbicides has resulted in reduced usage of these herbicides. In many vineyards repeat sprays of either systemic or contact herbicides are the basis of a weed control program.

Selection of an appropriate herbicide will depend on the target weed species, the growth stage and rate of growth of the weed species, soil type, vine age and the method of application. Only those herbicides registered for use in vineyards are permitted. Other factors which should also be considered are cost of the chemical, operator safety and potential off-target effects. Table 8.10 lists the herbicides currently used in Australian vineyards, some of their characteristics, and their recommended application rates. The list is continually evolving as new products are developed e.g. gluphosonate is proving a useful knockdown for summer weeds.

Problems associated with the use of herbicides include:

— Many herbicides have serious escape weed problems, often exacerbated by inadequate knowledge of herbicide activity and weed species response — for example, repeated glyphosate use has led to the establishment of willowherb (*Epilobium* spp - a woody shrub) as a weed problem on the vine strip in some Victorian vineyards.

— Potential phytotoxic effects on sandy soils, particularly with irrigation.

— Misconceptions regarding cost: weed control with the traditional broad spectrum herbicides such as simazine and amitrole is generally cheaper than cultivation. However, in vineyards where escape weeds are a problem, the addition of more expensive and specific herbicides, e.g. oryzalin and oxyfluorfen, may result in higher costs than cultivation. For example McCarthy (1985) noted that a total herbicide program (vine strip and alley) based on simazine and amitrole was 22% cheaper than total cultivation whereas a total herbicide program based on oryzalin, oxyfluorfen and amitrole was 120% more expensive.

Herbicide application also requires greater management and operator skill than cultivation as the consequences of incorrect calibration of spraying equipment and spray application may be disastrous for productivity.

Concerns about the long-term effects of herbicide residues on the environment and in grape products may lead to decreased use (see also 8.3.4). In Australia and California, some growers are no longer using residual herbicides for vine strip treatment, preferring to rely on contact or systemic herbicides alone. Others have abandoned herbicides entirely and are using other vine strip treatments such as mulch or mowing. At the same time, the use of low rates of systemic herbicide, applied with hooded, controlled droplet application (CDA) units, has become more popular for weed control in the alley space (Ludvigsen 1989), particularly to suppress winter-grown volunteer growth or cover crops in early spring (Figures 8.11, 8.12).

Mulch
Although mulch can now be applied to the vine strips by machines which dispense large hay bales (Figure 8.13), it is still an expensive option. Applied straw can be supplemented by, or replaced with, clippings (provided sufficient bulk can be grown) from alley sward which are directed onto the vine strip during mowing (Adem and Tisdall 1988, Macrae 1991). Most often mulches are organic materials such as cereal, pea straw or even paper — however inorganic materials, e.g. plastic film, woven plastic

Table 8.10. Characteristics and application rate of the main herbicides currently registered and used in Australian vineyards (adapted from Jenkins 1988).

Active Constituent	Main mode of action	Poison Schedule[a]	Application rate (L per sprayed ha[b])
Residual			
Diuron	Mainly root-absorbed but some foliage uptake. Long-term residual at high rates.	0	3.5 - 7.2
Napropamide	Absorbed by roots. Short-term residual.	0	4.5 - 6.7[d]
Oryzalin	Absorbed by roots. Residual activity for 4 to 8 months.	0	4.5 - 6.8
Oxyfluorfen	Absorbed by roots, and leaves of some seedlings. Medium to long-term residual.	7	3.0 - 4.0
Simazine	Mainly root-absorbed. Long-term residual.	0	2.3 - 4.5
Trifluralin	Absorbed by roots. Medium to long-term residual.	0	1.4 - 2.8
Knockdown			
Diquat	Absorbed by foliage. Inactivated by soil[c].	6	1.5
Paraquat	Absorbed by foliage. Inactivated by soil[c].	7	2.0 - 4.0
Systemic			
Amitrole	Absorbed by foliage[c]	5	9.0 - 24
Fluazifop	Absorbed by foliage. Selectively kills grasses. Short-term residual in soil[c].	5	1.0
Glyphosate	Absorbed by foliage, inactivated in soil.	5	1.5 - 9.0

[a] The Poison Schedule classification provides the user with an indication of the degree of hazard associated with a particular agrichemical. The user should comply with the safety directions on the label. 0 = low hazard; 5 = moderate hazard; 6 = moderate to high hazard; 7 = very hazardous.
[b] Sourced from product labels or various texts. Lower rates than those listed have been effective in some situations.
[c] The addition of a non-ionic surfactant is recommended.
[d] kg per sprayed ha.

fabric, may be used on vine strips, and are particularly useful for establishing young vines (Godden *et al.* 1982; Code 1990, Figure 8.14).

Cover crops and swards

There are many different ways in which cover crops are used in soil management systems (Ludvigsen 1987, 1992). In Australian vineyards, cover crops are mainly used in conjunction with cultivation. In this case, annual grasses and/or legumes are sown into prepared seedbeds in autumn. Seedbed preparation can involve one or more passes with tillage equipment to ensure weed-free conditions and a fine tilth for rapid establishment of the cover crop. A range of tillage equipment is used, the most common being the rotary hoe, disc or tine equipment. The development of sod-seeding equipment means the cover crop can now be planted with minimal soil disturbance. Grasses include oats, barley and cereal rye; legumes include peas, beans, vetches, clovers and medics (Table 8.11). Most commonly, the cover crop is incorporated into the soil by cultivation in spring, just before budburst. While incorporation of a bulky green manure crop does result in a rapid and significant improvement in organic matter, this advantage is lost with subsequent cultivation. A preferable alternative is to control subsequent weed growth with herbicides (McCarthy 1991). An alternative method of alley management is to grow a winter cover crop (usually a cereal which produces a large

Figure 8.13. Undervine straw mulch applied by machine.

Figure 8.14. Plastic mulch used for weed control in the vine strip during vineyard establishment.

Figure 8.15. Frost damage to young shoots.

Table 8.11. Cover crop and sward species for vineyards (compiled from Lodden 1990, Ludvigsen 1987, Sutherland 1986). All species are sown as early as autumn rains permit — usually March-April.

Type	Sowing Rate[a] (kg/ha)	Comments
Cover crops		
Cereal rye	80 - 100	Produces large amounts of organic matter. Can tolerate some water logging and drought.
Barley	80 - 100	Most cold tolerant cereal; slower breakdown in soil than cereal rye.
Oats	80 - 100	Often sown in mixture with peas or vetch.
Italian ryegrass	40 - 50	May be incorporated or mown; if allowed to seed may become a weed problem
Rape/Canola	20	Growth rate greatest in late winter - spring. Requires well-limed soils.
Faba beans	70 - 120	Earlier sowings are more susceptible to
Field peas	100 - 150	Fusarium root rot.
Vetch	10 - 20	Readily established; requires well-drained soils.
Mown sward		
Soft brome	6 - 10	Annual; prefers well-drained neutral or slightly acid soils.
Wimmera ryegrass	6 - 10	Annual; tolerates poor drainage and drought; inconsistent re-seeding.
Rose clover	10	Annual; most growth in spring; good for acid soils of low fertility. Poor competitor.
Sub clover	5 - 12	Annual; suitable for wide range of soil types but often used in alkaline soils.
Cocksfoot	9 - 10	Perennial; performs well in acid soils of low fertility.
Fescue	10 - 12	Requires minimum rainfall of 450 mm. Perennial; adapted to wide range of soil types; tolerates waterlogging.
Perennial ryegrass	6	Perennial; generally requires at least 650 mm rainfall but some cultivars suitable for drier sites.

a Suggested rates are higher than for broad-acre crops or pasture establishment as dense stands are required.

amount of organic matter by spring) which is then mown or rolled prior to budburst in frost risk areas. If frost is not a problem and there is adequate soil water, mowing can be delayed to allow more bulk to be grown. Clippings may be left in the alley or transferred to the vine strip. Subsequent regrowth is suppressed by a spray of systemic herbicide at low rate, usually with a CDA unit (Hodge 1985, McCarthy 1991. Figure 8.12). A further herbicide spray at a later date may be required. The resulting trash left on the soil surface has a mulching effect; the risk of erosion is decreased and infiltration is improved compared with cultivation. The dead root system of the annual cover crop eventually results in a significant increase in soil organic matter.

A variation of this system allows the cover crop or sward to set seed before final mowing and thus eliminate the need for herbicide and autumn sowing for one or more seasons. For this purpose, species, usually early seeding clovers or medics, should have good ability to compete with unwanted weeds, good reseeding ability, high seedling vigour, and good persistence; these requirements are, however, often difficult to meet. Soil pH and surface conditions influence the choice of species. Depending on the circumstances, low growth habit, drought tolerance, early seed production followed by rapid 'haying-off' is also desirable. Grasses used include soft brome, Wimmera rye, cocksfoot and fescues; legumes include clovers, medics and vetches (Ludvigsen 1987); commercial mixes are available. Deep-rooting species such as oil radish may be used to dry the soil (Perret 1987) and have been successfully used in Australia (McCarthy, pers. comm.). In districts with abundant spring rainfall and excessive vine vigour some success has been achieved using sward to reduce water availability to vines. When sufficient control of vigour has been achieved in late spring-summer the sward is mown and sprayed with glyphosate using a CDA machine. Carefully scheduled irrigations then ensure excessive vigour is not re-stimulated. This strategy is only suitable in frost-free areas or where over-canopy sprinklers are used for frost control.

8.3.3 Equipment
Vineyard soil management equipment is constantly evolving. The following are brief descriptions of some of the common types of equipment presently used for soil management in Australian vineyards.

Tillage equipment
Disc cultivator
The disc cultivator is probably the most commonly used tillage implement. It is used to incorporate herbage and prunings leaving a rough soil surface. Where a fine tilth is required such as for the preparation of irrigation furrows and for compaction for frost control, several discings a week or so apart may be required.

Rotary hoe
The rotary hoe consists of a series of rigid blades

attached to a revolving horizontal shaft which is driven by the tractor power-take-off. It can readily handle dense cover crops and bulky prunings. This implement can be more damaging to soil structure than others, especially if used when the soil is not at the correct water content.
A range of blades is available for specific purposes such as seed bed preparation, incorporation of cover crops or sward rejuvenation.

Tine cultivator
The tine cultivator is principally used to control seedling weed growth during the growing season after the vineyard has been initially disc cultivated or rotary hoed in spring. The tine cultivator is preferred for this operation as it produces less soil disturbance and is less destructive to soil structure. The two major types in use are rigid-tine or scarifier and the spring-tine.

Subsoil cultivators
Subsoiling or deep tillage refers to any tillage operation carried out below the normal working depth, ranging from relatively shallow (20 cm) disturbance without inversion using implements such as the AgrowPlow® and AgTill®, to deep ripping to 70 cm or more (Beckingham 1988). Subsoiling will be of most benefit in soils where there are compacted layers; some growers subsoil alternate rows one season and the other rows the next. Sod seeding can be done at the same time as subsoiling with some equipment (Ludvigsen 1988).

Blade ploughs
Blade ploughs skim just under the soil surface cutting weed roots and leaving the trash as mulch on the soil surface. Blade ploughs currently available are not particularly suited to vineyard use (Ludvigsen 1988).

Undervine tillage implements
Midmounted, hydraulically-operated undervine weeders are still widely used in Australian vineyards. Some types now include mechanical or electronic sensors which control movement of the weeder around vine trunks. They have largely

replaced the hand-operated 'silly plough' which is difficult to manipulate, often leaving areas of untreated soil near the vines and damaging trunks or roots. Undervine weeders can be fitted with three tillage heads: a plough share for 'ploughing-off'; a disc for 'throwing-on' and a knife for killing weeds on the undervine bank. They are often used in conjunction with a tillage implement in the alley.

Mowing equipment
Mowers may be either rotary slashers which throw the clippings to one side or cylindrical mulchers which spread the clippings evenly across the alley or, with special attachments, spread the clippings on the adjacent vine strip(s). Most are driven by the tractor power-take-off. Small mowers for towing by four-wheel-drive motor bikes are available (Ludvigsen 1988) as is mowing equipment suitable for use in contoured alleys (V-shaped row cross section) (Adem and Tisdall 1983, Macrae 1991). Mid-mounted, hydraulically-operated vine strip mowers are increasing in popularity — these can be operated in conjunction with alley mowers. Mowers with herbicide applicators are also available for alley mowing in conjunction with vine strip spraying (Ludvigsen 1988).

Herbicide applicators
For vine strip application, a mid- or front- mounted off-centre nozzle on a boom is used. Nozzles at each end of the boom allow two rows to be sprayed in a single pass. Undervine spot spraying is done with hand wands which, if hooded, can be safely used for knockdown herbicide application during the growing season. For herbicide spraying in alleys, a rear-mounted boom with several nozzles is most often used. Hooded CDA units are growing in popularity because they use low rates of both active ingredient and water, spray drift is minimized and rapid application is possible. Glyphosate rates as low as 1 L mixed with 10-15 L water per sprayed ha are common. The low weight of the unit results in minimal soil compaction and allows it to be towed by a light vehicle or a four-wheel motor bike at speeds up to 7-8 km per hr. Hooded CDA units are ideal for suppression of sward by herbicide ('chemical mowing'; Figure 8.11).

8.3.4 Soil management and organic viticulture
For many reasons the use of chemicals in Australian vineyards is likely to decrease in the future. More stringent controls on chemical residues in exported wine, increasing consumer demand for 'chemical-free' grape products and deregistration of existing chemicals are some of the factors that will contribute to reduced usage. At the same time, there is increasing acceptance of the principles of 'sustainable agriculture', i.e. the long term use of resources without their degradation. If growers can achieve lower levels of dependence on pesticides and herbicides, they will be better placed to respond to the requirements of future legislation/regulations controlling chemical use (Davidson 1990).

An Australian standard for organic and bio-dynamic produce is to be incorporated in the Australian Food Standards Code for the domestic market and in orders under the Export Control Act for fresh grapes, grape products and wine.

To achieve certification as an 'organic' vineyard, the fertility and biological activity of the vineyard and soil must be maintained by any one, or any combination, of the following:

— Elimination of artificial fertilizers: approved soil amendments and fertilizers include composted animal manures, blood and bone, seaweed, rock phosphate, gypsum, lime and dolomite. The cultivation of legumes, green manures or deep-rooting plants is encouraged. Jenkins (1991) listed the fertilizer value of some organic amendments and plant nutrition practices recommended by the California Certified Organic Farmers Inc. These include animal manures, seaweed and kelp extracts and grapemarc.

— Pests and diseases are handled by biological control and other natural means. The only sprays that are permitted are of non-synthetic substances such as pyrethrum, bordeaux mixture, lime sulphur, wettable sulphur, light mineral oils and soft soap. Jenkins (1991) detailed some possible ways of controlling pests and diseases without the use of synthetic chemicals.

With regard to pesticide and fungicide use, many Australian vineyards are currently operating in an 'organic mode' (Dry 1990). Soil management practices will, however, require some changes for vineyards to achieve full organic status as herbicides are not permitted. Cultivation is not an alternative as this practice is incompatible with the principles of sustainable viticulture. Limited cultivation (blade ploughing, subsoil tillage) together with mown sward and mulch will become the only acceptable practices, plus alternative methods of weed control such as 'flame weeding' (Davidson 1990). For mown sward, other plant species that compete less for water and nutrients will need to be found. In rain-fed vineyards, sward species that become dormant well before budburst will be desirable as will species that do not regenerate after the first mowing. Weed control in the vine strip will create the most difficult problem for organic vineyards, particularly during the establishment phase. Alternatives such as hand-hoeing, mulch or plastic film and matting are more expensive and viable alternatives are needed.

8.4 Frost and frost control

8.4.1 Frost damage

Frosts during the growing season can cause serious damage, reducing or eliminating the crop in that year. The potential yield in the following season may also be reduced. Frost injury is due to freezing of plant cells, with ice forming either within or outside the cell. During the course of freezing the ice expands, rupturing cell walls and disturbing the normal function of intracellular membranes. Internal freezing of cells kills them immediately; however, if freezing is confined to extracellular regions, damage is likely to be less serious (Westwood 1978). Young or immature tissues containing low levels of solutes are more prone to damage. Young vines may be killed outright whereas only immature canes may be damaged on older vines. Severe frosts or winter freezes have the capacity to split trunks allowing the opportunity for pathogen development, especially crown gall. Fortunately such frosts are uncommon in Australian grapegrowing areas. Depending on the stage of growth, spring frosts have the potential for severe damage to vines (Figure 8.15). Air temperatures of -3.5°C or less will damage vine buds at the woolly bud stage. Extended periods at these temperatures will normally kill the primary bud. However, secondary buds may still be

viable (see Volume 1, Chapter 4). Flowers are more sensitive than leaves and stems to low temperatures hence frosts can sometimes lead to little or no fruit on otherwise undamaged shoots. Autumn frosts prior to harvest can result in fruit breakdown and severe effects on fruit maturity because of premature leaf drop.

8.4.2 Frost types

There are two types of frost: advective and radiation. Advective frosts are generally associated with moderately strong winds and occur where large masses of cold air move into a locality. As advective frosts are commonly a problem at high altitude sites or at high latitudes they do not constitute a danger for most vineyards in Australia.

Radiation frosts occur on clear nights when long-wave radiation from the ground to the sky is not impeded by cloud cover or a high concentration of water vapour in the atmosphere and cooling of the air near the soil surface results. Strong temperature inversions can develop in calm, low humidity atmospheric conditions and if frost occurs under these conditions, they are called 'inversion' frosts (Rosenberg 1974; Figure 8.16). The most severe frosts occur when an inflow of a cold air mass, which significantly reduces temperature, is followed by a drop in wind speed. With a clear sky, subsequent cooling by radiation loss then results in a frost. The lowest and hence most damaging temperatures occur near dawn. Whilst atmospheric conditions are the major determinants of radiation frost risk (Table 8.12), local topography is important and should be considered when selecting sites for vineyards (see Volume 1, Chapter 10).

Reference is often made to 'white frosts' ('hoar frosts'). A white frost occurs when water vapour

Table 8.12. Effect of atmospheric conditions on the likelihood of radiation frost.

Atmospheric Conditions		Frost risk during morning after
Preceding day	Night	
Clear	Cloudy	Lower
Cloudy	Clear	Higher

condenses as ice crystals on plants or other bodies when the dew point is below freezing. A 'black frost' occurs when vegetation is frozen due to an air temperature drop without sufficient water vapour in the atmosphere to form a white frost (Rosenberg 1974).

8.4.3 Frost control

The best policy against frost is choosing a vineyard site where there is no (or minimal) frost risk. This question is discussed in Volume 1, 4.1.1 and 10.4.2. Frost control can employ both passive and active management of temperature and energy conditions in a vineyard. It may also involve manipulation of the vine to reduce its susceptibility to frost injury. Passive methods employ techniques to enhance solar energy input and retention by soil, to lessen vine exposure to cold conditions and to reduce long-wave radiation losses. Active methods employ energy consuming techniques to reduce long-wave radiation loss to the sky or to supply energy to directly warm the air.

Passive methods

Soil management
Factors influencing the receipt of short-wave radiation, transfer and storage of heat in the soil by day and its loss by long-wave radiation by night can be modified by soil management practices. Vegetation covering the soil surface will reduce soil heating and subsequent heat flow from the soil to the air. Bare, loose dry soil has low heat storage capacity and the air pockets in the soil insulate against heat input by day and output by night. On the other hand, bare, compacted wet soil (Figure 8.10) stores more heat by day and then re-conducts heat to its radiating surface by night because both moisture and compaction improve the thermal storage capacity and conductivity of the soil. In a clean cultivated vineyard on clear nights with minimum temperatures ranging from 20°C to -5.5°C, Bridley *et al.* (1965) found that rolling or irrigation alone increased air temperature at canopy height by 0.4°C compared with rolling or irrigation respectively. When rolling and irrigation were combined, air temperature increased by 0.6°C. In a Swiss study, clean cultivated, firm soil resulted in the highest grapevine bud temperatures (buds at 75-80 cm above ground were approximately 2°C higher than

surface temperature); low mown and high mown rye grass sward decreased bud temperature by 1°C and 2°C respectively. Thick mulch gave similar results to high-mown sward (McCarthy 1988). By comparison, bud temperature did not differ with straw mulch or herbicide under light frost conditions (McLachlan *et al.* 1989). A combination of herbicide vine strip and closely mown sward in the alley is not likely to present a significantly greater frost risk than herbicide plus cultivation. In summary, the above results show that the best soil management practice for frost reduction is bare (cultivated or herbicide), compacted, wet soil followed by closely-mown sward with a clean vine strip. Thick mulch or high sward are the worst options.

Trellis height
The closer the buds or shoots are to the ground, the greater the risk of frost damage. For example, a cordon at 1.4 m may be 0.5°C warmer than one at 0.9 m height. As mentioned above, bulky, high herbage cover increases the need for higher elevation of the buds.

Variety selection
Varieties with late budburst may avoid frost because the probability of frost declines as the season progresses (see Volume 1, Table 6.3).

Delayed pruning
Late pruning can delay budburst and thus provide a greater chance of escaping frost conditions (see 4.4 and Volume 1, Section 7.2.5)

Protective covering
Plastic covers, greenhouses/glasshouses and netting are used in some specialist applications. Apart from advancing ripening and protecting fruit from weather damage, significant avoidance of frost can also be achieved.

Reduction in ice nucleation active (INA) bacteria
These act as a 'seed' on which ice crystals can form. In their absence, water can cool to as low as -5°C without freezing (termed super-cooling) in many plants (Lindow and Connell 1984). INA bacteria include a number of naturally occurring bacteria such as *Pseudomonas syringae* (Lindow 1983) which may act as ice nuclei. Reduction in

the number of INA bacteria with copper compounds has the potential to reduce the risk of frost injury, particularly as bacterial numbers appear to be highest early in the growing season.

Active methods

Smudge pots
Artificial clouds of smoke generated by burning oil can reduce long-wave radiation loss under radiation frost conditions. They are usually ignited when the air temperature drops to 1°C and, depending on the nature of the inversion layer, may increase air temperature at canopy height by up to 3°C. When 150 pots, each of 5 L capacity are used per ha, about 260 L of fuel oil will be used every hour (Anon 1985). However smudge pots are no longer used in Australia due to both environmental and energy conservation considerations.

Air mixing
The presence of an inversion layer containing air warmer than that next to the soil surface offers an opportunity of frost control by mixing air layers to increase the air temperature near the soil surface. If this does not occur naturally, fans, wind machines or even helicopters may be used. Horizontally mounted fans are generally positioned 4-7 m above the ground and powered by electric, petrol or diesel motors. Vertical fans may also be used. The coverage of these machines will depend on the terrain and the ability to achieve adequate mixing of air layers. For a cherry orchard in Oregon, temperatures could be modified over about 5 ha, but adequate frost protection could be assured only for about 2 ha per wind machine (Bates 1972). Access to the inversion layer is most important: if it is too high (as under certain inversion conditions - Figure 8.16), the machine will not be able to produce a down-draught of warmer air.

Overhead sprinklers
Water applied through overhead sprinklers can be successfully used for frost protection. Frost protection results from the release of latent heat of freezing. It is effective for both radiation and advective frosts. Normal water application rate for frost protection is between 2.5 and 3.5 mm per hour although higher rates are sometimes used.

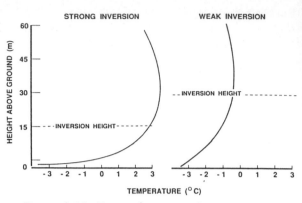

Figure 8.16. *Types of inversion layer.*

These rates are considerably lower than those used for over-canopy irrigation. A more detailed discussion of frost protection is given in Chapter 6. Water misting systems to generate artificial clouds have also been tried (Rosenberg 1974).

8.5 Concluding Remarks

Soil management in Australian vineyards has nearly come full circle since the exploitative cultivation systems brought with European settlement. The degrading effects of cultivating fragile shallow soils and other inappropriate methods are now more fully understood. Concurrent with these developments is the increasing acceptability of minimal chemical inputs to viticulture. There are many challenges that still face our soil managers; especially urgent are the needs for less competitive and early seeding species for swards in the rain-fed grapegrowing districts, and management systems which result in minimal soil compaction.

The causes, consequences, and control of vineyard soil acidification requires further research, especially the adaptation of their findings to vineyard soil management systems.

Adoption of the methods recommended for improving soil management is likely to result in increased vine capacity. This will lead to more vigorous shoots and shady canopies if vegetative growth and fruit production are not kept in balance and canopies are not adequately managed. A deliberate policy of avoiding soil improvement for the purpose of producing grapes for a particular end use must be carefully weighed against the eventual cost of rehabilitating the soil.

Further Reading

Auld, B.A. and Medd, R.W. (1987) Weeds: An Illustrated Botanical Guide To The Weeds of Australia. Inkata Press, Melbourne.

Bates, V. and Macgregor, A. (1991) Chemical Weed Control In The Vineyard. Department of Agriculture, Victoria.

Cornish, P.S. and Pratley, J.E. (eds) (1987) Tillage: New Directions In Australian Agriculture. Inkata Press, Melbourne.

Eadie, I.McL. (ed) (1985) Recommendations for Weed Control - Southern Australia. Weed Sc. Soc. of Vic.

Lee, T.H., Freeman, B.M. and Hayes, P.F. (eds) (1988) Vineyard soil and sod culture management. Aust. Soc. Vitic. Oen., Adelaide.

McCarthy, M.G. (1991) Vineyard soil management - who cares a sod? Aust. NZ Wine Ind. J. 5(1), 28-31.

Richards, D. (1983) The grape root system. Hort. Rev. 5, 127-68.

Skroch, W.A. and Shribbs, J.M. (1986) Orchard floor management: An overview. HortScience 21(3), 390-94.

van Huyssteen, L. (1990) The effect of soil management and fertilization on grape composition and wine quality with special reference to South African conditions. In Williams, P.J., Davidson, D.M. and Lee, T.H. (eds) 13-17 August 1989, Adelaide, SA, Aust. Soc. Vitic. Oen., Adelaide, pp 16-25.

van Zyl, J.L. (ed) (1988) The grapevine root and its environment. Tech. Comm. 215. Department of Agriculture and Water Supply, Republic of South Africa.

Other References

Abbott, T.S. and McKenzie, D.C. (1986) Improving soil structure with gypsum. Department of Agriculture, New South Wales. Agfact AC. 10.

Adem, H.H. (1988) The Tatura soil management system for vineyards. In: Integrated Pest Management for Orchards - proceedings of a seminar, 9-10 May, 1988, Mildura, Vic; Monsanto, Aust.

Adem, H.H. and Tisdall, J.M. (1983) Reconditioned soil: the key to better crops. Aust. Grapegrower and Winemaker 238, 18-19.

Adem, H.H. and Tisdall, J.M. (1988) Vineyard soil management - the Tatura way. In: Lee, T.H., Freeman, B.M. and Hayes, P.F. (eds) Vineyard Soil and Sod Culture Management. Aust. Soc. Vitic. Oen., Adelaide pp 5-12.

Anonymous (1985) The use of frost pots. Agnote 3181/85, Vic Department of Agriculture.

Atkinson, D. (1979) Effects (of herbicides) on soil with particular reference to orchard crops. Ann. Appl. Biol. 91, 125-29.

Baker, B. T. and McCarthy, M.G. (1981) Chemical weed control on new non-irrigated vineyards. Fact Sheet 11/81, SA Department of Agriculture.

Barnard C (1932) The root system of the Sultana. Council Sci. Ind. Res. J 5, 89-93.

Bates, E.M. (1972) Temperature inversion and freeze protection by wind machine. Agr. Meteorol. 9, 335-46.

Beckingham, C.R. (1988) Vineyard soil management. Aust. Grapegrower and Winemaker 292, 106-17.

Bhanghoo, M.S., Day, K.S., Sudanagunta, V.R. and Petrucci, V.E. (1988) Applications of poultry manure influences Thompson Seedless grape production and soil properties. HortScience 23(6), 1010-2.

Blackwell, J., Jayawardane, N., Muirhead, W.A. and Cassegrain, J.C. (1988) Soil slotting for existing and future vineyards. In: Lee, T.H., Freeman, B.M. and Hayes, P.F. (eds) Vineyard Soil and Sod Culture Management Aust. Soc. Vitic. Oen., Adelaide pp 27-38.

Bridley, S.F., Taylor, R.J. and Webber, R.T.J. (1965) The effects of irrigation and rolling on nocturnal air temperatures in vineyards. Agr. Meteorol. 2, 373-83.

Brown, A.J., Funk, K.H., Peverill, K.I. (1980) Manual on the soil testing service provided by the Division of Agricultural Chemistry. Technical Report 34, Department of Agriculture, Vic.

Christensen, L.P., Kasimatis, A.N. and Jensen, F.L. (1978) Grapevine Nutrition and Fertilization in the San Joaquin Valley. Univ. of Calif., Berkley Calif.

Cock, G.J. (1985) Soil structural conditions of vineyards under two soil management systems. Aust. J. Exp. Agric. 25, 450-4.

Cockcroft, B. (1978) Concepts of soil management. Proc. 3rd Aust. Wine Ind. Tech. Conf., 9-11 August 1977 Albury, NSW: Aust. Wine Res. Inst. pp 31-3.

Code, G.R. (1990) Weed control in vines - some experimental results and views. Plant Protection Quarterly 5(3), 110-2.

Damanakis, M.E. and Daris, B.T. (1981) Residues of triazine herbicides in a vineyard after a long-term application. Vitis 20, 329-34.

Davidson, D. (1990) Realistic alternative approaches to Australian viticulture - managing with fewer chemicals. Aust. NZ Wine Ind. J. 5(4), 328-30.

Dry, P.R. (1990) Some observations on disease and pest management in South Australian vineyards. Aust NZ Wine Ind. J. 5(3), 238.

Emerson, W.W. (1977) Physical properties and

structure. In: Soil factors in crop production in a semi-arid environment (eds) Russell, J.S. and Greacen, E.L. University of Queensland Press pp 78-104.

Flaherty, P.L., Jensen, F.L., Kasimatis, A.N., Kido, H., Moller, W.J. (eds) (1981) Grape Pest Management, University of California, Berkley.

Freeman, B.M. and McLachlan, G. (1988) Water use with a permanent sod in an irrigated vineyard. In: Lee, T.H., Freeman, B.M. and Hayes, P.F. (eds). Vineyard Soil and Sod Culture Management. Aust. Soc. Vitic. Oen., Adelaide pp 13-26.

Giulivo, C., Iannini, B., Levezzi, A. and Nuzzo, V. (1988) Effeti della technica colturale del terrono sullo stato nutrivo e sull'apparato radicale della vite. Rivista di Viticoltura e di Enologia 8, 335-50.

Glenn, D.M. and Welker, W.V.(1989) Orchard soil management and systems influence rainfall infiltration. J. Amer. Soc. Hort. Sci. 114(1), 10-14.

Godden, G.D. and Hardie, W.J. (1981) Comparison between grapevine response to polyethylene mulch and herbicide control of weeds. Gartenbauwissenschaft 46 (6), 277-84.

Godden, G.D., Hardie, W.J. and Witcombe, R.K. (1982) Plastic sheet mulch - a favourable alternative to herbicides during vineyard establishment. Aust. Grapegrower and Winemaker 224, 30-5.

Greaves, M.P. (1979) Long-term effects of herbicides on soil micro-organisms. Ann. Appl. Biology 91, 129-32.

Green, R. (1979) Soil structure in improving orchard soils. Agriculture Note Series 24, Department of Agriculture, Victoria.

Hardie, W.J. (1988) Practical experience with soil management - King Valley, Victoria In: Lee, T.H., Freeman, B.M. and Hayes, P.F. (eds). Vineyard Soil and Sod Culture Management. Aust. Soc. Vitic. Oen., Adelaide pp 13-26.

Haynes, R.J. (1980) Influence of soil management practice on the orchard agro-ecosystem. Agro-Ecosystems 6, 3-32.

Haynes, R.J. (1981) Effects of soil management practices on soil physical properties, earthworm populations and tree root distribution in a commercial apple orchard. Soil and Tillage Res. 1, 269-80.

Haynes, R.J. and Goh, K.M. (1980) Some observations on surface soil pH, base saturation abd leaching of cations under three contrasting orchard soil management practices. Plant and Soil 56, 429-38.

Hodge, D. (1985) Minimum tillage provides many benefits plus significant. savings. Aust. Grapegrower and Winemaker 224, 12-15.

Jenkins, A. (1988) Herbicide selection for vineyards - some considerations. Aust. Grapegrower and Winemaker 298, 15-17.

Jenkins, A. (1991) Review of production techniques for organic vineyards. Aust. Grapegrower and Winemaker 328, 133-41.

Kirchhof, G., Blackwell, J. and Smart, R.E. (1990) Growth of vineyard roots into segmentally ameliorated acid subsoils. In: Developments in Plant and Soil Sciences. Proc. 2nd Int. Symp. Plant-Soil Interactions at Low pH, June 24 - 29, 1990, West Virginia, USA. Kluever Acad. Publ. Dordrecht, Neth.

Lindow, S.E. (1983) Methods of preventing frost injury caused by epiphytic ice nucleation active bacteria. Plant Disease 67, 327-33.

Lindow, S.E. and Connell, J.H. (1984) Reduction of frost injury to almond by control of ice nucleation active bacteria. J. Amer. Soc. Hort. Sc. 109(1), 48-53.

Lodden, L. (ed) (1990) Sow what where - Pasture species for special purposes. Grassland Soc. of Vic. Inc.

Lombard, P., Price, S., Wilson, W. and Watson, B. (1988) Grass cover crops in vineyards. In: Smart, R.E. et al. (eds) Proc. 2nd Int. Symp. Cool Climate Vitic. Oen. 11 - 15 Jan 1988; Auckland NZ Soc. Vitic. Oen. pp 152-55.

Ludvigsen, R.K. (1987) Vineyard soil management: use of cover crops. Aust. Grapegrower and Winemaker 280, 102-8.

Ludvigsen, R.K. (1988) Machinery for new vineyard technologies. Aust. Grapegrower and Winemaker 292, 87-92.

Ludvigsen, R.K. (1989) A practical application: controlled droplet applicator use in the vineyard. Aust. Grapegrower and Winemaker 307, 23-4.

Ludvigsen, R.K. (1992) Growing a vineyard cover crop. Aust. Grapegrower and Winemaker 340, 106-9.

Macrae, I. (1991) The management of shallow and potentially unstable soils. Aust. NZ Wine Ind. J. 5(1), 32-4.

McCarthy, M.G. (1985) Herbicides and their problems. In: Lester, D.C., Cirami, R.M. and Lee, T.H. (eds) Chemicals in the vineyard. Aust. Soc. Vitic. Oen., Adelaide pp 25-30.

McCarthy, M.G. (1988) Some Swiss and South African experiences with soil management. In: Lee, T.H., Freeman, B.M. and Hayes, P.F. (eds). Vineyard Soil and Sod Culture Management. Aust. Soc. Vitic. Oen., Adelaide pp 43-50.

McLachlan, G., Sinclair, P. and Freeman, B.M. (1989) Soil moisture conservation using mulches. Aust. Grapegrower and Winemaker 311, 42-4.

Merry, R. (1990) Soil acidity and vineyard management in South Australia. Aust. Grapegrower and Winemaker 324, 11-12.

Pagliai, M., LaMarca, M., Lucamante, G. and Genovese, L. (1984) Effects of zero and conventional tillage on the length and irregularity of elongated pores in a clayloam soil under viticulture. Soil and Tillage Res. 4, 433-44.

Perret, P. (1987) Some ideas from Swiss viticulture. Aust Grapegrower and Winemaker 280, 95-101.

Perret, P. and Koblet, W. (1984) Soil compaction induced iron chlorosis in vineyards: presumed involvement of exogenous ethylene. J. Plant Nutrition 7, 533-39.

Pool, R.M., Dunst, R.M. and Lakso, A.N. (1990) Comparison of sod, mulch, cultivation and herbicide floor management practices for grape production in non irrigated vineyards. J. Amer. Soc. Hort. Sci. 115(6), 872-7.

Rice, E.L. (1984) Allelopathy, 2nd ed, Academic Press NY.

Richards, D. and Cockcroft, B. (1974) Soil physical properties and root concentrations in an irrigated peach orchard. Aust. J. Exp. Agric. Animal Husb. 14, 103-7.

Robinson, J.B. (1990) Some topical issues in vineyard soil management. Aust. NZ Wine Ind. J. 5(1), 14-6.

Rosenberg, N.J. (1974) Microclimate: The Biological Environment. J. Wiley and Sons, NY.

Saayman, D. and van Huyssteen, L. (1980) Soil preparation studies 1. The effect of depth and method of soil preparation on the performance of V. vinifera Chenin Blanc on Hutton/Sterkspruit soil. S. Afr. J. Enol. Vitic. 1, 107-21.

Smart, R.E. and Coombe, B.G. (1983) Water relations of grapevines. In: Water Deficits and Plant Growth. Kozlowski, T. (ed) Vol VII Academic Press NY pp 137-96.

Smart, R.E., Kirchhof, G. and Blackwell, J. (1991) The diagnosis and treatment of acidic vineyard soil. Aust. NZ Wine Ind. J. 5(1), 35-40.

Spurling, M.B. and Jennings, J.P. (1956) Frost: occurrence, prediction, control. J. S.A. Department of Agriculture. 60, 18-25, 53-4, 87-94.

Sutherland, J. (1986) Green manure crops for vegetable production. Agnote Series, Vic. Department of Agriculture.

Tan, S. and Crabtree, G.D. (1990) Competition between perennial ryegrass sod and 'Chardonnay' wine grapes for mineral nutrients. HortScience 25(5), 533-5.

Tisdall, J.M., Cockcroft, B. and Uren, N.C. (1978) The stability of soil aggregates as affected by organic materials, microbial activity and physical disruption. Aust. J. Soil Res. 16, 9-17.

Tisdall, J.M. and Oades, J.M. (1979) Stabilization of soil aggregates by the root systems of ryegrass. Aust. J. Soil Res. 17, 429-41.

Tisdall, J.M. and Huett, D.O. (1987) Tillage in horticulture. In: Cornish, P.S. and Pratley, J.E. (eds) Tillage - New Directions in Australia. Inkata Press, Melb., Aust.

van Huyssteen, L. (1988) Soil preparation and grapevine root distribution - a qualitative and quantitative assessment. In: The grapevine root and its environment. van Zyl, J.L. (ed) Tech. Comm. 215, Department of Agriculture and Water Supply, Republic of South Africa. 1-15.

van Huyssteen, L. and Weber, H.W. (1980) The effect of selected minimum and conventional tillage practices in vineyard cultivation on vine performance. Sth. Afr. J. Enol. Vit. 1, 77-82.

van Rooyen, F.C. (1980) The water requirements of tablegrapes. Decid. Fruit Grower 30, 100-5.

van Zyl, J.C. and van Huyssteen, L. (1984) Soil water management towards optimum grape yield and quality under conditions of limited or no irrigation. In: Lee, T.H. and Somers, T.C. (eds) Proc. 5th Aust. Wine Ind. Tech. Conf., 29 Nov - 1 Dec, 1983, Perth WA; Aust. Wine Res. Inst., Adelaide, pp 25-66.

Weir, R.G. (1987) Liming materials. Department of Agriculture, New South Wales. Agfact AC. 15.

Westwood, M.N. (1978) Temperate Zone Pomology. W.H. Freeman and Co, San Francisco.

Williams, R.D. (1981) Complementary interaction between weeds, weed control practices and pests in horticultural cropping systems. HortScience 16, 508-12.

Winkler, A.J., Cook, J.A., Kliewer, W.M. and Lider, L.A. (1974) General Viticulture. University of California Press.

Woodham, R.C. and Alexander, D.McE. (1966) The effect of root temperature on development of small fruiting Sultana vines. Vitis 5, 345-50.

CHAPTER NINE

Grapevine Nutrition

J.B. ROBINSON

Grapevines are able to grow and crop satisfactorily in a range of environments. In Australia in the past it was common to grow vines without added fertilizers unless very serious abnormalities occurred either in the form of symptoms of nutrient deficiency on leaves or as reduced crop production. During the last ten years there has been an increased understanding of the nutritional needs of grapevines. This has been stimulated in large part by the expansion of the industry into new areas with a wider range of soils than had previously been used. In all States there have been individual cases of nutritional deficiencies (see Figure 9.1) which have prompted research into specific fertilizer requirements, (e.g. zinc deficiency in SA and Vic.) Early, more general, experimental work on the need for the major nutrients was done in South Australia (in the Barossa Valley) and Victoria (in Sunraysia), but the usefulness of this work has been largely restricted to the area in which the experiment was done. More recently fertilizer trials have been carried out in WA and Victoria, and there has been wider use of tissue analysis survey techniques to identify potential regional nutritional problems and to spread the usefulness of information collected in fertilizer trials.

This chapter aims to lead the reader towards drawing up a fertilizer program based on logical decisions. A fertilizer program should be devised to complement the ability of the soil to provide nutrient elements (see Volume 1, Chapter 3) to the vine so that the vine can develop completely and crop efficiently. It is also important to recognize that nutrient elements should not be applied if the soil can supply them adequately. Nutritional effects on wine quality have also been identified which add another level of complexity to the subject. As rootstocks become more widely used there is no doubt that another set of nutritional problems will become obvious, related in part to the increase in vigour which many stocks induce in the scion.

The important questions that must be answered are:

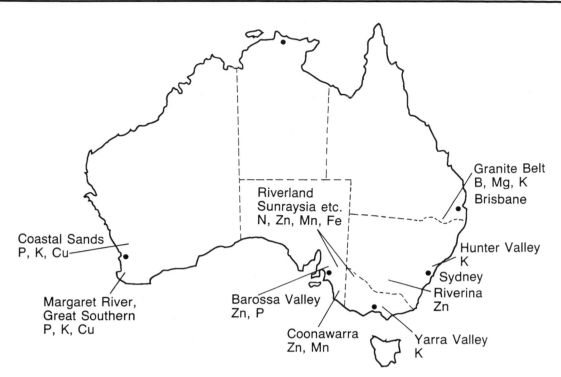

Figure 9.1. Many nutrient deficiencies in grapevines have been identified in the field in Australia. This map shows some of the areas in which they have occurred. Not all vineyards in these areas will necessarily be affected. The symbols used have their normal chemical meanings.

(i) What are the essential elements for growth and performance of vines?

(ii) How can the need for application of any of these elements in fertilizers be detected?

(iii) What fertilizers are available to provide these elements and what do they contain?

(iv) How are they best applied?

(v) How much should be applied?

9.1 Elements necessary for vine growth and development

In Australian viticultural areas, deficiencies of the elements nitrogen, phosphorus, potassium, magnesium, boron, zinc, manganese, iron and copper have been shown to influence vine health, growth, yield or quality. These elements all have unique properties as components of the living grapevine: some are part of the vine's structural framework, some are involved in trapping and using light energy and some are part of the enzymes which act as catalysts in chemical reactions in the cells of the plant. If one element alone is not available in sufficient quantities vine performance will be limited by the extent of the supply of that element. Individual deficiencies of each of these elements can result in characteristic growth restrictions or alterations in the colour of parts of leaves and in some cases the shape of leaves is changed. These are known as deficiency symptoms. Often deficiency symptoms observed in the greenhouse are different from those seen in the vineyard. It is possible to have 'hidden hunger', where vine growth or performance is reduced but no obvious symptoms can be found.

Traditionally the essential elements have been described as major and trace elements, or macro- and micronutrients. These names describe the quantities of the element needed by the plant. The macronutrients — potassium, nitrogen, calcium, magnesium, sulfur and phosphorus — occur in largest amounts in plant tissue, from about 0.2 to 3% of dry weight. The micronutrients are found in smaller amounts: iron and manganese at approximately 50 to 150 ppm dry weight and molybdenum, copper, zinc and boron at 0.5 to 40 ppm dry weight. Despite these differences, a deficiency of a micronutrient can be just as disastrous as a deficiency of a macronutrient. It is important to understand the part each element plays in plant growth and to know what the effects of deficiencies are likely to be.

9.1.1 Nitrogen

Nitrogen (N) makes up about 1-2% of the dry matter of grapevines and there are about 2 kg of nitrogen per tonne of grapes. It is a primary component of proteins, which have both structural and catalytic functions, and is also an important component of energy-transfer systems and of chlorophyll. The most obvious symptom of a shortage of nitrogen is reduced vigour—smaller leaves and shoots—and an all-over yellowing of leaves and other green tissues. Reddening (especially of petioles) may also occur when nitrogen is in short supply. The yellowing reflects a reduced chlorophyll content in leaves, which in itself is clear evidence of a reduction in the potential ability of the plant to trap light energy and thus to manufacture sugars. The reduced vigour brought about by a nitrogen shortage is the result of both a direct restriction of the synthesis of protein and an indirect reduction in photosynthesis which is essential for both protein and structural carbohydrate formation and to provide energy for other processes within the vine. Too much nitrogen may also have an adverse effect on the productivity of grapevines, leading to an increase in vigour which is associated with a reduction in both fruitset and bud fertility. High vigour may also lead to a disorder known as primary bud-axis necrosis (Figure 9.2a) which ultimately results in decreased yield potential. Excessive availability of nitrogen has also been implicated in the expression of the syndrome known as bunchstem necrosis (see Figure 9.2b).

9.1.2 Phosphorus

Phosphorus (P) makes up about 0.1 to 0.3% of the dry matter of the vine and there is about 0.6 kg of phosphorus in each tonne of grapes. It is a component of the fatty portion of cell membranes, of the compounds that take part in the fixation of carbon dioxide and the metabolism of sugars, and of the systems of energy storage and transfer within each plant cell which facilitate the living processes (metabolism). Phosphorus is also a vital component of the genetic material.

Table 9.1 Effect of superphosphate application on set of berries (1963-64 season)[a] at Nuriootpa
(from Tulloch and Harris 1970)

Variable	No superphosphate applied	Superphosphate
Berries per bunch	68.6	84.1[b]
Bunch weight (g)	71.6	93.4[b]

a. Treatments were begun in 1944.
b. Differences significant at $P = 0.001$.

The symptoms of phosphorus deficiency in grapevines are similar to those described for tree fruits: a gradual reduction in shoot growth occurs, sometimes without severe leaf symptoms. In the field, basal leaves may pale or turn yellow and fall before flowering time and red dots may form near the edges of mid or terminal lobes of basal leaves which later coalesce forming red bars at right angles to the veins (Cook et al.1983). Sultana grown in solution culture shows yellowing between the veins of recently matured leaves and dullness on older leaves as the phosphorus supply continues to be restricted. These symptoms have not been identified in the field. Yield reductions were reported as a consequence of phosphorus deficiency in the field in an experiment in the Barossa valley and these were traced to an effect on fruitset; when deficiency was corrected more berries were set in each bunch (Table 9.1) and vine vigour increased (Tulloch and Harris 1970). Reduced set and low bunch numbers per shoot were found in potted vines receiving restricted phosphorus (Skinner and Matthews 1989).

9.1.3 Potassium

Potassium (K) makes up a considerable part of the dry weight of the grapevine (up to 3%) and is an important component of grape juice: there are about 5 kg of potassium in each tonne of grapes. Potassium has a vital role in the internal vacuole of the plant cell where it is the most important positive ion (cation), providing electrical balance for organic and inorganic anions and indirectly maintaining the structure of the non-woody parts of the plant through an effect on turgor of cells. Unlike nitrogen and phosphorus, potassium does not enter into the structural molecules of plant cells and tissues.

A deficiency of potassium shows up first in the older leaves as it is very mobile within the plant and moves from older to younger tissue as the plant grows (see Figure 9.3). Older leaves of white varieties become yellowed near the margin and this chlorosis extends inwards towards the centre of the leaf. As the deficiency becomes acute marginal burning of the leaves occurs. In red varieties the leaves show red- rather than yellow-colouring prior to the onset of marginal burn. It is possible to confuse these symptoms with those of leafroll virus infection and salt- or moisture-stress. Defoliation may follow. The upper surface of younger leaves may become shiny, and an interveinal chlorosis (yellowing) similar to that caused by iron deficiency is seen. Another symptom associated with potassium deficiency under some conditions is a pronounced leaf blackening. Bunches are small and tight and berries ripen unevenly. Such symptoms are seen in Australian vineyards in some small areas in the Hunter Valley (NSW) and in the Granite Belt of Queensland (see Volume 1, Chapter 3) and in parts of WA and the Yarra Valley of Victoria.

9.1.4 Magnesium

Magnesium (Mg) is a component of the chlorophyll molecule. Deficiency shows as a yellowing between the veins of older leaves and red varieties show a red pigmentation in these areas (see Figure 9.4). In the Granite Belt of Queensland, symptoms that appear late in the season are not considered to be important but, where they occur before mid-summer, yields are seriously affected. The symptoms of magnesium deficiency can easily be confused with those of leafroll virus (which itself results in alterations of the distribution of Mg and K within the leaf blade and petiole); in South Australia a leaf colouring of Grenache resembles that caused by Mg deficiency but does not seem to be associated with low Mg concentrations. In tablegrapes grown in glasshouses at Murray Bridge (SA) severe magnesium deficiency is observed on shoots that grow in winter. This is probably induced by high residual concentrations of exchangeable potassium in the soil from previous tomato and cucumber crops.

9.1.5 Iron

Iron (Fe) is a micronutrient involved both in chlorophyll formation and energy trapping and transfer in photosynthesis and respiration. Its deficiency results in a diffuse yellowing of young leaves and new growth, rather as though these tissues had been bleached (Figure 9.5). When deficiency is not acute veins retain their green colour.

Soils that are truly deficient in iron are rare (leached or wind—blown sands). Most soils contain adequate iron but deficiency results from a bicarbonate inhibition of uptake of Fe ions at the root surface. High levels of bicarbonate are found in alkaline soils (due to free lime or sodicity), aggravated by poor aeration due to soil compaction and/or waterlogging. In the latter case symptoms of the deficiency often disappear if irrigation is withheld or as the season warms up and iron becomes available; vines and weeds gradually dewater the root zone and improve aeration. If alkalinity is inducing the chlorosis the severity of symptoms does not change much during the season. Variations in chlorosis tolerance will influence the usefulness of some of the root-stock cultivars derived from less tolerant American *Vitis* species (see Volume 1, Chapter 8).

9.1.6 Manganese

Manganese (Mn) is a micronutrient that is a component of catalysts involved in the synthesis of chlorophyll and in nitrogen metabolism. Symptoms of mild manganese deficiency are often seen in vineyards in the Mallee areas (calcareous earths) and in some higher rainfall areas. A yellowing occurs between the main veins in broad bands. This is seen first on the older leaves. If the deficiency is severe the younger leaves may also be affected. In water culture, shoot growth is retarded only when the deficiency is severe. Manganese deficiency symptoms can be confused with those caused by zinc deficiency and iron deficiency but symptoms of the latter deficiences tend to be exhibited first on younger leaves.

9.1.7 Zinc

Zinc (Zn) deficiency is often found in Australian viticulture. Zinc is a component of a catalyst involved in cell metabolic reactions. A severe deficiency results in 'little leaf' symptoms and

Figure 9.3. Symptoms of potassium deficiency in Muscat Gordo Blanco vines grown in sand culture. Edge burning and rolling of older and mid-shoot leaves is seen when the deficiency is severe. Young leaves show a chlorosis similar to that seen with iron deficiency. The shiny surface of the younger leaves is characteristic of the deficiency. A wide range of symptoms has been described from the field.

Figure 9.2. A. Twin shoots due to bud necrosis. The remains of the primary bud are visible between the shoots (Dry 1986). B. Bunchstem necrosis in Cabernet Sauvignon at Langhorne Creek; affected bunch on left, normal bunch on right. (See also 11.5.5).

Figure 9.4. Symptoms of magnesium deficiency usually occur in basal or mid-shoot leaves. The lower left photograph shows a leaf in a tablegrape glasshouse at Murray Bridge. The lower right photograph shows a mid-shoot leaf from a Shiraz vine grown in sand culture. The interveinal coloration is followed by necrosis as the leaves age. The symptoms are similar to those caused by leaf roll virus infection.

Figure 9.7. Symptoms of boron toxicity on a Muscat Gordo Blanco vine grown in sand culture. The spotty necrosis at leaf margins and between the veins on older leaves is characteristic. Leaf deformity similar to that caused by hormone sprays may also occur. Symptoms of boron deficiency are not easily displayed in a photograph.

Figure 9.5. Symptoms of iron deficiency. The upper photograph shows leaves of different ages from Shiraz vines grown in sand culture—note chlorosis evident on younger leaves. In the field (lower photograph) acute iron deficiency results in a golden chlorosis, stunted growth and eventually stem and leaf death.

Figure 9.6. Zinc deficiency symptoms on the leaves of Muscat Gordo Blanco developed in sand culture. Older leaf on right, younger on left. Note mottled chlorosis and widened petiolar sinus. In the field, mild zinc deficiency results in reduced set whereas severe deficiency leads to much reduced internode length and 'little leaf'.

Figure 9.8. The labelling if a fertilizer bag contains all the information needed to assess the value of the concentration and form of each nutrient which the bag contains and a shorthand summary of the concentrations of the major nutrients. The composition of each fertilizer on the market is registered with state authorities.

Table 9.2 Response in yield (kg dried fruit/3-vine plot) to zinc treatments of sultana at Red Cliffs[a].
(from Alexander and Woodham 1964)

Treatment	1959	1960	1961	1962	1963
No. zinc[b]	14.0	14.3	18.8	19.1	12.3
Zinc	15.3	16.7	18.6	21.9	14.1
LSD (P = 0.05)	1.1	1.6	1.5	1.9	1.6

a Vines in this vineyard showed no obvious zinc deficiency symptoms.
b Data taken from the set of treatments applied to plots that had received superphosphate.

stunted growth (Figure 9.6): the small leaves have a detailed mottling between the veins and have a widened petiolar sinus where the leaf stalk connects to the leaf. In the days before zinc treatment became routine the varieties Muscat Gordo Blanco, Pedro Ximines and Zante Currant were observed to be more susceptible than others grown in the Riverland of SA (Kemp and Beare 1944). More commonly, particularly in Riverland (SA), Sunraysia (Vic.), and the MIA (NSW) there is a less severe deficiency of zinc wherein symptoms are not obvious but yield is suppressed and good responses to treatment occur at least in some years (Table 9.2). Associated with this condition is the appearance on occasion of 'hen-and-chicken' berries (Morschel 1958). The routine treatment with zinc foliar sprays prior to flowering in many vineyards in South Australia and Sunraysia is based on awareness of this sub-symptomal yield suppression.

9.1.8 Boron
Boron (B) is a micronutrient that is perhaps more commonly toxic than deficient in vine growing areas of Southern Australia. Vineyards planted on Mallee soils (calcareous earths) or, less frequently, on land once used for vegetables sometimes show boron toxicity. The presence of boron in drainage water precludes its use for irrigation of grapevines. Boron appears to be involved in the internal regulation of growth by plant hormones. Boron deficiency symptoms have been reported in the field from the Granite Belt of Queensland (Jardine 1946). They include reduced set, a high proportion of seedless berries, death of the shoot tip, and yellowing between the veins of recently

matured leaves; rapidly expanding leaves may cup upwards and small areas between the veins become translucent. In very severe cases of boron deficiency longitudinal cracks develop along the canes.

Boron deficiency can be induced by drought conditions in areas with marginal boron status. Boron toxicity on the other hand shows first as a concave or convex cupping of the leaves near the shoot tip. This is followed by development of brown necrotic spots near the margins of leaves at the base of the shoot. The severity increases with time. Yellow streaks can appear between the veins of younger leaves (Figure 9.7). Recent data from petiole analysis services in Victoria suggest that boron deficiency may be more widespread than was previously believed, particularly in the higher rainfall areas.

9.1.9 Copper
Copper (Cu) is a micronutrient that is a component of the enzymes of oxidation. It is not normally expected to be deficient in vineyards as it is often applied to grapevines in copper-containing fungicidal sprays, e.g. Bordeaux mixture and copper oxychloride. In vineyards with acid soils and a long history of copper sprays copper toxicity is a possibility. Copper deficiency has been recorded at Gingin, Western Australia (Teakle,et al. 1943) (see Volume 1, Chapter 3): in this case vines were unthrifty, had short canes with shortened internodes; leaves were small, had only slight indentations and were pale in colour. Copper deficiency has also occurred in the coastal and Margaret River districts of WA.

9.1.10 Other elements
Deficiencies of a number of other elements may affect the health of grapevines but have not been reported from the field in Australia. Sulfur and molybdenum are worthy of mention since their deficiency is found in other plants in Australia.

Sulfur (S), a macronutrient, is a component of proteins and enzyme co-factors; the use of superphosphate but more importantly the use of wettable-, dusting- and lime-sulfur foliar applications in vineyards eliminates any chance of sulfur deficiency occurring.

Molybdenum (Mo), a micronutrient, is involved in nitrogen metabolism; molybdenum deficient

Table 9.3 Fertilizers that contain nitrogen

Fertilizer	Form of nitrogen and % N in each				Other nutrients contained (%)			Lime Requirement[a]
	Ammonium -N (Na)	Nitrate-N (Nn)	Urea-N (Nu)	Total-N (Nt)	Total-P Pt	Potassium (K)	Sulfur (S)	
Sulfate of ammonia	21			21			24	110
Ammonium nitrate	17	17		34				60
Mono-ammonium phosphate	10-11.2			10-11.2	22-23			43
Di-ammonium phosphate	18			18	20			55
Calcium nitrate		15		15				20
Potassium nitrate		13		13		38		26
Urea			46	46				84

[a]Approximate quantity of lime (kg) required to neutralize the acidity of 100 kg of each fertilizer (A.O.A.C. procedure).

soils are known in Australia but there are no documented responses of vines to molybdenum application.

9.2 Fertilizers

Fertilizers are carriers of plant nutrients. It is important to know: the elements which they contain and how much; the form of the element they contain; the manner in which the element in its various forms becomes available to the plant; and the way each form of element behaves in the container, after application to the soil surface and within the soil profile. These are the things that determine value for money and the best strategy of use (see e.g. Cook 1967).

The major sources of plant nutrients are detailed below. Much of this information is available on the labels of fertilizer containers (see Figure 9.8) and from the farm chemical registration authorities in each state.

9.2.1 Nitrogen-containing

Fertilizers contain one or more of three nitrogenous compounds, viz. ammonium-nitrogen, nitrate-nitrogen and urea-nitrogen. In Table 9.3 these are described in more detail. Urea is the most concentrated source of nitrogen. When applied to the soil it is broken down by the enzyme urease:

(urease)

Urea + water $\rightarrow$ ammonia + carbon dioxide

The ammonia formed in this reaction when dissolved in water forms the ammonium ion, unless the soil is alkaline in which case there is a chance of loss to the atmosphere as gaseous ammonia. Increased loss can occur if the urea is allowed to remain uncovered on the soil surface or is not washed into the soil with rain or irrigation. Up to 30% losses have been recorded.

Urea is thus effectively a source of ammonium nitrogen. Within the soil positively charged ammonium ions can be attached (adsorbed) to the negative clay and humus particles in the soil, be biologically incorporated directly into organic matter, or be converted, again biologically, to the negatively charged nitrate ion. Vines take up the nitrate form of nitrogen from the soil solution. Unlike ammonium-nitrogen, nitrate-nitrogen may be carried out of the soil profile in water percolating downward, i.e. the process of leaching. Generally it can be said that nitrate-nitrogen is immediately available to the plant while ammonium-nitrogen becomes available more slowly (after conversion to nitrate[3]); urea-nitrogen can be leached easily soon after application to the soil but reacts rather like ammonium-nitrogen.

If a choice is to be made between these forms of nitrogen it can either be made on the basis of price (urea is the cheapest per kg of N; ammonium nitrate and sulfate of ammonia are more costly) or on the basis of differences in the physical properties of the materials (urea unless specially granulated is not well suited to mixing with other materials as it takes up moisture and forms a solid cake; sulfate of ammonia is easy to handle and can readily be incorporated into mixed fertilizers (see below) but is the most acidifying (Table 9.3). The application method to be used should also be taken into account.

If broadcast and left on the surface of moist alkaline soils urea or sulfate of ammonia may incur significant losses as gaseous ammonia. These materials should be watered or cultivated into the soil profile shortly after surface application. The acid-forming properties of nitrogen fertilizers mean that in some areas lime must be used to keep the soil near neutral. This effect is not of great importance where soils are alkaline in pH, but on acid soils it is possible to reduce soil pH in a few years to the extent that the availability of other nutrients is affected.

The most significant effects of soil acidification are increased availability of manganese and aluminium (to the extent in some soils that toxicity can occur) and decreased availability of molybdenum and phosphorus. The quantities of lime required to counteract the acidification caused by various nitrogenous fertilizers are also presented in Table 9.3. Even on soils that are normally alkaline a regular check of the pH of the surface soil should be made when the more acid-forming materials are used (see Volume 1, Chapter 3).

A diagrammatic summary of the transformations of nitrogen in the soil is given in Figure 9.9.

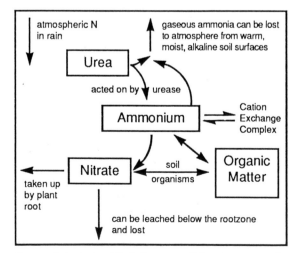

Figure 9.9. A simplified diagram of the nitrogen cycle.

Urea as a foliar-fertilizer

Urea can be used as a foliar-nutrient as it is taken up quickly by leaf tissue. If urea is used in this way its content of the toxic contaminant, biuret, becomes important. Biuret is formed as an impurity during the production process. If the concentration is much higher than 40 ppm in the solution in the spray-tank some damage will occur to sprayed leaves. This means that only urea that contains less than 0.4% biuret (in the urea as purchased) is safe for use at the normal spray-tank concentration of about 5-7.5 g/L. The effect of biuret damage on yield of grapes has not been determined and as damage is confined to those leaves present when the spray is applied it is possible that the danger has been over-emphasized. If the concentration of the urea in foliar sprays for grapes exceeds 10 g/L leaf burn caused by the urea itself is likely to be unacceptable. Some burn to expanding leaves occurs at concentrations as low as 5 g/L.

Urea in liquid formulations

Urea also finds wide application in liquid fertilizers applied to the soil (e.g. for injecting into drip irrigation systems as in Figure 9.10) because it is very soluble (up to 600 g/L can be used without danger of the urea crystallizing out at normal temperatures) and contains few sludge-like impurities that may block irrigation outlets. Used in this way it has a particular advantage over ammonium and nitrate forms of nitrogen. Ammonium ions tend to become concentrated on the soil cation exchange sites around the dripper outlet, while nitrate moves to the edge and bottom of the wetted zone and may easily be leached away and lost to the roots. Urea, however, is acted upon by urease as it moves through the soil and the ammonium ions so formed are distributed widely through the root zone. The long term effect of urea applied in this way may be to severely acidify the root zone (particularly when there is substantial leaching of nitrate from it), although the severity of this seems to depend on the composition of the irrigation water as well.

Urea is very soluble in water but, in the process of dissolving, it reduces the temperature of the water. It is thus difficult to dissolve urea quickly in a small volume of water.

Figure 9.11. Spotty regreening following a foliar spray which contained 1g/L of iron sulfate. Such a spray is a good way to check that iron deficiency is the cause of a chlorosis.

Figure 9.10. Fertilizer injector in use in a drip irrigated vineyard near Berri. Sophisticated equipment like this is not always used. Nutrients can be injected into irrigation lines with a gear pump or by using a pressure restrictor or a venturi device. Alternatively nutrients can be added on the pick-up side of the pump. Back flow protection may be required.

Nitrate-containing fertilizers

When soils are known to be strongly acidic there may be benefits in the use of nitrate fertilizers (calcium nitrate and potassium nitrate) through drip irrigation systems because they do not lead to further acidication.

Urea may enhance the rate of corrosion of metal pipes and sprinklers though not to the extent of ammonium forms of nitrogen. If urea or ammonium fertilizers are injected into irrigation lines it is important that the system be run for sufficient time after injection to ensure removal of the corrosive material from the pipelines.

9.2.2 Phosphorus-containing

The properties of the phosphorus fertilizers that are generally available are summarized in Table 9.4. Phosphorus is present in the form of calcium phosphates but with different solubilities. These forms are represented symbolically as: P_{ws} (denoting water soluble phosphate, which is readily available to plants), P_{cs} (denoting citrate soluble phosphate which is determined using a method which estimates the phosphate that is not

Table 9.4 Fertilizers that contain phosphorus

| Fertilizer | Form of phosphorus and % in each | | | | Other nutrients contained (%) | |
| | Water soluble-P | Citrate soluble-P | Acid soluble-P | Total-P | Sulfur | Total-N |
(Pws)	(Pcs)	(Pas)	(Pt)	(S)	(Nt)	
Superphosphate	7.6	1.0		8.6	11	
Double superphosphate	14.0	2.2	1.3	17.5	4.5	
Triple superphosphate	17.8	2.2	0.7	20.7	1.5	
Mono-ammonium phosphate	19.5-19.8	2.4-2.9	0.1	22-23		10-11.2
Di-ammonium phosphate	17.8	2.2	0.2	20.2	1.5	18
Ground rock phosphate			15.5	15.5		

immediately soluble but is slowly available to plants) and P_{as} (represents phosphate which is soluble in strong acid and largely unavailable to plants in neutral or alkaline soils and only slowly so in acid soils).

In most soils phosphate is strongly held near its site of placement by lime and clay particles; downward movement in the soil solution as it passes through the soil profile is slow (see Table 9.5). This behaviour of phosphorus explains the slow appearance of responses to superphosphate in a fertilizer experiment in Nuriootpa (see later). Soluble forms of applied phosphorus may be rendered insoluble in calcareous soils of high pH (greater than 8.0) and in very acid soils (pH below 5.5). These two aspects of the behaviour of phosphorus in soils are important in viticulture and affect the strategy of superphosphate use in vineyards. To avoid wastage in the cultivated layer of most soils, surface banding or subsurface placement of superphosphate is necessary. Special equipment has been developed for this (see 8.1.3).

If soils are strongly acid (e.g. have pH less than 5.5) rock phosphate rather than superphosphate may be worth using in the ripper furrow but rock phosphate is insoluble in neutral and alkaline soils and for these it is not a suitable fertilizer.

Superphosphate (single) is the phosphate carrier used in many mixed fertilizers. It is usually mixed

with sulfate of ammonia and a potassium carrier (see 9.2.5). Superphosphate also contains considerable quantities of gypsum and is thus a good source of sulfur (11% S). Gypsum is only slowly soluble. A few millimetres of rain are sufficient to leach the phosphate out of the fertilizer granule into the soil and it is gypsum which remains visible on the surface of a soil or in fertilizer bands for long periods after a superphosphate application. Phosphorus-containing fertilizers with concentrations of phosphorus higher than that in single superphosphate are now widely available (Table 9.4). Cost per unit of water-soluble phosphorus should determine which form is used. In areas where transport is an important component of fertilizer cost, high analysis forms may have an important cost advantage.

9.2.3 Potassium-containing

Muriate (chloride) and sulfate of potash are the generally used forms of potassium (see Table 9.6). On the basis of unit cost of potassium, the chloride form is the cheaper. However, before choosing the chloride form one should assess the risk of chloride damage to vines. This risk would not be great except where salty irrigation water has been used or where irrigation or rainfall is insufficient to leach the chloride from the fertilizer through the soil profile and hence away from the root zone. To provide an insight into this danger: 250 kg of muriate of potash would supply 125 kg of chloride; if this were applied to 1 ha of land and

Table 9.5 Concentrations of phosphorus[a] (mg/kg air-dry soil) in the soil profile of the under-vine bank in a vineyard at Padthaway three years after superphosphate had been applied. (from Robinson and McCarthy 1987)

Depth Interval (cm)	Rate of application[b] of superphosphate (t/ha)		
	0	0.5	1.0
0-15	10	56	188
15-30	4	10	6
30-45	4	3	8
45-60	2	3	8

a Phosphorus extracted in 0.5M sodium bicarbonate, 16h shake.
b Rate is expressed on a total vineyard area basis but the superphosphate was applied, in a single dressing, as a band to the undervine bank.

Table 9.6 Fertilizers that contain potassium

Fertilizer	Content of potassium (%)[a] Total-K (K)	Other nutrients contained (%) Sulfur (S)	Total-N (Nt)
Muriate (chloride) of potash	50		
Sulfate of potash	41.5	17	
Potassium nitrate	36.5		13

a Potassium is only available as the potassium ion

dissolved in a 50 mm application of water the increase in chloride concentration in the soil water would be approximately 250 ppm. Apart from this danger, it can be said that muriate and sulfate of potash are interchangeable.

There are other potassium fertilizers available, e.g. as by-products of cement manufacture. Their place in vineyard fertilization has not been assessed experimentally.

Potassium nitrate is usually considered to be too expensive for application to the soil when other forms of K and N are available but it can be used in foliar sprays, supplying both potassium and nitrate-nitrogen. It is also a form of K and N convenient for use in the formulation of liquid fertilizers (often in combination with urea) for use through dripper systems.

It is necessary to caution here that potassium deficiency is seen in Australian vineyards only in a few areas (the Yarra Valley of Vic., the Hunter Valley, NSW, the Granite Belt in Qld and in parts of WA). In fact, high K status in vines appears much more common in other parts of Australia. There is evidence that a high K concentration in juice can have a detrimental effect on the quality of red table wines (see Chapter 3) so local advice should be sought before K fertilizers are applied to vineyards.

9.2.4 Fertilizers for other elements.

Magnesium
Magnesium is available either in the form of dolomitic limestone (approximately 9% Mg), which can be used interchangeably with lime in acid soils, or Epsom salts (magnesium sulfate, 19% magnesium) which is used as a soil application or in foliar sprays (usually at 20 g/L).

Iron
Iron is available as iron sulfate or in a large variety of chelated forms. Unfortunately, it is not possible to correct iron deficiency easily. Soil conditions that lead to iron deficiency usually quickly render soil-applied iron compounds insoluble. Iron chelates can be used but are often too expensive. Iron chelates are forms where the iron is held in an organic complex which protects it against oxidation. If they are to be used, it is important to observe the conditions spelt out on the label, particularly concerning suitability for alkaline soils.

When applied in a foliar spray to grapevine leaves, iron does not move far from where it enters the leaf and spotty regreening occurs (see Figure 9.11). Subsequent growth remains chlorotic. Chelates can be used in foliar sprays but concentrations higher than 1 g/L are likely to cause severe leaf burn.

There are reports from Israel that sprays of iron sulfate at the high concentration of 100 g/L applied to fresh pruning cuts will correct iron deficiency. Swabbing pruning cuts with 250 g/L iron sulfate plus 50 g/L citric acid has also been used with success overseas. When any iron fertilizer is used, a portion of the vineyard should be left untreated to make certain that a spontaneous greening-up (which often occurs as the soil dries out and aeration improves in spring) is not confused with a cure as a result of treatment.

Manganese
Manganese is also applied as a foliar spray to grapevines (at about 1.5 g/L manganese sulfate). Crystalline manganese sulfate monohydrate (28.5% manganese), which is soluble in water, is used. Dissolved (liquid) forms are also available. Foliar application of solutions containing about 0.2-0.3 g/L of actual Mn are used unneutralized and these are achieved by dissolving manganese sulfate in water at 1-1.5 g/L or using an equivalent amount of already dissolved manganese sulfate. Some fungicides (e.g. Mancozeb) contain significant amounts of manganese.

Zinc
The forms of zinc that are commonly available are shown in Table 9.7. A number of approaches to the treatment of zinc deficiency have been used in Australia. Early work led to a recommendation for swabbing of pruning cuts or spraying of dormant vines with quite high concentrations (220 g/L) of zinc sulfate (e.g. Coombe 1964). More dilute foliar sprays with zinc oxide (2 g/L), zinc sulfate (1 g/L) or zinc chelate (as directed) are now used. Dissolved (liquid) formulations of zinc sulfate are available commercially and if chosen should be used as directed on the label. Comparative work has not been done in Australia but in California field studies have not shown any economic advantage of zinc chelates over other forms of zinc (e.g. Christensen and Jensen 1978).

Urea may be added to zinc foliar sprays at 5

Table 9.7 Forms of zinc that are commonly available

Form	Properties	Zn%	Comments
Zinc oxide	Insoluble powder (applied as a suspension)	80	Reacts slowly with moisture and carbon dioxide to supply zinc to leaves.
Zinc sulfate			
—monohydrate	Crystalline	36	Both forms are acid in solution and if used at
—heptahydrate	Crystalline	23	low concentration will not burn foliage.
Zinc chelate (EDTA)	Solution	Varies	Follow label directions.
Dissolved zinc sulfate e.g. Zincsol[R]	Solution	16.7 w/v[a]	Follow label directions.

a w/v means that the percentage concentration is expressed on a weight per volume basis; in this case 16.7 g per 100 mL.

to 7.5 g/L. Some fungicides (e.g. Mancozeb) contain significant amounts of zinc.

Boron

Boron is usually supplied as borax (12% B) or Sprayboron® (21% B) and applied to the soil at a rate of 10 g of borax or 5 g of Sprayboron® per ha every 1 to 3 years, or as a foliar spray (3 g/L) prior to flowering. As there is a thin dividing line between sufficiency and toxicity special care should be taken when deciding to use boron as a fertilizer.

9.2.5 Mixed fertilizers

The previous discussions have been confined to single fertilizers but it is also possible to use mixed or compound fertilizers. As the names suggest, such fertilizers are physical mixtures of some of the materials described above or fertilizers in which the components have been granulated together. The precise nature of the mixtures that are available varies from state to state in Australia. These fertilizers are best described by the percentage of each nutrient contained in them e.g. 10:4:4 contains approximately 10% total nitrogen, 4% phosphorus (water and citrate soluble), and 4% potassium. They are usually mixtures of sulfate of ammonia, superphosphate and sulfate or muriate of potash. More complex mixtures may also include small quantities of trace-elements. An example known to grapegrowers in South Australia is 'Blewitt Springs Mixture' formulated specifically for a group of vineyards on bleached sands (Uc2.2—see Volume 1, Chapter 3) near McLaren Vale, SA. It contains N 0%, P

4.7%, K 13%, S 10.9%, Cu 0.5%, Zn 0.45%, Mn 0.95%, B 0.15%, Mo 0.015%; it can be described as a 0:5:13 mixture plus trace-elements. Because the preparation of mixtures requires extra work on the part of the fertilizer companies, the nutrients contained in them cost more than when purchased singly. These extra costs can be computed as shown in Table 9.8.

There are also 'high analysis' versions of mixed

Table 9.8 Calculation of the money-value of a fertilizer mixture.

The easiest approach is to set the unit cost of N, P and K at the unit costs in their cheapest forms (e.g. urea, superphosphate and muriate of potash).

e.g. *Urea* contains 460 kg N per tonne

$$\frac{local\ price\ per\ tonne}{460} = \frac{unit\ cost\ of\ available\ N}{(\$A/kg).}$$

Superphosphate contains 86 kg P per tonne

$$\frac{local\ price\ per\ tonne}{86} = \frac{unit\ cost\ of\ available}{P\ (\$B/kg).}$$

Muriate of Potash contains 500 kg K per tonne

$$\frac{local\ price\ per\ tonne}{500} = \frac{unit\ cost\ of\ available}{K\ (\$C/kg).}$$

Now one tonne of a compound fertilizer described as 12:5:14 contains

120 kg N worth $A/kg or 120 x $A =	$D
50 kg P worth $B/kg or 50 x $B =	$E
140 kg K worth $C/kg or 140 x $C =	$F
Total =	$G

Whereas 1 tonne of 12:5:14 cost $H

$H – $G = the extra cost of buying the mixed fertilizer

fertilizers that contain components such as triple superphosphate (which is about 18% P) or one of the ammonium phosphates and granulated urea. Some are imported but locally manufactured versions are also available. In these, as in all fertilizers, it is important that the relative costs of the applied nutrients are calculated.

9.2.6 Organic fertilizers

Apart from the inorganic fertilizers described above a number of organic materials are available that can be used with advantage in vineyards (see also Chapter 8). They are listed in Table 9.9 together with the amounts of individual nutrients that they contain. Two points are important in the use of these materials:

1. The nutrients they contain are usually in an insoluble form (except for K) and in consequence organic fertilizers are best incorporated in the soil where micro-organisms can break them down and achieve a slow conversion of the nutrients to soluble forms and release N and P to the soil solution.

2. They are bulky and usually expensive to transport and spread. Consequently distant supplies are seldom worth considering.

The cost of the components of these materials should be compared with those in inorganic carriers (see 9.2.1-9.2.5 above) before decisions are made to use them. With a little super-phosphate, and perhaps nitrogen, considerable quantities of organic materials can be grown as

Table 9.9 The approximate nutrient content of commonly available organic materials suitable for use in vineyards

Material	Bagged fertilizer equivalent (N:P:K)	Actual Analysis N P K (kg per tonne of material)		
Winery marc	1.6:0.3:3	16	3	28
Fowl manure (deep litter)	2.5:1:1.5	25	12	15
Fowl manure (cage)	4:3:2	40	30	16
Blood and bone	4:4:0	40	40	—

a Organic materials are notoriously variable in nutrient content—analysis by a local laboratory is worth considering to determine the work of a particular material.

Table 9.10 Comparative petiole nitrate concentrations (%, dry weight basis)

Season	Organic matter applied	No organic matter applied	Probability P[a]
1979-80	0.76±0.13(20)[b]	0.39±0.06(29)	P<0.05
1980-81	1.30±0.19(15)	0.60±0.09(24)	P<0.01
1981-82	1.0±0.11(11)	0.46±0.07(40)	P<0.01

Petioles sampled from vineyards that had received organic matter dressings in the winter prior to sampling compared with those that had not (Robinson and McCarthy 1985).
a Mann Whitney U test.
b Mean ± s.e. (number of vineyards).

'green manure crops' and cultivated into the soil as a substitute for bagged organic materials (see Chapter 8). Survey work in the Barossa Valley has found that vineyards in which organic materials were used had higher petiole nitrate concentrations than did vineyards in which they were not used (Table 9.10). This may reflect the 'slow release' nature of organic nitrogen.

9.2.7 Foliar fertilizers

Many materials are most suited to application in foliar-sprays. Most of them are micronutrients (e.g. see zinc and manganese above) which, if allowed to come into contact with the soil, may under some conditions be rapidly immobilized and wasted. Nitrogen, potassium and magnesium can also be applied to grape foliage. Urea sprays (concentration 5-7.5 g/L) are often used in vineyards and potassium nitrate, at a rate of about 10 g/L, has also successfully corrected K deficiency. Epsom salts at a concentration of 20 g/L has also been used to correct magnesium deficiency and, in the treatment of bunchstem necrosis, concentrations as high as 50 g/L have been used.

Phosphorus is not absorbed easily by the leaves of grapevines — the spray solution needs to be acid (pH less than 4.6) (see Bester and Meynhardt 1968), and the technique has not been developed commercially. The concentrations of materials and the nutrient concentrations required in the spray-tank solutions for successful use of individual foliar nutrients are summarized in Table 9.11.

'Complete' foliar sprays are commercially available. These are often claimed to be suitable to correct macro- and micronutrient deficiencies

Table 9.11 Concentrations of nutrients in the spray-tank for successful foliar fertilization

Nutrient	Carrier	Concentration of carrier in spray Mixture (g/L)	Concentration of nutrient in spray Mixture (g/L)
Nitrogen	Urea	10	4.6
	Potassium nitrate	10	1.3
Potassium	Potassium nitrate	10	4.4
Magnesium	Epsom salts	20	2.0
Zinc	Zinc oxide[a]	2	1.6
	Zinc sulfate[a] (neutralized)	5	1.0
	Zinc sulfate (unneutralized)	1	0.3
Manganese	Manganese sulfate	2.5	0.2
Iron	Sequestrene[R]	1	0.06
Commercial foliar spray	N	(Manufacturer's recommended dilution 2.5-4 mL/L	0.37 (approx.)
	K		0.24 (approx.)
	Mg		— (approx.)
	Zn		0.0144 (approx.)
	Mn		0.0144 (approx.)
	Fe		

a These forms are slowly soluble on the leaf surface.

or to supplement other approaches to nutrition. However, it is worth comparing the concentrations of N, K, Mg, Zn, Mn and Fe achieved in the spray-tank using a typical example at the manufacturer's recommended concentrations with those rates known to be effective for individual nutrients (Table 9.11). These materials are costly and in general, if responses are achieved, it is likely that the vines would have been in a poor condition prior to the application.

The most successful time to apply nutrients to plant leaves is determined by the weather conditions. The longer the spray droplets or film remain unevaporated on the leaf surface the better the penetration of the nutrient. This is best achieved in the early morning or late afternoon, and on cool, overcast, still days when evaporation is low. Both surfaces of leaves should be wetted and a surfactant should be used. Most foliar nutrients can be applied together with insecticide or fungicide sprays but care should be taken if chelates are included; for example, copper may displace iron from the protecting molecule. When in doubt read the label or check with the manufacturer. Not a lot of work has been done

on the desirable spray volume but high volume sprays (1169 L/ha) were more successful than low volume (234 L/ha) sprays in treating zinc deficiency in California (Christensen and Jensen 1978).

When 'concentrate' spraying of insecticides or fungicides is carried out it is usual practice to apply the same rate of chemical on a per hectare basis as is used with high-volume equipment but in a smaller volume of water. If this approach is used with foliar nutrients, there is a small risk of leaf burn. It would be wise to check the label or with the manufacturer when deciding on the concentration of nutrient in the spray tank for use in 'concentrate' or low-volume spray machinery.

9.3 Determining the need for fertilizers

There are a number of quite diverse approaches to the matter of deciding if particular fertilizers are needed by grapevines in any given situation. The methods range from careful observation (foliage and fruit symptoms, plant associations, district practice), through field experiments, to chemical analysis of either grape tissue or of the soil. Usually several methods are employed together.

9.3.1 Symptoms of deficiency

In Section 9.1 the elements needed by grapevines and the symptoms that result from their deficiency were considered. Photographs of deficiency symptoms in Sultana vines have been published by Woodham and Alexander (1970). Knowing these symptoms, and observing closely the health of vines, it is possible to make decisions on the use of many nutrients—particularly zinc, manganese, boron and iron. However the following precautions may help avoid misleading conclusions:

1. Sporadic appearance of symptoms should not be taken seriously. Odd vines or arms of vines will often show symptoms but the cause may not be primarily related to nutrition—root or bark damage, and girdling with the trellis wire are examples.

2. It is important to differentiate between nutritional symptoms and those due to virus disease, e.g. leafroll virus causes symptoms that can be confused with potassium or magnesium deficiencies.

3. It is important to learn where changes of soil type occur within vineyards. Some areas may be shallow, some sandy, some limey, some poorly-drained, etc. Each of such soils may be associated with a different problem.

There are limitations to the usefulness of deficiency symptoms as a guide to the need for nutrients. Mild deficiencies may affect grapevine performance without displaying obvious symptoms e.g. for zinc deficiency, visible symptoms on leaves represent an acute part of the deficiency syndrome: 'hidden hunger' is more usual. Once symptoms have appeared, the damage has often been done. Multiple deficiencies (more than one deficiency present at the one time) are often difficult to diagnose from the symptoms. Symptoms developed in greenhouse vines may not match those seen in the field.

9.3.2 Soil/plant relationships

A knowledge of the soils within a vineyard and of their general and local properties often provides enough information to allow prediction of nutrient status. These points are detailed in Volume 1, Chapter 3, but some are worth emphasizing.

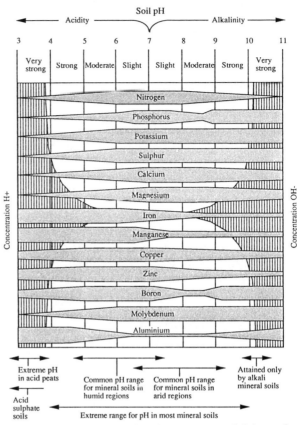

Figure 9.12. Effect of soil pH on availability of minerals. The width of each bar at any particular pH value shows relative potential availability. Most vineyard soils have pHs between 4.5 and 8.5. (Diagram by A.M. Alston)

1. Most Australian soils are low in both total and plant-available phosphorus.

2. Sands do not hold nutrients well against leaching by downward-percolating water. On these soils deficiencies of both macro- and micronutrients can and do occur (B in Qld, Cu in WA, Zn and Mn in SA and Vic.).

3. Acid soil conditions (pH less than 5.5) may render phosphates unavailable, whereas micronutrients are usually readily available and in some cases (Mn, Al) may be available to the plants in toxic quantities.

4. Alkaline soils (pH greater than 8.0) may also render phosphates insoluble and most micronutrients are converted to unavailable forms (see Figure 9.12).

5. If free lime is present in the soil, particularly if it is finely divided, iron deficiency may be

induced in vines. This is worse if the soil is badly drained or compacted and not well aerated.

6. Most Australian grape soils seem to provide adequate potassium except in isolated areas (see earlier).

This sort of information can be used to develop good rule-of-thumb fertilizer programs for many areas and has been the basis for the district recommendations that have evolved in each of the Australian grapegrowing areas.

9.3.3 District practice
District practice as a basis for making fertilizer decisions has the drawback that it tends to be a synthesis of probability and opinion and is often complicated by fashion and the influence of the salesman. A major difficulty is that usually growers do not know whether a nutrient that is being applied is necessary or superfluous. More objective methods are needed. One such method is to compare district practice with other practices in a replicated experiment, preferably within commercial vineyards. Another is to investigate comprehensively the nutrient element status of vines in a number of vineyards in the district. Both of these methods are considered below.

9.3.4 Field experiments
A few fertilizer experiments have been carried out on grapevines in Australia. The best known is the experiment at the Nuriootpa Viticultural Station of the SA Department of Agriculture and those carried out over many years by CSIRO research workers in Sunraysia (Vic., NSW) and the SA Riverland. Field experiments are currently in progress in South Australia, Victoria and Western Australia.

The Nuriootpa experiment is described by Tulloch and Harris (1970) and Seeliger and French (1971). It was laid out in 1944 in a non-irrigated vineyard on a Dr2.23 soil with a sandy/loam surface (Volume 1, Chapter 3). Annual dressings of sulfate of ammonia (3 cwt/acre = 375 kg/ha) superphosphate (2 cwt/acre = 250 kg/ha) and potassium sulfate (1 cwt/acre = 125 kg/ha) were applied separately and in combinations. No effects of treatment on yield were seen for 8 years; thereafter a significant yield increase in response to superphosphate occurred. This was maintained in subsequent years and the yield response was

found to be due to an increase in fruit set (Table 9.1). The delay in the response reflected the slow movement of phosphorus through the cultivated layer into the root zone. After 10 years of ammonium sulfate applications a reduction in vine vigour was seen and by 14 years yield was reduced. This is thought to be due to an indirect effect on phosphorus availability due to soil acidification which in turn was caused by repeated ammonium sulfate application. No responses to potassium fertilizer use were recorded except in one year.

In irrigated vineyards in the Murray Valley, on the other hand, trials set up by the CSIRO Merbein Research Station in each of the dried fruits districts along the Murray River of south-eastern Australia showed occasional yield increases following superphosphate application (Alexander and Woodham 1958). These increases were attributed to an indirect response due to improved cover crop growth, not to superphosphate directly, as had been shown by Walters (1942). Yield responses of about 10% were consistently achieved with 250-500 kg/ha applications of sulfate of ammonia. In other experiments long-term superphosphate applications in these areas were shown to induce zinc deficiency which, if left untreated, actually reduced yields (Alexander and Woodham 1964). The amounts of superphosphate applied were, however, extremely high.

These apparently conflicting results present an acute dilemma: to apply or not to apply superphosphate or nitrogen? In hindsight the problem is more basic. We do not know how well-supplied were the vines in the River districts or the Barossa with nitrogen, phosphorus and potassium at the time of these fertilizer trials. Furthermore responses to fertilizers in rainfall areas may be masked by drought and in all areas by pruning severity. No effort was made at the time to assess the general applicability of these fertilizer trials.

9.3.5 Tissue analysis
Tissue analysis provides the most promise for an objective guide to the nutrient status and fertilizer needs of grapevines, within and between districts, and between countries. Tissue analysis could have proved valuable in sorting out the above-

mentioned dilemma. The grapevines in the trial area at Nuriootpa may have been so well-supplied with N and K that no responses could have been expected; those on the Murray may have been well-supplied with P and K yet low in N due to soil characteristics and residual P availability. The lack of response to P in the specific vineyards in Sunraysia could have been because they had received adequate superphosphate before the experiments were started.

The first problem with any tissue analysis system is the choice of the organ or part to sample. Over the years some rules have been developed with woody perennial crops. The tissue:

— must be easy to identify and collect
— must provide easily reproducible results
— should be taken at a time when its chemical composition is changing slowly.

Viticulturists around the world or within Australia are not unanimous in their choice of tissue. The French Diagnostic Foliare laboratory at Montpellier relied upon two samples from each vineyard (one just at the end of flowering, the other at veraison) and compared a numerical average of the composition at the two sampling times with standards. They collected blade and petiole (leaf stalk) together from a node near the base of the cane. The Californian workers generally use petioles taken opposite a bunch at flowering which they term the 'bloomtime petiole'. Both these techniques are described in Cook (1966). In South Africa basal leaf blades are collected in January just before veraison (Beyers, 1962).

These three sampling methods were compared over a number of irrigated vineyards in the Loxton area by Robinson et al. (1978). The results pointed out the pitfalls in the too rigid use of tissue analysis in grapevines. The pitfalls relate to:

— differences in nutrient content from year to year,
— differences in nutrient content between varieties, and
— differences in interpretation between sets of standards.

If decisions had been based on the French method many vineyards would have been assessed as needing higher rates of nitrogen- and phosphorus-containing fertilizers. If the South African standards were used, most vineyards

Table 9.12   Collecting and handling grapevine tissue samples.

Sampling units (P or L)[a]:
  Petioles (leaf stalks, P) or Laminae (leaf blades, L) from basal leaves opposite bunches.
Sampling times (F or V)[a]:
  F: As near to full bloom (70% capfall) as possible;
  V: at veraison when berries begin to change colour.
To obtain a representative sample from the vineyard:
  Collect 100 petioles or laminae along a systematic traverse through each variety. An up and back track is followed selecting a leaf from vines evenly spaced along pairs of rows (see Figure 9.12a.)
  Areas with atypical soils, drainage problems, disease etc. should be excluded or sampled separately.
  Different varieties should be samples separately.
Sample handling:
  Petioles or laminae are held in paper bags in the icebox or refrigerator until they are packaged and mailed to the laboratory (where they are dried and ground to a powder). Samples should be collected early in the day (before leaves become stressed) and early in the week (so they can be processed by the laboratory before the weekend). Samples should not be taken immediately after overhead irrigation.

a P/F = petioles-at-flowering
   P/V = petioles-at-veraison
   L/F = laminae-at-flowering
   L/V = laminae-at-veraison

would have been assessed as receiving adequate quantities of N, P and K, but the standard ranges are very broad; and if those developed in California were used, the assessment would have been that adequate quantities of N and P and too large quantities of K were being used.

The conclusion drawn from the work was that the Californian method provided answers which correspond with local experience and with the results of the work of CSIRO, and can be used with some confidence. In dryland (rainfall) areas, data from the manurial trial on the Nuriootpa Viticultural Station also support the choice of petioles-at-flowering as the sampling unit. The untreated plots in that vineyard contained 0.14% P and 2.5% K, suggesting that a response to P and not to K might be expected. This is in fact what happened. After 20 years of fertilizer treatment the nutrient concentration in petioles-at-flowering from P treated plots was 0.45% P and from K treated plots 2.9% K. Nitrate (NO_3) analyses of petiole samples from this trial also

Table 9.13 Guidelines for nutrient concentrations in grapevine leaf tissue samples[a]

Nutrient (Units on dry weight basis)	Tissue (see Table 9.12)	Concentration Range					Toxic or Excessive	Comments
		Deficient	Marginal	Critical	Adequate	High		
NO₃-N (mg/kg)	P/F	<340	340-500		500-1200	>1200		Californian 'possibly toxic' range (> 2000 mg/kg NO₃-N) not supported by field observation in SA or WA. Field trials in progress. Data should be interpreted carefully. In many cases vigour may provide a more appropriate index of N status.
			OR					
NO₃(%)	P/F	>0.15	0.15-0.22		0.22-0.53	<0.53		
N (%)	L/F			2.9	3.9-5.0			
	L/V			1.6	2.2-4.0			
P(%)	P/F	<0.15	0.15-0.20	Approx. 0.2-0.3	0.2-0.46	>0.46		Responsive vines in SA had values above 0.1%, hence the critical value of 0.2%. Experience in WA shows vines with petiole P of 0.2-0.3% will respond to P fertilizer. High range (>0.46%) arbitrarily derived from single season's data at Nuriootpa, SA.
	L/F			0.18	0.25-0.4			
	L/V			0.12	0.15-0.3			
K(%)	P/F	<1.0	1.0-1.5		>1.5			Very high values (>4.0%) observed in SA do not suggest that toxicity is a valid concept. When deficiency is suspected, sample again 6-8 weeks later; select the blade of the most recently matured leaf. A value of <0.5% in petiole or 0.8% in blade plus petiole (WA) confirms deficiency. Work is in progress in WA and Vic.
	L/F			0.8	1.0-1.8			
	P/V	<0.6		1.0	1.2-3.0			
	L/V			0.6	0.8-1.6			
Ca(%)	P/F				1.2-2.5			
	L/V				1.8-3.2			
Mg(%)	P/F	<0.2	0.2-0.3		>0.3			
	L/F				0.3-0.6			
	L/V			0.2	0.3-0.6			
Na(%)	P/F						>0.5	
	P/V			0.5	0.1-0.4	0.5-0.6	>0.6	
	L/V			0.2	<0.1		>0.5	
Cl(%)	P/F						>1.0 or 1.5	Higher values than are used in California, based on survey work in SA.
	P/V			1.8	<1.5	1.8-2.0	>2.0	
	L/V			1.7	<1.3			

continued next page

Table 9.13 continued

Nutrient (Units on dry weight basis)	Tissue (see Table 9.12)	Deficient	Marginal	Critical	Adequate	High	Toxic or Excessive	Comments
Cu (mg/kg)	P/F	< 3	3-6		> 6			Contamination with foliar sprays is possible
	L/F			5	10-300			
	L/V			5	10-300			
Zn (mg/kg)	P/F	< 15	15-26		> 26			Contamination with foliar sprays is possible
	L/F			30	35-60			
	L/V	< 19		25	30-60			
Mn (mg/kg)	P/F	< 20	20-25		> 25			Contamination with foliar sprays is possible
	L/V			20	25-200			
B (mg/kg)	P/F	< 25	26-30		30-100		> 100	If a value in the toxic range is obtained, follow up with a blade analysis. (Value > 300 mg/kg confirms toxicity).
	L/V			25	35-100		> 300	

a These standards were established as follows:
P/F — Californian standards of Cook (1966) and Christensen *et al.* (1978) modified following survey work in South Australia by Robinson and McCarthy (1985). Other useful references include Cook and Kishaba (1956) and Robinson *et al.* (1978). Further work is in progress in Western Australia (J.E.L. Cripps and B.H. Goldspink personal communication; Goldspink 1987) and Victoria (K. Peverill personal communication; Brown 1987).
L/F and L/V — Synthesis of diagnostic records and unpublished survey results in NSW (R.G. Weir 1987).

support the choice of this organ: petioles from untreated plots contained about 0.8% NO_3 and from N treated plots 1.4%. No response to nitrogen would have been expected from vines with these levels (Cook's standard range is 0.25-0.75% NO_3) and the vines which had received nitrogen had NO_3 concentrations that could be considered toxic. N.B. The concentration of nitrate is expressed in two ways, % or ppm (see Table 9.13); ppm nitrate nitrogen equals 2258 × % nitrate; ppm and mg/kg are the same unit.

Further survey work in SA (e.g. Robinson and McCarthy 1985) has led to a development of some working standards based on samples of petioles collected during the flowering period (see Table 9.13). The major area of uncertainty in these standards is with nitrate-nitrogen as a measure of vineyard nutrient status. The variation between growers in their expectations of capacity and vigour of their vines may make it impossible to define a best nitrogen status that applies to all conditions. In any table of standards the footnotes are as important as the standard ranges (see, for example, the different critical value for phosphorus derived from work by Goldspink in WA).

Additional comparisons of some different approaches to diagnostic tissue analyses for grapevines have been made in NSW (Weir 1987). Samples of both leaf laminae and petioles were taken at flowering and at veraison. The standards for petioles-at-flowering agree with those obtained in SA. Petiolar tissue gave better assessments of potassium deficiency and chloride and sodium toxicities, lamina tissue for deficiencies of nitrogen, magnesium, zinc, boron (and toxicity), calcium, copper, manganese and iron (see Table 9.13). There has been renewed effort in recent years put into understanding the nitrogen needs of vineyards, stimulated by a need, in Europe at least, to minimize nitrogen losses from the vineyard eco-system. For a detailed up-to-date summary of this work, see the symposium proceedings edited by Rantz (1991).

Work is continuing on methods of sampling and standards for interpreting tissue analysis in vineyards in Australia (see Lee and Freeman 1987). Evidence is developing that standards will need to be refined to cope with differences between varieties, rootstocks and even with different irrigation, training methods and canopy exposure.

There are four ways in which tissue analysis is useful:

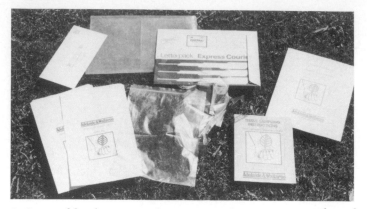

Figure 9.13. A typical commercial tissue analysis kit includes a mailer bag to send samples to the laboratory, paper bags to hold samples and field sheets which provide the background information to allow interpretation of the data. Items such as plastic gloves to minimize contamination while collecting the sample are optional.

1. In trouble shooting: when vine performance is below expectations yet problems in all other aspects of management have been ruled out (e.g. pests, diseases, soil conditions, irrigation frequency, etc.) it may point to a deficiency or toxicity which can then be treated. For this purpose a single analysis can be useful. Sometimes a comparison between 'good' and 'bad' areas of a vineyard is helpful.

2. To provide reassurance: alterations in cost structures, changes in irrigation systems and curiosity are among the reasons for deciding to check present fertilizer practice using tissue analysis. Sampling over two or three years may provide information which suggests an alteration in fertilizer practice or shows the need for the use of a fertilizer not previously considered necessary.

3. To monitor the effectiveness of a chosen nutritional program: normally two or more seasons of sampling are needed to take account of year by year variations. Data on tissue analysis should be obtained in all grape fertilizer experiments to permit extrapolation of the results to grapes in other soil types and other districts.

4. To define problems on a district-wide basis. The use of tissue analysis in surveys can identify problems not previously suspected.

A tissue analysis guide is outlined in Tables 9.12 and 9.13. The contents of a commercial tissue analysis kit are shown in Figure 9.13.

9.3.6 Soil Analysis

'Soil analysis' has been an attractive concept to horticulturists and soil scientists. Soil tests do not provide an absolute assessment of soil fertility, rather they give an index of the availability of particular nutrients which should be calibrated with crop response in fertilizer experiments. The difficulties involved in using soil analysis for the diagnosis of fertilizer needs are formidable even for an annual crop with a limited root system. For perennial plants like grapevines the task has been impossible. The main reason is that the roots of a grapevine explore a large volume of soil that can vary greatly in chemical composition even over short distances and it is not easy to obtain *representative* samples of this soil.

On the positive side, soil analysis has been helpful in predicting where acidity, alkalinity, salinity or toxic agents are likely to present hazards to grapevines. It has also allowed understanding of the P requirements of leguminous cover crops in Sunraysia and has explained the delayed appearance of a response to superphosphate at Nuriootpa. Soil analyses for pH (acidity/alkalinity), for salinity, for boron (with respect to toxicity) and for lime content have some direct predictive value for viticulture (see Chapters 7 and 8).

The potential availability of other nutrients is much more successfully assessed by watching for deficiency symptoms or by analysing the grapevine's tissues. There are a number of soil testing procedures in use in Australia. It is important to know which extraction method has been used before interpretation is attempted.

A sample of soil for analysis must be taken with care, otherwise results will be misleading. Surface samples (0-15 cm) are satisfactory for assessments of cover crop behaviour. They should be taken from the inter-row space with an auger or tube sampler and should be made up of at least 20 separate sub-samples taken along a zig-zag passage through the vineyard. If the soil type

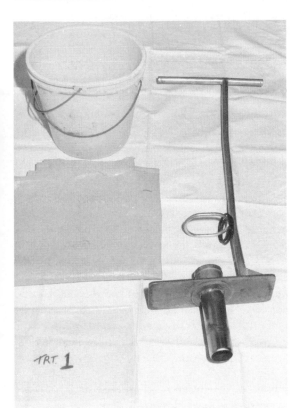

Figure 9.14. Equipment required for the collection of soil samples for testing includes a core sampler (15 cm depth × 50 mm diameter), a bucket in which to place the 20 or more cores collected, a plastic sheet for mixing and a plastic bag to hold the sub-sample which is to be sent to the laboratory. Thorough mixing is essential since as little as 1g of soil will be analysed. An auger is needed to take samples from depth in the rootzone.

the soil type varies across the vineyard, separate groups of samples should be taken from each area. The 20 or more sub-samples should be mixed thoroughly together on a plastic sheet (old fertilizer bags should not be used since contamination will give useless results) and a sub-sample of about 500 g removed and placed in a plastic bag (see Figure 9.14).

Samples representing the bottom of the root zone (e.g. for salinity) should be taken with an auger over the depth interval 90-100 cm in all but the shallowest soils. Again the larger the number of samples the better: 6-12 are usually taken to represent a problem area. They should be mixed in the field and sub-sampled as above

Table 9.14   Soil analysis values of relevance to viticulture

Phosphorus (P)	(a) In surface soil (0-15 cm) of Calcareous Earths and other soils (where pH is above 7.5-8.0) concentrations of 0.5M sodium bicarbonate-extractable P (Colwell, 1965 method)[a] above about 30 ppm are adequate for the growth of legume cover crops.
	(b) In the rootzone (15-30 cm) of neutral to acid soils, 50 ppm extractable P (Brays No. 1) is adequate for vine growth, but this figure is probably an over-estimate.
pH	Vines will grow over the range pH 4 to pH 8.5 but values lower than 5.5 may result in reduced yields through a depressing effect on P availability; aluminium and manganese toxicity is also possible. High pH (above 8.0) may be associated with zinc, manganese and iron unavailability.
Salinity	Electrical conductivity of the saturation extract (ECe) much above 4 dSiemens/m at the bottom of the rootzone poses a salinity hazard.
Boron	Boron levels in the saturation extract greater than 0.7 mg/L are dangerously high.
Lime requirement	Where cover crop behaviour is sub-standard and soils are acid, liming may be of value. There are various techniques for estimating lime requirements used in different parts of Australia. Soils officers with local knowledge should be consulted.

a N.B. The Colwell method involves a 16 h extraction time.

or, if finances allow, analysed separately. Some soil analysis values that are relevant to viticulture are tabulated in Table 9.14.

A wide range of commercial and government laboratories offer soil and plant analysis services. Interpretation should be done by someone familiar with the soils of the district in question. It is extremely important to know which soil analysis procedures are being used because the quantities of nutrients extracted by different methods vary widely, and should be compared with appropriate standard values.

9.4 Application of mineral nutrients in vineyards.

9.4.1 Methods of nutrient application.

The method of application should be chosen in light of knowledge of the behaviour of the nutrient (see section 9.2).

1. Broadcasting—involves manually or mechanically spreading the fertilizer material evenly over the surface of the soil. This method is used for nitrogen (applied for the vine) and superphosphate (applied for volunteer cover crops). Tractor-mounted equipment is available to carry out this operation. Contract spreading is available in many districts. Spreading by hand from truck or trailer can also achieve the even distribution required but at a higher labour cost.

2. Banding is a modification of broadcasting involving placement of the fertilizer in narrow bands (sometimes in opened furrows) adjacent to the vine row or to the undervine bank. Superphosphate and potassium fertilizers applied in this way saturate fixation sites in the surface of the soil and are able to move further through the soil profile resulting in higher concentrations of available nutrient in parts of the root zone. Machinery can be adjusted to do this.

3. Subsurface placement—involves ripping the fertilizer into the root zone to a depth of 15-30 cm below the surface to avoid wastage of nutrient in the surface horizons. Rippers have been developed to do this.

4. Drilling with seed—when the cover crop is sown, fertilizer may be applied through the fertilizer box on the drill, as with normal broad-acre crops.

5. Through sprinklers—urea and other soluble fertilizers may be applied through sprinkler systems either by pumping a concentrated solution into the delivery side of the irrigation pump (e.g. with the high pressure gear-pump on a spray tank), or by installing a venturi device to pick up the solution on the low pressure side of the pump. This method of application is the equivalent of broadcasting in that the material is applied to the whole vineyard area. Application should be stopped before the irrigation stops to ensure that the fertilizer is washed into the root zone but not leached past the roots, and that the fertilizer is not left in the irrigation lines at shutdown. A problem with this method is in achieving rapid solution of the fertilizer, but specially designed equipment is available. Uneven water distribution will result in uneven fertilizer distribution.

6. Through drippers—urea, potassium nitrate and other soluble fertilizer materials can be applied through drip systems. This method is of particular value during the establishment of a vineyard. Special equipment is available to meter concentrated stock solution into the irrigation stream. Cheaper devices can be made in the workshop, care being taken to make an apparatus strong enough to withstand the pressure in the irrigation lines. If the material is metered-in on the pickup side of the pump the dispenser does not have to withstand high pressure.

Fertilizer materials are classed as mildly toxic by water supply authorities. If there is a sudden pressure drop in the system (e.g. as a result of a power failure or a break in the main line) it is possible for concentrated nutrient stock solution to be sucked back down a supply line and find its way into potable water supplies drawn from the same system. To prevent contamination of this kind, backflow prevention is needed whenever nutrient injection is in progress. In some cases (e.g. where water supplies are drawn from the mains of public utilities) backflow prevention may be mandatory and the method and acceptable equipment prescribed in some detail.

7. Foliar sprays—dissolved material (e.g. urea, zinc and manganese sulfates) and fine suspensions (e.g. zinc oxide) can be applied to vine foliage alone or in combination with insecticides and fungicides. Concentrations higher than those specified may cause leaf burn. Early in the season 450 L/ha will adequately wet both sides of the foliage but as the season progresses proportionally more spray (up to 1500L/ha) will be needed. More concentrated solutions can be applied with air blast sprayers but as a rule-of-thumb care must be taken to apply about the same amount of nutrient per unit area as with high volume sprayers (see earlier comment). The weather conditions suited to successful foliar applications are described above (9.2.7).

8. Expression of rates of nutrient applications—

different methods are used to express rates of application of nutrients as follows:

— For broadcasting, deep placement and banding rates are expressed as quantity of nutrient or fertilizer per unit area (hectare) of vineyard.

— For treatment of cover crops rates are expressed per unit area sown (i.e. in relation to the drill setting) and are thus about 1/3 lower if expressed per unit area of vineyard.

— For foliar sprays concentrations are expressed as concentration of material in the spray-tank or mass of material applied per hectare.

9.4.2 A fertilizer program

From this chapter and also Volume 1, Chapter 3 it should be clear that there can be no single fertilizer program that is suited to all viticultural areas in Australia. Within each area soils vary and hence fertilizer programs must vary. Examples of specific fertilizer programs have been given by Hawson (1971) and Hawson and Webber (1971) for Sunraysia, by Taylor and Winks (1976) for Queensland and by Robinson and McCarthy (1984) for South Australia. Local extension literature is the best place to find these specific recommendations.

It is important to distinguish two approaches to fertilizer use, viz. the corrective approach where a large quantity of a nutrient is applied to provide a reserve of the nutrient in the soil sufficient to last for many years, and the maintenance approach where enough nutrient is supplied regularly (e.g. annually) to supply the on-going needs of the plant. The best example of a corrective approach is that which is taken with superphosphate when 1-2 t/ha is ripped into the planting line or applied as a band along a permanent undervine bank and no more phosphate is applied for many years. An example of a maintenance application is the routine zinc spray that is applied before flowering.

The approaches that should be used for each nutrient are tabulated briefly in Table 9.15 and discussed below.

Nitrogen

In most areas of Australia, except those with high rainfall or sandy soils, legume-rich cover crops or volunteer winter growth will supply the vines with sufficient nitrogen. Nitrogenous fertilizers should then only be used as follows:

1. New vineyards. It is vital to keep the newly planted rootling growing vigorously—nitrogen applications during this period are essential (see Chapter 2). The young vine has a small root system and is probably getting more water than it needs so its roots are growing in a leached soil. Nitrogen must therefore be applied regularly. The equivalent of about 3 g of actual N per vine per month is needed (reference to Table 9.3 will aid calculation of the amount of each N fertilizer this represents). This nitrogen can be applied daily or weekly with drip systems and less frequently but prior to irrigation where sprinkler or furrow systems of watering are used. It should be applied to a square metre or so around the base of the vine.

2. Established vineyards. In Europe, nitrogen has been applied routinely at high rates, e.g. 100 kg N per ha; such high rates are quite unnecessary in Australia. In the Sunraysia/Riverland and other areas nitrogen is needed in some situations—30-40 kg of N per hectare will give small yield responses in some years. In sandy soils responses are likely to be more predictable and it is in these situations elsewhere in Australia that nitrogenous fertilizers should be considered (see also drip irrigation). Where good legume-based winter cover crops are grown extra nitrogen is not likely to be needed.

Excess nitrogen is detrimental to grapevines as it may reduce set and induce vigorous vegetative growth which may indirectly reduce fruitfulness and cause disease build-up in bunches. The acidifying effects on the soil of some nitrogenous fertilizers should also be remembered (see 9.2.1). Foliar application of urea at 5 g/L, particularly in the pre-flowering zinc spray, is common in South Australia in the belief that it assists in the uptake of zinc. Where vines are well-supplied with N this practice is of doubtful value. Unthrifty vines may benefit, but where N levels are adequate the extra nitrogen may cause problems.

3. Drip irrigation. It is clear that vines irrigated with drip systems quickly become nitrogen deficient if N is not supplied through the irrigation system. Fertilizer trial work has not been done, but a constant feed of about 30 ppm actual N in the irrigation stream or monthly applications to an annual total of about 30-50 kg actual N per hectare per year seem to be satisfactory. Work is currently underway on the timing of nitrogen fertilizer. There is a good argument for postharvest applications in addition to those made during rapid growth, but the results to date have been conflicting.

Table 9.15 A summary of vine fertilizer requirements

Nutrient	Main considerations	Strategy	Preplanting	Young vines
Nitrogen	Easily leached in sandy soils May reduce soil pH when used over a number of years	Maintenance (annually or more frequently)	Nil	Apply 3g of actual nitrogen per vine (see p.201) per month to soil near base of rootling. or Use about 30ppm actual N in drip feed
Phosphorus	Most Australian soils are natively low in phosphorus. Phosphorus is relatively immobile in most soils. Where fertilizers have been used in the past, residual phosphorus may be high enough to supply vines for many years.	Corrective (as required)	If needed deep place 0.5-1.0 tonne of superphosphate per hectare. Rip into planting line 15-40cm deep or apply 0.5 to 1.0 tonne of superphosphate to the undervine bank in a narrow band.	Nil
Potassium	Adequate K present in most soils. Excessive K can have a detrimental effect on red wine quality. Potassium fertilizer is needed in specific areas.	Corrective or maintenance	If needed deep place 1-2 tonne of sulfate of potash into planting line on K fixing soils, otherwise side-dress.	Nil except where light sands mean maintenance K dressings are needed. Then use a mixed fertilizer to apply both N and K e.g. 8:4:8 or equivalent at about 40g/vine/month.
Magnesium	Adequate Mg is present in most soils. In glasshouses previously used for tomatoes etc. high soil K status may induce Mg deficiency.	Corrective or maintenance	Apply dolomite and incorporate into soil. The rate should be determined on the basis of a lime requirement or soil test.	Nil
Zinc	Zinc is rendered unavailable in many calcareous soils, and is absent in leached soils. Zinc deficiency may reduce fruitset without causing deficiency symptoms on leaves.	Maintenance (annually)	Nil	Zinc sulfate sprays (1g/L) or zinc incorporated into compatible insecticide and fungicidal sprays.

Mature vines	Special considerations
In some areas e.g. Riverland/Sunraysia and leached sands elsewhere annual dressings of 30-60kg/ha of actual nitrogen can be used to maintain vigour. This can be applied as a broadcast application or in frequent doses via a drip irrigation system. Foliar sprays of 5g urea/litre are used with micro nutrients in some areas. In areas with loams and clay soils vigour may be satisfactory with lower rates of N or no applications at all. However, if drip irrigation is used watch vigour closely.	Higher rates of N may help where vigour is poor due to other factors (e.g. nematode attack). If the legume component of winter growth in the vineyard is high this may supply enough nitrogen for the vines. Drip irrigated mature vines need N to compensate for the leaching effect of the point source irrigation.
If vines have received deep-placed P or have had regular applications of superphosphate over many years there may be no need to supplement the supply. Need can be determined with petiole analysis. If they have not, then apply 0.5 to 1.0 tonne of superphosphate to the permanent undervine bank or 1-2 tonne of superphosphate per hectare can be ripped into the mid row area to a depth of 15-40 cm.	A check should be made on the residual value of P before heavy super dressings are applied i.e. If planting is taking place in improved country, plant vines, analyse petioles for P, then decide to apply superphosphate if needed. If vineyard is long established, periodically check vine P status with petiole analysis. If phosphate fertilizer is banded to the undervine bank, some broadcast fertilizer may be needed to supply the cover crop. Check the inter-row space with an agronomic soil test.
Heavy corrective dressings of K_2SO_4 (1-2 tonne per hectare) can be used on a trial basis if symptoms appear and are confirmed with petiole analysis, but only on soils which are known to be K-fixing (seek local advice). Foliar sprays of potassium nitrate at 10-20g/L can be tried. Maintenance dressings of K at rates of 50 to 100kg/ha (actual K) can also be used.	Take care that K is needed as high K supply can lead to reduced wine quality. Obtain specialist local advice about the K fixing ability of the soil before deciding on application rates and methods. The corrective approach (see 9.4.2) has not been tried experimentally in Australia.
Maintenance sprays of Epsom salts (20g/L) can be applied annually. In glasshouses previously used for tomatoes or cucumbers both soil applications (up to 0.5kg/m²) and foliar sprays of Epsom salts (20g/L) can be tried.	Bunch stem necrosis has been linked with low Mg in Europe. Bunch sprays at veraison of Epsom salts at 50g/L can be tried.
Routine maintenance sprays (zinc sulfate at 1g/L) applied annually prior to flowering or zinc sulfate swabbing of bleeding pruning cuts. In some cases Zineb or Mancozeb sprays may provide sufficient zinc.	A past history of extremely heavy superphosphate use can be associated with Zn deficiency. A past history of heavy animal manure application (e.g. sheep camps) is associated with Zn deficiency.

Table continued next page

Table 9.15 (continued)

Nutrient	Main considerations	Strategy	Preplanting	Young vines
Manganese	Deficiency occurs in leached soils or those containing lime.	Maintenance (annually)	Nil	Manganese sulfate sprays if needed (1g/L)
Iron	Symptoms of iron deficiency are often related to waterlogging and soil compaction. Free lime in soil induces deficiency	Corrective or maintenance	If waterlogging is likely install tile drainage	Iron chelates can be considered if symptoms are severe.
Boron	Adequate in most soils. May cause toxicity if water or soil concentrations are high	Corrective or maintenance	Apply a basal broadcast dressing of Sprayboron® at 5 kg per ha or equivalent rates of borax or boric acid	Boron foliar sprays if needed (3g/L borax, or 1.25 g/L of Sprayboron®
Copper	Usually controlled with copper fungicides	Maintenance	Nil	In suspect situations copper fungicides can be used.

Phosphate

If phosphorus is deficient, good responses are obtained when the applied phosphate moves into the rootzone. The original recommendation for mature vineyards drawn from the Nuriootpa work was for deep placement of about 600 kg/ha of superphosphate in every third vine row for three years (so that the whole vineyard was treated after 3 years), and then a maintenance dressing of about 100 kg/ha of superphosphate every third year except in soils where strong fixation could be expected. However, the need for a maintenance dressing has not been demonstrated experimentally. The Nuriootpa work also led to a general recommendation for a pre-planting application of superphosphate of about 1 tonne/ha, ripped into the planting line before new vineyards were established (Seeliger & Loder 1969). Recent work at Padthaway shows that surface application of superphosphate to the herbicide treated undervine bank is more efficient than subsurface placement in the mid row (Robinson and McCarthy 1987).

Two pieces of information are still missing about the use of phosphorus in vineyards. The first concerns the need for a maintenance dressing after subsurface or band applications of quite large amounts of superphosphate. The second concerns the residual value of superphosphate applied in previous cropping phases before vineyards are developed (e.g. pasture or cereal crop) and thus the need for deep-placed superphosphate where vines are planted in 'improved' country. These points are more important now than they were in the late 1960s as the cost of superphosphate is now relatively much higher. The following strategies are recommended for superphosphate use:

1. New vineyards. If a total of 1-2 tonnes of superphosphate per hectare have been applied in a previous cropping phase, apply no more superphosphate than is needed for the establishment of a legume-based cover crop (use your local soil analysis service to check that there is sufficient available phosphorus present in the soil surface). When the vineyard is bearing, have a petiole analysis carried out. If the P concentration in the petioles-at-flowering is below

Mature vines	Special considerations
Maintenance spray can be applied with zinc spray or at other times of the year. In some cases Mancozeb may provide sufficient manganese.	Manganese deficiency has been observed on heavily limed (previously acid) Adelaide Hills soils.
Correction can often be achieved by close control of irrigation in spring and by installing tile drains. Iron chelates as a soil dressing (30-50g/vine) or a foliar spray (1g/L) can be tried but the economics of their use should be checked.	Economics of correction with chelates should be checked.
10 kg of borax/hectare or 5 kg of Sprayboron® every year will correct the deficiency. The US literature suggests a higher rate every 3 years. Annual borax or Sprayboron® foliar sprays can be used in place of a soil dressing.	There is only a small margin for error with B. Take care to calculate rates accurately.
In suspect situations use copper fungicides in preference to organics.	Use of superphosphate supplemented with copper is possible but in crops on which copper fungicides are used there is a risk of copper toxicity through a build-up of soil copper concentration.

0.20% (or 0.30% in WA) apply superphosphate at a rate of 500-1000 kg/ha to the undervine bank.

2. Established vineyards. If 1-2 tonnes of superphosphate have been applied per hectare (either broadcast or deep-placed), phosphorus deficiency is unlikely to develop quickly. Check the need for phosphorus for the legume cover crop or volunteer winter legume by having an available phosphate test by your fertilizer company or soil testing service. If superphosphate is needed for the legume it should be applied at the agronomic rate of 100-200 kg/ha and this should also provide a maintenance supply for the vines. For reassurance have a petiole analysis for phosphorus done every 3-5 years to check that concentrations of about 0.2% (or 0.3% WA) and above are maintained.

Potassium

In those areas of Australia where potassium is known to be needed, two approaches to K fertilization can be used. In sandy soils a maintenance dressing of about 40 kg of potassium per ha per year is usually recommended (e.g. in the Granite Belt of Queensland and on the sands of West Australia). The corrective approach (where about 2 tonnes of potassium sulfate per hectare are applied in opened furrows adjacent to the undervine bank) is used in California where soils strongly fix applied potassium. It may be suited to isolated situations in Australia, but there has been no reported testing of this approach.

Micronutrients

As micronutrient deficiencies are often caused by immobilization of the nutrients in the soil by adverse soil conditions rather than by complete absence from the soil, a maintenance approach involving annual applications is most useful. Zinc, manganese and copper deficiencies are all treated with foliar sprays. Zinc is particularly involved with fruitset so is best sprayed prior to flowering. Manganese and copper deficiency can be treated with more latitude in the timing of the sprays. Urea can be included in trace element foliar sprays (see nitrogen above). Where needed, boron can be applied as a maintenance foliar spray of borax or Sprayboron® or as a corrective soil dressing.

9.4.3 Fertilizer timing

Nutrients such as potassium and phosphorus which are held in slowly exchangeable or slowly soluble forms in the soil can be applied at virtually any time of the year. It is always helpful if rain or irrigation closely follows the application and can move the nutrient into the rootzone in the season of application and thus prevent any delay in correction of a deficiency. (See the corrective approach to fertilizer use, 9.4.2.)

Nitrogen on the other hand is more labile in the soil profile and can be leached through the rootzone. Annual single or split applications are used to compensate for this behaviour. In the past nitrogen has usually been applied early in spring to ensure availability as the soil warms up and root growth commences, or split between a spring and a summer application. A number of studies have suggested that nitrogen uptake occurs only slowly during the spring growth flush and the uptake rate increases around flowering time and it continues until well after the crop has been harvested. A better strategy may be to apply nitrogen in late spring and immediately postharvest in vineyards where vigour is low and nitrogen fertilizer is clearly needed. With drip irrigation timing of early season applications is largely determined by the need to irrigate. Micro-nutrient (foliar spray) applications should be made during the period of most vigorous growth when demand will be greatest.

9.5 Concluding remarks

9.5.1. Effect of canopy on nutrition

During the last decade two types of canopy change have been instituted: on the one hand formal shoot placement has been adopted, especially in cool areas, and on the other machine and minimal pruning has been widely adopted. Approaches to fertilizer use that have been developed for more traditional vineyards may have to be subtly altered to maximize the potential offered by these changes. This may be particularly important in the case of nitrogen nutrition which can so markedly affect shoot vigour. As yet, there has been insufficient research or field experience to assess whether altered nutrition recommendations are needed.

9.5.2 Effect of rootstocks

If rootstocks are used in new plantings or for the replanting of old vineyard land the decisions regarding fertilizers are much harder to make. For the most part, grapevines in Australia have been grown on their own roots and little experience has been gained on the nutrition of vineyards on rootstocks. It is probable that some extra lime-sensitivity can be expected. The greater vigour induced by many stocks means that adjustment in N usage (particularly in the irrigated areas) will be one way to control vine size. There is also the possibility that special strategies will be needed to keep K concentrations low in grapes produced by vines on rootstocks (e.g. Downton 1977). It is possible that tissue analysis standards suited for use with heavily-pruned, nematode-infested vines will need to be changed for clonal vines on vigorous rootstocks and trained on large trellises.

9.5.3 Alternatives for assessing nitrogen status

Kliewer and Cook (1974) in California have found a good relationship between the level of arginine in grape juice and the nitrogen status of the vineyard; work is continuing on this approach in Australia (e.g. Freeman 1986) but the results do not look promising. Test strips are available that can rapidly detect nitrate in sap squeezed from grape petioles. If this method is to be used with confidence proper calibration work will be needed.

9.5.4 Nutrition with drip or micro-jet irrigation

There are indications from commercial vineyards that relatively immobile nutrients like phosphorus applied through drip irrigation systems are made use of more efficiently than those applied by broadcasting onto the soil surface. In particular the movement of phosphorus into the rootzone may be faster than expected. If this field experience is confirmed in experiments more work will be needed to determine the minimum rates of nitrogen and phosphorus required. In contrast, mobile nutrients like nitrogen are more easily leached through the rootzone and to drainage with drip irrigation. Fertilizer behaviour with microjet irrigation systems is not yet understood.

9.5.5 Mycorrhiza

The roots of grapevines and hybrids growing in the field are commonly infected with vesicular-arbuscular mycorrhizae. These fungi are known to enhance the ability of plant root systems to take up phosphorus and zinc from the soil (e.g. see Possingham and Groot Obbink 1971). Seedlings and explants from tissue culture have been artificially inoculated with various mycorrhizae and increases in growth have been demonstrated. Differences in the effectiveness of different species of fungi have also been demonstrated (see, for example, Schubert *et al.* 1988). The technique of inoculation with mycorrhizal fungi may be useful in commercial viticulture in the future particularly when propagation is carried out in soil-less mixes or fumigated nursery soil, but more research will be needed before it can be adopted widely.

9.5.6 Organic viticulture

There is an identifiable demand for agricultural and horticultural products grown without input from manufactured fertilizers and agricultural chemicals (Zuur 1988). We have seen earlier that grapevines are capable of at least limited growth and production in a wide range of soils and climates without substantial inputs of fertilizers, except where severe deficiencies (especially of phosphorus or zinc) occur. Animal manures or winery marc can be used to raise vineyard nitrogen status although there is some doubt that sufficient nitrogen availability could be maintained if a full drip irrigation schedule is adopted. A program of animal manure application will also apply some P and K as a bonus. No experiments have been done, but finely ground rock phosphate could provide phosphorus on acid soils. In any case if an organic strategy is pursued it would be wise to monitor vineyard nutrient status using tissue analysis.

9.5.7 Nutrition and wine quality

Somers (1975) has pointed out that the quality of dry red table wine in Australia is related to its pH. He has further shown that pH is associated with the K concentrations in the juice and that these tend to be higher in Australian wine than in that from the high quality red wine areas in France. The mechanisms governing the potassium content of Australia grapes are being examined

and methods sought to control its concentration by changing practices in the vineyard.

Another aspect of wine quality affected by nutrition of the grape vines is the availability of sufficient nutrients to allow proper growth of the yeast. 'Stuck' fermentation of must in West Australia has been related to a low level of nitrogen nutrition in the vineyard (Goldspink 1987).

Further reading

Christensen, L.P., Kasimatis, A.N. and Jensen, F.L. (1978) Grapevine Nutrition and Fertilization in the San Joaquin Valley, Bulletin 4087, Division of Agricultural Sciences, University of California, Berkeley

Cook, J.A. (1966) Grape nutrition. In: Temperate to Tropical Fruit Nutrition (N.F. Childers Ed.) Horticultural Publications, New Brunswick, N.J.

Cook, J.A. and Kishaba, T. (1956) Petiole nitrate analysis as a criterion of nitrogen needs in California vineyards. Proc. of the Amer. Soc. of Hortic. Sci., 68, 131-40.

Delmas, J. (1971) Fertilisation of the Vine (French). In:Sciences et Techniques de la Vigne Vol. 1 eds. J. Ribereau-Gayon et E. Peynaud, Ch. 9, Dunod, Paris.

Lee, T.H. and Freeman, B.M. eds. (1987) Vine Nutrition. Proc. Aust. Soc. of Vitic. and Oenol. seminar, 31 July 1987, Aust. Wine Research Inst., Glen Osmond, SA

Leece, D.R. (1976) Diagnosis of nutritional disorders of fruit trees by leaf and soil analysis and biochemical indices. J. Aust. Inst. Agric. Sci. 42, 3-19.

Rantz, J. (Ed.) (1991) Nitrogen in Grapes and Wine. Proc. Int. Conf., Seattle July 1991. Amer. Soc. Enol. Vitic. Davis, California.

Reuter, D.J. and Robinson, J.B. eds. (1986) Plant Analysis — An Interpretation Manual. Inkata Press, Melbourne.

Robson, A.D. (ed.) (1989) Soil Acidity and Plant Growth. Academic Press, Sydney.

Other references

Alexander, D. McE, and Woodham, R.C. (1958) 'Available' phosphorus in alkaline soils in relation to the grown of tick bean (Vicia faba L. car. minor Beck) Aust. J. of Agric. Res. 9, 633-9.

Alexander, D. McE, and Woodham, R.C. (1964) Yield responses to applications of zinc and superphosphate. Aust. J. of Exp. Agric. and Animal Husb. 4, 169-72.

Bester, A.J. and Meynhardt, J.T. (1968) A study of some factors influencing the foliar uptake of phosphorus by grape vines. South African J. of Agric. Sci.. 11, 477-81.

Beyers, E (1962) Diagnostic leaf analysis for deciduous fruit. South African J. of Agric. Sci.. 5, 315-29.

Christensen, L.P. and Jensen, F.L. (1978) Grapevine response to concentrate and to dilute application of two zinc compounds. Amer. J. of Enol. and Vitic., 29, 213-6.

Colwell, J.D. (1965) An automatic procedure for the determination of phosphorus in sodium hydrogen carbonate extracts of soils. Chem. Ind. Part 1, p. 893.

Cook, G.W. (1967) The Control of Soil Fertility. Crosby Lockwood and Son Ltd., London.

Cook, J.A., Ward, W.R. and Wicks, A.S. (1983) Phosphorus deficiency in California Vineyards, Calif. Agric. 37, 16-8.

Coombe, B.G. (1949) Zinc treatment of Sultana vines. J. Dep. Agric. S. Australia 53, 59-61.

Coombe, B.G. (1964) The winter treatment of grapevines with zinc and its interaction with time of pruning. Aust. J. Exp. Agric. Animal Husb. 4, 241-6.

Downton, W.J.S. (1977) Influence of rootstocks on the accumulation of chloride, sodium and potassium in grapevines. Aust. J. of Agric. Res. 28,- 879-89.

Dry, P. (1986) Primary bud-axis necrosis of grapevines. M. Ag. Sc. thesis, University of Adelaide.

Freeman, B.M. (1986) Arginine as a selection criterion. In: Aspects of grapevine improvement in Australia (T.H. Lee Ed.) (Aust. Soc. Vitic. Oenol., Glen Osmond).

Goldspink, B.H. (1987) Grapevine nutrient analysis — services and basis for standards in Western Australia — In: Lee and Freeman (1987) loc. cit. 5-19.

Hawson, H. (1971) Getting the best from young vines. Mallee Hortic. Digest 18 (3), 7.

Hawson, J. and Webber, R.T.J. (1971) Another look at vine nutrition. Mallee Hortic. Digest. 18 (3), 5-7.

Jardine, F.A.L. (1946) The use of borax on Waltham Cross grapes in the Stanthorpe district. Queensland Agric. J. 62, 74-8.

Kemp, H.K. and Beare, J.A. (1944) Little leaf in deciduous fruit trees and vines. J. Dep. of Agric., S. Australia, 47, 470-9

Kliewer, W.M., and Cook, J.A. (1974) Arginine levels in grape canes and fruits as indicators of nitrogen status of vineyards. Amer. J. Enol. Vitic. 25, 111-8.

Morschel, J.R.G. (1958) Vine diseases on the Murrumbidgee Irrigation areas — a summary of spray trials. Agric. Gaz. N.S.W. 69, 36-42.

Possingham, J.V., and Groot Obbink, J. (1971) Endotrophic mycorrhiza and the nutrition of grape vines. Vitis 10, 120-30.

Robinson, J.B. and McCarthy, M.G. (1984) Vine fertilizers for the Barossa district for the 1980's. Aust. Grapegrower and Winemaker No. 244, 45-7.

Robinson, J.B. and McCarthy, M.G. (1985) Use of petiole analysis for assessment of vineyard nutrient status in the Barossa district of South Australia. Aust. J. Exp. Agric. 25, 231-40.

Robinson, J.B. and McCarthy, M.G. (1987) Method of application of superphosphate in vineyards. In: Lee and Freeman (1987), loc. cit. pp. 73-8.

Robinson, J.G., Nicholas, P.R. and McCarthy, J.R. (1978) A comparison of three methods of tissue analysis for assessing the nutrient status of plantings of Vitis vinifera in an irrigated area in South Australia. Aust. J. of Exp. Agric. Animal Husb. 18, 294-300.

Schubert, A., Cammarata, S. and Eynard, I. (1988) Growth and root colonization of grapevines inoculated with different mycorrhizal endophytes. Hortic. Sci. 23, 302-3.

Seeliger, M.T., and French, R.J. (1971) Changes in soil chemical properties in a long term fertilizer trial in a non-irrigated vineyard. Aust. J. Agric. Res. 22, 931-40.

Seeliger, M.T., and Loder, M.A. (1969) Fertilizers for vines in non-irrigated areas. J. Dep. of Agric. of S. Australia 73, 74-9.

Skinner, P.W. and Matthews, M.A. (1989) Reproductive development in grape (Vitis vinifera L.) under phosphorus-limited conditions Sci. Hortic. 38, 49-60.

Somers, T.C. (1975) In search of quality for red wines. Food Tech. in Aust. 27, 49-56.

Taylor, D.E. and Winks, C.W. (1976) Grape growing in Queensland. Queensland Dep. of Primary Ind., Horticulture Branch Advisory leaflet H,18-76.

Teakle, L.J.H., Johns, H.K., and Turton, A.G. (1943) Experiments with micro elements for the growth of crops in Western Australia IX. Copper deficiency of currants at Gingin and its correction. J. Dep. Agric. W. Australia. 20, 171-84.

Tulloch, H.W., and Harris, W.B. (1970) Fertilizer responses with non-irrigated Shiraz grapevines. 1944-1966. Aust. J. Agric. Res. 21, 243-52.

Walters, D.V. (1942) Manurial trials with irrigated sultana vines in the Murray Valley, Australia. Empire J. Exp. Agric. 10, 77-88.

Weir, R.G. (1987) Grapevine nutrient analysis — services and basis for standards in N.S.W. Department of Agriculture. In: Lee and Freeman (1987) loc cit. pp. 41-7.

Woodham, R.C. and Alexander, D. McE. (1970) Foliar symptoms of malnutrition in the sultana vine. CSIRO Div. Hortic. Research Technical Paper No. 1.

Zuur, D. (1988) Alternative viticulture in Europe. Ruakura Agric. Centre, Hamilton, N.Z. 88 pp.

CHAPTER TEN

Grape Pests

G.A. BUCHANAN and T.G. AMOS

10.1 *Common pests of established vines*
1. *Lightbrown apple moth*
2. *Grapevine moth*
3. *Longtailed mealybug*
4. *Grapevine scale*
5. *Grapeleaf blister mite (Erinose mite)*
6. *Grapeleaf rust mite*
7. *Bunch mite*

10.2 *Pests restricted in distribution or sporadic in occurrence*
1. *Grape phylloxera*
2. *Fruit flies*
3. *Rutherglen bug*
4. *Cicadas*
5. *Weevils*
6. *Fig longicorn*
7. *Fruit-tree borer*
8. *Grapevine hawk moth*
9. *Locusts and grasshoppers*
10. *Thrips*
11. *Snails*
12. *Birds*

10.3 *Pests of drying grapes*
1. *Raisin moth*
2. *Driedfruit beetles*
3. *Vinegar flies*

10.4 *Pests of young vines*
1. *African black beetle*
2. *Cutworms*
3. *Rabbits and hares*

With few exceptions, insect and mite pests of agricultural crops can be controlled with pesticides. It is the cost of control, in both financial and environmental terms, that constitutes the main problem of control programs based solely on the use of pesticides. With the notable exception of grape phylloxera, the pests present in Australian vineyards seldom pose a serious threat to the crop and are relatively easy to control. Consequently, grapegrowers have been able to avoid most of the environmental problems associated with the intensive use of pesticides that occur in some other fruit crops.

The prime objective of pest control is to prevent pests causing economic injury, that is, a loss in excess of the cost of controlling them. In Australian vineyards, regular control programs arc feasible only for the relatively few common and consistently damaging pests, and the many sporadic pests must be dealt with as they occur. Ideally, there should be precise knowledge of the relation between pest numbers and injury so that the grower would know, for example, whether or not it was economic to spray for an average of eight caterpillars of lightbrown apple moth per vine at berry set. In practice, such precision is possible for a few pests only (Baker 1987) and the judgements are usually based on the experience of the grower or vineyard manager.

The level of pest abundance at which economic damage does occur is influenced by both the nature of the damage and the market outlet for the grapes. Pests that attack grape bunches cause a downgrading of appearance, in addition to loss of yield. With tablegrapes, the appearance of the bunch is important, and costs associated with the cosmetic aspect of pest damage, such as sorting and trimming damaged bunches, may be far greater than those due to reduced yield. Thus for tablegrapes, there is a lower tolerance of pests that attack fruit than for dried fruit or winegrapes. The difference should be reflected in the approach to pest control.

Environmental problems that are associated

with the use of pesticides, and which are of direct concern to the grower, are the initial and residual toxicity, the development of resistance in pests, and the rapid build-up of pest populations due to the elimination of natural enemies, i.e. parasites and predators. The solution to pesticide toxicity problems lies in observing recommended safety precautions and withholding periods. Resistance and effects on natural enemies can be minimized by the more effective use of pesticides. The approach to control of regular pests should be such that the need for additional control of sporadic pests is reduced, wherever possible. Sometimes this can be done by applying a pesticide that controls several pests simultaneously. This approach is particularly useful for tablegrapes, where little damage can be tolerated. In other cases, however, it may be desirable to use more selective pesticides to avoid affecting natural enemies of grape pests.

The above matters are discussed in 11.6.

It is the purpose of this chapter to describe the pests of the grapevine in Australia, and to provide a guide to methods for their control. The scientific and common names of pests in this chapter are as recommended by Carne *et al.* (1987). Recommendations for insect control may differ between states and are subject to frequent review; therefore growers should contact their local Department of Agriculture office for current recommendations.

10.1 Common pests of established vines

This section deals with those grape pests that are common to most grapegrowing areas of Australia and for which regular control programs are applied. Although the relative importance of the pests may differ, methods for their control are similar. An approach to control known as integrated control is applicable to these pests, particularly where they attack dried fruit and winegrapes. Integrated control is a pest management system that utilizes all suitable techniques and methods in as compatible a manner as possible in order to maintain pest populations below the level at which they cause economic injury. For further details see entomological works such as Huffaker (1971). In practice, this means that emphasis is placed on

the use of relatively selective insecticides, such as the microbial insecticide *Bacillus thuringiensis* for caterpillars, so that there is minimum effect on the natural enemies which assist in control of lightbrown apple moth, grapevine moth, longtailed mealybug and grapevine scale. The practical benefit to growers is that fewer sprays should be required for these pests. Increasing development of this approach is likely in the future as knowledge concerning the natural enemies of grape pests and the effects of differing pesticides on them is accumulated.

10.1.1 Lightbrown apple moth

Lightbrown apple moth *Epiphyas postvittana* is a native leaf-roller which feeds on a wide range of native and introduced plants. It is an important pest of pome and stone fruits, as well as of grapevines, and a minor pest of other horticultural crops such as citrus. It is now present in all Australian states, being indigenous to eastern Australia and having recently become established in Western Australia. Lightbrown apple moth is a more serious pest in cooler than in warmer areas, and is favoured by conditions that cause lush growth in its host plants.

Appearance and biology
The moths are pale brown, with a wingspan of about 10 mm. Males are smaller than females and have dark brown markings on the hind portion of the forewing. After mating, the female lays several egg masses during her life span of approximately two weeks. The egg masses usually contain 20-30 eggs and are laid on the upper surface of vine leaves. They are inconspicuous, since the eggs are green to yellow in colour, small and flat.

After hatching, the young larvae (caterpillars) wander on the vine until they locate a suitable feeding site, such as the growing tip of a shoot or near a leaf vein on the undersurface of a leaf. The larvae are slender and green, with a brown head capsule, and when fully grown measure 15-20 mm in length. They typically feed in protected locations, initially beneath a silken webbing, but later they roll leaves, web leaves together, or web berries, to form a shelter in which they feed (Figure 10.1). When disturbed, they wriggle backwards rapidly, and may hang suspended from the feeding site by a silken thread.

210

Figure 10.1. Typical damage by lightbrown apple moth to a vine shoot during spring. The shelter formed by webbing of the leaf and developing bunch has been partially opened to show the lightbrown apple moth larvae.

The pupa is brown, about 10 mm long, and is usually found at the larval feeding site. After emergence of the moth, the pupal case often remains protruding from the pupation site.

Lightbrown apple moth normally has 3-4 generations per year. It overwinters as larvae which feed in the vineyard on broad-leaved weeds, such as dock, capeweed and clovers. Although some overwintering larvae migrate to vines at budburst, vines are mainly infested when moths that develop from overwintering larvae lay eggs on vine foliage during October. Larvae hatching from these eggs feed on vine foliage and bunches during November and reach the moth stage during December. A second generation then develops on the vines during summer, the larvae of this generation still being present at harvest of most vine varieties. In some seasons at least, another generation may develop on the grapevines during late summer. Moths then lay eggs on alternative host plants, or occasionally on senescing vine foliage, and the winter is passed in the larval stage.

Damage

Larvae of the overwintering generation that migrate to vine foliage at budburst can cause damage by chewing off whole shoots or the developing bunches. However, unless lightbrown apple moth is unusually abundant, the damage incurred at this stage does not warrant insecticidal control.

Damage to foliage by larvae is of little consequence, but feeding on bunches during late spring and summer can result in crop losses of up to 10%, sometimes more. Larvae of the spring generation reduce the potential size of the crop by feeding on the flowers and berries. Damaged berries usually drop, and little evidence of damage remains visible at harvest.

Damage by larvae of the summer generation consists of both surface feeding on, and penetration into, berries (Figure 10.2a). The feeding wounds provide a site for infection by bunch-rotting organisms, such as the fungi *Botrytis cinerea* and *Aspergillus* spp., which can lead to further crop loss. Because of lightbrown apple moth's preference for feeding in protected locations, vine varieties with compact bunches tend to be more severely damaged than those with more open bunches.

Control

Lightbrown apple moth is attacked by native predators and parasites, as well as a virus disease, but these are seldom sufficient to prevent economic damage occurring. The main predators are spiders and lacewings, while common parasites include the egg parasite *Trichogramma*, larval parasites *Apanteles tasmanica* and *Voriella uniseta*, and the pupal parasite *Brachymeria phya*.

In vineyards prone to frost, it is a sound practice to remove weed growth prior to budburst as a means of frost protection. As larvae overwinter on weed growth within the vineyard, removal of this vegetation prior to budburst will reduce subsequent infestation of vines. Where weed growth infested by larvae is destroyed after budburst, a protective spray may be warranted in order to prevent transfer of larvae onto vine foliage.

Due to its habit of feeding in protected locations, precise timing and thorough application of insecticides are necessary for effective control. The main spray is applied in early November to protect bunches from attack by spring generation larvae during the flowering and setting period. A further spray is often necessary during early January for control of larvae of the summer generation.

Control of lightbrown apple moth is possible with a selective insecticide, e.g. *Bacillus thuringiensis*, or broad spectrum insecticides, e.g.

Figure 10.2a. Damage to table grapes by a lightbrown apple moth larva. Feeding wounds on grape berries often become infected with bunch-rotting fungi.

Figure 10.2b. Section through a Waltham Cross bud showing damage by Colomerus vitis. The mites appear as white, elongate objects scattered throughout the bud.

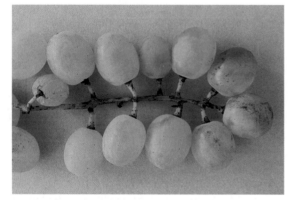

Figure 10.2c. The black scarring on the berry stems is typical of damage by bunch mite.

Figure 10.2d. Phylloxera galls on the leaves of a rootstock planting at Rutherglen.

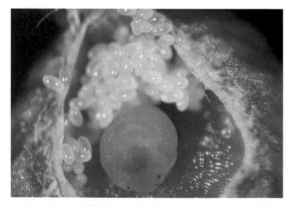

Figure 10.2e. Phylloxera leaf gall cut open from below to show the insect and eggs.

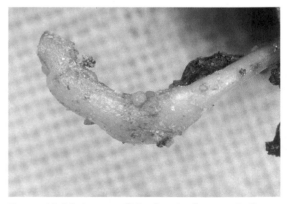

Figure 10.2f. A root gall (nodosity) of grape phylloxera on the root of the rootstock 3309. Note the insects in the curve of the gall.

carbaryl and chlorpyrifos. The broad spectrum insecticides are appropriate for tablegrapes, where there is little tolerance of pests. Continued spraying, however, with broad spectrum insecticides may aggravate mealybug and mite problems in vineyards.

In winegrape and dried fruit vineyards, control of lightbrown apple moth is best achieved with *Bacillus thuringiensis*. Sprays should be timed to coincide with egg hatch, which can be predicted with computer-based models and/or monitoring of populations in vineyards. The advantage of *Bacillus thuringiensis* is that it encourages biological control of both lightbrown apple moth and other grapevine pests, with the practical result that few if any insecticide sprays are required in many Australian vineyards.

10.1.2 Grapevine moth

Grapevine moth *Phalaenoides glycine* is a native insect which has become a widespread and common pest of grapevines in Australia and New Zealand. In addition to its native foodplants and grapevines, it also feeds on Fuchsia and Virginia creeper (*Parthenocissus quinquefolia*). It is most problematic in rainfall vineyards, where it is often the most abundant insect pest present.

Appearance and biology
The day-flying moths are black, with attractive markings of pale yellow on the wings and orange beneath the body. They live for two to three weeks, and are often seen visiting flowers to feed on nectar.

Each female moth is capable of laying several hundred eggs. Eggs are laid singly, usually on the underside of vine leaves or on stems, and hatch in one to two weeks. The larvae feed mainly on leaves, but may also cause damage to bunches in spring. There are six larval stages, of which the first two feed on the undersurface of leaves and skeletonize them, while later stages chew irregular portions of whole leaves. The larvae are easily recognized, as they have distinctive greenish-yellow and black markings with some red near the hind end. The distribution of larvae within the vineyard is usually patchy, with only isolated vines or groups of vines carrying high numbers. When fully fed, larvae may wander for a day or two before pupating in a cell excavated

Figure 10.3. The predatory shield bug Oechalia consocialis *feeding on a grapevine moth larva. The bug has inserted its mouthparts into, and is sucking the contents from, the body of the larva. Photograph courtesy of Dr C. Cordingley, Waite Agricultural Research Institute, Glen Osmond, SA.*

by the larva, either in soil, the wood of vines and trellis posts, or in debris.

The grapevine moth overwinters as a dormant pupa, and emerges as a moth in early spring. Two to three generations occur each year, with larvae generally being abundant during spring, and again in autumn.

Damage
Although mainly leaf feeders, larvae can ruin bunches by chewing off the flowers and young berries during spring. They are voracious feeders and if not checked are capable of defoliating vines. Complete defoliation is common on household vines, but extensive defoliation does not often occur in commercial vineyards, even when control measures are not implemented.

Control
Despite its potential for destruction grapevine moth is a minor pest of commercial vineyards. As it is susceptible to the insecticides commonly applied for control of lightbrown apple moth, grapevine moth is seldom a problem in vineyards where these insecticides are regularly applied. In vineyards where few if any insecticides are used, grapevine moth is checked by native parasites, predators and a virus disease. The most important

natural enemy appears to be the predatory shield bug, *Oechalia consocialis* (Figure 10.3). Both nymphs and adults of this bug feed by sucking the body contents from grapevine moth larvae. Of the parasites, *Euplectrus agaristae* attacks the larvae of grapevine moth, while *Echthromorpha intricatoria* and *Lissopimpla semipunctata* are pupal parasites (Cordingley 1975).

Outbreaks of grapevine moth are obvious due to the conspicuous nature of the larvae and the damage it causes. When damaging infestations do occur, they can be readily controlled by sprays of *Bacillus thuringiensis*, which cause little harm to natural enemies of grapevine moth.

10.1.3 Longtailed mealybug

Longtailed mealybug *Pseudococcus longispinus* is a cosmopolitan pest of temperate and subtropical fruit crops, and of ornamental plants. Although present in all grapegrowing areas, it is most prevalent in the irrigated vineyards of the Murray Valley. Sporadic outbreaks affecting all varieties may occur, but it is the late-harvested varieties that are damaged most regularly.

Appearance and biology
The adult female is wingless and slow-moving, with a rather flat oval-shaped body about 3 mm in length. It is covered with a fine coating of white powdery wax, which is formed into filaments at the sides of the body. The name of the insect refers to the characteristic pair of tail filaments, which are normally longer than the body (Figure 10.4).

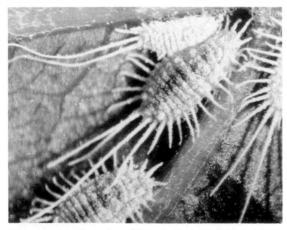

Figure 10.4. Females of long-tailed mealybug on the underside of a vine leaf.

Each adult female produces over 100 offspring. Eggs are laid singly and hatch almost immediately they are laid. The newly hatched nymphs may spend several days sheltering beneath the mother's body before wandering off to commence feeding. Female mealybugs pass through three nymphal stages before reaching adulthood, and the males four. The males cover themselves with a white cottony cocoon during the second nymphal stage, and pass through a prepupal and pupal stage within the cocoon before emerging as an adult. The adult male is a delicate winged insect with a pair of waxy tail filaments.

Longtailed mealybug normally has three generations per year in southern Australia. It overwinters beneath the bark of vines (Browning 1959) and in cracks and crevices of trellis posts. Furness (1973) reports that it also overwinters on cover crops and weeds in the vineyard. Young mealybugs produced in autumn are the prevalent overwintering stage, and infest vine foliage shortly after budburst. They become mature and reproduce in late October and November. During spring, mealybugs are found feeding on the undersurface of leaves at the base of shoot. Grape bunches become infested during summer, especially in late January and February when the mealybug population again reproduces.

Young mealybugs are killed by hot, dry conditions, and are particularly susceptible during the wandering phase between leaving the mother and commencement of feeding. Thus climatic conditions during summer, particularly in late January and February, influence the severity of mealybug infestation. Due to the unfavourable effect of low humidity, longtailed mealybug tends to be most abundant on vines with dense foliage. Mealybug populations typically increase during autumn, with the result that late-harvested grapes are often infested more severely than those picked earlier.

Damage
Longtailed mealybug feeds by sucking plant fluids, but normally this does not result in significant damage. The economic importance of longtailed mealybug is due to its excretion of a sugary liquid called honeydew. The presence of honeydew on grape bunches makes them sticky and unsightly, thus rendering them unsuitable for fresh fruit

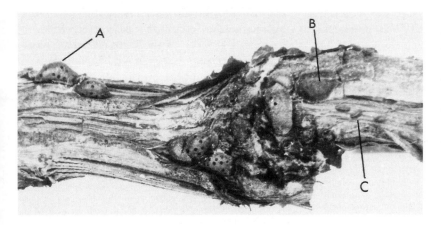

Figure 10.5. Various stages of grapevine scale on a cane during winter. A. scale killed by parasitic wasps, showing the emergence holes made by the adult wasps. B. Dead adult scale. C. Young overwintering scale.

markets. Where fruit is dried, honeydew retards the drying of affected bunches. With winegrapes, heavy infestations of longtailed mealybug may lead to the grapes being suitable only for distillation.

Control
Longtailed mealybug is attacked by native parasites and predators, of which the predatory ladybird *Cryptolaemus montrouzieri* and the parasite *Anarhopus sydneyensis* have been used with some success in California for the biological control of mealybugs infesting citrus. In Australia, *C. montrouzieri* has been reported as an effective predator in New South Wales, Queensland and Western Australia. *Cryptolaemus montrouzieri* and *A. sydneyensis*, however, are not present in the Murray Valley; here the ladybird *Rhizobius ruficollis* is the main predator and the wasp *Anagyrus fusciventris* is the most common parasite. A recent attempt to establish the parasites *A. sydneyensis* and *Hungariella peregrina* in the Murray Valley was not successful (Furness 1977).

On most varieties, insecticidal control is not warranted in many seasons, and sporadic outbreaks are dealt with as they occur. In some cases, such outbreaks have been associated with the use of broad-spectrum insecticides for the control of other vine pests (Furness 1976). However, in vines which are particularly prone to damage, a schedule of preventative sprays is necessary. Control by means of insecticides is difficult due to the waxy body coverings and sheltered locations of the insects. Best results are obtained with thorough coverage and when applications are timed to coincide with the emergence of young mealybugs. In Western Australia, a pre-budburst spray is often applied, but in the eastern states sprays are normally applied in November and January.

10.1.4 Grapevine scale
Grapevine scale *Parthenolecanium persicae* occurs on grapevines, and on some deciduous fruit trees, throughout Australia. Although a potentially serious pest, it is well controlled in most areas by natural enemies, and only occasionally becomes severe enough to warrant control. Infestations of grapevine scale are most common in irrigated areas and on older grapevines.

Appearance and biology
The adult females are dark-brown, oval-shaped scales about 7 mm in length, and are found on canes and amongst bark of older wood during spring (Figure 10.5). There is only one generation a year, the young being produced in October-November. Numerous, pale-yellow eggs are laid beneath the mother's body, so that when egg production has finished the cavity beneath the adult scale is filled with eggs. The adult scales die after reproducing, but the dead scales may remain on the vine for several months.

The young scale crawlers that hatch from the eggs move onto new growth, usually settling and feeding on the underside of vine leaves. The young scales are difficult to find on foliage, as they are small, flat, and yellow in colour. In autumn the partly grown scales move onto the canes and old wood where they overwinter. During winter the scales are brown in colour and relatively small, but during early spring they grow rapidly into adults.

215

Damage
Grapevine scale feeds by sucking sap, and heavy infestations may affect vigour to the extent that vines are severely weakened. The scales also excrete honeydew, and where infested leaves are in close proximity to bunches, the bunches may be fouled by honeydew. A black, sooty mould fungus often develops on the honeydew. The distribution of grapevine scale within a vineyard is typically patchy, with only a few vines being heavily infested (May 1952).

Control
Grapevine scale is difficult to find in newly established vineyards, possibly due to the use of clean planting material. In older vineyards it is normally held under satisfactory control by natural enemies, the most effective of which appears to be a parasitic wasp *Metaphycus lounsburyi*. In New South Wales, predators such as the ladybird *Cryptolaemus montrouzieri* and a moth larva *Catoblemma dubia* are also reported to assist control. Where ants attend the scales to obtain honeydew, they can interfere with biological control by driving away parasites and predators. The control of ants may thus be necessary to avoid persistent infestation of grapevine scale.

When damaging infestations do occur, the main control measure is a dormant oil spray applied during July. The extent of scale infestation is best judged during winter, and it is often convenient to mark infested vines during pruning. Due to the patchy distribution of grapevine scale it is economic to spot spray the infested vines only, a procedure which is also less harmful to natural enemies of the scale.

For reasons of convenience, some growers tend to delay oil applications until well after pruning, and even to combine oil applications with the lime-sulfur treatment for mite control. This procedure has the disadvantage that the scales become larger and more difficult to kill, and the risk of phytotoxic effects from oil sprays becomes greater as budburst approaches. Where winter control of severe infestations of grapevine scale has been omitted, a thorough application of a contact insecticide during spring will assist in control.

10.1.5 Grapeleaf blister mite (Erinose mite)

Although the common leaf-galling form of *Colomerus vitis*, i.e. erinose or grapeleaf blister mite, has been known in Australian vineyards for many years, a physiologically distinct, bud-inhabiting strain of this mite also occurs, i.e. bud mite. The two strains are identical in appearance, being distinguished only by their behaviour and the damage they cause. The only known host of both strains of the mite is *Vitis vinifera*, but the relative prevalence of the two strains appears to differ between grape varieties.

Appearance and biology
Colomerus vitis is a tiny mite with a white elongate body and two pairs of legs. It cannot be seen with the unaided eye. Development from the egg to adult may occur in as little as two weeks, and there are many generations per year. Both strains of the mite overwinter in grape buds, most often just beneath the outer bud scales, but occasionally they occur throughout the bud (Figure 10.2b). In most vine varieties the basal buds of a cane are infested more often than the distal buds. The mites remain active and feed on the bud scales during winter. Although the adult is the predominant overwintering stage, egg production usually commences before the buds have burst. At budburst, mites that have penetrated to inner leaf scales are carried up the developing shoot, while those beneath the outer bud scales are found at the base of the shoot.

Feeding on the underside of young, expanding leaves by the grapeleaf blister strain of the mite

Figure 10.6. Leaf galls formed by grapeleaf blister mites. The galls appear as irregular bulges on the upper surface of the leaf (left), while on the lower surface the concavity of the gall is lined with a dense growth of plant hairs (right).

causes the formation of the characteristic gall (Figure 10.6). New galls are not developed on mature leaves. The galls are hemispherical in shape, with the concavity opening on the lower leaf surface, a characteristic which readily distinguishes them from the galls of grape phylloxera. The concavity of the gall is densely lined with plant hairs, initially white but turning reddish brown later in the season. The mites live amongst the plant hairs, feeding on the epidermal cells of the lower leaf surface. In severe infestations the whole leaf surface can be galled, and occasionally the upper leaf surface, flowers or young berries may be affected. Leaf galling is most severe when humid weather, which favours mite survival, coincides with rapid shoot growth when there are abundant susceptible leaves. During autumn, the mites leave the leaf galls and migrate to overwintering sites within the buds.

The bud strain of *C. vitis* differs from the grapeleaf blister strain in that it does not form leaf galls, but spends almost the whole year living within grape buds. After budburst, bud mites are found in protected sites on the cane, often under the stipular scales at the base of the leaf petiole. As the buds develop at the leaf axils, the mites infest the outer bud scales. Feeding by the mites within buds results in a range of abnormal growth symptoms, which may vary with the degree of infestation and the position of mites within the bud. Symptoms attributed to bud mite in California include distorted basal leaves, short basal internodes, dead overwintering buds, dead terminal buds on new canes, witches-broom growth of new shoots, zigzagged shoots, bunch drop and scarification of the green bark of shoots (Smith and Stafford 1948, Smith and Schuster 1963). Symptoms of bud mite damage, however, tend to be sporadic, and can be confused with similar symptoms caused by other pests and diseases, e.g. fanleaf virus may cause zigzag growth and shortened internodes. Barnes (1958) showed that symptoms similar to bud mite injury in some Californian vineyards were related to pruning time and could be remedied by the application of boron.

Damage
Damage by grapeleaf blister mite differs between vine varieties; some, such as Muscat Gordo Blanco, Trebbiano and Muscadelle, are particularly susceptible. Leaves galled by the mite tend to drop prematurely, and in severe cases berries are liable to sunburn, and the following season's crop affected. In young vines, extensive damage to leaves and ensuing leaf drop can seriously affect vigour. With mature vines, however, significant losses are unlikely even when control measures are omitted. Freeman (1988) found that photosynthesis was not affected until 75% of the leaf surface was blistered.

The extent of damage by bud mites is not known, and there is no conclusive evidence that spraying with a miticide will improve yields. Although bud mite appears to infest all varieties, it is uncommon to find a large proportion of buds heavily infested, and it is doubtful that it causes economic loss. Varieties such as Waltham Cross and Ohanez, however, may be exceptions (May and Webster 1958).

Control
The traditional control measure for grapeleaf blister and bud mites has been lime-sulfur applied at the advanced woolly-bud stage. Although control of grapeleaf blister and bud mites may not be required in some varieties, lime-sulfur is also effective against bunch mite and grapeleaf rust mite. Thus it is usually applied as a preventative spray, the timing of which is aimed at killing mites when they are most exposed, before they move to protected sites on the cane (bud mite) or within leaf galls (grapeleaf blister mite). The timing can be flexible, as McLachlan (1969) showed that lime-sulfur is just as effective against grapeleaf blister mite when applied to dormant vines as it was with semidormant vines. Colloidal sulfur sprays applied for powdery mildew control during spring and summer also assist in mite control.

Postharvest sprays have also been used for mite control, especially where climatic or cultural conditions prevent the application of lime-sulfur in spring. The postharvest sprays are aimed at intercepting mites, i.e. grapeleaf blister mite, grapeleaf rust mite and bunch mite moving to overwintering sites. They are however, not likely to be effective in controlling bud mite, unless systemic miticides are used.

Predatory mites, especially *Typhlodromus*

doreenae, *Amblyseius victoriensis* and *A. loxtoni*, can provide good control of the pest mites on grapevines (James and Whitney, 1991). *Amblyseius victoriensis* is the major predator of blister and rust mites, while *T. doreenae* is considered the key biological control agent for bunch mite. The predatory mites are particularly effective in wine or dried vine fruit vineyards where copper and wettable sulfur are the main fungicides applied.

10.1.6 Grapeleaf rust mite

Grapeleaf rust mite *Calepitrimerus vitis* is a tiny torpedo-shaped mite, cream in colour, with two pairs of legs. As with the related *Colomerus vitis*, it cannot be seen with the naked eye, is specific to grapevines, and has many generations a year. Although the mite is widespread, it tends to be most common in the more humid coastal vineyards.

Grapeleaf rust mite overwinters beneath the outer bud scales of dormant buds, but does not appear to cause significant damage to buds. Egg-laying commences in spring, and the mites move onto the foliage to feed after budburst. The mites live exposed on both sides of the leaf, but are found mainly on the upper surface.

The mites feed on epidermal cells of the leaf, often alongside the main veins. Affected areas turn reddish brown, with the area along the main veins showing the deepest brown discoloration. In severe cases the majority of leaves on a vine may be discoloured, but yields do not appear to be affected. Damaged leaves tend to drop earlier than normal. As the mites live openly on the leaf surface, they are exposed to the action of sprays, and are normally controlled by the chemicals applied for control of grapeleaf blister mite, or by predatory mites.

10.1.7 Bunch mite

Bunch mite *Brevipalpus californicus* has been known as a pest of grapevines and citrus in Australia since the early 1940s. However, in the Sunraysia district at least, the *Brevipalpus* mite causing bunch mite damage is *B. lewisi* (Buchanan *et al.* 1980). As there appears to be little difference in their biology and the damage caused to grapevines, the term bunch mite is used here to include both species. Bunch mite infests all varieties and is prevalent in the hotter inland, grapegrowing areas.

Appearance and biology
The adults are small, flat mites, just visible with the naked eye, and red (*B. californicus*) or brown (*B. lewisi*) in color. Development from egg to adult takes 20-30 days at field temperature, and there are 4-6 generations a year. The mites overwinter as adults beneath outer bud scales, in cracks in bark on the canes, or in the basal whorl of debris at the base of the cane. They do not feed during winter.

After budburst the adult mites move to the base of new shoots, where they commence feeding and laying eggs. Feeding by both adult and juvenile mites at the base of the shoot results in a black scarring at the affected areas. As the population increases, the mites move up the new canes, and by berry set all green portions of the vines are usually infested. Feeding by mites on leaves does not result in discernible damage, but on bunches it results in a black scarring of bunch and berry stems (Figure 10.2c). Damage to bunches is usually most extensive on late-harvested, spur-pruned grape varieties such as Doradillo.

Damage
The effect of bunch mite scarring on bunch and berry stems is to render grapes unsuitable for the fresh fruit market. In grapes used for wine or drying, scarring of bunches is of no economic consequence. Occasionally, a reduction in yield due to shrivelling of berries at the apex of the bunch or berry drop, has been associated with bunch mite damage.

Control
In most vine varieties, bunch mite is controlled adequately by lime-sulfur applied for grapeleaf blister mite or by colloidal sulfur applied for powdery mildew. Predatory mites, in particular *Typhlodromus doreenae*, provide adequate biological control of bunch mite in wine or dried vine fruit vineyards. Where additional control is required, such as for tablegrapes, miticides can be applied during summer.

10.2 Pests restricted in distribution or sporadic in occurrence

Although pests included in this section may be regarded as minor in terms of the total vineyard area regularly damaged by them, the damage to individual properties can be extensive. Grape phylloxera and fruit flies are restricted in distribution by quarantine barriers, while the distribution and abundance of other pests is influenced mainly by climate and the presence or absence of alternate host plants.

10.2.1 Grape phylloxera

Grape phylloxera *Daktulosphaira vitifolii* is the most destructive insect pest of grapevines. It is an aphid-like insect indigenous to eastern North America, where its native host plants are various American species of *Vitis*. In the period from 1860 to 1900 it was accidentally transported to most viticultural areas of the world. It was first recognized as a pest in France, where its introduction resulted in the destruction of over one million hectares of grapevines and almost destroyed the wine industry in that country (Ordish 1967).

In Australia, grape phylloxera was first discovered at Fyansford near Geelong, Victoria, in 1877. Several vineyards in the Geelong district were subsequently found to be infested, and a policy of destroying vineyards was adopted in an effort to eradicate the pest. In 1893 phylloxera was found in the Bendigo district, and again a policy of eradication was followed. de Castella (1920) stated that the cost of eradication and compensation at Geelong was £50,375 ($100,750) and at Bendigo £37,391 ($74,782). During the late 1890s, however, phylloxera was discovered at Heathcote in the Goulburn Valley, in replanted vineyards at Geelong, and in the Rutherglen district. By 1902, 275 of the 10394 ha of vines in Victoria were affected by phylloxera and at least 600 ha had been previously uprooted during attempts at eradication (Dubois 1902). Phylloxera was also found in areas near Sydney and in Brisbane, but the main vine-growing areas in New South Wales and Queensland were not infested. In Victoria, the only districts that remained free of phylloxera were Lilydale, Great Western and the irrigated vineyards of the north west.

The effect of phylloxera at Rutherglen, at that time the principal grapegrowing area in the Commonwealth, was to reduce the vineyard area to less than one-quarter of its previous size.

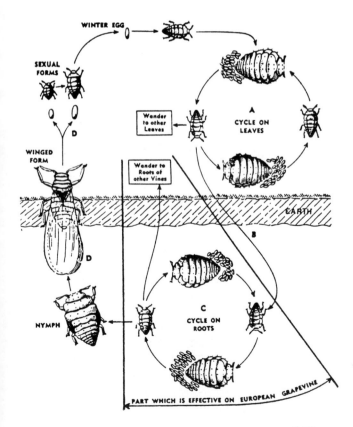

Figure 10.7. The life cycle of grape phylloxera (after Coombe, 1963). All stages in this diagram are to scale except that eggs are too small; the eggs should be just smaller than the insects that hatch from them. A. Cycle of 4-7 generations of leaf-galling phylloxera on leaves of American vines during summer; showing eggs, nymphs and adults. B. During late summer an increasing proportion of nymphs migrate to the roots, instead of forming leaf galls. C. Cycle of 4-7 or more generations of root-feeding phylloxera on both American and European vines; it is the decay of root galls that results in death of European vines. D. A winged form develops on American vines during autumn, flies, and lays eggs which hatch into sexual forms. These mate, and the female lays a winter egg, which initiates the cycle on leaves in the next season. This part of the cycle is rare and always abortive on European vines.

Appearance and biology

On *Vitis vinifera*, the only above-ground symptoms of grape phylloxera are dead, dying or weakened vines (Volume 1, Figure 8.1). A pattern of infestation termed oil-spotting often occurs, where vines are weakest in the centre, and vine vigour increases towards the periphery of the spot. Oil-spotting arises from the slow spread of the root-feeding forms of phylloxera outwards from the source of infestation. The only reliable method of confirming the presence of phylloxera on *Vitis vinifera* is to examine the roots of weakened vines for the insects. Coombe (1963) recommends that this be done during summer, when the insects are numerous, large-bodied and light in colour. Adults are about 1 mm long and greenish yellow in colour (Figure 10.2f).

Life cycle

The life cycle of grape phylloxera is complex, and differs between American, e.g. *Vitis riparia* and *V. rupestris*, and European, i.e. *V. vinifera*, vines. On European vines the life cycle is limited to root-living forms, whereas on American vines and their hybrids leaf-galling forms may also be present (Figure 10.2d).

With American vines, the life cycle on leaves is initiated by the hatching in spring of the overwintering egg. The young nymph commences feeding on the upper surface of a young leaf, which causes a pocket-like gall to form around the insect. The gall opening is on the upper surface of the leaf, slit-like, and rimmed with plant hairs. The nymph develops within the gall to a wingless adult female that reproduces parthenogenetically, i.e. without mating, laying up to 500 eggs (Figure 10.2e). Nymphs hatching from these eggs leave the parent gall and commence feeding, and produce further galls (Figure 10.7a). As the season progresses, an increasing proportion of young nymphs move to the roots instead of forming galls on leaves (Figure 10.7b). Leaf galls occur on the leaves of American vines and some of their hybrids, such as the rootstocks 3309 and 101-14, at Rutherglen. They are most prevalent in seasons with a high summer rainfall (Coombe 1963).

The life cycle on grapevine roots occurs with both European and American vines. Young nymphs are the normal overwintering stage on European vines, but on American vines both overwintering nymphs and the winter egg (which gives rise to the cycle on leaves) may occur. Overwintering nymphs shelter in crevices and beneath bark on the older roots, but are difficult to discern because of their small size and brown colouration. They commence feeding on the roots in spring, and develop to wingless adult females that reproduce parthenogenetically. Up to 200 eggs may be laid, and the ensuing nymphs wander through cracks in the soil to infest other roots, or to the soil surface and thence to roots of neighbouring vines. Several generations of root-feeding phylloxera may occur during a season (Figure 10.7c).

On American vines, some of the root-feeding phylloxera develop into winged insects during late summer and autumn (Figure 10.7d). The winged phylloxera leave the soil and lay eggs on the underside of leaves or on bark. The eggs are of two types, some developing to females, and some to males. These sexual stages do not feed. Mating occurs, and the female lays a single, winter egg beneath the bark of the vine. In spring, this egg hatches to initiate the leaf-galling cycle. On European vines this part of the life cycle does not often occur, and if it does, it is not carried through to the stage that normal leaf galls are formed.

Dispersal

Natural spread of grape phylloxera is by the winged form and through the wandering of root-living forms. The winged form could be carried several kilometres by wind, but is reliant on the presence of suitable leaves, i.e. of American vines, to establish an infestation. Consequently it is of little importance as an agency of spread in areas where European vines predominate, and of no importance where such vines are planted on their own roots. Spread of grape phylloxera through the wandering of root-living forms in cracks in soil, or on the soil surface, is comparatively slow, and appears limited to a few metres a year under favourable conditions. In sandy soils, which do not crack, the spread of root-living phylloxera is retarded to the extent that vines in very sandy soils are little affected.

King and Buchanan (1986) showed that phylloxera crawlers move up vine trunks onto the vine canopy from where they can be easily dispersed by wind or viticultural machinery in contact with the canopy. Spread of phylloxera up to 103 m in a season in the direction of the prevailing wind was recorded within one vineyard. Transport of crawlers on viticultural machinery was likely where a large population of phylloxera developed on roots, where environmental conditions such as high humidity favoured survival of crawlers, and where there was a high level of mechanization of vineyard operations.

The main method by which grape phylloxera has been spread to grape areas throughout the world is by transport of infested grapevine rootlings. The importance of this method of spread is illustrated by the fact that the distribution of phylloxera in Australia has changed little since quarantine measures have been in operation (Buchanan 1987). Other methods of artificial spread are in soil adhering to stakes, picking boxes, cultivation equipment, etc., or by water flowing through infested land.

Damage
The feeding by grape phylloxera on roots of both European and American vines results in the formation of root galls. Where phylloxera settle on growing rootlets, they cause the root to swell and curve around the feeding puncture, resulting in a characteristic hook-shaped gall termed a nodosity (Figure 10.2e). The diameter of the nodosity may be six times that of the normal root, and its formation stops growth of the rootlet. Where the insect settles on older roots it causes a rounded swelling to form, which gives the root a roughened or warty appearance. The swellings on older roots are term tuberosities. It is the decay of the root galls, usually about a month after their formation, which results in the injury to the vine.

On established, susceptible vines, and with conditions favourable to phylloxera, above-ground symptoms such as stunting of of cane growth may appear in the third year of infestation, followed by death of the vine in the fifth or sixth year. Young vines, with a more limited root system, may be killed even more rapidly. Generally, vines in heavy shallow soils that crack readily are more susceptible, whereas vines in sandy soils and possessing a well-developed root system may withstand phylloxera for several years (Davidson and Nougaret 1921).

Control
There are two established methods used to control grape phylloxera in Australia: quarantine and resistant rootstocks. Quarantine measures are organized on a state basis, and aim to prevent spread of phylloxera to non-infested areas by prohibiting removal of grapevine material from infested areas. Where phylloxera is already present, the only satisfactory method of control is to graft vines onto resistant rootstocks. These rootstocks are derived from American species of Vitis which can tolerate the presence of phylloxera on their roots. A range of rootstocks resistant to grape phylloxera is available (see Volume 1, Chapter 8).

In contrast to most other insect pests, satisfactory control of grape phylloxera has not been obtained with chemicals. Soil has been fumigated with carbon disulfide in Europe, but the treatment is expensive and only temporary suppression is achieved. The effects of phylloxera may be delayed or partially alleviated by frequent, light irrigations, foliar application of nutrients, and other cultural treatments (e.g. light cropping) that reduce stress on vines.

10.2.2 Fruit flies
The Queensland fruit fly *Dacus tryoni* and the Mediterranean fruit fly *Ceratitis capitata* are major pests of soft fruits in Australia. Queensland fruit fly occurs in coastal and subcoastal areas of Queensland and New South Wales, extending into eastern Victoria, while Mediterranean fruit fly is restricted to Western Australia. Attack on grapes by Queensland fruit fly is comparatively rare and control measures are seldom required. Mediterranean fruit fly, however, damages late table grapes in Western Australia, and government regulations make it compulsory to control Mediterranean fruit fly in the infested area of that state.

Appearance and biology
The fruit flies are similar in size to the housefly. The thorax of Mediterranean fruit fly is black with irregular white markings, and the rest of the body yellowish to light brown in colour. Queensland fruit flies are reddish to dark brown in colour, with attractive yellow patches on the thorax.

The life cycles of both species are similar. The female fly punctures ripe or ripening fruit with her ovipositor and forms a chamber within the fruit, in which several eggs may be laid. In warm weather the eggs hatch in 2-4 days, and the young larvae commence burrowing and feeding within the fruit. Full-grown larvae are 8-10 mm in length, and creamy white in colour. When removed from fruit and placed on a smooth surface, the larvae jump. After feeding, the larvae drop to the ground and burrow into the soil where they pupate. In warm weather, the adults emerge from the soil in about two weeks. They are relatively long-lived provided that water and suitable food, such as honeydew produced by scale insects and aphids, are available. Several generations occur each year. Fruit flies are usually abundant in areas having a warm climate, a sequence of favourable host fruits, and abundant summer rainfall.

Damage

In grapes, the puncture marks made by the female fly appear as black irregular-shaped spots on the skin. Tunnelling in the berry by young larvae leads to the appearance of fine thread-like, black lines radiating from the puncture marks (Figure 10.8). Grapes are however, not a favourable host for fruit flies, and often larvae do not develop to maturity (May 1958, Jenkins *et al.* 1967). Although the proportion of berries damaged may be low, the presence of larvae is a problem in grapes produced for local or export fresh fruit markets.

Control

In vineyards, fruit flies are controlled by cover sprays of systemic insecticides. These insecticides are not only effective against flies but also penetrate the fruit to kill eggs and larvae. In Western Australia, Mediterranean fruit fly is established in an area around Perth, which includes the Swan Valley vineyards, and grapegrowers in this area are required to control this pest.

The main fruit-growing areas in the south-west of Western Australia are substantially free of Mediterranean fruit fly, and any grapes transported into this area must be treated to prevent spread of the fly. Restrictions on movement of fruit from areas infested by Queensland fruit fly are imposed also in the eastern states. Eradication programs based on control of flies with bait sprays of maldison and protein hydrolysate, and/or mass releases of sterile male fruit flies, are used in

Figure 10.8. Grape berries infested by Mediterranean fruit fly. The black markings are due to tunnelling by young larvae. Photograph courtesy of A.N. Sproul, Department of Agriculture, Western Australia.

conjunction with the quarantine measures to restrict the distribution of fruit flies in Australia.

10.2.3 Rutherglen bug

Rutherglen bug *Nysius vinitor* is a native insect which occurs in all states but is particularly troublesome in hot, dry areas. Normally it is of little importance but, in seasons with an unusually hot spring and summer, Rutherglen bug may occur in plague numbers, invading and causing extensive damage to fruit and vegetable crops.

Appearance and biology

Rutherglen bugs are about 4 mm long, dull grey or brown in colour, with clear wings that life flat on the body when at rest. They are very active, and when numerous are readily seen both on vines and on the ground between vines. The adult is the stage most noticeably present in vineyards during outbreaks.

The normal habitat of Rutherglen bug is in paddocks containing weed species of the families Compositae, Gramineae and Cruciferae. Development may also occur on other plants. Eggs are laid in the soil, foliage or flowering heads of its host plants, and both the nymphs and adults feed on the flowers and seed. Development to the adult stage is completed in 3-4 weeks during spring and summer, several generations occurring each year. Each female may lay over 500 eggs, and under hot conditions population increase is extremely rapid. Both nymphs and adults require almost continuous access to water for survival, the water being obtained form plants, dew, ground moisture or free water (Kehat and Wyndham 1972a,b).

When its host plants dry off during summer, migration by flight of adult bugs into horticultural crops is liable to occur. Generally, Rutherglen bugs does not reproduce on cultivated fruits and vegetables, and its presence in vineyards is probably due to the need of water for continued survival. Reproduction can, however, take place where suitable food plants, e.g. capeweed and paspalum, occur as weeds in the vineyard. Rutherglen bug quickly becomes numerous in fruit crops under favourable conditions, but has been observed to disappear just as rapidly after rain.

Damage
Rutherglen bug attacks all green parts of the vine, but is mainly found sucking fluid from shoots, stems and berries. Affected berries shrivel and dry out, and exudations of gum may appear at the feeding punctures. Attack on shoots can result in wilting and death of the shoot when the bugs are numerous.

Control
Control of Rutherglen bug relies on the application of contact insecticides to vines and to the ground beneath the vines. Removal of weed growth in and around vineyards will prevent reproduction of the bug in these areas. Where hot, dry weather conditions persist, migration of adults into vineyards may continue, necessitating repeated insecticide application.

10.2.4 Cicadas
Cicadas are plant-feeding bugs that spend their nymphal life in soil, feeding on the roots of native trees and shrubs. Full-grown nymphs, which may take several years to develop, leave the soil and climb up the host plant, where they change to the adult. Adults of *Melampsalta* are black in colour and, as with other cicadas, the male is capable of sound production.

In the Hunter Valley, adults of *Melampsalta* spp. have been reported damaging grapevine canes and shoots through their egg-laying activities (Greenup 1967). The females possess a spear-like ovipositor which is used to form an egg chamber in wood. The egg chambers have

circular openings and extend into the pitch of the cane at an angle. Several eggs are placed in each chamber. The effect of numerous oviposition holes in canes is to cause dieback and to render the canes susceptible to breakage.

The cicada eggs hatch after several weeks, the young nymphs dropping to the ground and burrowing into the soil. It is not known whether nymphs injure grapevines, and there are no recommended control measures for either adults or nymphs.

10.2.5 Weevils
Apple weevil (also known in South Australia as curculio beetle) *Otiorhynchus cribricollis* is the most common of the weevils attacking grapevines, particularly in South Australian and Victorian vineyards. It is a cosmopolitan pest, thought to be a native of Europe, that also attacks fruit trees, lucerne and various weeds.

Appearance and biology
The weevils are dark brown in colour, and about 1 cm long. They are flightless and reproduce parthenogenetically, i.e. without mating, each weevil laying 50-60 eggs. Eggs are laid during autumn, and hatch in about 3 weeks under favourable conditions. The larvae, which are legless white grubs, burrow into the soil where they feed on the roots of weeds and cover crops during winter and early spring. They are usually found between 8 and 40 cm below the soil surface. Pupation occurs in a cell excavated by the larva in the soil, and the weevils emerge during late November and early December.

The weevils remain in the soil or other sheltered sites by day, ascending the trunk of grapevines to feed at night. Although the weevils are long-lived, there is a period in mid-summer (January to mid-February) when they do not feed. Most of the weevils die after laying their eggs in autumn, but a few overwinter and cause damage in the following spring (Andrewartha 1933).

Damage
Damage to grapevines is due to the feeding of the weevils on above-ground parts of the vine, particularly during December. Feeding on leaves results in a saw-toothed margin of affected leaves. The weevils also feed on the surface of shoots and

bunchstems, causing wilting and death of the shoot or bunch through a ring-barking effect. Although damage is of most importance on young vines, at times the weevils do cause economic damage to older plantings.

Other weevils

In addition to apple weevil, the garden weevil, vine weevil, elephant weevil and fruit tree root weevil may occasionally attack grapevines.

The garden weevil *Phlyctinus callosus* is indigenous to South Africa where it has been known as a pest of grapevines from 1896. Since its introduction to Australia, the adult has become a pest of garden plants and apples, but as yet it has not become an important pest of grapevines. Its biology and behaviour is similar to that of apple weevil, and it damages leaves, shoots and bunch stems in a similar manner. The adult is greyish brown in colour, with a light-coloured, V-shaped line across the posterior end.

The vine weevil *Orthorhinus klugi* is a native insect which feeds mainly on wattles. On grapevines, the larval stage bores into canes, eventually pupating within the tunnel. Vine weevil is, however, not as common as the related elephant weevil *Orthorhinus cyclindrirostris* the larvae of which also bore into canes. Elephant weevil and vine weevil can also cause damage by feeding on the buds and bark of canes. The fruit-tree root weevil *Leptopius squalidus* is another native weevil which feeds on buds and foliage of grapevines and fruit trees. Its larvae feed on the roots of fruit trees causing dieback of aerial portions, but are not known to attack vine roots.

Control

Where weevils require specific control measures in established plantings, cover sprays of a contact insecticide are used. Infestations of vine weevil, elephant weevil and fruit-tree root weevil often originate from native trees, so the early clearing of land and removal of infested native trees in the vicinity of vineyards will help avoid attacks. For vine weevil and elephant weevil, the removal and destruction of infested prunings would also assist in control. With apple weevil, the normal cultivation practices in vineyards probably aid in suppression, although Andrewartha (1931) suggests this may cause them to feed on the roots of the crop plant.

10.2.6 Fig longicorn

The fig longicorn *Dihammus vastator* is primarily a pest of cultivated figs, but occasionally attacks grapevines in the Hunter Valley (Anon. 1958). The beetles lay eggs singly on bark, and the larva tunnels into the wood. It may tunnel upwards in canes or down through the roots. The larva is whitish in colour, up to 4 cm in length, and has a dark-brown head with well-developed jaws. It pupates at the end of the tunnel. Effective control can be obtained with contact insecticides provided they are applied when young stages of the longicorn are exposed on the vine.

10.2.7 Fruit-tree borer

The fruit-tree borer *Crytophasa melanostigma* is a native moth that feeds on wattles, but also attacks fruit trees and occasionally grapevines. Eggs are laid on bark, and the larvae feed on the bark. On fruit trees they make surface tunnels covered with silk and excrement, and on grapevines they bore into spurs and lower canes, causing die-back and loss of vigour. The reddish-brown larvae are about 4 cm long when fully grown, and pupate in the tunnel. Control, if warranted, relies on the physical removal and destruction of affected parts, or on injection of insecticides into the feeding tunnels. In South Australia, the larvae of *Echiomima* spp. also cause damage in a similar manner to fruit-tree borer.

10.2.8 Grapevine hawk moth

Although widely distributed in Australia, grapevine hawk moth *Hippotion celerio* is rarely of concern in commercial vineyards. The larvae feed on foliage and can rapidly defoliate grapevines, but are readily controlled by

Figure 10.9. The larva of the grapevine hawk moth Hippotion celerio.

insecticides applied for other vine pests. Grapevine hawk moth larvae are green in colour, with two conspicuous eyespots, and possess a dorsal spine-like process characteristic of hawk moth larvae (Figure 10.9). Pupation occurs in the soil or in fallen leaves underneath the vine. The adult is brown in colour, attractively marked with silver stripes on the forewings and a red area on the hindwings. They are strong fliers, and feed on nectar. In Queensland, the larva of the hawk moth *Theretra oldenlandiae* is also known to feed on grapevines.

10.2.9 Locusts and grasshoppers

Several species of native locusts and grasshoppers occasionally increase to plague proportions and may invade horticultural crops when pastures dry out. The term locust applies to species that occur as dense, strongly-migratory swarms, whereas grasshoppers are species that never form swarms, or else form only loose swarms that migrate little. The species liable to threaten vineyards are the Australian plague locust *Chortoicetes terminifera*, the small plague grasshopper *Austroicetes cruciata*, the spur-throated locust *Austracris guttulosa* and the wingless grasshopper *Phaulacridium vittatum*.

The major pest in eastern Australia is the Australian plague locust. Populations build up in outback New South Wales and Queensland, giving rise to dense flying swarms which appear suddenly in horticultural areas. The spur-throated locust does not swarm in southern Australia; invasion of vineyards by this insect, the small plague grasshopper, and the wingless grasshopper usually originate from nearby pastures. Locusts and grasshoppers are foliage feeders, and when pastures dry out are liable to invade grapevines and other crops that provide green feed. Although grapevines appear not to be a favoured host plant, the large numbers of insects present may lead to extensive damage, particularly on border rows.

Control of locusts and grasshoppers relies on the spraying of swarms with a contact insecticide such as maldison, usually by aircraft or ground mister. Treatment of small groups of flying adults is not normally economical. Where hoppers are invading vineyards from adjacent grass paddocks, an insecticide barrier should be applied across the line of advance.

10.2.10 Thrips

Thrips cause concern to growers when they become abundant in grape flowers during spring. Common species in inland areas are plague thrips *Thrips imaginis* and tubular black thrips *Haplothrips victoriensis*. They are tiny (1-2 mm long) insects with a narrow body and wings. Plague thrips are light brown to grey, while *H. victoriensis* is black, as implied by the common name.

Thrips are sometimes blamed for poor berry set and scarring of grape berries. Available evidence shows that there is no measurable improvement in berry set where thrips are controlled with insecticides.

Thrips feed on plant tissue by puncturing the epidermal cells and sucking liquid from the damaged cells. Plague thrips will also lay eggs in the plant tissue, which leaves a small swelling at the site of oviposition. In California, western flower thrips cause scarring of Thompson Seedless berries by feeding under persistent flower caps, and 'halo spots' by laying eggs in young berries (Jensen *et al.* 1981). Similar symptoms on grapes in Australia have been attributed to plague thrips. The scarring is not significant where grapes are dried or used for wine, but downgrades the appearance of table grapes.

Thrips are readily controlled with contact insecticides, but no specific treatments have been registered due to the lack of obvious benefits through controlling thrips.

10.2.11 Snails

The common garden snail *Helix aspersa* and the sand dune snail *Theba pisana* are introduced pests of European origin which attack many cultivated plants. The common garden snail is the more common and widely distributed, having been present in Australia since 1888. Although usually not important, in wet seasons snails may become sufficiently numerous to warrant control measures.

Appearance and biology
The shell of a full-grown common garden snail is about 2.5 cm in diameter and made up of four to four-and-a-half whorls. It is greyish yellow and brown in colour, the brown usually occurring in four bands. The shell of the sand dune snail is about 2 cm in diameter when full grown,

whitish in colour with fine dark bands.

Snails are hermaphroditic, i.e. each individual possesses male and female organs, and during mating mutual fertilization occurs. Individual garden snails may lay eggs several times, producing several hundred eggs. The clutches of eggs are buried in moist soil at a depth of 2.5 to 4 cm. The eggs hatch in a few weeks to produce young snails, which possess a tiny shell at hatching. The young snails then make their way to the soil surface and commence feeding. The growth rate depends on the availability of food and moisture, but usually the snails are mature and breed within a year of hatching.

Snails favour moist conditions, and normally feed at night. The main feeding organ is a tongue-like radula, consisting of rows of very small teeth which are used to rasp food. During dry conditions the snails aestivate, i.e. become dormant, and usually seal themselves down to hard surfaces or seal the shell opening with a hard calcareous epiphragm.

Damage

In vineyards snails are mainly a problem in early spring, attacking vine foliage shortly after budburst. The snails feed on the leaves and shoots causing distortion or total failure of the shoot and destroying the developing bunches. Also, snails that are present on vines at harvest are a potential contaminant of wine and dried fruit, especially where the fruit is harvested mechanically, and may cause either the fruit to be rejected or increase the cost of processing it.

Control

Weed growth in and around vineyards provides ideal sites for snails to feed and shelter. Removal of weed growth, preferably well before budburst, is normally sufficient to control snails. Wet seasons are favourable to snails, in addition to making cultivation difficult, and in such seasons chemical control may be necessary. Snail baits, containing methiocarb or metaldehyde, give effective control when placed beneath vines during periods of snail activity. The effectiveness of metaldehyde is, however, reduced if weed growth is present or if wet weather persists, as it acts by immobilizing snails and rendering them susceptible to desiccation. Some of the pesticides used on vines affect snails, of which the copper-based fungicides are particularly effective because they both repel and kill snails.

10.2.12 Birds

In vineyards adjacent to forest or bushland, the prevention of damage by birds can be the most difficult problem facing the grower. Damage is generally less in large areas of vines or where vineyards are surrounded by open land, but may still be significant where large flocks of birds occur near harvest. The greatest incidence of bird attack on grapes is in boundary rows, and often damage is most severe near trees or bushes that provide refuge sites for birds. The removal of such shelter is often a useful method of reducing bird depredations.

Of the introduced birds, the Common Starling *Sturnus vulgaris* and the House Sparrow *Passer domesticus* are the most important pests. Native birds that damage grapes include the Silvereye *Zosterops lateralis*, Australian Raven *Corvus coronoides* and Little Raven *C. mellori*. Several other species of native birds may occasionally feed on grapes, but usually they do not cause economic damage.

Figure 10.10. Bird damage to wine grapes. Both pluck-damage and peck-damage has occurred.

Feeding on grapes may commence well before the berries are ripe. Thomas (1957) reported that starlings may feed on currants in mid-December, before the berries have coloured. Depending on the species of bird, and variety of grape, the berries may be damaged by pecking, and remain on the bunch, or be removed by plucking (Figure 10.10). In addition to direct loss of fruit, bird damage may result in higher picking costs, mould infection of the bunches and, with table grapes, extra costs in preparing the bunches for market.

Prevention of damage relies principally on devices that keep birds away from vineyards rather than cause their destruction within the vineyard. Control of birds solely by killing is seldom successful, is liable to arouse the indignation of the public, and renders the grower liable to prosecution where protected birds are involved. Growers should consult the appropriate Wildlife Officers where native birds are a problem, as most or all of these are protected species in the different states. A permit must be obtained before protected species can be destroyed.

A variety of chemical, visual (scarecrows, dead birds, models of predatory birds, streamers, flags, etc.), and acoustic (gas-guns, firecrackers, starting pistols) methods have been used to repel birds in vineyards. A common problem is that the birds become accustomed or habituated to the devices, sometimes within a few days. Consequently, it is often necessary to use a combination of methods, and to vary the position and use of scaring devices, in order to maintain their effectiveness for the required period. As it becomes difficult to repel birds once they have been feeding in a vineyard for several days, it is important that control measures are implemented before grapes become attractive to birds.

There has been little research on methods of preventing bird damage in Australian fruit crops, and grower experience is the only way of determining the best method or methods for a particular area. The most common method of bird control is gas-guns, supplemented by shotgun patrols. This method gives good results against ravens and starlings. Distress and alarm calls have been used in other countries to repel starlings (Frings and Frings 1967, Bouddreau 1972) but little interest has been shown in Australia for this technique. An example of the acoustic devices is 'Av-Alarm' which is claimed to interfere with bird communication and provoke anxiety in birds. This has been used in vineyards with apparent success against starlings and ravens, and to a lesser extent, against silvereyes. However, the usefulness of this and other acoustic devices in closely settled areas is limited, unless neighbouring families are either exceptionally tolerant or hard of hearing.

Rooke (1984) found that silvereyes in Western Australia preferred nectar from Marri trees, nightshade berries, figs and saltbush berries to grapes. He suggested the planting of figs or nectar-bearing plants such as *Banksia occidentalis* may attract silvereyes away from grapes. Similarly, the use of sacrificial border rows, separated from the main inner part of the vineyard by 3-4 rows from which grapes have been prematurely harvested can limit bird damage.

Table grapes and other high value crops may be protected by netting. The net needs to totally enclose the fruit, and the mesh size should be less than 15 x 15 mm to protect against silvereyes.

10.3 Pests of drying grapes

The insects of major importance during grape drying are the raisin moth *Ephestia figulilella*, the dried fruit beetles *Carpophilus hemipterus* and *C. dimidiatus* and vinegar flies, various *Drosophila* species. These insects not only reduce yields, but also contaminate the dried fruit. Vinegar flies and driedfruit beetles are especially prevalent during wet seasons, when splitting of grapes and relatively long drying periods predispose the grapes to insect attack.

Insecticide treatments of drying grapes are not desirable because of the likelihood of excessive insecticide residues in dried vine fruit. Preharvest sprays can control insects (Buchanan *et al.* 1984) but are of doubtful economic value. The most effective treatment for dried fruit beetles and vinegar flies is to hasten drying, e.g. by artificial dehydration. The incidence of raisin moth can be reduced by boxing fruit in the late afternoon so that the chance of raisin moth eggs being killed by high temperature is increased. Vineyard sanitation is important. All dried grapes should be handled in thoroughly cleaned boxes and delivered promptly to the processors.

10.3.1 Raisin moth

Although the raisin moth *Ephestia figulilella* is primarily a pest of drying and fallen fruits, it is known to feed on ripening grapes and on damaged or mouldy clusters of grapes. It is of particular concern because of its ability to infest grapes that are almost completely dried. The raisin moth lives and develops mainly out-of-doors, but is often brought into storages with infested fruit in which it will continue to develop.

Appearance and biology
The moth is about 10 mm long and has a wingspan of 15 mm. The forewings are drab grey and the hind wings whitish without distinct markings. Female moths are capable of laying several hundred eggs, most of which are deposited on drying grapes in the first few hours of darkness during the daily flight period. After hatching, the larvae start feeding on the surface ridges on the grapes and later may bore into the flesh. Larvae moult about six times and may be carried into the packing shed on the dried grapes and complete their development there. Larvae in the vineyards, however, pass the winter in cocoons in the upper layer (5 cm) of soil near the vine trunks, under the rough bark of the grapevines, or in cracks and crevices of trellises and the structure of the drying racks. These larvae pupate in the spring and moths start emerging in late spring, reaching a peak in early to mid-summer. Moths live for about two weeks, and development from egg to adult is completed in 32-45 days at 30°C. There may be several overlapping generations each year.

Damage
The mass of excreta, cast skins and webbing resulting from the presence of this insect lowers the quality of the fruit. During processing, however, these contaminants are reduced substantially in the fruit.

Control
Sanitation is of greatest importance. All fallen and waste fruit should be collected and destroyed. Dried grapes should be delivered to the processors as soon as possible, since holding the fruit in the vineyard increases the risk of further infestation.

10.3.2 Driedfruit beetles

The driedfruit beetles *Carpophilus hemipterus* and *C. dimidiatus* are attracted to and breed in overripe, fermenting and partly rotted fruit, particularly those with bunch rot. Grapes that are very dry or completely rotted are not attractive to these beetles. However, larvae that begin in overripe fruit may continue their development after the fruit is almost dry. Fallen fruit under trees, vines and drying racks provide excellent breeding sites, particularly where frequent irrigation keeps the soil surface moist.

Appearance and biology
Carpophilus hemipterus beetles are about 4 mm long, oval in shape and dark brown in colour with two, amber-brown spots on each wing cover, one near the tip and a smaller one at the outer margin of the base. The wing covers are short, leaving the tip of the abdomen exposed. Adults feed in rotting fruit, and a female can lay more than 1000 whitish eggs scattered on the grapes. After hatching, the larvae feed on the grapes and when fully grown are about 5 mm long, sparsely hairy and white yellowish in colour. The mature larvae enter the soil to pupate. Pupae are about 4 mm long, and white or pale yellow in colour. *Carpophilus hemipterus* usually survives the winter as pupae in cells in the upper 5 cm of soil near the food source in which development took place, such as under drying racks. Under favourable conditions *C. hemipterus* breeds rapidly, developing from egg to adult in about 19 days at 30°C. Adults may live for more than 100 days and are strong fliers, but only fly during daytime when the temperature is higher than about 18°C.

Carpophilus dimidiatus is 2-4 mm long and resembles *C. hemipterus*, except that it has no spots and its colour ranges from brownish yellow through brown to black tinged with red. Its feeding habits and biology are similar to those of *C. hemipterus*, and it may be seen flying at any time of the day, particularly in the afternoon.

Damage and control
Damage from direct feeding on the flesh of the grapes, together with the excrete and cast skins, spoils the appearance of the fruit and thereby reduces its quality. In addition, these beetles carry yeasts and mould spores in and on their bodies.

Thus they assist in spreading bunch rots of ripe and drying grapes. The main controls are rapid drying of grapes and sanitation to reduce breeding sites for driedfruit beetles.

10.3.3 Vinegar flies

Vinegar flies, also called ferment flies, include species of *Drosophila* that are common wherever damaged or overripe fruit and vegetable waste accumulate. They are attracted to damaged grapes and other fruits, in addition to fermenting fruit waste.

Appearance and biology

Drosophila melanogaster is a common species and is a small fly with bright-red eyes, transparent wings, and a shining black abdomen, which has a yellow band on each of the first three segments. The body is about 2-3 mm long. The microscopic eggs are white. The larva is dusky or whitish, without legs or eyes, and its head is pointed with a pair of dark-coloured mouth hooks at the end. Larvae pupate in a yellowish-brown pupal case near the drier edges of the food. Vinegar flies are only active during the day and can travel distances of more than 8 km. They have the most rapid reproductive rate of any dried fruit insect, D. melanogaster taking only about 7 days to complete development from the egg to the adult. Female flies may lay as many as 2000 eggs and live for about 70 days at 20°C. Under the same conditions males live for about 43 days.

Damage and control

Vinegar flies may carry yeasts and mould spores on their bodies when they leave rotting fruit and thereby contribute to the spread of various bunch-rotting organisms which attack grapes. In addition they contaminate the drying grapes with their cast larval skins and pupal cases. These are difficult to remove during processing of the fruit, and thus may lower fruit quality. Control measures are as indicated for dried fruit beetles.

10.4 Pests of young vines

The main pests of young vines in Australia are African black beetle, cutworms, rabbits and hares. These pests are damaging in the period from planting until shoots are trained to the trellis wire, sometimes killing vines but more often retarding growth to the extent that young vines do not reach the wire in the allotted time, and must be retrained in the following year. Some pests of established vines, particularly erinose mite and the weevils, may have a similar effect when they attack young vines.

10.4.1 African black beetle

The African black beetle *Heteronychus arator* is a native of South Africa that has become a pest of pastures, cereals and other crops in New South Wales and Western Australia. The beetle is a typical cockchafer, glossy black in colour, and about 1.5 cm in length. Although possessing wings, the beetle spends most of its time on or under the ground (Jenkins 1965).

There is only one generation a year, the beetles being the overwintering stage. Eggs are laid in soil during spring and the larvae feed on organic matter in the soil. Final-stage larvae may feed on grass roots, damaging pastures. Damage to grapevine rootlings and other crops, however, is due to the feeding of the beetles after their emergence in mid-January and in the following spring. They feed on plants at or below ground level, ring-barking or injuring the main shoot or root, and cause wilting and collapse of the plant.

Control

As pasture land is the main habitat of the beetles, infested pastures should be cultivated and kept weed-free, especially during summer when larval stages are present, before planting vines. An insecticide applied to the ground before planting, or jetting insecticides into soil at the base of infested vines, will also control the beetle.

10.4.2 Cutworms

Cutworms, which are larvae of moths belonging to the genus *Agrotis*, attack many cultivated plants and weeds. The moths are stout-bodied, brown in colour, and lay their eggs on the foliage of the host plant. The larvae are 3-4 cm in length when full grown, are cream, green, or brown in colour, and when disturbed usually curl into a tight spiral. They feed at night, and can be found sheltering in loose soil during the day. There are several generations a year. On young vines, cutworms feed on the foliage, sometimes cutting through leaf stems or shoots, and are capable of defoliating vines when they are numerous.

Control

Cutworms are controlled by spraying young vines and the ground beneath the vine with a contact insecticide.

10.4.3 Rabbits and hares

Rabbits, and less commonly hares, are present throughout the vineyard areas of southern Australia, and can cause extensive damage by stripping leaves and bark from young vines. Rabbits live gregariously and usually occupy well-defined territories. They require some form of cover to survive, such as that afforded by burrows, hollow logs and heavy undergrowth. In contrast hares are solitary animals that do not have permanent homes and range over a wide area. In isolated vineyards or on the fringes of a settlement rabbits are the main problem, but in large areas of grapevines hares are often the most persistent pest.

Control

The rabbit control measures carried out by farmers and graziers, e.g. poisoning with 1080®, destruction of warrens, together with myxamatosis, aid in suppressing rabbit populations, but specific control measures are still required during vineyard establishment in many areas. Where rabbits are abundant, the most satisfactory method of control is to enclose the proposed vineyard site with a rabbit-proof fence and exterminate any rabbits within the fence area. Fencing the vineyard will also assist in exclusion of other grazing animals. The wire netting of the fence should be buried about 15 cm in the ground, and a bed log laid into the ground between gate posts. Advice on methods of exterminating rabbits can be obtained from the organizations that deal with vermin control in the various states, e.g. Department of Lands and Pest Control Board.

In vineyards that are not fenced, repellents give some protection against rabbits and hares. Thiram sprays are commonly used, but lime-sulphur sprays or blood and bone fertilizer sprinkled at the base of young vines also give protection for a limited period. Where hares are a persistent problem, shooting can be an effective method of protecting young vines.

Further reading

Hely, P. C., Pasfield, G., and Gellatley, J.G. (1982) Insect Pests of Fruit and Vegetables in NSW. Inkata Press, Melbourne.

Huffaker, C.B. (ed.) (1971) Biological Control. Plenum Press, New York.

Ordish, G. (1967) Biological Methods in Crop Pest Control. Constable, London.

Other references

Andrewartha, H.G. (1931) The apple curculio. J. Agric. West. Aust. 8, 106-14.

Andrewartha, H.G. (1933) The bionomics of *Otiorrhynchus cribricollis*. Gryll. Bull. Ent. Res. 24, 373-84.

Anon. (1958) Tree borers. Agric. Gaz. N.S.W. 69, 252-8.

Baker, G. (1987) How to combat lightbrown apple moth. Aust. Grapegrower and Winemaker No. 285, 27-8.

Barnes, M.M. (1958) Relationships among pruning time response, symptoms attributed to grape bud mite, and temporary early season boron deficiency in grapes. Hilgardia 28, 193-226.

Boudreau, G.W. (1972) Factors related to bird depredations in vineyards. Am. J. Enol. Vitic. 23, 50-3.

Browning, T.O. (1959) The long-tailed mealybug, *Pseudococcus adonidum* (L.), in South Australia. Aust. J. Agric. Res. 10, 322-9.

Buchanan, G.A. (1987) The distribution of grape phylloxera *Daktulosphaira vitifolii* (Fitch), in central and north-eastern Victoria. Aust. J. Exp. Agric. 27, 591-5.

Buchanan, G.A., Bengston, M. and Exley, E.M. (1980) Population growth of *Brevipalpus lewisi* McGregor (Acarina: Tenuipalpidae) on grapevines. Aust. J. Agric. Res. 31, 957-65.

Buchanan, G.A., McDonald, G., and Evans, P.W.C. (1984) Control of *Drosophila* spp., *Carpophilus* spp., and *Ephestia figulitella* (Gregson) in Sultana grapes grown for dried fruit. Aust. J. Exp. Agric. Anim. Husb. 24, 440-6.

Carne, P.B., Cantrell, B.K., Crawford, L.D., Fletcher, M.D., Galloway, I.D., Richards, K.T. and Terauds, A. (1987) Scientific and common names of insects and allied forms occurring in Australia. C.S.I.R.O., Melbourne.

Coombe, B.G. (1963) Phylloxera and its relation to South Australian viticulture. Dep. Agric. South Aust. Tech. Bull. No. 31.

Cordingley, C. (1975) The grape-vine moth (*Phalaenoides glycine*). Australian Grapegrower and Winemaker 136, 44-8.

Davidson, W.M. and Nougaret, R.L. (1921) The grape phylloxera in California. U.S. Dept. Agric. Tech. Bull. No. 903.

de Castella, F. (1920) Twenty years of reconstitution. J. Agric. (Victoria) 20, 481-92.

Dubois, R. (1902) Report of the director of the viticultural station. J. Agric. (Victoria) 1, 764-75.

Freeman, B.M. (1988) Effect of grape leaf blister mite on grapevine photosynthesis. Australian Grapegrower and Winemaker No. 289, p. 20.

Frings, H., and Frings, M. (1967) Behavioural manipulation (visual, mechanical and acoustical). In Pest Control. Biological, physical, and selected chemical methods (eds.) W.W. Kilgore and R.L. Doutt. Academic Press, New York.

Furness, G.O. (1973) The ecology and control of the long-tailed mealybug in the Riverland area of South Australia. M.Ag.Sc. Thesis, University of Adelaide.

Furness, G.O. (1976) The dispersal, age-structure and natural enemies of the long-tailed mealybug Pseudococcus longispinus (Targioni-Tozzetti), in relation to sampling and control. Aust. J. Zool. 24, 237-47.

Furness, G.O. (1977) Apparent failure of two parasites, Anarhopus sydneyensis (Hymenoptera: Encyrtidae) and Hungariella peregrina (Hymenoptera: Pteromalidae) to establish on field populations of Pseudococcus longispinus (Hempitera: Coccidae) in South Australia. J. Aust. Entomol. Soc. 16, 111-2.

Greenup, L.R. (1967) Cicadas as pests in New South Wales. Agric. Gaz. N.S.W. 78, 42-6.

James, D.G. and Whitney, J. (1991) Biological control of grapevine mites in inland Australia. Aust. N.Z. Wine Ind. J., 6(3), 210-4.

Jenkins, C.F.H. (1965) The black beetle. J. Agric. West. Aust. 6, 39-42.

Jenkins, C.F.H., Shedley, D.G., and Sproul, A.N. (1967) The Mediterranean fruit fly. Dep. Agric. West. Aust. Bull. No. 2668.

Jensen, F.L., Flaherty, D.L. and Luvisi, D.A. (1981) Thrips. In 'Grape Pest Management'. Ed. Flaherty et al. Publication No. 4105. University of California, Berkeley, pp. 176-86.

Kehat, M. and Wyndham, M. (1972a) The influence of temperature on development, longevity and fecundity in the Rutherglen bug, Nysius vinitor (Hemiptera: Lygaeidae). Aust. J. Zool. 20, 67-78.

Kehat, M., and Wyndham, M. (1972b) The effect of food and water on development, longevity, and fecundity in the Rutherglen bug, Nysius vinitor (Hemiptera: Lygaeidae). Aust. J. Zool. 20, 119-30.

King, P.D. and Buchanan, G.A. (1986) The dispersal of phylloxera crawlers and spread of phylloxera infestations in New Zealand and Australian vineyards. Am. J. Enol. Vitic. 37, 26-33.

May, A.W.S. (1952) The grape scale. Queensl. Agric. J. 75, 105-7.

May, A.W.S. (1958) Fruit fly control in deciduous orchards. Queensl. Agric. J. 84, 493-6.

May, P. and Webster, W.J. (1958) The bud strain of Eriophyes vitis (Pgst.) in Australia. J. Aust. Inst. Agric. Sci. 24, 163-5.

McLachlan, R.A. (1969) Control of grape leaf blister mite (Eriophyes vitis) (Pag.) in the Stanthorpe district, Queensland. Queensl. Dep. Primary Ind. Div. Plant Ind. Bull. No. 459.

Rooke, I.J. (1984) Research on reducing damage to grapes by silvereyes in south-western Australia. Proceedings of the 5th Aust. Wine Industry Technical Conference, Perth, W.A., pp. 177-89.

Smith, L.M. and Schuster, R.O. (1963) The nature and extent of Eriophyes vitis injury to Vitis vinifera L. Acaralogia 5, 530-9.

Smith, L.M., and Stafford, E.M. (1948) The bud mite and erineum mite of grapes. Hilgardia 18, 317-34.

Thomas, H.F. (1957) The starling of the Sunraysia district, Victoria. Part II. Distribution. Emu 57, 131-44.

Editors' note: (1995 printing)
The reader is also referred to the following recent publication: Nicholas, P.R., Magarey, P.A. and Wachtel, M.F. (1994) Diseases and Pests, (Grape Production Series No. 1), Winetitles, Adelaide.

CHAPTER ELEVEN

Grape Diseases and Vineyard Protection

R.W. EMMETT, A.R.HARRIS, R.H. TAYLOR and J.K. McGECHAN

The introduction of most diseases of grapevines into Australia was, in retrospect, inevitable. When the first grapevines were introduced from Europe, downy mildew and the insect pest phylloxera were absent from European viticulture. Virus diseases were probably localized in Europe before grafting became essential in the latter part of the nineteenth century to combat phylloxera; hence the early grapevine introductions into Australia were virus-free or carried only mild strains of viruses. Furthermore, as most introductions were probably made as non-rooted cuttings, they would have been free of nematodes.

However, because of a lack of understanding of grapevine diseases and the absence of quarantine facilities, diseases such as powdery mildew and downy mildew were spread from North America to Europe and in due course to Australia. Thus the cost of production of grapes in Australia was increased substantially by the need for disease control programs and for research to develop these programs. Fortunately, in most grapegrowing areas of Australia, the climate does not favour the development of fungal diseases every year and disease occurrence is usually sporadic. Nevertheless, growers are faced annually with a choice of insuring against disease by applying routine spray schedules or taking calculated risks and applying the minimum number of sprays possible. Until recently, the latter course of action was a rather dangerous philosophy, although it was not without justification, both economically and with regard to minimizing chemical contamination of the environment. The recent introduction of fungicides with eradicant ability has increased the flexibility of control programs for some diseases, but it has also made the development of appropriate disease control strategies more complex.

In this chapter, the diseases of grapevines known to occur in Australia are described. Aspects of vineyard protection are also discussed to help viticulturists develop and apply efficient integrated pest management programs in their vineyards.

11.1 Fungal diseases

The major diseases of grapevines in Australia caused by fungi are downy mildew, powdery mildew, Botrytis rot, black spot or anthracnose and Phomopsis cane and leaf spot.

11.1.1 Downy mildew

Downy mildew (*Plasmopara viticola* (Berk. & Curt.) Berl. & de Toni) is indigenous to north-eastern North America where it spread from wild grapes into cultivated vineyards. The disease was probably introduced to Europe when North American native grapes were being tested in the search for phylloxera-resistant rootstocks.

In Australia, downy mildew was first recorded at Rutherglen, Vic. in 1917 and by the 1920s it had spread through most of eastern Australia except Tas. where it was not recorded until 1959. It has not been recorded in WA where the growing season is hot and dry.

Damage caused
In seasons when above average rainfall occurs in late spring and early summer, district crop losses may reach 10–20% or more when control programs are not applied thoroughly.

Symptoms
All green parts of the vine can be affected by downy mildew. Leaves are usually first to be infected. Prominent circular spots 1–2 cm in diameter with a translucent oily appearance (Figure 11.1a) develop on their upper surface. Later the spots turn yellow. The characteristic white downy growth with spores of the fungus (sporangia) may appear under the 'oil spots' on the lower surface of the leaf (Figure 11.1b). In warm wet conditions, favourable to growth of the fungus, the spots may enlarge or coalesce to cover most of the leaf. Otherwise, the spots dry out and become brown and papery; later, during humid conditions, further sporulation of the fungus may occur around their outer edges.

On fully mature leaves, infections are usually confined by minor veins, and a patchwork of yellow-brown diseased and green healthy tissue results. Severely infected leaves shrivel and fall prematurely.

Bunchstems may also become diseased and, if infection occurs before berry shatter, losses can be severe. The characteristic downy growth of the fungus may cover infected bunches (Figures 11.1c and 11.1d) which later shrivel and fall. From berry shatter onwards, the extent of bunch infection and losses are progressively reduced. Berries are most susceptible to infection until they are 5–6 mm in diameter. After this stage infected berries stop growing, harden and become bluish-green before turning brown, withering and falling from bunches. Although maturing berries are resistant to infection, they may be killed when pedicels and bunchstems become diseased. Severely diseased vines may be defoliated and exposed fruit may sunburn and fail to ripen properly. Cane dieback and delayed budburst can occur in the following year.

The presence of downy mildew can be confirmed by incubating moist leaves in a polyethylene bag held in darkness overnight at 20–25°C. If the disease is present, white fungal growth will be seen on the lower surface of leaves the following day.

Varietal susceptibility
Varieties of *Vitis vinifera* differ only slightly in susceptibility, Sultana and Pinot Noir being particularly susceptible while Cabernet Sauvignon and Semillon are less susceptible. Hybrids of *Vitis vinifera* and other *Vitis* species (e.g. *V. riparia* or *V. rupestris*) are much less susceptible and some are relatively resistant.

Life cycle

The downy mildew fungus overwinters in leaf debris as thick-walled resting spores (oospores) which may survive in soil for at least 2 years. Each oospore germinates to produce a sporangium which releases motile zoospores. Air-borne sporangia or splash-dispersed zoospores infect through stomata while vine foliage is wet. Symptoms appear after an incubation period varying from 5–21 days. Secondary sporangia which induce further infections are produced through stomatal openings on warm wet nights following oil spot development. The life cycle is completed when oospores develop within infected ageing leaves during late summer and autumn.

Predisposing factors

During winter, rainfall and persistent soil moisture favour the maturation of oospores. During late spring, summer and autumn, warm wet weather favours disease development. Primary infection occurs during the growing season mostly when soils are wet for 24 hours or more, rainfall exceeds 10 mm and minimum temperatures are 10°C or more. The optimum temperature for infection is about 25°C, the minimum about 9°C and the maximum about 28°C. Sporulation on infected vine tissues occurs at night within 4–6 hours when temperatures are 13°C or more and humidity is high (usually 90% or more). Secondary infection mostly occurs when vine tissues are wet for at least 2–3 hours during the early morning and temperatures are 11°C or more. More humid areas of vineyards are often the foci of downy mildew infection.

Control

Control may involve prevention and protection. Prevention is achieved through management practices that increase air movement and decrease wetness in vineyards (see 11.6.2). Protection consists of either applying fungicides regardless of weather conditions or spraying on the basis of forecasts of infection and disease appearance. In most routine schedules, protectant fungicides are applied every 2–3 weeks (Table 11.1) when tissue is most susceptible to infection and damage (i.e. from 4 weeks after budburst until 2–3 weeks after

berry set). Further sprays may also be needed when weather conditions favour disease development.

Where grapegrowers have access to downy mildew advisory services or monitoring devices, spray timing may be aligned with predicted downy mildew infection periods (see 11.6.4b(vii)). The availability of eradicant fungicides in recent years has made this approach safer. Most eradicants will control the disease when applied up to 5–7 days after infection (Margarey 1985, Margarey et al. 1985).

For many decades Bordeaux mixture was widely used to control downy mildew, but in recent years copper oxychloride, mancozeb, cupric hydroxide and dithianon have been preferred. Increasingly, mixtures of eradicant (post-infection) fungicides (e.g. metalaxyl, benalaxyl, ofurace or potassium phosphite) and protectant (pre-infection) fungicides (e.g. copper oxychloride or mancozeb) are being used.

11.1.2 Powdery mildew (Oidium)

Powdery mildew (*Uncinula necator* (Schw.) Burr, syn. *Oidium tuckeri* Berk.) is thought to be indigenous to North America or Japan (Bulit and Lafon 1978). It first appeared in European vineyards between 1840 and 1850. By 1866 it was present in Australia and is now endemic.

Symptoms

All green tissues of grapevines can be infected. Some varieties such as Chardonnay, Zante Currant and Sultana produce occasional shoots partly or entirely covered with powdery mildew. These 'flag shoots' (Figure 11.2a) are most evident 2–4 weeks after budburst, before they are hidden by the rest of the vine canopy (Emmett et al. 1990).

More commonly the first symptoms detected are small yellow-green blotches, up to 1 cm in diameter, on the upper surface of leaves (Figure 11.2b). On the lower leaf surface, the web-like growth of the powdery mildew fungus can be seen with a hand lens (×10). These infected areas expand and become ash grey and powdery as spores of the fungus are produced. The dusty films gradually darken as surface cells of infected vine tissues die and blacken. Dark fern-like patterns of dead cells can be seen when the fungus is rubbed off infected tissue. As the disease spreads, leaves develop a mottled appearance and their

Table 11.1 A typical spray schedule for Sunraysia, Vic. and NSW

Spray No.	Timing	Diagram No.*	Primary target	Secondary targets affected	Treatment
1	Advanced woolly bud	C	Erinose mite	Leaf rust mite Bunch mite Bud mite Restricted growth	Lime sulfur
2	Budburst	D	Black spot	Phomopsis cane and leaf spot	Ziram
3	2 weeks after bud-burst	E-F	Black spot	Phomopsis cane and leaf spot	Ziram
			Lightbrown apple moth		*Bacillus thuringiensis*
4	Shoots 20 -30 cm or 4 weeks after bud-burst	G	Downy mildew	Black spot, Phomopsis cane and leaf spot	Mancozeb
			Powdery mildew	Bunch mite	Sulfur
5	Shoots 30 -40 cm (Approx. 6 weeks after budburst)	H	Downy mildew	Black spot, Phomopsis cane and leaf spot	Mancozeb
			Powdery mildew	Bunch mite	Sulfur
6	Bunch protection (a) Late capfall	I	Botrytis bunch rot	Powdery mildew	Benomyl
	(b) Immediately after fruit set	J	Downy mildew	Black spot	Mancozeb
			Botrytis bunch rot	Powdery mildew	Benomyl
			Powdery mildew	Bunch mite	Sulfur
			Lightbrown apple moth	Grapevine hawk moth Vine moth	*Bacillus thuringiensis*

Table continued next page

Table 11.1 continued

Spray No.	Timing	Diagram No.*	Primary target	Secondary targets affected	Treatment
7	Follow on treatments— (a) immediately after rain or— (b) as required—		Downy mildew Powdery mildew Lightbrown apple moth	Powdery mildew Bunch mite	Copper oxychloride Sulfur *Bacillus thuringiensis*
8	2-3 weeks before harvest—		Botrytis rot		Iprodione

* Diagram codes as indicated in Volume 1, Chapter 7, Figure 7.3.

upper and/or lower surfaces become covered in powdery fungal growth. When young leaves are severely infected, their growth slows and they crinkle, become brittle and eventually fall.

Patches of dusty ash-grey fungal growth also develop on infected leaf petioles, tendrils, canes and bunchstems. On mature canes, red-brown to black dappled patches (Figure 11.2c) indicate earlier infection. Severely infected canes mature irregularly and die back from their tips.

Infection of inflorescences may reduce fruit set. Infected berries develop web-like blemishes and are eventually covered with ash-like growth. Often berry development is retarded. Severely infected berries are scarred, distorted and may split exposing their seeds (Figure 11.2d). Severely infected bunches are retarded in maturity and black fruited varieties may colour unevenly.

Late in the season tiny black specks (fruiting structures known as cleistothecia) often appear on the surface of heavily infected leaves, bunches or canes. These spherical structures with whisker-like appendages are just visible and are readily seen with a hand lens.

Damage caused
Unsightly markings and staining of berries and bunchstems downgrades the quality of table grapes. Severely infected bunches are also prone to bunchrot and may create 'off' flavours in wine. A series of severe seasonal infections by powdery mildew reduces the vigour and productivity of vines.

Varietal susceptibility
The most susceptible varieties of *V. vinifera* include Muscadelle, Chardonnay, Crouchen, Riesling, Frontignac, Semillon, Palomino, Muscat Hamburg and Zante Currant. Grenache and Shiraz are much less susceptible. Hybrids with other *Vitis* species may be resistant.

Life cycle
In some varieties, the powdery mildew fungus overwinters as dormant fungal strands (mycelium) in buds. In spring, infected buds produce the 'flag' shoots on which the fungus rapidly produces spores (conidia) which spread infection.

Overwintering fruiting structures (cleistothecia), first observed in Australia in 1984 (Wicks *et al.* 1985), may also be a source of primary infection each season. Cleistothecia are dispersed into crevices in the bark on vines or other sheltered places where they mature and overwinter. They may also survive in leaf litter in some seasons. In spring, cleistothecia produce ascospores immediately after rain or overvine irrigation. These ascospores create new primary infections. Ascospore infections may lead to sexual variation in the powdery mildew fungus and the development of strains that are more virulent or more resistant to fungicides.

As powdery mildew colonies develop, feeding tubes (haustoria) of the fungus enter vine tissues, absorb nutrients and slowly kill surface cells. After 5 to 12 days, depending on temperature, the fungus produces further conidia. These are spread

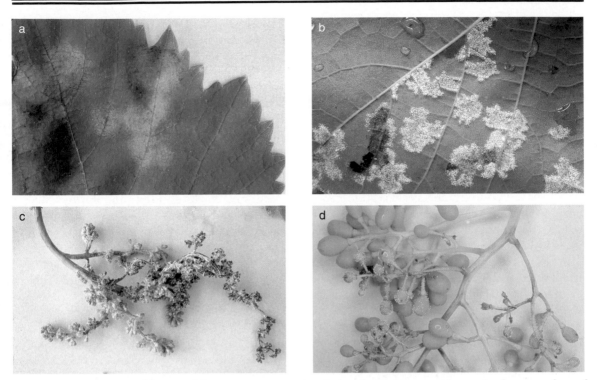

Figure 11.1. Downy mildew. a. Oil spots on young vine leaves. b. Downy growth on the lower surface of a mature leaf. c. Rot of an inflorescence caused by downy mildew. d. Young berries infected with downy mildew.

Figure 11.2. Powdery mildew (Oidium). a. A powdery mildew 'flag shoot' (right) arising from an infected bud. b. Blotches on the upper surface of an infected leaf. c. Dappled reddish patches on mature canes just after leaf fall resulting from powdery mildew infection. d. Distortion and splitting of severely infected berries (Waltham Cross).

by wind and may cause secondary infection within 24 hours if conditions are favourable. The fungus may go through at least three cycles of infection before symptoms are first detected.

Predisposing factors
Infection from ascospores released from cleistothecia is most likely to occur between budburst and flowering following rains or irrigations of 2.5 mm or more at temperatures of 10–30°C (Gadoury and Pearson 1990). But apart from this, mild weather favours powdery mildew development. It grows most rapidly on vines in late spring, early summer and autumn. Conidia germinate at leaf surface temperatures from 6° to 32°C, the optimum being 25°C. Germination and growth are rapid at 20°C to 27°C. At leaf surface temperatures above 35°C, spore germination is inhibited. In vineyards in north-west Vic. and south-west NSW for example, powdery mildew colonies on foliage exposed to bright sunlight are likely to be killed when air temperatures exceed 39°C for 6 hours. However, sheltered colonies may survive.

Conidium release occurs during daylight and is promoted by sharp changes in relative humidity. Moisture however, has less impact on powdery mildew development than temperature and solar radiation. Although high relative humidity increases sporulation, the disease can develop under relatively dry conditions. Free water from rains, dew or irrigation may cause poor and abnormal germination of conidia or wash them from the vine surface. However, colonies often survive because they are slightly hydrophobic or are sheltered by the vine canopy. Water on vines may lower the temperature in the canopy and encourage rather than discourage the development of infections (Sall and Teviotdale 1981). As moderate temperature and low to moderate light are most favourable for powdery mildew, localized microclimates may affect disease incidence and development. Often there are sheltered localities in vineyards where powdery mildew persists and flourishes each season.

Control
Preventative programs give good control. In most schedules, fungicides are applied every 2–3 weeks commencing 2-4 weeks after budburst (Table 11.1). For more than a century sulfur formulations have been used for control; dusting sulfur has been widely used but sulfur sprays are now preferred. However, sulfur may damage vines if applied when temperatures exceed 32°C; it may also taint wine if applied within one month of harvest and leave undesirable residues on tablegrapes. For these reasons systemic fungicides such as fenarimol, propiconazole or triadimefon are often preferred (Wicks *et al.* 1984). Copper fungicides (particularly Bordeaux mixture) used for downy mildew control, and benomyl, used for the control of Botrytis rot, also offer some protection against powdery mildew.

Once powdery mildew infections are well established, preventative treatments fail to achieve good control and grapevines must be drenched with wettable sulfur combined with a wetting agent at rates of 1,500–4,500 litres per hectare, or alternatively, drenched with systemic fungicides. Most eradication programs are less effective than routine protection programs for powdery mildew control (Emmett *et al.* 1984). Cultural practices such as keeping the canopy open (see 11.6.2) may also reduce disease incidence.

11.1.3 Black spot (anthracnose)
Black spot or anthracnose (*Elsinoe ampelina* Shear) appears to have spread to Australia from Europe where it has occurred since ancient times (De Castella and Brittlebank 1918). Before the introduction of downy mildew, black spot was regarded as the most serious disease of grapevines in Australia. Drastic control measures were used; for example, vines were swabbed with 10% sulfuric acid, 50% iron sulfate or mixtures of both in the winter, followed by spring applications of Bordeaux mixture (De Castella and Brittlebank 1918). In the early 1950s early spring applications of ziram or thiram were found to be effective (Coombe 1953, Taylor 1954). At about that time it was recognized that sprays of Bordeaux mixture early in the season were toxic to grapevines. Ziram was so effective that within 3-5 years black spot ceased to be an important problem.

Symptoms
Small brown pin-head sized spots (1–3 mm) are the first signs of leaf infection (Figure 11.3a).

These spots quickly enlarge into circular greyish-black patches with reddish-brown margins. With time the margins of spots darken and their centres tear away, giving leaves a tattered appearance.

On shoot stems, small indentations quickly turn brownish-black and develop slightly sunken centres and raised borders. Gradually these spots elongate and develop grey centres. When spots merge, girdling and death of stems may occur as shoots twist and distort.

When bunches are infected before or during flowering, girdling may cause withering and shedding. On berries, round sunken brown spots enlarge to form 'bird's-eye spots' with grey centres and dark-red margins. Young immature berries tend to remain attached like dried mummies after they have been attacked. As affected berries ripen, spots on their skins become hard crusts (Figure 11.3b).

Scars or cankers with pitted or cracked centres gradually form as infections on canes mature. Frequently these cankers are deep enough to expose the inner wood of canes, while the surrounding bark and wood often become blackened and burnt in appearance (Figure 11.3c).

Damage caused
Crop loss can result from severe infections on canes and flower clusters and also from the loss of potential fruiting wood available for the next season.

Varietal susceptibility
Sultana is highly susceptible to black spot. Table-grape varieties such as Muscat Hamburg, Waltham Cross, Muscat Gordo Blanco and Ohanez are less susceptible and most winegrape varieties are relatively tolerant.

Life cycle
The black spot fungus overwinters and survives for some years as a resting mass of fungal tissue (sclerotium) within cankers on canes or spurs (De Castella and Brittlebank 1918). In spring, the cankers produce spores (conidia) which, during rain or heavy dews, are splashed or carried in water by insects onto young vine shoots where infection takes place. Infection of wet host surfaces can occur within 3–10 hours depending on the temperature (Brook 1973). Further sporulation

produces secondary spread within 5–14 days, development being more rapid at high temperatures.

Generally the spread of black spot within vineyards is slower and more localized than that of downy and powdery mildew as it occurs only when free water containing spores is splashed or carried from existing infections.

Predisposing factors
Only young and succulent vine tissues are susceptible to infection. Resistance increases as tissues age. Surface moisture is essential for spore dispersal and infection. Moist conditions also favour sporulation within cankers. Temperature appears to be less important although it influences the rate of disease development. Cool wet weather during spring and early summer are particularly favourable for disease outbreaks. Hot dry conditions retard the spread of the disease.

Control
Black spot control programs rely on the routine application of fungicides so that vine foliage is protected over periods of active growth when conditions are favourable to disease. Fungicide applications are recommended at 10–14 day intervals, from late dormancy or at 50% budburst to post-flowering (see Table 11.1). Ziram is very effective when used in this way. Other organic fungicides such as mancozeb or dithianon are also useful protectants. Copper fungicides (e.g. Bordeaux mixture, cupric hydroxide, copper oxychloride and copper oxychloride-zineb) are relatively ineffective. It is essential to maintain regular spray programs to prevent the establishment of persistent infections.

11.1.4 Eutypa dieback
Eutypa dieback or 'dying arm' was a disease of unknown cause of grapevines in SA for more than 50 years (Wicks 1975). It is now known that this disease is caused by *Eutypa lata* (Pers:Fr.) Tul. (syn. *E. armeniacae* Hansf. & Carter; anamorph, *Cytosporina* sp.). It occurs in all major grapegrowing areas of SA and has also been recorded in those of other states. Eutypa dieback is an insidious disease and few growers recognize its importance, particularly in non-irrigated vineyards.

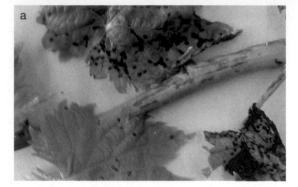

Figure 11.3. Anthracnose or black spot. a. Indentations on young shoot stems and brown-black spots on young leaves. b. Black spot blemishes on maturing berries. c. Canker on a dormant cane.

Figure 11.4. Eutypa dieback. a. Stunted shoots from an infected cordon. b. A Eutypa canker extending from an old pruning wound, exposed by removing the bark on an infected cordon (Grenache).

Figure 11.5. Phomopsis cane and leaf spot. a. Phomopsis leaf spot. b. Scarring at the base of stems caused by Phomopsis. c. Bleached areas on a dormant infected cane.

Symptoms

Shoot symptoms are most noticeable during early spring. Shoots are stunted to about one-third of their normal length and usually have shortened internodes. Their leaves are small and chlorotic, cupped, tattered, speckled and marginally necrotic (Figure 11.4a). Inflorescences on stunted shoots are of normal size but if the shoot is severely affected they may shrivel and die.

Frequently only one arm of a vine develops stunted shoots. In subsequent seasons, however, affected arms decline and die as the disease spreads to other parts of the vine. Gradually adjacent arms become affected until the entire frame of the vine dies.

First signs of disease are areas of dead wood (cankers) around pruning wounds or below dead spurs extending towards the crown of the vine. Often the bark over cankers is depressed and distorted with longitudinal cracks and the canker is more distinct when the outer bark is removed (Figure 11.4b). Internally, zones of stained dead wood can also be seen extending away from infected spurs or wounds. Severely affected vines often produce watershoots that are healthy and can be trained to replace a dead arm. However, after a number of years, the new arm also produces stunted shoots and eventually dies.

Symptoms of Eutypa dieback are rare on vines less than ten years of age and there is no particular pattern of distribution within vineyards.

Damage caused

Economic losses from Eutypa dieback have not been determined because many other complicating factors affect yield loss. In irrigated areas, Eutypa dieback is usually of little importance because the loss of an arm on a vine is soon offset by vigorous growth from arms of the same or adjacent vines. In non-irrigated areas however, dead arms are rarely replaced by new growth from adjacent arms.

Varietal susceptibility

All *Vitis vinifera* varieties in Australia are susceptible. Disease symptoms are most pronounced on Grenache but Muscadelle, Chenin Blanc, Palomino, Mataro, Shiraz, Cabernet Sauvignon, Doradillo, and Pedro Ximenes are also frequently affected (Wicks 1975).

Life cycle

Apart from vines, *E. lata* infects apricots, almonds, plums, apples, pear, tamarisk and a wide range of ornamentals including common garden plants such as Pittosporum and Ceanothus (Bolay and Carter 1985). These hosts may act as sources of infection.

Spores (ascospores) of *E. lata* are produced within masses of small black fruiting structures (perithecia) which create a black layer (stroma) on infected woody tissues two or more years after their death. Perithecia form most readily in districts where the mean annual rainfall exceeds 350 mm, or where wood of infected vines or trees is regularly exposed to overhead irrigation. Each winter, a new generation of perithecia is produced and when mature, abundant spores are discharged during or just after each rainfall or overhead irrigation of 2 mm or more. The spores are carried by wind onto vines and washed or splashed into new pruning wounds. Some spores enter open xylem cells and germinate. The fungus then grows slowly down the xylem at 10–12 cm a year, until the arm of the vine is killed. When the infection reaches the trunk, the vine eventually dies. As the disease is slow to develop, early symptoms (cankers around infected wounds) are not usually seen for two or more years after the time of infection.

Predisposing factors

As *Eutypa* infection occurs when spores enter wounded tissues, the greater the exposed area and the newer the wound, the greater the chance of infection. Vines are most susceptible to infection on the day of pruning or wounding. Resistance to infection increases as healing proceeds and other organisms become established in wounds.

Pruning in wet weather during late autumn and spring increases the risk of infection as most abundant spore releases occur during rains in this period. Although spores can travel many kilometres once airborne, vines are at greatest risk when sources of spores are in close proximity either within the vineyard or within nearby orchards or vineyards. Losses from Eutypa dieback mostly occur in young plantings when large pruning wounds are left unprotected and in older plantings where vine vigour has declined.

Control

Control measures involve protection of wounds from infection by *Eutypa* and the eradication of existing infections. Wound protection is a better prospect than eradication.

Pruning in early winter (June), when spore production is low will minimize the risk of infection although no time of the year is completely safe. The application of benomyl to wounds appears to protect tissues from infection. Large cuts into two-year or older wood should be thoroughly treated. The benomyl solution can be applied with a small, hand operated spray bottle or by using manual or pneumatic spraying secateurs specifically developed for the purpose (Carter 1985, Carter and Perrin 1985).

Immediate treatment of large trunk wounds is very important as the infection of these is most likely to reduce vineyard life. Treatment of pruned one-year-old spurs is not warranted as these are unlikely to become infected (Magarey and Carter 1987).

At an early stage, *Eutypa* infections can be eradicated from vines by careful surgery. Diseased parts of vines should be located in spring before they are masked by adjacent healthy growth. To avoid overcutting, a series of successive saw cuts should be made at the base of the diseased arm until there is no evidence of dead wood. After surgery, the cuts should be protected to prevent new infections.

All infected wood that is removed should be burnt. If diseased vines are cut down, no parts of the diseased stump should be left above soil level as these may become sources of *Eutypa* spores. The same precautions apply to diseased woody plants (particularly apricots) adjacent to vineyards.

11.1.5 Phomopsis cane and leaf spot

Phomopsis cane and leaf spot (*Phomopsis viticola* (Sacc.) Sacc.) was formerly known as grape dead arm. The use of the latter name has been discontinued as similar symptoms are caused by Eutypa dieback (Moller *et al.* 1981) (see 11.1.4).

Phomopsis cane and leaf spot is widely distributed throughout the world. It was first recorded in Australia before 1930 but its presence

and significance were not appreciated until 1955–1960 when black spot was almost completely controlled by ziram and thiram. The occurrence of *Phomopsis* is sporadic. It appears to have occurred in the mid-Murray and the north-east of Vic., the MIA and around Forbes, Dubbo and Sydney (NSW) for many years. More recently it has been recorded in all states except Tas.

Symptoms

All green parts of grapevines can be infected by *Phomopsis*. The most obvious symptoms occur on spring shoots and are usually confined to the basal 20–30 cm. On leaves, first signs of infection are tiny dark brown to black spots rarely more than 1 mm in diameter, irregular in shape and usually surrounded by pale green or yellow halos extending up to 2–3 mm beyond each spot (Figure 11.5a). Leaf distortion without tearing occurs and portions of leaves may be killed when spots are numerous. Even mildly affected leaves, particularly those with spots on their petioles, turn yellow and fall. Heavily infected basal leaves may also be stunted.

On shoot stems, small spots with black centres are first signs of disease. Gradually these spots may expand into brown to black oblong markings (up to 5 cm long and 2 cm wide, Figure 11.5b) and their surface cracks and becomes roughened as canes swell and harden. In severe cases, the scabby lesions may merge to form large cankered areas. When shoot stems are partially or entirely girdled, shoots are stunted or killed. During strong winds, severely scarred shoots may break off at the base. Occasionally, on stems of inflorescences or bunches, spots similar to those on shoot stems also develop. If infection is extensive, inflorescences or bunches may wither and die.

During winter, severely infected canes or spurs discolour and develop irregular dark brown to black patches intermingled with bleached areas. White canes in winter are distinctive for this disease; infected tissues, particularly around nodes and adjacent to original scars, whiten as they dry out and become speckled in appearance as tiny pimple-like, black fruiting bodies (pycnidia) of the *Phomposis* fungus develop (Figure 11.5c).

Damage caused

When infections are severe, vine bunch number and yield are reduced when shoots are girdled and break off near the base. If canes weakened by infection are retained at pruning time, they are also more susceptible to frost damage and are less productive than healthy canes. As infected canes are often difficult to see, pruning to select sound, unaffected canes is time consuming and pruning costs are increased. Circumstantial evidence suggests that one of the major factors contributing to the great increase in yield per hectare in the MIA during the 1960s was the diagnosis and development of control measures for Phomopsis cane and leaf spot.

Varietal susceptibility

Many tablegrape varieties are susceptible to damage including Waltham Cross, Purple Cornichon, Muscat Hamburg, Sultana, Ohanez and Cardinal. Among the winegrape varieties, Grenache, Palomino and Muscadelle are particularly susceptible.

Life cycle

Phomopsis overwinters as fungal growth (stroma) and pycnidia within infected vine tissues especially canes and mummified bunches. Water-borne conidia released from pycnidia during rains are washed, splashed or spread by insects onto young vine foliage or bunches where they initiate infections through wounds or stomata. After an incubation period of three to four weeks symptoms appear on leaves. Stem symptoms usually take longer to develop. During summer, fungal growth is relatively inactive in vine tissues but activity resumes in autumn and winter as canes discolour and pycnidia develop. Infected canes and spurs may continue to produce pycnidia and conidia for at least three seasons.

Predisposing factors

Infection requires long periods of cool wet weather. In Australian vineyards, primary infection mostly occurs in spring during prolonged, heavy rain when shoots are at an early stage of development. At least 10 hours of rain are usually required to promote spore production from pycnidia and, after spore dispersal, a further 8–10 hours or more of very high relative humidity or surface moisture are usually required for infection. The optimum temperature for spore germination and fungal growth is 23°C. Growth of Phomopsis within infected vine tissues is temperature-dependent and is inactivated by hot summer weather.

Control

Where practical, diseased canes or spurs should be removed and destroyed. Use of canes or spurs damaged by Phomopsis in the framework of vines should also be avoided.

The treatment of completely dormant wood and canes with sodium arsenite (0.38%) was used to inactivate over-wintering pycnidia and to supplement spray programs during the growing season, but these sprays are now discouraged. Protectant fungicides such as dithianon applied at 10–14 day intervals commencing at budburst are reasonably effective. If conditions favouring disease persist, up to five sprays may be required and of these, the first two are the most important. Fungicides used for the control of black spot (e.g. ziram) and/or downy mildew (e.g. mancozeb) also offer protection against Phomopsis when used in routine spray schedules (Creecy and Emmett 1989) (Table 11.1). When establishing new vineyards, care should be taken to select cuttings for propagation from vines free of Phomopsis.

11.1.6 Botrytis rot or grey mould

Botrytis rot of grapes is caused by Botrytis cinerea Pers., a ubiquitous fungus which attacks many plants. Usually soft or succulent tissues are infected, particularly those of floral parts or ripening fruit. Dried material may also be colonized after it has been wet.

In the Hunter Valley districts of NSW, in southern and south west Vic. and in south-eastern SA, losses can be substantial in winegrape varieties with tight bunches. In the Murray River districts of NSW, Vic. and SA and in areas like Stanthorpe Qld., losses mainly occur in late-maturing wine and tablegrape varieties. Botrytis often causes post-harvest losses of tablegrapes during transit and cool storage, unless adequate control measures are applied.

In certain situations, under specific conditions of temperature and humidity, winegrapes infected with Botrytis decay slowly. As berries desiccate,

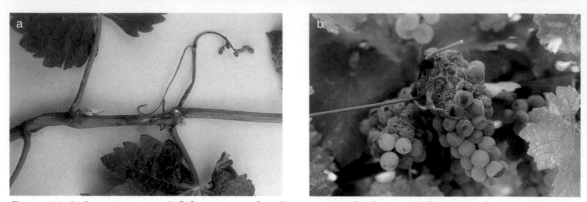

Figure 11.6. Botrytis rot. a. Soft brown rot of a shoot stem and adjoining inflorescence b. Rotting berrries in a bunch of Sauvignon Blanc grapes infected with **Botrytis**.

Figure 11.7. Rhizopus rot of rain damaged Sultana berries just prior to harvest.

Figure 11.8. Black mould or Aspergillus rot of Sultana grapes.

Figure 11.9. Ripe rot on Calmeria berries.

Figure 11.12. Leafroll. a. Interveinal purplish-red tints on leaves of Cabernet Franc infected with leafroll virus. b. Leaf symptoms of leafroll on Sultana. (Figure 11.12b courtesy CSIRO Division of Horticulture).

their acid and nitrogen content decrease while their sugar content increases. Ultimately, this results in a condition known as 'noble rot' that is highly prized by winemakers because infected grapes can be used to produce unique aromatic wines with residual sugar. However, climatic conditions leading to 'noble rot' development are uncommon and most *Botrytis* infections cause bunch rot and crop loss.

Symptoms

In favourable conditions *Botrytis* infects young succulent shoot growth early in the season causing patches of soft brown rot at any position on shoot stems (Figure 11.6a). Infected shoots often break at the nodes revealing a brown discolouration of internal tissues. Shoot stems are usually girdled at the point of infection and their extremities either wilt and die or break off. When infection occurs at the base, entire shoots are killed. When young leaves are infected, the fungus usually grows from the edge of the leaf into the main veins producing a brown, V-shaped area of dead tissue. Infected inflorescences develop patches of brown, mushy rot that spread along the main stalk (peduncle) until the inflorescence is completely rotted.

Berries and bunches also rot after *Botrytis* infection. In some seasons, occasional immature berries in bunches develop a soft brown rot in early summer (mid-season rot). During favourable conditions, grey-buff coloured spore masses of the *Botrytis* fungus develop on infected berries. More often, however, bunch rots caused by *Botrytis* develop in late summer and autumn as grape berries mature, or after harvest when grapes are cool-stored. First signs of infection in mature grape berries are small circular water-soaked spots. On coloured grapes, these spots may be faintly cleared and relatively indistinct. When berries are rubbed, the skin over these spots cracks and slips freely, revealing the firm inner berry pulp. Gradually affected berries soften and turn brown, but they may remain turgid as the rot spreads within them. Later, grey to buff coloured tufts of fungal growth grow from splits in skins of the infected berries. In compact bunches, the rot may spread rapidly from berry to berry until entire bunches are rotted with a matted grey-velvet-like appearance (Figure 11.6b). If dry conditions follow infection, berries

dry up and become raisin-like but remain attached to bunches.

Black structures (sclerotia), up to 6 mm in diameter, may develop on parts of vines that have been colonized by *Botrytis* (e.g. dead canes and mummified berries) when conditions are unfavourable for fungal growth. Sclerotia may also develop on decayed berries in cool storage.

Damage caused

In most districts, shoot damage is of little or no importance. Mid season rots may cause up to 10% crop loss in some varieties when favourable conditions prevail in regions such as the Hunter Valley, NSW (Nair 1985a). However, most substantial crop losses (often exceeding 40%) usually result from reductions in fruit quality and the loss of fruit weight when bunches are rotted either at or just prior to harvest. Losses may also occur when juice leaks from damaged bunches during transport. When wet weather persists after infection, undesirable secondary fungi, yeasts, bacteria and vinegar flies may also colonize mouldy bunches leading to 'off-flavours' in wines. Wines made from rotted grapes are difficult to process and are subject to faults.

With tablegrapes, the early development of *Botrytis* on occasional bunches in storage and its subsequent spread to other bunches may lead to the loss of entire consignments of fruit.

Varietal susceptibility

All varieties are susceptible but those with thin-skinned berries and/or tight bunches are most susceptible. These include Riesling, Traminer, Chardonnay, Ondenc, Chenin Blanc, Semillon, Grenache, Pinot Noir, Pedro Ximenes and Mueller-Thurgau. Varieties such as Shiraz are more tolerant.

Life cycle

B. cinerea overwinters on grapevines as sclerotia on or within canes (Nair 1985a) or on residues of rotted bunches. Sclerotia frequently persist in grape mummies left on vines after previous harvests (Sall *et al.* 1981). In damp conditions, spores (conidia) are produced on the surface of sclerotia and are spread by wind to sites of potential infection such as developing shoots or inflorescences. During flowering and setting, senescing flower parts (caps, stamens and aborted berries) are colonized. Occasionally individual berries are also penetrated through their stigmas (McClellan and Hewitt 1973). After a period of inactivity, fungal growth within infected berries resumes when conditions are favourable and berry sugar content has increased to 6–8° Brix or more (Nair 1985a). Eventually these infected berries rot.

Spread of infection is by growth from infected berries into adjacent berries at points of contact or from air-borne conidia produced on infected berries or on other decaying plant material present in vineyards. Ripening berries are infected from conidia through their skins or through wounds. Ultimately, sclerotia are produced in or on remnants of vine tissues that have harboured *Botrytis*.

Predisposing factors
Wet conditions in early spring are required for sporulation on overwintering sclerotia. Wet windy weather, frost or hail damage followed by at least 12–24 hours of free moisture, are usually required for leaf and shoot infection (Wicks *et al.* 1988). Colonization of senescing flower parts, aborted berries and developing berries at berry set and the formation of spore masses on rotting infected berries is also favoured by prolonged wet weather.

Infection of intact berries depends on their sugar content, the persistence of free moisture on berry surfaces, and prevailing temperatures. Periods of wetness required for infection range from 15 hours at 23°C to 30 hours or more at 10°C or 30°C (Sall *et al.* 1981). Generally cool wet weather favours *Botrytis* development and fungal growth ceases when temperatures reach 35°C or more. Red varieties often contain compounds that retard *Botrytis* development. Grapevines with dense canopies are more susceptible to disease.

Control
Botrytis control involves the application of well-timed fungicide treatments integrated with vineyard sanitation and vine canopy management practices. Sources of *Botrytis* within vines can be reduced by removing dead canes and grape 'mummies' from vines at pruning and burying them. As moisture and temperature on the surface

flowers and berries influence *Botrytis* infection and development, vineyard management practices that ensure that vine canopies and bunches are well aerated also contribute to disease control (Sall *et al.* 1981, Savage and Sall 1984) (See 11.6.2). Applications of protectant fungicides in spring (e.g. when shoots are 10–20 cm long) may be necessary to reduce the incidence of shoot infection and the loss of inflorescences. However, in most districts bunch rot control primarily depends on preventing *Botrytis* from becoming established within bunches during the flowering period. Consequently fungicide applications at pre-flowering and approximately 10–14 days later (during flowering) are worthwhile on susceptible varieties.

Additional preharvest applications, particularly for tablegrapes destined for storage, may be necessary. In most routine schedules, sprays are applied just before bunch closure and/or at veraison and 1–2 weeks before harvest.

Effective protectants include benzimidazole fungicides (e.g. benomyl, carbendazim, thiophanate methyl) and dicarboximide fungicides (e.g. procymidone, vinclozolin, iprodione). The rotation of fungicides of these different groups is recommended to discourage the development of fungicide-resistant strains of *Botrytis* (see 11.6.4,b(iii)).

Postharvest control of *Botrytis* on tablegrapes relies on preharvest control measures employed in vineyards and fumigation with sulfur dioxide during storage.

Other bunch rots
Apart from *Botrytis cinerea*, other micro-organisms may cause rots of ripening grapes and the spoilage of stored grapes or grapes on drying racks. These include *Rhizopus stolonifer* (Ehrenb.:Fr.) Lind. or *R. arrhizus* Tesher, the cause of *Rhizopus* rot, *Aspergillus niger* v. Tiegh., the cause of black mould or Aspergillus rot, *Penicillium* spp., *Cladosporium* spp. and several other fungi. Various yeasts and bacteria also cause sour rots and pungent sour rots respectively (McGechan 1978, Barbetti 1980, Nair 1985b). Rhizopus rot and Aspergillus rot are the most common rots of ripening early maturing grapes in the warmer Murray River districts of Vic., NSW and SA.

Symptoms

Berries infected by *Rhizopus* become soft and watery and covered with whisker-like fungal growth that is initially white but later develops dull-black spherical spore-heads (Figure 11.7). Berries infected with *Aspergillus* become watery with a foul odour and develop a coating of black or chocolate-brown powdery spores (Figure 11.8). After complete decay, only shells of berries covered with dusty spores remain.

Varietal susceptibility

Thin-skinned tablegrape and dried fruit varieties (e.g. Sultana) with berries that split readily as they mature are most susceptible to Rhizopus and Aspergillus rots. Wine varieties with tight bunches are also readily infected, particularly if berries split as bunches fill out.

Biology

Infection mostly occurs after fungal spores germinate within cracks or splits in berry skins following heavy rain or overhead irrigation. Ripening berries damaged by insects may also be infected. After germination, colonization of damaged fruit is rapid and substantial losses can occur on vines or on drying racks. The rotting of berries often involves a progression of colonizing fungi and bacteria. The activity of insects such as vinegar flies and Carpophilus beetles may also hasten berry decay. Warm, wet or humid conditions are particularly favourable for the development of Rhizopus or Aspergillus rots.

Control

Management practices that minimize berry damage are the basis of control measures. With fruit for drying on vines, summer or harvest pruning (May and Kerridge 1967) can be used to promote berry dehydration or reduce berry splitting immediately after heavy rains just before harvest. Careful control of irrigation is also essential. However, summer rainfall when berries are mature can negate the effects of good irrigation programs. Berry thinning to reduce the tightness of bunches is worthwhile in high value tablegrapes. The control of other pests or diseases that may cause berry damage (e.g. lightbrown apple moth and powdery mildew) can also be helpful. Generally fungicides applied to bunches following rain damage are not effective because damaged berries weep and fungicide concentrations in wounds are difficult to maintain at high enough levels to prevent the development of rots associated with a wide range of micro-organisms.

11.1.8 Minor fungal diseases

Ripe rot

Glomerella cingulata (Stonem.) Spaulding & Schrenk (anamorph:*Colletotrichum gloeosporioides* (Penz.) Penz. & Sacc.) has a world-wide distribution and causes ripe rots of many different kinds of fruit. In Australia, ripe rot of grapes usually appears in seasons when other rots are prevalent and causing heavy losses.

Cool-stored fruit as well as fruit on the vine can be affected. On individual berries, small sunken circular spots 5–10 mm in diameter are the first signs of disease. On white-fruited varieties, the diseased flesh turns pale red or brown. As the affected areas gradually expand in size, characteristic dark coloured fruiting bodies (acervuli) of the fungus develop, rupturing the berry skin in concentric rings (Figure 11.9). High moisture and high temperatures favour disease development. Incidence of ripe rot can be reduced by removing berry mummies and bunch residues (sources of inoculum) from vines during pruning.

Bitter rot

Melanconium fuligenum (Scrib. & Viala) Cav. (syn. *Greeneria uvicola* (Berk. & Curt.) Punithalingam) causes bitter rot. As the name implies, a characteristic of the disease is the unpleasant burnt bitter taste it imparts to fruit, a flavour which can be carried into wines.

Individual berries or groups of berries are infected as they ripen. First signs of disease on berries are discolourations at their point of attachment. As the rot spreads through each berry, small raised structures (acervuli), irregular in shape and size, rupture the berry skin and rapidly produce masses of wet glistening brown to black spores. On white-fruited varieties, the disease is obvious but on black- and red-fruited varieties it may be masked because the fruit has often coloured by the time infection occurs. The disease is usually a more significant problem on over-mature fruit. Small black-brown necrotic flecks may also develop on leaves, stems and immature berries earlier in the season.

M. fuligenum overwinters within infected vine tissues and on the surface of old canes and vine bark. Warm, wet conditions favour infection and disease development. Routine spray programs with fungicides, such as mancozeb and dithianon used to control downy mildew, usually control bitter rot.

White rot

Grapevine white rot is caused by *Coniella diplodiella* (Speg.) Petrak & Sydow. Infection of fruit usually follows injury by hail or berry splitting after heavy summer rains. Most outbreaks in Australia follow hail storms. Although all green parts of vines can be affected, bunches are usually damaged more than shoot stems and leaves. When bunch stems are affected, brownish depressed scars or cankers form and may enlarge until the stems are girdled. Entire bunches or portions of bunches beyond the girdled area eventually wither and die. Infected berries become very juicy before turning whitish-grey and drying up. Brown or brownish-black fruiting bodies (pycnidia) of the fungus develop under the skin of withered berries.

Persistent high relative humidity and moderate to high temperatures (24–27°C) following hail or rain storms favour disease development. Bunches nearest the ground are more prone to infection. In Australia, the incidence of white rot is spasmodic and no fungicide treatments are usually applied for its control.

Armillaria root rot

Armillaria spp. cause root rots of perennial shrubs and trees in many parts of the world. Occasionally grapevines are also affected. In Australia, incidence on vines is often associated with tree fruit orchards (especially apple and peach) either adjacent to plantings or as the previous crop.

Infected vines show premature autumn colouration and progressively decline in vigour over a period of several years as their main roots and crown are rotted. When their trunk is girdled vines eventually die. A fan-like sheath of white fungal growth is revealed when the bark is stripped from affected parts of the trunk. Black-brown boot-lace-like rhizomorphs (root-like aggregations of fungal tissue up to 1 mm in diameter) can also be observed on the rotting root systems which have a mushroom-like odour. Toadstools of the *Armillaria* fungus may also appear around the base of infected vines in autumn.

Spread of disease occurs when rhizomorphs of *Armillaria* grow slowly through the soil from infected roots or stumps to adjacent vines. To prevent spread, visibly affected vines should be removed together with vines within two metres of the affected area. All old root pieces should also be thoroughly removed from the soil before further vines are planted. Soil fumigation with methyl bromide is the best control method where outbreaks are isolated but is only worthwhile if the affected area is small.

Pythium crown rot

Young vines up to two years of age are most susceptible to crown rot caused by *Pythium ultimum*. This disease can cause annoying delays during vineyard establishment.

Infected vines develop a wet, sour-smelling rot which may girdle the vine at or just below ground level. Only the cortex and phloem are destroyed by the fungus; the xylem vessels remain intact. Shoot growth on affected vines is poor and foliage may turn yellow. In severe cases, wilting may occur, particularly with the onset of warmer conditions. If the rotted area at ground level is not extensive, the wound may heal over after the surrounding soil has dried out. Most diseased vines gradually recover after being stunted in their early stages of growth.

Cool, wet conditions in spring, excessive soil moisture and rank weed growth around young vines favour disease development. Incorporating large quantities of green plant material into the soil, ploughing wet soils against the butts of young vines or the placement of drip irrigation outlets too close to vine stems also promotes crown rot. Fungal activity, however, is greatly reduced when soils dry out in summer.

Removing soil from around infected plants and allowing the rotted area to dry out usually inhibits disease development. The soil can be replaced later during the summer when further infection is unlikely. The drenching of soils around affected plants with fungicides, such as metalaxyl, may

Figure 11.10. Pseudocercospora leaf spot on Vitis labrusca.

also reduce disease development, but is costly; it is more appropriate for the treatment of affected vine rootlings in nurseries.

Phytophthora root rot

Phytophthora cinnamomi Rands causes root rot diseases of woody plants including grapevines.

Infected vines are stunted and show premature autumn colouration in mid-summer. Leaves on white-fruited varieties turn yellow, whilst those of red-fruited varieties redden. Some defoliation may also occur. Infected vines usually die during the following winter. In late spring and summer the new roots produced on infected vines become discoloured. Although the epidermis of these roots remains intact, their internal tissues change from the healthy cream colour to grey. The root rot may progress up into the perennial roots and eventually into the butt of vines before they collapse and die.

Grafted vines are most commonly affected, particularly those on the rootstock *Vitis rupestris* or its hybrids. Most varieties of *Vitis vinifera* appear to be resistant.

Phytophthora root rot develops when soils are saturated for long periods. Control consists of avoiding heavy, poorly-drained soil types when planting. In established vineyards, the improvement of soil drainage using tile or other types of sub-surface drains reduces the disease incidence.

Black root rot

Thielaviopsis basicola (Berk. & Br.) Ferraris occasionally causes root rot of grapevine rootlings, particularly in nurseries.

Vines with black root rot show premature autumn colouration. Fibrous roots and the crown of infected vines turn dark brown to bluish black. Severely infected roots develop a mushy, decayed cortex and lack root hairs (Canter-Vischer and Over De Linden 1972).

Most *Vitis* species, particularly those used as rootstocks (e.g. *V. rupestris, V. riparia*) appear to be susceptible to black root rot. As disease development occurs when soils are excessively wet, the problem is reduced by improving soil drainage.

Pseudocercospora leaf spot

This disease is caused by *Pseudocercospora vitis* and is mostly confined to *Vitis labrusca* and *V. labrusca* hybrids. Although of very minor importance, it can cause considerable defoliation of these varieties during wet summers, particularly in the high rainfall districts of coastal NSW. Infected leaves develop small (1–4 mm) brown or red-brown angular-shaped spots before falling prematurely (Figure 11.10). Sprays applied for downy mildew control are usually sufficient to control the disease.

11.2 Bacterial diseases

Only one bacterial disease, crown gall, is of any significance in Australian vineyards. Fortunately quarantine procedures have excluded other important bacterial diseases such as bacterial blight and Pierce's disease.

11.2.1 Crown gall

Crown gall

Crown gall was probably introduced to Australia along with early grapevine introductions. Prior

Figure 11.11. Crown gall. Galls at the base of a vine infected with the crown gall bacterium.

to the early 1970s it was regarded as a minor disease of *Vitis vinifera* varieties grown on their own roots. However, with the increasing use of American varieties as rootstocks coupled with improvements in irrigation techniques, the incidence of crown gall has increased and it is now regarded as a potentially significant disease.

Symptoms
Galls (callus-like outgrowths) form at the base of hardwood cuttings, at the crowns of vines (on the trunk just below or at ground level) (Figure 11.11), at bud or graft unions or at disbudding sites. Occasionally, aerial galls also develop where hardened canes or cordons have been damaged or where vines have been top-worked. Galls do not develop on the foliage or generally on the roots of grapevines.

At first, galls are small, pale, irregularly-shaped lumps of tissue with a relatively smooth surface. As they enlarge, their surfaces become dark and rough. One or more galls usually develop on each vine. They vary in size (from 1 cm to 10–20 cm in diameter) and in growth rate. The galls are cancerous in nature and mostly consist of soft disorganized tissues, unlike galls produced by nematodes (see 11.4.1) and some insects. As galls age, they break down and rot, except at their point of attachment where they may remain soft,

moist and cream in colour. In hot dry conditions, old galls, especially those above ground level, become dark, brittle and cracked and may break off.

Damage caused
As the undifferentiated cells in galls develop at the expense of normal host differentiation, the yield and growth of vines with substantial galls may be reduced by up to 40% (Schroth *et al.* 1988). Young vines, in particular, become stunted and unthrifty and may eventually die when stressed. Patches of soft brown rot on young vine roots may also develop but the importance of this is uncertain at this stage.

Varietal susceptibility
Some widely-used rootstocks (e.g. Ramsey, K51–40 and Schwarzman) and scions (e.g. Pinot Noir, Merlot, Shiraz, Chardonnay, Riesling and Cabernet Sauvignon) are infected (Ophel *et al.* 1988). In the field, galling is often observed on Muscat Gordo Blanco, Sultana, Zante Currant, Schwarzmann and Dog Ridge.

Biology and predisposing factors
Crown gall disease is caused by the bacterium *Agrobacterium vitis* (Ophel and Kerr), formerly known as *Agrobacterium tumefaciens* (Smith and Townsend) Conn. biovar 3. Tumour-forming strains of this bacterium may incite gall formation and root decay on grapevines while non-tumour forming strains do not cause galling. *A. vitis* differs from the bacteria causing galls on other hosts such as stone fruit, pome fruit and ornamentals. These diseases are caused by *A. tumefaciens* biovars 1 and 2. In Australia, *A. tumefaciens* biovar 1 occasionally occurs on grapevines but causes little or no damage.

Tumour and non-tumour forming strains of *A. vitis* survive for long periods in the vascular tissue of grapevines as systemic symptomless infections. The bacteria may also survive in vine roots and in soil adjacent to infected roots but after roots die or are removed from the soil bacterial populations decline substantially. *A. vitis* differs from other bacteria in that it is specifically associated with grapevines. In contrast, *A. tumefaciens* biovars 1 and 2 readily survive in contaminated soils which can become a significant source of infection.

Galls usually develop where infected vine tissues have been wounded. Moist conditions favour disease development. Galls are usually more prolific in sandy soils that are constantly wet due to frequent drip or undervine irrigation. Mist propagation in association with budding, grafting, transplanting and root trimming in nurseries also provides good conditions for gall formation. On nursery stock, galls usually appear in late spring on infected cuttings planted earlier in the season and are most noticeable when rootlings are lifted for transplanting or budding. Occasionally, aerial galls also develop on established vines where vine wood has been damaged by severe frosts.

Control

Although inoculation with the related bacterial species *Agrobacterium radiobacter* Strain K1026 (registered as No Gall®) provides a successful biological control of crown gall on other crops such as stonefruit, it is not effective against *A. vitis* on grapevines. When establishing new vineyards, only planting material from indexed vines that are certified as free of crown gall should be used. If certified planting material is not available, material from the healthiest and most vigorous vines available should be used.

The use of shoot tip culture is effective in eradicating *A. vitis* from infected vines (Burr *et al.* 1987). Hot water treatment (50°C for 30 minutes) of dormant grapevine cuttings decreases the inoculum level of *A. vitis* in infected cuttings (Burr *et al.* 1989) and can reduce crown gall incidence in a nursery (Ophel *et al.* 1990). However, complete eradication of the pathogen is not achieved by hot water treatment.

After a vineyard has become contaminated, the crown gall bacteria persist within infected vines until they die or are removed. Even after removal, bacteria may remain in the soil until all grapevine roots have died. Clean rootlings planted into soil 1–2 years after contaminated vines have been removed may still become infected.

To prevent the spread of bacteria during budding and grafting, implements should be dipped in a chlorine solution (500 mg/L; diluted sodium hypochlorite) and rinsed in a very dilute chlorine solution (5 mg/L).

11.3 Virus and virus-like diseases

Virus and virus-like diseases are, almost without exception, systemic throughout plants and are readily transmitted by grafting. Virus diseases are caused by viruses (extremely small particles, mostly 30–2,000 nm in size), while the causal agents of virus-like diseases have not been observed.

About 30 virus or virus-like diseases occur in grapevines throughout the world. At least 8 of these have been observed in Australia. They include leafroll, fanleaf, fleck, yellow speckle, stem pitting (legno riccio), enation, vein necrosis and summer mottle. Of these leafroll, yellow speckle and fanleaf are the most widespread and leafroll is the only one of major importance.

Virus or virus-like diseases cause a gradual reduction in yield and a lowering of fruit quality. They are nearly always systemic within grapevines and are spread by man during vine propagation. Only fanleaf is naturally spread by its nematode vector (see 11.4.4).

The relatively low number of virus diseases present in Australian vineyards reflects the history of grapevine introductions and subsequent quarantine policies. Early importations from Europe and South Africa, except for Sultana, Waltham Cross and Zante Currant, were relatively virus-free. Viruses became widespread after it became essential to graft vines onto phylloxera-resistant rootstocks to combat the world-wide phylloxera outbreak in the period 1870–1900. Virus-infected rootstock vines were frequently and unwittingly used during propagation, resulting in a rapid spread of viruses through European vineyards and nurseries. The spread of fanleaf occurred when nurseries became infested with its nematode vector. As a result, later importations into Australia, made at the turn of this century, mainly to replace areas destroyed by phylloxera, were often infected with virus.

Following the discovery of phylloxera in the east of Australia in the late 1890s, rigid quarantine measures were introduced which restricted the importation of grapevines from overseas and the movement of grapevines within Australia. This minimized the spread of virus diseases. Today, when grapevines are imported from overseas, they are only released from quarantine when they have been shown to be free from known harmful viruses (Barlass *et al.* 1987).

Figure 11.13. Yellow speckle disease on leaves of Waltham Cross.

Figure 11.14. Fanleaf virus. a. Leaf distortion symptoms of the fanleaf strain. b. Leaf symptoms of the yellow mosaic strain. c. Leaf symptoms of the veinbanding strain. d. Grapevine fanleaf virus particles.

Figure 11.15. Vein necrosis. Leaf symptoms on Richter 110. (Photo courtesy of G. Fletcher).

Viroids differ significantly from viruses. They lack a protein coat and are simply units of nucleic acid that 'live' in the nuclei of plant cells. Virtually all *vinifera* vines contain viroids. Viroid-free material has recently been developed which will permit assessment of the effects of infection. The present general view, however, is that they are not directly involved in any major grapevine disease. The best-documented viroid disease is yellow speckle (GYS) which is widespread in Australia (see below), but seems only mildly damaging. From analogy with their effects on other plants, e.g. cucumber and citrus, it is possible that viroid infection affects growth and development of grapevines (e.g. by shoot dwarfing). In that respect, their effects may even be beneficial and yield useful clones (Semancik *et al.* 1992).

11.3.1 Leafroll

Leafroll (GLRV) is the most important and widespread virus disease of grapevines in Australia and throughout the world. Severe strains may reduce grape yields by as much as 50%, and some mild strains reduce yield by 20% in some years (Woodham *et al.* 1984). Reductions in yield are associated with reduced annual vine growth and less bunches per vine. The sugar content of berry juice may be reduced by up to 30%, particularly in cool climates, while the acidity of berry juice is increased. Fruit maturity may be delayed by up to four weeks.

In Australia, GLRV occurs in all tested clones of Sultana and Waltham Cross, and in some clones of wine varieties such as Cabernet Sauvignon, Grenache and Shiraz (Handreck 1974). Although GLRV symptoms can often be readily recognized in the field, latent strains are present in several varieties (e.g. clones of Sultana, Waltham Cross and Shiraz). Rootstock varieties may also carry symptomless infections.

Diagnostic leaf symptoms start to appear in autumn on mature leaves near the base of shoots and gradually extend along each shoot. The margins of affected leaves curl or roll down only in some varieties. Leaves of infected black- and red-fruited varieties develop a purplish-red or reddish colouration between veins, while the main veins remain green (Figure 11.12a). In white-fruited varieties, the leaves yellow prematurely with main veins and veinlets remaining green (Figure 11.12b), and some strains can cause areas of dead tissue between veins. In red-fruited varieties, GLRV may cause poor development of fruit colour.

Symptoms that may be confused with those produced by GLRV are caused by the strangulation of shoots or by the constriction of leaf petioles, by normal colouration in red-juiced varieties, by abnormal cool breaks in weather, and by iron deficiency associated with high levels of calcium carbonate in the soil (lime-induced chlorosis). The latter symptom, which is more common in spring and early summer, may also occur in autumn. It is usually evident on leaves towards the shoot tip, whereas GLRV symptoms first appear near the base of shoots.

As shown recently by use of the technique of double stranded RNA (dsRNA) analysis (Rezaian *et al.* 1992), GLRV is a complex disease involving more than one virus, and is a widespread disease. Specific dsRNAs are found in low-yielding clones of Sultana, but not in healthy indicator vines nor in clean vines generated by tissue culture techniques. This means that dsRNA analysis, combined with a tissue culture method, can be used as a means of rapid generation of virus-tested clean stocks of important clones.

11.3.2 Yellow speckle

Grapevine yellow speckle (GYS) is widespread in Australia. It occurs in all Sultana and Waltham Cross vines tested and in vines of numerous other varieties (Shanmuganathan and Fletcher 1980); it is prevalent but often symptomless in clones imported from California. Symptoms of GYS rarely develop on infected vines grown elsewhere in the world; hence the disease was first described in Australia (Taylor and Woodham 1972).

Typical leaf symptoms are small, irregular speckles ranging in size from a pinpoint to about 1 mm in diameter on exposed mature leaves on the main shoot or small lateral shoots. The speckles, situated along the main vein and/or veinlets may be isolated, or may be grouped together forming conspicuous areas of diseased tissue (Figure 11.13). Symptoms, which may appear on only two or three leaves per vine and rarely occur on more than about twenty, are most frequently seen on young vines. They usually develop in January-February and may intensify in

February-March, although in unusual seasons they may develop strongly in late spring. The colour of the speckles is at first yellowish-green and usually intensifies to chrome yellow or whitish yellow by March. When severe, leaf symptoms of yellow speckle cannot be readily distinguished from those of the vein banding strain of fanleaf virus (Figure 11.14c).

GYS may reduce the yield of some grape varieties (e.g. Muscat Gordo Blanco) by up to 9%. When mild strains of leafroll virus are also present, effects on vine growth are compounded and yields may be reduced by up to 24%, annual growth may be decreased by up to 50% and the sugar content of berry juice may also be depressed (Emmett and Fletcher unpublished).

Although GYS is graft-transmissable, there is also some evidence of a low rate of natural spread in field vines (Woodham and Krake 1982), but the vectors involved, if any, are unknown. The causal agents of GYS are considered to be viroids (Koltunow *et al.* 1989) that cannot be eliminated by heat therapy (Resaian *et al.* 1992). Hot conditions favour disease expression.

11.3.3 Fanleaf virus

There are at least three strains of grapevine fanleaf virus (GFV) (sometimes referred to as infectious degeneration) and each causes a disease with distinct symptoms. The strains include true fanleaf (the type strain), yellow mosaic and vein banding (Taylor and Hewitt 1964). Enation (see 11.3.4) may also be part of the fanleaf complex.

Fanleaf diseases are caused by a soil-borne virus (nepovirus) that is transmitted in Australia by the dagger nematode, *Xiphinema index* (see 11.4.4). Symptoms of the fanleaf and yellow mosaic strains are most pronounced in spring, whereas the symptoms of vein banding develop in autumn.

The fanleaf strain (Figure 11.14a) causes stunting of early growth and the development of abnormal canes which may zig-zag at the nodes. Internodes are abnormally variable in length and in some cases are so reduced that double buds occur directly opposite each other. The canes may also divide to produce 'Y' branches. The leaves are often leathery in texture, asymmetric in shape and tend to clasp. The structure of the leaf around the stem (the petiolar sinus) is abnormal and opens out, giving the leaf a fan-shaped appearance. Some strains cause the leaf to be more deeply serrated than normal and have nettle-like margins.

The yellow mosaic strain (Figure 11.14b) is characterized by yellow blotching or sheet yellowing of the leaves. In severe cases the yellow colouration extends into the veins and shoots. However, the symptoms are very variable, with the yellow colour being confined to a few spots on a few leaves or in extreme cases to all the leaves and shoots. The affected areas are bright chrome yellow at first and diseased vines are often visible from a distance. As temperatures rise in the summer, the colour either bleaches or regreening occurs. Often the bleached areas burn and the grapevine has a desiccated, unthrifty appearance in the summer and autumn.

The vein banding strain (Figure 11.14c) causes yellow banding along the veins of the leaves late in summer. The yellowing does not extend into the veins, which remain green.

GFV is common only in the Rutherglen-Corowa area of north-east Vic. and south-east NSW where its vector *Xiphinema index* also occurs. The fanleaf strain is more prevalent than the yellow mosaic and vein banding strains which, although spectacular, are relatively uncommon. Although GVF is widespread, the most common form is a mild one which is very difficult to detect by visual observation. GVF is found only rarely in areas other than Rutherglen; it has been detected only a few times in tests on hundreds of grapevines.

Mite injury may be confused with the mosaic symptoms caused by some fanleaf strains but can be distinguished by the malformation of the veinlets and pinpoint sized areas of dead tissue killed by the mites.

In addition, some herbicides can cause symptoms rather similar to some strains of grapevine fanleaf virus. Terbacil or diuron injury, for example, somewhat resembles vein banding disease but differs because veins and veinlets become translucent in appearance. Vine reactions to 2,4-D may also be rather similar to symptoms caused by the fanleaf strain of GFV or by enation.

GFV may kill vines in some situations, but in Australia, infected vines usually live for long periods and progressively become unproductive. On susceptible varieties, average yield losses may exceed 50%. The quality of fruit on infected vines is also reduced because of poor fruit set and the development of loose bunches that may have excessive numbers of 'shot' berries.

11.3.4 Other virus-like diseases

Enation

Grapevine enation is comparatively rare in Australia. It has been observed on Black Frontignac, Traminer and Doradillo (McGechan 1970). Symptoms consist of small, leaf-blade-like outgrowths (enations) on the lower surface of basal leaves (up to about the sixth node). Outgrowths, or 'hemming', are roughly parallel to the main veins which can be abnormally close together, and cause mis-shapen basal leaves. Symptoms occur in early spring, but leaves that develop on affected shoots after spring are normal.

Fleck

Although grapevine fleck is widespread in Europe it is relatively rare in Australia. It occurs in clones of some fruiting varieties, always in a symptomless form, and apparently always in combination with one or more of the other diseases. Infected vines of the rootstock *Vitis rupestris* var. St George (syn. du Lot) develop prominent symptoms in late spring consisting of small, yellowish, translucent areas in the veinlets of young leaves. Fleck can cause a marked depression of growth in this variety.

Stem pitting

Grapevine stem pitting or 'legno riccio' (rugose wood or bark and wood pitting disease) is also uncommon in Australia. To date, it has only been recorded in the Murray River irrigation districts on Muscat Gordo Blanco scions grafted onto *Vitis rupestris* var. du Lot (St George) rootstocks (Sarooshi *et al.* 1982). Affected scion-rootstock combinations exhibit varying degrees of graft incompatibility. In extreme cases scions will graft successfully but later show delayed budburst, poor spring growth, low fruitfulness and a progressive decline back to the rootstock (although, subsequently, rootstocks remaining after scion decline may grow away quite normally).

Wood pitting symptoms can be observed on rootstocks or scions more than 2–3 years old. These consist of numerous longitudinal grooves in the inner-wood corresponding to ridges on the inside of the bark. Considerable disruption of xylem tissues in the vicinity of the graft union may also be evident.

Stem pitting is graft transmissible but little is known about its causal agent except that a virus (closterovirus) may be associated with the disease (Conti *et al.* 1980). There is no known vector of stem pitting and, although the disease may spread through the soil, it is mostly spread by using symptomless scions or rootstocks carrying the causal agent.

Vein necrosis

Grapevine vein necrosis was first observed in Australia at Merbein, Vic. in 1974 on the hybrid rootstock Richter 110. It was subsequently detected in clones of Ramsey, Harmony and Schwarzmann (Woodham and Krake 1984). The disease is graft-transmissable and may also spread naturally. It occurs on vines in other parts of the world but its economic importance is unknown.

Symptoms of vein necrosis first appear on basal leaves of shoots during late spring (mid-October to mid-November). Parts of minor veins become necrotic and brown in colour. The affected veinlets soon turn black and during summer the extent of leaf veinlet necrosis increases (Figure 11.15). The number of leaves with symptoms also extends along shoots. Symptoms are most prominent on the lower leaf surface, particularly when the necrotic veinlets become numerous and create a black net-like effect on leaves. From mid-November onwards, discrete small, brown, necrotic spots (less than 1 mm in diameter) may also appear randomly in interveinal areas of mid-shoot leaves with or without necrotic veins. Severely affected basal leaves may die prematurely and fall during summer. Vein necrosis can be symptomless in some varieties and rootstocks.

Summer mottle

Grapevine summer mottle was first reported on Sideritis, a tablegrape variety of Greek origin, at Merbein, Vic. (Krake and Woodham 1978). It is a minor graft-transmissible disease that may also spread naturally.

Symptoms usually develop in early summer on young expanding and recently matured leaves and remain systemic on actively growing shoots until autumn. They are most pronounced on Sideritis but may also develop on other varieties. However, some varieties remain symptomless when infected.

Initial symptoms on individual leaves range from a mild yellowish feathering from main veins or veinlets to yellowish mottling developing uniformly in patches delineated by main veins or sometimes in areas that almost cover entire leaves. Later, small red-coloured patches may appear on severely affected parts of leaves of black-fruited varieties.

11.3.5 Control of virus and virus-like diseases

As most virus diseases have a detrimental effect on vine performance, avoiding these diseases by not propagating from infected vines can greatly improve grape production and quality. With time, virus and virus-like diseases should become a decreasing problem provided that growers support vine improvement schemes and use only recommended virus-tested planting material when establishing vineyards. Selection, heat treatment, indexing on sensitive indicator vine varieties and other plants, along with tissue culture techniques developed and adopted during the past two decades, are now producing relatively virus-free, high-yielding planting material.

Virus-free vines should remain that way unless they are grafted with virus-infected grapevines or planted into virus-infested soil (e.g. soil with the nematode, *Xiphinema index* carrying fanleaf virus). In Australia, the latter is unlikely to occur unless the virus-free material is used to replant vineyards in the Rutherglen district of north-east Vic.

Unfortunately indexing to detect viruses in grapevines is an expensive and/or time consuming process. Conventional indexing procedures, using grafted woody grapevine indicator plants, may take 18–30 months to confirm the presence or absence of viruses. Although other more rapid diagnostic methods (e.g. those based on nucleic acid analysis) are being adopted for some viruses, most involve the use of costly reagents and equipment. Hence indexing for virus detection is only justified and used for screening clones selected by research establishments or vine improvement groups or to check the virus status of imported grapevine material before it is released from quarantine.

11.4 Nematodes

The importance of plant parasitic nematodes (eelworms) in grape production has only been recognized since the mid-1950s. Nematode attack results in either a general decline of the vineyard or slowly spreading patches of stunted, unthrifty vines. Thus, the symptoms caused by nematode infestation may be confused with other diseases or conditions which restrict the uptake of nutrients and water by the roots. There are several different nematodes that damage grapevines by feeding on their roots.

11.4.1 Rootknot nematodes (*Meloidogyne* spp.)

Damage caused

The four recognized species infecting grapevines in Australia are *M. javanica*, *M. incognita*, *M. arenaria* and *M. hapla*. Of these *M. javanica* is the most important and occurs in all the major viticultural areas. *M. javanica* predominates in warmer regions, while *M. hapla* occurs in some cool districts (Seinhorst and Sauer 1956, Stirling 1976). Infestation of a vineyard causes continuing loss of production. Young vines, which have small, shallow root systems, are most severely affected, and may even fail to establish.

Symptoms

Infected vines are stunted, low-yielding, pale and sensitive to stress. The feeding female rootknot nematode stimulates grapevine roots to produce swellings or galls (Figure 11.16a), which vary in size and number according to vine variety, nematode species and the number of nematodes present. If a gall is broken open carefully, a tiny, round, glistening white body of a mature female may be seen with a hand lens. The galls on small lateral roots may resemble a string of beads, and severe infestations may produce so many galls that whole rootlets become rough and thick. The abnormal growth of cells in the galls disrupts the uptake of water and nutrients. In severe cases, the galls and adjacent root tissue rot due to secondary infections.

Life cycle

The life cycles of the four species are similar. At optimum temperatures, rootknot nematode second-stage juveniles hatch soon after the eggs

A

B

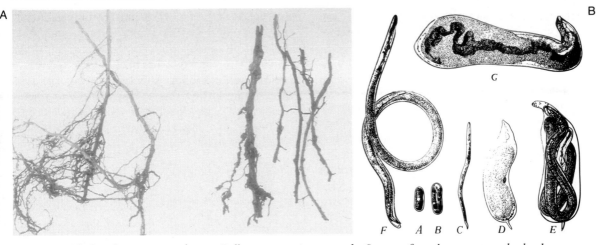

Figure 11.16. Rootknot nematodes. a. Galls on grapevine roots. b. Stages of rootknot nematode development (×70). A. Unsegmented eggs, B. Egg containing larva, C. Migratory larva free in soil. D. Larva sedentary in root, E. Larval moult containing fully developed male, F. Adult male, G. Young female.

are laid. The microscopic, eel-shaped juveniles (0.4 to 0.5 mm long) move through the soil to vine roots which they enter near the tip and penetrate to the cortex. The juveniles moult quickly three more times and develop into either sedentary females, or occasionally into migratory males which are slightly larger (Figure 11.16b). Males leave the root and fertilize the females, although mating is not essential for reproduction. Females stimulate the root to produce giant cells, on which they feed. The female swells and lays 500 to 2000 eggs into a jelly-like material which may remain within the gall, or protrude from the root.

The life cycle is completed in 25 days at 27°C, but is quicker at higher soil temperatures. There are usually four to six generations per year, most of them in summer, but in warm climates there may be eight.

11.4.2 Citrus nematode (*Tylenchulus semipenetrans* Cobb)

Damage caused

Citrus nematode is widespread in most citrus growing areas in Australia. It was first reported as a parasite of grapevines in Sunraysia, Vic. (Seinhorst and Sauer 1956), where citrus groves are interspersed with vineyards, but it also has been found in vineyards in the MIA, NSW and in SA (Stirling 1976). The close proximity of citrus and vines in irrigation areas along the Murray River probably accounts for the wide distribution and large populations of citrus nematode in these

vineyards, even on heavy soils where citrus has never been grown. Citrus nematode can reduce the growth of roots and shoots of potted vines. In the field, large populations, which are commonly attained, apparently cause slow vine decline.

Symptoms

Infested vines show reduced vigour and yield, sometimes with a slight loss of feeder roots. In heavy infestations, jelly-like material secreted by adult females causes soil particles to stick to rootlets, making them appear dirty.

Life cycle

Citrus nematode is relatively small, the mature female being 0.4 mm long. The first-stage juvenile develops within the egg and moults once. At 24°C, eel-shaped second-stage juveniles hatch from eggs in twelve to fourteen days, and males may mature within seven more days. Males can survive for eight months without feeding, but females fail to develop without a host plant. Female juveniles feed on surface cells, and immature females penetrate to the cortex, where they establish permanent feeding sites each with several specialized nurse cells. The posterior portion of the female, which protrudes from the root, swells to a kidney shape, and when she matures she lays several hundred eggs in a jelly-like mass at the root surface. The adult female causes most damage, and may reproduce without fertilization. The life cycle is completed in six to eight weeks, and populations can multiply rapidly on grapevines.

11.4.3 Lesion nematodes (*Pratylenchus* spp.)

Damage caused
Lesion (or root-lesion) nematodes are widespread in grapegrowing areas, but their economic importance is uncertain. *P. vulnus* is considered the most important of the lesion nematodes on grapevines in Vic. (Meagher 1969), but *P. scribneri* can also cause severe damage (Seinhorst and Sauer 1956).

Symptoms
The only above-ground symptoms are low vigour and yield, and possibly slight potassium deficiency symptoms. Lesion nematodes penetrate to the centre of the vine root, where small lesions develop and enlarge. Invasion by large numbers of nematodes may cause sufficient lesions to girdle the root, causing death of the tip. The vine responds by producing more lateral roots above the lesions, but these too may be destroyed. Serious root-rotting by secondary organisms is common, and this also reduces the number of feeder roots. The characteristic symptom of lesion nematode attack in vines is the tangled mass of short, branched lateral roots.

Life Cycle
Lesion nematodes are migratory parasites, unlike rootknot and citrus nematodes; all stages move from root to root and the adult females lay eggs singly in the soil or within the roots. Second-stage juveniles hatch from the eggs, and there are three more moults. The eel-shaped juveniles and adults move mostly between cortical cells in the root, feeding around the conducting tissues and killing cells as they migrate. Males are common for *P. vulnus* although the female may reproduce without fertilization. The life cycle is completed in five to eight weeks depending on temperature.

11.4.4 Dagger nematodes (*Xiphinema* spp.)

Damage caused
Xiphinema index Thorne & Allen (fanleaf dagger nematode) is important, not only for the damage it causes directly to vines, but also because it transmits grapevine fanleaf virus (GFV) from infected to healthy vines during feeding. This nematode and GFV were apparently introduced to the Rutherglen (Vic.) area from Europe, but quarantine measures for phylloxera have fortunately restricted its spread (Meagher *et al.* 1976, Harris 1983a). Although *X. index* has not been found further than 10 km from Rutherglen, eradication is not feasible and its presence poses a threat to Australian viticulture. In many viticultural areas overseas, it is the most damaging nematode.

Little is known of the significance of other dagger nematodes found in Australian vineyards (e.g. *X. pachtaicum, X. monohysterum,* although nematodes of the *X. americanum* group are widespread (Sauer 1962, Stirling 1976, Harris 1983a).

Symptoms
Poor growth and low yield are the only above-ground symptoms of infestation by *Xiphinema* species. Where GFV occurs with *X. index*, the grapevines are usually weak and the yield is greatly reduced. *X. index* suppresses growth of rootlets of young vines, and the tips become dark, curved and slightly galled. Some feeder roots die, causing proliferation of other feeder roots above the feeding site. A dense mass of branched, swollen, dark roots is produced when large populations are present.

Life cycle
Dagger nematode adults and juveniles feed from the outside of roots and migrate between roots. They feed only at or near the root tip, penetrating the central vascular system with their long stylet (feeding spear). Males are rare, and female *X. index* usually reproduce without fertilization. Eggs are laid singly in the soil, and first-stage juveniles hatch in six to eight days. For *X. index* to develop, the four juvenile stages and the long (over 3 mm) adult must feed. The life cycle takes between five weeks and nine months, depending on temperature, but individuals survive for several years.

11.4.5 Other parasitic nematodes
Several other parasitic nematodes are common in Australian vineyards, but their economic importance is unknown. These include ring nematode (*Criconemella* [= *Macroposthonia* = *Criconemoides*] *xenoplax*), spiral nematode (*Helicotylenchus dihystera*) and stubby-root

nematode (*Paratrichodorus minor*). Pin nematode (*Paratylenchus hamatus*) also feeds and reproduces on vines but probably causes little damage.

11.4.6 Ecology

Plant-parasitic nematodes can damage grapevines under a wide range of climatic conditions, but populations generally increase most rapidly and are most active at high temperatures. Rootknot nematodes are more common and more damaging to grapevines in sandy, alkaline soils and in warmer regions. Citrus, lesion and dagger nematodes are prevalent in both clayey and sandy soils. Although nematodes are susceptible to desiccation, juveniles of citrus nematode and eggs and juveniles of rootknot nematode can survive for several years in dry soil in the absence of a host crop. *X. index* can survive in waterlogged or frozen soils, and can persist in dry soil without plants for at least six years.

The natural spread of plant-parasitic nematodes is limited, most spread being dependent on any agent which moves soil. Nematodes are spread mainly by the introduction of infested plants into new vineyards (Meagher 1969). In the past, nematode-infested grapevine rootlings were distributed from nurseries in the Murray Valley. Recycling of sub-soil drainage water into the irrigation system also spread large numbers of viable citrus nematode juveniles and eggs, as well as smaller numbers of rootknot and lesion nematodes (Meagher 1967). Nematodes are also spread by the movement of infested soil in flood water and on machinery, humans or animals.

11.4.7 Control measures

Strict precautions should be taken to prevent the introduction of plant-parasitic nematodes into new vineyards because once a vineyard or nursery becomes infested there is no known way to eradicate the nematodes. When nematode damage makes a vineyard uneconomic, the best palliative is to replant on nematode-resistant roostocks.

Prevention
Only healthy nursery stock should be planted. Rootknot nematode infection can often be detected by the presence of root galls, and all galled rootlings should be discarded. The nematodes can be virtually eradicated from bare-rooted grapevine rootlings by careful hot water treatment at 52°C for five minutes.

Control in established vineyards
Despite many experiments in Australia and overseas (Harris 1986), no chemical has been found that can replace the fumigant DBCP, which became unavailable in 1980. Research on biological control of nematodes shows some promise, but no commercial control measure is envisaged in the near future. A bacterial parasite of rootknot nematodes is widespread in Riverland (SA) vineyards over 25 years old, where it may be reducing nematode populations, but natural increase of the parasite is slow (Stirling and White 1982).

Replanting in nematode-infested soil
The capital costs of replanting an infested vineyard are high but replanting gives the viticulturist an opportunity to incorporate new technologies. Before replanting, the residual root fragments should be removed and the soil should be deeply cultivated, particularly in summer. Pre-plant fumigation with 1,3-D (1,3-dichloropropene) temporarily reduces nematode numbers and is usually advantageous even when nematode-resistant rootstocks are to be planted. Soil fumigation and crop rotation, however, have given poor control of *X. index* and GFV because the nematode can survive for many years at great depths in soil in the absence of a host plant.

Nematode-resistant or tolerant rootstocks should be used where vines are to be planted in an infested area (Volume 1, Chapter 8). 'Resistant' grapevine rootstocks are not completely resistant (immune), because some nematodes can feed and reproduce on their roots, but they are able to tolerate the nematodes. Tolerance is a type of resistance, but describes the ability of the plant to grow satisfactorily despite feeding by nematodes. A tolerant plant suffers little injury even when heavily infested. If replanting in soils heavily infested with a particular nematode, it may be prudent to select rootstocks that have resistance as well as tolerance to that nematode (Table 11.2) to reduce nematode numbers.

Much Australian research has enabled selection of nematode-resistant or tolerant rootstocks suitable for particular situations (Sauer 1974, 1977, Stirling and Cirami 1984, Wachtel 1986,

Table 11.2 Resistance [1] and tolerance[2] to some *Vitis* rootstocks to four types of parasitic nematodes

Rootstock	Nematode			
	Rootknot[3]	Citrus	Lesion[3]	Dagger
ARG 1 (syn. AXR 1)	S, I	?	S, I	S, I
Dog Ridge	R, T	R, T	R[3], T	S, I
Freedom	R, T	R, T	S, ?	R, ?
Harmony	MR[3], I[3]	?	S, I	R, T
K51-32	R, T	R, I	?	S, I
K51-40	R, T	R, T	?	?
5 BB Kober	MR, I	?	?	S, I
Ramsey	R, T	R, T	R, T	S, I
Rupestris du Lot (syn. St George)	S, I	?	S, ?	S, I
Schwarzmann	R, T	R, T	?	R, T
SO 4	MR[3], T	?	?	S, I
101-14	MR, I	S, ?	?	S, I
110 (syn. 110 R)	MR, I	S, ?	S, ?	S, I
420 A	S, I	?	S, ?	S, I
1202	S, I	?	?	S, I
1613	MR[3], I[3]	?	S, I	S, T
1616	R, T	R, T	?	S, I
3306	S, I	?	R, ?	S, I
3309	S, I	?	R, ?	R, T

1. Effect of grapevine on nematode reproduction.
R = resistant (little or no nematode reproduction)
MR = moderately resistant (intermediate nematode reproduction)
S = susceptible (uninhibited nematode reproduction)

2. Effect of nematode on grapevine:
T = tolerant (little or no injury)
I = intolerant (much injury)

3. Resistance or tolerance may differ according to nematode species, soil temperature and other factors.

Goss and Cameron 1981, Harris 1983b, 1988). As more vineyards are replanted, rootstocks are likely to become more popular as a long term solution to nematode problems.

11.5 Disorders of unknown cause

In addition to the well recognized diseases of grapevines caused by fungi, bacteria, viruses, virus-like agents and nematodes, a number of other disorders occur in Australia for which the cause is still unknown or is inadequately defined. These are briefly described in the following section.

11.5.1 Grapevine yellows

Grapevine yellows was first observed in 1976 on Riesling grapevines in South Australia. Since then it has been found on other white wine varieties and in other states. The disorder or disease is more prevalent in warmer viticultural regions such as the Riverland (SA), Sunraysia (Vic., NSW), and the MIA and Hunter Valley (NSW). It occurs to a lesser extent in other grapegrowing areas although it has not been observed in Western Australia (Magarey and Wachtel 1985).

Figure 11.17. Yellows disorder. a. A shoot with leaves overlying each other as their margins curl downwards, early signs of yellows on Chardonnay. b. A yellows affected shoot at a more advanced stage (Riesling).

Figure 11.19. Bunchstem necrosis and similar disorders. a. Early bunchstem necrosis on an inflorescence of Sultana. b. Bunchstem necrosis on Sultana showing necrosis of the peduncle, lateral stems and berry stems (pedicels). c. Water berry or bunch-stem necrosis on Ohanez where necrosis is mostly confined to berry pedicels (See also Figure 9.2b).

Figure 11.20. Restricted growth. Affected Sultana shoots in spring.

Symptoms

In most seasons, the disease does not appear until flowering or after flowering and is confined to individual shoots. These may be solitary although they often occur on adjacent spurs, on the same cane or on the same cordon. At first, affected shoots stop growing and their leaves tend to overlie each other and curl downwards slightly at their margins. Gradually leaves assume a dull, slightly yellow-green appearance (Figure 11.17a) and with time distinct irregular yellow patches develop firstly at leaf margins and later near main veins (Figure 11.17b). Chlorosis is usually followed by necrosis along leaf margins and in patches elsewhere on leaves. As the season advances, leaves fall prematurely.

Entire bunches or portions of bunches on affected shoots usually shrivel and die (Magarey and Wachtel 1985). Stems of affected shoots become brittle, develop a bluish appearance and fail to lignify. They die back progressively from their tips either during the growing season or during the following winter. Some spurs with affected shoots may also die but death of cordons is rare.

In the following season, budburst is delayed on surviving spurs or canes that carried affected shoots in the previous season. Shoots and bunches from these buds may be either normal but reduced in size or again be affected. A remission of symptoms on affected shoots may also occur during the growing season following extended periods of hot weather. Symptomless lateral shoots may grow from the nodes of declining shoots.

Damage caused

Yield losses are associated with the loss of bunches on affected shoots, the frequency of affected shoots per vine and the number of affected vines per vineyard. The latter may vary widely from season to season. Losses of up to 50% have been recorded on some varieties.

Varietal susceptibility

Symptoms are most pronounced on Riesling, Chardonnay, Traminer and Montils. Hybrids of these and of Sylvaner and Semillon are also affected.

Biology and predisposing factors

Vines that are heavily cropped and slightly stressed nutritionally are more likely to develop yellows,

particularly in warmer regions. Symptoms may be masked within the canopies of vigorous vines.

In many ways grapevine yellows in Australia is similar to some European grapevine yellows diseases, particularly 'flavescence doree'. The latter is caused by a phloem-inhabiting, leaf-hopper-borne, mycoplasma-like organism. There is some evidence that Australian grapevine yellows may also be associated with a mycoplasma-like organism.

Control

Although grapevine yellows in Australia can be controlled by pressure injecting dormant vines with tetracycline (Magarey and Wachtel 1986), no commercially acceptable control measures are available at this stage. In Europe, insecticide sprays are applied during the growing season to control leaf-hopper vectors of 'flavescence doree' and reduce disease incidence. However in Australia, the significance of potential leaf hopper vectors (Osmelak *et al.* 1989) in relation to the development of grapevine yellows is poorly understood and there is no indication that insecticide spray programs will reduce disease incidence.

11.5.2 Grapevine decline

Grapevine decline mostly occurs in the Lower Murray River Irrigation Districts of SA, Vic. and NSW. Although incidence is erratic, production losses in affected vineyards may be as high as 60%. Declining vines have a number of non-specific symptoms such as delayed budburst in spring, reduced shoot growth, poor root development and general unthriftiness later in the season. Vigour and yields of individual vines may fluctuate from season to season before they eventually decline.

A complex of factors are often associated with grapevine decline. These include poorly drained soils, the presence of Pythiaceous fungi (e.g. *Pythium ultimum*, *Pythium irregulare* and *Pythium aphanidermatum*) and the subsequent breakdown of root systems (Bumbieris 1972). Root damage caused by nematodes and careless cultivation may also be aggravating factors.

Varieties such as Doradillo, Muscat Gordo Blanco, Pedro Ximenes and Grenache are most severely affected. Good management with particular attention to drainage and irrigation appears to be the only method of control.

Figure 11.18. Measles. a. Leaf symptoms.
b. Spotting on fruit of affected vines.

11.5.3 Grapevine measles

A disorder resembling a mild form of black measles in California (Moller and Sall 1981, Pearson and Goheen 1988) has been observed in some vineyards in the Coomealla Irrigation District (NSW), near Adelaide (SA) and occasionally in other areas.

In mid-summer interveinal areas on leaves become chlorotic. Later necrotic patches develop which are irregular in shape and may enlarge to cover most of each leaf (Figure 11.18a). Affected leaves fall prematurely. On red-fruited varieties, the margins of the necrotic areas are reddish-brown. Occasionally numerous small spots (0.5–2 mm in diameter) appear on fruit of affected vines (Figure 11.18b). When the arms and butt of affected vines are sectioned, a large zone of necrosis is often observed with brown to black staining extending away from it along the vascular tissue. Once vines have developed symptoms they continue to be diseased in subsequent years although the intensity of symptom expression may vary from season to season. In California, the cause of black measles is unknown although fungi such as *Phellinus igniarus* (L.:Fr.) Quel. and *Cephalosporium* sp. are often present in the wood of diseased vines (Pearson and Goheen 1988). *Cephalosporium* sp. and other fungi have also been found in vines with measles-like symptoms in Australia.

11.5.4 Young vine collapse

Young vine collapse refers to a disorder that is most common in the Lower Murray River Irrigation Districts of Vic., NSW and SA. Vines up to four years old that appeared healthy in the previous season die or dieback to ground level during winter. Occasionally later in the next growing season, new shoots are produced at soil level where a crown is still alive but by this time the vine has suffered a serious set-back. Sometimes, sudden collapse also occurs during the growing season. As a result of young vine collapse, vineyard establishment can be hampered considerably depending on the number of vines affected. Most susceptible varieties are Grenache, Ohanez, Doradillo and Mataro; Sultana is occasionally affected. Occurrence appears to be associated with factors in the previous season which have severely depleted carbohydrate reserves in young vines (e.g. premature overcropping or severe defoliation caused by downy mildew).

11.5.5 Bunchstem and bud necrosis

Bunchstem necrosis (BSN) is a physiological disorder that gives lesions on grape peduncles and pedicels. Synonyms are numerous and include 'water-berry', 'shanking' and 'Stiellähme'.

BSN develops during and after veraison as pronounced zones of tissue breakdown (up to 3-6 mm long) which become soft and water-soaked

Figure 11.21. Black speck. Specking on bunchstems of Calmeria.

Figure11.22. Vineyard spray machinery. a. Protective clothing, advisable for many spray operations. b. Air-blast sprayer. c. Aerial spraying using a fixed winged aircraft and rotary atomizer equipment (photo courtesy of G. Buchanan). d. A boom-nozzle system mounted on a helicopter. e. 'Maxi' ducted air sprayer (photo courtesy of Hardi Spraying Equipment Ltd.) Note protective clothing.

before they turn brown. Parts of the bunch beyond the zones of breakdown may wilt, die and drop off. Sites of breakdown vary although they are usually located on bunchstems and/or at the junction of bunch stalks (Figure 11.19b, 9.2b), or on berry pedicels (Figure 11.19c). Berries beyond the zones of breakdown do not ripen properly and often wilt and wither. In severe cases, flabby berries fall when bunches are shaken. Wine made from BSN-affected grapes often has quality defects.

BSN appears to develop more frequently in cooler regions (Coombe and Allan 1953) on more vigorous vines but its incidence is sporadic and erratic, between regions, seasons, varieties and even vineyards. Occurrence appears to be greater in Orange-Mudgee districts in NSW and the SA grape regions south of Adelaide. Losses of up to 80% have been reported in Cabernet Sauvignon and Muscat Hamburg and in Flame Seedless grown in glasshouses.

BSN appears to be associated with conditions that lead to competition between developing fruit and vigorous vegetative growth. Vine nutritional status and prevailing environmental conditions are often implicated as predisposing factors. BSN has been promoted by applying excess ammonium nitrogen to vines (Christensen and Boggero 1985) and reduced by applying magnesium sulphate sprays at veraison and 10 days later (Theiler 1985). In Australia, no procedures for preventing BSN have been developed.

Early BSN was so-named by Jackson and Coombe (1988) because of its general resemblance to BSN but its different timing. It affects inflorescences at any time from their early appearance (i.e. when they are about 2 cm long) until flowering. It differs from poor setting associated with heavy abscission of flowers and young berries. First signs of early BSN are shrivelled brown necrotic areas at the base of pedicels of flower buds which subsequently fall. Sections of the peduncle or entire peduncles then turn brown, shrivel and die (Figure 11.19a). Affected parts of flower clusters may or may not abscise and fall (Jackson and Coombe 1988). When the disorder develops extensively, berry set and vineyard yield are greatly reduced. Some varieties appear to be affected more by early BSN than others and incidence is greater in cooler regions and especially within shaded vine canopies. To date no control measures have been developed.

Bud necrosis (BN) is a widespread disorder of grapevines causing reduced shoot fruitfulness and yield. The central axis of the bud, i.e. the main shoot primordium, becomes necrotic while the lateral (secondary) axes remain healthy. The effect is that, at budburst, only the twin lateral shoots develop and these have few inflorescences (Figure 9.2a). Necrosis commences soon after flowering but is most apparent in buds sectioned during the next winter. Incidence of BN is highest in basal nodes on vigorous shoots; it is promoted by any factor that enhances shoot vigour, e.g. high levels of nitrogen or application of gibberellic acid (Perez-Harvey 1991). Shoot thinning, topping and defoliation, particularly in spring, also promote BN incidence (Dry 1986). The condition has been attributed to low light incidence on the buds (Perez-Harvey 1991) and high levels of endogenous gibberellins in the buds (Dry 1986).

11.5.6 Restricted growth

'Restricted growth' is a spasmodic phenomenon that mostly occurs on Sultana in Vic. and NSW although it has been observed in the Riverland (SA). Budburst on affected vines is delayed and when it does occur, shoot development in the first two to three weeks of growth is dramatically retarded. Affected shoots are 'celery-like' and although stem thickness is normal, leaves are usually reduced in size, chlorotic and sometimes mildly necrotic (Figure 11.20). However, it is not uncommon for affected shoots to recover rapidly within a period of two to three weeks so that they cannot be distinguished from shoots that were unaffected. But if shoot development remains retarded, maturity of fruit is delayed and yields may be reduced. Although the cause of restricted growth is unknown, lime sulphur sprays applied at the woolly-bud stage appear to provide good control.

11.5.7 Black speck

'Black speck' is a minor disorder that occurs spasmodically on young vine growth in the lower Murray River irrigation areas of NSW and Vic. although it has also been observed in other inland districts of NSW and SA. Symptoms are black-brown pinhead size specks (rarely exceeding 1 mm in diameter) surrounded by a pale yellow-green halo on leaves and small black slightly raised scabs on young stems, bunchstems and berries (Figure 11.21). Black speck does not appear to affect fruit yield even though shoots severely affected just after budburst may be temporarily distorted and stunted. Occasionally, however, the disorder is severe enough to lower the quality of tablegrapes.

Black speck development appears to follow periods of wet weather that occur while shoot stems, leaves, bunch stems and/or berries are young and succulent. The disorder is usually more prevalent on well established minimal-pruned vines that develop dense canopies. No control measures for black speck have been developed at this stage.

11.6 Vineyard protection and pest management

In this section, the term 'pest' refers to fungi, bacteria, nematodes, insects, mites or other undesirable organisms and animals, but not weeds. The term 'pesticide' refers to a substance (chemical), or mixture of substances, used to prevent, destroy, repel or reduce the harmful effects of pests.

The efficient management of pests in vineyards requires an understanding of pest biology and involves processes such as the correct definition of targets, the setting of economic injury levels for individual pests, the monitoring of pest levels over periods when control is required and the selection of appropriate control strategies. The latter may incorporate cultural, biological and chemical control measures and the integration of these for important (key) pests. Cultural control measures embrace knowledge of host resistance, along with knowledge of canopy and vineyard management techniques that foster pest control. Biological control strategies require an understanding of the biology of biological control agents, their interaction with pests and their management in vineyards. With chemical control measures, knowledge of pesticides and correct strategies for their use is needed along with knowledge of application procedures and equipment. In the following sections, these aspects are briefly discussed in relation to the development of efficient integrated pest management programs in vineyards.

11.6.1 Target definition
The accurate definition of targets for treatment is essential before efficient strategies for the control of pests in vineyards can be developed. Target definition draws on knowledge of pest identification, pest biology and economic thresholds for damage and treatment on grapevines or grapes and knowledge of appropriate pesticides to be used in control programs for the treatment of targets.

Pest identification
Correct identification of the pest that is the target of each control program is essential so that appropriate treatments are prescribed. Inaccurate identification may lead to the use of control measures that are not only ineffective but also a waste of time and resources.

Pest biology
A good understanding of the biology and ecology of pests often indicates stages of their development that can be targeted for effective treatment. With most pests, some stages are accessible to treatment while others are not.

Grapevine biology
The definition of targets for treatment, particularly when applying pesticides, can also be influenced by the development of the grapevine host that supports the pest. Knowledge of grapevine vegetative and reproductive growth patterns and the rate of development of new tissue is needed (Volume 1, Chapter 7). When protectant fungicides are used for example, the frequency of applications is influenced by the rate of production of new unprotected vine tissue. Often pest activity is also closely related to grapevine development.

Economic damage levels and action thresholds
In reality, the control of a pest is warranted only if the additional return from the crop resulting from the application of control measures exceeds the cost of control. When appraising the importance of pests and deciding whether they should be targets for control programs, economic injury or damage levels and action thresholds should be defined. The economic damage level for a pest is the population density or the severity level where economic damage occurs and expenditure on control is warranted. At levels

above the economic damage level for each pest, the potential cost of damage is greater than the cost of control measures.

The action threshold for a pest is the pest population density at which control measures must be initiated to prevent pest levels exceeding the economic damage level. Hence most action thresholds are lower than economic damage levels and are determined on the basis of the expected rate of pest development and the time required for the application of effective pesticides or other control procedures.

Unfortunately, economic damage levels and action thresholds are not clearly defined for most pests of grapevines. Action thresholds, for example, may fluctuate from district to district to account for factors such as climatic conditions, time of year, stage of grapevine development, varietal differences, vineyard management practices, marketing requirements and expected returns on produce. The stage of pest development can also be important. Furthermore, with many pests precise and/or reliable sampling techniques to estimate levels of pest populations are still being developed.

In some situations, scope for delaying the application of pesticides is also limited. With tablegrapes, a blemish-free product is usually required and most pests must be controlled either before they appear or before they cause visible damage. The rapid development of some fungus diseases may also dictate the need to apply fungicides to protect vine tissues before disease appearance, particularly where weather conditions restrict vineyard accessibility and the timing of pesticide applications.

Pesticide characteristics
Where the choice of pesticides is limited or where one pesticide is preferred because of efficacy or cost, the characteristics of a pesticide used in a control program (e.g. persistence, mode of action, etc.) may also influence target definition. Knowledge of these characteristics is needed when determining the most suitable method of application and the timing of applications.

11.6.2 Cultural practices
Approaches to vineyard establishment and management can influence the development of

pests each season. Choice of planting material, vineyard layout and topography, trellis design, canopy management, weed management and soil and water management are some of the aspects that warrant careful consideration because of their potential impact on pest management.

Choice of planting material
Where possible, grapevine varieties that are resistant to pests should be planted to minimize the long-term need for costly pest control programs. When establishing new vineyards, planting material free of pests should also be used. Apart from virus and virus-like organisms that can have long term effects on vineyard yield (see 11.3), diseases such as Phomopsis cane and leaf spot, black spot and crown gall can be readily introduced into vineyards on or within planting material along with the costs associated with the management of these diseases in future years.

Vineyard layout and topography
Sheltered areas in vineyards with poor air drainage may develop microclimates favourable for disease when the macroclimate is mostly unfavourable. When planning vineyards, careful attention to spacing vines, row direction and placement of wind-breaks in relation to prevailing winds can ensure maximum air drainage and a minimum duration of foliage wetness.

Canopy management
Microclimates can be manipulated by canopy management (Smart 1984, 1985; Chapter 5). Cultural practices can be employed to change the microclimate and thus minimize pest development. The removal of leaves from around bunches increases air movement and reduces the duration of humidity and wetness within bunches, thus making conditions less favourable for diseases such as Botrytis rot (Gubler et al. 1987).

Practices that maximize air movement and light penetration within the canopy will also reduce Botrytis rot (Savage and Sall 1983, 1984) and may discourage the development of diseases such as powdery and downy mildews: an added benefit is improved spray penetration. Management practices that maximize the distance between the soil and susceptible vine foliage may also discourage infection by diseases where the soil is a source of primary inoculum (e.g. downy mildew).

Soil and water management
Efficient soil drainage in vineyards is important as the pooling of water in low lying areas can favour disease development. Pythium and Phytophthora root rots, for example, develop readily in waterlogged soils. Prolonged soil wetness may also promote downy mildew primary infection by encouraging the maturation and germination of overwintering soil-borne oospores. Because of their more favourable microclimates, wet low lying areas in vineyards are often sites for the early development of other diseases such as powdery mildew and Botrytis rot.

Irrigation practices can also influence disease development. With overvine irrigation, the duration of foliage and bunch wetness should be kept to a minimum especially at night or in association with dews or rains to reduce the risk of creating conditions favourable for sporulation and infection by diseases such as downy mildew and Botrytis rot. Prolonged irrigation of vines just before harvest should also be avoided as this may split grape berries and encourage the development of bunchrots or moulds.

Weed management
Aspects of ongoing vineyard management such as weed control can have an effect on pest incidence in vineyards. Apart from modifying the environment, weeds present in vineyards may harbour insect pests and snails (see Chapter 10).

11.6.3 Biological control
Pest populations on grapevines in vineyards co-exist with a wide range of other organisms. Some of these organisms may exert a natural control on the pest population through parasitism or predation. This particularly applies to insect pests such as lightbrown apple moth (Chapter 10.1.1), longtailed mealy bug (Chapter 10.1.3) and grapevine scale (Chapter 10.1.4), and mites (James and Whitney 1990). The recognition and fostering of natural biological control agents is an important aspect of vineyard pest management. In particular, it warrants special consideration when planning chemical control strategies for pests.

11.6.4 Chemical control
An understanding of pesticides and their characteristics is essential when planning and conducting chemical control programs for pests in vineyards. For this reason some aspects of pesticide technology are briefly summarized in this section. For a more detailed treatment see more comprehensive papers such as Behncken (1983) and Emmett (1985).

a. Pesticides
Most pesticides consist of an active chemical constituent prepared in a concentrated form, or in a formulation, by a manufacturer. They are suitable for use after mixing with a recommended diluting agent (e.g. water). Pesticides are classified according to their principal use (e.g. as miticides, insecticides, nematicides, fungicides, bacteriacides, etc.) and their of mode action (Behncken 1983).

(i) Types of pesticides
While most pesticides have a principal mode of action, many have more than one mode of action and can be effective against more than one type of pest.

Contact insecticides are pesticides that kill insect pests by direct contact. They enter the insect's body by absorption following direct contact of the insect with pesticide particles, droplets or pesticide-contaminated surfaces. Organochlorine, organophosphorus and carbamate insecticides and synthetic pyrethroids are typical pesticides in this group. Some pesticides that have a residual contact action and act as stomach poisons, must be ingested by the insect to be effective. Some 'biological insecticides' such as *Bacillus thuringiensis* must also be eaten by the insect to cause death.

Systemic insecticides are absorbed by the roots or leaves of plants and translocated systemically to other plant tissues. They are effective against insects that feed on plant sap even when feeding occurs at sites well away from the point of insecticide application. Dimethoate and demeton-s-methyl are typical systemic insecticides.

Fumigant insecticides (e.g. methyl bromide) enter the insect's body through natural openings (spiracles) in a gaseous state.

Protectant fungicides prevent infection by inhibiting fungal development on the plant surface.

They are applied before infection occurs and most have a broad spectrum of activity. Protectant or pre-infection fungicides include copper compounds (e.g. copper oxychloride), mancozeb and dithianon.

Eradicant fungicides either partially or totally kill fungi already present on or in the plant or prevent these fungi from contributing to further disease development. They are effective when applied after infection has occurred. A principal feature of most eradicants is their ability to penetrate plant tissues and become systemic. Some examples of eradicant or post-infection fungicides are metalaxyl and potassium phosphite used for downy mildew control.

Systemic fungicides have the ability to penetrate the plant surface and move within plants. Movement may be relatively localized, such as across leaves from one side to the other, or extensive, via the plant's vascular system. Systemic fungicides include benomyl and metalaxyl.

(ii) Pesticide formulations

Pesticide formulations are prepared by chemical manufacturers so that the active ingredient can be safely and easily applied. Most formulations used in vineyards consist of an active ingredient either in a non-diluted form (fumigants) or, dissolved or suspended in diluents such as water or oil (solutions, suspensions or emulsions), inert solids (wettable powders dusts or granules) or a gas (aerosols). To improve the efficiency of application of formulations, chemical additives such as wetting agents are often included. Mixtures of active ingredients may also be formulated to take advantage of synergistic effects or to increase efficacy e.g. the protectant fungicide copper oxychloride is mixed with the eradicant fungicide metalaxyl to create a more versatile formulation for downy mildew control.

(iii) Wetting agents

Wetting agents reduce the surface tension of the spray mixture and improve its ability to wet the target surface by inducing droplets to spread. Their use can improve coverage and hence pest control, particularly with solutions of relatively insoluble wettable powder formulations. Non-ionic wetting agents are preferred as there is less risk of phytotoxicity.

(iv) Water quality

Water is the most widely used diluent for pesticides. However, variations in water quality can create problems when applying pesticides. Ideally, the water used with pesticides should have low levels of total solids and salt, be of neutral pH and be relatively 'soft'.

(v) Pesticide compatibility

Two or more pesticides are often combined in spray mixtures to save time, labour and machinery costs. However, problems associated with incompatibility (e.g. reduced efficacy or increased phytotoxicity) may arise when different pesticides are mixed. Mixing may increase the concentration of wetting agents and other additives with harmful effects on the plant surface. Information about pesticide compatibilities may not be readily available but can usually be obtained from chemical manufacturers on request. Where possible, the mixing of pesticides should be avoided unless recommended by pesticide manufacturers or unless the pesticides involved have been shown to be compatible through extended use.

(vi) Pesticide toxicology

Pesticides are toxic chemicals and their potentially harmful effects should be considered when they are used. Pesticides may enter the body by absorption through the skin, by oral ingestion or by inhalation.

One measure of the relative toxicity of a pesticide to humans or mammals is reflected by its median lethal dose (LD_{50}). This is a statistical estimate of the dose of the pesticide needed to kill 50% of the test animals used in toxicology studies (e.g. rats, mice or rabbits).

A generalized classification of comparative toxicity of some pesticides is presented in Table 11.3. As LD_{50} decreases, toxicity increases.

(vii) Pesticide residues

Residues are pesticide deposits or by-products that persist in plant or animal tissues or in soil, water or air after the use of a pesticide. The amount of pesticide residue is expressed in parts by weight of the pesticide chemical per million parts by weight or volume of commodity (mg/kg or mg/L = p.p.m.). Although some pesticides are rapidly inactivated after application, others (or their by-

Table 11.3. Classification of comparative toxicity of pesticides.
Note that the lower the LD_{50} the higher the toxicity.

Toxicity level[1] (Example pesticides)[2]	Oral LD_{50} (mg/kg)	Dermal LD_{50} (mg/kg)
Extremely toxic	< 5	< 10
Highly toxic (e.g. methidathion)	5-50	10-100
Moderately toxic (e.g. carbaryl)	50-500	100-1000
Slightly toxic (e.g. benomyl)	500-5000	> 1000
Practically non-toxic (e.g. chlorothalonil)	5000-15000	—
Relatively harmless	> 15000	—

1. From Behncken 1983.
2. Based on acute oral LD_{50} values for rats.

products) may persist for years in a biologically active form. Such residual contamination may affect human or livestock health, subsequent crop growth and pollute the environment. As a result, acceptable levels of pesticide residues in plant and animal products (i.e. maximum residue limits or MRLs) are defined by government legislation. Excessive or illegal pesticide residues may lead to rejection of the produce for sale and may occur as a result of the use of inappropriate pesticides, careless application or application with faulty equipment, spray drift or spraying too close to harvest.

The concept of a 'withholding period' has been adopted as a practical way of ensuring that pesticide residues do not exceed the MRL when food products are sold. The withholding period is the recommended interval that should elapse between the last application of the pesticide and harvest. It is determined on the basis of knowledge of the rate of degradation of the pesticide under normal conditions when the pesticide is applied at the recommended rate and in the correct manner. Details of withholding periods are included in 'the directions for use' on pesticide labels.

(viii) Handling pesticides
As most pesticide formulations are toxic, safety is a very important consideration. The hazards of pesticides should be considered in all aspects of

pesticide use such as storage, measuring and mixing, application and disposal of containers. As a result, the instructions on the labels of all pesticide containers should be followed precisely.

b. Pesticide use strategies
A number of aspects should be considered when planning and adopting strategies for pesticide use in vineyards. Apart from cost and efficacy, these include registered use patterns and rates for pesticides (which are conditional upon their sale), the potential development of pesticide resistance and potential effects on non-target organisms and biological control agents. Use patterns may involve routine application schedules for vineyard protection or more flexible strategies that rely on pest warning services and/or the monitoring of pest activity. The latter are often adopted to minimize pesticide use.

(i) Registered pesticide use patterns
All Australian States have legislation that requires pesticides to be registered for specific uses prior to their sale. The registration process is designed to prevent the sale of ineffective chemicals, ensure that only minimum effective doses are recommended, and that health and residue hazards are minimized.

(ii) Pest resistance
Like other biological organisms, pests constantly

adapt to their environment. The heavy use of some pesticides may result in a dramatic increase in the proportion of 'resistant' individuals in the pest population that can survive exposure to the pesticide. In some cases, resistance may develop to a group of related chemicals (cross resistance) or worse, to chemicals with different modes of action (multiple resistance). In all cases valuable chemical control options are lost.

(iii) Anti-resistance strategies

When using pesticides it is important to plan use patterns or strategies so that the evolution of resistant pest populations is prevented or delayed as much as possible. Generally, the type of anti-resistance strategy developed depends on the characteristics of the pest concerned and the mode of action of the pesticides available for use in the pest control program.

Strategies that delay or prevent the development of pest resistance mostly involve the early use of treatment programs designed to avoid long term exposure of the pest to a single or group of pesticides with a particular mode of action. With fungicides for example, this can be achieved by using chemicals with different modes of action in mixtures and/or in rotations (Delp 1981).

Most protectant fungicides used in viticulture have a non-specific toxicity to fungal growth and inhibit many sites in fungal metabolism. With these fungicides, it is highly unlikely that a fungal pest will accomplish the large number of changes required to achieve resistance at all sites of chemical action. Hence the chance of development of resistant strains is remote. For this reason, protectant fungicides (e.g. sulfur, copper compounds, mancozeb and dithianon) have been used widely in viticulture for decades without any significant decrease in efficacy.

In contrast, systemic and/or eradicant fungicides have specific toxicity to fungal growth (i.e. they specifically inhibit only one or a few sites in fungal metabolism) and they are more likely to be rendered ineffective when strains of fungi appear with slightly different reactive sites or metabolic pathways. Groups of fungicides of this type commonly used in viticulture include the benzimidazoles (e.g. benomyl, thiophanate methyl), the phenylamides or acylalanines (e.g. metalaxyl, benalaxyl, ofurace), the phosphonates (e.g.

potassium phosphite), the dicarboximides (e.g. procymidone, vinclozolin, iprodione) and the demethylation or ergosterol biosynthesis inhibitors (e.g. fenarimol, triadimenol, propiconazole). Although each of these fungicide groups has a different mode of action, fungicides within each group have a similar mode of action.

As many systemic and/or eradicant fungicides are vulnerable to loss of efficacy because of the development of resistance by fungal pests, most are sold in pre-packed mixtures with protectant fungicides. Minimal use as curative treatments is also recommended in most cases.

(iv) Other undesirable side-effects of pesticide use

Apart from the development of pest resistance, the use of pesticides may have other undesirable side effects on populations of beneficial organisms such as earthworms and bees or naturally occurring biological control agents of pests (parasites or predators). Pesticides that leave persistant residues or by-products are more likely to have a long-term effect on these non-target organisms than short-term contact pesticides.

The careless use of broad spectrum pesticides may not only lead to resurgences in pest populations but also to the emergence of new or potential pests that were not a problem previously. This may result from the decimation of the complex and interacting populations of natural enemies that, prior to pesticide application, were controlling populations of the non-target species so that they did not cause economic damage and require control, e.g. the development of spider mites as major pests of grapevines in some viticultural regions overseas (James and Whitney 1990).

(v) Strategies for timing pesticide treatments

Pesticide treatments can be applied either in routine schedules that are implemented regardless of seasonal conditions or, in treatment programs that are initiated because of a reasonable probability that pests have appeared or will appear. Various treatment strategies can be adopted depending on pest prevalence, regional conditions and available resources.

(vi) Routine treatment schedules

A conventional strategy for pest control is to apply

a routine schedule of pesticide treatments each season. The principal aim is to prevent pest development. They are planned so that a protective cover of pesticide is maintained on grapevines as they grow, particularly over periods when the crop is susceptible and losses are likely to occur. They are applicable, in particular, to the control of fungal diseases and principally designed for the use of protectant fungicides. Usually in these cases, eradicant fungicides are used only in critical circumstances such as when the fungal disease has not been satisfactorily contained because of the mistiming or inadequacy of protectant applications. Protectant fungicides are also used because most are less expensive than eradicants.

The timing of treatments in routine schedules is based on the risk of pest incidence as perceived from past experience. Average seasonal climatic conditions and associated pest activity, the residual persistence of pesticides previously applied and vine growth (or the development of unprotected susceptible foliage) are taken into account. Treatment timing is usually prescribed according to calendar date or according to stages of vine growth. With schedules of fungicide treatments, the latter approach is more effective (Kable 1977). Usually, particular emphasis is placed on the protection of inflorescences and young bunches (berries up to 5–6 mm diameter) to prevent crop losses. Intervals between treatments range from 10–28 days (mostly 12–14 days) depending on the pesticide used, regional and vineyard conditions and expected pest pressure.

The timing of treatments in routine schedules may also be influenced by other management practices. For example, in over-vine irrigated vineyards (especially those irrigated at night), downy mildew disease pressure is greater than in furrow irrigated vineyards and treatment schedules need to be more intensive.

When designing an efficient spray schedule to control a number of target pests, the objective is to achieve satisfactory pest control with as few sprays as possible thereby maximizing cost-effectiveness. This can be done by choosing multipurpose pesticides where possible and timing treatments so that a number of pests are controlled with each application. An example of the integration of treatments for a range of pests into a routine schedule designed to protect grapevines grown in the Lower Murray River districts of Vic. and NSW is outlined in Table 11.1.

(vii) More flexible treatment strategies
Although routine schedules provide effective pest control in most seasons, programs more aligned with pest activity (or expected activity) on a seasonal basis are usually more efficient especially over periods when vine growth is rapid and pest pressure is high. This particularly applies in regions where the seasonal development of pests is sporadic. Here routine schedules are inefficient because pesticides may still be applied in seasons where there is little or no pest development and there is no need for control.

Efficiency is improved by aligning treatments with timely assessments of pest risk so that they are more likely to be applied when really required. This approach also offers more scope for using post-infection or post-infestation treatments with eradicant pesticides. Ultimately, the efficiency of treatment timing is dependent on the accuracy of estimates of pest risk each season. In some regions, assessments of pest risk are provided through warning services operated by State Departments of Agriculture or commercial interests in conjunction with State Departments of Agriculture.

Pest risk assessments are usually derived from the initial level of pest activity (either as primary activity resulting from overwintering populations or secondary activity reflecting the level of pest populations already active up to a particular time) and subsequent pest development in the prevailing environmental conditions. Various techniques are used to relate these factors and develop estimates of pest risk. Increasingly computer-based simulators of pest development are being employed in conjunction with the monitoring of climatic conditions and pest incidence in vineyards. Recent advances in computer technology have led to the development of automatic weather monitoring devices.

With pests such as lightbrown apple moth, computerized day-degree models based on daily temperature records can be used to predict moth flights and the subsequent timing of insecticide treatments to kill larvae infesting the foliage each season (Madge and Stirrat 1991). With downy mildew, the likelihood of primary and secondary infection periods can be computed from detailed records of rainfall, leaf wetness, humidity and temperature using a computerized simulator of downy mildew epidemiology (Magarey et al. 1991). The date on which symptoms (oil spots) will appear and the likely severity of infection can then be forecast and recommendations for disease management can be prescribed. Alternatively, the approximate end of the latent period (or time of appearance of oil spot symptoms) can be forecast from an incubation calendar in which the duration of the latent period (mostly 7–10 days) is determined in relation to average temperature patterns for that time of the season (Magarey et al. 1985). Spray warnings can then be issued before the end of the predicted latent period. They may involve two options.

The first is to stop the appearance of disease by applying an eradicant fungicide before the end of the latent period (usually 0–7 days after the rain that created the infection period). The second, where the first option cannot be achieved because of limited vineyard accessibility after rain or for other reasons, is to treat the vineyard with a protectant fungicide at a later date to prevent secondary spread of the downy mildew fungus after sporulation occurs on the oilspots that developed after the infection period. The susceptibility of leaves and fruit and the ratio of unprotected to protected foliage must also be taken into account when making decisions about spraying. The latter is influenced by the timing of previous sprays.

Sampling procedures for estimating pest populations are an integral part of vineyard monitoring and the adoption of more flexible pest treatment strategies. These procedures are of particular importance where it is necessary to efficiently determine pest presence or absence or pest action thresholds.

Ultimately pest simulators and climatic data logging systems may be incorporated in small, inexpensive computerized devices for use in individual vineyards. The advantage of these systems is that they could greatly improve the accuracy of pest risk assessment because they not only account for regional macroclimate, but also individual vineyard microclimates. Greater input into pest monitoring may be required for viticulturists but in the long term this is not expected to offset the savings achieved from improved treatment timing particularly in regions where pest incidence is sporadic.

c. Pesticide application

Pesticides may be applied with high, low or ultra-low volume ground spraying machines, by aircraft (using fixed wing aircraft or helicopters) or by other methods. The method chosen will depend on available financial resources and agricultural services, vineyard size, location, vineyard terrain and topography and other factors.

(i) Spray application

Spray application involves four basic processes— droplet generation (by the spray machine), movement of the droplet cloud (by the machine to the target), droplet deposition (onto the target), and the kill efficiency of deposited droplets (on the target organism) (Campbell 1987).

Droplet generation in spray machines is achieved using atomisers such as hydraulic nozzles, rotary atomisers (rotating cages and spinning discs) or air shear nozzles. The latter two can be electrostatically charged or uncharged. Hydraulic nozzles produce droplets of variable size while rotating cages or spinning discs can produce droplets of optimum size for efficient spray deposition.

The droplet cloud will penetrate the canopy or be lost as drift. Energy to move the droplet cloud is generated by spraying equipment (e.g. atomiser pressure). Regardless of the volume of carrier used, most spray machines achieve good coverage only on the top and outside of grapevine canopies.

Droplet deposition (the impaction and retention of droplets on the target) is influenced by drop size and velocity and by the type and size of the target (Campbell 1987). With grapevines, the canopy (target) changes through the season. In most pest control programs, deposition of pesticides is required on foliage and bunches at all stages of growth. It is more difficult to achieve good coverage on bunches than on leaves. Droplet size appears to be particularly important and good deposition on all parts of vines is more likely to be achieved when droplet size is optimal and the range of drop sizes is extremely narrow.

The efficiency of spray application can be checked by the use of fluorescent tracers (Campbell 1985, 1987). The deposit of spray solution onto the target changes from a continuous film to discrete droplets as the volume of carrier (water) is reduced (Campbell 1987). With high volume (HV or dilute) spraying, prescribed amounts of pesticide per unit area of crop are mixed with relatively large volumes of water and applied to the point of surface runoff. Volumes of spray used vary from 550 L/ha early in the growing season to more than 1100 L/ha when the vine canopy is fully developed. With low volume (LV or concentrate) spraying, the same prescribed amount of pesticide per unit area of crop is mixed with much lower volumes of water (e.g. 50–400 L/ha). With ultra-low volume (ULV or high concentrate) spraying, pesticides are mixed in only 50 L/ha or less. Low volume and ULV techniques are usually more efficient (Campbell 1987).

The kill efficiency for a specific pesticide/target pest combination is influenced by droplet size, droplet density and by pesticide concentration (Campbell 1987). The kill efficiency of spray deposits is also influenced by weathering (erosion) of the deposit on the plant surface and depends on the nature of the surface, the ability of the pesticide deposit to adhere to the surface (related to pesticide formulation) and prevailing environmental conditions. Some protectant fungicides are particularly prone to weathering.

(ii) Spray machinery

Inadequate pest control may be a consequence of poor maintenance and/or incorrect operation of spray machinery. To operate effectively, spray machines must control the volume rate, break the spray liquid into droplets of the correct size, adequately distribute the droplets through the canopy and achieve the required rate of pesticide deposition. Spray machines are efficient if they provide acceptable pest control at minimal cost.

Spray equipment available for use in vineyards includes hand-held spray guns, boom sprayers and air assisted (air-blast) sprayers (Figure 11.22b). Aerial spraying from either fixed wing aircraft (Figure 11.22c) or helicopters (Figure 11.22d) is also used in some regions, particularly where ground spraying operations are inefficient because of vineyard size or terrain.

Hand-directed spray guns can be highly effective but are slow and costly. Boom sprayers have higher capital costs but lower operating costs. Over-the-row boom sprayers are more efficient than one-sided types because they spray two rows at once and travel alternate rows instead of every row in the vineyard. Most boom sprayers give acceptable coverage providing ground speed is relatively low (not more than 6 km/hour), volume rates are kept relatively high (at least 500–800 L/ha) and vine canopies are not excessively dense (Campbell 1987). Hooded booms (i.e. over-the-row booms shielded on the top and sides) have been used occasionally and warrant further development because they improve spray coverage of the foliage and offer a means of recovery and recycling of spray mixture. The Trinova multi-purpose unit for pruning, harvesting and spraying is another interesting development (Intrieri and Poni 1990).

Air-assisted spray machines apply sprays at low volume and at higher ground speed than boom sprayers; some machines also achieve excellent coverage (Campbell 1987). Most air-assisted sprayers have lower operating costs than boom or hand sprayers.

During aerial spraying operations, pesticide distribution and deposition is influenced by aircraft speed, spraying height (ideally 1.5–3 m above vines), atomiser design and spacing and by wind speed and direction. When spraying from fixed winged aircraft, slight turbulence, particularly cross-winds of 1–9 km/hour, are desirable for good penetration. When helicopters are used, sprays can be applied in winds up to 16 km/hour (Beckingham 1977). However, excessive winds cause substantial drift and decrease deposition on the target. Poor deposition may also occur in calm conditions with a high inversion layer (Anon. 1976).

One advantage of aerial spraying is that treatments can be applied quickly despite adverse soil conditions that may prevent ground spraying. Labour costs with aerial spraying are also much less than with ground spraying operations. A disadvantage of aerial spraying is that spray penetration is not usually as good as that achieved with ground spraying, particularly when vine canopies are fully developed (Clingeleffer *et al.* 1975, Kable 1977).

For a more detailed review of spraying techniques and spray machinery used in vineyards, see Emmett (1988).

(iii) Dust application
The application of pesticides as dust formulations to grapevines has declined over recent decades although occasionally sulfur dusts are still applied for powdery mildew control in some districts. For a detailed account of the operation of dusting machines, see Behncken (1983).

(iv) Soil fumigation
The application of fumigant pesticides to vineyard soils for the control of fungal, insect or nematode pests is a specialised operation. To be effective, particular attention must be given to soil preparation, placement of the fumigant and sealing of the soil surface. For a detailed account of soil fumigation methods, see Behncken (1983).

(v) Other application methods
In vineyards, pesticides for the control of fungal, insect or nematode pests, especially when soil-borne, may also be applied as drenches or via irrigation systems.

11.7 Concluding remarks
The many diseases and disorders that occur on grapevines in Australia have a considerable impact on grape production. Apart from the losses they cause, costs associated with their control exceed many millions of dollars annually. Increasingly, a more professional approach to the management of pests (diseases, insect pests, etc.) is needed not only because of economic constraints but also because of environment, health and marketing considerations. A good understanding of pest biology and control options is a necessary prerequisite as highlighted by the information presented in this chapter. A flexible attitude to pest control is also essential when developing safe and efficient pest management programs.

Increasingly consumers are demanding that grapes and grape products should be free of artificial substances. As analytical techniques for the detection of pesticides become more precise, tighter controls are being placed on pesticide use. The challenge facing Australian viticulture now is to increase the efficiency of pest management and reduce the use of pesticides and other resources and still maintain sustainable production.

Further reading
Behncken, G. (Ed.) (1983) Pesticide Application Manual, Queensland Dept. Primary Industries Brisbane, Australia. 232 pp.
Lester, D.C., Cirami, R.M. and Lee, T.H. (Eds) (1985) Chemicals in the Vineyard. Aust. Soc. Vitic. Oenol., Glen Osmond, SA. 112 pp.
Emmett, R.W. (1988) Fungicide and pesticide spray application: An overview. Aust. Grapegrower and Winemaker No. 297, 39–45.
Flaherty, D.L. Jensen, F.L., Kasimatis, A.N., Kido, H. and Moller, W.J. (Eds) (1981) Grape Pest Management. Univ. Calif. Publ. No. 4105. Uni. Calif. Berkeley, Calif. USA. 312 pp.
Pearson, R.C. and Goheen, A.C. (1988) Compendium of Grape Diseases. APS Press, American Phytopathological Soc., St. Paul, Minnesota, USA. 93 pp.

Other references
Anon. (1976) Aerial application of agricultural chemicals. U.S.D.A. Agricultural Handbook No. 287.
Barbetti, M.J. (1980) Bunch rot of Rhine Riesling grapes in the lower south west of Western Australia. Aust. J. Exp. Agric. Anim. Husb. 20, 247–51.
Barlass, M., Newman, H.P., and Possingham, J.V. (1987) Grapevine quarantine at Merbein, Victoria. Aust. Grapegrower and Winemaker No. 286, 15–7.
Beckingham, C.R. (1977) Aviation—What it can do for horticulture. Seed and Nursery Trader No. 75, 31–3.
Bolay, A. and Carter, M.V. (1985) Newly recorded hosts of *Eutypa lata* (=*E. armenicacae*) in Australia. Plant Protection Quarterly 1, 10–2.
Brook, P.J. (1973) Epidemiology of grapevine anthracnose caused by *Elsinoe ampelina*. N.Z. J. Agric. Res. 16, 333–42.
Bulit, J., and Lafon, R. (1978). Powdery mildew of the vine. In: The Powdery Mildews. D.M. Spencer (ed.) Academic Press, New York, USA. pp. 525–48.

Bumbieris, M. (1972) Observations on some Pythiaceous fungi associated with grapevine decline in South Australia. Aust. J. Agric. Res. 23, 651–7.

Burr, T.J., Katz, B.H., Bishop, A.L., Meyers, C.A. and Mittah, V.L. (1987) Effect of shoot age on systemic infestations of *Agrobacterium tumefaciens* biovar 3 and production of pathogen free vines. Am. J. Enol. Vitic. 39: 67–70.

Burr, T.J., Ophel, K., Katz, B.H. and Kerr, A. (1989) Effect of hot water treatment of systemic *Agrobacterium* biovar 3 in dormant grape cuttings. Plant Disease 73, 242-5.

Campbell, M.M. (1985) Efficiency of machine application of agricultural chemicals to grapevines: Machinery available on the Australian market. In: Chemicals in the Vineyard. D.C. Lester, R.M. Cirami and T.H. Lee (eds) Aust. Soc. Vitic. Oenol., Glen Osmond, SA. pp. 49–58.

Campbell, M.M. (1987) Evaluation of equipment and methods for applying agricultural chemicals. In: Proc. 6th Aust. Wine Industry Tech. Conf., T.H. Lee (ed). Aust. Industrial Pub., Adelaide. pp. 180–3.

Canter–Visscher, T.W. and Over de Linden, A.J. (1972) Root and basal stem rot of grapevine caused by *Thielaviopsis basicola* (Berk. & Br.) Ferraris. N.Z. J. Agric. Res. 15, 184–5.

Carter, M.V. (1985) Evaluation of a manual spraying secateur for protecting trees and grapevines against wound-invading pathogens. Aust. Plant Pathology 14, 43–4.

Carter, M.V. and Perrin, E. (1985) A pneumatic-powered spraying secateur for use in commercial orchards and vineyards. Aust. J. Expt. Agric. 25, 939–42.

Christensen, L.P. and Boggero, J.D. (1985) A study of mineral nutrition relationships to water berry in Thompson Seedless. Am. J. Enol. Vitic. 36, 57–64.

Clingeleffer, P.R., Trayford, R.S., May, P. and Holt, G.E. (1975) Contrasting fungicide deposits by aircraft and ground machines in a vineyard. Proc. 5th International Agric. Aviation Congr. Kenilworth, England 1975 pp. 313-20.

Conti, M., Milne, R.G., Luisoni, E. and Boccardo, G. (1980) A closterovirus from a stem–pitting–diseased grapevine. Phytopathology 70, 394–9.

Coombe, B.G. (1953) Control of black spot on grapevines. J. Dept. Agric. S. Aust. 56, 562–4.

Coombe, B.G. and Allan, H.R. (1953) Grape bunch stalk rot. J. Dept. Agric. S. Aust. 56, 418 & 422.

Creecy, H. and Emmett, R.W. (1989) Evaluation of fungicides for the control of Phomopsis cane and leaf spot on grapes, 1986. Fungicide and Nematicide Tests 44, 81.

De Castella, F. and Brittlebank, C.C. (1918) Anthracnose or black spot of the vine. Dept. Agric. Vic. Bull. No. 42.

Delp, C.J. (1981) Strategies for dealing with fungicide resistance problems. Proc. 11th British Insecticide and Fungicide Conf. British Crop. Protection Council, Croydon, UK pp. 865-71.

Dry, P.R. (1986) Primary bud-axis necrosis of grapevines. M.Ag.Sc. thesis, University of Adelaide.

Emmett, R.W. (1985) Fungicides and their use in vineyards. In: Chemicals in the Vineyard. D.C. Lester, R.M. Cirami and T.H. Lee (eds) Aust. Soc. Vitic. Oenol., Glen Osmond, SA. pp. 11–24.

Emmett, R.W., Wicks, T.J. and McQuinn, D. (1984) Control of grapevine powdery mildew in Southern Australia: II Evaluation of fungicides applied after infection. Agric. Record 11, 16–8.

Emmett, R.W., Wicks, T.J., Magarey, P.A. and Madge, D.G. (1990) Recent developments in grapevine powdery mildew management. Aust. NZ Wine Indust. J. 5, 213–7.

Gadoury, D.M. and Pearson, R.C. (1990) Germination of ascospores and infection of *Vitis* by *Uncinula necator* Phytopathology 80, 1198-1203.

Goss, O.M. and Cameron, I.J. (1981) Rootstocks beat nematodes in grapevines. J. Agric. West. Aust. 22, 34–5.

Gubler, W.D., Marois, J.J., Bledsoe, A.M., and Bettiga, K.J. (1987) Control of Botrytis bunch rot of grape with canopy management. Plant Disease 71, 599–601.

Handreck, K.A. (1974) Grapevine virus diseases—What are they? Aust. Grapegrower and Winemaker No. 122, 6-7.

Harris, A.R. (1983a) Distribution of parasitic nematodes in vineyards in central and north–eastern Victoria. Aust. J. Exp. Agric. Anim. Husb. 23, 221–4.

Harris, A.R. (1983b) Resistance of some *Vitis* rootstocks to *Xiphinema index*. J. Nematol. 15, 405-9.

Harris, A.R. (1986) Comparison of some nematicides on *Vitis vinifera* cv. Sultana in Victoria, Australia. Am. J. Enol. Vitic. 37, 224–7.

Harris, A.R. (1988) *Xiphinema index*-resistant *Vitis* rootstocks screened for comparative field performance in a Chasselas vineyard replant site. Vitis 27, 243-51.

Intrieri, C. and Poni, S. (1990) A new integrated approach between training systems and mechanical equipment for full mechanization of quality vineyards. In Proc. 7th Aust. Wine Industry Tech. Conf., P.J. Williams, D.M. Davidson and T.H. Lee (eds) Aust. Industrial Publ., Adelaide. pp. 35–50.

Jackson, D.I. and Coombe, B.C. (1988) Early bunchstem necrosis—a cause of poor set. Proc. 2nd Int. Cool

Climate Vitic. Oenol. Symposium, Auckland, New Zealand. pp. 72–5.

James, D.G. and Whitney, J. (1990) Biological control of grapevine mites. Aust. Grapegrower & Winemaker No. 321, 37–43.

Kable, P.F. (1977) Practical management of crop diseases. Winston Churchill Memorial Trust Report. Dept. Agric. NSW 142 pp.

Koltunow, A.M., Krake, L.R., Johnson, S.D. and Rezaian, M.A. (1988) Two related viroids cause grapevine yellow speckle disease independently. J. Gen. Virol., 70, 3411–9.

Krake, L.R. and Woodham, R.C. (1978) Grapevine summer mottle: a new graft–transmissible disease. Vitis, 17, 266–70.

Madge, D.G. and Stirrat, S.C. (1991) Development of a day-degree model to predict generation events for lightbrown apple moth *Epiphyas postvittana* (Walker) (Lepidoptera:Tortricidae) on grapevines in Australia. Plant Protection Quarterly 6, 39-42.

Magarey, P.A. (1985) A disease management system for viticulture. Aust. Grapegrower and Winemaker No. 256, 6–7.

Magarey, P.A. and Carter, M.V. (1987) Eutypa dieback in apricots and grapevines. Dried Fruit News NS 14, 8–9.

Magarey, P.A. and Wachtel, M.F. (1985) A review of the present status of Australian grapevine yellows. Agric. Record 12, 12–18.

Magarey, P.A. and Wachtel, M.F. (1986) Australian grapevine yellows. Int. J. Trop. Pl. Dis. 4, 1–14.

Magarey, P.A., Wachtel, M.F., Weir, P.C. and Seem, R.C. (1991). A computer-based simulator for rational management of grapevine downy mildew (*Plasmopara viticola*). Plant Protection Quarterly 6, 29-33.

Magarey, P.A., Wicks, T.J. and Weir, P. (1985) Some new guidelines for the control of grape downy mildew. Aust. Grapegrower and Winemaker No. 256, 13–8.

May, P. and Kerridge, G.H. (1967) Harvest pruning of Sultana vines. Vitis 6, 390–3.

McClellan, W.D. and Hewitt, W.B. (1973) Early Botrytis rot of grapes: time of infection and latency of *Botrytis cinerea* Pers. in *Vitis vinifera* L. Phytopathology 63, 1151–7.

McGechan, J.K. (1970) Important virus diseases of grapevines in New South Wales. Aust. Grapegrower & Winemaker No. 81, 4–5.

McGechan, J.K. (1978) Bunch rot of grapes. Farmer's Newsletter No. 139, 18–22.

Meagher, J.W. (1967) Observations on the transport of nematodes in sub–soil drainage and irrigation water. Aust. J. Exp. Agric. Anim. Husb. 7, 577–9.

Meagher, J.W. (1969) Nematodes and their control in vineyards in Victoria, Australia. Int. Pest Control 11, 14–8.

Meagher, J.W., Brown, R.H., Taylor, R.H. and Harris, A.R. (1976) The distribution of *Xiphinema index* and other parasitic nematodes associated with grapevines in north–eastern Victoria. Aust. J. Exp. Agric. Anim. Husb. 16, 932–6.

Moller, W.J. and Sall, M.A. (1981) Measles. In: Grape Pest Management. Univ. Calif. Publ. No. 4105. D.L. Flaherty, F.L. Jensen, A.N. Kasimatis, H. Kido and W.J. Moller (eds). Univ. Calif. Berkeley, Calif. USA. pp. 74–5.

Moller, W.J., Kissler, J.J. and Leavitt, G.M. (1981) Phomopsis cane and leaf spot. In: Grape Pest Management. Univ. Calif. Publ. No. 4105. D.L. Flaherty, F.L. Jensen, A.N. Kasimatis, H. Kido and W.J. Moller (eds). Univ. Calif. Beverley, Calif. pp. 70–3.

Nair, N.G. (1985a) Bunch rot of grapes caused by *Botrytis cinerea*. In: Chemicals in the Vineyard D.C. Lester, R.M. Cirami and T.H. Lee (eds). Aust. Soc. Vitic. Oenol., Glen Osmond, SA. pp. 59–66.

Nair, N.G. (1985b) Fungi associated with bunch rot of grapes in the Hunter Valley. Aust. J. Agric. Res. 36, 435–42.

Ophel, K., Burr, T.J., Magarey, P.A. and Kerr, A. (1988) Detection of *Agrobacterium tumefaciens* biovar 3 in South Australian grapevine propagation material. Aust. Plant Pathology 17, 61–6.

Ophel, K., Nicholas, P.R., Magarey, P.A. and Bass, A.W. (1990) Hot water treatment of dormant grape cuttings reduces crown gall incidence in field nursery. Am. J. Enol. Vitic. 41, 325-9.

Osmelak, J.A., Emmett, R.W. and Pywell, M. (1989) Monitoring potential leafhopper vectors of the causal agent of Australian vine yellows. Plant Protection Quarterly 4, 8–10.

Perez-Harvey, J. (1991) The influence of nitrogen fertilization on bud necrosis and bud fruitfulness of grapevines. Proc. Int. Symp. on nitrogen in grapes and wine. Amer. Soc. Enol. Vitic. Davis, Calif. pp. 110-5.

Rezaian, M.A., Habili, N., Krake, L.R. and Scott, M.S. (1992) Viruses, viroids and grapevines. Aust. Grapegrower & Winemaker. No. 340, 37-41.

Sall, M.A. and Teviotdale, B.L. (1981) Powdery mildew. In: Grape Pest Management. Univ. Calif. Publ. No. 4105. D.L. Flaherty, F.L. Jensen, A.N. Kasimatis, H. Kido and W.J. Moller (eds). Univ. Calif. Berkeley, Calif. pp. 46–50.

Sall, M.A., Teviotdale, B.L. and Savage, S.D. (1981) Bunch rots. In: Grape Pest Management. Univ. Calif. Publ. No. 4105. D.L. Flaherty, F.L. Jensen, A.N.

Kasimatis, H. Kido and W.J. Moller (eds). Univ. Calif. Berkeley, Calif. pp. 51–6.

Sarooshi, R.A., Bevington, K.B. and Coote, B.G. (1982). Performance and compatibility of Muscat Gordo Blanco grape on eight rootstocks. Sci. Hortic. 16, 367–74.

Sauer, M.R. (1962) Distribution of plant parasitic nematodes in irrigated vineyards at Merbein and Robinvale. Aust. J. Exp. Agric. Anim. Husb. 2, 8–11.

Sauer, M.R. (1974) Yields of sultanas on rootstocks. J. Aust. Inst. Agric. Sci. 40, 84-5.

Sauer, M.R. (1977) Nematode resistant grape rootstocks. Aust. Dried Fruits News NS 5 (1), 10-4.

Savage, S.D. and Sall, M.A. (1983) Botrytis bunch rot in grapes: The influence of selected cultural practices on infection under Californian conditions. Plant Disease 67, 771–4.

Savage, D.S. and Sall, M.A. (1984) Botrytis bunch rot of grapes: influence of trellis type and canopy microclimate. Phytopathology 74, 65–70.

Schroth, M.N., McCain, A.H., Foott, J.H. and Huisman, D.C. (1988) Reduction in yield and vigour of grapevine caused by crown gall disease. Plant Disease 72, 241–6.

Seinhorst, J.W. and Sauer, M.R. (1956) Eelworm attacks on vines in the Murray Valley Irrigation Area. J. Aust. Inst. Agric. Sci. 22, 296–9.

Semancik, J.S., Szychowski, J.A. and Welpert, J.A. (1992) Viroids in grapevines: a threat or an opportunity? Practical Winery and Vineyard. In press.

Shanmuganathan, N. and Fletcher, G. (1980) Indexing grapevine clones in the Fruit Variety Foundation of Australia for virus and virus–like diseases. Aust. J. Exp. Agric. Anim. Hus. 20, 115–8.

Smart, R.E. (1984) Canopy microclimates and effects on wine quality. In: Advances in Viticulture and Oenology for Economic Gain. Proc. 5th Aust. Wine Indust. Tech. Conf. T.H. Lee and T.C. Somers (eds). Univ. Western Australia, Perth. pp. 113–32.

Smart, R.E. (1985) Principles of grapevine canopy microclimate manipulation with implications for yield and quality. A review. Am. J. Enol. Vitic., 36, 230–9.

Stirling, G.R. (1976) Distribution of plant parasitic nematodes in South Australian vineyards. Aust. J. Exp. Agric. Anim. Husb. 16, 588–91.

Stirling, G.R., and Cirami, R.M. (1984) Resistance and tolerance of grape rootstocks to South Australian populations of root-knot nematodes. Aust. J. Exp. Agric. Anim. Husb. 24, 277-82.

Stirling, G.R. and White, A.M. (1982) Distribution of a parasite of root–knot nematodes in South Australian vineyards. Plant Disease 66, 52–3.

Taylor, R.H. (1954) Black spot of the vine–new recommendations for control. J. Dept. Agric. Vic. 52, 370–4.

Taylor, R.H. and Hewitt, W.B. (1964) Properties and serological relationships of Australian and Californian soil–borne viruses of the grapevine and arabis mosaic virus. Aust. J. Agric. Res. 15, 571–85.

Taylor, R.H. and Woodham, R.C. (1972) Grapevine yellow speckle—a newly recognized graft–transmissible disease of *Vitis*. Aust. J. Agric. Res. 23, 447–52.

Theiler, R. (1985) Stiellähme–Befallsprognose. Schweizerische Zeitschrift fur Obst–und Weinbau 121, 474–7.

Wachtel, M.F. (1986) Resistance and tolerance of grapevine rootstocks to citrus nematode (*Tylenchulus semipenetrans*). Aust. J. Exp. Agric. 26, 517-21.

Wicks, T.J. (1975) The dying arm disorder of vines of South Australia. Agric. Record 2, 14–20.

Wicks, T.J., Emmett, R.W., Magarey, P.A. and Fletcher, G.C. (1984) Control of grapevine powdery mildew in southern Australia: I Evaluation of protectant spray programmes. Agric. Record 11, 12-5.

Wicks, T.J., Magarey, P.A., Emmett, R.W., Baker, G.J. and Baker, B.T. (1988) Practical management of grapevine diseases and pests. Aust. Grapegrower and Winemaker No. 297, pp. 13–23.

Woodham, R.C. and Krake, L.R. (1982) Grapevine yellow speckle disease—studies on natural spread observed in the field. Vitis 21, 337–45.

Woodham, R.C., Antcliff, A.J., Krake, L.R. and Taylor, R.H. (1984) Yield differences between Sultana clones related to virus status and genetic factors. Vitis 23, 73-83.

Woodham, R.C. and Krake, L.R. (1984) Grapevine vein necrosis disease detected in rootstocks in Australia. J. Aust. Inst. Agric. Sci. 50, 58–60.

Editors' note: (1995 printing)

The reader is also referred to the following recent publication: Nicholas, P.R., Magarey, P.A. and Wachtel, M.F. (1994) Diseases and Pests, (Grape Production Series No. 1), Winetitles, Adelaide.

CHAPTER TWELVE

Special Cultural Methods for Tablegrapes

R.M. CIRAMI, I.J. CAMERON and P.R. HEDBERG

The commercial production of tablegrapes is a highly specialized field of viticulture catering for both the domestic and export markets. Whilst accounting for only 5% of fresh grape production in Australia it is rapidly gaining prominence as one of Australia's leading fruit exports. In 1987-88 it was estimated that 46,100 t of grapes were produced in Australia for tablegrape consumption. In the same year 21,801 t of tablegrapes, valued at $41.7m were exported, mainly to Singapore, the United Kingdom, Hong Kong, New Zealand, Europe and the Pacific Islands. The development of the industry is recounted in Volume 1, Chapter 1.

A tablegrape must be attractive to the eye as well as the palate. Berry characteristics such as shape, size, colour and evenness of bloom are important. In addition to the natural differences between varieties, cultural practices have a large effect on appearance of fruit at harvest. The berries should be free of blemishes such as those caused by wind damage, spray residues, insects, birds or fungal disorders. The natural bloom on the berries should be disturbed as little as possible. It is also an advantage if the berries are of uniform size and colouring and are well distributed on the bunch. Bunches should be medium in size, well filled and not too tight or straggly. Other factors affecting the sale of tablegrapes are the eating qualities, the shelf-life and the suitability for handling and transport. Eating qualities are judged by the ripeness, flavour and texture of the berry and the presence or absence of seeds (see Chapter 15).

Seedless grapes such as Sultana and Flame Seedless are proving to be increasingly popular in Australia. Unfortunately, seedlessness is often associated with small berry size, though such berries can often be enlarged by the growth regulator gibberellic acid (see 12.2.3). The flavour of a particular variety varies considerably according to seasonal conditions, soil type and irrigation practice. For instance the distinctive and popular flavour of muscat varieties can be intensified by limiting irrigation prior to harvest. Berry texture is a prominent component of eating quality and is important for the handling, transport, storage and shelf-life of the grape. The 'foxy' flavour associated with *Vitis labrusca* varieties has not been popular in Australia.

The principal Australian varieties are listed in Table 12.1 and discussed in Section 12.3. It

279

Table 12.1 Tablegrape varieties used in Australia with their approximate harvest period* and storage life** in Griffith, NSW (from Hedberg 1985b)

SEASON / Variety	***	**	Early Dec	Jan	Mid Feb	Mar	Late Apr	May	Storage Life (Weeks)
Early season									
Beauty Seedless	B	S		O-----------					N.R.
Cannon Hall Muscat	W			O-----............					4-6
Cardinal	R			O-------					N.R.
Chasselas	W			O--------					N.R.
Delight	W	S		O--------					N.R.
Early Muscat	W		O-----------						N.R.
Flame Seedless	R	S		O---------					4-6
Fresno Seedless (32-68)	W	S		O--------					N.R.
Gold	W			O--------					N.R.
Madeleine	W		O--------						N.R.
Monukka	B	S		O------------					N.R.
Perlette	W	S	O---------						N.R.
Queen of the Vineyard	W			O------------					4-6
Mid-season									
Black Hamburg	B				O------.............				4-6
Black Malaga	B				O-------------				8-12
Carolina Blackrose	B			O--------------					—
Emerald Seedless	W	S			O----------				—
Exotic	B				O------.........				4-6
Flame Tokay	R				O-------.....				4-6
Golden Muscat	W			O--------------					N.R.
Italia	W				O-------.......				6-10
Muscat Hamburg	B			O--------------					4-6
Marroo Seedless	B	S		O--------------					—
Olivette Blanche	W				O---------				—
Queen	R				O----------				4-8
Red Malaga	R				O--------------				8-12
Red Prince	R			O------------					—
Ribier	B				O--------......				8-14
Royal Ascot	B			O------------					N.R.
Ruby Seedless	R	S			O-----------				—
Sultana	W	S		O--------------					6-10
Sultana Moscata	W	S		O--------------					4-6
Waltham Cross	W			O--------------					4-8
Wortley Hall	B				O----------------				8-12
Late Season									
Aledo	W					O-----............---			8-12
Calmeria	W					O-----............---			8-16
Cornichon	B					O-----------------			6-12
Emperor	R					O------............------			12-20
Muscat Gordo Blanco	W					O---------			—
Nyora	B					O--------------------			6-14
Ohanez	W					O-----............-----			8-16

*   O - indicates the approximate date of reaching 16° Brix
**   N.R. - not recommended for storage
*** Berry Colour: W = White, R = Red, B = Black; S = Seedless
—   Storage life unknown

should be noted that other varieties of promise are being tested and may find a place in the industry. Tablegrapes are grown commercially in all mainland States with a trend for the early areas to specialize in early varieties and the later areas to specialize in mid- and late-season varieties.

12.1 The culture of tablegrapes

12.1.1 Soils

Tablegrapes are adapted to a wide range of soil types but preferences for certain types of soils have developed. In Western Australia mid and late-season tablegrapes are generally grown on the best alluvial soils near the Swan River. Very early varieties such as Madeleine and Chasselas are often planted on deep sands or gravel soils to encourage earliness; careful selection of soil type can advance ripening date by at least one week. In the Murray River areas, light sandy soils are preferred for early varieties such as Perlette and Cardinal. However there are some varieties, for example Red Malaga, which do not perform well on light soils, having poor set and poor yields. Vines on rich fertile soils which have excessive vigour must be carefully managed so as not to produce large crops of 'watery', poorly-coloured fruit. Slightly less fertile soils that favour extensive root development are preferred. Vines grown on such soils often produce grapes with excellent flavour and keeping quality. Rootstocks are often used to overcome specific soil problems (Volume 1, Chapter 8).

12.1.2 Tablegrape row orientation and vine spacing

Row orientation is most influenced by the direction of the prevailing winds and solar aspect. Strong winds at right angles to the row will open up the vine on one side. This can be an advantage, particularly for early varieties, as the openness on that side may promote colour development and earlier ripening.

In heat waves, however, openness is a disadvantage as excessive sunburning of fruit can occur. Rows which parallel the direction of the prevailing winds have a more uniform distribution of foliage, although additional handwork is needed to keep the vine open. The slope of the ground must also be considered in row orientation for reasons of surface drainage and irrigation. Another factor to consider in row orientation is the path of the sun. Grapes develop better colour when ripened in bright, diffuse light but are liable to burn if exposed directly to the hot afternoon sun, particularly in the warmer regions. Correct selection of row orientation and trellis can minimize such problems.

The usual spacing between vine rows is 3.4 to 3.7 m, which provides ample room for vine growth and vineyard equipment. Spacing within the row is generally wider for tablegrapes than for winegrapes; vine spacings of 2.4 to 2.7 m are common for vigorous varieties like Waltham Cross, Sultana, Red Malaga, Italia and Cardinal; the wider spacing permits development of a larger vine framework. Vines with less vigour like Cornichon and Muscat Hamburg are planted closer—1.5 to 1.8 m. Vines trained to an overhead pergola trellis are spaced at about 3.0 to 4.0m square. For the overhead pergola used on headlands in Western Australia the spacing is 5.5 × 3.4 m; the pergola height is 2.0 to 2.2 m (Figure 12.1).

Figure 12.1 *The overhead pergola trellis used on headlands of vineyards in the Swan Valley, Western Australia.*

12.1.3 Trellising

The quality and productivity of tablegrape plantings is intimately linked with the type of trellis employed. In addition to the normal trellis functions (Chapter 3), a tablegrape trellis should permit the following:

(i) Facilitate the even distribution of foliage, spaced so as to permit adequate light penetration to basal buds, and thereby improving bud fruitfulness, and at the same time aiding pest and disease control by improving ventilation.

(ii) Improve conditions for pollination and fruit set, and for the development of pigment in the skin of red and black berries.

(iii) Allow the bunches to hang free of foliage, canes or cordons and be in a convenient position for handwork and harvesting.

(iv) Protect against sunburn.

The trellis design used on a particular site must be related to the variety, vine spacing and vine vigour. The mismatching of trellis size and vine vigour may be detrimental. On trellises that are too large, fruit exposure and water demand can be excessive; and on those that are too small bud fruitfulness, fruit ripening and colour development may be hindered. The basic rule is that vines of high capacity demand larger trellises than those of low capacity.

In places with a long tradition of tablegrape culture it is common to find elaborate and specialized trellises. In South Africa, for example, perold, herringbone, overhead, slanting, factory-roof and double-slanting trellising systems are used. The slanting trellis (the length of the slanting section varies between 1.5 to 2.5 m and is set at an angle of 45⁰ to 55⁰ with wires spaced 30 cm apart) is the most widely used (Evans *et al.* 1973) while overhead pergolas (tendones) are most common in Italy.

Australian tablegrape trellises have, in the past, been quite simple, consisting of low, single-wire cordons with added foliage wires for canopy support. A narrow T-trellis has been used extensively in the Murray Valley regions and pergolas have been effective in some situations with some varieties (Figure 12.1). With increasing specialization in tablegrape culture more sophisticated trellises are being used to improve quality and production efficiency, such as those shown in Figure 12.2. The slanting trellis is proving economical and effective in the hot Murray Valley region. Various types of Y-shaped or factory-roof trellises are excellent designs providing for easier vine management with high quality grape production.

12.1.4 Nutrition

Nutrition is a controversial subject in the management of tablegrapes as, indeed, it is of all vineyards (see Chapter 9). As a general rule the nutritional level needs to be higher with tablegrapes than with winegrapes and requires more frequent guidance from tissue analysis standards (see Chapter 9).

Large applications of nitrogen are used on vines of low vigour, however Kliewer (1977) has shown that high levels of nitrogen can reduce fruit colour and soluble solids in the variety Emperor. Phosphorus is used in areas of known or suspected deficiency; and potassium is often applied to red or black varieties in the belief that it improves colouring, despite the lack of experimental evidence.

The Granite Belt (Queensland) has soils of low fertility and here the maintenance of productivity is thought to depend on a program of fertilizing plus green manuring. Official recommendations are to plant oats as a cover crop using 200 kg/ha of superphosphate and 100 kg/ha of urea. The cover crop is incorporated about six weeks before budburst. In addition, 150 kg/ha of 8:8:27 NPK mixed fertilizer is suggested for late winter application. Boron, zinc and magnesium deficiencies also occur and may need remedial applications (see Section 9.1). When levels of soil magnesium are low, tablegrapes can exhibit a physiological disorder which causes the bunchstems to dry out (bunchstem necrosis — BSN, 'shanking' or rachis desiccation). BSN has been severe in glasshouse tablegrapes near Murray Bridge, South Australia.

In Western Australia, most tablegrape growers apply heavy rates of fertilizer. Blood-and-bone and/or a balanced artificial fertilizer are applied near budburst and side dressings of a mixed fertilizer, usually high in potash, are given during the growing season. The side dressings are often applied before irrigating in early summer.

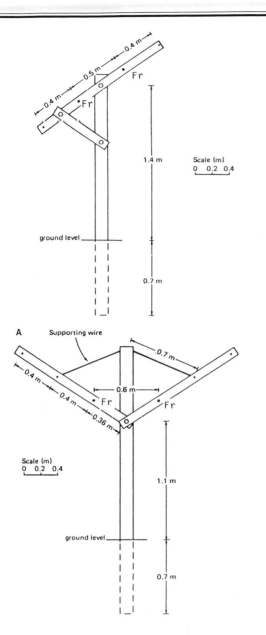

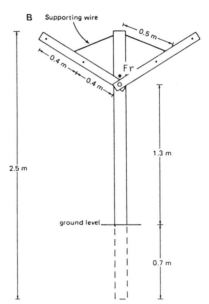

Figure 12.2 Improved tablegrape trellis designs.

Left: Slanting trellis. Fr = fruiting wire.

Below: 'Y'-shaped trellis for (A) vigorous, irrigated vines or (B) less vigorous, unirrigated vines. Fr = fruiting wire.

Slanting trellis (Loxton, SA).

Y-shaped trellis (Berri, SA).

283

12.1.5 Irrigation

In the production of tablegrapes, vines must never suffer from a shortage of soil moisture. Although the fruit produced from non-irrigated vines can have outstanding flavour and keeping quality and can mature earlier than irrigated vines of the same variety, these qualities are at risk: in drought years, or during lengthy summer heatwaves, non-irrigated vines may produce wilted bunches with soft, immature, poorly-sized berries. Irrigation of tablegrapes should therefore be regulated so that the growth rate of the berries is kept moderate and uninterrupted. Excessive irrigation is likely to give large, 'watery' berries lacking in flavour; such fruit does not pack, travel, keep or eat well and usually brings poor prices. In temperate areas the last irrigation should be completed at least ten days before harvest begins. In low rainfall areas irrigation should be reduced before harvest, but with care that water stress does not develop, especially if harvesting is prolonged.

Undervine methods of irrigation are preferred for tablegrape culture (see Chapter 6). Whilst spray irrigation is often easier, it may cause softening and splitting of ripening berries, as well as increasing the risk of fungal diseases.

The amount of irrigation required varies between regions and the season (natural rainfall), the variety and the soil. Summer rainfall regions will require less irrigation than those regions without summer rain. For example the MIA has 400 mm of rain each year, but the high summer temperatures requires that about seven furrow irrigations of 0.8 ML/ha are applied, adding an extra 560 mm each season. In the Swan Valley however, with an annual rainfall of 875 mm, soil water levels are usually adequate until early December. Mid-season and late varieties are given one to three irrigations, each of 75 to 125 mm. Different soil types require different levels and frequencies of irrigation. As discussed in Chapter 6, light sandy soils need less water more frequently, compared with heavier clay soils.

12.2 Techniques to improve tablegrape quality

The statement made by Winkler *et al.* (1974) that

.... good quality in tablegrapes represents a combination of medium-sized clusters of uniformly

large, perfect berries with the characteristic colour, pleasing flavour, and texture of the variety . . .

applies equally for Australia. In addition to the above-mentioned establishment and maintenance aspects, there are several practices that help achieve this ideal, for example: regulating crop load, adjusting the setting performance, manipulating foliage, and using plant growth regulators to improve berry size and colour development. Table 12.2 shows the operations and timing that can be used to improve grape quality.

12.2.1 Adjusting crop load

Fruit quality varies considerably with the amount of crop carried by the individual vines. The aim in tablegrape culture is to maximize yields while maintaining high fruit quality. Crop load can be adjusted by dormant pruning and shoot and crop thinning.

Pruning
The level of pruning should be adjusted according to the variety and the vigour of individual vines to achieve a desired balance between crop and foliage. If the vines are pruned too heavily, shoots will be excessively vigorous with associated poor set, poor disease control and inferior colour development. On the other hand, light pruning leads to overcropping, substandard fruit and a tendency towards biennial bearing.

Most tablegrape varieties grown in Australia bear satisfactory crops when spur-pruned. Spur numbers are increased or decreased until a satisfactory level is reached as indicated by crop load and shoot vigour (see Chapters 4 and 5); with most varieties this is achieved with 10 to 16 well-spaced 2-node spurs per vine. Varieties that initiate an inadequate number of bunches with spur pruning need longer pruning. Emperor and Ohanez are normally pruned to short-canes of 6 to 10 nodes in length, whilst Sultana vines are pruned to longer, 14-node canes. Replacement canes for these cane-pruned varieties are usually provided from spurs left for this purpose.

Shoot thinning
Removal of unwanted shoots, generally watershoots (i.e. those other than from clear buds—count nodes—left at pruning) is called shoot

Table 12.2 Cultural operations used in Australia to improve tablegrape quality

Period	Action	Reason
June-September	Pruning	Basic crop adjustment
October/November	Shoot thinning and placement	• opens up vine • provides shoot selection • provides crop reduction
October/November	Inflorescence thinning	Improves set on hard-to-set varieties
November (pre-flowering)	Shoot topping and tipping, CCC Gibberellic acid	Improves set Lengthens bunches
November (flowering)	Pollination Girdling Gibberellic acid	Improve set Improve set Thins berries, promotes seedlessness
November (post-flowering)	Gibberellic acid Bunch thinning	Increases berry size Selection of well-set bunches
December	Berry thinning	Improves tight bunches
December-March	Shoot adjustment Bunch adjustment Leaf removal Ethephon Girdling	Improves foliage exposure Ease of harvesting Improves colour Improves colour Advances ripening

thinning (the term de-suckering has been commonly used but this is incorrect because a sucker is a shoot arising from below ground). The main purpose of shoot thinning is to open up the vine canopy and improve the ventilation and exposure of the remaining shoots. Some crop thinning is also achieved if bearing shoots are removed (see 12.2.3). Shoot thinning is generally started when the shoots have reached Stage G (i.e. about ten visible internodes) and is continued until soon after set (i.e. Stage J when there are about 20 visible internodes). If shoot thinning is carried out too early, new shoots may be forced from buds on the cordon. Generally speaking, all shoots other than those growing from the spurs retained at pruning are removed; in the case of cane-pruned varieties such as Sultana and Ohanez, and where replacement spurs are needed on old spur-pruned cordons, all barren shoots are removed unless they are needed for shading or as replacement canes in the following season. There are some varieties which may not be suitable for shoot thinning: Italia, for example, produces succulent growth in spring and any shoot thinning appears to aggravate

the problem of shoots blowing off during periods of high wind.

It is thought that a moderate degree of shoot thinning is an advantage in vineyards with limited water supply because it reduces the vines' water needs but this may not be true. Also excessive shoot removal might weaken the vine, especially if it is young.

Crop thinning
Of all the methods available for crop regulation, thinning offers the opportunity for greatest selectivity and quality improvement. There are three types of crop thinning: inflorescence, bunch and berry.

a. *Inflorescence thinning* (called flower cluster thinning by Winkler) is carried out before flowering. It is practised on varieties that tend to set straggly bunches, e.g. Cardinal, Ribier and Muscat Gordo Blanco. The inflorescences that remain are better nourished and set is thereby increased giving more attractive bunches. The earlier the thinning is done the greater the benefit

Figure 12.3 Inflorescence thinning. Whole inflorescences are removed.

Figure 12.4 Bunch thinning. Excessively and poorly set bunches are removed.

to the remaining inflorescences. With Cardinal and Ribier the basal inflorescence is usually wide-branching and poorly shaped and should be removed (Mostert 1976). In contrast, the basal inflorescences of Waltham Cross and Barlinka have a better structure than the apical inflorescences (Figure 12.3) (Anon. 1979). One important advantage of inflorescence thinning is that the inflorescences are readily visible and the operation is rapid.

Inflorescence tipping is practised to improve the appearance of the bunch in some varieties. The practice is particularly important with varieties that set large bunches and/or have poor set and berry size. Cardinal, Ribier, Ruby Seedless and some others are now routinely inflorescence-tipped to improve berry set and berry size and to give earlier and more uniform ripening.

b. *Bunch thinning* (called cluster thinning by Winkler) is done after flowering and generally after set; the operation is basically a culling or sorting of bunches at an early stage of berry development

whereby undersized, poorly-set or tangled bunches are removed (see Figure 12.4). It is especially useful during the first few bearing years when fruitfulness is high but reserves are low due to the limited development of stem and root framework. In non-irrigated vineyards, young vines may require further bunch thinning just prior to harvest, particularly if adverse weather has been experienced during the growing season. Crawford and Greenhalgh (1975) showed that thinning of Muscat Hamburg advanced the date of maturity, increased the colour and percent soluble solids of the berries, allowing earlier marketing when premium prices are paid for well-coloured, sweet fruit.

Bunch tipping is the removal of parts of bunches after set to regulate crop load and improve bunch shape and size. Sultana bunches destined for export (designated as Thompson Seedless) are tipped heavily, often leaving only three or four shoulder sprigs to give a 'chunkier' bunch of about 600 g weight. The varieties Flame Seedless and Ruby Seedless also need heavy bunch tipping to produce a smaller bunch that is more marketable (Figure 12.5). Varieties such as Cardinal or Ribier may also have their shoulder

Figure 12.5 Bunch tipping. Part of the bunch is removed after set.

branch tipped to produce a more attractive bunch.

c. *Berry thinning* is sometimes necessary to thin berries on varieties that set over-compact bunches. Berry thinning is carried out on individual bunches soon after berry set and must be completed before the berries are large enough to touch each other (i.e. during the first growth phase). If done well it gives looser bunches, larger berries, better colour development in red or black varieties and reduces the risk of bunch rot at harvest. Red Prince, Barlinka, Wortley Hall, artificially-pollinated Ohanez and GA-treated Perlette and Sultana benefit from berry thinning. Berry thinning can also be used on Emperor, Ribier and Cardinal to remove undeveloped berries.

The operation is time-consuming and labour-intensive but the results are rewarding; bunches that have been well-thinned in the spring or early summer require very little cleaning at harvest and packing rates are considerably improved. To obtain a well-formed bunch, more than half the berries on the bunch may have to be removed. A degree of berry thinning can be achieved quickly by the process called 'milking'; this consists of running thumb and forefinger (or a hairbrush) quickly down the bunchstem to remove a proportion of berries and bunch laterals just prior to shatter.

12.2.2 Treatments which affect setting

Girdling

Girdling (cincturing) is the removal of a 3-6 mm ring of bark down to the cambium in a complete circle around the trunk or arms (Figure 12.6). The girdle severs the phloem and interrupts the normal movement of carbohydrate to the roots thus increasing the amount of food material and hormones in the portion of the vine above the cut. Girdling improves set, increases berry size, advances ripening (see 12.2.9) and improves colouring. Girdling used to be commonly practised on Currants but is now rarely used in Australia. Specialist growers catering for particular markets may find it a useful practice. Madeleine vines are often girdled when the berries reach 2.5mm diameter (about the size of this letter O or of mustard seed), four to five days before GA treatment (see 12.2.3). This combination of girdling and gibberellic acid has been well

Figure 12.6 Girdling a vine to improve set and/or berry size and shape.

researched and ample experimental evidence supports the value of the practice. Repeated girdling over a number of years may reduce bunch size and the life expectancy of the vine.

Artificial pollination

Unlike most other varieties of grape, Ohanez and Bridal (Olivette Blanche) are not self-pollinating and require some form of cross pollination. The Ohanez flower, for example, has well developed female parts but ineffective male parts with recurved stamens and low vigour pollen (Avramov 1954). Artificial pollination can be achieved by rubbing the bunches with a sprig of newly opened flowers from another pollen-producing variety.

In 1939 two vignerons in Western Australia pioneered the technique of pollinating Ohanez by spraying the flowering bunches with a suspension of pollen in water. Hale and Jones (1956) showed that Black Malaga, Muscat Gordo Blanco, Cornichon and Wortley Hall were suitable pollinizer varieties. Today all Ohanez and Bridal grapes grown in Western Australian are artificially pollinated. Bunches of Black Malaga or Muscat Gordo Blanco are picked when in full bloom and agitated vigorously in a bucket of water; the mixture is then sieved and the pollen suspension is hand-sprayed on to each flowering bunch (Figure 12.7). The bunches are sprayed with fresh suspension every 2-3 days during the 10-14 days of flowering. Elsewhere pollinizer varieties such as Muscat Gordo Blanco, Waltham Cross or Emperor are interplanted, one pollinizer for every eight vines as follows:

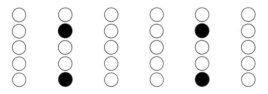

or entire rows of the pollinizer in every fourth row of the block.

Topping and tipping

Topping (removing 10 cm or more of the shoot tip) and tipping (removing less than 10 cm of the shoot tip) have long been held to improve the set of grapes. The improved set is achieved by reducing competition for food materials between the shoot tips and the developing ovaries. For this purpose, the operation is normally carried out 4-7

Figure 12.7 Pollination by the spraying of a pollen suspension.

days before the peak of flowering. Effects of topping vary from year to year and the treatment can be harmful to vines of below-average vigour. Topping of very vigorous vines, particularly vines grafted on to rootstocks, may lead to the development of considerable amounts of second crop which rarely develops to full maturity and can have a detrimental effect on the primary crops. Topping and tipping are not widely practised; growth retardants such as CCC and Alar can more easily achieve a similar result (Coombe 1965, 1967, 1970, Peterson 1974 a and b).

Zinc deficiency

A deficiency of zinc may seriously affect the set and development of grape berries. Zinc deficient vines produce straggly bunches with many undeveloped or shot berries. Varieties such as Muscat Gordo Blanco, Cardinal, Ribier and Red Malaga are particularly susceptible to zinc deficiencies, especially when grown on sandy soils and on vigorous rootstocks such as Ramsey and Dog Ridge (see Chapter 9 for treatments to correct zinc deficiency).

Growth regulators

Two types of growth regulators are used to influence grape setting, the promoter gibberellic acid (GA) and the retardant CCC [(2-chloroethyl)-trimethylammonium chloride].

Figure 12.8   Gibberellic acid used on Sultana grapes to increase berry size.
Left: GA treated   Right: Untreated

a. GA

With seedless grapes, GA (5-15 mg/L) sprayed on flowers as they are beginning to open reduces the number of berries set. If applied later, this thinning effect is lost (see 12.2.3). On the other hand, GA can improve set and berry size of male-sterile varieties like Madeleine. The yield and bunch appearance of Madeleine can be greatly improved with the application of 15-20 mg/L GA just before the shatter stage (stage H). Madeleine (see Section 12.3) is the earliest tablegrape grown in Western Australia and is marketable by mid- to late-December.

b. CCC (chlormequat)

Application of CCC to either the foliage or the bunch, from one to three weeks before bloom, may increase fruit set by more than 20% in several seeded and seedless *vinifera* grape varieties (Coombe 1965, 1967, 1970). Peterson (1974 b) found a similar result with the growth retardant Alar (N-dimethylaminosuccinamic acid).

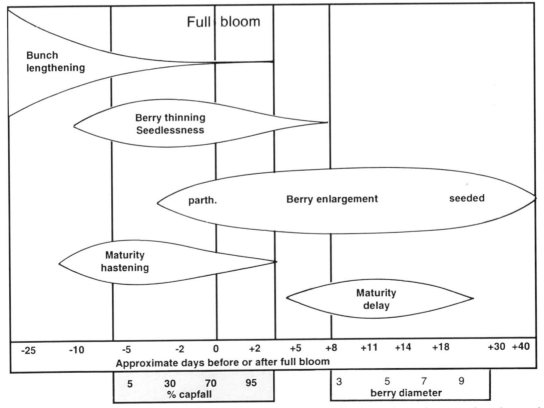

Figure 12.9   Effect of time of GA treatment on the numerous responses shown by grape bunches and berries. Berry enlarging treatments are generally applied later than thinning treatments but their timing is influenced by ovule and seed growth. (Diagram by B.G. Coombe after Turner 1972)

12.2.3 Increasing berry size with gibberellic acid

During the last few decades there has been widespread interest in the use of plant growth regulators for viticulture. Gibberellic acid (GA), is the most widely used growth regulator in Australian tablegrape growing, as in all other countries.

GA is used to improve bunch size and berry development of seedless grapes, especially Sultana (Weaver 1972, Boehm 1960; Figure 12.8 and 12.9). GA has several divergent effects on seedless grapes depending on time and rate of application, as illustrated in Figure 12.9.

(i) *Bunch elongation.* GA sprayed onto bunchstems when bunches are a half to two thirds of their final length causes them to grow longer than normal and helps prevent excessive compactness.

(ii) *Thinning.* GA sprayed on flowers as they are beginning to open reduces the number of berries on the bunch, i.e. it has a thinning effect. If applied later, this thinning effect is lost. These treatments also inhibit seed development and may produce seedlessness in normally seeded varieties e.g. Delaware and Cardinal; such berries may then be enlarged by further GA treatment as in (iii).

(iii) *Berry size.* GA increases berry size when applied after the commencement of flowering. The effect is generally greatest when applied as berries approach 3 mm diameter (small wheat grains) at which stage cells are actively dividing in the pulp. Earlier treatments, at 80-100% capfall, are better for enlarging small parthenocarpic berries

(presumably to trigger cell division) and late treatments, at 30-40 days after full bloom, for enlarging seeded berries in the few varieties that do respond to GA (Considine 1983). The earlier the treatment the greater the berry lengthening effect.

(iv) *Maturity.* GA, applied in the period between the beginning of flowering and full bloom, advances maturity. If applied after full bloom, maturity is delayed.

(v) *Berry drop.* GA treatment of Sultana increases the tendency for berries to drop after shaking the bunch. (This is called 'shatter' in the USA.) The severity of this effect is influenced by time of GA treatment in parallel with the berry enlarging effect, especially by later treatments (Ben-Tal 1990).

The application of GA to seedless grapes varies according to variety and desired berry size and maturity. Table 12.3 shows the range of GA treatments used in seedless tablegrape culture. Correct timing of spraying and a thorough wetting of bunches are critical. Often multiple spraying is used (up to 4 or 5 in succession) especially if flowering is asynchronous. Spraying of all foliage and heavy total dosages are to be avoided, otherwise bunch numbers may be reduced during the next season; some growers limit the total GA applied in each year to less than 100 mg/L e.g. 7 + 15 + 30 + 40.

In California, very few fresh seedless grapes are produced without GA treatment. The response of other seedless varieties such as Perlette, Beauty Seedless, Monukka and Flame Seedless to GA is similar to that of Sultana although the

Table 12.3 Schedules showing timing and gibberellic acid concentration (mg/L or ppm) for treatment of seedless tablegrapes (after Hedberg 1985a)

Purpose	% capfall of most bunches				Berry diameter (mm)				
	20	40	60	80	4	5	6	7	8
Earliest ripening (Sultana)	6		10		10				
Mid-season larger berries (Sultana)	6				10				
Largest berry size									
• Sultana, Perlette			10-15*		30-40		30-40		
• Flame Seedless		3-10							20-30†

* Or 2 to 3 separate sprays between 30 and 80% capfall using lower ppm sprays.
† Repeated 1 week later.

concentration and timing of the sprays may need to be varied for optimum results. Perlette, for example, has a tendency to set significant numbers of shot berries following bloomtime sprays. Some seedless varieties do not respond well e.g. Autumn Seedless, Blush Seedless, Centennial Seedless, Dawn Seedless, Fiesta and Ruby Seedless.

GA is not recommended for use on most seeded varieties as a vine spray. Stannard *et al.* (1974) showed that GA sprays applied to Waltham Cross between full bloom and shatter increased the 'hen-and-chicken' problem, reduced yield, caused abnormal shoot development, fasciation and dead buds the following season. Bud fruitfulness in the year following GA sprays can also be markedly reduced. However, Combrink *et al.* (1974) did show that dipping bunches in solutions of GA or GA plus PCPA (para chloro phenoxy acetic acid) improved the quality of Waltham Cross. The Japanese have a large tablegrape industry that is based mainly on the *Vitis labrusca* seeded variety Delaware; individual bunches are dipped in GA to produce very large seedless berries. The method is also successful on Waltham Cross but not Italia (Dry and Smart 1986).

12.2.4 Foliage manipulation

In addition to shoot topping and tipping, foliage can be manipulated in other ways to improve fruit coloration and quality, reduce disease or simply improve accessibility.

Leaf removal

Leaf removal is mainly used on coloured varieties, many of which require light for colour formation, but can be used on all varieties. Two or three mature leaves and sometimes whole laterals are removed from the vicinity of bunches near veraison, especially on the shady side of the vine. Excessive leaf removal may hinder fruit ripening and encourage sunburn, although removing a few old leaves near the bunches at harvest time is not detrimental to bunch nutrition (May *et al.* 1969, Kliewer and Antcliff 1970). Leaf removal allows the bunches to hang freely, thus reducing wind scarring and bloom removal. It also facilitates harvesting by removing leaves that may interfere with bunches and by making the fruit more visible.

Removal of the interior leaves may sometimes by useful for preventing bunch rot development in very late varieties following rain (Winkler *et al.* 1974). The practice allows sun and air to penetrate the vine and speeds evaporation of moisture from the berry surface.

Tucking-in, wrapping-on, rolling-on and folding-up

These are local terms for hand placement of new

Figure 12.10 The hand placement of shoots into the vine canopy or trellis to increase grape exposure. Larger trellises are preferable alternatives to this practice.

shoots on to the foliage wires (see Figure 12.10). The extra layers of foliage on top of the vine may reduce sunburn, but greatly aggravates disease control problems. In Western Australia, where rows are generally oriented east-west, shoots of all varieties are folded-up on to the foliage wires after setting. The southern sides of the vine are left open and the canes hang over the north side to provide additional shade protection against sunburn. Bunches are untangled and poorly set bunches are removed at this time. Higher and better trellises should provide many of the advantages achieved by foliage manipulation, without the cost of hand labour.

12.2.5 Improvement of berry colour

Many red and black tablegrape varieties have less pigmentation than desired for maximum consumer appeal. This may be due to the effects of leafroll disease, or to deficiencies in light, temperature, soil moisture or nutrition (Winkler *et al.* 1974, Kliewer 1977). Treatment of bunches with ethephon may enhance colour development in Emperor (Jensen *et al.* 1975) and Red Malaga (Peacock *et al.* 1977). Jones and Cameron (pers. comm.) demonstrated that ethephon significantly hastened colour development in Emperor in Western Australia without causing any softening of the fruit (Table 12.4); application of ethephon at 300 mg/L when the bunches showed 5-10% colour development gave the quickest and most consistent results.

Hedberg (1979) indicates that ethephon will improve and hasten grape colouring with the varieties Barlinka, Cardinal, Emperor, Red Malaga, Muscat Hamburg and Black Prince but has no effect on the colouring of Cornichon or Ribier. Table 12.5 shows suitable rates of ethephon.

12.2.6 Hastening of ripening

In their desire to produce early ripening tablegrapes, growers are planting vines in 'early' districts—localities like northern Queensland, Central Australia near Alice Springs, the River Darling in west—central New South Wales and Kununurra and the Kimberleys in the far north of Western Australia (Volume 1, Section 1.4). In regions that lack winter cold, such as northern Queensland, the methods of tropical viticulture are employed i.e. pruning twice each year—July

Table 12.4 Effect of ethephon applied at early veraison on the percentage of marketable coloured bunches of the variety Emperor at four stages after treatment

Concentration of ethephon (ppm)	Days after spraying			
	15	20	28	35
0	0	2	3	21
100	7	19	33	65
200	9	20	47	67
300	29	38	46	65

Source of data: Jones and Cameron (pers. comm.).

Table 12.5 Rates of ethephon to improve and hasten grape colour (Hedberg 1979)

Variety	Rate
Barlinka	100ppm (20mL*/100L water)
Cardinal) Muscat Hamburg) Emperor)	200ppm (40mL*/100L water)
Red Malaga) Black Prince)	
Cornichon) Ribier)	no benefit

* Volume of commercial preparation, 50% active ingredient.

and January—the first growth cycle from August to November being the main crop production period.

Vines can be manipulated in various ways to allow a hastening of ripening to obtain early grapes for specialized markets:

Vine covers
Vine covers may advance ripening by up to 25-30 days, as has been shown on the varieties Ribier, Chasselas and Cardinal (Chamayou 1975, Vryonides 1976 and Manzo 1976). The use of plastic covers not only hastens ripening but reduces disease and pest problems and enhances quality. Yields are lower under plastic but higher prices for early grapes make the operation highly profitable (Vryonides 1976).

Standard vegetable glasshouses (Cirami *et al.* 1986) and fibreglass houses are used in South Australia and Victoria to gain protection from frost, wind and bird damage permitting production of unblemished fruit that ripens four to six weeks earlier than vines grown out of doors.

Cameron (1986) found that a plastic cover over Perlette grapes from late winter hastened maturity by up to eleven days and even more when early budburst was stimulated with 2% hydrogen cyanamide. Similar results were found with Cardinal and Ribier although fruitfulness was reduced in the following season.

Hydrogen cyanamide

The ability of cyanamide to stimulate earlier and more uniform bud burst is well documented. Manipulating pruning dates and treating with cyanamide has hastened maturity in central Australia (McColl 1986) and in S.E. Queensland (George *et al.* 1988). Providing sufficient warmth exists, budburst can be stimulated three weeks after vines are pruned, generally in June, and

Figure 12.11 Serious bird damage on ripening fruit.

sprayed immediately after pruning with 1 to 5% cyanamide (plus wetter). Such vines may flower as early as September and ripen fruit in November. The bursting effect is slowed if pruning/spraying is delayed into the winter period (Dry 1992).

Girdling

Girdling (see 12.2.4) can hasten ripening by improving coloration and sugar accumulation. Best results are obtained from vigorous vines having only a light to moderate crop and the girdle should be made just before ripening begins (Weaver 1976, Winkler *et al.* 1974).

Ethephon

Ethephon (see 12.2.8) can also be used to advance ripening. Blommaert *et al.* (1974) advanced the ripening of Barlinka; treated vines had fruit with higher sugar content, lower acid and better colour than untreated vines. Similar results were obtained with Cardinal (Jensen and Andris 1977) and Sultana (El-Banna and Weaver 1979).

12.2.7 Pest and disease control

The standard disease and pest control measures outlined in Chapters 10 and 11 are used for tablegrapes. However, because of the importance of the appearance of the fruit and the fact that the end product is eaten fresh from the vineyard, certain pests and diseases create additional problems for the tablegrape grower.

The major pests are birds, mealy bug, lightbrown apple moth and bunch mites. Mediterranean fruit fly can be a problem in Western Australia unless adequate control measures are taken, and mice and foxes can also be a serious problem in some districts. Downy mildew, oidium and black spot are perennial problems for all grapegrowers, and botrytis can seriously affect the storage life of late-ripening varieties such as Ohanez and Emperor. The use of pre-harvest fungicides to improve shelf-life is discussed in Chapter 15.

Bird damage can cause severe losses (Figure 12.11) and unfortunately control measures are not always successful. Small vineyards planted near tree-lined watercourses or adjacent to citrus orchards are especially liable to bird damage. Silvereyes (*Zosterops literalis*) are perhaps the worst bird pest of tablegrapes in Australia. Flocks of these birds gather early in the season as the fruit is softening and attack the fruit before it has reached a marketable stage. Late-maturing varieties are also liable to serious damage by silvereyes. Gas guns, nets, shooting and various scare devices have all been tried with variable success. Knight and Robinson (1978) have successfully used acoustic signals to protect grape crops from silvereyes. They found that vocal communication was necessary for the cohesion of groups of silvereyes and disruption of this communication over specific wavelengths acted as an effective deterrent and forced birds to move to unprotected areas. The starling, crow, galah and parrot all respond to the range of control techniques mentioned above. The secret of success seems to be in starting a variable pattern of protection early, before the fruit begins to soften, and then continuing to the end of harvest.

Some tablegrape growers are resorting to the use of complete net protection against birds, as are cherry growers; the adoption of this practice needs careful balancing of costs and returns. The reduced risk of bird damage is one of the favourable aspects of glasshouse production.

12.2.8 Rain damage

Use of the best cultural technology to improve grape quality can be offset by rain falling close to harvest. The increased turgidity of the berries that results after rain can cause susceptible varieties to crack or split, allowing fungal infection and rendering the fruit unsuitable for table use (Figure 12.12).

Physically covering the vine to protect the fruit from light showers has been shown to reduce rain damage to fruit, but the high costs have to be balanced against the benefits. Many of the cultural methods described earlier in this chapter help mitigate the fungal infection following rain damage.

12.3 Special cultural methods for particular varieties

Many of the tablegrape varieties have to be treated in special ways to produce a distinctive, quality product. An array of diverse and interesting practices have been developed over the years by innovative growers. Some special cultural practices

Figure 12.12   Berry splitting caused by wet weather.

are described below, together with some general comments on recently introduced varieties. Additional information on varieties can be found in Volume 1, Chapter 6.

Barlinka
A large-berried, late-ripening black grape. The variety is very susceptible to summer rain wherein it splits badly. Berry thinning, when carried out soon after setting, allows for full bunch and berry development and tends to minimize the effects of rain damage. The berries turn uniformly black well before they are palatable. Barlinka is the principal tablegrape grown in South Africa; the selection grown in Australia appears to differ from the South African variety, though this could be due to environment. This variety is not suited to commercial production.

Beauty Seedless
An early, black seedless grape. It responds to GA and berry thinning but is susceptible to berry splitting and tends to wilt in storage. This variety is not suited to commercial production.

Black Malaga

A mid-season black grape with medium-sized, slightly elongated berries. Generally considered to be a shy bearer but yields can be improved by leaving longer spurs (four to five buds), or leaving a short 6- to 8-node cane at the end of each cordon arm. Setting and bunch shape are improved by removal of the bunch tail during flowering. The variety is often used as a source of pollen for the pollination of Ohanez.

Blush Seedless

This red, crisp grape has the general characteristics of Emperor, but is earlier-colouring and earlier-ripening. It has a brighter red colour than Emperor and is similar in storage and shipping qualities. It is essentially seedless with only soft, greenish seed rudiments present. The bunches are well-filled to compact. The berries are oval and of uneven size. The vines are susceptible to powdery mildew and the fruit rots if vines are overcropped. The fruit matures in late February-early March.

Shoot thinning when growth of latent buds reach 15 to 20 cm appears necessary. Only a few lateral shoots develop and these should be removed. Bunch thinning (removal) is required to reduce overcropping. The basal bunch on the shoot develops a good size 'wing' while the upper bunch has a small 'wing' or tendril. Wings and tendrils should be removed when thinning. Vines can be spur-pruned.

Calmeria

A late-ripening, open-pollinated, vigorous variety which is replacing Ohanez as an export variety. Berries are large, white, elongated and seeded with tough skins. Bunches set well but berries are prone to 'wind-suck' (thumb mark indentation on the berries following temporary moisture stress; this may be related to BSN). Calmeria can be cane- or spur-pruned.

Cannon Hall Muscat

An attractive white grape with large, slightly elongated berries having a distinctive muscat character. The variety sets poorly following cold, wet weather at flowering. Grapes maintain high acidity when ripe and harvest for export does not begin until 17° Brix is reached. Antcliff *et al.* (1976) regard this variety as identical to the Cannon Hall Muscat of England and not a tetraploid sport of Muscat Gordo Blanco.

Cardinal

This variety has performed well throughout Australia and is popular because of its early maturity, large berry and bunch size, and attractive red colour. Its berries are inclined to crack in wet seasons or following sprinkler irrigation after veraison. Excessive vine vigour may reduce fruit set and fruit colour and should be avoided by attention to irrigation, rootstocks and fertiliser practices. Cardinal is a very fruitful variety often producing three bunches per shoot. Vines are normally pruned to short spurs and up to two thirds of the bunches are removed well before flowering in order to regulate cropping and improve setting. Ethephon can also be used to enhance colour development (see 12.2.8) and under some circumstances GA enlarges its berries.

Centennial Seedless

This white variety has large berries with only occasional seed traces. Berry colour is dull, obscured by a heavy bloom. The skin is thin but crack resistant and the flesh is firm with a very mild muscat flavour. Grapes ripen 3-4 weeks before Sultana and one week after Perlette. It is a self-thinning variety at flowering and produces a naturally loose and well-filled bunch. It shatters less than Sultana and produces an excellent raisin with a large berry size.

Generally only two shoots develop per spur so shoot thinning in spring is not necessary. The fruit develops generally as one bunch per shoot. The bunches are 25-30 cm long. If a wing is present, it is usually small. The berry is somewhat pointed and may have two small soft seed coats inside. Exposed fruit develops a dull amber colour while shaded fruit remains a uniform green colour. Centennial Seedless appears to develop problems with browning of berries when they are packed and this may make the variety less desirable for commercial marketing. GA treatments for thinning and sizing are not particularly effective and are discouraged in California.

Chasselas

An early-ripening variety which can be used for both tablegrape and wine production. Red and white selections are available but as the flavour is poor it is not widely grown in Australia.

Christmas Rose

This variety has large to very large bunches with large, well-coloured, red seeded berries with tear-drop shape. Colouring begins earlier and is completed by the time the first colour appears in Emperor. It is less dependant on light for colour development than Emperor. Berries have thin tender skin, but are crack resistant. Berries are crisper than Emperor with a higher sugar content and better acid balance and neutral flavour.

Berry size is uneven and fruit ripens in mid-March. Neither shoot thinning nor bunch thinning are required. Generally only one bunch develops per shoot. Bunches are large and loose and should be tipped.

Cornichon (Olivette Noir)

A late-maturing variety with purple-coloured, elongated berries. All known clones of this variety grown in Australia are infected with leafroll virus giving poor colouring, especially under hot irrigated conditions. Cornichon is cane-pruned in Queensland. In other states spur-pruning is normal with short 6- to 8-node canes being left at the ends of the cordons.

Dawn Seedless

An early-maturing, attractive, white seedless variety with medium size oval berries. While it resembles Perlette it has bunches which do not require berry thinning and are more uniform in size with larger berries. Skin is tougher than Perlette with berry flesh firm and meaty, but not as crisp as Perlette. The fruit is palatable at a low sugar content.

Vines are low to medium in vigour and produce many shoots from latent buds. Shoot thinning is required when growth reaches 15-20 cm. Generally two shoots per spur develop with one bunch on each shoot. The bunches do not develop tendrils or wings. The fruit ripens in late January and begins to breakdown rapidly. Dawn Seedless does not respond to bloom sprays or sizing sprays of GA. The variety does set a fairly tight bunch.

Delight

A pleasant, slightly muscat-flavoured, early white seedless grape. The bunch is less compact than Perlette and the berries have a larger natural size. The berries have a thin skin that splits easily in wet weather but have a pleasant crisp texture with a distinctive attractive flavour. The vines crop well with spur pruning. Berry size can be enhanced with GA but berry thinning treatments are less reliable.

Early Muscat

A very early, white, seeded variety with tough skin, firm pulp and a heavy aromatic muscat flavour. It has been reasonably useful as an early variety in Queensland.

Emerald Seedless

A recently introduced large-berried, white seedless variety with large bunches. Ripens later than Sultana.

Emperor

A large-berried, late-ripening, red variety which is suitable for cold storage and export. The vines are vigorous and should be trained on a high, wide trellis. The variety responds to light pruning; this is achieved by using 3- to 4-node spurs or a combination of 2-node spurs and short canes. Cropping is best regulated after light pruning, rather than using pruning as the main method of crop regulation. Overcropping can result in poorly coloured underdeveloped berries and weak bunchstems. Bunches are not normally berry-thinned. Early removal of poorly set bunches can reduce labour costs at harvest time. Ethephon can be used to even out and hasten colouring of Emperor (see 12.2.6).

Exotic

A variety noted for its large berry size, crisp firm texture and thin, tender, black skin. It is very susceptible to cracking and splitting and thus not particularly suited to commercial production.

Flame Seedless

An increasingly popular variety in Australia. Its medium-sized berries are bright red, seedless and crisp, ripening about the same time as Cardinal. Spur pruning is normally used. The current GA program is for two 3 mg/L GA thinning sprays at 40-50% and 80-90% flowering followed by two 30 mg/L GA sizing sprays when berry diameter is 5-8 mm (Leamon 1988). The upper shoulder branch of the bunch is also often removed.

Fresno Seedless (32-68)

A recently imported variety from the USA with medium-sized, yellow seedless berries. The vines crop well with spur pruning. The use of GA on this variety is not usually recommended but large quality improvements are achieved with bunch thinning and trimming. Berry shatter can be a problem during marketing.

Hunisa

A red, seeded variety with large bunches of large, attractive, elongated berries. The fruit ripens late mid-season. The variety is female flowered (male sterile) and needs pollination and cane pruning.

Italia

A large-berried, attractive, white, mid-season variety which has a pleasant muscat flavour. Italia is considered easy to grow; it responds to spur pruning and requires only minimal thinning after fruit set. The berries are susceptible to bruising and vines should therefore not be planted in windy, exposed situations.

Kishmishi

A red, seeded variety with very large, elongated berries which are firm and very crisp. Its large bunches are very loose. The flowers are male sterile and need pollination. (The name Kishmishi resembles one of the synonyms of Sultana).

Madeleine (Madeleine Angevine)

A very early, white grape which is grown mainly in Western Australia. The seedlessness is apparently due to lack of fertilization as the variety has female (male-sterile) flowers (like Ohanez). Gibberellic acid sprays (15-20 ppm) to improve set and berry size are applied just prior to the shatter stage. Girdling may also be used.

Marroo Seedless

A mid-season, large, black seedless grape bred by the CSIRO. Pruning is to 2-node spurs and inflorescences are thinned to one bunch per shoot before flowering. The remaining bunches are further trimmed in half after fruitset. GA should not be used on Marroo Seedless as it tends to produce abnormal growth in the season of application and reduces crop levels in the following season.

Muscat Gordo Blanco

A medium-sized, white, mid-season variety which has a distinctive muscat flavour. Overcropping, overwatering and excessive vigour severely reduce flavour development in the berry. Flavour is all-important with this variety since the bunch does not have an attractive appearance. Poor setting and uneven berry development are problems in most areas where the variety is grown, but clonal selection has lessened these detrimental effects. Inflorescence tipping at flowering time usually improves set and berry development.

Muscat Hamburg (Black Muscat)

An attractive, early mid-season, black grape with a delicious muscat flavour. It is popular with growers, particularly in Victoria and New South Wales, since it is tolerant of rain damage and can double as a winegrape. Uneven ripening of berries within the bunch can cause concern in some years and crop regulation by hard pruning, bunch thinning and leaf removal are often practised. Very tight and non-marketable bunches are removed after set.

Nyora

A Cornichon x Ohanez cross, Nyora was looked to as a possible replacement for Cornichon. Pruning is to 2-node spurs. The variety tends to crop erratically but the grape colour is much darker than Cornichon. Bunch trimming after fruit-set is a normal practice.

Ohanez (Almeria)

A late-maturing, white variety suitable for cold storage and export. Ohanez has male-sterile flowers and adequate cross pollination is necessary to produce a crop. Hand pollination is used in Western Australia (see 12.3.4), but growers in other states rely on interplanted varieties that flower at the same time; Muscat Gordo Blanco, Muscat Hamburg, Waltham Cross, Purple Cornichon and Semillon have been used for this purpose. Ohanez must be cane-pruned as the fruitful buds occur well out on each cane. A large framework of permanent wood seems necessary for successful cropping. Overhead trellis systems are preferred.

Olivette Blanche

Known as Bridal in Western Australia, Olivette Blanche is a mid-season variety with large, white, elongated berries and large, well-filled bunches. It requires artificial pollination in Western Australia but sets well in other States. The berries are thin-skinned and easily bruised, and require careful handling.

Perlette

An early, white, seedless variety with a mild, aromatic flavour. GA, bunch and berry thinning are required to achieve satisfactory berry size and bunch looseness. Spur pruning is mostly used. Current recommendations for GA suggest a 10 mg/L GA thinning spray at 50% flowering (or two sprays at 40-50% and 80-90% flowering if flowering is slow) followed by a 30 mg/L GA sizing spray at 100% shatter (Leamon 1988). Bunch thinning to one bunch per shoot is common with bunch trimming and berry thinning after set. The berries are prone to splitting and the vines are very susceptible to nematodes.

Queen

A red, mid-season grape with large oval berries, neutral flavour and large bunches. Bunches should be thinned to one per shoot and trimmed by half within one week of fruit set. Vines are pruned to 2-node spurs.

Queen of the Vineyard

An early to mid-season, white, seeded variety that is widely grown throughout the world. The vines crop well and produce a robust, medium-large berry that has a pleasant, mild muscat flavour.

Red Globe

This variety has very large, pinkish-red, seeded berries with outstanding eye appeal and large to very large bunches. The fruit stores well. Red Globe appears to be superior to Emperor in having higher and more consistent yields. It produces full colour earlier and has a larger berry size. Berries have thin skin with firm flesh and are crack resistant. The brush is very resistant to detachment. Berry flavour is insipid. Vines are weak and few shoots develop from latent buds and no shoot thinning is required. Generally only one bunch develops per shoot.

Red Malaga

A mid-season variety with medium-sized berries and large loose bunches. Berries are crisp and neutral in flavour and tender-skinned.

Red Prince

An early to mid-season, crisp, red variety. Red Prince sets over-compact bunches which must be berry-thinned to produce an acceptable, export-quality product. Berry thinning is carried out just after setting. Chemical thinning has not been satisfactory.

Ribier (Alphonse Lavallee)

An attractive, large-berried black grape which ripens mid-season. Ribier is one of the finest of the European hothouse varieties and performs well in Queensland. Growers on the River Murray have found that removal of the bottom 7 cm of the bunch just prior to flowering produces a well-set bunch with well-sized berries, thus greatly improving quality. Ribier is spur-pruned. Overcropping must be avoided if fruit quality is to be maintained. Only the second bunch is usually retained on each shoot.

Royal Ascot

An older variety grown mainly in Queensland. It is a black, seeded, medium sized, oval-shaped grape with small-medium compact bunches. Although it looks similar to Muscat Hamburg it has little muscat flavour and ripens a little earlier.

Ruby Seedless

A recently introduced mid-season variety with crisp, red seedless berries and a large bunch. Bunch thinning is essential as is bunch trimming leaving only 3-4 shoulder sprigs. Pruning is usually to clear single-node spurs. GA sprays are not recommended for this variety.

Sultana (syn. Thompson Seedless)

A white, mid-season variety with medium-sized, slightly-elongated, seedless berries. Because of its seedlessness and attractive though neutral flavour, the Sultana is the most popular tablegrape in Australia. The enlarged 'cultured' Sultana is now exported as Thompson Seedless. Sultana must be cane-pruned (4-6 canes) for satisfactory crops. A range of cultural operations will increase berry size and bunch quality. Latest recommendations (Leamon 1988) for large-berried Sultanas are:

— Thin bunches to one per shoot before flowering.

— Thinning sprays of 10 mg/L GA when bunches are at 40-50% flowering (with a few bunches at full flowering). This spray is followed by 15 mg/L GA at 80-90% flowering which helps berry lengthening.

— Sizing sprays of 30 mg/L GA when 50% of bunches have reached 4-6 mm berry size.

— Trim bunches within 2 weeks of shatter to 3-4 shoulder sprigs.

Sultana Moscata
An attractive yellow-green, oval, seedless, grape. The medium-sized berries are significantly larger than the natural Sultana berry. The berry skin is crisp and the pulp firm and juicy. Berries have a pleasant, neutral flavour but no real muscat character as the name may imply. Bunches are well-filled and attractive. Vines are of moderate vigour and bear well with spur pruning. Response to GA is minimal, however the natural berry size is quite adequate for marketing. The fruit appears to handle well, looks very attractive, and is more rain tolerant than Sultana.

Waltham Cross
A popular, mid-season, white tablegrape grown throughout Australia. The vines have a delicate balance between vegetative growth and fruit development; excessive vigour usually leads to 'hen-and-chickens' (large and small berries) and poor vigour leads to overtight bunches. Light pruning is desirable and long spurs at the ends of cordons, and cane pruning, have all been used with beneficial results. A system of late pruning has been found to reduce 'hen-and-chicken' wherein the vines are not pruned until three weeks after budburst. The technique causes the bunches to flower later, and the fruit ripens during the cooler period of mid to late March.

Wortley Hall (Heptakilo)
A vigorous, mid-season variety with large, conical bunches of large, black berries. The vines consistently produce second- and third-crop on lateral shoots. Growers prefer the second crop as the bunches ripen later and are more uniform in size, set and colour. A white selection is also grown in Western Australia but it has less vigour, little second crop and has very large bunches which require berry thinning.

12.4 Concluding Remarks

The economic production of quality tablegrapes requires the careful selection of vineyard site (climate, soil and topography), the choice of suitable varieties, and the use of improved cultural techniques. Sound harvesting, storage and marketing methods (see Chapter 15) are needed to sell profitably a high quality, perishable product in widely scattered markets. In the past the Australian tablegrape industry has been hampered by antiquated growing and selling methods but there are distinct signs of change. Tablegrape production has increased dramatically in recent years such that in 1988 and 1989 tablegrapes were Australia's most important fresh fruit export. Similarly the development of new growing areas and storage technology enable tablegrapes to be available on Australian markets for almost the whole of the year.

Further reading
Hedberg, P.R. (1985a) Production and marketing of tablegrapes. Department of Agriculture, NSW, Agfact H7.1.4. (Agdex 243/00).
Hedberg, P.R. (1985b) Tablegrape varieties. Department of Agriculture, NSW, Agfact H7.2.2. (Agdex 243/30).
Malan A.H. and Carstens W.J. (1971) The cultivation of tablegrapes in South Africa, Department of Agriculture Technical Services Pamphlet No 388.
Possingham, J.V. (1975) Tablegrape growing in Australia. World Crops 27, 217-221.
Weaver, R.J. (1972) Plant Growth Substances in Agriculture, W H Freeman and Company, San Francisco.
Winkler, A.J., Cook, J.A., Kliewer, W.M., and Lider, L.A. (1974) General Viticulture, 2nd Edition, University of California Press, Berkeley.

Other references

Anon. (1979), Monthly Seasonal Reminders. Deciduous Fruit Grower, 29, 292.

Antcliff, A.J., Skene, K.G., Possingham, J.V. (1976) The Cannon Hall Muscat grape. Vitis 15, 1-4.

Avramov, L. (1954) Flower drop in the more important indigenous and some foreign vine varieties in Serbia, Trans. title Ark, Poljpor, Naak, 7, 62-84.

Ben.-Tal, Y. (1990) Effects of gibberellin treatments on ripening and berry drop from Thompson Seedless grapes. Amer. J. Enol. Vitic. 41, 142-146.

Blommaert, K.L.J., Hanekom, A.N. and Theron, T. (1974) Effect of Ethephon on the maturation of Barlinka grapes. Deciduous Fruit Grower, 24, 263-265.

Boehm, E.W. (1960) Cultured Sultanas. Journal of the Department of Agriculture of South Australia, 63, 481-483.

Cameron, I.J. (1986) The effect of cyanamide and modified environments on the production of premium quality table grapes. Second National Tablegrape Industry Technical Conference, Stanthorpe, Queensland, Australia, Queensland Department of Primary Industries, Agdex No 243-10.

Chamayou, C. (1975) Tablegrape growing trials under plastic. Part III, Progres Agricole et Viticole, 92, 255-260.

Cirami, R.M., Furkaliev, D.G. and Hodge, D. (1986) Glasshouse growing of table grapes: The Virginia experience. Aust. Grapegrower and Winemaker 268, 101-2.

Combrink, J.C., Malherbe, W.S., Ginsburg, L. and Truter, A.B. (1974) Treating Waltham Cross grapes with growth regulators. Deciduous Fruit Grower, 24, 146-149.

Considine, J.A. (1983) Concepts and practice of use of plant growth regulating chemicals in viticulture. In L.G. Nickell (ed.) 'Use of Plant Growth Regulators in Agriculture'. CRC Press, Boca Raton. Volume I, 89-183.

Coombe, B.G. (1965) Increase in fruit set of Vitis vinifera by treatment with growth retardants. Nature 205, 305-306.

Coombe, B.G. (1967) Effects of growth retardants on Vitis vinifera, Vitis 6, 278-287.

Coombe, B.G. (1970) Fruit set in grape vines: the mechanism of the CCC effect. J. Hort. Sci. 45, 415-425.

Crawford, D.E., and Greenhalgh, W.J. (1975) The effect of bunch thinning on Black Muscat tablegrapes. University of Sydney, Department of Agronomy and Horticultural Science, Research Report No 3.

Dry, P. (1992) Hydrogen cyanimide — a useful tool in grapegrowing. Aust. Grapegrower and Winemaker No. 340, 29-33.

Dry, P.R. and Smart, R.E. (1986) How to get rid of the seed in seeded table grapes. Aust. Grapegrower and Winemaker 274, 22.

El-Banna, G.I. and Weaver, R.J. (1979) Effect of ethephon and gibberellin on maturation of ungirdled Thompson Seedless grapes. Amer. J. Enol. Vitic. 30, 11-13.

Evans, E.P., Erasmus, G.M.M., Meynhardt, J.T. and Alberts, A.J. (1973) The cultivation of tablegrapes in the summer rainfall area: Trellis-systems for tablegrapes. Tablegrape Series D1/1973, Department of Agricultural Technical Services., Pretoria.

George, A.P., Nissen, R.J. and Baker, A.K. (1988) Effects of hydrogen cyanamide in manipulating budburst and advancing fruit maturity of tablegrapes in South-eastern Queensland. Aust. J. Exp. Agric. and An. Husb. 28, 533-8.

Hale, C.R. and Jones, L.T. (1956) The pollination of Ohanez grapes. J.Agric. Western Australia 5, 565-567.

Hedberg, P.R. (1979) Improved grape colour with ethephon. Farmers' Newsletter No. 145, 27-28.

Jensen, F.L., Kissler, J.J., Peacock, W.L. and Leavitt, G.M. (1975) Effect of Ethephon on colour and fruit characteristics of Tokay and Emperor Tablegrapes. Amer. J. Enol. Vitic. 26, 79-81.

Jensen, F. and Andris, H. (1977) Ethephon has mixed effects on tablegrapes. California Agriculture 31, 18.

Kliewer, W.M. and Antcliff, A.J. (1970) Influence of defoliation, leaf darkening, and cluster shading on the growth and composition of sultana grapes. Amer. J. Enol. Vitic. 21, 26-36.

Kliewer, W.M. (1977) Influence of temperature, solar radiation and nitrogen on coloration and composition of Emperor grapes Amer. J. Enol. Vitic. 28, 96-103.

Knight, T.A. and Robinson, F.N. (1978) A preliminary report on an acoustic method of protection of crops from damage by silvereyes Zosterops lateralis in South Western Australia. Technical Memorandum No 14, CSIRO Division of Wildlife Research.

Leamon, K (1988) Guidelines for producing quality table grapes - 1988. Table Grape News 25, Spring 1988.

Manzo, P. (1976) Covering with plastic to hasten the ripening of Cardinal grapes and to delay the harvest of Italia. Vignevini 3, 21-24.

May, P., Shaulis, N.J. and Antcliff, A.J. (1969) The effect of controlled defoliation in the Sultana vine. Amer. J. Enol. Vitic. 20, 237-250.

McColl, C.R. (1986) Cyanamide advances the maturity of tablegrapes in central Australia. Aust. J. Exp. Agric. and An. Husb. 26, 505-9.

Mostert, E.W. (1976) Summer treatments for tablegrapes. Deciduous Fruit Grower 26, 323-325.

Peacock, W.L., Jensen, F., Else, J. and Leavitt, G. (1977) The effects of girdling and Ethephon treatments on fruit characteristics of Red Malaga. Amer. J. Enol. Vitic. 28, 228-230.

Peterson, J.R. (1974a) A bunch position effect on response to CCC on Cabernet Sauvignon grapevines. Aust. J. Exp. Agric. and An. Husb. 14, 122-125.

Peterson, J.R. (1974b) Effect of N-dimethylaminosuccinamic acid on Cabernet Sauvignon grapevines. Aust. J. Exp. Agric. and An. Husb. 14, 126-128.

Stannard, M.C., Peterson, J.R. and Sproule, R.S. (1974) Effects of gibberellic acid on fruit, hen and chicken condition and vine development in the following season of Waltham Cross grapes. Aust. J. Exp. Agric. and An. Husb. 14, 256-261.

Turner, J.N. (1972) Practical uses of gibberellin in agriculture and horticulture. Outlook on Agriculture 1, 14-20.

Vryonides, P. (1976) New findings on the culture of tablegrapes. Growing Cardinal under plastic. Bulletin OIV, 49, 965-978.

Weaver, R.J. (1976) Grape Growing. (John Wiley & Sons: New York).

CHAPTER THIRTEEN

Harvesting of Winegrapes

R.P. HAMILTON and B.G. COOMBE

Grapes have been harvested and made into wine for at least 5,000 years. Wine quality was no doubt extremely variable in early times. Inconsistency in wine quality has been greatly reduced by empirical development and by research work. Two important aspects that have contributed significantly to the improvement are discussed in this chapter: (1) the understanding of the process of grape ripening (2) harvesting and handling operations.

13.1 Grape berry development

Winegrape harvesting in Australia extends from early January, in Alice Springs, to June with late varieties in Tasmania and in some regions of Victoria and South Australia (Figure 13.1). Despite the range in time, the principles underlying the physiological, morphological and chemical development of the fruit of grapevines remain the same.

13.1.1 Physiology of berry development
After flowering, the grape berry shows two successive sigmoid growth cycles (Figure 13.2A). During the first growth cycle — designated the 'vegetative' phase by the French — there is a rapid increase in size. The phase consists of a 3-4 week period of cell division which grades into 4-6 weeks of cell enlargement (Harris *et al.* 1968). The berries have a high chlorophyll content, are quite hard and accumulate large amounts of organic acids.

Towards the end of this cycle the berry's growth slows, giving what is called the lag phase; this is brief in early-ripening varieties but might occupy 4 weeks or even longer in late varieties or under certain growing conditions (Coombe 1980). Seeds complete most of their development during this cycle.

The second growth cycle is the ripening phase of 5–8 weeks. It begins at veraison, which marks several dramatic developmental changes: berries soften, change from a green colour, accumulate sugars, lose acidity, and expand in volume (due entirely to cell enlargement). A feature of this growth is that the rate of sugaring exceeds that of water accumulation and hence sugar concentration increases, often at strikingly high rates. The sugar that accumulates comes into the berry via the phloem tubes in the vascular bundles; it originates from photosynthesis in green tissues, chiefly leaves, and from mobilization of stored reserves in woody tissues (up to 40% according to Kliewer and Antcliff 1970). The amounts of sugar accumulated per berry vary with berry size, from 5 mg per berry per day in small berries to over 50 mg per berry per day in large berries.

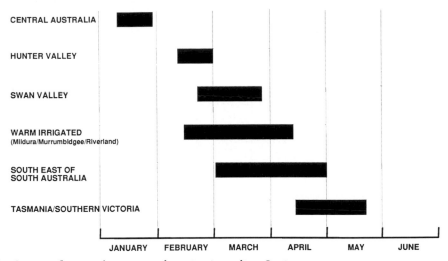

Figure 13.1 Range of grape harvesting dates in Australian Regions.

13.1.2 Chemistry of berry development

Berry development after veraison includes accumulation and metabolism of a range of compounds. Their fluxes are influenced by several factors including:

Variety: The genotype determines the rate of progress of phenological stages (Volume 1, Chapter 6), and the types and amounts of compounds present.

Climate: The macro-, meso- and micro-climates all influence canopy development with consequent effects on berry development. Berries may be affected directly or indirectly by weather factors including temperature, rainfall, humidity, wind, hail and frost.

Soil: Soil type influences water availability, nutrition and root development all of which affect vegetative growth.

Shoot growth: The vine integrates all environmental factors in the way its shoots and bunches develop. Shoot vigour, crop load and fruit exposure all affect berry development and composition; high crop load, in particular, has a major effect in lowering the Brix plateau and the content of flavour compounds.

The chief components of grape juice are shown in Table 13.1. However it is known that there are over 700 compounds present in ripe grapes. Variations in the relative amounts of these compounds, that is, grape composition, directly determines wine quality.

Water content

The major component in the berry is water, and its amount closely parallels berry volume (Figure 13.2A). Berry volume is largely determined by daily increments of inflow balanced with outflow. Inflow is mainly phloem water during the 2nd cycle. Outflow is mainly of xylem water and transpiration through the cuticle (Lang and Thorpe 1988). Relative to total berry weight, water is at its highest percentage during December, midway through the first growth cycle. It is lower earlier due to high tartrate levels in ovaries at flowering, and decreases later, firstly because of malate accumulation until veraison, and thereafter because of sugaring. Overripe berries may have a dry weight of up to 30%; the high Brix readings of such berries are often due to water loss by continued transpiration from the berries, which eventually shows as shrivelling.

Sugar

The majority of soluble solids in grape juice are sugars (90%). The remainder consists of organic acids, polysaccharides, pectins, potassium, proteins and other compounds (Table 13.1). About 99% of the sugars are glucose and fructose, with small amounts of sucrose, raffinose and some others. Sugars increase in concentration during ripening so that at harvest about a quarter of the berry weight consists of sugar. The ratio of glucose to fructose shows characteristic changes as berries develop. At veraison glucose considerably exceeds fructose concentration but, as sugaring proceeds,

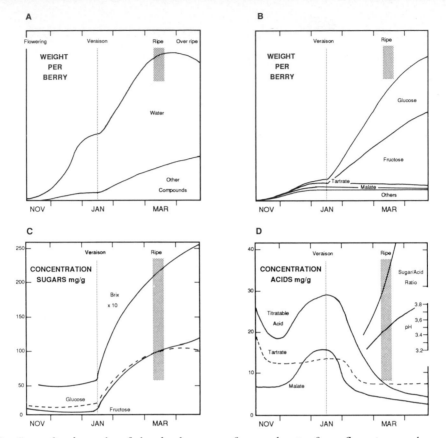

A

Flowering   Veraison   Ripe   Over ripe

WEIGHT
PER
BERRY

Water

Other
Compounds

NOV   JAN   MAR

B

Veraison   Ripe

WEIGHT
PER
BERRY

Glucose

Fructose

Tartrate
Malate
Others

NOV   JAN   MAR

C

Veraison   Ripe

CONCENTRATION
SUGARS mg/g

Brix
x 10

Glucose

Fructose

NOV   JAN   MAR

D

Veraison   Ripe

CONCENTRATION
ACIDS mg/g

Sugar/Acid
Ratio

Titratable
Acid

Tartrate

pH

Malate

NOV   JAN   MAR

Figure 13.2   Generalized graphs of the development of grape berries from flowering to the over-ripe stage. A. Changes in berry weight apportioned to water and the total of other compounds. B. Changes in the weight per berry of sugars (glucose and fructose), acids (tartrate and malate) and other compounds. C. Concentrations of glucose and fructose, and changes in Brix of the juice. D. Concentrations of tartrate and malate, titratable acidity and pH, and changes in the sugar/acid ratio of the juice. (From Coombe 1975).

the ratio glucose/fructose tends towards unity; occasionally, in over-ripe grapes, the metabolism favours formation of fructose and the ratio glucose/fructose exceeds unity (Figures 13.2 B and C). Note that fructose is much sweeter than glucose.

Acid

The major acids in grapes are tartaric and malic acid, comprising over 90% of total acids, with citric and a number of others making up the balance (Table 13.1). During their first growth cycle, grape berries are large accumulators of acid and, by veraison, acids are the predominant components. Tartrate, which is a stronger and more stable acid than malate, is at a high concentration in grape ovaries; it is accumulated during early berry growth and, thereafter, weight

per berry remains constant. Malate is accumulated strongly as veraison approaches, reaching concentrations of 10 to 20 g/L, often higher than those of tartrate (Figure 13.2D). After veraison, titratable acidity declines steadily due to three factors:

(i) A net decrease in malate per berry due to its respiration. High temperature hastens malate respiration and, in some berries, malate decreases to very low levels. Tartrate is respired slowly, if at all.

(ii) Dilution by water due to berry growth.

(iii) Conversion of acids to salts and metal-acid salts which are weakly acidic. Further, potassium forms potassium acid tartrate which precipitates readily from water (as does calcium tartrate and calcium oxalate). The amount of potassium increases during ripening, especially in the skins.

Table 13.1: Concentration (g/L and mM) of some components of free-run juice from grapes of average ripeness

Component	Range of g per L			mM
	Low	Mid	High	Mid
Water	700	**750**	800	—
Carbohydrates				
Glucose	80	**105**	130	**580**
Fructose	70	**95**	120	**530**
Sucrose	Trace	**1**	5	**3**
Pectin	0.1	**0.5**	1	—
Inositol	0.2	**0.5**	0.8	**3**
Acids				
TA as tartaric	3	**7**	12	—
Tartrate	2	**6**	10	**40**
Malate	1	**5**	9	**40**
Citrate	Trace	**0.3**	0.5	**2**
Nitrogen (N)				
Total—N	0.2	**0.8**	2	—
Amino acid—N	0.1	**0.4**	1	**3**
Ammonia	0.01	**0.06**	0.12	**3.3**
Phenolics Total	0.1	**0.5**	1	—
Minerals — Ash	2.5	**3**	6	—
Potassium	1	**2**	3	**50**
Phosphate	0.2	**0.35**	0.5	**4**
Sulphate	0.03	**0.2**	0.35	**2**
Magnesium	0.1	**0.2**	0.25	**8**
Calcium	0.04	**0.14**	0.25	**4**
Boron	Trace	**0.03**	0.07	**3**
Manganese	Trace	**0.03**	0.05	**0.5**
Iron	Trace	**0.02**	0.03	**0.4**
Copper	Trace	**0.002**	0.003	**0.03**
Zinc	Trace	**0.002**	0.005	**0.03**

Note that EU limits for Australian wines include: chlorides < 1g/L, sulfates < 2g/L and phosphates < 0.4g/L.

The decline of titratable acidity and the rise in pH are shown in Figure 13.2D.

Other compounds

Compounds other than water, sugars and acids make up a minor proportion of a grape berry's weight, but they are the source of most of the interest, pleasure and value by which winegrapes and wine are judged. Their number and variety is enormous. An expanded list might extend Table 13.1 to nearly 10 pages of this book, and, within a decade, another page might become necessary. A brief account is given below of some of these groups - phenolics, volatiles, vitamins, minerals and N-containing chemicals - with reference to their significance in the harvesting of winegrapes.

Phenolics

Phenolics embrace compounds that contribute colour, astringency and flavour, and are crucial ingredients for wine. Catechins, procyanidin condensation products (tannins), anthocyanins and flavonols have complex sensory effects in wine (and also in table grapes). These and the simpler chlorogenic, hydroxybenzoic and hydroxycinnamic acids (e.g. caffeic and coumaric acids and their tartrate esters, caftaric and coutaric acids) are often bound with sugars forming reserves; these reserves may later be metabolized to other compounds, some of which have sensory significance. Many compounds are more abundant in skin and seed. Like so many components of the berry, phenolic compounds increase during ripening, but with differences between parts of the berry and in response to varied growing conditions. For example, cool night temperatures stimulate skin colour formation in Flame Tokay table grapes. An even more potent effect is that of increased light incidence on individual berries, which stimulates the production of phenolics on a per berry basis (Crippin and Morrison 1986). This type of reaction has become significant since the discovery by Somers and Evans (1974) of a correlation between ionized anthocyanin concentration of red winegrapes and the quality of young red table wines made from them.

Volatiles

There are a large number of compounds of high vapour pressure that contribute to the aroma and flavour of grape juice in particular ways. The strongest *vinifera* aroma is found in muscat varieties, due to a distinctive mixture of volatile acids, alcohols, esters, terpenoids and other compounds (Williams *et al.* 1987). In contrast, an extract of free volatiles of the free-run juice of Shiraz grapes, a non-floral variety, showed more than 100 compounds, the majority being norisoprenoid or shikimate-derived and present in minute amounts (< 1 ppb) (Abbott *et al.* 1990); similar compounds were found in grape skin extracts. Hydrolysis of the residual non-volatile fraction produced larger amounts showing the presence of a reserve of bound forms.

As a general rule, aroma becomes detectable, quite suddenly, during specific stages of berry ripening e.g. McCarthy (reported in Coombe and Iland 1987) found that aroma of Riesling berries reached a peak after sugar levels passed 12-14° Brix. Knowledge of aroma development is crucial in the choice of harvest date and for decisions on vinification of the harvest. The principle is now being used for these purposes by some winegrowers who assess the aroma of juice from a succession of berry samples (e.g. Jordan and Croser 1984; see also under 13.1.3).

Vitamins

Vitamins are not thought to be factors that influence time or method of harvesting grapes, although they influence yeast metabolism during fermentation. The amounts in grapes are not large — 15-150 ppm for Vitamin C, 1 or more ppm for vitamin A, niacin, pyridoxine and pantothenic acid, 0.1 ppm for thiamine and riboflavin, and 0.001–0.01 ppm for biotin and folic acid. Alleged vitamin P, a flavone form, is abundant in grape juice but its credentials as a vitamin are contentious. The concentration of most vitamins increases with ripening (Winkler *et al.* 1974).

Minerals

The components of grape juice listed in Table 13.1 include those minerals that are essential for plant growth (see Chapter 9). Potassium (K) is by far the most abundant mineral. Its high level has important implications in winemaking; the dicarboxylic anions, malate and tartrate, form acid salts as well as salts with various cations having different solubilities. Thus, with increasing K levels in grape juice, pH increases because of the formation of salts and also the insolubility of potassium acid tartrate (KHT, also called potassium bitartrate). There are many reasons why high pH in grape must is detrimental in making wine; its effect in lowering the ionization of anthocyanins is particularly important (see above in the section on phenolics). Due to the nature of clay minerals in many soils used for viticulture (Volume 1, Chapter 3), Australian musts often have higher K content than those in Europe. The concentration of K increases several-fold as berries ripen, reaching especially high levels in grape skin (Iland and Coombe 1988). Another component with significance in vinification is nitrogen (see heading below); one of its major effects is in the provision of nutrition for yeast growth. Grapes from vineyards with vigorous grass swards in South Africa have given poor fermentation rates due to low nitrogen content (van Huyssteen and Weber 1980).

Nitrogen-containing compounds

Practically all nitrogen (N) in grape berries occurs in the reduced state. N-containing compounds enter into the metabolism of most classes of compound, some yielding forms that have sensory significance. The total N in must ranges from 0.2 to 2 g per L, but higher concentrations occur in skin and seed. Ammonium is the predominant form of N in immature berries but declines as ripening progresses. In ripe grapes, amino acids make up more than half of the total N, most of them being formed during the latter half of ripening.

Concentrations vary greatly between individual members of this group, with proline, arginine and glutamate often predominating; others that are prominent include alanine, α-aminobutyric acid, aspartate, serine and threonine. The levels of amino acids vary between varieties, climate and growing conditions. Some, but not all, are assimilated by yeast during fermentation.

Compositional changes during ripening

Sugar accumulation commences at veraison; sugar concentration increases steadily during ripening even though the water content of the berry increases at the same time. Brix levels can be extrapolated with some accuracy from successive measurements as ripening progresses and, during the early phases, they provide a good basis for indexing the rate of change of other components. The rate of increase in sugar concentration is affected by, among other things, the water supply to the vine; water stress accelerates the rate of increase while rain or irrigation decelerates it or may even cause a temporarily reduced level.

Some compounds decrease with ripening, especially malic acid. It has been suggested that malate decline is due to respiration in the vascular bundles (Coombe 1987). Many components increase in roughly the same manner as sugar, e.g. potassium. With others, the increase is influenced by different factors so that their relativity to sugar is not constant. Yet others, such as flavour volatiles and some amino acids, show most of their accumulation later in ripening when sugar increase is slowing. There are indications that aroma may decline again after reaching a maximum; the details of these relativities are not certain and remain to be investigated more thoroughly.

13.1.3 Harvest indices for winegrapes

Winegrapes are usually picked in one pass and the choice of picking date has important influences on wine quality. The determination of time of harvesting is a complex compromise between availability of harvesting labour or a mechanical harvester, the weather, the likelihood of pest and disease damage, and the stage of ripeness of the grapes. Since wine quality depends on grape composition, and composition changes as grapes ripen, it is profitable to choose a harvest date that gives an optimum mix of compounds for wine making. The specification of ripeness may be made for the grower by the purchaser; for example, Shiraz can be harvested at 14°Brix for sparkling wine production at one extreme through to more than 25°Brix for fortified material at the other. Whatever the circumstances, the more the grower understands about the course of ripening, the more likely it is that the prices paid for the grapes may be maximized. du Plessis (1984) refers to the lack of objective data to guide picking date. The following are some harvest indices that have been suggested for maximizing quality:

Total soluble solids (TSS)

TSS is the most common guide to ripeness. The TSS level chosen varies with wine style as well as the known performance of a given patch of vines. The higher the TSS, the higher the potential alcohol (or alcohol plus residual sugar) of wine made from the juice. Grape TSS as low as 14% is used in some countries, giving wine with 8% alcohol which is the Australian legal minimum; but normally the range of TSS is from 18 to 24% which yields wines with 10 to 13.5% alcohol; most yeast types cannot survive at alcohol levels greater than 14%. Overripe or botrytis-affected grapes with TSS values approaching 30% are used for sweet table wines.

Acid

Acid and pH have important effects on the course of the fermentation through their influence on oxidation-reduction potential, microbial metabolism and on colour and flavour. Acidity makes an important contribution to wine palatability; an intermediate level is needed as a low-acid wine is 'flat' and uninteresting while a high-acid wine is sharp and indigestible. Titratable acidity (TA) is often in the range of 6 to 10 g per L in Australian grape musts. Lower values may occur in grapes from hot regions, and higher from cool regions or in green grapes.

307

pH

pH is the negative log of the concentration of hydrogen ions (H^+) and generally correlates inversely with titratable acidity (TA). High levels of an alkali metal in a juice, especially K, reduce H^+ concentration and elevate pH for a given level of TA. There are examples of Australian musts that have acceptable acidity as judged by TA (e.g. 6.5 g/L) but unacceptable pH (e.g. 3.8 or higher); invariably, K is found to be high in these musts. High K, and hence high pH, causes more problems with red wines than with white because of the large amount of K that is extracted from skins together with the red pigments. Somers and Evans (1974, 1977) showed the detrimental effects on quality of red wines that result when fermentations occur at pHs greater than 3.7. While acid addition and ion exchange procedures reduce this problem, the methods are costly; natural acidity is preferred.

Sugar-acid indices

Since both sugar and acid are important bases for choosing the stage of ripeness of a grape crop it is useful to combine them into one value. Sugar divided by acid is the most successful index since the ratio increases sharply as berries ripen (Figure 13.2D) and the date of a specified ratio may be readily estimated by extrapolation from a sequence of measurements made as harvest approaches. Values vary with wine style and need to be specified by the winemaker, but, for dry table wines in much of Australia, ratios calculated as ^{0}Brix $\times$ 10/TA (as expressed above) vary from 20 to 40 . Similar values are found in California and South Africa (du Plessis 1984).

Where high pH is likely, as in musts with high K levels, indices of sugar and pH have been suggested, either ^{0}Brix $\times$ pH or ^{0}Brix $\times$ pH^2 (Coombe *et al.* 1980). These have not been widely adopted — instead winemakers have set limits for each factor separately.

Phenols and colour

Makers of red wine have taken note of the observation by Somers and Evans (1974, 1977) that subjective quality scores of young red table wines were correlated directly with values of ionized anthocyanin concentration. Cootes (1984) has adapted these results to the measurement of a colour/phenol ratio on an acidified skin extract (E520 nm/E 280 nm at pH 1) and has found that the ratio is highest in fruit from vineyards with the highest red pigment levels; ratio limits have been set for light-, medium- and full-bodied styles of red table wine. P.G. Iland (pers. comm.) is currently investigating some of the factors affecting the Potential Total Anthocyanin (PTA) levels of red winegrapes from which harvest indices may emerge.

Aroma and flavour of the juice

The foregoing indices provide guides to the basic composition of the grapes destined for wine but they indicate little about actual quality. In vineyards with favoured climate, 'terroir' and viticultural practices, and a long history of consistent high quality production, experience is clearly the best guide. But growers and makers not in this position need more information. Analyses of nitrogenous compounds such as proline or ammonia, and other groups of compounds, have not provided useful harvest indices (du Plessis 1984). Research is therefore emphasizing those compounds that are more directly related to aroma and flavour. The analysis of monoterpenes was regarded as a possible guide for the harvest of varieties with floral characteristics because this group has many compounds with floral aroma (Williams *et al.* 1987, Strauss *et al.* 1987); this approach has given variable results (P.J. Williams, pers. comm.). Another method being considered is to measure the concentration of total glucosides in juice (the glycosyl-glucose assay); preliminary work on this idea has shown a promising correlation with juice flavour in Shiraz, a non-floral variety (Abbott *et al.* 1991).

Inadequacies of objective methods have led some winegrowers to experiment with systems of organoleptic assessment of quality in juice samples — by smell and taste. Useful results have been obtained. For Riesling grapes, Cootes (1984) has described a procedure for sampling, juice preparation and assessment of aroma; a good correlation was found between wine quality and aroma score, far superior to that with Brix, titratable acidity and pH. Disciplined aroma scoring of serial samples from a vineyard has revealed when aroma becomes evident in the juice; it is suggested that sugar, acid and pH standards should only be used after aroma has developed (Jordan and Croser 1984). The methods are described in these two papers.

13.2 Grape sampling and testing

A vineyard is sampled to gauge yield and the collective composition of the field at that time (Wolpert and Vilas, 1992). It is therefore important that the sample, and the way it is processed, provides a good estimate of the composition of the total crop after it has been crushed. A sample may also serve to provide an estimate of berry size which is important for the diagnosis of compositional differences relating to the quality and for calculating yield components to enable comparisons between vineyards and seasons (see 13.2.5)

An important source of error in the sample arises from the way in which the sample is taken in the vineyard because of variability between vines, between bunches on each vine, and between berries on each bunch.

13.2.1 Vineyard variability

Coping with the variation between vines in a vineyard is a matter of judging the type and amount of each variation in composition and making an appropriate adjustment in the sampling method. The major effects of variation are on the amount of crop per vine, exposure of the fruit and its stage of development. These differences are often attributable to the following factors:

— genetic mixing of the vines in the patch to be sampled, due to rogues/'strangers' or mixed clones;
— mixing of vine ages, a problem in the early years in slowly established vineyards;
— mixed topography and soil types which can cause variation in rate of fruit development;
— variable soil water status between vines leading to ripening differences between vines; herbage growth interacts with soil water availability;
— crop size variability between vines which causes fast (light crop) or slow (heavy crop) ripening;
— vine canopy variability which influences fruit exposure with consequent differences in fruit development and composition (Chapter 5);
— edge vines and misses contribute to variability;
— pests and diseases which, if of patchy distribution, contribute greatly to variation.

13.2.2 Sampling procedures

Vineyard sampling has to make allowance for variations in the berry population to be tested and apply a standardized method of sampling. Vineyard variation is not confined to differences between vines but includes variations between bunches (exposed/protected, inside/outside, shoulder/tail) and between berries (top/middle/bottom, large/medium/small, early/late).

An optimal sampling scheme includes an assessment of the variation within each component of vine variability. Sampling methods used in Australia include:

Whole vine — all fruit from each selected vine
Bunch — whole bunches
Sprig — a segment of the bunchstem with attached berries
Berry — individual berries from each selected bunch.

Each method has its advantages. The following factors influence the choice of sampling method: the size of the samples for processing; the speed with which the sample can be collected; understanding, gained from experience and good records, of the relationship between results from the sample and those from the crusher; and the accuracy required from the sample.

The procedure of whole vine sampling presents a problem in the ability to select vines representative of the block being sampled. Bunch, sprig and berry sampling help reduce this problem as a wider range of vines may be covered within a reasonable sample size. Bunch and berry sampling are the main methods used. Comparisons of sampling methods (Rankine et al. 1962) indicated that, provided the sample size is appropriate, the difference between bunch and berry sampling is small, particularly as the crop ripens. These authors found that berry samples tended to show greater ripeness than the actual must composition.

In a small, uniform vineyard (less than 1 ha for example), a 200-berry sample taken from vines evenly distributed through the vineyard (3 berries per vine and about 5% of vines sampled) is sufficient to provide an accuracy to within 1°Brix of the must after crushing. If greater accuracy is required, or the vineyard has a significant range in vigour, a larger sample should be taken. In larger vineyards, a reduction in the number of vines sampled is possible with an increase in the number of berries taken per vine (5 berries per vine, 3% of vines sampled). In very large vineyards (greater than 10 ha), with little variation in vine vigour across the vineyard, every tenth pair of rows may be traversed with every tenth vine sampled from alternate sides (1% of vines sampled). Rather than specifying a method for a specific area, there is merit in taking one sample for each fermentation lot e.g. 20 tonnes of fruit, or several lots after experience has shown the degree of variation between them.

There are several references to protocols for berry sampling. All refer to standard methods for sampling i.e. bunch selection and number and position of berries in the bunch. As an example, Jordan and Croser (1984) advocated sampling 1% of vines (every tenth vine in every tenth row) taking 10 berries per vine using two randomly selected bunches, with 5 berries from the inside of one and 5 from the outside of the other. The berries taken comprise 2 from the top, 2 from the middle and 1 from the tail of the bunch. The key to successful sampling is to standardize a method, apply it throughout the ripening period, and check the harvest sample with that of the crushed must.

For best results, samples are taken at the same time of day, preferably in the morning or the same part of the day when harvesting is done; note that dew on the fruit may alter the results. The fruit is stored in sealed polythene bags at 2-4°C and processed within 24 h.

13.2.3 Preparation of samples for testing

The aim in preparing a sample for testing is to simulate the extraction operation of the winery crusher. Several methods can be explored and the most satisfactory selected for a particular winery's routine use so that valid season-to-season comparisons can be made. Since the distribution of compounds within berries varies from compound to compound, as well as stage of development, it is necessary to check that the matching of method with the winery practice remains valid with all samples. Grape samples may contain berries in varying stages of development, ranging from hard and unripe to raisined and shrivelled; the relative contribution of these types of berries needs to match that in the winery. If a bunch-sampling method is used, the handling of the bunchstems also needs to be mimicked; it may be useful to strip the berries from the stems before crushing them. Another useful precaution is to anticipate any post-harvest changes which may occur.

Juice is obtained by pressing, blending or crushing of the sample by various means as follows:

Pressing

At the simplest, grape samples may be crushed by hand either in the bag in which the sample is collected or in a muslin bag. Care is needed to crush all berries. 'Bag' or lever presses are a further development (Figure 13.3). They are readily cleaned but the extraction percentage can be variable; Cootes *et al.* (1981) found that Sultana juice obtained by a bag press had a pH 0.2 units lower than the commercial crush. P. Perret at Wädenswil (pers. comm.) has constructed a mobile juice sampling device for field operation. It uses a pair of small, thin-rubbered Willmes presses and a portable air compressor; samples of 5 kg fruit yielding 2 L juice gave results that match the winery crush and about 250 samples can be handled in a day.

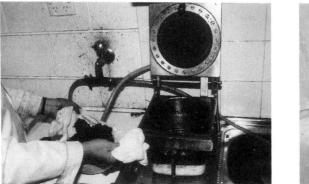

Figure 13.3 Extraction of juice from grape samples. Examples of two extraction methods; the water-bag press (left) and a cone press (right).

Blending/mincing

These are difficult to clean but give good samples provided the blending or mincing time is kept constant and short.

Crushing

Roller crushers do not macerate the berries and are readily mechanized, however cleaning is a problem. The Cone Crusher (Figure 13.3) can give good results. Its action is intermediate between crushing and pressing, with a degree of control exercised by the user, and provides a preliminary filtration (Jordan and Croser 1984, Cootes *et al.* 1981).

In the case of varieties with pigmented skin there are measurements that will permit the quantification of anthocyanins, both total and ionized. For these the juice preparations described above are unsuitable. Cootes (1984) describes a method in which macerated berries are treated with pectinase, acidified to pH 2.8, sonicated, centrifuged, acidified again to pH 1.0 and the optical density measured at specified wavelengths. Iland (1988) describes a similar method which has since been simplified by using a skin preparation based on discs punched from the berries (P.G. Iland, pers. comm.).

13.2.4 Grape testing

The tests made on juice samples include measurements of total soluble solids, titratable acidity and pH and, less frequently, colour, aroma and flavour. Measures of some chemical components such as malate, tartrate, potassium, amino acids, etc. are obtained after crushing to guide vinification methods, but these are not considered here.

Total soluble solids (TSS)

Solute concentration is a colligative property measured, in the grape industry, by hydrometry or refractometry.

Hydrometers (Figure 13.5a) are closed glass 'floats' weighted at one end so that they float to a depth proportional to the solute concentration. The level is read against a scale in the narrow stem by lining up the bottom of the meniscus of the juice. For most hydrometers, 0.2 –0.5 L of juice are needed.

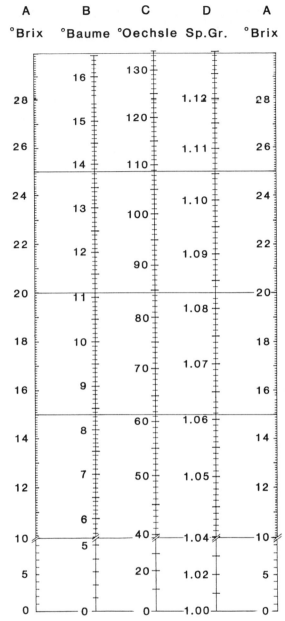

Figure 13.4 Nomogram of scales for measuring solute concentrations in aqueous solutions at 20°C. A °Brix (g solute per 100 g solution); B °Baumé, modulus 145; C °Oechsle; D Specific gravity, 20/20°C. A, B and D from Bates et al. 1942; A and C agree with AOAC 1960 list, but not B. Oechsle values (C) were obtained from Arnold (1957) by matching with Brix values. Comparisons of Oechsle scale by hydrometry and refractometry can be found in Jacob and Schrodt (1973). (Drawn by B.G. and M.F. Coombe)

Figure 13.5 Testing grape juice. In the vineyard, juice is expressed (A) and its soluble solids concentration measured by a hand refractometer (B). In the laboratory, soluble solids is measured by refractometry (hand or machine) or by hydrometry (C), and pH and titratable acidity by meter and titration, or by automatic titrator (D).

Errors in reading may be caused by suspended solids in the solution or bubbles attached to the hydrometer. The temperature of the juice is measured at the same time and corrections applied from appropriate tables.

Refractometers are also widely used. Refraction of light depends on temperature, solute concentration and specific refractive index of the solvent. In many commercial refractometers, the scale provided is already calibrated to a useful 'sugar' scale such as Brix, Baumé, Oechsle, Balling, Twaddle and others. Of these, the first two are the most commonly used in Australia; their scales are compared against Oechsle and specific gravity in Figure 13.4. Brix approximates % TSS (including sugars, acids, ions and other solutes) and, in ripe grapes, is close to per cent sugar by weight. Baumé scale approximates potential alcohol % v/v after complete fermentation of the juice.; this is not a strict relationship - with Baumé readings less than 10, actual alcohol is slightly lower, and those greater than 10 give alcohol greater than the Baumé reading. Winery staff tend to use Baumé and grapegrowers use Brix. Balling resembles Brix but is calibrated at 15.5ºC, not 20ºC. Oechsle is a German scale and equals (Specific Gravity − 1.000) x 1000. Hand refractometers (Figure 13.5b) can be operated with as little as one drop of juice and are useful for spot checking in the vineyard as well as in the laboratory. Abbé refractometers are more accurate instruments. Whatever the type, careful correction for temperature is needed either by using tables of correction factors based on the temperature of the juice, or by adjusting the zero of the scale using distilled water at the same temperature as the test solution.

Titratable acidity (TA)
TA is one indicator of acid level. It measures the sum of anions and metal-acid anions by alkali titration expressed as grams tartaric acid equivalents per litre juice. (Note that sulfuric acid equivalents, used in France, have lower values). NaOH 0.1 N is titrated to a phenolphthalein or pH 8.2 endpoint (pH 7.0 gives lower values). Automatic titrators give rapid and accurate readings (Figure 13.5D).

pH
Good pH meters are available commercially, some being small and portable. They need periodic calibration against buffers of standard pH (often 7.0 and 4.0) and adjustment for temperature.

Organoleptic assessment of juice samples
For success with this method, it is essential that oxidation be minimized to reduce the alteration of aroma and flavour. A suitable method of preparation is described by Jordan and Croser (1984) as follows: add SO_2 (to give 25−30 mg per L free SO_2), erythorbate (50 mg/L) and pectic enzyme (as recommended by the manufacturer) to the juice receival vessel; the chilled grapes (< 2ºC) are crushed, sparged with N_2 to remove dissolved O_2, SO_2 adjusted, and the sample then sieved into a CO_2-filled bottle, sealed, and let settle for 24 h; the clear juice is siphoned or decanted

into another CO_2-filled bottle and sealed. Such samples, are suitable for aroma assessment for several months when stored at 0ºC. These authors also describe the subsequent methods used for aroma and flavour assessment.

13.2.5 Measuring grape size
The methods described above are aimed at providing the winemaker with an indication of the current composition of the crop. A sample could also serve to determine berry size, which is valuable information: it is essential for the calculation of the components of yield (crop weight/berry weight gives berry number) and also permits conversion of juice concentration values to amounts-per-berry which, in turn, permits determination of the basis of compositional differences. Unfortunately the berry sampling methods described for analysis of composition often give over-estimates when used for berry size; whole-bunch, bunch-lateral or bunch-segments are preferred. After sampling, berries are carefully separated from the stems—any loss via the brushes is worth estimating and correcting for—then

counted and weighed. Counting can be aided by electronic counting machines (as used in small grain research) or by counting grids with, say, 100 wells. The use of a grid system also makes it possible to get information on size distribution which is valuable for diagnosing compositional differences: small berries often contribute a different mix of components to the crush. Other counting methods are to freeze the bunch- or bunch-segment samples and, at a convenient time, break up the sample (berries break away without leaving a brush) and count berries or pedicels. It should be possible to further mechanize sizing and counting of such samples by adapting the methods used commercially for apple and soft fruits.

13.3 Harvesting

13.3.1 Previntage planning
Spray program
The spray chemicals used for protection against pests and diseases may cause problems if applied at a stage when residues interfere with health

Figure 13.6 Hand picking equipment. Kerosene tins (A) and Bryce buckets (B) are being replaced by high-density plastic buckets (C), preferably with plastic handles. A range of picking snips is shown: note the long-nosed pair which facilitates access to bunchstems. Photograph D depicts one form of crate used to aid transfer of fruit in pallet lots.

regulations or vinification. Many spray compounds have specified 'withholding periods' which provide a guide to the planning of a suitable spray program. Late sulfur applications, on red grapes in particular, have been known to adversely affect wine quality.

Irrigation and rain

Excessive water stress impairs leaf function and ripening and should be avoided. However, irrigation close to the time of harvesting needs careful management to avoid interference with vineyard access, especially with flood and furrow methods as well as overhead sprinklers. Irrigation of every second row may be helpful with some irrigation methods. Drip irrigation is least complicating. Heavy rains are a special problem for which the main preparation is the provision of adequate surface drainage and canopies that dry out quickly. Management practices using reduced cultivation or permanent grass swards may also improve access in wet conditions. Excess water, whether from irrigation or rain, may lower sugar levels and cause splitting of berries giving potential for mould development.

General preparation

Equipment to be used during harvest needs to be checked and prepared to avoid lost time during harvest. Factors to be considered for a harvest schedule include:

— the logistics of handling the harvested grapes;
— the winery's capacity to process them;
— estimation of the rate of ripening and date of optimum ripeness for each vineyard unit (see Section 13.2.1)

Harvesting at optimal ripeness is achievable in small vineyards; in larger vineyards it is usually necessary to compromise by straddling the estimated optimum date. Harvest scheduling becomes easier with experience of each vineyard block, although there is always a need for vigilance over the course of ripening and a preparedness to adjust plans.

Vine skirting

Trailing canes, particularly in vigorous vineyards, interfere with harvesting and increase costs, therefore 'skirting' of vines is usually cost effective. It is particularly valuable in mechanically harvested vineyards as it reduces blockages and loss of fruit.

Figure 13.7 Front-end loader as an intermediate transport. Grapes are transferred from picking containers (top) to the front-end loader bin (middle) which then takes the fruit out of the vineyard to the transport vehicle (bottom).

Canes are trimmed to 50 cm from the ground, preferably in the week before harvest. Note that the trimmed canes can have sharp ends which present a hazard to pickers.

13.3.2 Containers and transport

Grape berries are not robust and need to be handled carefully to reduce splitting and crushing

Figure 13.8 Pallet handling systems. These are used especially for premium fruit. A. One form of pallet which may be folded flat when empty. B. An apple-bin alternative; note the use of plastic liners in both types. Two methods of unloading pallets: forklifts (C) modified with frames and holding lugs at the front of the forks, or tipping frames (B & D) used in conjunction with gantry-mounted hoists.

that leads to oxidation and spoilage. Berry damage may be reduced by:

— minimizing transfer of grapes from one container to another,
— use of shallow containers, to reduce pressure on the berries,
— protection of exposed metal surfaces with tough, chemically inert and easily-cleaned compounds,
— strong and watertight construction of containers,
— designs that conform with processor's handling facilities (e.g. easily transported, both empty and full, and compatible with winery unloading capabilities),
— multipurpose lifting points to facilitate

unloading with a wide range of equipment, e.g. provision of both slots and handles for forklifts, as well as crane lifting points.

Handpicking containers

The use of tins, wooden boxes and similar containers has largely been replaced by plastic containers of 15 to 25 L capacity (Figure 13.6); the smaller containers suit low-yielding vineyards. Stackable round or rectangular buckets of durable high-density plastic are available. Plastic handles reduce the potential for metal contamination of juice. In small vineyards, containers are stacked (with care to avoid crushing of berries) and transported to collecting points or bins or directly to the crusher.

Figure 13.9   Slapper-mounted harvester discharging fruit into a gondola. The observer is ensuring even load distribution and acceptable levels of 'material-other-than-grapes' (MOG). The inset shows unloading of a gondola.

Grape bins

There are a wide range of methods used to hold fruit for transfer to the winery.

One system employs front-end loaders with specially designed 'buckets' (½ tonne lots) as an intermediate container between the picking bucket and the transport vehicle in the headland or loading area (Figure 13.7). In large vineyards fruit is simply transferred from picking buckets directly into a transport bin or tip truck.

An alternative for large vineyards with premium fruit is the transfer of harvested grapes from the picking-container into specially modified wooden bins (with pallet bases for forklift handling) of 250-500 kg capacity (Figure 13.8). These are transported in pallet form, then unfolded, locked and lined with heavy duty plastic film. Bins of metal construction holding 1-2.5 tonnes, are widely used in the Australian winegrape industry for both hand and machine harvesting. Bin designs vary but generally of a width to match row spacings and a dept convenient for the tipping of buckets (or deeper for mechanical harvesting). The bins are transported within the vineyard on tractor-drawn unsprung trailers.

Gondolas

Gondolas were developed for mechanical harvesting where rapid handling of large quantities is essential. Gondolas, which are deeper and narrower than bins, hold up to 2.5 tonnes and are towed by tractors. Unloading is by side tipping (Figure 13.9) using the tractor hydraulics, either into a transporter (tip truck or bins on a truck tray) or directly into the crusher hopper if nearby.

Tip trucks

A useful alternative to grape bins is that of tip trucks with modifications to the tailgate using rubber seals and small outlet or a hose fitting permitting drawing-off of free-run juice before the grapes are transferred to the crusher hopper (Figure 13.10). This method is gaining increasing acceptance in the industry particularly for short haulage and for grapes destined for bulk wine.

Transport

The distance from vineyard to winery and the volume of fruit being processed determine the method of transport. In all cases there is a need for sufficient capacity in containers to ensure that

Figure 13.10 A typical tipper system: A. excess juice is released through a small outlet before opening the tailgate; B & C. the fruit being tipped; note the baffles in the trailer tray to reduce grape movement during haulage; D. the fully extended tipping system being cleaned on the receival apron.

harvesting may continue whilst grapes are transported. Where the rate of picking and the distance to be covered is reasonable, bins on picking trailers and gondolas may be transported directly to the winery. For greater distances, heavier transport vehicles permit greater flexibility. Tip trucks may be used in both applications with 'semi-tippers' prevailing for long-distance haulage (Figure 13.10).

Loading/unloading systems
Where it is not possible to unload fruit directly into the crusher hopper or on to a transport, a bin system offers scope for flexibility in fruit handling. The components of this method include the bins, a loading area and a lifting mechanism.

Loading areas are best sited either in or near

the vineyard and need to be well drained, firm and dust free. Availability of a good lighting system will facilitate loading at night. Bins may be unloaded from the picking trailers either directly on to the transport or 'queued' in position to wait until the next truck. Picking trailers that allow full bins to be slid off the trailer to the ground are useful. Loading may be done by either mobile cranes, forklifts or gantries.

Unloading at the winery is achieved by a range of systems:
(i) Bin lifting and tipping. A mobile or gantry crane is used to lift the bin from the transport and transfer it to a tipping point which engages with either two pins on the bin or a tipping frame holding the bin, over which the whole bin pivots and is emptied into the crusher (Figure 13.11).

Figure 13.11   A mobile gantry system with details of the cradle for the grape bin shown in the inset. This system is capable of handling most bins fitted with lifting points.

(ii) Side tipping bins. Bins are loaded from the vineyard onto a transport trailer with one side of the bin located into a hinging structure, e.g. locating pins or chain. For unloading, the trailer is positioned next to the crusher pit and a mobile or gantry crane lifts one side of the bin, tipping its contents without removing the bin from the trailer (Figure 13.12).

(iii) Rotating-head forklifts. Development of large forklifts with rotating heads (360°) has greatly increased flexibility and capacity in the handling of grapes. These units allow unloading of grape bins from transports either for direct tipping into the crusher, or for collation of varieties, particularly with mixed loads, by storage on the crusher apron. The forklift empties the bin by positioning the bin over the pit and rotating the forks. The head may then be shaken to remove any bunches caught on the forks and the forklift then moved to a washing apron for rinsing of the bin, a process not possible with the other systems (Figure 13.13).

13.3.3 The harvesting operation

In a perfect winegrape harvest, no berries are pierced or squashed, and no leaves, dirt or other materials are present when the fruit is delivered to the crusher, preferably at a low temperature. Ideally the harvest is not extended nor too costly. Harvesting can be done by hand or by machine, both of which have different sorts of problems.

Mechanical harvesting was developed in response to two major influences (May 1977);

— the costs of grape production,

— labour shortage.

Districts with large vineyards and scarce labour (e.g. Coonawarra, SA), have been at the forefront of development of mechanization of vineyards in Australia.

Mechanization of grape harvesting was explored initially in USA in the 1950s using a cutter-bar principle, and then later by shaking methods. The first commercial harvesters were introduced in Australia in 1972 after about five years of development (see May, 1975, 1976). By 1974, 23 harvesters were in use covering 2,500 ha (6% of Australian vineyards). Today almost all regions utilize machine harvesters, the exception being some of the most recently developed districts. e.g. the districts near Melbourne with

Figure 13.12 Side tipping of grape bins. Bins are either loaded directly from gondolas (see Figure 13.9) or by use of a forklift. In this example a chain is installed to hitch the bins to the trailer tray. The inset shows one method for lifting the bins for tipping; others include mobile gantry cranes or forklifts.

small vineyards and wineries. The usage of mechanical harvesters is probably more widespread in Australia than in any other grapegrowing country (e.g. about 75% of the total harvest, compared with about 50% in USA and 20% in France) but it is difficult to estimate the number of machines in operation.

A single machine with 2—4 operators can harvest up to 0.5 ha per hour which is approximately 20—50 times faster than hand-picking. In the larger regions, with continuous harvesting, this means that a machine could harvest up to 700 ha in one season, easily justifying the high capital cost. In addition to the many machines operated by large individual properties, there are a significant number owned by contractors. A proportion of these are transported from early to later ripening districts to increase their workload e.g. from regions on the Murray River to the South-east of South Australia. (Note Chapter 11.2.1 and 11.5 of the dangers transportation presents to the spreading of pests.)

The development and refinement of mechanical harvesting has provided a successful alternative to hand harvesting and countered the difficult problems of both the scarcity and high costs of labour. The first machine harvesters were efficient in fruit removal but compromised grape quality by damaging fruit. Improvement of the mechanics of mechanical harvesting, together with the advantages of being able to pick at night to gain the benefit of cooler fruit (10–20°C), particularly if coupled with rapid winery processing, now means that decisions on the method of harvesting depends on the cost and the logistics of winery handling and not so much on the effects on the quality of harvest. The final product can be very similar whether hand or machine picked (see Fetter *et al.* 1982, Lott 1982). In a recent evaluation of machine ('slapper') versus hand-harvesting of Chardonnay in the Napa Valley, California (Clary *et al.* 1990), machine harvesting gave fewer bunchstems, a higher proportion of primary berries and also of second crop berries, a greater juice loss, and a higher proportion of non-grape matter. The admixture of second crop produced a lower Brix (-2%) and a higher malate concentration (+12%); however no wine quality differences were discerned. The authors concluded

Figure 13.13 A. A rotating head forklift in the process of tipping into a receival hopper. B. Front view of the forklift head and (C) details of the forks and the loading/unloading process. D. Washing of the bins on the receival apron while the bin is inverted.

that the greater juice loss with the slapper was offset by the lower costs.

There are a few soft-skinned varieties, which are generally difficult for current machines to harvest e.g. Semillon. Most modern vineyards are designed and managed to facilitate machine harvesting. Problems arise when attempts are made to harvest older, poorly-managed vineyards.

Good communication between the harvesting team, the transport and the winery is an essential element for a smooth vintage, especially with machine harvesting, much of which is done at night.

The details of hand harvesting are dealt with below but those of mechanical harvesting are considered in the next section (13.3.4).

Hand harvesting

Hand harvesting is laborious. Each bunch must be located and held, and the bunch attachment snapped or cut. The characteristics of the variety

strongly influence the rate of harvest. A few varieties have bunchstems that break readily and may be simply pulled from the vine, e.g. Shiraz. Usually however, this method damages the fruit and cutting of each bunchstem is necessary. Varieties with bunches that tend to tangle within the canopy (e.g. Traminer) are particularly difficult, often requiring several cuts to free all of the berries. Berries of some varieties shatter readily when being harvested (e.g. Cabernet Sauvignon, Sultana) and extra care is required to reduce losses.

Apart from these variety factors the rate of hand harvest is determined by;
— the method by which the vines were pruned,
— crop load,
— bunch size,
— trellis type,
— canopy density and shape,
— conditions for pickers, including temperature, humidity, ground conditions and vineyard access.

A good picker may harvest from as little as 750 kg (e.g. small, tangled bunches of Traminer) up to 5,000 kg (e.g. large bunches of Pedro) per 8 hour day.

Hand harvesting seems unlikely to be replaced by machine harvesting where picking is required that is selective and precise for the production of specialist premium wines that justifies the extra cost. However, development of machines for small, narrow-rowed vineyards may alter this situation.

Pickers use small pairs of secateurs or grape-picking snips which have long narrow blades to help access to bunch stalks (Figure 13.6). Picking knives with short curved blades and thick handles are sometimes used. Attention should be given to skin protection, water supply and toilet needs of pickers. Strong footwear and first-aid kits are advisable to counter injuries from snips, insects, weed seeds and sharp protruding canes. Well organized picking teams can enhance the speed of the harvest. A good team has a leader, pickers and transporters. The leader helps time-tabling, recording and maintenance of standards. The transporters transfer fruit from the picking buckets to the tractor and bin trailer and facilitate the return of buckets to the pickers. The number of rows picked at each pass depends on the numbers of pickers and collecting bins as well as the size of the crop. At the end of each day the collection and cleaning of buckets, and fuelling and servicing of tractors, helps the progress of the next day's harvest.

The method of payment for pickers varies according to the range of factors that influence the cost of harvest. Payment on a time basis is expensive if pickers are unskilled or unmotivated. Contract picking enables a fixed cost per volume or weight of fruit harvested. This may either be at a piece-work rate per unit of fruit picked (e.g. a bucket) or by teams sharing a rate per tonne which can be recorded at the weighbridge.

13.3.4 Mechanical harvesting

Harvesting by machine is now an established part of Australian viticulture. Experience has been gained on the requirements in the vineyard and in the harvesters, and in the way the mechanical harvesting operation is carried out (see Volume 1, Figure 1.12 and Plate 1).

Vineyard set-up and variety influences

For mechanical harvesting, a vineyard needs row and headland width sufficient for passage and turning of the machine, with obstructions (e.g. power poles, trees, etc.) kept to a minimum and well-marked. Clear marking of row numbers helps reduce confusion for operators, particularly at night. Most harvesters can cope with varied terrain except where large differences in the levels of the vineyard floor occur on either side of the trellis. Ideally the trellis height (0.5-2.0 m) and width (up to 1.5 m) in a particular vineyard should be consistent and the vines pruned and maintained to conform with this framework. Uneven fruit distribution along the trellis requires careful adjustment of the machine by the operator.

The physiology of the variety has a strong influence on the success of machine harvesting. Ideal varieties have tough berries and weak peduncles and pedicels (e.g. Cabernet Sauvignon) or a tendency to abscise at the pedicel junction. Soft-skinned varieties (e.g. Semillon) tend to burst during harvesting giving the potential for large juice loss and exposure to oxidation; if these are excessive, hand harvesting may have to be substituted. Generally, however, most varieties may be consistently machine harvested.

The stage of ripening also influences the success of mechanical harvesting. Varieties harvested early in maturity for use as a sparkling wine base can be difficult to dislodge from the vine (e.g. Pinot Noir) resulting in bud damage and a significant reduction in fruit potential for the next season (Dry *et al.* 1990). Late picked fruit tends to have soft, weakly-attached berries, particularly when bunch rot is present, causing berries and bunches to fall before the collector plates surround the vine. In contrast, some varieties tend to shrivel (e.g. Shiraz) and more energy is required to remove the fruit.

Harvester configuration

The main requirements for a machine harvester are that it be highly manoeuvrable and have sufficient power capacity to operate a picking head.

There are two main types of grape harvesters — towed and self-propelled. Towed machines offer the cost advantage of using an existing tractor as the power plant (rather than having a machine which may only be used during vintage). However, it is likely that the utility of self-propelled harvesters will be extended by using the frame for other vineyard operations, including pruning and both fungicide and herbicide application (Intrieri and Poni 1990).

Machine harvesters need to be highly manoeuvrable to cope with a multiplicity of vineyard layouts and topography. Modern self-propelled machines have four-wheel drive with hydraulic steering on all wheels allowing both fine control down the rows and sharp turning at row ends. Hydraulic drive assists reversing and "point"-turning. Hydraulic adjustment of the height of the picking head, together with independent rams on each wheel to adjust height and level, helps the harvester cope with variable terrain. Older machines may have two-wheel drive and manual levelling. Other useful design features include: wide tyres to reduce soil compaction; position-adjustment of the delivery or discharge chute to distribute fruit evenly in the collecting bin and to avoid obstacles; and good lighting for night harvesting (covering ahead, the machine area and the delivery chute). A means of communication between the machine operators is also needed to cope with the high noise level.

The machine operates with the picking head over a single vine row, leaving as few gaps as possible for fruit to be lost whilst minimizing cane damage. All surfaces contacting the fruit need to be chemically inert and all machinery in the fruit-conveying systems be designed for maximum isolation from the fruit e.g. closed lubrication systems and protective skirts. The use of food grade oils also reduces the risk of fruit contamination.

Individually sprung 'fishplates' are opened by the passage of the vine trunk while retaining a tight fit around the trunk; they are angled to divert fruit to the conveyors. As the picking action is vigorous, a curtain is used on the long axes of the machine to catch all fruit and drop it back onto the conveyors. Fruit thrown forward and backward is largely deflected within the head by the surrounding canopy.

Endless-belt conveyors made from inert materials incorporate ribs to lift fruit from the fish-plate level to the delivery chute height. Recent developments for reducing juice losses include endless bucket systems with strong deformable material to reduce fruit buffeting.

Harvesting dislodges large numbers of leaves with the fruit as well as a range of other material (MOG — material-other-than-grapes) including vine parts (e.g. canes and arms), trellis components (e.g. staples and drippers) and anything else sheltering in the vine (e.g. snails and insects). Fans are used at the first junction of the elevators to extract as much leaf material as possible whilst minimizing fruit loss. The volume of juice adhering to the discarded leaves is relatively small. It has been found that leaf contamination greater than 5% affects wine quality adversely. The amount of leaf in the harvest is minimized by fine control of fan speed. Easy and safe access to the fans is needed to clear blockages. Strong magnets are placed at the end of the delivery shutes to capture any metal dislodged from the trellis by the harvester.

Picking heads
There is a great diversity of trellis types in Australia (Chapter 3). Most of the harvesters and picking heads were initially designed to handle a particular trellis type e.g. the wide-T trellis with the impactor head. Picking heads transfer energy to the vine fruiting area in order to remove the majority of the fruit whilst minimizing damage to both the fruit and the vine structure. The fruit is removed from the vine by breakage at the base of the bunch, giving whole bunches, or at various points along the peduncle/pedicel system giving bunch parts, or by tearing at the pedicel or brush giving individual berries. The proportion of these components varies.

The following factors may be modified in setting up the harvester for a particular vineyard:

Picking head width — set to minimize damage to the vines by allowing a clearance of 10–25 cm

Height — adjusted to cover the majority of the fruit on the trellis

Picking head frequency/amplitude — regulated to remove the majority of berries

Ground speed — variation permits fine tuning of the energy input to remove the majority of fruit and minimize damage (0.5-1.5 km per hour)

Present pickings heads are of several types: slapper, impactor, pulsator and others.

a. Slapper
The slapper head comprises two paired banks of

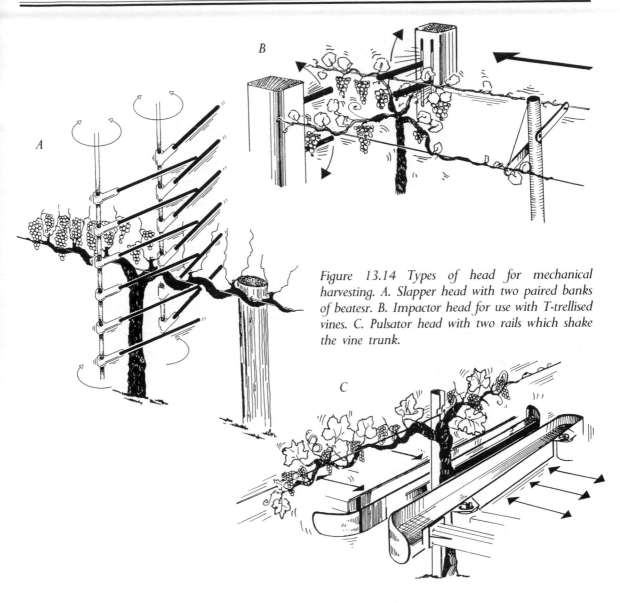

Figure 13.14 Types of head for mechanical harvesting. A. Slapper head with two paired banks of beatesr. B. Impactor head for use with T-trellised vines. C. Pulsator head with two rails which shake the vine trunk.

beaters, presented to the vines in tandem (Figure 13.14a). Its action is to 'slap' the fruiting area of the vine, although it applies energy by swinging the vine components and the flexible parts of the trellis at an amplitude and speed sufficient to release the fruit.

Replaceable fibreglass rods make up the operating part of the slapper and are attached by means of adjustable brackets on the beater banks. Changes in the number, length, weight (e.g. by use of stainless steel ferrules) and the angle of the rods, adjust picking efficiency for a particular trellis. Performance may also be modified by adjusting beater speed (150–350 rpm) or by using

the beaters either in- or out-of-phase. In early designs the beating action was in the fruit zone, but presently it has a swinging action, either in- or out-of-phase, helping reduce the level of damage both to the fruit and the vine. The most recent developments have included adjusting the angle of the heads for the beaters to reach up into the vine from below and hanging the head from the harvester with gravity positioning it vertically over the vine (as compared to a fixed head which is held over the vines at the angle at which the harvester moves).

The slapper has proved to be the most versatile of the picking heads. The combination of head-width and angle adjustment, allowing both single-wire and T-trellis to be harvested, and the adjustment of the beater rods, permits a greater harvesting efficiency in a wide range of varieties and pruning methods (Botting and Dry 1989). Some fruit damage occurs through the slapper harvesting method. Apart from damage through the catching and conveying arrangement, which occurs with all harvesters, fruit can be caught and broken by the beaters. However, with skilled operation, the majority of fruit is undamaged, often with whole bunches in the sample.

b. Impactor

Two pairs of cam-driven fingers work with an action that produces an efficient transfer of energy to T-trellised vines with flexible T-heads (Figure 13.14b). The fingers have a motion which includes a long cyclic plucking action through a distance of some 20 cm. The fingers lift and drop the trellis wire in applying energy to the vine via the trellis. The amount of energy applied to the vine may be modified by adjusting the speed of the fingers and the ground speed.

The impactor is not as versatile as the slapper in that it requires carefully trained vines on a well-maintained trellis for efficient harvesting. Apart from adjusting the head height through machine levelling during harvesting, the impactor can only accommodate small changes in trellis height. Further, all energy transfer is through the trellis wire so that, unless the vines are well trained with the fruit concentrated in its vicinity (maximum of 25 cm for the bunch stalk to the wire), the impactor may harvest poorly. The flexibility of both the trellis and the vines is vital to efficient picking and any wood on the trellis wires older than three years does not have sufficient flexibility and can seriously affect harvest efficiency and the degree of vine damage.

The fruit obtained by impactor harvesting has a high percentage of whole bunches. The major damage occurs in passage through the fruit handling system as well as bunches that are damaged by contact with the fingers.

c. Pulsator

Two rails, positioned at two-thirds of the height of the vine trunks, apply energy to the trunk by oscillating sideways through an amplitude of up to 10 cms (Figure 13.14c). With no direct contact between the energy transfer system and the shoots this method offers the advantage of the least damage of all the harvesting methods, other than to the trunk itself. The harvest mainly consists of whole bunches. This method relies heavily on efficient energy transfer through the vine aided by provision of a stake at each vine. Pruning systems are needed that ensure all fruit is close to the training wire otherwise there is insufficient force to dislodge all bunches. Results with this method in Australia have been generally disappointing and, of the three methods described, it is least used.

d. Other heads

The picking heads listed above have been described in order of current popularity in Australia. Other head types that have been tried or used in other countries include:

'Combination'/pivotal pulsation heads — these combine pulsator and slapper actions.

Spur wheels — operate as beaters in a circular motion, plucking bunches from the vine.

Rotating fingers — a similar principle to the spur wheel but using long flexible fingers.

Suction — exposed bunches are harvested by negative air pressure inducing 'suction'.

As with all machines, continued improvements are being made and competitive models are available from many countries, in particular, USA, France and Italy.

Harvester operation

The high cost of machine harvesters necessitates good maintenance and a preference to operate for an extended season. The majority of harvesters in Australia are owned by large company vineyards where vineyard size and the spread of harvest dates readily justifies their purchase. Trends in labour cost and availability mean that smaller vineyards are also able to justify machine ownership. Another owner-category includes contractors, many of whom operate similarly to large companies by moving their harvesters through the vintage from the warmer to the cooler districts to lengthen the operating season.

Because of the complexity of machine harvesters, their effective use requires a skilful operator and capable mechanical support. During harvesting, an observer is required to check the efficiency of harvesting and advise the operator accordingly, as well as keep the belts and blowers free from blockages. Other workers maintain the supply of bins to collect the harvest. During each harvesting shift the machine should be monitored for signs of mechanical problems and the hydraulic system watched for leaks that might contaminate the fruit. Any break in harvesting can be used to check for alignment and tension in the fruit collecting system.

If there is a change in varieties picked during a harvesting session the harvester collection system will need to be washed down, particularly when changing from red to white varieties when pigment contamination is likely. Washing down is best commenced in the picking head region and continued through to the final delivery chute with the belts running slowly throughout to remove dislodged material. Care is needed to avoid directing water on to hot hydraulic components.

At the end of a harvesting session the harvester needs to be thoroughly cleaned in order to avoid build-up of sugars, grit and tartar. Detergents and scrubbing brushes may be needed. After cleaning, all moving parts require oiling or greasing to counter the effects of sticky, acidic grape juice and the large amounts of cleaning water. Thorough cleaning is of special importance where there is the possibility of transferring pests (e.g. phylloxera) or diseases (e.g. downy mildew) between districts (Chapter 11.2.1 and 11.5).

13.3.5 Protection of harvested grapes

Grapes degrade physically and chemically after harvesting. Some of this degradation can be reduced or delayed by protective compounds. Since many of the compounds can be harmful in high concentrations they need to be evenly distributed through the fruit.

Handling and temperature
Minimal handling of the grapes after harvest reduces damage caused by juicing and breakdown. The type and degree of movement of the container and the duration of the handling directly affects the amount of damage. The breakdown processes of oxidation and enzymatic activity, as well as the activity of wild yeasts, are directly related to both grape temperature and the length of time between harvesting and processing. Harvesting during the coolest part of the day, together with rapid cooling of the grapes if required, minimizes this damage.

Sulfur dioxide
The addition of compounds that form sulphur dioxide (SO_2, preservative 220*) protects grapes by SO_2 antiseptic action on yeasts and bacteria, its anti-oxidant effect and by enzyme inhibition. SO_2 may be formed by the addition of sulfurous acid (SO_2 pressurized and in liquid form), as a freshly-prepared SO_2 solution at a lower concentration, or as metabisulfite salts which yield about half their weight as SO_2. Potassium metabisulfite (PMS) is the preferred salt; sodium is cheaper but is less desirable in wine. The salts may be applied in solution form particularly with machine harvesting where it is metered at the delivery chute. The salts may also be applied as a powder which offers the advantages of both ease of addition as well as being more stable than a low concentration liquid. However, the powder should be fresh as it also breaks down in storage. The administration and dosage needs adjustment to obtain SO_2 concentrations that are appropriate for the type of wine to be made and to avoid excessive amounts that may result in bound sulfur compounds.

Other fruit protectants
Ascorbic acid (antioxidant 300*), or its isomer erythorbic acid (antioxidant 310*), can be used to augment the anti-oxidant properties of SO_2. The displacement of air with denser, chemically inactive gases such as nitrogen and carbon dioxide effectively reduces non-enzymic oxidation. Gas purity needs checking as does adequacy of closure of the container to reduce gas loss. In dusty conditions, and with long haulage or exposure to diesel exhaust, tarpaulin use is recommended. This also shades the grapes from heat; note however that bins should be able to 'breathe' to reduce condensation and to permit heat loss.

13.3.6 Post-harvest vineyard management

Because of the corrosive action of acids in grape juice and the damaging effects of other compounds, especially sugar, harvesting equipment needs stripping, cleaning, oiling and painting after each season. Trellises may need attention to repair damage caused by machinery. Similarly, attention to the vines themselves is simpler while the vines

*NH&MRC Approved Food Additive Numbers.

are actively growing as damaged shoots are readily identifiable; pulling-out of damaged shoots assists all pruning, especially cane-pruning. Finally, an assessment of the degree of bud damage permits a compensating adjustment to the bud level for next season's pruning.

A post-harvest irrigation, which encourages the retention of leaves without inducing active growth, may allow the vine to increase its potential productivity the following season by continuing active photosynthesis, thus enhancing inflorescence development and carbohydrate storage.

13.4 Concluding remarks

High costs, and problems with the availability of skilled labour for Australian vineyards, have been a catalyst for the mechanization of vineyard activities. For instance the availability of mechanical harvesting opened up alternative approaches to vine pruning: it made possible the harvesting of small, scattered bunches which were difficult to handle by normal picking methods. As a consequence, various types of mechanical pruning methods have been developed and introduced, the ultimate of these being the non-pruning method called 'minimal pruning' (see Chapter 4). These developments have revolutionized vineyard management (Baldini and Intrieri 1984).

Advances in harvesting technology have resulted in the ability to mechanically harvest grapes in a condition rivalling that of grapes harvested by hand. No doubt, further improvements will eventuate. Associated development of winery capability to handle large quantities of grapes for both bulk and premium end-use has allowed exploitation of optimum harvest conditions.

Continued research on the compounds that give the best indication of grape quality will allow achievement, in the near future, of the ability to harvest an entire vineyard when the grapes are at optimum ripeness.

Further reading

Amerine, M.A. and Ough, C.S. (1980) Methods for Analysis of Musts and Wines. Ed. 2., J. Wiley, New York.

Baldini, E. and Intrieri, C. (1984) Meccanizzazione della Vendemmia e della Potatura. Macchine e Systemi di Allevamento. Coop. Libr. Univ. Editrice, Bologna.

Lee, T.H. (Ed.) (1981) Grape quality: assessment from vineyard to juice preparation. Proceedings of seminar; Aust.Soc. of Vitic. and Oenol, pp.39-56.

O.I.V. Symposium on 'Quality of the Vintage' (1977). Oenol. and Vitic. Res. Inst., Stellenbosch, S. Africa.

Other references

Abbott, N.A., Coombe, B.G., Sefton, M.A. and Williams, P.J. (1990) The secondary metabolites of Shiraz grapes as an index of table wine quality. Proc. 7th Aust. Wine Industry Tech. Conf., Adelaide, 1989. Australian Industrial Publishers, Adelaide, SA. 5064. pp 117-120.

Abbott, N.A., Coombe, B.G. and Williams, P.J. (1991) Development of a rapid analytical technique for the estimation of the concentration of potential volatile flavour compounds and hence quality of Vitis vinifera Shiraz grapes. Provisional Patent No. PK7216, 16 July 1991.

Arnold, A. (1957) Beitrage zur refraktometrischen Methode der Mostgewichtsbestimmung. Vitis 1, 109-120.

Bates, F.J. et al. (1942) Polarimetry, saccharimetry and the sugars. Natl. Bur. Stand. (U.S.) Circ. No. C440.

Botting, D. and Dry, P. (1989) Mechanically harvesting the wide tee-trellis: some recent developments. Aust. Grapegrower and Winemaker, No. 310, 39-40.

Clary, C.D., Steinhauer, R.E., Frisinger, J.E. and Peffer, T.E. 1990) Evaluation of machine- versus hand-harvesteed Chardonnay. Amer. J. Enol. Vitic. 41, 176-81.

Coombe, B.G. (1975) Development and maturation of the grape berry. Aust. Grapegrower and Winemaker. No. 136, 60-66.

Coombe, B.G. (1980) Development of the grape berry. I. Effects of time of flowering and competition. Aust. J. Agric. Res. 31, 125-131.

Coombe, B.G. (1987) Distribution of solutes within the developing grape berry in relation to its morphology. Amer. J. Enol. Vitic. 38, 120-127.

Coombe, B.G. and Iland, P.G. (1984) Grape berry development. Proc. 6th Aust. Wine Industry Tech. Conf., Adelaide 1983. Australian Industrial Publishers, Adelaide, SA, 5064. pp 50-54.

Coombe, B.G., Dundon, R.J. and Short, A.W.S. (1980) Indices of sugar-acidity as ripeness criteria for winegrapes. J. Sci. Food Agric. 31, 495-502.

Cootes, R.L. (1984) Grape juice aroma and grape quality assessment used in vineyard classification. Proc. 5th Aust. Wine Industry Tech. Conf., Perth, 1983. Aust. Wine Res. Inst., Glen Osmond, SA, 5064, pp 275-292.

Cootes, R.L., Wall, P.J. and Nettlebeck, R.J. (1981) Grape quality assessment. In 'Grape Quality.

Assessment from vineyard to juice preparation'. ASVO seminar proceedings. Aust. Wine Res. Inst., Glen Osmond, S.A., 5064, pp 39-56.

Crippin, D.D. and Morrison, J.C. (1986) The effects of sun exposure on the phenolic content of Cabernet Sauvignon berries during development. Amer. J. Enol. Vitic. 37, 243-247.

Dry, P., Weatherall, M. and Noack, A. (1990) Long-term effects of mechanical harvesting of Pinot Noir and Cabernet Sauvignon. Aust. Grapegrower and Winemaker, No. 316, 25-26.

du Plessis, C.S. (1984) Optimum maturity and quality parameters in grapes: A review. S. Afr. J. Enol. Vitic. 5, 35-42.

Fetter, K., Schreiber, R. and Seifert, O. (1982) Vergleichende Betrachtungen zwischen Hand- und Maschinenlese aus kellerwirtschaftlicher Sicht. Deutsche Weinbau. 21, 950-952.

Harris, J.M., Kriedemann, P.E. and Possingham, J.V. (1968) Anatomical aspects of grape berry development. Vitis. 7, 106-119.

Iland, P.G. (1988) Leaf removal effects on fruit composition. Proc. 2nd. Int. Cool Climate Vitic. and Oenol. Symposium, Auckland, N.Z. Soc. Vitic. Oenol., Auckland, N.Z. pp 137-138.

Iland, P.G. and Coombe, B.G. (1988) Malate, tartrate, potassium and sodium in flesh and skin of Shiraz grapes during ripening: concentration and compartmentation. Amer. J. Enol. Vitic. 39, 71-76.

Intrieri, C. and Poni, S. (1990) A new integrated approach between training systems and mechanical equipment for full mechanization of quality vineyards. Proc. 7th Aust. Wine Industry Tech. Conf., Adelaide, 1989. Aust. Wine Res. Inst., Glen Osmond, SA, 5064. pp 35-50.

Jacob, L. and Schrodt, W. (1973) Vergleich refraktometrischer und densimetrischer Methoden der Mostgewichtsbestimmung. Die Wein-Wissenschaft 28, 169-180.

Jordan, A.D. and Croser, B.J. (1984) Determination of grape maturity by aroma/flavour assessment. Proc. 5th Aust. Wine Industry Tech. Conf., Perth, 1983. Aust. Wine Res. Inst., Glen Osmond, SA, 5064, pp 261-274.

Kliewer, W.M. and Antcliff, A.J. (1970) Influence of defoliation, leaf darkening and cluster shading on the growth and composition of Sultana grapes. Amer. J. Enol. Vitic. 21, 26-36.

Lang, A. and Thorpe, M. (1988) Why do grape berries split? Proc. 2nd Int. Cool Climate Viticulture and Oenology Symposium, Auckland, N.Z. N.Z. Soc. Vitic. Oenol., Auckland, N.Z. pp 69-71.

Lott, H. (1982) Der Einfluss des Traubenvollernters auf die Weinqualitat. Deutsche Weinbau. 21, 958-960.

May, P. (1975) Mechanical harvesting of grapes in Australia. Aust. Grapegrower and Winemaker 139, 4,6,11.

May, P. (1976) Workshop on mechanical harvesting of wine and drying grapes. Aust. Grapegrower and Winemaker No. 148, 16-18, 20.

May, P. (1977) Mechanical harvesting of grapes in Australia with special reference to its effects on grape quality. OIV Symposium proceedings on 'Quality of the Vintage'. Oenol. Vitic. Res. Inst., Stellenbosch, South Africa. pp. 425-434.

Rankine, B.C., Cellier, K.M. and Boehm, E.W.(1962) Studies on grape variability and field sampling. Amer. J. Enol. Vitic. 13, 58-72.

Somers, T.C. and Evans, M.E. (1974) Wine quality: Correlations with colour density and anthocyanin equilibria in a group of young red wines. J. Sci. Food Agric. 25, 1369-1379.

Somers, T.C. and Evans, M.E. (1977) Spectral evaluation of young red wines: anthocyanin equilibria, total phenolics, free and molecular SO2, 'chemical age'. J. Sci. Food and Agric. 28, 279-287.

Strauss, C.R., Wilson, B. and Williams, P.J. (1987) Flavour of non-Muscat varieties. Proc. 6th Aust. Wine Industry Tech. Conf., Adelaide, 1986. Aust. Industrial Publ., Adelaide. pp 117-120.

van Huysteen, L. and Weber, H.W. (1980) The effect of selected minimum and conventional tillage practices in vineyard cultivation and vine performance. S. Afr. J. Enol. Vitic. 1, 77-83.

Williams, P.J., Strauss, C.R., Aryan, A.P. and Wilson, B. (1987) Grape flavour — a review of some pre- and post-harvest influences. Proc. 6th Aust. Wine Industry Tech. Conf., Adelaide, 1986. Aust. Industrial Publ., Adelaide. pp 111-116.

Winkler, A.J., Cook, J.A., Kliewer, W.M. and Lider, L.A. (1974) General Viticulture. Univ. California Press, Berkeley, 710 pp.

Wolpert, J.A. and Vilas, E.P. (1992) Estimating vineyard yields: introduction to a simple two-step method. Amer. J. Enol. Vitic. 43, 384-388.

CHAPTER FOURTEEN

Harvesting and Drying of Grapes

J.R. WHITING

Drying of fruit is a process by which fresh fruit, which has a relatively short shelf-life, is changed into a product that is preserved for future use. The low moisture content (10-15%) and high sugar concentration (70-80%) of dried fruit is unfavourable to the survival of most food spoilage organisms. Storage space is also reduced because the large amounts of water removed during drying reduces the volume of the fruit. Drying of fruit occurs naturally *in situ* on plants. Harvesting of fresh grapes, combined with natural or artificial drying methods, enables control over the drying process. Many methods to facilitate the drying of grapes have been developed and a wide range of product types are available.

In prehistoric times it is probable that dried grapes were collected and stored for subsequent use. Records of dried fruit have been found in Egypt dating back to 3000 years BC and further records of dried grapes are found in biblical times and through the early Greek and Roman days. Today world production of dried grapes is about 1.15 million tonnes, of which 75% is produced by drying without pre-treatment to disrupt the waxy layer surrounding the berry ('naturals'). Up to 20 countries now produce dried grape products.

In Australia, grape varieties suitable for drying were amongst the earliest introductions of vines. However it was not until the dry hinterland was opened up and irrigation settlements developed that substantial quantities of dried vine fruit were produced (see Volume 1, Chapter 1). Since the early 1900s Australia has developed its own cold alkaline oil emulsion treatment to produce a particular type of light amber-coloured sultanas that have found favour in certain markets. Australia now has approximately 15,000 ha of vines used for drying producing on average 80,000 tonnes p.a. of dried fruit, about 7% of world production. The production level can vary considerably due to seasonal influences and fluctuating diversions to the winery or tablegrape trades. The production of dried grapes accounts for about 95% of the total dried fruits production in Australia.

This chapter describes the principles of the drying of grapes, the range of products that can be produced and details the techniques used to produce high quality dried vine fruit.

14.1 Climatic conditions for dried vine fruit production

14.1.1 Regions throughout the world

Climate is the major determining factor influencing the selection of regions suited to dried vine fruit production. The drying rate for grapes closely follows the evaporation rate for a particular region and season. Thus climatic conditions that produce a high evaporation rate (low rainfall, low relative humidity, high temperature and rapid air movement) are most suitable for fruit drying. Suitable regions are classed as hot or very hot (Smart and Dry 1980) with heat summations exceeding 2000°C days and mean temperature of the hottest month exceeding 23°C. Annual rainfall is usually below 650 mm and frequently below 350 mm, with minimal rain and low humidities during summer and early autumn. These regions are generally situated between 25° and 40° latitude in both hemispheres. The low rainfall regions usually require irrigation to

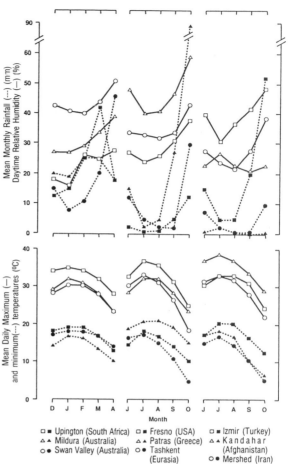

Figure 14.1 Mean monthly maximum and minimum temperature, mean monthly rainfall and daytime percentage relative humidity during the ripening and drying period for the major dried fruit producing areas of the world. Source: Meteorological Office, HMSO (1958-1976).

supplement the natural rainfall, for example in Australia, USA and South Africa.

The climate of various locations representing the major dried fruit producing regions of the world are compared in Figure 14.1. Being the hottest and driest, the dried fruit producing areas in Afghanistan have the most favourable climate for dried fruit production with the California production area in the USA and areas in Iran almost as good. South Africa has hot summer temperatures but sporadic seasons with high rainfall can be a problem in the dried fruit producing areas. The (former) USSR dried fruit producing areas have very low rainfall during the drying season but temperatures are not as high

Table 14.1 Dried vine fruit planting and production figures in Australia 1987-88 and a comparison with the mean for the previous 10 years.

State	Region	Total Vineyard Area (ha)	Estimated area producing dried vine fruit (ha)	Grape production—estimated fresh tonnes used for drying		
				Sultana	Currant	Raisin
NSW	Sunraysia	3586	2435	43615	1279	2451
Victoria	Sunraysia	11854	9278	178010	7241	5869
Victoria	Mid Murray	4495	1859	26783	327	2065
Victoria	Rest of State	2414	67	365	8	24
S.A.	Riverland	10195	1297	16186	5049	703
S.A.	Rest of State	12837	15	8	116	—
W.A.	Total State	1765	269	25	1299	206
	Other	9725	56	612	61	169
Australia	Total	56871	15276	265604	15380	11487
Total production — tonnes dry wt. 1987-88				71245	4631	2596
Mean production — tonnes dry wt. 1979-88				70437	5699	4663

Sources: Australian Bureau of Statistics; Australian Dried Fruits Corporation

as some other countries. The Murray River Valley areas in Australia may receive some rain during the summer period and the temperatures are lower than most countries.

The Swan Valley, Ismir (Turkey) and Patras (Greece) regions are all close to the coast and are characterized by high humidities right through the drying season and high rainfall late in the season. These conditions have led to the almost exclusive growing of Zante Currant, an early ripening variety, in Greece and the Swan Valley.

14.1.2 Regions within Australia
Over 99% of the total dried vine fruit production in Australia occurs in the Murray River Valley (Table 14.1). The Swan River Valley in Western Australia is the only other significant producing area. The remaining production comes from remnants of former small producing areas, e.g. McLaren Vale and Clare Valley in South Australia. About 27% of the total vineyard area in Australia is utilized for dried vine fruit production. The 1987-88 dry weight production of about 71,000 tonnes of sultanas was about average for the previous ten years, the range being from 51,138 to 87,140 tonnes.

Currant production also varies markedly between seasons (range 4195 to 7275 tonnes in the last 10 years) but there has been a general decline in dried currant production in the 1988 and 1989 seasons. Raisin production was less than average in 1987-88 due to greater diversions to wineries and annual raisin production has fluctuated markedly (range 1030 tonnes to 8505 tonnes in the last 10 years). Over the 1979-1988 period, 87% of the dried fruit produced was sultanas, 7% was currants and 6% was raisins. *(Definitions used by the Australian industry: sultanas are the dried grapes of Sultana and Merbein Seedless, currants are from Zante Currant and Carina, and raisins (lexias) from Muscat Gordo Blanco and Waltham Cross. Worldwide, the term 'raisin' refers to any dried product of grapes).*

Murray River Valley
The predominant dried vine fruit producing areas in Australia occur along the Murray River extending to the west from the Swan Hill area in Victoria and New South Wales into the Riverland area of South Australia. Annual climatic data for Mildura to represent this region is shown in Volume 1, Chapter 2. Additional climatic data

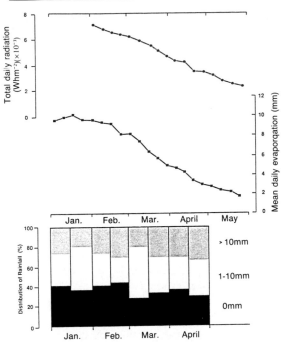

Figure 14.2   Mean total daily radiation, mean daily evaporation and distribution of rainfall for Mildura, Victoria. Sources: Clingeleffer (1984), Rural Water Commission, Victoria, and Considine (1973).

for the ripening and drying period is presented in Figure 14.2. The main features of the harvesting and drying season are the less favourable conditions for drying as the season progresses. The general deterioration in drying conditions is due to decreasing day length and consequently less solar radiation energy. This decreases the mean air temperature and the mean daily evaporation rate; the latter is proportionate to the rate of water loss from berries during drying. There is a high frequency of rainfall likely to cause damage near harvest or to retard the drying rate during the full length of the drying season. However the incidence of rainfall does not become greater through the drying season.

The seasonal variability in rainfall is quite large and this has been shown to play a significant part in the seasonal variability in the quantity and quality of dried vine fruit (Considine 1973). Nearly half of the seasonal variation in sultana production from year to year is caused by rainfall during March. The production of currants (from the Zante Currant variety) can also be significantly affected by rain during the first half of January, causing berry splitting, and February, causing

bunch rot and breakdown. Lexia raisin production has also been significantly affected by rain in late March.

The rain does not usually become more frequent or heavier during the drying season (Figure 14.2). Light falls of rain (< 2 mm) generally have little effect on splitting or on drying rates. However heavy falls, above about 10 mm, may split susceptible varieties and affect the drying rate, especially if the weather remains humid.

The main effect of rain on Sultana prior to or during harvest is to split the fruit, resulting in damaged berries which dry a darker colour. This produces a mixed sample of light- and dark-coloured berries. Rain during drying will reduce the overall colour of the fruit to an evenly darker brown. Persistent wet weather through the drying period can result in mould and insects attacking the partially dried fruit and producing an unsavoury product. Dehydration greatly reduces the incidence of mould.

It would be expected that, as a rule, the greater the rainfall during the drying season the poorer the fruit quality, but exceptions are common. For instance, two years with a similar pattern and total rainfall for February, March and April (about 62 mm) were 1955 and 1960, yet the proportion of fruit graded 2 crown or lower was far higher in 1955 (97% of ADFA production) than in 1960 (3% of ADFA production). Thus differences in the ripening of fruit, the timing and duration of inclement weather and in the drying technology between seasons can influence the effects of rain damage.

Swan River Valley
This is the only significant dried vine fruit producing region in Australia under the influence of coastal conditions. The mean monthly maximum temperatures are higher than for Mildura but the daytime humidity is higher and substantial amounts of rainfall occur from April onwards. Zante Currant, an early maturing variety, is the major variety grown for dried fruit.

14.2 The principles of grape drying

14.2.1 The grape berry
The bulk of the grape berry consists of flesh in which the cells have very thin walls and the very

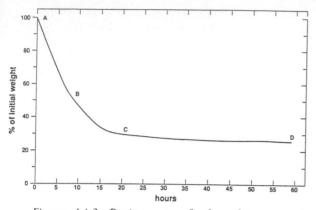

Figure 14.3 Drying rate of oil-emulsion treated Sultana grapes dried in a 50°C oven. Source: Martin and Stott (1957).

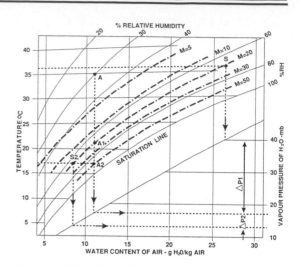

Figure 14.4 Mollier diagram for air with sorption isotherms of Sultana grapes (—·—). S = Sultanas of 20% moisture content (M = 20) at 36°C. A = air at 35°C and 30% relative humidity (dry weather). △P1 = 24mb of vapour pressure difference, i.e. rapid drying will occur. If air temperature decreases to A1 (21°C, 69% RH) equilibrium is reached and no further drying occurs. If air temperature is lowered further, e.g. at night, to 17°C the vapour pressure of Sultanas at S2 will fall below that of air at A2 and a small negative vapour pressure gradient (−4mb) results and the Sultanas absorb water from the air. Source: Szulmayer (1973).

large vacuoles contain primarily water, sugars and acids. Water movement from these cells can be rapid initially but during the later stages of drying the osmotic effects of the sugars hinder water loss (Martin and Stott 1957). Surrounding the flesh is the skin tissue with thick-walled cells and relatively smaller vacuoles, the sap of which is rich in phenolic compounds. The outermost layer of the berry is a waxy cuticle consisting of a non-cellular cutin material overlain with wax platelets. The cuticle provides a firm barrier to water movement from the berry. Further water movement is to the atmosphere by evaporation and removal by air movement.

14.2.2 Drying stages

There are three main stages of water loss from grape berries (Martin and Stott 1957) (Figure 14.3). The first phase (A-B) involves an overall contraction of the berry but the berry retains its shape and the skin does not wrinkle. A period of equalization of temperature with the environment occurs (dependent on berry size) before water loss commences. The surface of berries treated with oil emulsion can be regarded as equivalent to a water surface with water moving to the surface by liquid capillary flow. The main influence on drying during this stage is the relative humidity and flow rate of air, and it has been proposed that pan evaporation rates could be used to calculate the drying rate of berries (Wilson 1962).

The second stage of drying (B-C) commences when the skin begins to wrinkle at about 20% to 50% loss of the initial fruit weight. The loss

of weight required to cause wrinkling of the skin decreases as the season progresses. Water loss during this period is initially limited by water removal from the surface of the berry. The rate of water loss can be increased by: (a) increasing the fruit temperature, which increases the permeability of the cuticle, (b) decreasing the relative humidity of the ambient air which allows greater water movement into the air, and (c) increasing the air speed to remove moisture laden air. These responses effectively raise the partial water vapour pressure deficit. In the field these parameters of climate fluctuate markedly and drying does not occur at a steady rate (Martin and Stott 1957).

Szulmayer (1971) has demonstrated that heat absorbed directly by the fruit causes the vapour pressure to rise within the fruit. The resultant greater difference between the fruit interior and ambient air increases the flow of moisture even at low air flow rates. Thus, drying of hot fruit

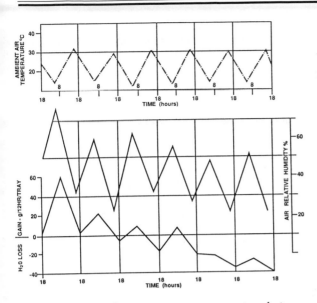

Figure 14.5 Ambient air temperature, air relative humidity and weight fluctuations of dry Sultana grapes over 6 days. Source: Szulmayer (1973).

with cold air produces more rapid drying than drying of cold fruit with hot air. A series of sorption isotherms (Figure 14.4) have been derived for Sultana grapes by Szulmeyer (1973). These are useful in predicting such things as (a) the atmospheric conditions for efficient drying, (b) to what moisture content a product can be dried, (c) when drying comes to a standstill, and (d) when resorption of water will occur. The drying rate decreases markedly toward the end of the second phase since water loss is then regulated by the rate of water diffusion through the flesh and skin cells.

Drying ceases when the moisture content of the berry and the air are at equilibrium. Under field conditions the equilibrium is not always constant and water movement from berries to air is reversible. The uptake of water by berries is particularly evident during periods of high moisture content after rainfall or at night (Figure 14.5). Szulmayer (1973) has characterized these movements, which can be quite considerable; it is possible for berries to regain during one night, all of the moisture lost during the previous day.

The third and final stage of drying (C-D) occurs when about 95% of the total loss of weight has occurred and all 'free' water has been removed. This stage of drying does not occur under field drying conditions.

14.2.3 Factors affecting drying rate

Water movement within the berry
Within the grape berry, water moves by diffusion from the vacuoles of the cells and by capillary action along the cell walls during the first two stages of drying. The drying rate is faster with smaller berries because of a shorter distance of water movement. Riva and Peri (1986) compared the drying rates of several grape varieties and found the drying rate was inversely proportional to the square of the radius of the berry as well as the skin thickness. Immature berries dry faster because of the lower osmotic pressure from the lower sugar concentration.

The cuticle
The skin of the berry contains very few stomata and the waxy nature of the cuticle is a major barrier to water movement. Cutin is the base material of the cuticle and is made of hydroxy fatty acid polymers that are permeable to water. The wax platelets on the cuticle are composed of 'hard' (mainly oleanolic acid) and 'soft' (mixture of alcohols, esters, acids and aldehydes) waxes (Grncarevic and Radler 1971) in an overlapping platelet structure (Chambers and Possingham 1963). The thickness of the cuticle is 2 to 3 μm and the platelets are about 0.1 μm wide.

The surface waxes of untreated grapes comprise overlapping platelets orientated in all directions, to give the berry its 'bloom' appearance, and with pores or holes between the platelets (Figure 14.6). After treatment with drying oil emulsion the platelets change orientation and became adpressed to the cuticle and take on a shiny, reflective appearance. It has been suggested that the change in reflectivity influences the absorption of radiant energy by the berry and hence drying rate, but this would mainly apply to fruit dried in the direct sun.

The waxes of the grape berry are composed of about 70% 'hard' wax and 30% 'soft' wax (Radler 1965). Research has shown that the 'hard' wax and the cutin material have minimal influence on water loss and that the 'soft' wax component of the cuticle is the main barrier to water loss. Experiments on model membranes demonstrated that the main constituent of grape cuticular wax, oleanolic acid (a 'hard' wax), had no effect on water evaporation but the esters of long chain fatty acids and alcohols ('soft' waxes) were effective in

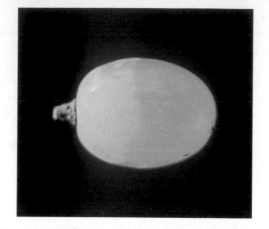

Figure 14.6 Sultana grape berry with undipped upper portion showing the waxy bloom and the shiny reflective appearance of the oil emulsion treated lower portion.

preventing evaporation (Grncarevic and Radler 1967). The precise nature of the hydrophobic properties of the grape cuticle is unknown.

Evaporation of water from the cuticle
Evaporation depends on ambient climatic conditions and is enhanced by high temperatures, low relative humidity and high air speed to remove moisture-laden air. The majority of fruit is shaded from the direct sun during rack drying and direct radiation to heat the berries is not a major influence on drying rate for fruit dried on racks.

The relative humidity is largely influenced by climate, although humidity is important where fruit is densely clumped and humid air movement is restricted. Improving air movement to remove moisture-laden air is one area in which growers can influence natural drying rates. Drying areas should not be shielded by buildings or trees and fruit should not be placed too densely on the rack, to allow air movement to remove moist air.

14.2.4 Browning in grapes
There are obvious benefits in drying the fruit rapidly to minimize the length of time of exposure of the fruit to the weather. However another effect is the lighter colour of the fruit due to less browning. Grape berries contain high levels of phenolics that can condense to form brown pigments (polyphenols, tannins). The condensation of phenolics can occur by the activity of enzymes or by non-enzymic means.

Enzymic browning
The enzyme polyphenol oxidase is largely responsible for enhancing the condensation of the phenolics to brown pigments. The phenolics and the enzyme are separated in different compartments of the cell and in an undisturbed state no oxidative browning occurs. However, once the vacuole (containing the phenolics) ruptures, brown pigments can be formed by the polyphenol oxidase which is located in the cytoplasm of the cell. The vacuole can rupture during the drying process at about 50% water loss or from physical damage to the berry.

The activity of polyphenol oxidase is greater in the skin of the grape berry than in the flesh and activity in both skin and flesh declines as the grapes mature (Radler 1964). To prevent browning, rapid dehydration is required to produce conditions inside the berry that will inhibit the enzyme. Radler (1964) has shown that the quality of the fruit is related to the rate of drying, and has attributed this to the rapid increase in sugar concentration during the drying of fruit, which greatly reduces the activity of polyphenol oxidase. However polyphenol oxidase activity may also be inhibited by other factors such as low oxygen concentrations (Joslyn and Ponting 1951).

Rehydration of fruit also stimulates browning, presumably by creating conditions under which polyphenol oxidase becomes active again. Untreated fruit dried in a partial vacuum in the absence of oxygen will produce fruit that does not brown. Fruit dried in the dark will also show no browning (Bottrill and Hawker 1970) whereas fruit dried in the direct sun produces a darker colour than fruit dried in indirect light. The precise nature of the influence of light on browning has not been determined.

Non-enzymic browning
Several volatile compounds associated with non-enzymic browning reactions have been found in naturally dried Sultanas (Ramshaw and Hardy 1969). These grapes, dried in direct sun without pre-treatment by an oil emulsion to enhance drying, produce a very dark purple/brown coloured fruit with a distinctive caramelized flavour. Another form of non-enzymic browning is the condensation of sugars with amino acids (Maillard Reaction). This occurs at a slow rate,

particularly during storage. McBean *et al.* (1971) also cite a third form of non-enzymic browning in which the chlorophyll, present in fruit dried in the shade, changes to the brown coloured pheophytin.

14.3 Treatments to enhance drying

Many treatments have been developed to enhance the rate of drying of grapes and one of these — the cold alkaline oil emulsion treatment — has been emphasized in Australia because of its ease of use in producing light coloured sultanas. Most of these treatments involve a modification of the berry cuticle or skin, or changes in drying conditions to enhance rapid water loss. In this chapter the term 'drying' will be used to describe water loss under natural conditions while 'dehydration' will be used to describe water loss under controlled conditions of airflow, temperature and humidity (Phaff 1951).

Alkaline oil emulsion

The use of alkaline oil emulsion (cold dip) has been known since early Roman times in the Mediterranean area and was initially formulated using olive oil and wood ash. In Australia the process was first attempted in the early 1900s but was discarded in favour of the traditional hot dip method (Henshilwood 1950). However the general use of cold dips began in the 1920s after encouragement by Greek settlers. The alkaline oil emulsion is now prepared from specially formulated drying oils ('dipping oils') and food grade potassium carbonate (K_2CO_3) (Table 14.2).

There is very little removal of wax from the cuticle by the alkaline oil emulsion (Grncarevic and Radler 1971). The alkaline oil emulsion disrupts the waxy cuticle to enhance drying but the actual mechanism of the action of the oil emulsion has not been determined. It has been proposed that the oil emulsion solution re-orientates the wax platelets to decrease the

Table 14.2 Composition of various oil emulsion treatments for the drying of grapes

Product treatment	Rate per 100 L water			Approximate volume required per tonne of fresh fruit (L)	Immersion time (mins)
	Drying oil (L)	Potassium carbonate (kg)	Potassium hydroxide (kg)		
Sultana raisins					
Standard dip[1]	1.5	2.4	—	30	3
First rack or trellis[2] spray	1.0	1.8	—	60 (rack) 200 (trellis)	—
Second rack or trellis[3] spray	0.5	0.9	—	15 (rack) 100 (trellis)	—
Lexia raisins					
Standard cold dip	1.5	2.4	—	30	15
Modified cold dip	1.5	2.4	1.0	30	15
First and second rack[2] spray	1.5	2.4	—	60	—
Third rack spray[4]	1.0	1.8	—	15	—

1. Solution pH should be maintained at pH 10 using potassium hydroxide additions.
2. In unfavourable drying conditions a first spray using the rates for standard dip can be used.
3. Applied about 4 days after the first spray. Also used to 'touch up' standard dipped fruit wetted by rain.
4. Also used as a 'touch up' spray for cold dipped fruit wetted by rain.

Source: Agnotes No. 17/79 and 18/79, Department of Agriculture, Victoria.

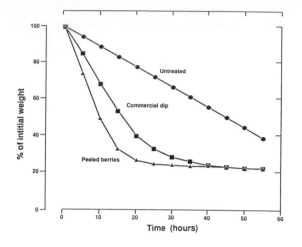

Figure 14.7 *Relative drying rates of dehydrated Sultana berries after peeling the skin and oil emulsion treatment compared to untreated grapes. Source: Grncarevic (1963).*

distance between adjacent platelets, effectively bringing hydrophilic groups of platelets together to facilitate water movement (Possingham 1972). Although Barnett (1980) disputed this theory, no alternative explanation was proposed.

The drying rate of berries with the skin removed would reflect the greatest achievable drying rate (Figure 14.7). The relative drying rate of untreated berries shows a steady rate of water loss limited by the intact cuticle. The commercial dip mixture treatment has a relative drying rate approaching that of peeled berries.

The drying oil used for drying grapes is derived from animal tallow or vegetable oil base and replaces the olive oil used originally. A drying oil contains about 60-70% ethyl esters (primarily as ethyl oleate and oleic acid) and about 30% emulsifiers. In California the small amount of drying oil used is based on methyl esters. In recent years oils have been developed specifically for rack or trellis spraying and these contain lower levels of emulsifiers (10-20%). These mixtures do not need to remain stable for long periods of time as is the case for bulk dipping methods. The tallow and vegetable base drying oils produce similar drying rates (Figure 14.8a), while drying oils containing lower proportions of emulsifier (higher concentrations of drying oil) tend to produce faster drying rates. Drying rate can also be influenced by the concentration of drying oil and potassium

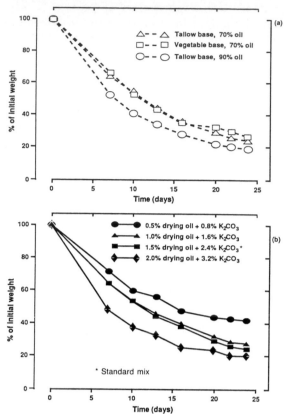

Figure 14.8 *(a) The influence of drying oil extract (tallow or vegetable) and concentration of oil (tallow base) in an oil emulsion mixture on the drying rate of field dried Sultana berries. (b) The drying rate for a standard mixture of a commercial drying oil and potassium carbonate by comparison with 1/3, 2/3 and 4/3 strength solutions using Sultana grapes.*

carbonate (Figure 14.8b) but the optimum concentration may vary from season to season.

The ethyl esters have been clearly demonstrated to be the active component of the dipping oil (Radler 1964, Ponting and McBean 1970). Ethyl oleate used alone without the potassium carbonate is effective in increasing the drying rate but the fruit retains an oily appearance. Off-flavour residues of ethyl or methyl oleate can be detected at about 200 mg/kg of dried fruit and emulsifiers may also contribute to off-flavours (Guadagni and Stafford 1979). Free fatty acids have reportedly been detected in oil formulations (Radler 1965) and a role in assisting drying has been proposed (Barnett 1980). However Fogerty and Burton (1981) could not detect free fatty acids in a

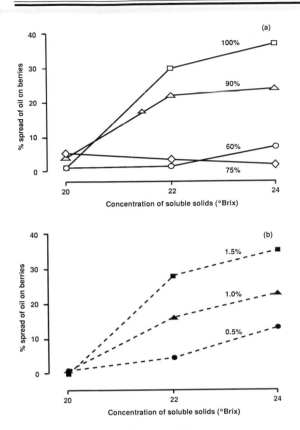

Figure 14.9 (a) Influence of fruit maturity and percentage ethyl oleate in the drying oil (60, 75, 90 and 100% ethyl oleate) and (b) the effect of fruit maturity and concentration of drying oil (0.5, 1.0 and 1.5% of 100% ethyl oleate) in the emulsion mixture on the spread of oil emulsion on partly dipped Sultana grape berries. Source: Schache, Mattschoss and Hayden (unpublished).

number of commercial drying oils and proposed that previous reports of fatty acids were due to interference by acidic emulsifiers in the method of determination.

Potassium carbonate used alone has also been demonstrated to have some effect on drying rate by some workers (Grncarevic 1963), but not by others (Radler 1964, Ponting and McBean 1970). The berry retains its waxy appearance after potassium carbonate treatment, in contrast to the effect of oil or oil emulsion which 'cuts' the bloom to produce a 'wet' appearance. Ponting and McBean (1970) reported that sodium carbonate used in an oil emulsion was much less effective on drying than potassium carbonate. Fogerty and Burton (1981) have, however, found sodium

carbonate just as effective as potassium carbonate in forming a stable emulsion, although drying rates were not evaluated.

The concentration of ethyl esters on the berry surface (from the drying oil emulsion) can decrease during drying (Barnett 1978). Also, if the oil emulsion is washed off the berry within about 24 hours of application, the berry reverts to a matte appearance and does not dry quickly (Grncarevic and Radler 1971). This early work indicated that the emulsion needs to be applied to the whole berry surface to obtain uniform colour. However it has since been demonstrated in laboratory studies using dehydration at $40^{\circ}C$ that, above a maturity level of about 22° Brix, partial immersion of the berry in oil emulsion can produce an acceptable product (May *et al.* 1983). With dipping treatments about 37 μL of oil emulsion adheres to berries weighing about 1.5 g. This volume can be reduced to 1.5 μL per berry if the berry is sprayed evenly with fine droplets of 190 to 440 μm diameter. Such low application rates would be impractical to apply evenly to fruit in the field and comparable results have yet to be demonstrated under field conditions.

The ethyl ester concentration can influence the spread of oil on a berry depending on the fruit maturity. Fruit at 20° Brix shows very little spread of the drying oil, but at 22° Brix or higher the spread of oil on a berry is greater at the higher ethyl ester concentrations (Figure 14.9a). Also the made-up strength of the drying oil influences the spread of oil at maturity levels of 22° Brix or greater with 2/3 and 1/3 strength solutions of 100% ethyl ester having less oil spread on a berry than a full strength mixture (Figure 14.9b).

Hot dip
A hot lye dip of wood ash, quicklime ($Ca(OH)_2$) and caustic soda (NaOH) was the traditional method used to treat Muscat Gordo Blanco grapes in Spain. In Australia a solution of 0.5 kg of caustic soda per 100 L of water heated to $85^{\circ}C$ and fruit dipped for 4-5 seconds has been used on the Waltham Cross and Muscat Gordo Blanco varieties. This treatment partly removes the wax (Grncarevic and Radler 1971) and splits the skin of the berry to increase drying rate. The dried fruit, however, can become quite brown and very sticky in storage due to leakage of sugars. This

method is no longer used due to the high labour input and poor fruit quality. Other variations of hot dips have been used in the past, such as a combination of potassium carbonate, caustic soda and drying oil heated to 80°C, but the 'cold' oil emulsion treatment has replaced them.

Sulphite dip

A pale yellow, sulphur-bleached product is produced after the fruit is treated in a boiling solution of 0.3 kg caustic soda and 2.5 kg sodium sulphite per 100 L of water for 4 seconds and then dehydrated. Only a small amount of fruit is produced in this manner, in California.

Tunnel drying

A small tonnage of grapes is dehydrated in enclosed dryers to produce speciality products in Australia. The dehydraters operate at 60°C and the fruit takes about three days to dry. This is an expensive process and the dried fruit is sold at a premium.

Other methods

Air or steam blanching treatments have been used on other food products to reduce drying time but have received little commercial attention for grapes. A dry-blanch-dry method has been developed experimentally for grapes (Lazar *et al.* 1963) to overcome losses from sugar leakage observed in steam blanching (Ponting and McBean 1970).

Other alternative drying methods, such as freeze drying, have not been adopted by the grape industry. However a recent development in California using a Microwave Vacuum Drying System has demonstrated that an alternative dried product, termed a 'grape puff', can be produced and its future potential is being investigated.

14.4 Types of raisin products

The age-old method of fruit drying using 'natural' methods still accounts for most of the dried fruit produced in the world. An additional range of products has been produced using alternative drying techniques and varieties. However the market penetration of many of these products is low due to resistance to change by consumers and the lack of market development by producers.

Particular products, such as the Australian sultana, have developed niches in certain markets but other products of lower price and quality are entering the market. The four basic types of dried vine fruits produced in Australia are shown in Figure 14.10. This section describes the various dried vine fruit products available and their basic methods of production.

14.4.1 Dried without pre-treatment

'Naturals'

By far the greatest amount of 'naturals' is dried from the variety Sultana (known as Thompson Seedless in USA, Sultanina in the Near East, Oval Kishmish in Asia). The fruit takes about 3 weeks to dry and retains a smokey-grey bloom, is characteristically a dark purple-brown colour and has a caramelized flavour. The fruit is dried in direct sun (sun-dried) being placed on wooden or paper trays, as in California, or on concrete or clay slabs, as in South Africa, Afghanistan, Turkestan and Iran. After about 10 to 14 days the fruit is turned over to complete the drying on the underside of the bunch. In California the dried product is known as Thompson Seedless Raisins (TSR's).

In Australia small quantities have been produced either by drying on concrete slabs, trellis drying or with the assistance of dehydration. Problems with climate and late maturity of fruit in Australia have precluded the production of optimum quality 'naturals' (Kerridge and Grncarevic 1965, Hayes 1985b).

In Afghanistan, Sultana grapes are also dried slowly in the shade in drying sheds to produce a light coloured, greenish-yellow 'natural' called 'soygi' (Grncarevic 1969). These have a delicate and distinctive flavour and are preferred in Pakistan and India, and interest in them as a speciality product has also been shown in Europe.

Currants

Currants are distinguished by the small berry size (approximately 0.1 g dry weight) and the dark blue colour of the fruit with a smokey-grey bloom. Greece is the traditional country for currant production where the main variety is Zante (known as Zante Currant in Australia, Black Corinth in California). The fruit can be dried on trays, on drying racks or trellis-dried and typically

Figure 14.10 The four basic types of dried vine fruit produced in Australia (a) 'naturals', (b) currants, (c) sultanas and (d) lexia raisins.

takes about 3 weeks to dry. Currants dried in the direct sun produce a lower quality product than trellis-dried fruit or rack-dried fruit (Whiting and Morey 1988).

In Australia almost all currants are dried on racks. The main variety used is Zante Currant, but the berries split easily following rain at or prior to harvest. A new hybrid variety, Carina, has been released in Australia (Antcliff 1975) (Figure 14.11). It has the advantage of being resistant to berry splitting from rain. However it has other differences to the traditional Zante Currant variety (uneven berry size, larger berry size and later maturity) which diminish its popularity for planting. Attempts to hasten the drying of Carina grapes harvested late in the season, by using oil emulsion sprays, produced a loss of bloom and difficulties in processing and storing the fruit.

Muscatels
Raisins produced as 'naturals' from large-berried, seeded varieties, usually Muscat Gordo Blanco, are called muscatels in Australia, muscats in California and malagas in Spain. They may be marketed loose

or with berries still attached to the bunchstem (as 'clusters' or 'layers'), and with or without seeds.

Others
Many varieties of grapes can be dried to produce speciality products. For example, the Black Monnuka variety produces a distinctive-tasting, finely-wrinkled attractive fruit. Dried Shiraz grapes have been used in the past to produce fruit

Figure 14.11 Bunches of Carina with larger berries, uneven berry size and looser clusters than Zante Currant.

muffins. A large range of hybrids, selections and varieties are under evaluation in many countries, and in Australia, several large-berried varieties for seedless raisins and speciality market products have been described (Barrett *et al.* 1969, Newman and Clingeleffer 1987). Alternative grape products are also of interest. In California, a 'grape puff' is being developed (see 14.3) and locally a sultana essence by-product used as a flavourant in food and drink has been released.

14.4.2 Dried with pre-treatment

Sultanas

The use of alkaline oil emulsion treatments to assist the drying of grapes produces a light-coloured, golden-brown fruit which has become commonly known in Australia as 'sultanas' (more correctly, sultana raisins). This product is predominantly produced from the seedless variety Sultana, although a new hybrid variety, Merbein Seedless (Antcliff 1981), is being tried in Australia and overseas. Merbein Seedless has the advantage of being relatively more resistant to splitting after rain near maturity than Sultana, but it is more readily damaged during handling and produces a slightly darker dried product than Sultana (Newman *et al.* 1985). Products similar to sultanas are produced in Turkey, Greece, Iran, South Africa and California.

Golden bleach

Golden-yellow raisins are produced from Thompson Seedless (Sultana) grapes in California (see 14.3). The fruit is either dehydrated or sun-dried and the product has a distinctive sulphur dioxide taste many consumers find objectionable when the fruit is eaten without cooking.

Lexias

Large-berried, seeded grapes treated in a hot caustic dip or an oil emulsion produce a light brown to dark brown coloured raisin. These are commonly produced from the Muscat Gordo Blanco and Waltham Cross varieties in Australia and are called lexias. A similar product sun-dried in Spain is sold as 'valencias'. Lexias are mostly deseeded and sold in Australia as 'Seeded Raisins'!.

14.5 Fruit ripening and preparation for harvest

Grapes ripen during the late summer and autumn, a period of decreasing radiation and air temperature. High yields and certain management techniques may delay maturity, therefore the time of harvesting is crucial to produce adequately dried fruit of high quality at the maximum possible cropping levels. If grapes ripen later in the season the risk of not getting them dry increases and greater costs using dehydration techniques are incurred.

14.5.1 Ripening

Grape berry growth follows a double sigmoid pattern with a rapid influx of sugar during the second phase. However due to variations in climate ripening can vary markedly between seasons (Figure 14.12). For instance the level of 20° Brix was reached on 27 January in 1978, an early season compared to the average date of 17 February. In reality, harvesting is usually delayed until mid February even in early years such as 1978 to take advantage of the extra yield gain in weight of sugar. The average rate of ripening is about 2° Brix per week up to early February, but this decreases to about 0.5° Brix per week by mid February and thereafter the rate of sugar accumulation slows considerably.

The increase in mean berry weight usually slows down before the rate of sugar increase does, suggesting that berries may be losing water. For example in 1959 from 17 February to 24 February the gain in berry weight was 0.02 g, (Figure 14.12b) yet the gain in total soluble solids per berry (sugars) between those dates was 0.04 g (Figure 14.12c). Thus the berry lost 0.02 g, presumably as water. The total weight of soluble solids per berry is therefore a useful index to determine when sugar accumulation has ceased. Jacob (1944) determined that above 24° Brix little further increase in total sugar is likely for Sultana and Muscat of Alexandria (Muscat Gordo Blanco). Delaying the harvest of grapes to gain extra weight through sugar accumulation must be weighed up against the poorer drying conditions and hence poorer fruit quality more likely to occur later in the drying period.

Despite the variation in maturity most varieties are harvested at approximately the same time each

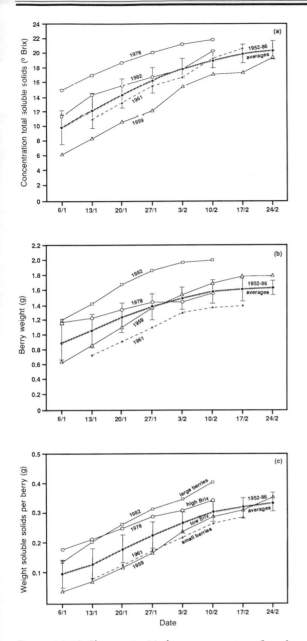

Figure 14.12 Changes in (a) the concentration of total soluble solids (° Brix), (b) berry weight (g) and (c) total soluble solids per berry (g) of Sultana grapes for a range of seasons compared to the averages (and standard deviations) obtained over 35 seasons (1952-1986). Source: Department of Agriculture, Victoria.

year. In the Murray Valley, Zante Currants are harvested in the first week of February at a maturity of about 24⁰ Brix. In Western Australia Zante Currants are picked in late January. Sultana

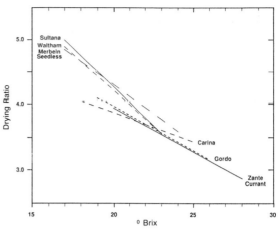

Figure 14.13 Drying ratios (fresh weight to dry weight) for Waltham Cross, Muscat Gordo Blanco, Sultana, Zante Currant, Merbein Seedless and Carina at various sugar contents. Sources: Grncarevic (1973) and Whiting and Morey (unpublished).

harvesting for dried fruit generally begins in the third week of February at a maturity of about 20⁰ Brix. Carina currants are harvested in late February to early March at a maturity of 24⁰ Brix and lexias are harvested at about 22⁰ Brix in mid March. Acid level is not used as a guide to determine harvesting but the acid concentration can contribute to the overall flavour of the dried product.

Regular sampling of properties near Mildura by the Department of Agriculture, Victoria, has been useful in comparing ripening between seasons on a district basis (Figure 14.12). However, with changes in management and cropping levels between properties the results are becoming less meaningful for comparison with past seasons and growers are now encouraged to assess maturity on their own properties.

The maturity of the fresh grapes relates closely to the quality of the dried fruit and the weight of dried product per tonne of fresh grapes. Immature grapes produce shrivelled light-weight berries without the meatiness desired by consumers. The drying ratio of fruit is higher with immature fruit and the lower the ratio the better the yield of dried fruit. The drying ratio for various varieties is shown in Figure 14.13. With Sultanas an increase in sugar level of 1⁰Brix at a cropping level of 25 tonne/ha fresh weight results in a dried

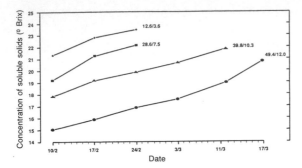

Figure 14.14 Rate of Brix development of Sultana grapes at a range of cropping levels. The final fresh and calculated dried yield as tonne per hectare are shown in each case.

weight increase of approximately 300 kg/ha. The concentration of sugar is usually measured by hydrometer or refractometer as described in Section 13.2.4

High cropping levels usually delay the maturity of the crop. Figure 14.14 shows the rate of sugar accumulation in Sultana with a range of cropping levels. Although high yields are economically sound, the associated delay in maturity shifts the drying period into less favourable climatic conditions. This slows the drying rate and usually produces a dark brown coloured fruit that requires extra dehydration to reach an acceptable moisture content.

Attempts to enhance ripening using ethephon have had mixed results. El-bana and Weaver (1979) demonstrated enhanced maturity with Sultana, but other trials have shown inconsistent results (Andris *et al.* 1981).

With black-berried varieties, such as Zante Currant and Carina, a uniformly dark blue-black colour is desired. Lighter coloured red berries in currants reduce the grade of the fruit. It is desirable that an even colour should have developed on the berry before picking is started. Trials with Carina have shown that with crops over about 10 tonne/ha dry weight the colour becomes uneven and lower grade fruit results.

14.5.2 Preparation of vines for harvesting
Setting sprays are required for the production of small, even-sized currants with the Zante Currant and Carina varieties. Traditionally trunk girdling at flowering has stimulated berry set on Zante Currant, a parthenocarpic variety. This process is

now substituted with a spray of 1 mg/L gibberellic acid plus 100 mg/L chlormequat chloride (CCC) applied at full capfall. In the past, treatment with parachlorophenoxyacetic acid (PCPA) was also effective in increasing set but it produced thick berry pedicels, a high proportion of seed traces, and greater splitting after rain near harvest.

Carina is a stenospermocarpic variety that has female flowers (no viable male pollen). Whilst the setting of Carina can be enhanced by the spray treatment used for Zante Currant, a split spray of chlormequat chloride at two weeks prior to flowering and gibberellic acid at full capfall has produced better results than the combination spray in some seasons.

No setting sprays are required for Sultana, although the lexia variety Muscat Gordo Blanco has responded to treatment with dilute solutions of chlormequat chloride to increase berry set. The fresh and dried yield of Sultana can be increased by the application of low concentrations of gibberellic acid after full capfall but the associated increase in berry weight may be undesirable (Antcliff 1967).

Particular attention is required to control certain weeds such as three cornered jack (*Emex australis*), caltrop (*Tribulus terrestris*) and gentle annie or innocent weed (*Cenchrus echinatus*), to prevent weed seed contamination of the dried fruit. In the vineyard, weed growth in the undervine area may be controlled by residual and knockdown herbicides and the inter-row area by frequent cultivation, mulching or herbicides. The racks and drying areas should also be kept free of troublesome weeds. The drying areas are best grassed and closely mown prior to drying operations to minimize dust contamination of the fruit. Racks and harvesting equipment should be checked prior to use and rendered operational.

Many growers cease irrigating during the harvest period with the aim of producing high sugar concentrations; however, severe water stress usually restricts total sugar production. Postharvest irrigations are applied to reduce accumulated soil water deficits and to promote growth of cover crops. The overhanging shoots on the vines can be trimmed to improve access to the fruit for harvesting.

14.6 Harvesting and drying of fresh grapes

The proper handling of fresh fruit is critical for the production of high quality dried fruit. Any broken or squashed berries stimulate the browning reactions and dark berries will result, and any weed seed or other contaminant will produce problems for processors and consumers. The techniques used in Australia to produce dried vine fruits differ from those in other countries and several stages of the process require careful attention. The majority of the dried fruit is produced by hand harvesting and rack-drying. A small proportion of growers (10-15%) use trellis-drying (see section 14.7).

14.6.1 Harvesting

Harvesting in the Murray Valley is mainly done by itinerant workers and the co-ordination of labour for the region is undertaken by the Commonwealth Employment Service.

Inexperienced pickers require training as the correct harvesting procedure is important to maintain quality.

The picking is usually done by two people per row of vines, one on either side. Empty buckets are placed along the rows beforehand within easy reach of the pickers. The fruit should be placed (not dropped or dragged) into a bucket after cutting the bunchstem with a knife or clippers or carefully snapping the bunch stem at the abscission point (node). Fruit to be bulk dipped is placed in perforated 'dip tins' holding about 8 kg and care must be taken to prevent dirt entering the buckets through the holes. If rack spraying is used, un-perforated buckets holding 8 kg (shrub tubs) or 10 kg (Bryce buckets) can be used which decreases soil contamination of the fruit (Figure 14.15). The buckets should not be overfilled, to reduce squashing of fruit by other buckets stacked on top of them during transport to the drying area, and the buckets should be regularly washed to clean off any dirt adhering to juice on the bucket. About 1 tonne of fresh grapes is collected per load.

The buckets of fruit are harvested at piece rates of between $0.32 and $0.64 per bucket of 8 kg, depending on the variety (1989 rates), which equates to an average picking rate of about 150 buckets of Sultana grapes per day for six days a week to earn the award weekly wage.

Figure 14.15 Hand harvesting of Sultana bunches into plastic unperforated buckets.

14.6.2 Bulk dipping

For bulk dipping, a steel frame is used upon which the buckets are placed, and this is winched off the trailer (using electric, hydraulic or manual winches) and placed into the 'dip tank'. Several variations of this procedure have been adopted, such as submerging the trailer frame plus the buckets of fruit. The 'dip tank' contains about 3,000 L of oil emulsion solution ('cold dip') and the fruit is fully submerged for several minutes to allow penetration into all bunches (Figure 14.16). Excessive dipping time induces berry splitting. The fruit is then raised, drained for about five minutes and transferred back to the trailer to be carted to the rack.

The standard drying solution for Sultana grapes consists of 2.4 kg potassium carbonate and 1.5 L of drying oil per 100 L of water (Table 14.2). The pH should be checked regularly with litmus paper and maintained above pH 9.5 using

Figure 14.15 Dipping of Sultana grapes into a bulk dip tank of oil emulsion using perforated 'dip' tins.

additions of potassium carbonate or potassium hydroxide. Sugar from squashed berries reduces the pH. A removable tray in the bottom of the tank is desirable to collect accumulated mud and debris.

A dip tank is often made from corrugated galvanized iron or mild steel (dimensions approximately 2.1 × 1.5 × 1.0 m) but concrete tanks both above and below ground level are also used. A smaller volume of drying solution is usually kept in reserve to top up the main tank on a regular basis. About 30 L of drying emulsion is removed per tonne of fresh fruit.

An alternative to bulk dipping is the Obst dip. This consists of a trailer with a central tank running the full length of the trailer containing the oil emulsion. The grapes are placed into one end of the tank as they are collected from the vine rows and a conveyor system moves the buckets towards the front of the trailer. The fruit is submerged for about 10 seconds and after this time buckets are withdrawn and placed on the sides of the trailer to drain. This system is rarely used now. Lexia raisins are bulk-dipped as are sultanas, but with longer periods of immersion and in some cases modified by the addition of potassium hydroxide to the drying emulsion (Table 14.2).

14.6.3 Drying rack

In most countries fruit is primarily placed on the ground or trays for drying and it was originally done this way in Australia. During the early 1900s drying racks were developed in Australia, and other countries such as South Africa now use them. Racks evolved from 6-8 tiers up to the common 10-12 tier rack. Originally built from wooden components, most racks are now constructed from steel. The racks are variable in length (46-92 m) and are generally 1.5 m wide and 2.4-3.0 m high (Figure 14.17). There is usually 3.0 m between intermediate posts and galvanized wire netting (rabbit wire) 1.2 m wide with 5 cm mesh size is tensioned from each end with wooden cross pieces as well as with wires along each side. Wooden or steel cross pieces are inserted at 1.0 m intervals to prevent wire sag and form a firm surface for placement of fruit.

Racks are usually orientated north-south to take advantage of the prevailing west winds and to promote more even exposure of fruit to the sun. Racks can be spaced 5 m apart to allow access for shaking, but wider spacings of 9-12 m allow better air movement. A 70 m rack contains approximately 840 m² of drying area which can hold about 20 tonne of fresh fruit (about 5 tonne when dry). In South Africa racks are commonly erected in pairs, 3 m apart with a concrete floor and a common roof. The addition of roofs to racks in Australia prevents the top layer of fruit discolouring in the direct sun and protects the fruit from rain.

Before fruit is placed onto a rack a sheet of hessian or plastic mesh is placed on top of the bottom wire and suspended above the ground. This hessian serves to catch berries that drop off the bunches during loading onto the rack. Grapes placed on the rack should be carefully spread by hand to cover the netting about one bunch thick. Any damaged or mouldy berries should be removed along with leaves and other material.

14.6.4 Rack spraying

This method avoids the use of a bulk dip and is quicker. All fruit is loaded directly onto the rack after being collected from the vineyard. In many vineyards it takes a day or two to fill a rack, after which the rack is sprayed with drying oil emulsion using a wand or a series of nozzles attached to a spray unit (Figure 14.18a). A drying oil emulsion of 1.8 kg of potassium carbonate and 1.0 L of drying oil per 100 L of water is applied at a rate of 60 L per tonne of fresh fruit (Table 14.2). The drying oils are usually specially formulated for rack spraying and contain lower levels of emulsifiers. After about 5 days, when bunches have partly shrivelled, a second application of drying emulsion of 0.9 kg potassium carbonate and 0.5 L of drying oil per 100 L of water is used to wet berries missed by the first spray. Rack spraying must be thorough to avoid uneven drying and fruit colour.

The rack spraying method permits the use of non-perforated buckets which reduces grit contamination, as does the washing effect of the application methods. The removal of drying emulsion by rain within 24 hours of application reduces the effect of the drying emulsion (Grncarevic and Lewis 1976) and hence the emulsion should be reapplied. Clingeleffer (1986) has suggested the reversibility effect lasts up to the final stages of drying but this may depend on the maturity of the fruit. With roofed racks plastic curtains may be attached to the side to exclude direct rain.

If rain is persistent moulds may develop on the fruit. Rack dehydration can prevent this problem, but growers without such dehydraters have resorted to applying metabisulphite or burning sulphur. These methods are not considered appropriate as the maximum acceptable level of sulphur in dried vine fruit may be exceeded. In California a commercial preparation of 2% potassium sorbate has been effective in reducing moulds in 'naturals'. With lexia raisins, rack sprays need to be repeated, often up to three times, to ensure adequate drying.

Fruit may be left on the rack during good drying conditions until it reaches an acceptable moisture content to be received by the packing shed, i.e. 13% moisture or less. However if drying conditions are poor, drying should be continued until the fruit reaches at least 18% moisture to permit successful shaking from the racks. Fruit should be shaken off and not rubbed with sticks as this crushes the berries. Fruit on the berry hessian at the bottom of the rack usually contains many damaged, and hence dark, berries and these should be handled separately. Mechanical shakers attached to tractors have now replaced this once manual task (Figure 14.8b).

14.6.5 'Naturals'
Both currants and naturally-dried sultanas and raisins are harvested by hand in a similar manner to fruit treated with drying oil emulsion. Currants are harvested early and can be dried on racks to produce a good quality product. Sultana fruit produces a better quality product and dries faster if it is dried in the direct sun, for instance on concrete slabs (Figure 14.19) or plastic sheeting, by comparison with rack or trellis drying (Hayes 1985a). Fruit dried in the direct sun must be turned after about 10-14 days to permit even drying of the bunch.

The consistent production of high quality 'naturals' is difficult in Australia, compared with other countries, because of the relatively late maturity of Sultana and the lower temperatures during the drying season. Most naturally-dried

raisins require dehydration to achieve adequate drying.

14.6.6 Solar technology
To produce high quality dried fruit consistently, procedures that overcome the influence of poor weather are essential. An early version of solar technology, utilizing a solar collector in conjunction with a rack, was unsuccessful (Wilson 1962). Subsequently Szulmayer (1971) described various types of solar driers. More recent research has included tests of solar collectors on the roof of the rack, rockpiles, plastic curtains and ducted air heating (Fuller et al. 1989). Initial results indicate that a system using a solar air heater (collector) mounted on the roof of the rack combined with forced air circulation and plastic side curtains (Figure 14.20) is a practical and economic system.

14.6.7 Mechanical harvesting of fresh fruit for drying
The adoption of technology for the mechanical harvesting of fresh fruit for drying has not occurred in Australia despite promising research results (May et al. 1974). The critical factor is berry damage during harvesting, because any broken berries dry darker and reduce the quality grade. Also the complete fruit handling system needs to be changed to handle single berries; this embraces the need for small containers to hold the fresh fruit after harvest and a smaller rack mesh size to prevent berries dropping down through the tiers on the rack.

The mechanical harvesting of partly dried berries has been examined in California (Studer and Olmo 1971). The canes are cut as in the harvest pruning operation (see Section 14.7.2) but the fruit is not sprayed with drying emulsion and is harvested within about 5-7 days, in a partly dried state, and placed on sheets of paper on the ground to finish drying.

14.7 Production and harvesting of trellis-dried fruit
Trellis-drying is an alternative method for the commercial production of dried vine fruit. The system was first used experimentally in 1956 (May and Kerridge 1967). It has largely been used as a method of salvaging rain affected grapes in

Figure 14.17 Drying rack used for the production of dried fruit in Australia, also showing fruit drying on polymesh sheeting and a 'sweat' box used in the past to send fruit to the packing shed.

Figure 14.18 (below) Rack dried Sultanas showing (a) the application of oil emulsion using high volume spray equipment and (b) a tractor mounted rack shaker to remove dried fruit.

A

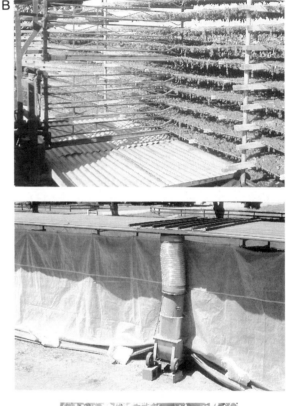

B

Figure 14.19 (above) Drying 'natural' Sultana grapes on a concrete slab, also showing the 'bulk' bins now used to send fruit to the packing shed.

Figure 14.20 (above right) Solar air heating system to assist the drying of grapes showing the roof mounted solar flat plate collector, fan and ducting to distribute the heated air and plastic curtains to control air flow.

Figure 14.21 (right) Trellis system for the mechanization of dried Sultana production using alternating sides of the trellis and cane positioning for mechanical harvest pruning and harvesting of the fruit. (Developed by I. Shaw, South Merbein).

wet seasons but now a proportion of growers use the method as a standard management system. Although it has been assessed as a more economic system of production, it requires significant changes to the trellising and handling of fruit.

Trellis-drying has been adopted to some extent in the production of sultanas and currants in Australia and California. In this system the fruit is 'harvested' by cutting canes much as they are during winter pruning; the shoots, foliage and fruit are left *in situ* on the trellis wires where they dehydrate. This is called 'harvest pruning'. Drying oil emulsion is applied to Sultana fruit soon after cutting and, when almost dry, the fruit is machine-harvested and 'finish-dried' if necessary.

14.7.1 Setting up the vines

Only cane pruned vines can be used and Sultana is the main variety used commercially. Whilst the traditional trellis systems can be used, they are not as suitable as specially prepared vines. Older vines suffer from the debilitating effect of continual harvest-pruning and the older trellis systems are generally too close to the ground for successful harvesting.

The primary aims of setting up are to have strong vigorous vines that withstand the harvest-pruning effect, to have fruit readily accessible for quick cutting, and to be able to readily eliminate crown bunches. Vigorous grafted vines on a narrow-T trellis with foliage wires, a wide-T trellis or a hanging cane system are most suitable. The undervine area should be free of weeds.

Several training methods have been developed to facilitate mechanization of the cutting process. These include split cordons, cane-spur systems, split systems, hanging cane and swing-arm systems (May and Clingeleffer 1982). Several of these systems are being evaluated by growers. The swing-arm trellis (Clingeleffer and May 1981) has been further developed into an experimental production system with a multi-purpose machine to harvest-prune, spray and harvest the fruit (Gould and Whiting 1987). A similar system has also been developed in California (the alternating duplex) to facilitate mechanical cane severance (Studer 1984) and another version using similar principles is also being developed in Australia (Shaw 1986) (Figures 14.21 and 14.22).

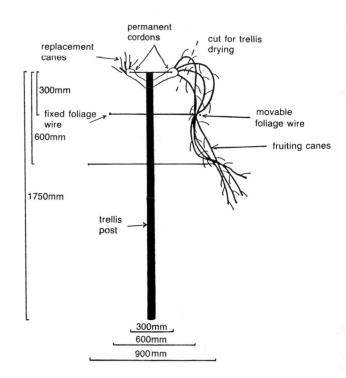

Figure 14.22. Commonly used dimenstions for the 'Shaw' trellis shown in Figure 14.21.

14.7.2 Cane cutting

The canes need to be cut at the correct place to ensure that most of the fruit will be dried on the trellis and yet adequate leaf area is retained to prevent debilitation of the vine (Figure 14.23). It has been assessed that a minimum of 40% of the leaf must be retained to maintain vine vigour (Scholefield *et al.* 1978). The harvest-pruning should be completed by early March; later cutting is associated with slower drying rates and darker fruit of lower quality (Sarooshi and Roberts 1978). The cutting is usually done by hand but mechanical cutting methods are being developed. Approximately 0.4 hectare can be cut by one person per day. Bunches not severed from the vine (crown bunches) could be removed as inflorescences (Sarooshi and Roberts 1979) but growers prefer to harvest them separately when mature. Fresh grapes must not be allowed to remain on the vine since harvesters remove and squash them and the sticky juice causes leaf fragments to adhere to the dried fruit.

Figure 14.23 Harvest pruned Sultana vines showing fruit drying in situ *on the trellis.*

14.7.3 Spray application

The application of the drying oil emulsion to trellis-dried fruit is the most critical aspect in producing high quality dried sultanas. Various spray application units have been developed to enhance penetration of the drying emulsion into the bunch which is often surrounded by leaves. The initial development of a star-wheel sprayer (Clingeleffer *et al.* 1977) has not been pursued commercially nor have efforts to use micro-sprayers been successful, particularly in vines of moderate to high vigour.

Almost all sprayers now utilize high volumes of the drying emulsion delivered through low pressure (300 kPa) jets with the run-off solution collected and recycled (Figure 14.24). Approximately 20,000 L per hectare is applied with about 7000 L per hectare remaining on the vine. These levels are approximately three times the volumes per tonne of fruit used for rack spraying. It is critical to apply adequate volumes of drying emulsion and to correctly position the jets to thoroughly wet the interior of the bunch (Hayden 1988). Clumping of fruit on the trellis makes spray penetration difficult and trellis systems that spread the distribution of fruit enhance wetting. Trimming of excessive growth prior to spraying also assists spray penetration.

Sprays are best applied just before or within two days of cutting, although a delay of up to one week can still be effective. Grncarevic and Hawker (1971) have demonstrated that satisfactory quality fruit can be produced even when the drying

emulsion application is delayed until the fruit has lost 50% of its weight. Generally an initial application of a two-thirds strength drying emulsion is applied and a follow-up spray of one-third strength mixture after about five days. The effect of the drying oil emulsion on active leaves is believed negligible (Clingeleffer *et al.* 1977) but application to leaves should be minimized.

Figure 14.24 Hooded spray shield for the application of oil emulsion to trellis dried Sultana grapes.

348

Figure 14.25 Harvesting of trellis dried fruit using a low powered, tractor drawn harvester.

14.7.4 Harvesting trellis-dried fruit

Harvesting by hand or machine should not commence until the fruit is below 18% moisture, and preferably 16%. The dried fruit is easier to remove in the afternoon or evening after the moisture absorbed by stems during the night has dried off. However fruit should not be harvested when it is too hot since the softer berries are more prone to damage.

Conventional winegrape harvesters can be used, but local manufacturers have produced harvesters that can be tractor-mounted or towed (Figure 14.25). All harvesters can operate at a high level of efficiency with correct setting of beater speeds and ground speeds, most of which are determined by operator experience. Up to 0.8 hectare per hour can be harvested by machines compared to about 0.02 hectares per hour for hand harvesting. Improvements to harvesting machines are continually being made, with the emphasis on producing a stalk- and leaf-free sample of undamaged fruit.

14.7.5 Postharvest handling

Fruit above a moisture level of 13% is unacceptable for processing and should be dried further. Trellis-dried fruit could be finish-dried on ground sheets in direct sun but it is a labour intensive process, vulnerable to inclement weather and not suitable for large quantities of fruit. Some growers have opted for large bin-drying systems using fuel-fired heaters. These systems are often partly or totally mechanized to assist transfer of fruit from the vines to the bins. These systems are large enough to handle a day's harvesting and the fruit is dried overnight and cleared away next morning ready for the next afternoon's harvesting.

14.7.6 Long term effects of trellis drying

The combined effect of several years of severing about 60% of the canopy from the vine at grape maturity has a depressing effect on vine yields and growth. Most work indicates a yield reduction of about 10%, although there are other reports of higher losses (Christensen *et al.* 1970, Whiting 1982) in cases where the proportion of cane severance exceeded 60% or the vines were not healthy. The level of removal of 60% of the canopy is critical and should not be exceeded. The main effect of trellis drying on yield is to reduce the bunch weight. This has been associated with fewer flowers per bunch (Scholefield *et al.* 1977), and with Zante Currant similar results have been found despite the use of setting sprays (Whiting 1982). The use of vigorous grafted vines should produce high crop levels.

Other alternatives for lessening the impact of harvest pruning, such as reducing the frequency of harvest pruning and using different trunk configurations, are not successful (May *et al.* 1978). At present, several hybrid varieties that dry while still attached to the vine are being assessed in South Africa and California and these may produce dried fruit on the vine without having to cut the canes.

14.8 Finish-drying and dehydration

Fruit cannot always be dried to the moisture level of 13% required by packing sheds and finish-drying is required. The drying process involves the evaporation of water from the berry surface and the removal of the water vapour by air movement. The simplest form of drying is to spread fruit onto sheets on the ground; the sun provides the heating to evaporate the water and the wind removes the vapour (sun drying). Dehydration on the other hand involves the heating of air by fuel-powered burners and increasing the air velocity using fans.

14.8.1 Sun drying

With sun drying, fruit is placed onto water-proof sheeting, mainly a polylined mesh, on flat ground and spread out to absorb sun radiation (Figure 14.26). In clear warm weather fruit dries quickly, for example 2-3 days to dry fruit down from 16-17% moisture to below 13%. The capital cost of such methods is low, but the labour input may be high and the rate of drying is entirely dependent on the weather.

Fruit should be spread to a depth of about 25 mm, or no more than three berries thick, to ensure the drying rate is not slowed unduly. A layer of fruit of 50 mm or 75 mm reduces the rate of drying (Clingeleffer 1984). The increase in berry temperature in the direct sun produces a higher vapour pressure deficit for fruit than on racks where fruit mainly dries under ambient conditions. Although the vapour pressure difference decreases markedly as the season progresses, due to lower radiation intensity and less sunlight hours, water movement out of the

Figure 14.26 Finish-drying of fruit with sun drying using plastic sheets on the ground.

berry still occurs. Also, despite increases in fruit moisture content caused by overnight dew, fruit can be rapidly dried by the direct heat from the sun early the next day. However, under unfavourable weather conditions, fruit should be covered over at night and re-opened when conditions are suitable.

Exposure of fruit to the sun also removes the green tinge that often appears in fruit dried in the shade. Green tinge is due to the presence of chlorophyll that has not been broken down by sunlight (Bottrill and Hawker 1970). Wetting the fruit with water at a rate of 1 L per m² and then covering the fruit for several hours promotes the breakdown of green pigments upon re-exposure to the light.

Heaping and mixing the fruit while hot (e.g. while on a ground sheet) can be used to even up the moisture content of the fruit where some semi-dried bunches (mainly from incomplete drying oil emulsion coverage) have been mixed in with the dried fruit. These semi-dried 'blobs' cause problems with the cleaning and sorting in the packing shed. The hot moist fruit 'sweats' after covering over and the moisture is absorbed by the drier berries. Trellis-dried fruit can have a greater proportion of 'blobs' due to poor spray penetration and the presence of undried crown bunches.

14.8.2 Dehydration

Fuel-fired dehydrators can also be used to finish-dry the fruit. These systems are used when weather conditions are poor or when rapid finish-drying is required. The most commonly used fuels are kerosene and propane gas. The burners are required to heat the air to 50º-60ºC with an airflow of about 280 m³/min.

Fruit on a rack can be dehydrated by enclosing the rack with curtains (usually plastic) and ducting the heat from the burner along the rack (Figure 14.27a). Operation at 60ºC for 6-8 hours is generally sufficient to finish drying of the fruit. The capital costs are high and fuel usage is moderate but the fruit can be made ready for sending direct to the packing shed (Berrett and Weste 1979).

Fruit can also be dried in 'bin dehydrators'. The bins are usually 6 x 2.4 m and 0.5 m high with a mesh covered wire bottom about 0.15 m above the ground. The fruit is placed in the bin

Figure 14.27 Dehydration of fruit (a) on a rack and (b) in a bin dryer.

to a depth of 100-150 mm and the unit is covered and sealed with a plastic sheet (Figure 14.27b). The heated air, using fuel-fired heaters, is forced through the fruit and vented below the layer of mesh. Temperatures of 50-60°C for 6-10 hours are used to remove the moisture in the fruit, followed by a cooling period without heat. Recycling of warm, vented air can reduce fuel consumption. A recent development employs a tunnel of a double plastic skin to utilize solar heating of the air passing between the plastic layers. The major cost with conventional dehydraters is the labour to load and unload the bins, but mechanized systems have been developed by some growers to decrease this cost.

The packing sheds also have facilities for drying fruit that is delivered above the maximum moisture content. These are large tunnel dryers where the fruit is spread onto trays. The charges for this drying process are quite high.

14.8.3 Delivery
All fruit is sent to packing sheds in bulk bins or sweat boxes. A bulk bin, 1.2 × 1.2 × 0.6 m made from 5-ply timber, holds about 500 kg of dried fruit, while a 'sweat box' of 0.95 × 0.64 × 0.20 m holds about 60 kg of fruit. Fruit delivered promptly to the packing shed is less likely to be contaminated by insect pests. Upon receival at a packing shed all fruit is weighed and a sample collected for grading and assessment of other quality characteristics. This sample is kept for some weeks in case of appeals by growers against the grading.

14.9 Classing, processing and marketing of dried vine fruit

14.9.1 Classing system
Whilst classing systems are often directly associated with 'quality' there is not a clear definition of quality and expectations vary depending on the end use of the product and the consumer requirements. For instance, with the baking trade, a darker coloured, small berried type may be satisfactory but for direct eating an attractive, meaty berry is desired. The present system of grading is adequate provided it correlates with the types of products consumers are demanding.

The grading system in Australia is primarily based on colour grade standards set subjectively each year by the Australian Dried Fruits Association's (ADFA) grade fixing committee comprising statutory authorities, growers and packers. These grade standards may vary from season to season. Each packing shed receives a subsample of the grades for classing. State Dried Fruits Boards have been established as independent bodies under state acts. Their function is setting grade standards, inspecting fruit, classing of fruit, arbitrating on appeals against grade, registration of packing sheds and the inspection of on-farm drying areas (see Volume 1, Section 1.3). Although samples for classing are taken from just the top of bins delivered to the packing shed this method is considered adequate. Bins containing uneven grades of fruit may be detected during tipping into the processing line. In South Africa a bin tipping system allows a representative sample to be collected from throughout a bin.

The basic grades are defined by Acts of Federal Parliament and are published under the Commonwealth of Australia, Exports (dried fruits) Regulations (1938) and subsequent amendments.

Table 14.3 Requirements for the grading of currants for export (from Export Control (Dried Fruits) Orders, No. 12 of 1988, Commonwealth of Australia).

Crown grade	6	5	4 (Fancy)	3 (Choice)	2	1 (Standard)	MF
Full bodied berries (bold)	++	++	+	−	−	−	−
Typical flavour and texture	++	++	++	++	+	+	+
Absence of shot/pin-head berries	+	+	+	+	+	+	+
Berries with seeds, max. % by count	3	3	3	3	3	3	5
Red berries, max. % by count	0	5	15	25	35	40	70
Colour of berries	dark	dark	dark	dark	dark	dark	dark
Retains bloom	++	++	+	−	−	−	−
Upper size limit (mm)	10	10	10	10	10	10	15
Lower size limit (mm)	7	4	4	4	4	4	4

++ = required, + = desirable, − = not required, MF = manufacturing

Table 14.4 Requirements for the grading of sultanas for export (from Export Control (Dried Fruit) Order, No. 12 of 1988, Commonwealth of Australia).

Crown Grade	7	6	5L	5B	4L	4B	3L	3B	2L	2B	1	MF
Full bodied berries (bold)	++	++	−	−	−	−	−	−	−	−	−	−
Typical flavour and texture	++	++	++	++	++	++	++	++	++	++	+	+
Dark berries, max % by count	0	5	10	10	15	15	20	20	50	50	−	−
Colour of berries	bright golden	bright amber	light amber	dark amber	amber	dark amber-brown	amber-light brown	brown light brown	light brown	dark brown	−	−

Size categories	Extra Small	Small	Large	Extra Large	Jumbo	Unspecified
Maximum riddle size (mm)	8	10	15	15	20	15
Minimum riddle size (mm)	5	5	10	12	12	5

++ = required, + = desirable, − = not required
L = light, B = brown, MF = manufacturing

The main requirements of dried fruit are that they shall be manufactured from sound, reasonably mature fruit, be practically free from foreign matter, not have mineral impurities exceeding 75 mg per 100 g and not have excessive moisture. The major components of the grading system are summarised in Tables 14.3 to 14.6.

High quality currants are to have a uniformly smokey-blue appearance with a low proportion of red coloured berries (Table 14.3). Currants with a black appearance (bloom removed by damage) or a high proportion of poorly coloured red berries are of low quality. Currants in Greece are graded firstly by appearance, then size; this is done within each region with its own trademark. In California a three grade system is used based on criteria similar to Australia's.

Sultanas in Australia are graded into categories based on overall colour ranging from amber to dark brown (Table 14.4). Fruit may be further divided within light or brown types depending on the main colour of the sample. Further limits are

Table 14.5 Requirements for the grading of lexia raisins (from Export Control (Dried Fruit) Order, No. 12 of 1988, Commonwealth of Australia.

Crown Grade	6	5	4	3	MF
Typical flavour and texture	++	++	++	+	+
Dark berries, max. % by count	0	20	30	—	—
Colour of berries	bright amber	brown–brownish green	brown–dark brown–brownish green	—	—

Size Categories	Extra Large	Large	Small	Midget	Unspecified
Maximum riddle size (mm)	—	20	14	10	—
Minimum riddle size (mm)	20	14	10	6	10

++ = required, + = desirable, − = not required, MF = manufacturing

Table 14.6 Requirements for the grading of 'natural' sultanas and lexia raisins (from Export Control (Dried Fruit) Order, No. 12 of 1988, Commonwealth of Australia).

	Sultanas			Lexia Raisins		
	Fancy	Choice	Standard	Fancy	Choice	Standard
Typical texture and flavour	++	++	++	++	++	++
Retain natural bloom	++	+	—	++	+	—
Light coloured berries, max. % by count.	10	15	50	0	10	30
Colour of berries	blue-brown	blue-brown	dark blue-brown	blue-brown	blue-brown	blue-brown

++ = required, + = desirable, − = not required.

placed on the samples for criteria that incur penalties. In Greece and Turkey the grades are mainly based on colour and berry size.

Lexia raisins are classed mainly on uniformity of colour and size, and also flavour (Table 14.5). In California lexias are sorted into four classes mainly according to size. 'Natural' sultanas and lexia raisins are classed in Australia as Fancy, Choice and Standard depending on the proportion of light and off-coloured berries (Table 14.6). In California, the 'naturals' are classed into four

grades based on the content of grit, capstems, stems, and of damaged, sugared, discoloured, mouldy, and underdeveloped berries.

Financial penalties are imposed for fruit with excessive moisture, grit, leaf matter, mould, waste, stalks, trash, 'blobs', weed seeds and chemical residues. The maximum permissible defect limits for various dried vine fruit grades are summarized in Table 14.7. There are financial bonuses for light coloured fruit and higher grade fruit.

Airstream sorting is used to calculate the

Table 14.7 Maximum permissible defect limits for dried vine fruit (from Export Control (Dried Fruits) Orders, No. 12 of 1988, Commonwealth of Australia).

	Currants				Sultanas					Lexia Raisins			
	6 Cr	5 Cr 4 Cr 3 Cr	2 Cr 1 Cr	Mf	7 Cr	6 Cr 5 Cr Fan[B]	4 Cr Ch[B] 3 Cr	2 Cr 1 Cr Std[B]	Mf	6 Cr Fan[B]	5 Cr Ch[B]	4 Cr 3 Cr Std[B]	Mf
Pieces of stalk, per sample of fruit[A]													
— total pieces more than 15 mm in length	3	3	3	10	3	3	3	3	10	5	5	5	5
— total pieces of stalk	6	6	12	20	6	6	6	12	20	5	5	10	15
Pieces of fruit material or foreign fruit per sample of fruit.	10	10	10	10	10	10	10	10	10	10	10	10	10
Capstems, % by number	2	2	4	8	1	1	2	2	6	4	5	5	15
Immature berries, % by number	0.5	1	4	15	0.5	1	2	3	10	0.5	1	1	10
Damaged berries, % by number	0.5	2	3	n.a.	0.5	1	2	3	n.a.	0.5	1	2	n.a.
Mouldy berries, % by number	0.5	1	2	4	0.5	1	1	2	5	0.5	1	2	5
Leaf adherence to berries, % by number	1	1	1	10	0.5	1	2	2	10	—	—	—	—
Pieces of other foreign matter per sample of fruit	1	1	1	1	1	1	1	1	1	1	1	1	1

A. Sample fruit weights — Currants 12.5kg, Sultana 15kg, Raisins 10kg.
B. Classification for natural type raisins.

Cr = Crown   Mf = Manufacturing   Fan = Fancy
Std = Standard   Ch = Choice

proportion of waste in the Thompson Seedless Raisins in California. The air-stream sorter has been evaluated in Australia (Hayes 1985a) but has yet to be adopted by the industry. Differing results with air-stream sorting have been found between Australia and California, and this has been attributed to a difference in the surface texture of Thompson Seedless Raisins and Australian sultanas.

The measurement of external colour of dried sultanas in Australia by a Hunter Colour Difference Meter (Model D25L) has demonstrated a general correlation between grade and colour measurement (Grncarevic and Lewis 1973) but the industry has not yet taken up the use of such instruments.

14.9.2 Storage
Very little on-farm storage is attempted and almost all fruit is stored in large sheds by the packing companies. This fruit is stored at ambient temperature, but many studies have shown that colour and flavour changes are reduced at lower storage temperatures (McBean et al. 1971, Stafford and Guadagni 1977). Packing sheds are regularly fumigated with pyrethrum or methyl bromide to control insect pests. The main pests are raisin moth (Ephestia figulilella), Indian meal moth (Plodia interpunctella) and saw toothed grain beetle (Oryzaephilus sarinamensis). The use of chlorpyrifos on fresh or partly dried fruit significantly reduces the incidence of the major raisin pests (Buchanan et al. 1984). The incorporation of a drying emulsion treatment hastens the degradation of the chlorpyrifos (McDonald et al. 1983) though there is very little further loss of the chemical during processing.

14.9.3 Processing
The desirable quality parameters for good processing are freedom from 'blobs', moisture content less than 13%, no compacted leaf matter on berries and freedom from stalks and other contaminants. Damage to berries can be assessed using a ferrous sulphate test for polyphenolics (Lewis and Simmons 1978).

The processing of dried fruit involves separating the fruit from stalks and other foreign matter using riddles. The berry capstems (pedicels) are removed in a spinning cage and separated by riddles and

air blowers, along with light-weight, undersized berries. The fruit is then washed, dried and sorted by hand. A dressing oil, usually a stabilized vegetable oil, is used to reduce sugar crystallization in the berry, to improve the free running properties of the fruit, to extend the shelf life of the fruit and to improve the appearance of the fruit by a glossy sheen.

Paraffin dressing oil was previously used but due to the rejection of paraffin by other countries, hydrogenated vegetable oils (triacylglycerols), such as Durkex 500®, are now in use. These vegetable oils have higher melting points, are more difficult to apply and can produce off-flavours due to oxidative rancidity. This illustrates a need for more acceptable dressing oils. Dressing oils are not applied to fruit dried without the aid of a drying emulsion, e.g. currants and 'naturals'.

Fruit is usually stored in cardboard cartons with a total weight of 15 kg. The cardboard must have a low chlorophenol content to eliminate musty off-flavours. Stickiness and clumping of fruit into solid blocks are problems that may appear in packed fruit. This problem is due to the presence of sugar on the berry surface caused by berry damage. Techniques that reduce berry damage, e.g. trellis-drying and correctly adjusted recleaners and destemming cones in the processing line, along with optimal dressing oil rates and lower pack weights (12.5 kg per carton) may reduce the clumping problem (Tarr 1989). At the packaging stage, fruit is also inspected by the Commonwealth Department of Primary Industries and Energy for export clearance.

14.9.4 Marketing
The Australian Dried Fruits Association provides orderly marketing by setting minimum prices for the sale of all dried fruits under exemption from the Trade Practices Act. A separate statutory body, the Australian Dried Fruits Corporation is responsible for controlling the export marketing. The Commonwealth Department of Primary Industries and Energy is responsible for enforcing quality and trade description requirements for export markets.

Three main marketing groups are responsible for the sale of dried vine fruit and two of these are members of the ADFA, hence the industry has a large influence on the marketing of its products. Some agents in overseas countries are wholly or partly owned by the industry, whilst others are not. For further comments on the industry organization see Volume 1, Section 1.3.9.

Returns to growers are averaged over the domestic and export returns by a statutory equalization scheme. Unlike the wine and table grape industries, the dried fruit industry is obliged to receive all dried fruit. This leads to large imbalances between supply and demand and large fluctuations in returns to growers. An underwriting scheme is also available to protect growers from sudden downfalls in returns. The pricing is set by the ADFA and various costs are deducted. These include assessors brokerage, bank charges, ADFA levy, insurance, freight, equalization levy, promotion, packing costs, state board levies, sales commission and local levies.

Export marketing is controlled by the Australian Dried Fruits Corporation, a statutory authority consisting of representatives from growers, packers and government. Its function is to promote and control the export of dried fruits; it acts as a controlling agency only, not as a sales agent. The Corporation is involved in agency arrangements, allocations, export prices and terms, promotion market survey, overseas shipping, quality control and cooperation with other producing countries. Australia exports dried fruit to nearly 50 countries but the majority of the product goes to Germany, Canada, New Zealand, Japan, Great Britain, France and India.

The marketing and payment schemes to growers are currently under review and changes are anticipated.

14.10 Concluding remarks

In the past 100 years, since the commencement of large scale drying of grapes in the irrigation colonies of the Murray River Valley, the dried vine fruits industry has seen immense changes in the production, processing and marketing of its produce. The early pioneers in dried fruit culture typically followed the patterns of production in the traditional dried vine fruit countries of Greece and Spain. Later, different cultural techniques and varieties were adopted by the industry to suit the local conditions.

Countries such as Turkey and Chile with low cost labour will provide strong price competition for Australian dried fruit. To maintain market share the industry in Australia must strive to produce a consistently high quality product without the seasonal variations due mainly to rain during the harvest and drying period. The predicted adverse consequences of the greenhouse effect (e.g. less winter chilling, increased summer rainfall) may influence the budburst, ripening, disease pressure and drying conditions. Such changes will require further technological advancements to produce disease and rain-damage resistant cultivars and a better use of solar energy. In the future the dried vine fruits industry will need to continually adapt in response to inevitable political, social, environmental and technological changes.

Further reading

Anonymous (1982) Grape Drying in Australia. Australian Dried Fruit Processing Committee. 20p.

Barnett, D. (1980) Dried grapes — the involvement of lipids in their production. CSIRO Food Research Quarterly 40, 16-22.

Berrett, J.C. and Weste, H.L. (1978) Dehydration of vine fruits. Aust. Dried Fruits News NS6(2), 4-7.

Chambers, T.C. and Possingham, J.V. (1963) Studies of the fine structure of the wax layer in Sultana grapes. Aust. J. Biol. Sci. 16, 818-25.

Clingeleffer, P.R. (1986) Grape drying principles in relation to trellis drying. Aust. Dried Fruits News NS14(2), 14-16.

Grncarevic, M. and Lewis, W. (1976) Drying of grapes in Australia Food Technol. Aust. 28, 66-7, 69-71, 76.

Martin, R.J.L. and Stott, G.L. (1957) The physical factors involved in the drying of Sultana grapes. Aust. J. Agric. Res. 8, 444-59.

Other references

Andris, H.L., Jensen, F.L. and Beede, R.H. (1981) Ethephon is of doubtful value on Thompson Seedless Table Grapes. Calif. Agric. 35 (9/10), 10.

Antcliff, A.J. (1967) Increasing the yield of dried fruit from the Sultana with growth regulators. Vitis 6, 288-93.

Antcliff, A.J. (1975) Four new grape varieties released for testing. J. Aust. Inst. Agric. Sci. 41, 262-3.

Antcliff, A.J. (1981) Merbein Seedless: a new white seedless grape for drying. J. Aust. Inst. Agric. Sci. 47, 167-8.

Barnett, D. (1978) Determination of lipid residues resulting from treatments used in the processing raisins and sultanas. Food Technology in Australia 30, 498-502.

Barrett, H.C. Kerridge, G.H. and Antcliff, A.J. (1969) The drying characteristics of several Sultana clones. Food Technology in Australia 21, 516-7.

Bottrill, D.E. and Hawker, J.S. (1970) Chlorophylls and their derivatives during drying of sultana grapes. J. Sci. Food Agric. 21, 193-6.

Buchanan, G.A., McDonald, G. and Evans, P.W.C. (1984) Control of Drosophila spp., Carpophilus spp., and Ephestia figulilella (Gregson) in Sultana grapes grown for dried fruit. Aust. J. Exp. Agric. Anim. Husb. 24, 440-6.

Christensen, P., Lynn, C., Olmo, H.P., and Studer, H.E. (1970) Mechanical harvesting of Black Corinth raisins. Calif. Agric. 24(10), 4-6.

Clingeleffer, P.R. (1984) Effects of time of season, fruit depth and covering at night when ground drying, on acceptable moisture content of Sultana raisins. J. Sci. Food Agric. 35, 173-181.

Clingeleffer, P.R. and May, P. (1981) The swing-arm trellis for Sultana grapevine management. S. Afr. J. Enol. Vitic. 2, 37-44.

Clingeleffer, P.R., Trayford, R.S., May, P. and Brien, C.J. (1977) Use of the starwheel sprayer for applying drying emulsion to Sultana grapes to be dried on the trellis. Aust. J. Exp. Agric. Anim. Husb. 17, 871-80.

Considine, J.A. (1973) A statistical study of rain damage of grapes grown for drying in Victoria. Aust. J. Exp. Agric. Anim. Husb. 13, 604-11.

El-Bana, G.I., and Weaver, R.J. (1979) Effect of ethephon and gibberellin on maturation of ungirdled Thompson Seedless grapes. Amer. J. Enol. Vitic. 30, 11-3.

Fogerty, A.C., and Burton, D.E. (1981) Analysis of drying oils used to reduce the drying time of vine fruits. CSIRO Food Res. Quarterly 41, 80-5.

Fuller, R.J., Schache, M.J. and Kaye, D.R. (1989) Improved technology for solar drying of vine fruit. Department of Agriculture and Rural Affairs, Victoria. Research Report Series. No. 86, 46p.

Gould, I.V., and Whiting, J.R. (1987) Mechanization of raisin production with the Irymple Trellis System. Transactions of the Amer. Soc. Agric. Eng. 30, 56-60.

Grncarevic, M. (1963) Effect of various dipping treatments on the drying rate of grapes for raisins. Amer. J. Enol. Vitic. 14, 230-4.

Grncarevic, M. (1969) Drying and processing grapes in Afghanistan. Amer. J. Enol. Vitic. 20, 198-202.

Grncarevic, M. (1973) Drying ratios — dried vine fruits. Aust. Dried Fruits News NS1(2), 6.

Grncarevic, M. and Hawker, J.S. (1971) Browning of Sultana grape berries during drying. J. Sci. Food Agric. 22, 270-2.

Grncarevic, M. and Lewis, W. (1973) External colour of dried sultanas. Food Technology in Australia 25, 562-5.

Grncarevic, M. and Radler, F. (1967) The effect of wax components on cuticular transpiration — model experiments. Planta 75, 23-7.

Grncarevic, M. and Radler, F. (1971) A review of the surface lipids of grapes and their importance in the drying process. Amer. J. Enol. Vitic. 22, 80-6.

Guadagni, D.G. and Stafford, A. E. (1979) Factors affecting the threshold of methyl and ethyl oleate emulsions in raisins and raisin paste. J. Food Sci. 44, 782-4.

Hayden, O. (1988) Wetting machines for trellis drying. Aust. Dried Fruits News NS16(2), 14,16.

Hayes, R.J. (1985a) Aspects of dried vine fruit quality and processing. Department of Agriculture and Rural Affairs, Victoria. Research Project Series. No. 209, 45p.

Hayes, R. (1985b) Producing natural sultanas and slab drying. Aust. Dried Fruits News NS13(2), 14-5.

Henshilwood, J. (1950) Pioneering Days in Mildura. Sunnyland Press, Red Cliffs. 44p.

Jacob, H.E. (1944) Factors influencing the yield, composition, and quality of raisins. California Agr. Exp. Sta. Bull. 683, 1-43.

Joslyn, M.A. and Ponting, J.D. (1951) Enzyme-catalysed oxidative browning of fruit products. Adv. Food Res. 3, 1-44.

Kerridge, G.H. and Grncarevic, M. (1965) Production of dark coloured sultanas by sun-drying in Australia. Food Technology in Australia 17, 328-9, 331.

Lazar, M.E., Barta, E.J. and Smith, G.S. (1963) Dry-blanch-dry (DBD) method for drying fruit. Food Technology 1201, 120-2.

Lewis, W.J. and Simmons, I.D. (1978) A test for skin damage of dried grapes. Food Technology in Australia 30, 391-2.

May, P. and Clingeleffer, P.R. (1982) Mechanizing the production of Sultana (Thompson Seedless) raisins. In:University of California, Davis. Grape and Wine Centennial Symposium Proceedings Ed. Webb A.D. University of California, Davis. 191-4.

May, P. and Kerridge, G.K. (1967) Harvest pruning of Sultana vines. Vitis 6, 390-3.

May, P. Clingeleffer, P.R. and Simmons, I.O. (1983) Effects of varying the method of applying alkaline emulsion on the drying of Sultana grapes. J. Sci. Food Agric. 34, 1215-28.

May, P., Clingeleffer, P.R., Brien, C.J. and Scholefield, P.B. (1978) Harvest pruning of young Sultana vines under various training systems. Aust. J. Exp. Agric. Anim. Husb. 18, 847-54.

May, P., Scholefield, P.B., Clingeleffer, P.R., and Smith, L. (1974) Experiments on the mechanical harvesting of Sultanas for drying. J. Sci. Food Agric. 25, 541-52.

McBean, D.M., Joslyn, M.A., and Navy, F.S. (1971) Dehydrated fruit. In: Biochemistry of Fruits and their Products, Vol. 2. Ed. Hulme, A.C. Academic Press, London 623-52.

McDonald, G., Buchanan, G.A. and Griffiths, G.R. (1983) Insecticide application and degradation in Sultana grapes grown for drying. Pestic. Sci. 14, 528-36.

Newman, H.P., and Clingeleffer, P.R. (1987) Preliminary evaluation of alternative drying varieties. Food Technology in Australia 39, 294-5.

Newman, H.P., Clingeleffer, P.R. and Possingham, J.V. (1985) Update on experimental results with Merbein Seedless. Australian Dried Fruits News NS13(2), 17-8.

Phaff, H.J. (1951) Fruit and vegetable dehydration principles and advances (1864-1945). Chronica Bot. 12, 306-29.

Ponting, J.D. and McBean, D.M. (1970) Temperature and dipping treatment effects on drying rates and drying times of grapes, prunes and other waxy fruits. Food Technology 24(12), 85-8.

Possingham, J.V. (1972) Surface wax structure in fresh and dried Sultana grapes. Ann. Bot. 36, 993-6.

Radler, F. (1964) The prevention of browning during drying by the cold dipping treatment of Sultana grapes. J. Sci. Food Agric. 15, 864-9.

Radler, F. (1965) The surface lipids of fresh and processed raisins. J. Sci. Food Agric. 16, 638-43.

Ramshaw, E.H. and Hardy, P.J. (1969) Volatile compounds in dried grapes. J. Sci. Food Agric. 20, 619-21.

Riva, M. and Peri, C. (1986) Kinetics of sun and air drying of different varieties of seedless grapes. J. Food Technol. 21, 199-208.

Sarooshi, R.A. and Roberts, E.A. (1978) Effect of date of pruning, timing, number and composition of oil emulsion sprays on harvest pruned Sultana. Amer. J. Enol. Vitic. 29, 233-8.

Sarooshi, R.A. and Roberts, E.A. (1979) Effect of trellising, crown bunch handling, and the number of oil emulsion and gibberellic acid sprays on harvest-pruned Sultanas. Aust. J. Exp. Agric. Anim. Husb. 19, 122-8.

Scholefield, P.B., May, P. and Neales, T.F. (1977) Harvest pruning and trellising of Sultana vines. 2. Effects on early spring development. Sci. Hortic. 7, 123-32.

Scholefield, P.B., Neales, T.F. and May, P. (1978) Carbon balance of the Sultana vine (Vitis vinifera L) and the effects of autumn defoliation by harvest pruning. Aust. J. Plant Physiol. 5, 561-70.

Shaw, I. (1986) Development of specialised trellis drying systems. Hanging cane. In:Trellis drying and mechanical harvesting of grapes. Eds. Ballantyne, I. and Macrae, I. Department of Agriculture and Rural Affairs. Conference Proceedings Series No. 7, 93-4.

Smart, R.E. and Dry, P.R. (1980) A climatic classification for Australian viticultural regions. Aust. Grapegrower and Winemaker 196 8,10,16.

Stafford, A.E. and Guadagni, D.G. (1977) Storage stability of raisins dried by different procedures. J. Food Sci. 42, 547-8.

Studer, H.E. (1984) The Alternating Duplex:A vine training system for mechanized raisin production. Transactions of Amer. Soc. Agric. Eng. 27, 986-9.

Studer, H.E. and Olmo, H.P. (1971) The severed cane technique and its application to mechanical harvesting of raisin grapes. Transactions of the Amer. Soc. Agric. Eng. 14, 38-43.

Szulmayer, W. (1971) From sun-drying to solar dehydration 2. Solar drying in Australia. Food Technology in Australia 29, 494-5, 497, 499, 501.

Szulmayer, W. (1973) Thermodynamics of sun-drying. In:Sun in the Service of Mankind. Proc. Int. Congress, Unesco House, Paris 1973. V24, 1-9.

Tarr, C.R. (1989) Investigations into stickiness and compaction of dried vine fruit. Department of Agriculture and Rural Affairs, Victoria. Research Report Series No. 99. 37p.

Whiting, J.R. (1982) Response of Zante grapevines to cane and harvest pruning. Amer. J. Enol. Vitic. 33, 185-90.

Whiting, J.R. and Morey, B.G. (1988) Drying of Carina grapes. Aust. Dried Fruits News NS15(3), 13.

Wilson, B.W. (1962) The role of solar energy in the drying of vine fruit. Aust. J. Agric. Res. 4, 662-73.

CHAPTER FIFTEEN

Harvesting and Handling of Tablegrapes

R.M. CIRAMI, I.J. CAMERON and P.R. HEDBERG

In Australia, tablegrapes are produced for both the domestic and export market (Volume 1, Section 1.4). Most of the production areas are located hundreds of kilometres from domestic markets and export exit points, therefore careful handling, packing, cooling and transport are essential to ensure that the grapes arrive at their destination in good condition.

The marketing period extends mainly from late October to April with stored tablegrapes being available right through the winter months. Tablegrapes are grouped into three harvest categories—early season (October to late January), mid season (early February to late March), and late season (April to May) (see Table 12.1).

15.1 Maturity of tablegrapes

Tablegrapes are considered ripe when they have attained an attractive appearance and are pleasant to eat. As grapes ripen, the flavour and colour characteristics of the variety develop and the berries soften. Grapes do not ripen appreciably after picking, so an acceptable level of palatability must be reached at the time of harvest.

15.1.1 Maturity standards

The importance of harvesting grapes at the best stage of maturity is well recognized. Legal minimum standards for maturity based on total soluble solids concentration of the berries (^{0}Brix) and titratable acidity have been established. ^{0}Brix can be readily determined with a refractometer or a hydrometer (see 13.2.4); acidity is measured by titration with sodium hydroxide (O.1N) to a phenolphthalein or pH 8.3 endpoint. The minimum standards vary considerably for different varieties and between States, and whether the grapes are for export or sale in Australia.

Tablegrapes for export were required by legislation to have minimum Brix levels, specified by variety, and to be sound, clear and free of external moisture, foreign smells or tastes and free of sulfur damage. They were further classified into Extra Class, Class 1 and Class 2 according to berry size (see 15.1.3). Present legislation simply specifies that the grapes be true-to-label, but uses the former specifications as a guide; Table 15.1 summarizes the indicated Brix levels.

Minimum maturity standards have been operated by several Australian States to prevent unripe grapes from reaching the consumer. Combrink *et al.* (1977) state that the relationship between Brix level and palatability remained virtually constant every year; they felt Brix was the best maturity index and could be determined readily.

The Brix/acid ratio (the ratio of °Brix to titratable acid as tartaric acid, g/100 mL of juice) is widely used as a maturity index for tablegrapes in other countries; and is a specified standard for some export grapes (see Table 15.1) and also in some states of Australia. Sultana, for example, has excessively high acidity early in the season and can be unpalatable even though the fruit meets the minimum Brix requirements.

Judging the minimum acceptable level of maturity is always a problem with early ripening varieties as there is a strong desire by growers to harvest as early as possible in the expectation of receiving high prices for new season fruit. However, if unripe grapes are allowed to be sold, an adverse reaction by consumers may depress subsequent sales until recognizably ripe fruit reaches the market. Conversely over-ripe berries are prone to handling injuries, disease and shrivelling due to water loss. The tendency for berries to separate from their pedicels (shatter) is also increased in some varieties when the fruit is over-ripe; gibberellin-treated Sultanas (Thompson Seedless) are a notable example.

The grower may assess ripeness by observing colour of fruit, colour or condition of bunch stems (straw-yellow or woody) and berry taste. Black and red varieties usually exhibit a characteristic bright berry colour when ripe. White varieties develop a semi-translucent appearance. Taste is an important guide to ripeness, but should always be related to the appearance of the bunch and the sugar content of the berries, as repeated tasting can dull taste perception making it difficult to distinguish less ripe berries.

15.1.2 Maturity levels for cool storage
The effects of cool storage upon maturity

Table 15.1. Standards of minimum °Brix levels specified in the 1991 Export Control Regulations — Schedule No. 2 for tablegrapes.

Minima	Varieties
15 °Brix	Barlinka, Cardinal, Early Madeleine, Fresno Seedless, Redglobe, Ribier
16 °Brix	All other varieties
17 °Brix	Cannon Hall Muscat
18 °Brix	Thompson Seedless (syn. Sultana)

A minimum Brix/acid ratio is accepted as an alternative to a minimum Brix level for five varieties. The ratios are: 18/1 for Cardinal, Emerald Seedless and Flame Seedless: 19/1 for Thompson Seedless: and 26/1 for Sugraone (this variety, called Superior Seedless in USA, may develop off-flavours at Brix levels above 18-20°)

standards have been outlined by Dahlenberg *et al.* (1979). For immediate marketing or short term storage (up to three weeks) the flavour and sweetness/acidity of the grapes will change little from harvest to marketing. However, for long term storage, the best tasting grapes at harvest may not be the best flavoured grapes after six or more weeks storage. During storage the acid content of the grapes slowly declines, but at a greater proportional rate than the sugar content. Some acidity is an essential part of the characteristic taste of many varieties and late storage may result in grapes with a sweet but flat dull taste. A slight 'tartness' in the fruit is required for long term storage, but this has to be associated with an adequate sugar content. Grapes with a high acid content and inadequate sugar content may develop a bitter 'off flavour' during storage.

15.1.3 Size Grades
Minimum diameters of berries were prescribed in legislation for the classification of export tablegrapes. The sizes varied for different export grades; for example, Class 1 of group A varieties (e.g. Cardinal) had a minimum diameter set at 20 mm, other grapes had smaller diameters. This requirement has been changed to a trueness-to-label system as mentioned in 15.1.1.

15.2 Pre-harvest protection

Botrytis rot (*Botrytis cinerea*) is a major fungal disease of grapes both in the vineyard and in storage (see Chapter 11). It occurs in all major grape-producing regions of the world following late season rains. McClellan and Hewitt (1973) reported a variant of this disease which they called 'early botrytis rot'. They observed that bunch rots due to *Botrytis cinerea* developed in mid season in the absence of rain. Infected berries turned brown, lost moisture and shrivelled. They established that the infection takes place during flowering, the fungus then remains latent until veraison or later when it resumes growth and rots the berry.

A range of fungicides can be used to control botrytis. They are most effective when applied at early and late flowering, before bunch closure and prior to harvest. Fungicides are best used in rotation to reduce the build-up of resistance by the botrytis fungus (Chapter 11). Canopy management techniques to reduce vine humidity and berry spitting also aid in control (see Chapter 5).

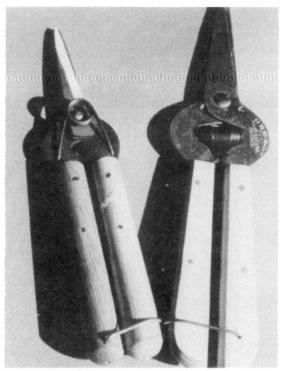

Figure 15.1 Light weight, slim-profile snips for trimming tablegrape bunches.

15.3 Harvesting tablegrapes

High harvesting costs are a feature of the tablegrape industry as picking, trimming and packing operations are highly labour intensive. In an effort to reduce costs some tablegrape vineyards in Australia are family enterprises with a minimal amount of outside labour employed, however with the current expansion in tablegrape production, some large enterprises and centralized packing facilities have been developed.

15.3.1 Selective harvest

Only attractive bunches that have good eating, shipping and keeping qualities should be harvested. As all the bunches on the vine rarely mature together, more than one picking may be required to harvest all of the marketable fruit. Selective picking helps reduce bunch trimming. Bunches requiring excessive trimming are often left on the vine for eventual picking and delivery to wineries or distilleries.

Ideally, harvesting should be done during cool conditions, preferably in the early morning; the heat content (field heat) of the grapes will then be at a minimum, hence reducing the amount of water lost from stems and berries.

The bunch is harvested with picking snips or secateurs, the cut being as close to the supporting stem as possible. Grapes should be held by the bunchstem during picking and trimming to minimize loss of bloom. If rain or irrigation occurs when the grapes are ripe it is best to delay harvesting for 2-5 days; the sudden increase in berry volume caused by uptake of water may lead to berry splitting but this needs several days to become clearly evident.

15.3.2 Bunch trimming

Bunch trimming is the removal of immature, diseased, split, shrivelled, poorly coloured or undersized berries to improve the appearance of the bunch. The amount of trimming required varies according to the variety, seasonal conditions, cultural techniques used (see Chapter 12) and the market being supplied.

More trimming is often required to meet export standards than for the local market. Light weight, slim-profile trimming snips (Figure 15.1) are used for this purpose.

Figure 15.2 A well-organized tablegrape packing shed.

15.4 Packing tablegrapes

15.4.1 Packing Sheds
Many tablegrapes in Australia are picked in the field and then trimmed and packed in grower-owned sheds. The grapes are picked, carefully placed in polystyrene boxes, shallow plastic trays or wooden picking boxes for transfer to the packing shed and subsequent trimming and packing. Packing sheds vary greatly in design depending upon the size of the packing operation. Adequate lighting and ventilation, ample room for storage of packaging materials and packed fruit, and convenient receival, dispatch and working areas are essential to ensure a smooth flow of grapes with minimum handling (Figure 15.2). Pre-cooling and cold-storage rooms are also becoming an essential feature of a tablegrape enterprise (Figure 15.3).

The trimming and packing of tablegrapes in a packing shed has the advantage of good working conditions, easier supervision and allows the use of semi-skilled labour for the trimming operation. The major disadvantages are high capital costs and increased handling of the fruit.

15.4.2 Field packing
In field packing the grapes are harvested, trimmed and packed directly from the vine (Figure 15.4). Experienced labour is required for this operation but it has the advantage of limiting the loss of bloom and damage to berries. The packed boxes are left under the vine and a tractor forklift with pallet is used to collect the fruit and deliver it directly into a cold room or to a transport area. Field packing is often used for early maturing, easily-damaged varieties.

15.4.3 Packing for the domestic market
Grapes are packed for the domestic market in a range of containers using varying methods of presentation. Different packing styles have been developed over the years as growers have attempted to capture a specific section of the market, or have tried to lower their costs of production. Generally, fruit is packed by variety and is graded as either Extra Class, Class 1 or Class 2 grade.

Bunches are placed in the box or carton either with bunchstems up or bunchstems down. Many growers use a 'face-pack' (Figure 15.5) with all

Figure 15.3 Pre-cooling and cold storage rooms are an essential feature of modern tablegrape production.

Figure 15.4 Field packing of tablegrapes

the stems hidden. This system produces an attractive pack with an even layer of grapes facing the buyer. Peggie (1975) reported that the 'face-pack' has lost favour in California and has been replaced by the 'stems-up pack' which allows buyers to remove packed bunches by the stem, minimizing berry damage (Figure 15.6). This is now widely used in Australia.

The main function of a package is to contain, to protect and to identify the contents. It should also add sales appeal and have minimal cost. In Australia the most widely used is the standard half-case or carton with approximate internal dimensions 450 mm long, 290 mm wide and 135 mm deep. The package can be constructed of timber, fibreboard or polystyrene and holds about 10 kg of grapes. Timber cases are lined with paper and are usually fully lidded. Cartons are the preferred packaging, although, compared with timber cases, greater care is required where long distance transport or storage is involved. The cartons are marketed with a fully telescopic lid.

Polystyrene boxes were introduced and used for tablegrapes in Europe in the mid-1960s and in Australia since 1977. The Australian polystyrene box has internal measurements, 454 mm long,

290 mm wide and 165 mm deep. The boxes have excellent insulating properties but are fragile and require large storage areas to hold stocks since they cannot be transported in a dismantled form as can timber cases or cartons (Figure 15.7). For these and environmental reasons, polystyrene boxes are less favoured now; they are rarely used for export. Returnable plastic crates can also be used for the direct sale of grapes to supermarkets and other retail outlets. Two sizes are in general use: 36 L which holds 18 kg of grapes, and 22 L which holds 10 kg of grapes. Both crates are compatible for stacking.

15.4.4 Packing for the export market

The major export markets for Australian grapes are Singapore, the United Kingdom, Hong Kong, Europe, New Zealand and the Pacific Islands. Keenan (1980) states:

Tablegrapes are one of the premium fruits imported into Southeast Asia and as such are considered to be a luxury item. The principal suppliers are the United States, Australia, Chile and South Africa with cheap local grapes being supplied by Thailand, mainland China and Taiwan. Japan is also a supplier of premium gift-pack type grapes. In Asia the style of grape preferred has:

Figure 15.5 A 'face-pack' of tablegrapes with a 'window'.

Figure 15.6 A 'stems-up pack' for easy bunch access within a polythene lined telescopic cardboard carton.

Figure 15.7 A 'face-pack' within a polystyrene box.

(i)   a sweet, low-acid, seedless berry,

(ii)   berries and bunches of even light red colour which is a Chinese symbol of prosperity,

(iii) large sized berries (20-30 mm),

(iv) fresh green stalks and capstems,

(v)   medium sized bunches (500 - 600 g), and

(vi) a reasonable maturity which will not result in 'berry shatter'.

'Berry shatter' is very important as grapes are sold as bunches which are generally displayed by hanging on hawker's stalls and in fruit shops . . . . . . these outlets still comprise the majority of the fruit business in Southeast Asia. 'Shatter'-prone varieties such as Purple Cornichon have limited appeal in Southeast Asia. In addition, the stalk length is important as long stalks enable the bunches to be tied easily for display.

Importers, particularly in Singapore and Indonesia, traditionally preferred a wooden package filled with cork for sea freight of grapes from Australia. This package, known as the 'cork pack', was ideal for re-export to other countries in Southeast Asia and for distribution over long distances by road (Tugwell 1978). The cork provided excellent protection for grapes during transportation but has been phased out due to its expense and its spoilage of the natural bloom of the fruit.

The export of grapes in fibreboard packages without cork became popular in Australia after 1978 when air freight and containerized vessels became a significant part of the tablegrape industry. Fibreboard packages are less expensive, easier to assemble and cheaper to air-freight than wooden boxes. Fibreboard cartons are the most commonly used grape package carrying about 10 kg of grapes, although a 5 kg package is normally used for European destinations. The fibreboard packages used in Australia have a wide variety of internal dimensions designed to meet the preference of each market. The telescopic packages have a waxed inner surface to minimize the absorption of moisture from the grapes and the environment.

Figure 15.8 Cooling packed grapes before lid closure.

15.5. Postharvest handling

15.5.1 Cooling

Cooling is necessary to remove field heat rapidly from the grapes; it is particularly important for grapes transported to distant markets and for grapes destined for long term cold storage. The rapid reduction of temperature has three advantages:

(i) It greatly reduces the grape's rate of respiration; the slower this rate the longer the storage life.

(ii) Germination and development of decay-causing fungal spores is slowed by low temperature.

(iii) The loss of moisture from the grapes is reduced and this lessens wilting, stem desiccation and browning, and berry shatter (Ginsburg and Truter 1976).

To preserve quality, grapes should be cooled immediately after harvest to below 10°C. Ideally, grapes are packed then forced-air cooled down to 0 – 2°C prior to lid closure and shipment (Figure 15.8).

Rapid movement of cool air around the fruit is needed for effective and economical cooling. While well-ventilated or evaporative-cooled packing sheds (or even wet hessian bags placed over grape picking containers) are beneficial, rapid cooling requires specially designed cooling rooms equipped with forced-air coolers. Forced-air cooling can remove most of the field heat within four hours of placing packed grapes in the cool room. Cooling times may be four to ten times longer in a conventional cool room in which air circulates mainly around the packages rather than the grapes.

15.5.2 Cold Storage

Cold storage is used for holding fresh grapes under conditions that will prolong their saleable life by reducing water loss, fungal infection and fruit deterioration. Cold storage brings many advantages: it helps maintain continuity of labour during harvest; helps regulate orderly supplies of fruit to market; and permits the continuation of marketing after the end of the grape season, thereby increasing total sales.

To achieve the desired results, cool stores for grapes should be correctly designed and constructed; professional assistance is advisable. The specifications will be determined by the total quantities of grapes to be stored, the daily rates of loading, the temperature of the grapes going into store, the desired rates of cooling, the required relative humidity, storage temperature and the need for protection against corrosion by sulfur dioxide. More specific information on cooling and cool storage can be found in Mitchell *et al.* (1972), Anon. (1977), Dahlenburg *et al.* (1979) and Nelson (1979).

Storage

After sound, mature grapes have been properly packed and pre-cooled, the factor which then determines success or failure in their preservation is the storage environment. Factors in the storage environment that affect grape quality are temperature, relative humidity, air movement, and fumigation with sulfur dioxide (Ryall and Harvey 1959).

a. Temperature

The lower the temperature the longer the fruit can be stored. The recommended range is −1°C

Figure 15.10 A 10 kg grape package with sulfur dioxide generator destined for storage.

Figure 15.9 Fungal rots of stored tablegrapes.

to 0°C. Grapes will freeze near −1.5°C.

b. Relative humidity
As relative humidity increases, water loss from the grapes decreases. A high relative humidity, near 96%, is recommended.

c. Air movement
High velocity cooling air (60 to 90 air changes per hour) speeds the removal of field heat during cooling but, during storage, air movement should be reduced to 5% of the above rates to prevent stem and berry desiccation. Only enough air movement need be provided to remove respiratory heat and maintain adequate levels of oxygen; this can be achieved by cycling fans with the compressor so that they do not operate continuously, or by using the plastic jacket system of storage (Dahlenburg *et al.* 1979).

d. Fumigation with sulfur dioxide
Various fungi such as *Botrytis cinerea, Cladosporium*

herbarium, Penicillium, and *Alternaria* spp., may cause serious losses in grapes even under the low temperatures at which grapes are stored (Figure 15.9). Fumigation with relatively low levels of sulfur dioxide destroys fungal mycelium and spores on the surface of the berries. Nevertheless, any mycelium located within the berry will continue to develop during storage and regular applications of sulfur dioxide are necessary to prevent the spread of infection to adjacent sound berries. In addition to reducing decay, sulfur dioxide prevents bunchstems from turning brown or black in storage, reduces berry shatter and reduces the rate of respiration of the grapes (Ryall and Harvey 1959).

Sulfur dioxide treatment methods
The grapes may be fumigated with sulfur dioxide gas or by sulfur dioxide-releasing chemicals. The alternative sulfur dioxide treatments are:

a. In-package sulfur dioxide generators
A two-stage sulfur dioxide generator was developed by Nelson and Gentry (1966) for in-package fumigation of tablegrapes. The generator is a pad containing sodium metabisulfite glued between paper strips of differing permeability. Moisture within the package of grapes is absorbed and reacts with the sulfite releasing sulfur dioxide. The first stage of the generator begins releasing sulfur dioxide during the first few hours of initial cooling and reaches maximum release by the second day. This provides the initial kill of fungi residing on the surface of the fruit. The second stage begins acting slowly after the fifth day and continues to generate for the next two months.

The slow-release second stage is designed to kill spores germinating from any internal infection. A single storage or quick-release generator is also available for short-term storage. Both generators, developed in the USA in the late 1960s as Grape-Guard[©], are now manufactured in Chile.

A 10 kg package destined for short storage (0-2 weeks) may only require the first stage sulfur dioxide generator on top of the package. A 10 kg package destined for longer storage is usually packed within an unvented polyethylene bag (Figure 15.10) with a full two-stage pad placed on top after the grapes are cooled and before closing. The 5 kg export package only requires half a Grape-Guard pad. Long term storage requires a new Grape-Guard (2nd stage) generator to be inserted into the package at 8-10 weeks. The polyethylene liner inside the package contains the sulfur dioxide gas and maintains high humidity. This helps to retain maximum freshness (Leamon 1986). Good temperature control is necessary to prevent the excessive release of sulfur dioxide that will occur if fruit temperatures are allowed to rise (Nelson 1979, Dahlenburg et al. 1979).

b. Whole room flush systems
For this system a 0.5% (by volume) concentration of sulfur dioxide gas is injected into the cold room initially. After 20 minutes the room is ventilated. At intervals of no more than seven days 0.1 percent (by volume) is injected into the room and then vented after 20 minutes. The main problems with this system are the retention and maintenance of high humidity and the corrosive effects of sulfur dioxide on the cold room and associated equipment (Ryall and Harvey 1959, Dahlenburg et al. 1979, Nelson 1979). Grapes are packed in plastic liners or pallets covered with a plastic cover to reduce dehydration of stems during storage.

c. Daily shot dosing
An alternative to weekly fumigation of grapes with sulfur dioxide is the injection of smaller quantities into the room every one or two days. Two injection systems can be used. In the first, liquid sulfur dioxide is measured into a glass sight-tube then allowed to flow into the room, after first vaporizing it with heat. The second uses a timer switch to automatically open a valve to gas the room once a day. The timer shuts off

the valve after a pre-set time to give a concentration of 60 mg/L sulfur dioxide for daily fumigation or 230 mg/L if fumigated every other day. One hour after fumigation a second timer can be set to operate a fan to exhaust excess sulfur dioxide from the room. Other alternatives include allowing the sulfur dioxide to escape slowly through leaks in the coolroom or using the water sprays in high humidity refrigeration equipment to absorb the gas.

d. Whole room trickle system
A flow of sulfur dioxide into the room is maintained at 10 mg/L continuously by a metered trickle of gas (DeSwart and Louw 1968). The system was further developed and used commercially in South Australia in 1978. A plastic jacket is constructed inside the cold room. A fan and ducts within the jacket provide air circulation and sufficient venting to provide a complete change of air through the room every four to five hours. sulfur dioxide gas is trickled into the jacketed room and this balances the loss through ventilation and maintains a constant 10 mg/L concentration of sulfur dioxide inside the jacket. This system provides excellent control of fungi with minimum damage to the cold room and equipment. A full description of the trickle system, including construction, venting and sulfur dioxide metering is presented by Dahlenburg et al. (1979).

Storage life of grapes
Keeping quality varies with variety. Some varieties, even under optimal storage conditions, show significant losses in only four to six weeks, whereas other varieties can be maintained for six months in near-perfect market condition. The storage life expected for some of the main varieties is given in Table 12.1. The figures relate to sound, well-trimmed fruit stored under optimal storage conditions.

Storage faults vary with variety. The Italia grape develops a distinct browning of the skin in cold storage which intensifies after removal. The berries remain sound and firm but the browning gives the fruit a dull, imperfect appearance; Nelson (1979) attributes this discoloration to tannins in injured or senescent cells. Waltham Cross stores well with the berries remaining in near perfect condition during long storage; however the stalks

Figure 15.11 Careful stacking of pallets gives a more stable unit and reduces damage in transit. Stacked pallets are further protected by an enclosing mesh and corner guard strips.

Figure 15.12 A refrigerated sea container being loaded with export tablegrapes.

tend to desiccate at an early stage. There is evidence that some varieties, particularly those with Muscat character, lose flavour during storage (A.P. Dahlenburg, pers. comm). During storage of Ohanez, individual berries and even whole bunches sometimes develop a scald-like discoloration of the skin, giving a generally dull appearance or a distinct brown discoloration which is confined to the skin; flavour of the affected berries remains normal (Hall and Scott 1977). Ohanez grapes stored for more than eight weeks should be inspected regularly for discoloration.

15.6 Marketing

Tablegrapes must be handled with great care to avoid a loss of quality. A low temperature/high humidity regime should be maintained throughout the whole marketing chain if quality is to be preserved. Excessive condensation on warm fruit will aggravate fungal rots. Conversely a low humidity will cause rapid dehydration of the fruit, particularly if air velocity is high. Increased temperature and humidity levels may also stimulate an excessive SO_2 release from in-package generators causing bleaching and tainting of nearby grapes. Correct stacking of pallets and containers is critical for a good out-turn of fruit. Figures 15.11 and 15.12 show a good technique for stacking pallets and containers. Compression damage may occur when the load is cool-stored for any length of time or stacked more than two pallets high.

15.7 Concluding remarks

The harvesting and handling of tablegrapes requires more care, time and energy than for other grape usages because the final product is destined to be consumed fresh, and must be attractive, clean and palatable. It is not sufficient merely to grow quality fruit. The specialist tablegrape grower's job must continue through harvest, trimming and packaging and even into cool storage and transport of his produce to market. Long-term success depends upon the quality of the product in the market. A reputation for good quality, gained by self-imposed standards of growers and packers brings rewards in market volume and price. The spectacular increase in the volume of export earnings of Australian tablegrapes — increasing 25-fold from 1984 to 1988 — suggests that good methods have been adopted.

Further reading
Anon. (1977) Tablegrapes and refrigeration Proc. Int. Inst. Refrigeration, Commission C2, Paris.
Anon. (1988) Commonwealth of Australia Export Control (Orders) Regulations. Schedule 2. Grape.
Chesterfield, I. and Smith, P. (eds) (1990) Table Grapes. A Product Quality Manual. Victorian Department of Agriculture, Melbourne.
Dahlenburg, A.P., Gillespie, K.J. and Jarrett, L.D. (1979) Post harvest handling of tablegrapes. Hort. Notes No. 4 (1979). Department of Agriculture, South Australia.

Mitchell, F.G., Guillou, R. and Parsons, R.A. (1972) Commercial cooling of fruits and vegetables. Calif. Agric. Exp. Sta. Ext. Serv. Manual 43.

Nelson, K.E. (1979) Harvesting and handling California tablegrapes for market. No. 4095. Agricultural Sciences Publications, University of California, Berkeley.

Winkler, A.J., Cook, J.A., Kliewer, W.M and Lider, L.A. (1974) General Viticulture. University of California Press, Berkeley.

Other references

Combrink, J.C., Ginsburg, L., Truter, A.B. and Van Der Westhuizen, A.J.M. (1977) A comparison of various maturity indices for tablegrapes. Tablegrapes and refrigeration Proc. Int. Inst. Refrigeration, commission C2, Paris. 27-32.

DeSwart, G.H. and Louw, A.I. (1968) Factors affecting the successful long-term cold storage of tablegrapes. Deciduous Fruit Grower 18, 23-26.

Ginsburg, L. and Truter, A.B. (1976) Cold Stores for Grapes. Fruit and Fruit Technology Research Institute, Stellenbosch.

Hall, E.G. and Scott, K.J. (1977) Storage and market diseases of fruit. CSIRO, Australia.

Keenan, S.R. (1980) Market situation and outturn report in South East Asia. Australian Dept. Primary Industry.

Leamon, K. (1986) The Australian tablegrape market in Europe 1986. Second national table grape industry technical conference. Stanthorpe, Qld. Queensland Dept. of Primary Industries Agdex No. 243-10.

McClellan, W.D. and Hewitt, W.B. (1973) Early botrytis rot of grapes: time of infection and latency of *Botrytis cinerea* Pers. in *Vitis vinifera* L. Phytopathology 63, 1151-1157.

Nelson, K.E., and Gentry, J.P. (1966) Two stage generation of sulphur dioxide within closed containers to control decay of table grapes. Amer. J. Enol. Vitic 17, 290-301.

Peggie, I.D. (1975) Report on the tablegrape industry in California. Department of Agriculture, Vic.

Ryall, A.L. and Harvey, J.M. (1959) The cold storage of vinifera tablegrapes. Agriculture Handbook No. 159. United States Department of Agriculture, Washington, D.C.

Tugwell, B. (1978) Report on the quality of Australian fruit and vegetable exported to South East Asia. Australian Dept. Primary Industry.

INDEX